Raymond Selkirk

Chester-le-Street and
Its Place in History
by
Raymond Selkirk

The author at Usworth Aerodrome (Sunderland Airport) just before an archaeological survey flight. The aircraft in the background is the airfield's gate guardian, an ex RAF Vickers Valletta.

Chester-le-Street and Its Place in History

by

Raymond Selkirk

Written on behalf of the Northern Archaeology Group of County Durham & Tyne & Wear

We shall not cease from exploration
And the end of all our exploring
will be to arrive where we started
And know the place for the first time.
(T.S. Eliot)

The book has been made possible by a grant from the Heritage Lottery Fund.

Supported by the
Heritage Lottery Fund

The accuracy of facts and research data, by the very nature of historical research and archaeological search, is always open to question and debate. Questions on facts and data, and any contributions should be addressed to:

> The Northern Archaeology Group
>
> Columbia Old School
>
> Washington
>
> Tyne & Wear

First published in January 2001

ISBN 1-900456-05-02

This book is available from:

> Casdec Printcentre
>
> 21/22 Harraton Terrace, Birtley, Co. Durham DH3 2QG
>
> Tel: (0191) 410 5556 Fax: (0191) 410 0229

By the same author:

> *The Piercebridge Formula*, Patrick Stephens Ltd, 1983
>
> ISBN 0-85059-621-1

> *On the Trail of The Legions*, Anglia Publishing 1995
>
> ISBN 1-897874-08-01

Printed by

> Casdec Printcentre

Chester-le-Street and Its Place in History

Contents

Page

Acknowledgements

My thanks are due to the following people who assisted with this book.

All the landowners and farmers who have allowed our teams access to their land.

The members of the Northern Archaeology Group of County Durham.

Members of the Association of Northumberland Local History Societies who assisted with excavations of unknown Roman roads at Bywell, Hartburn and Brinkburn Priory.

The students of the "Chester-le-Street Project 2000 Class."

James Alder, artist, for his picture of the Viking ship.

Elizabeth Anderson, researcher, field-walker, and who grew rice outdoors in her Sunderland garden.

Neville Andison, excavator and engineer.

David Armstrong B.Eng, C.Eng. for research on Roman dams.

The late Captain David Armstrong, RN, for his assistance with the research of the history of Northumberland.

Brian Atkinson for his model of the Roman bridge-pier.

Professor Richard Bailey, who taught me about the Saxons.

Dr John Banham, Chester-le-Street District Council, who suggested that this book be written; also co-author of Chapter 15.

Chief Superintendent Ken Barritt, MBE, for information on advanced Roman mathematics.

JA Biggins, geophysical surveyor.

Librarian Anne Birtle, Durham Constabulary Headquarters, Aykley Heads, for her help with the County war diaries.

Alan Bowlam, metal detectorist.

Don Bowman, coal industry and wagonway expert, co-author of Ch15.

Ken Brown, field team transportation, NAG Treasurer.

Sue Brown for her translations of Professor Grenier's works.

Bill Burdus, BDS, excavator of Cong Burn Roman bridge.

Richard & Sue Cansdale, experts on Hartburn village.

Fiona Cassidy, translator of European languages.

Joe Cassidy, excavator, librarian & researcher.

Norman Cassidy, pilot, historian.

Dr John Chapman, Hexham historian.

Dr Eric Clavering for his information on the River Wear.

Steve Clinton, metal detectorist.

Ray Colley, for his staunch help with a very arduous excavation on a Roman road south of Chester-le-Street.

Dennis Coulson, researcher.

John Curry, historian.

Andy Davison for his excellent finds of Roman roads.

The Mayor of Equilines, for his information on the Roman navigation weir at Montignies St Christophe, Hainaut, Belgium.

John S Fenwick, geologist.

Professor Sheppard Frere of Oxford who awarded me the Martin Harrison Prize at Newcastle University, for my dissertation on "The Lost Roman Roads of Durham and Northumberland."

Dr Peter Gill and Norma Gill, excavators and researchers.

Chris Goldsmith, colliery and waggonway historian.

Bob Goodings, BA(Hons), excavator of Cong Burn Roman bridge.

The late Tom Gray, ex-RAF pilot, later history graduate, for his assistance with fieldwork, and for persuading me to become a professional archaeologist.

Hilary Green, BA, researcher.

Professor Dennis Harding, archaeologist, pilot/air photographer.

Peter Harvey, retired miner and team's geologist.

Gordon Heald, Institution of Civil Engineers, Northampton, for his advice on the construction of Roman weirs and spillways.

John and Wendy Hedges, researchers and PR work.

Gordon Henderson, specialist on the Binchester Roman fort.

Mike Hodgson, logistics man, crane driver, marine historian.

Reg Holdsworth, excavator of Cong Burn Roman bridge.

Chief Engineer Peter Houldey and Thelma Houldey, excavators.

Imperial War Museum for the picture of the WW1 RNAS airship.

Ian & Beryl Johnson, finders of Page Bank Roman bridge remains.

Pat Jones, former Commodore of the Ripon Motor Boat Club, for his vast information on ancient and modern inland waterways.

Dr Ian King, researcher.

Robert King, proof reader, modern historian.

Harry Lawson, pilot.

Brenda Locke, aircraft co-pilot/observer, fieldwalker.

Len and Brenda Ludvigsen for their expertise at fieldwork and the discovery of many Roman roads. Also proof readers.

John Maddison, local historian.

Pauline Magee, BA(Hons), archaeologist. Many finds & much work.

Steve Marchant for his photographic expertise, also assistant secretary of the Northern Archaeology Group.

Vivien Matthewson-Dick, proof-reader, public relations officer.

Divers, Rolfe Mitchinson and Bob Middlemass, who found the great Roman treasure on the river bed at Piercebridge, the Corbridge Roman navigation weir and the Corbridge Roman slave-chain.

Don Mitchinson, marine researcher.

Fred Mitchinson, researcher and field walker.

Ian Moss, metal detectorist.

George Nairn for his pictures of old Chester-le-Street.

RB Nelson and PW Norris for their drawings of ancient warships.

The Newport Museum for info on the Barland's Farm Roman boat.

Alan Oliver, researcher.

Captain Dennis Ord, sailing ship master.

Graham Outterside, metal detectorist.

Chief Engineer Neil Pattison, rugged territory field explorer.

The late Joe Relph, pilot and former flying comrade.

Inspector Alan Richardson, historian, communications expert and editor of NAG Newsletter, Chairman of the Northern Archaeology Group of County Durham; for internet information contact: nag @ summerhouse 71.freeserve.co.uk Fax/phone 0191 5840791.

Acknowledgements

Robert Richardson, Chester-le-Street historian.

Dennis Ridley, pilot.

Dr Irene Robinson, expert metal detectorist.

Liz Robinson (BBC), PR and metal detectorist.

The late, Bob Robson MBE, bridge-builder, for his vast amount of information on Roman and other bridges in Northumberland.

The Rolex Company of Geneva who awarded me an International Award for Exploration for my 1983 book, "*The Piercebridge Formula.*"

Ken and Jake Rollings, researchers and excavators.

Carole Ross BA(Hons), archaeologist.

Elizabeth Rowell, for her information on the Tyne Valley.

The late Ward Rutherford, editor of "Ancient Magazine," and former author and war correspondent.

Robert Ryle, farmer, pilot, airstrip owner and operator.

Terry Shaw, historian, researcher & fieldwalker.

Dr Grace Simpson, archaeological consultant.

Dr DJ Smith who taught me about Roman art and who showed me that there were other ways of studying the Romans than looking for them with an aeroplane.

Joe Smith of Grassington for advice on Roman roads of Yorkshire.

The late Ernest W Sockett, university lecturer and archaeologist, for his help with Latin translations.

Rev Rodney Thomas and Michelle Thomas for the use of their church as the headquarters of the Northern Archaeology Group of County Durham.

James Tilt, historian, excavator.

Phil Tweedy DFM for the loan of his "goolie chit."

Kapitein Ruudi Verschoor of the Netherlands Ammunition ship *Singelgracht,* who drew the cartoon of the Roman ox-wagon, while our ship was in a minefield during the Gulf war.

Elizabeth Waller of Piercebridge, who brought my attention to the post holes of the hitherto unknown Roman weir (W4) in the rock river bed of the River Tees opposite Holme House Roman villa.

Robin Walton of Coxhoe for his information on the lost Roman roads of County Durham.

Norah Wanless, for her information on the "*Chester Volunteers.*"

Alan Ward, C.Eng, researcher.

Captain Harry Whitelaw and Lois Whitelaw, numismatists.

Margaret Whyte, New College, Durham, my former boss and present historical advisor.

Dr Joan Wilkinson BDS, researcher. fieldwalker and excavator.

Fred Wood, researcher and fieldwalker.

Tom Wright, air photographer/observer, engineer, historian and former Chairman (now Deputy Chairman) of the Northern Archaeology Group of County Durham.

Monica Young, researcher.

All those people I have met in the countryside who have expressed interest in our work and have given me help and encouragement without me learning their names.

All those hundreds of people who have written to me with enthusiasm and support.

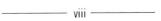

Foreword

In 1983, Raymond Selkirk wrote a book entitled *The Piercebridge Formula*. It was inspired by the author's experiences as an air survey pilot for a professor of archaeology. Because of his background and training, Raymond Selkirk was able to locate and identify evidence missed by most archaeologists, both ground searchers and airborne observers. This experience included several years as a ship's officer. He served on all kinds of merchant ships and also in naval auxiliaries. Part of his sea-time was spent moving troops and heavy military equipment around the world. He served on captured German passenger liners which had been pressed into use as British troopships.

After a few years at sea, he transferred to commercial aviation and flew for several airlines in most parts of the world. During this period he also flew photographic survey aircraft in Central Africa.

His interest in archaeology led him to take a B.A. honours degree in the subject, and his dissertation on the Lost Roman Roads of Northumberland won the Martin Harrison Prize at Newcastle upon Tyne University.

His first book,*The Piercebridge Formula*,won a Rolex International Prize for Exploration. This was presented in London by Sir Vivian Fuchs, the Antarctic explorer. The book sold at £9.95 but it is now worth £120 on the second-hand market (1999 prices).

His next book was entitled *On the Trail of the Legions,*and in 1995, entered the top ten best-sellers at position No.7 with Margaret Thatcher's memoirs at number 8.

When he retired from commercial aviation, he returned to sea on an occasional free-lance basis and served in the Falklands, and also on an ammunition carrier during the entire Gulf War. During this time, further studies gained him a B.Sc honours degree in nautical studies.

As the secretary of the Northern Archaeology Group, he has trained dozens of amateur archaeologists who are now beavering away around our countryside, adding a tremendous amount of hitherto unknown evidence to the meagre discoveries of the last hundred years. Much of this new evidence relates to the Roman period when Chester-le-Street was a staging post in the huge and powerful Roman Empire.

Also the study of our town's short but glorious Saxon cathedral days takes us to Lindisfarne and Iona. Other researches take readers far beyond our town's boundaries. The author says that: "in order to understand Chester-le-Street, we must see it in its much wider context". In the Saxon cathedral days, the see of our ancestors' church stretched from the Tees to the Firth of Forth and from the North Sea to the Irish Sea. We must mark our home town's rightful place in history and also geography, hence the size of this volume which has been financed by the Heritage Lottery Fund, and actively supported by the Chester-le-Street District Council.

Tom Wright,

Chairman of the Northern Archaeology Group of County Durham.

Chester-le-Street and its Place in History

Introduction

Two-hundred-and-sixty miles from London, the Newcastle upon Tyne & Edinburgh express train speeds northwards through County Durham. A few minutes earlier, the train has passed across the viaduct overlooking Durham City and given the passengers a magnificent view of the cathedral and castle which sit on a rocky peninsula, the ancient "Dunholm," formed by an almost complete loop of the River Wear. Very shortly, the driver will begin to apply the brakes for the approach to Newcastle, the River Tyne, and the old Roman frontier of nearly two-thousand years ago.To the north of Durham and eight miles south of Newcastle, a curious tourist might look out of the right-hand carriage window and wonder about the identity of a bold, four-towered story-book-type medieval castle on a hill, and the modest town below, from which protrudes an elegant and lofty church spire. Few trains stop here now and most of the south-north traffic is carried by the busy A1(M) motorway which bypasses the town on its east side.The town is the one-time Saxon cathedral-city of Conceastre or Cuneceastre and its modern name is Chester-le-Street. The earliest written records tell us that the place was inhabited in AD883 by Saxon monks who fled from the Holy Island of Lindisfarne on the Northumberland coast, where Viking raiders had caused death and destruction. The Saxon monks had carried the body of their Saint Cuthbert with them, and on arrival in Conceastre, built a simple wooden church-shrine in the middle of the ruinous Roman fort of Concangis which had lain deserted since the evacuation of the Roman army almost five hundred years previously. At fourteen miles from the sea, the Saxon refugees, who had wandered for seven years in search of a secure retreat, thought that they were safe at last from the Viking sea-raiders.It is extremely likely however that there was a Saxon settlement outside the disused Roman fort well before the arrival of the monks as there is a reference to St Cuthbert visiting the place on one of his missionary journeys from Lindisfarne.I know this town well because I was born in it not long after the Great War of 1914-18. My schooldays were spent there and after half a century of wandering around the world, I am back in the same house where I played as a five-year-old child. My long years of absence were spent as both a mariner and aviator but during my duties in distant places, some fascinating, and others horrific, I never lost the love for my home town and its surrounding countryside, especially the valley of the River Wear, the former *"Vedra Fluvius"* of the Romans.The town wasn't always bypassed by a main road; towards the end of the first century AD, the Romans built their fort on a slight rise above the confluence of their "Vedra" and a much smaller river, the "Con *Fluvius*" (modern Cong Burn). The fort is situated one day's march south of the River Tyne. Strangely, in their fort name (Concangis), the Romans used the name of the tributary, the "Con" instead of the dominant river, "Vedra," and the later Saxons, with the name "Conceastre" followed suit. During leaves from my airline, I would discover the reason for the selection of the minor stream's name when I flew as a part-time air survey pilot for a doctor of archaeology.The

Norman-French conquerors changed the name of the town first to "Ceastre" and then to "Chester" (fort). This later became "Chester in the Street" and "Chester-le-Street" (fort-on-the-road). This Roman road had run from Brough-on-Humber (Petuaria) to Newcastle upon Tyne (Pons Aelius). It passed right by the Concangis Roman fort, the site of which is now occupied by the existing parish church and surrounding school complexes. The same site was used by the late Saxon stone church and the earlier Saxon wooden cathedral-shrine. The ground research for my archaeological survey flights would reveal to me the reason for the Saxon selection of ex-Roman sites for their churches and it wasn't because of the free building stone lying around - the early Saxon churches were built of timber; but more of this later. This book will attempt to cover the history of Chester-le-Street and surrounding area from the melting of the great ice sheets about ten-thousand years ago, to present times. My old friend Mr H W Harbottle MA, in 1976, wrote an excellent little book entitled *Chester-le-Street*. He began by saying: "The history of Chester-le-Street is the history of England in miniature." I have followed his lead and in order to enable readers to understand fully the history of our town, I have spent time on looking at all the influences which forged this story. I have started at what I think is an appropriate beginning for our home location which after the melting of the last great ice sheet, was the bed of a huge lake of glacial melt-water. Sometimes I have had to delve deeply into various subjects. For example it is not sufficient to read about a few odd finds of Roman artefacts recovered in the area. We must understand WHY the Roman fort was built here at all. Much research and many recent archaeological excavations are giving us the answers. Some of these results have been unexpected but nevertheless fascinating. We have to look at other aspects too. Just as no story about the Battle of Britain in 1940 could be told without mentioning the German *Luftwaffe* or Hitler's regime, nor can we explain why the Saxon monks sought refuge here in our town and later Durham, without looking at the Vikings who caused the monks to flee from Lindisfarne in the first place; and so it goes on - one subject brings out others, hence the seemingly large volume.

Raymond Selkirk, BA(Hons) BSc(Hons)

Archaeologist and former survey pilot

Chester-le-Street 1999.

Chapter 1
Prehistoric Period

Time, like an ever-rolling stream,
Bears all its sons away;
They fly forgotten, as a dream
Dies at the opening day.

John Wesley.

Let us go back two-million years in time and four-thousand miles distance to the East African shores of the Indian Ocean. This seems a very strange place to begin the History of Chester-le-Street, but it was there, about that time, that man learned to make stone tools, and with improved weapons, was able to hunt wild animals more efficiently. Also at some uncertain time, man had learned how to make and control fire, and the latter was an important factor in the human beings' increasing longevity due to the various benefits of cooking. Fruit and vegetables can be eaten raw but if certain uncooked or insufficiently cooked meats are consumed, organisms which live in fish and animals may enter human bodies and cause diseases. The best known example is "trichinosis," which humans get from uncooked or undercooked pork products. Tapeworm and other parasitic conditions can be caught by eating undercooked fish of certain kinds.

Early Man probably discovered cooking by accident, by dropping meat into a fire and after recovering it, noticing how much better it tasted. Other accidental uses of fire such as the clearing of woodland, the production of pottery, and later, the discovery of metals also resulted, but these subjects will be dealt with shortly.

The human hunting creatures spread slowly over a very long period from Africa and India into the inhospitable climates of Asia and Europe, and knowledge of fire allowed their caves and other dwellings to be warmed artificially. Their skins lost the dark colour which was caused by the action of the ultra-violet rays of tropical sunshine on the pigmentation "melanin" which is an ingredient in the skins of all human races.

The arrival of these human hunters into Northern Europe was delayed however, by an Ice Age - not the last one, but the one before that, which ended around 250,000 years before our present Christian era.

In order to produce a comprehensive history and pre-history of our home area, we must start with the melting of the last great ice sheet which covered Northern Europe until about twelve-thousand years ago. The causes of these Ice Ages are not fully understood, and there have been at least four of them; the last one, known as the "Devensian" formed about 120,000 bc (bc = inexact version of BC). When the two-mile-thick glacier finally melted about

10,000 bc, it left our topography much the same as it is now except for a few gravitational adjustments which will be mentioned shortly, the ravages of the human race, and the drying-up of post-glacial lakes. In this residual landscape, shaped by the ice-cap, the archaeological evidence we seek lies in the top few feet of soil.

As mentioned above, the causes of the Ice Ages are still poorly understood but let us say that over extremely long periods, the polar ice-caps expand and contract. During the expansions, tremendous volumes of water become locked-up as ice over the land masses and the resultant sea levels are very low. During the subsequent melting of the ice-sheets, sea levels rise. This is why there are ancient raised beaches on some of our mountain sides and these were formed in warm periods or "interglacials"; and sunken beaches below the waves were formed during glaciations.

The remnants of our last Northern Hemisphere glaciation are the two-mile-thick ice-sheets over Greenland. From time to time, similar ice-sheets covered most of Britain.

Due to a warming climate causing melting, the release of tremendous weights of ice, causes the Earth's surface to spring back very slowly to its former shape. This is called "isostasy" and is a very slow process, in Northern Britain taking a thousand years to spring back up about one foot. Geological forces and weathering also alter the Earth's masses over millions of years but that is beyond the scope of this book.

The last Ice Age-but-one retreated a quarter million years ago and the sea levels fluctuated. This was well before the period of history we are concerned with here. The ice would however return closer to our time and begin to chisel and wash out the landscape to a close approximation of what it is today.

This last ice-sheet advanced about 70,000 bc and drove our remote ancestors to the south of the Thames. What was to become Scotland and Northern England, was once again covered by an ice-sheet thousands of feet thick. In this slowly southerly-moving ice was embedded billions of tons of soil and boulders scraped from the hills of the north; so the future Scotland lost a large percentage of fertile soil to the lands of the future England.

These last ice-sheets retreated from the British Islands about twelve-thousand years ago, and during the melting, the billions of tons of ice-transported debris were deposited. One of these "melt-dumps" was of sand, and this formed the hill now called Newcastle Bank at the north end of the present Chester-le-Street. The modern Civic Centre and the Police Station stand on this ridge.

Before the last Ice Age, the River Wear had flowed along Team Valley and was a tributary of the River Tyne. The ice-deposited sand of Newcastle Bank blocked the channel of the River Wear, and the site of our future Chester-le-Street became the bed of a large lake which had a surface level of 140m above the present Ordnance Survey Datum. This is well above the contour of Newcastle Bank, but an extra barrier-dam was a huge retreating glacier just off the line of the present coastline of Durham.

The huge glacial lake, "Lake Wear" as it is known to geologists, had two main overflows: one to the south through the Ferryhill Gap which was cut by raging floods from melting ice, and the Ryhope Gap, formed in the same manner.

About 8,000 bc, the rising North Sea broke through the present Dover area and formed what is now known as the English Channel. Britain thus became an island, cut off from Europe by a shallow sea. About the same time, over on the other side of the North Pole, the land bridge between Asia and Alaska became submerged, forming the Bering Strait between the Asian and North American continents. No doubt, the early inhabitants of North America had crossed this land bridge before its inundation.

The North Sea is still very shallow, and mammoth and reindeer bones have been trawled-up from the Dogger Bank. The English Channel is also shallow except for the Hurd Deep which is a trench north of the Channel Islands and the Cherbourg Peninsula. This trench has the typical shape of a sub-glacial valley rather like the channels under Greenland's ice which have been sounded from the surface of the ice-cap by sonar equipment. It is now thought that Greenland may be two, or even three, islands.

Although our hills and valleys are almost the way the last ice left them, some changes have taken place to coastline shapes, with losses to erosion (take the case of Marsden Rock). There are also gains elsewhere with siltation and shingle deposits. There are slight changes in the elevation of the land surfaces due to the slow return to equilibrium ("isostasy") after the release of the tremendous weight of ice. This vertical flexing is very slow but continues to date. In Norway, some of the Vikings' landing stages have risen several feet out of the water. In Britain, the movement is much smaller and not uniform over the whole country. North of the Bristol-Humber line, the land is rising extremely slowly while in south-eastern England, for some reason, it is still subsiding. The whole subject is very complex.

The changes in shorelines due to erosion and siltation must be taken into account when we study coastal archaeological sites. As will be seen later, of great importance to the history of our home area and Chester-le-Street in particular, will be the migration of rivers and scouring actions, which seem to be poorly understood by many historians and archaeologists.

During glaciations, the sea levels are low, therefore the gradients of the rivers are increased and as the ice melts, deeper river beds are scoured-out. During the intervening periods of high sea levels (such as the present post-glacial period), the rivers are comparatively sluggish and are depositing gravel. Due to a misunderstanding of the subject, the opposite is often claimed, but positive proof of a general lack of river bed-cutting in the last few thousand years is that the bases of two-thousand-year-old Roman bridge-pier bases remain intact in our rivers with not even the Roman tool-marks scoured from the stones.

On occasion, on the line of these Roman bridges, jammed between river bed boulders, lie Roman artefacts in pristine condition just where the Romans dropped them as offerings to the river gods. Over two-thousand such artefacts have been recovered recently by expert divers, from the line of the Tofts Field Dere Street Roman bridge at Piercebridge.

Now let us return to the peoples who occupied the land after the formation of the North Sea and the English Channel.

The Mesolithic (Middle Stone Age) people had no knowledge of farming, and continued their hunting, fishing and food gathering. One of their sites has been identified at Star Carr, in the Vale of Pickering which was a huge lake at the time. Star Carr was an island then. Artefacts have been radio-carbon-dated to c7500 bc. The mud deposits on the site preserved wooden objects as well as bone arrow-points and small harpoon-heads. This former great lake of Yorkshire was the result of the melt-waters of the glacier collecting in a valley which had been blocked by ice-deposited debris.

We are now fairly sure that this lake which we call "Lake Pickering" still existed in Roman times and was used as an inland transport waterway by the Roman bargemen as at many places around the 23 metre contour line, thousands of Roman ship and barge copper rivets have been found by metal dctectorists. The wooden hulls have rotted away. It is likely that the lake still lingered into Viking times as there is a place called "Flotmanby" which is Old Norse for: "The place of the ferry-boatman," but that is leaping ahead...

The edge of Greenland's icecap. Further inland, the snow becomes ten-thousand feet deep and the mountains are hidden. Fifteen-thousand years ago, 90% of Britain was covered by a similar icecap. This photograph was taken by the author on the ferry flight of an air taxi from Sunderland Airport to the Piper aircraft factory at Lock Haven, Pennsylvania, for a major overhaul.

About 4,000 bc, significant changes took place in Britain when settlers with a knowledge of agriculture and animal husbandry arrived.

These "Neolithic" (New Stone Age) peoples are classified under this heading because their improved polished stone axes, with holes drilled for hafts, show their advancing technology. They also used pottery but it was their ability to farm the land which allowed them to follow a totally different life-style from the nomadic hunter-fishers who had been forced to follow herds of wild animals. This significant change is often termed the "Neolithic Revolution" and happened in Western Asia about 10,000 bc, but a few thousand years later in Western Europe and Britain.

The new arrivals must have made the Channel crossing in skin boats, bringing their animals and seed with them. They were from Celtic tribes which spread right across France and southern Europe. Don't forget, there was no such thing as an Englishman in Britain. The

Nordic Angles, Saxons and Jutes, who would become the first members of the "English" race did not arrive until the end of the Roman occupation, about five-thousand years into the future.

The Neolithic farmers built rectangular timber huts and buried their dead communally in elongated burial mounds which we call "long barrows." While thousands have been destroyed, a great many survive and provide the most obvious evidence of the period. They are sometimes built of earth piled over an artificial cave of huge stones, or thousands of smaller stones piled over a similar megalithic chamber.

Neolithic (New Stone Age) tools.

Some of these "long barrows" are extremely complex and a vast number of man-hours must have been spent in their creation. This tells us that the workers lived in an organised society which could support tasks other than essential ones of food production, habitation-building and forest clearance.

Perhaps these burial mounds were more than mere tombs. It is thought in some circles that the human remains were taken out at intervals for rituals. Intact skeletons are seldom found and piles of bones are usually intermixed. Maybe the barrows were the first pagan religious monuments in our countryside. The practice of barrow-burial continued for several thousand years. New designs appeared and there were switches from communal to single burials; inhumations to cremations and vice-versa. Neolithic enclosures known to us as

A Nineteenth Century view of the remains of a Neolithic burial mound. The stone chamber was once covered by a huge mound, part of which survives on top of the capping stone. Location: Bryn Celli Ddu, Anglesey. It is thought that there are burial mounds on Waldridge Fell but these have yet to be verified by excavation. The nearest proven one is at Copt Hill, Houghton-le-Spring.

"causewayed camps" have been found in southern England, dated to the Fourth Millenium BC, and these consist of a number of concentric ditches and internal banks. The ditches are seldom continuous, with uncut ground forming causeways. Their purpose is unclear as there is little evidence for occupation. Windmill Hill in Wiltshire is the best known example and has been dated to c3300 bc.

Late Neolithic Man (and early Bronze Age Man too) built monuments known to us as "henges," which are found only in the British Isles. In addition to the famous "Stonehenge" which had later additions in the Bronze Age, many crop marks are seen from the air, of circular ditched and banked enclosures, some with one entrance, and others with two diametrically opposed. Henges often have extra features such as circles of upright stones, as at Stonehenge and Avebury, or timber posts which at one time graced Durrington Walls and Woodhenge. Other features include burials, pits, and occasionally a long avenue-type enclosure known to us as a *cursus*. Henges usually produce Neolithic pottery.

In the early 1970s, I was flying as Professor Dennis Harding's air survey pilot and on one flight, we were just preparing to join the landing pattern at Sunderland/Usworth Airport after a long search, when we noticed a most spectacular crop mark of the oval shape of the

*The remains of a Neolithic "Henge" monument near RAF Dishforth, Yorkshire. The Pilot,
Squadron-leader A. Moffat, demonstrates how low-angle sunlight reveals the contours of
ancient sites, with highlights and shadows.*

buried ditches of what we thought might be a "henge monument," just to the south of
Hastings Hill (NZ 353 542) near Sunderland. In addition there was a second crop mark of an
elongated rectangle of the *cursus* type (because it was thought at one time that they resembled
race-tracks!). There is a prominent example at Stonehenge. Our Hastings Hill *cursus* ran due
south and was lost under the A19(T) motorway but seemed to be lined up on the distant
ancient burial mound at Copt Hill (NZ 353 493) near Houghton-le-Spring, which contains both
Neolithic and Bronze Age remains. There has been a second burial mound at Copt Hill just a
couple of hundred yards to the south-west of the surviving Copt Hill tree-covered barrow,
but it has been ploughed away. The site is still visible from the air.

Our "henge monument" lacked the usual opposite entrances and this was puzzling.
Professor Anthony Harding of Durham University, an expert on the Stone and Bronze Ages,
now tells me that our "henge monument" is actually a Neolithic "causewayed camp," an
equally mysterious Neolithic structure.

There are other suspected burial-mounds in the same area. Two prominent ones are large
tree-covered mounds at Warden Law (NZ 374 503). It was argued at one time by some
academics that these were merely "drumlins" which are heaps of debris deposited through
holes in melting ice-sheets. A few years ago however, a small boy was throwing stones at a

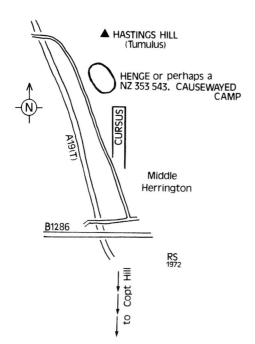

▲ HASTINGS HILL
(Tumulus)

HENGE or perhaps a
NZ 353 543. CAUSEWAYED
CAMP

CURSUS

A19(T)

Middle
Herrington

B1286

RS
1972

to Copt Hill

In 1972, Professor Dennis Harding and the author, while preparing to join the air traffic control circuit at Usworth-Sunderland, spotted a "Henge" monument, or possibly a "Causewayed Camp," just to the south of Hastings Hill. Hastings Hill is a natural hill but has been used as a ready-made burial mound by Neolithic people. To the south of the oval crop mark was a "cursus," of the type which can be seen approaching "Stonehenge." These avenues were so-named because old antiquarians thought they were race-tracks. They are still not understood, but probably served a pagan religious function. This is up to now, the only known cursus in the north of England.

pot in a pond at the foot of one of these mounds, fortunately without breaking the vessel. His curiosity persuaded him to fish it out of the pond and it was subsequently proved to be a Bronze Age burial urn which contained cremation ashes. All mention by "experts" of "drumlins" ceased.

With regard to the Hastings Hill henge and *cursus*, Professor Dennis Harding's aerial photographs have appeared in many magazines and history books. There are suspected Bronze Age burial mounds on Chester-le-Street's Waldridge Fell. The most prominent one is at map ref NZ 247 497, to the north of the Waldridge - Edmondsley road. A Bronze Age shield was found near Edmondsley at Broomey Holme Farm and an Iron Age burial was found in 1889 when a grave was being dug in St Peter's churchyard Sacriston. The Iron Age body had been contracted into a cist (pronounced kist) which was a stone-lined roughly cubic chamber. The bones were much decayed, with a beaker of food or water beside them. The remains are now in the British Museum.

Britain's first roads seem to have been constructed in the Neolithic period: in Somerset, corduroy timber trackways dating to the late-Neolithic have been found preserved in peat. The trackways had crossed marshy areas, linking settlements on higher ground.

There has been much publicity about the astronomical alignments of stone circles and henges. At first, archaeologists resisted the new theories (as they invariably do), but now, to varying degrees, under the weight of computer-derived calculations, the celestial orientations of ancient structures are being accepted.

Elsewhere, old academic theories are being exterminated and a prime example of this is the discovery by engineer Bauval that the three Pyramids at Giza form a facsimile in plan of Orion's Belt in the constellation of Orion (the ancient Egyptian sky-god). The Great Pyramid was not merely a tomb: it had more important functions - two rectangular shafts (previously assumed to have been ventilators) connect the King's Chamber to the outside faces of the pyramids - one to the north face and the other to the south. Two similar shafts join the Queen's chamber to north and south faces. Due to a gyroscopic precession of the Earth's axis which takes 25,800 years to complete one "wobble," the stars

The plan-view of the Iron Age oppidum (large developed hillfort) at Maiden Castle, Dorset. The Romans captured this citadel in spite of its complex entrances and multiple defences and moved the survivors to the Roman town of Dorchester. The nearest known Iron Age hillfort to Chester-le-Street is another "Maiden Castle" NZ 283 417, north of Shincliffe, on the opposite side of the River Wear to the suspected Roman site at Old Durham Farm.

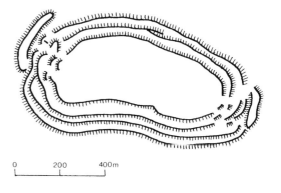

```
0        200       400m
└────────┴─────────┘
```

are no longer in the same directions in the sky, but a highly sophisticated astronomical calculator has shown that in the year 2450 BC, the southern King's shaft was lined-up exactly at the meridian crossing (due south) on the star which is the left hand marker of Orion's belt. The Great Pyramid represents this star Alnitak on the ground plan. The King's northern shaft was lined up on the Pole Star of ancient Egyptian times, which was Thuban in the Constellation of Draco.

The southern Queen's shaft was lined-up on Sirius (Egyptian sky-goddess Isis) at the meridian crossing, and the northern shaft on Thuban. Thus the Great Pyramid was not just a tomb but also a long-range "gun battery" which fired the souls of the dead Kings and Queens to the holy spots in the sky. The international Egyptologists are mortified at the discoveries, and across the world many academic "experts" have lapsed into a sullen silence. It seems that the ancient peoples were far cleverer mathematicians and astronomers than has been thought hitherto. We cannot therefore regard the builders of Stonehenge and our own more modest Hastings Hill complex as the work of backward savages.

We do not know how early man discovered how to manufacture pottery but it is extremely likely that a piece of clay was dropped accidentally into a fire. The resultant terracotta may have sparked off experiments. In the relatively low temperatures of the fires of early mankind, the clay would have been "baked" rather than "fired" and this baked clay is termed "terracotta" by modern archaeologists. It looks as if the Neolithic farmers were the first people in Britain to master the art of pottery-making, although in the early part of this period, experts describe them as "Aceramic" or "Pre-pottery Neolithic." This gives us a rough starting point for pottery production in Britain and Northern Europe.

The main constituent of pottery is pot clay and this term mainly describes the size of the particles in the clay which is usually the mineral kaolinite. The tiny crystals of kaolinite are flat and plate-like. When the clay is wet, these crystals have a film of water between them, and the clay can be moulded by hand or on a potter's wheel. The clay is then dried out until the crystals are no longer free to move. When this drying reaches "leather hardness," the vessels can have decorations incised, impressed or burnished into them, or lugs and handles added with a sticky clay adhesive. When even drier, a "slop" which is a thin slurry of clay for decoration or a good finish can be added. When the pots are completely dry, they are fired in a kiln. The purpose of firing is to weld the clay particles together.

The kaolinite group of clays melts at about 1770 degrees Centigrade but this temperature would have been far beyond the reach of early kilns. However if certain impurities act as fluxes, the clay particles will "sinter" together (coalesce into a single mass under the influence of heat, without actually liquefying) at temperatures between 1000 to 1200 degrees Centigrade for most ancient pot clays. It is however unlikely that early kilns reached these temperatures and much of the clay was unsintered and is thus termed "baked terracotta".

The discovery of the production of metals also probably began accidentally when rocks containing ores, possibly acting as a fire surround, reached melting point in a draught or a wind. The later improved kilns of the Bronze Age reached higher temperatures and the production of "fired" clay may have started as a by-product of metal working.

Significant changes occurred in Britain around 2,500 bc with the arrival of the "Beaker Peoples." This name is derived from their distinctive beaker-shaped pottery drinking-vessels. These utensils are usually found beside burials in barrows which had now become circular in shape. These new-style barrows showed no signs of the dead having been disturbed for rituals, as in earlier Stone Age long barrows.

Some archaeologists argue that there was an "invasion" of Beaker People, but others think that the artefacts arrived by trade, or a transfer of manufacturing techniques. Skulls found in burials are round, unlike the ones from earlier periods, so the "invasion theory" holds favour at the moment. The importance of the Beaker Period is that metallurgy was introduced into Britain at this time, proof of which are copper daggers and ornaments found with the beaker burials. The Bronze Age was dawning. Bronze is an alloy of copper and tin and is a much harder material than copper. It is also easier to handle and pour than pure copper. Pure molten copper has an affinity for oxygen and is what modern foundry workers call "wild" because its thirst for oxygen causes it to become filled with air bubbles. A small percentage of tin gets rid of this problem as well as producing the hard alloy, bronze.

It is likely that the discovery was made accidentally by using copper ore which contained tin as an impurity.

A further influx of settlers known as the "Wessex Culture" arrived in Britain in the Second Millenium BC. No settlements have been found but further changes in barrow fashions identify the culture. The circular tombs have several variations such as "bell," "disc," "saucer," and "pond" barrows. Inhumations predominate in the early Wessex barrows, and cremations in the later ones. Rich grave-goods are found with the burials. These include objects of gold, copper, bronze, amber, faience, shale, bone, and various pottery vessels. Most of these materials are not available in Wessex and demonstrate that the inhabitants were extensive traders.

It is possible that the missing settlements of this period are hidden under the later Iron Age hillforts as it is now thought that this type of defended enclosure was used in the late Bronze Age. Radio-carbon-dating has shown some surprisingly early origins for some hillforts. Examples are: 1470 BC at Mam Tor in Derbyshire and 1100 BC at Dinorben in Denbighshire.

The various fashions of Bronze Age barrows remain in our landscape although thousands have been destroyed by later agriculture. Even so, circular burial mounds usually had ditches around them and these ditches, even though infilled, often manifest themselves as crop marks, easily visible from an aircraft.

Barrows are often on high ground but the builders have seldom selected the peaks as sites. Quite often the peaks are out of sight of the immediate valley so the builders have placed their mounds on high shoulders which are easily visible. They would not have been visible if the valleys had been heavily wooded and this is just one more pointer towards extensive early forest clearance.

Small circular copses frequently cover burial mounds but care must be taken not to confuse them with round, tree-covered fox-coverts of fairly recent times. Medieval artificial rabbit warrens can also resemble barrows. Other "false barrows" may be "drumlins" which as previously mentioned are heaps of ice-transported spoil, dropped during the melting of the glaciers; spoil-heaps from lead-mining; and other such activities which can on occasions, also leave earthworks which resemble the genuine ancient evidence.

The square and rectangular field-systems called "Celtic lynchets" by the famous aerial archaeologist, Major O G S Crawford of the Royal Flying Corps, (later Professor), have been in use during the Bronze Age and possibly earlier. Crawford was correct when he said that these fields were pre-Roman, but it looks as if they were also pre-Celtic.

It took a long time for man to discover how to produce and use the metal, "iron." The Iron Age began in the later Second Millenium in western Asia, and in Europe during the early 1st millenium BC. It seems that the knowledge of iron-working spread westwards from the Middle East after the collapse of the Hittites which allowed the secret to escape. The Romans were an Iron Age people but British historians use the term "Iron Age" to describe the people between the Bronze Age and the Roman occupation of Britain. Technically, we are still in a kind of Iron Age, but perhaps it would be more accurate to call our present status, the Aluminium-alloy/Plastic/Microchip Age.

Because our establishment has divided ancient man's development into the "Three Age System" - Stone Ages, Bronze Age and Iron Age, it does not mean that on the change from stone to bronze, all stone artefacts became redundant, and an immediate switch to bronze was made. The Romans in Britain were still using sharp flint blades and scrapers in cooking, and to prepare animal skins for clothing. Bronze, gold and lead have continued to be used ever since the Bronze Age right up to our present time.

The gradual change to the use of iron implements was beneficial to the natives of Britain because, not only is iron a very hard durable and useful metal, the ores are extremely common in these islands. According to the historian Longstaffe, there was in his time, evidence of ancient Iron Age, Roman and possibly Viking extraction of iron ore near our home town of Chester-le-Street, up the valley of the Con/Cong/Cone, through Whitehill and up across the fells. This was borne out a few years ago when we excavated a small Roman bridge across the Cong Burn at the foot of Pelton Fell Bank. This bridge had carried a Roman road to Concangis (Ch-le-Str) which ran directly from Ebchester Roman fort, via Stanley. The road in the vicinity of the bridge was built almost entirely of iron slag. This was quite common in Roman roads: a farmer in central England reported that during a thunderstorm, a lightning flash struck a Roman road in one of his fields and the strike exploded about a quarter-mile of ancient slag-constructed road out of the ground.

Pure iron melts at 1535 degrees Centigrade, a temperature which was unobtainable artificially before the 19th century AD.

However if iron is smelted with carbon as a fuel, the iron absorbs some of this carbon from the fire and when the carbon content reaches 3 to 4.5 per cent, the melting point falls to 1150 degrees Centigrade - not much higher than the melting point of copper (1083 degrees C), or the temperature of an efficient pottery kiln. However, the resulting alloy, "cast iron" or "pig iron" is brittle, hard and useless for the manufacture of tools and weapons. If the Romans got the temperature of their furnace too high, the resultant cast iron was thrown away into refuse pits. The ancient peoples therefore did not let the iron become molten - they took it from the furnace as a spongy red-hot mass called a "bloom." This was then worked into shape by hammering. Unknown to our ancients, this hammering also got rid of most of the carbon. The sparks flying away under the blacksmith's hammer are particles of carbon being driven out. Thus when our ancient peoples' blooming iron masses were beaten into shape, when the carbon content dropped to near one per-cent, they had unwittingly produced an excellent iron which was almost steel. The latter is a compound which contains 0.3 to one per-cent carbon.

People often wonder why in ancient times, charcoal was so important. In later times, if it had not been for the discovery that "coke," a product of coal, could do the same job, there would be no trees left in Britain.

Lead, because of its low melting point, would probably have been one of the first metals to come to the notice of ancient peoples, but because it was so soft, it was virtually useless until man used it as an alloy with copper and therefore produced lead-bronze as well as the more common tin-bronze.

The Romans however used thousands of tons of lead. They extracted silver which is commonly found with lead. This silver was used for coinage. Pigs of Roman lead, often found by archaeologists, are marked *"Ex-Argentium"* (silver removed). This label reduced theft of lead pigs from mines which were usually operated by convict or prisoner of war labour because slaves were too valuable to be given a slow death in this manner.

After the extraction of silver, the Romans exported countless thousands of tons of lead from Britain for the manufacture, all over their empire, of miles of lead pipes, cisterns, and also on occasion, sheets of roofing material for high class buildings. The Romans knew all about lead-poisoning but they also understood that if water pipes of lead were allowed to grow an oxide on the insides, the danger of contaminated water from them was greatly reduced.

Although silver is found on its own on occasion in some parts of the world, it is mostly obtained from the LEAD ore "galena" in which silver sulphide occurs as an impurity. After smelting the ore, silver was recovered by the process of cupellation. This involves the melting of the lead and its oxidation leaving the silver behind. Silver is soft and could be "cold-worked" but was usually alloyed with other metals.

Air pollution is a very old curse and in their quest for lead and silver, the Greeks and Romans poisoned their air from belching conical-shaped smelters. How do we know about this ancient pollution? The two-mile-thick Greenland ice-cap holds each season's unmelted snow in layers similar to tree-rings. All deposits from the atmosphere sit in varying thicknesses in the annual layers, each of which has been identified by counting, comparing and labelling drilled cores.

Between 500 BC and AD 300, enough lead precipitated onto Greenland to equal 15% of the lead deposited there by the burning of leaded petrol from 1930 to 1990.

The Greenland ice holds accurate data from most of the world's weather and volcanic disturbances. The thickness of layers of ash from the eruption of Vesuvius in AD 79 can be measured, and the explosion of the volcanic island of Krakatoa in the Sunda Strait (Java/Sumatra) in 1883, is marked by a significant band of debris.

In their heyday, the smelters of the Roman Empire produced about 90,000 tons of lead ingots per year. Roman Britain contributed to this.

Pliny the Elder in AD 77 told us that: "the lead refiners cover their faces, otherwise noxious and deadly vapours are inhaled".

Trading probably introduced iron objects into Britain but a comprehensive knowledge of iron production arrived with the coming of the "Belgae," a wave of invaders of Celtic origin. Their home had been northern France in the last few centuries BC, but many of them were evacuating Gaul ahead of the Roman conquest of that land.

It is not possible to state a firm date for the arrival of the first iron-workers in Britain. It looks as if the same tribes had begun immigration into Britain in the Bronze Age as there was a continuation of use of farmland and cemeteries.

The new arrivals brought with them, in addition to the latest skills in iron-working, more sophisticated weaponry, coinage, and the potter's wheel.

From Roman sources, we know that their fortified administrative settlements were known as *oppida*. Some of them, such as Maiden Castle in Dorset, were extremely complex. The *oppidum* at Maiden Castle was the fourth feature on the same site, having been preceded by a Neolithic causewayed camp, a long barrow, and an Iron Age hillfort. The hillfort had developed into the more complex *oppidum*.

Right throughout Britain, hundreds of these hillforts survive, most of them on well-selected, easily defended positions. They are generally circular in shape but often follow a hill-contour which produces an oval or perhaps irregular perimeter. The design is usually a ditch surrounding a timber-revetted earth-and-stone rampart. Sometimes dry-stone walling was used to revet the ramparts. Where there were high sea-cliffs, promontories have been formed into forts by digging ditches over narrow necks of land.

The entrances of hillforts were cunningly constructed but were not as complex as those of the larger *oppida*.

The buildings inside the hillforts were circular huts. It seems that Iron Age Britain was a very warlike place with one tribe against the next. When the Roman occupation took place, inter-tribal conflict was discouraged and evidence of this can be seen from the air in the form of hut circles outside the ramparts of the hillforts.

Pax Romana would render the fortifications obsolete, but we will come to that before long.

We have an eye-witness account of Iron Age Britain of about 320 BC: the great navigator Pytheas, from Massilia (Marseilles), evaded the Carthaginian blockade, passed through the Straits of Gibraltar and headed north. Perhaps he was trying to find the trading secrets of the Carthaginians, such as the source of the tin they obtained from an island in north-western Europe.

Pytheas talked of the islands of "Albion" and "Ierne" and described chariots which he saw in operation in Belerium (Cornwall), and bread, cake and mead which he tasted in Kent. He mentioned several geographical peculiarities, notably the large tides. He circumnavigated Ireland and then pressed on northwards to an island which he called "Thule" (probably Iceland), six days sailing from Britain and one day south of "the great frozen sea." So much for the myth that ancient navigators hugged the land.

There is evidence that the Iron Age tribes used a network of roads which often followed the high ground and are known as "ridgeways." These roads probably originated in much earlier periods. The Romans who would shortly enter the scene in Britain, paved some of these tracks and incorporated them into their military network, thus explaining why a straight Roman road suddenly meandered for a few miles in a most un-Roman fashion.

From the air, I have counted over sixty Iron Age hillforts in Northumberland and southern Scotland. There is also a large number in Yorkshire but there are few in Durham. If there were coastal cliff-top promontory forts, they will have gone due to the soft nature of Durham's sea cliffs which are eroding at a fast rate. Also, our county is very difficult for archaeology due to the amount of damage by industry. Although the scars are healing now, the pit-heaps and their subsequent removals; open-cast mining; quarries; lead mines and spoil heaps; railways; shipyards; and factories have obscured the scene for airborne searchers. Nevertheless, extensive new information about our ancient history is there, even if well camouflaged.

The nearest Iron Age hillfort to Chester-le-Street is Maiden Castle, between Durham and Shincliffe. Surely there must have been one on Penshaw Hill before the monument was

The crop mark of an Iron Age hillfort at Grinsdale on the River Eden to the west of Carlisle, map ref NY 375 585. The Romans may have occupied this site as a Roman road appears to run to the riverside entrance of the hillfort from the corner of the field centre-left. Bonnie Prince Charles also camped here in 1745. The search continues for Iron Age sites in County Durham.

constructed, but I will mention that peculiar hill in due course when other subjects are discussed.

There is an Iron Age settlement on the hill to the south of Shildon at NZ 229 233. A newly-discovered Roman road from Mordon to Staindrop, via the spot height of 208m in Toytop Plantation, passes just to the north of this native fortification. Just to the west of Mordon, the Romans have crossed an ancient lake via a ferry.

Before we move on to the Roman invasions of Britain and the subsequent quest for the purpose and siting of Chester-le-Street's Roman fort, we must spend a little time on archaeological techniques to enable students to understand better the methods used to obtain information.

Aerial view of Maiden Castle Iron Age oppidum (tribal-hillfort)

The forthcoming chapter deals with archaeological techniques which range from aerial surveys to electronics. The most important archaeological technique however is fieldwalking and this requires only an experienced eye for reading the landscape. Skill comes from practise and it is astonishing how much hitherto unknown information can be gained without excavations.

This photograph shows three archaeologists of the Northern Archaeology Group standing on the tomb of an important Roman official. The location is one mile south of the Roman fort of High Rochester (Bremenium). The Roman road Dere Street runs right past this graveyard. Several high-class tombs have had their stonework robbed out for field walls etc but a sharp-eyed observer can detect about fifty lesser graves which show up as small mounds. The latter probably contain cremation urns.

Bremenium is located at a Roman crossroads and there is also a little-known aqueduct system in the area, a branch of which passes close to the above graves.

The archaeologists shown here are: from left to right, Norman Cassidy, pilot; Rolfe Mitchinson, diver, and Tom Wright, chief engineer of the Seaham Habour Dock Company, and former chairman of NAG. This view is to the north towards the Roman fort.

An old painting of the Roman tombs; the square ones have now gone. This view is to the east and the Roman road runs along the base of the hill.

Chapter 2
Archaeological Techniques

Operta Aperta
(Hidden things are revealed)
Motto of 16 [Air Reconnaissance] Squadron, Royal Flying Corps

Nature's archaeological target markers

It is well known that under certain conditions, tell-tale marks manifest themselves in open country and if viewed from above, the shapes of these marks often reveal the location and identity of buried features. These give-away marks can be seen as differential colouring of vegetation above buried features (crop marks); white-outlined shapes produced by a thin dusting of snow collecting in slight hollows, or drifting along ridges (snow marks); shapes visible in bare ground where the farmer has filled in an old ditch with a different coloured soil (soil marks); and shadowy shapes produced by low angle sunlight outlining undulations almost imperceptible at ground level (shadow marks).

The manifestations were observed long before the development of aeroplanes: about 1740, the antiquarian, William Stukeley was ridiculed when he said that from a hilltop, he could see the distinctive shape of a Roman temple in a field of corn. Pioneer balloonists also reported similar sightings but it was not until the tremendous expansion of aviation in the 1914-18 World War that serious notice was taken of the phenomena. The various types of marks are explained as follows:

Crop marks

For crop marks to show, two conditions must be met. Firstly, the right type of crop must be planted in the field which contains the hidden archaeological site (cereal crops give the best results by far), and secondly, a drought or period of dry weather be experienced. The ancient peoples were enthusiastic ditch-diggers and even though infilled, these deep cuttings in the subsoil retain water, and during dry weather, the roots of a cereal easily penetrate the loose infill with the result that the crop over the ditch grows taller, thicker and of a deeper shade of green. This is known as a "positive crop mark." Where the hard subsoil has not been disturbed, the crop's roots reach the level of the subsoil and stop, resulting in a uniform shade of medium green.

Over old foundations or road metalling, the crop grows stunted and of a yellow-green colour. This is a "negative crop mark." When a cereal crop is ripe, the positive crop mark is still visible as a deeper gold colour and the negative mark as a more watery yellow.

Upper diagram

A. *Roman ditch outside fort wall;* **B.** *Fort wall;* **C.** *Earth rampart behind fort wall;* **D.** *Topsoil in Roman times;* **E.** *Subsoil BC.*

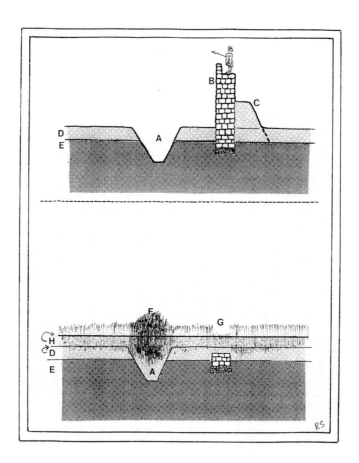

Lower diagram

A. *The Roman ditch is still there but full of topsoil, and the fort and rampart have gone.*

F. *During a dry spell, the cereal crop can send its roots into the deeper topsoil in the old Roman ditch and the crop grows thicker and higher causing a positive crop mark.*

G. *The crop's growth is stunted over wall foundations, causing a negative crop mark.*

H. *The present level of the surface, due to earthworm action and debris etc, is about two feet higher than the surface in Roman times (D).*

What Stukeley had seen from his hilltop was the crop mark of a Roman temple. About the same period, negative crop marks were reported in France over the ploughed-out remains of circular burial mounds. On these, plant growth was sparse and they were known locally in northern France as *danses de fees* (fairy dances).

Even after the crop is harvested, the thick growth over the infilled ditch can be seen as a deeper colour in the remaining stubble and a suitable name for this would be a "stubble mark." Crop marks can show up in plants other than cereals, such as peas and beans or sugar beet, but the contrasting marks in these, and other crops are much inferior to those produced by wheat, oats and barley.

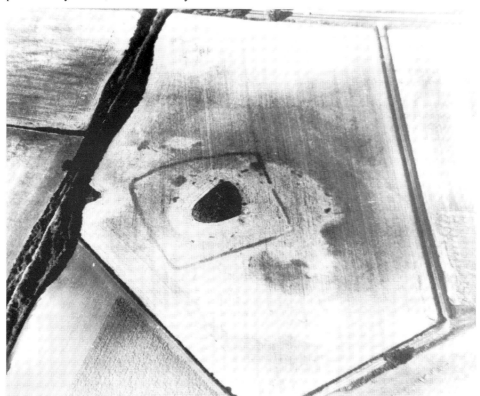

A Roman-period Iron Age enclosure at Dene House Farm, Thornley, Co. Durham, NZ 354 388. These settlements were simple Celtic native farmsteads and are usually termed: "Romano-British settlements" (or RB sites). This one is known to pilots as "The Fried Egg site." The yolk of the egg is a rocky outcrop which presumably provided an excellent foundation for a large circular hut. The single entrances to these Celtic farms were nearly always in the eastern sides, probably to face the rising Sun. There are scores of these sites in County Durham. It looks as if the natives tried to copy the Roman square shape but seldom got it right.

Crop mark of a previously unknown Roman fortlet, NZ 143 162, (above centre) at Winston, on the top of the cliff above the River Tees. Dr Gale reported a Roman road here; he was correct. The Roman road can be seen descending the hill to the left of the modern road, just right of bottom centre. The mirror image of the Roman road (a Roman surveyor's trademark) can be seen on the opposite side of the river, running from centre to left centre. The Romans must have had a bridge or ford in this vicinity. The ditch of the fortlet is too regular for that of a native RB site and there is an entrance on the south side.

A suspected Roman fort, previously undiscovered, showing as a soil mark at Elstob, Co. Durham, NZ 338 240. The modern road in the background is on top of, or in close proximity to Cade's Roman road. This Roman road runs from Newcastle upon Tyne to Brough on Humber passing Chester-le-Street en-route.

A suspected Roman fort in Scotland at map ref NT 883 653 on the hill to the east of Press Mains Farm, 2 miles west-north-west of Eyemouth. The site is showing as shadow marks in the field on the right, and crop marks in the field on the left. The marks are the characteristic Roman "playing card" shape, and if the site proves to be Roman, then the Ordnance Survey map of Roman Britain which shows the Roman road, the "Devil's Causeway", ending at Berwick-upon-Tweed, will have to be amended. This view is to the west across Press Mains Farm.

Identification of sites

The identity of the site is determined by the shape of the crop/snow/shadow/soil mark. If it is square or rectangular with rounded corners, it is highly likely that the constructors were from the Roman army. If it is an irregular quadrilateral with a gateway on the eastern side, then the originators were Roman-period British (Celtic) farmers. Circular ditches usually surrounded the defended pre-Roman Iron Age Celtic settlements. Other archaeological sites such as prehistoric religious monuments (henges) and burial mounds (barrows) had their own distinctive shapes.

Old foundations of walls are buried not because the stonework is sinking but by earthworm action. Every night, the worms push up their casts and the end result is approximately an extra foot of soil above the ancient ground level for every thousand years of elapsed time. Windblown debris also assist the build-up. This rate of burial refers to open

An unknown Roman temporary camp beside the known Roman road across Wheeldale Moor, North Yorkshire, SE 797 976. After a heath fire, the new heather is growing thicker over the ancient ditch.

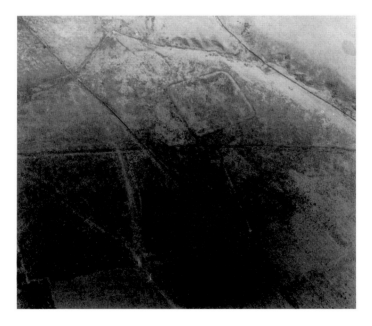

A Roman temporary camp on Haltwhistle Common, a quarter mile south of Turret 47A on Hadrian's Wall. This camp, at map ref NY 646 654, shows the characteristic shape of a marching camp, and the defensive tutelae can be seen in front of each gateway.

country. In towns where each generation flattens buildings and starts again on top of the rubble, the ancient habitation-layers can be twenty or thirty feet below the modern surface. In the Middle East, this continuous elevation of habitation-levels is exaggerated in the *tells* (Arabic for mound or hill) which rise above the plains as artificial hills, produced by a long accumulation of mud bricks. New villages are constantly erected on the remnants of the old.

With regard to earthworm action; as the level of the soil rises, the Earth does not increase in diameter; gravity keeps it in shape. Therefore, billions of earthworm activities are not increasing our planet's size.

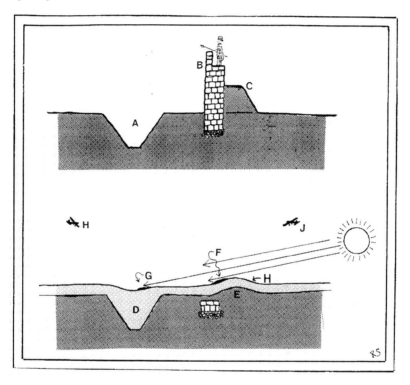

Upper diagram: Roman defences with ditch A, fort wall B and earth rampart C.

Lower diagram: The same site almost 2,000 years later. The fort wall B, has been robbed for building materials. The ditch D has been filled in, but a slight depression, difficult to detect at ground level, still exists. The earth rampart has almost gone but leaves a slight ridge E, also difficult to see at ground level. In low-angle sunlight, shadows are cast by the remains of the rampart at F and by the lip of the slight depression at G. The opposite side of the slight depression is also highlighted. An observer in the aircraft at J does not see the shadows but as the aircraft circles into the down-sun position at H, the whole shape of the Roman fort is revealed by shadows and highlights.

Soil marks

These marks are useful in winter and do not rely on a combination of cereal crops and a drought. Quite often, when a farmer has infilled an old ditch, the soil he has used is of a different colour and is easily visible from an aircraft. Sites which show-up as soil marks in bare fields in winter invariably produce crop marks in the other seasons if the right conditions are met.

Shadow marks

Many fields are in permanent pasture and have not been cultivated for hundreds of years or even longer. If the surface of such a field contains very slight undulations such as the last remnants of ancient earthworks and ditches, these may be invisible to the observer at ground level, but when viewed from an aircraft in low-angle sunlight in early morning or late evening and especially in winter and spring when the grass is short and the Sun's altitude small, the shape of the whole habitation appears as if by magic. One side of the almost flattened earthwork is highlighted and the other is in shadow. The almost invisible ditch likewise has one side highlighted with the other in shadow. Thus the whole shape of the site is revealed. The marks show best when the aircraft is down-sun of the site, so searches for shadow marks should be conducted with the aircraft being flown in a series of advancing circles.

The British archaeologist Sir Leonard Woolley (1880-1960), who excavated Ur in 1922-9 had been attempting earlier to locate an ancient Egyptian cemetery below the Second Cataract of the Nile near Wadi Halfa. This site had eluded Sir Leonard and the expedition leader, D R MacIver, but one evening, after a hard day's search, the two men climbed a hill to view the sunset. In the low-angled sunlight, strange circles, invisible at ground level, appeared at the base of the hill. As Sir Leonard descended, the circles disappeared, but MacIver, who had remained behind was able to direct him to the positions with hand signals. Sir Leonard marked them with small cairns. Next day, workers excavated the marked positions and found a tomb at every one.

When crop mark conditions are present, the corn or barley grows higher over the infilled ditch and in low-angle sunlight, this casts a shadow, and an excellent combination of crop marks and shadow marks is obtained.

During the nineteenth century, soldiers who had served at Gibraltar said that when they looked from the top of the rock, towards the Spanish border to the north, they could see the remains of the old Spanish lines which were invisible at ground level.

Snow marks

Snow marks are rather like shadow marks etched with a white paint brush. Faint traces of earthworks are necessary, and in a light dusting of snow, the ditch is painted with a bright white band. A bank, even a slight one, causes drifting, and a combination of snow marks and low-angle-sun shadow marks can produce a most striking result.

Heavy snow obliterates all signs of the site. During the thaw, the snow remains in the ditch long after the remainder of the field is clear. Possibly the latter would be better called

*The Roman complex at Blakehope, on Dere Street, near Elishaw, Northumberland,
NY 859 945, showing as snow marks. The fort and annexe occupy the
centre of an earlier temporary camp. The Roman features are covered with later medieval
rig-and-furrow strip cultivation. Towards the River Rede,
the rig-and-furrow has been destroyed by modern ploughing.*

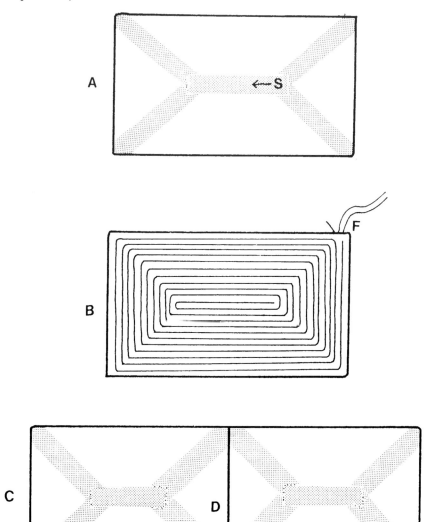

Many fields have in them what is usually referred to as an "envelope pattern." This is caused by the farmer starting ploughing at point S on diagram A. The farmer ploughs round and round the central furrow, and the four diagonal lines where the plough has been lifted to turn are usually clearly visible from an aircraft. In diagram B, the farmer has finished ploughing and left the field at F. In diagram C, two adjoining fields have envelope marks showing as soil or crop marks, and the unwary or inexperienced aerial observer may think that he has located a square archaeological site at position D.

"melt marks." Closely related to melt marks are "frost marks": when a field is covered with frost, ancient stonework below ground level retains heat better than the surrounding soil and the line of the foundation is revealed by the absence of frost, and shows as a dark line.

Parch marks

Crop marks do not normally show up in grassland, but during a period of hot dry weather, lawns and pastures which hide buried roads or stone foundations, reveal their secrets when the grass above the stonework or metalling becomes scorched and turns brown.

Plant marks

Some wild flowers and weeds like to grow over old stonework, and quite often, a field with a buried line of stone develops a prominent line of flowering weeds above invisible foundations. Poppies have an affinity for wetter infilled ditches outside the ramparts of Iron Age British hillforts.

Wind marks

When positive crop marks are present, the cereal growth above the ditch is higher than that over the rest of the field. Strong winds can strike the projecting tops, and the end result is that the corn is flattened along the lines of the ditches.

Spurious marks

Where horses or goats have been tethered, they may have grazed circles of grass which can look like the marks of Iron Age huts when viewed from an aircraft.

Circular bands of dark grass caused by fungi (fairy rings) can also look like the marks left by ancient rondavels.

A straight track of stunted grass across a field need not be evidence of an ancient road. It may be an animal path, the cattle having been kept in a straight line by a thin electrified wire, invisible to the airborne searcher.

A few years ago, strange circles appeared in fields of corn. These were not crop marks but corn flattened with boards strapped to the feet of practical jokers. The surprising thing is that many people, some of academic standing, were taken in by them.

Summary

Wherever the hand of man has disturbed the soil, the resulting differences of soil density or colour, water content, undulations (humps and bumps), heat retention etc, periodically show some kind of phenomena which are visible to an airborne observer.

Our search areas can be likened to a "palimpsest." That is a manuscript on which the original script has been effaced to make room for a second writing. Parts of the surface of lowland Britain, for example Celtic field systems, are overlain by signs of Roman occupation and the area in turn is almost obliterated by medieval rig and furrow strip-fields. Modern agriculture camouflages all three except for occasional crop marks. Shadow marks in permanent pasture sometimes show traces of all periods, and then it is up to the photographic interpreter to identify and separate the evidence.

Dilston, NY 976 635 from the air. Bottom centre, with tractor marks bisecting it, is the faint trace of a Romano-British farmstead. Right centre is a field with a typical "envelope pattern" caused by the plough turning. Top right on the hill to the right of the farm is the slight earthwork of a suspected Roman fortlet. A little-known Roman road (Forster's Road)crossed the Devil's Water just below the fortlet and headed west past Dilston Park Farm. At 11 o'clock to the farm is a medieval road curving down the hill towards the modern A695. This view is to the south-east.

There follows a few stories about pioneer aerial archaeologists:

In 1918, a crew-member of a two-seater British reconnaissance aircraft on the Western Front was a certain Major Osbert Guy Stanhope Crawford of the Royal Flying Corps. Major Crawford was the aeroplane's "observer" and this was the old name for the crewman who was a combined navigator/photographer/radio operator/bombardier and gunner. Before his military service, Crawford worked for the Ordnance Survey and had become very interested in ancient monuments. His flying career had introduced him to the phenomena now known as "crop marks" which allowed, under certain conditions, the shapes of the foundations of buildings and other works from past historical occupations, to manifest themselves as lines of different shades in acres of overall spring-green or harvest-gold cereals.

This method of detection of archaeological sites was regarded by most of the "establishment" of the period as what would now be termed "fringe archaeology"; but the appearance of the botanical facsimiles of past human works had been noted long before the advent of powered aircraft: in 1740, as mentioned previously, the Rev Dr Stukeley had looked down from a hill in southern England and was astonished at the shape of a Roman temple in the corn below. His report was ridiculed.

Various early aeronauts who ventured aloft in balloons also mentioned the sightings of ghostly shapes of ancient architecture in the farmlands. Their reports were likewise ridiculed.

Unfortunately, activists in all fields of exploration have always been denigrated by cloister-bound self-confessed "experts." The German explorers of East Africa, in the 19th century were lampooned when they reported snow-capped, twenty- thousand-foot mountains almost on the equator. The sages in London said it was impossible for ice-caps to exist in the tropics.

Experts in Paris also criticised the flying priest, Pere Poidebard when he reported that while he was being flown over Syria in 1925, looking for ancient irrigation channels, which could possibly be refurbished for modern cultivation, he spotted a whole network of unknown Roman roads, forts and signal stations. When he landed, these became invisible on the surface and he couldn't find them. He was a resourceful man and discovered a unique method of locating buried Roman roads from ground level - he drove a train of camels across the area of the invisible road, and when the beasts intercepted the line, they turned along it. The Roman writer, Vegetius, had also known of camels' trail-finding abilities: he wrote: "These animals seem to have a natural instinct for following in the steps of their long-departed kin."

An aircrew, about to depart from Sunderland-Usworth aerodrome on an archaeological survey flight c1968. Harry Lawson left, the author right. The aircraft is a Piper Cherokee and the field car, a VW181, civil version of the WW2 German "Kubelwagen."

Not all archaeological survey flights went smoothly. The author took off in this single-seater "Turbulent" aircraft intending to explore some Roman roads in County Durham but on take-off the starboard undercarriage fell away due to a sheared pin. A one-wheeled landing had to be made and when speed was lost, the starboard wing-tip struck the ground and the aircraft slewed off the runway into a drainage ditch. The airport fire truck and a large part of the Sunderland Fire Brigade were on hand waiting for the crash landing.

Poidebard used to get his pilot to skim along lost Roman roads at a height of fifteen feet, while he tried to photograph inscriptions on Roman milestones which whizzed past. If the surface of the desert allowed, his plane would land to allow him to dig a quick *sondage* (trial trench) across a buried feature.

Poidebard's subsequent books remain the standard reference works for the Roman Empire's eastern frontiers.

In 1918, a crop mark probably saved the lives of Major OGS Crawford and his pilot: they became lost behind enemy lines in bad visibility. Major Crawford then spotted the double tell-tale lines of the crop marks over the drainage ditches of a Roman road. He recognised this feature as one he had noticed previously and was able to guide the aircraft back to the allied lines.

On a later sortie, he was shot down by a German aircraft and spent some time in a German POW camp where he studied books on archaeology.

After the war, he returned to Flanders and excavated some of his crop marks, thus proving his techniques. He eventually became a university professor and is now recognised as one of the pioneers of "aerial archaeology."

Also during the 1914-18 war, a certain Lieutenant-Colonel GA Beazley of the Royal Engineers, was carrying out an aerial survey of the Tigris-Euphrates plain, when about sixty-five miles north-west of Baghdad, he sighted the outlines of canals, and the square grid system of an ancient city. He had discovered the Ninth Century "Old Samarra." Beazley continued to investigate these sites, both from the air and on the ground, but in May 1918, the searches were cut short when he was shot down by an enemy aircraft. Thus another flying archaeologist was awarded ample study time in a prison camp. After the war, Beazley's accounts were published in the *Geographical Journal* of 1919 and 1920. In 1925, Squadron Leader GSM Insall, who had been awarded the Victoria Cross in the war, was on a flight out of his base at Netheravon, and from a height of two-thousand feet, he looked down on what was thought by antiquarians to be the mutilated remains of a very large "disc barrow." To Insall, it looked very much like a much-eroded version of the famous Stonehenge just a couple of miles away. The following year, when the site was under wheat, Insall took a photograph of the crop marks of the so-called "barrow" and the result caused a stir among archaeologists. Insall's photograph suggested that the site had been a wooden version of Stonehenge, and excavations confirmed this and it became known as "Woodhenge." Further monuments of this type, hitherto unknown, were found throughout Britain and dated to the Neolithic and early Bronze Ages.

About the same time, OGS Crawford received help from a kindred spirit, Alexander Keiller, who had been a pilot in the Royal Naval Air Service during the war. An aircraft was hired from the De Havilland company at the RAF base at Weyhill, and a captured German camera installed in the observer's cockpit. The results of the Keiller/Crawford survey were published in *Wessex from the Air* in 1928.

In the 1930s another amateur aerial surveyor was Major George WG Allen, an engineer who owned his own aircraft. His photography was mostly of the Oxford and Thames valley areas, and he must be admired for the excellent results he obtained while flying his De Havilland Puss Moth solo, handling a large, unwieldy and complex camera while gripping the aircraft's stick between his knees.

During the subsequent 1939-45 war, OGS Crawford lost many of his photographs when a German bomb hit his office at the Ordnance Survey during the blitz. One of Crawford's last speaking engagements before the outbreak of war had been to a group of *Luftwaffe* officers! Allen's large collection at the Ashmolean Museum partly compensated for Crawford's loss,

In 1945, an amazing French air force pilot, Colonel Jean Baradez, became a temporary archaeologist when he searched North Africa for evidence of the Roman occupation. Baradez had been inspired by Pere Poidebard but he used modern military methods. Baradez had no knowledge of the Romans but he was a reconnaissance pilot and was used to searching for camouflaged enemy camps, roads and fortifications. He used the same technique in his search for the Romans. On his very first flight, from his American-built 300 mph Martin Marauder bomber with two x 2,000 hp Pratt & Whitney engines, he photographed from high altitude, 150 square kilometres in one hour. Although the area had been well studied by experts, the Colonel confounded all concerned with the discovery of an unknown wall and ditch system similar to Hadrian's Wall in Britain. This first grid of photographs also produced a hundred kilometres of unknown Roman roads, a Roman fort, thirty fortlets and other buildings associated with the roads; also sixty stone towers along his *Fossatum*, many integral with his frontier-wall.

The Algerian war of independence prevented further work. One day the task may be completed, possibly from cameras in orbitting satellites.

Aerial searches continue world-wide and it is now thought by British survey pilots including the author that more than half of the Roman roads in Britain have yet to be found.

Resistivity surveys

This is the most commonly used of the geophysical surveying methods. The electrical resistance of the ground is measured with a resistivity meter. Readings are taken in a grid pattern. The resistance between probes varies with high levels through buried stone walls and low levels across infilled and wet ditches. When the readings are plotted on a plan, an outline of the buried site is produced.

The magnetometer

This instrument measures the strength of the Earth's magnetic field. In the tail of an anti-submarine aircraft, an indication is received when the aeroplane passes over a submerged craft. Likewise, buried stonework and old ditches cause fluctuations of magnetic fields, which can be measured by a suitable surface-crawling machine. When plotted, the readings outline the buried features.

Radar (R-adio A-ngle D-irection A-nd R-ange)

Since the beginning of the 39-45 war, ships and aircraft have been detected by reflections of transmitted radio waves. The archaeological version of this equipment detects buried features with a beam transmitted down into the ground. In maritime and aviation work, the radio pulses are sent out in space from a rotating antenna and the echoes are displayed electronically in plan form on a fluorescent screen. Airfield and ships' radars suffer from a minimum range problem because the same antenna is used for transmission and reception. A radio wave travels at 186,000 miles per second, (300,000,000 metres/second) or 300 metres in a millionth of a second (microsecond). The leading edge of a microsecond-duration pulse will extend outwards from a ship for 300 metres before the trailing edge leaves the antenna. Thus a dead space, devoid of echoes, extends for a radius of 150 metres around the ship. Shorter pulses are selected for close range work such as river navigation in fog.

With archaeological ground-probing radars, pulses can be shorter but advanced electronic technology must be used to overcome the minimum range problem. This technology is beyond the scope of this book. Let us just say that the device is pulled across the ground like some kind of super (and very expensive) lawn-mower. A computer print-out displays the buried features.

Laboratory-based dating methods

When a site is under investigation by various archaeological authorities, there are many scientific methods of dating the artefacts found. Most of them are extremely expensive processes and are beyond the scope of the amateur archaeologist who is interested in the actual discovery of the site. A brief mention of them follows before we move into the countryside where the site must be found before the boffins can tell us how old it is.

Coin and pottery dating

Scientific dating methods are superfluous if we find Roman coins. Unlike our modern ones, these coins do not carry dates, but the period of reign of the emperor depicted is known. Likewise, the periods of manufacture of various types of Roman pottery are known and this provides an excellent method of dating the layer of soil in which the ceramics are found.

Radiocarbon dating

All living things, both animal and vegetable absorb carbon. Plants take in carbon dioxide from the atmosphere and retain some carbon in their tissues.The plants are eaten by herbivorous animals, some of which are in turn eaten by carnivores.

Carbon dioxide contains a very small proportion of the radioactive isotope, carbon 14, so called because it has two more neutrons in its nucleus than the normal carbon 12 atom. C14 has eight neutrons, and C12, six. Both carbon 12 and carbon 14 have six protons and six electrons, the electrons in two distinct orbit-shells. Carbon 14 is constantly produced in the upper atmosphere by a reaction involving cosmic radiation. All radioactive materials release energy. In a nuclear bomb, it all happens at once and whole cities can be destroyed. Left on its own, the radioactivity of a substance decays at a known rate for that substance over an extremely long period. Thus uranium becomes LEAD when it finally loses all its radioactivity.

For carbon 14, its radioactivity is halved every 5,736 years.

When an animal or plant dies, it ceases to absorb carbon and the carbon 12 remains in the dead material while the radioactive carbon 14 decays to carbon 12 at a known rate. Thus the ratio of carbon 12 to carbon 14 can determine the time elapsed since death.

The production rate of carbon 14 in the upper atmosphere has not been constant over the last few thousands of years and a correction has to be made to readings. The upper case letters BC or AD denote a calibrated radiocarbon date or a date derived from historical sources that needs no scientific confirmation. The lower case letters bc or ad represent uncalibrated radiocarbon years. BP(calibrated) or bp(uncalibrated) mean "before present" but the "present" refers to the year 1950, the latest date that the atmosphere was sufficiently uncontaminated to act as a standard for radiocarbon dating.

Dendrochronology (tree ring dating)

It is well known that the age of a tree can be determined by counting the rings. One new ring is grown every year. Depending on the weather experienced during the year, the ring growths vary in thickness so that all trees in the same area will have been affected in a similar manner. Using present-day trees, and specimens of progressively older timbers from churches and archaeological sites, each with overlapping ring sequences, a table of tree-ring widths has been established, and this extends back in time for several thousand years. The Bristlecone Pine of California is particularly long-living and has yielded a sequence of rings extending back to c9000 BP. In Ireland, oak preserved in bogs has produced a table of ring thicknesses going back to c5950 BP.

If wood is kept wet, it can last for thousands of years and the above method of dating can be of considerable use when we examine surviving Roman bridge timbers and piles which lie in our river beds. Pieces of timber structures from other periods can be similarly dated.

Thermoluminescence

This is a method of dating pottery and other clay-fired artefacts. All objects, both above and below ground are being constantly bombarded by cosmic rays. Minerals absorb this radiation and store up energy in their crystal lattices. This energy is released in the form of light when the mineral is heated. When pottery is fired, the energy is released and the build-up process starts all over again. If the ancient pottery is re-heated, the energy picked up since its original firing will be released and the amount will tell us how long ago the original firing took place.

Other sophisticated laboratory tests

There are many other methods such as Potassium/argon dating, Fission track dating, and Magnetic dating. The reader who is interested in the whole subject of scientific dating should consult the many and varied specialist books available.

Metal detectors

In the right hands, metal detectors are very useful archaeological tools. I always use them on my own excavations as ancient coins and other small artefacts are usually covered with rust and soil and are missed by students. All buckets of spoil pass by the head of a metal detector and the find-rate in my excavations rose by a thousand per-cent when I invited experts with these devices to participate.

If an archaeologist wants to protect a site from nocturnal visits by unwanted searchers, he can spread powdered domestic coke over the site and this produces a blanket spurious signal which defeats all metal detectors.

Illustration taken from Sebastian Minster's Cosmographiae Universalis, published in Basle in 1550. It shows miners at work in an Alsace silver mine. On the top of the hill is a diviner (dowser) using a hazel twig. Divining/dowsing is an ancient art and in spite of ridicule from some quarters, astonishing results can be obtained by certain gifted people.

Dowsing

This subject causes more controversy than metal detectors. Let me say that it definitely works though I am not very good at it myself. Hidden roads and walls produce signals. Electrical cable repair men use this system all the time. Also drain repairers, as well as the normal and well-known water-finders.

The serious student of our town's history should now have a good idea about how archaeologists discover new evidence.

We can now move on from "prehistory" which is the period (in Britain) before the Roman invasions, to "history" which begins with written records made by that race of excellent civil engineers and first class soldiers, who invaded Britain twice under Julius Caesar in 55 BC and 54 BC. Caesar's ships on both occasions became stormbound or damaged due to Atlantic depressions racing up the Channel and the land activities had to be cut short. (Low pressure weather systems did not begin with BBC weather forecasts.) In AD 43, the Romans, came again and occupied most of mainland Britain for four-hundred years.

Our home area which had probably supported a few humble Celtic Iron Age farmsteads would become a Roman fortified town with links with the rest of the huge and powerful Roman Empire. The next chapter goes into the importance of our town in Roman times in great detail, and much new evidence is published for the first time.

A very important way to understand the history of our countryside is to learn to read the landscape by field-walking. Much practise is needed but the end result is extremely rewarding.

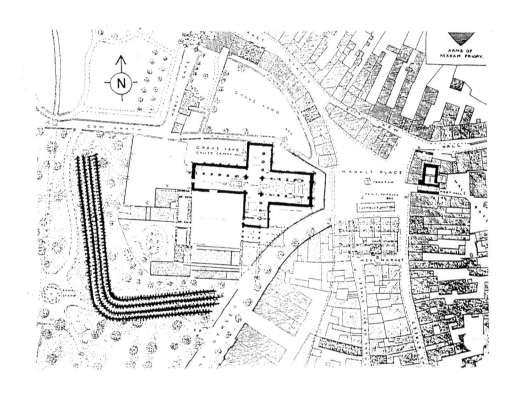

Antiquarians of old were sure that there was a Roman fort under Hexham Abbey. Many suspected Roman roads converge on the Abbey and these will be excavated in due course. An early Roman frontier also intersects the Abbey site. In 1986, expert dowser Andy Davison carried out a dowsing grid-search of the lawns around the abbey. Archaeological students of Newcastle University plotted his signals as he marched back and forth and the surprising result was four parallel Roman-type ditches. Electronics experts from York University followed this up with a resistivity survey to the north-west of the abbey in the area called "Campey Hill." A large artificial-looking earthwork was detected undergound, and plans are in hand to conduct further investigations, hopefully an excavation.

Stereoscopic (three dimensional) photography can be useful in archaeology. The aircraft flies in a straight line and takes two photographs of the same target area, from positions A and B. The two photographs are identical except that on photo A, the top of the tall chimney at E is seen at C, and on photo B, at D. When the photographs are placed side-by-side and viewed through a stereoscope with the left eye looking at the left photo A and the right eye, the right photo B, the human brain sees just one photograph. The top of the chimney, however, appears as a double image, and the eyes cross slightly dozens of times per second to merge the chimney-top into a single image. This constant flexing of the eyes signals a three-dimensional image to the brain, because the human brain uses the inward convergence of the eyes as a range-finding device. In practice, stereoscopic photography can work for objects just a few inches high if the interval between photographs is increased: a slight bump in a field, hardly visible at ground level, can look like a six-feet-high wall.

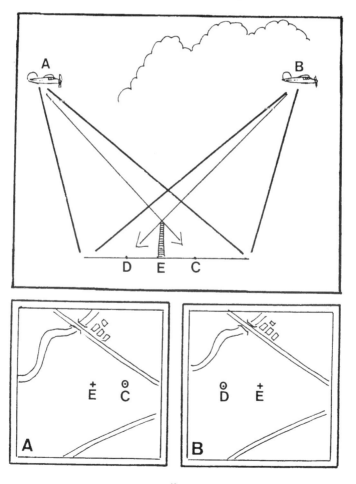

Underwater searches are extremely useful to archaeologists. Here a Zodiac dinghy is being lowered into the water prior to a search for submerged Roman remains.

SIDE SCAN SONAR

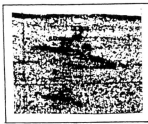

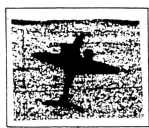

ACTUAL   ENHANCED

KLEIN HYDROSCAN SIDE SCAN SONAR
RECORD SHOWING WORLD WAR II AIRCRAFT
PROBABLY A PBY CATALINA, LYING IN 30
METERS OF WATER IN LOCH NESS.

Not only are ancient remains found underwater. This illustration shows a World War 2 aircraft, probably a PBY "Catalina" flying boat, lying in 30 metres of water on the bed of Loch Ness. The instrument which detected this is a development of the depth-finding echo-sounder but the "Side-scan sonar head" is towed at depth behind the boat and its signals are sent out sideways but also inclined downwards.

A Vickers "Wellington" bomber was recovered from Loch Ness some years ago and is now on display at a museum on the factory site where it was built - Weybridge, Surrey. The RAF has no record of the PBY in the illustration.

A Roman mosaic from Ostia showing a Roman merchant ship thought to be depicted arriving at Narbonne.

A Roman mosaic showing merchant ships and lighthouse at Ostia.

Chapter 3
Portus Concangis: A Roman Port?

I would only add one remark, that nowhere else does the sea make its power more felt: the tide causes long stretches of the rivers alternately to ebb and flow, nor does it simply rise and sink upon the shore, but it runs far inland, and winds about and makes its way into the very heart of the hills and mountain chains, as if the sea were the lord of all.

Tacitus, speaking of Roman Britain.

To trace the Wear upwards or downwards is like ascending or descending the stream of English history.

Rivers of the East Coast, 1829

Vedra *et* Con + tidal limit + Hinegan's Pond = *Portus*?

The main object of this chapter will be to establish why a Roman fort and a *vicus* (civil settlement) were built at all in Chester-le-Street. For that we must look at the Roman communications system, and some quite remarkable information has been revealed in recent years by aerial surveys, research, and excavations. Because of this extensive new evidence, the District Council asked me to write this book.

We must investigate with all available methods, why the Romans built a fort and town on the site of what would become later, our home town of Chester-le-Street.

In medieval times, after the post-Roman short but glorious Saxon cathedral-city period, Chester-le-Street became a small village with hardly any contact with the outside world. An occasional affluent gentleman on horseback, or a string of pack-horses led by a trader, travelled across the area, along ruinous Roman roads which had not been repaired for the best part of a thousand years; but in the main, the average inhabitant of Chester-le-Street never left the locality.

In the four-hundred years that Britain had been part of the Roman Empire, things were different. Our Roman fort and town were linked by a complex system of roads to other Roman bases. These roads were built initially as a swift police action network, but more important for heavy cargoes, Roman Chester-le-Street was linked by river and sea to all ports and inland waterways of the whole Empire. We think that the name of our Roman fort was "Concangis" and it was a supply base manned by second or third rate troops. Their function was to rest and feed fighting troops which were on their way to and from the frontier zones facing Caledonia, the land of the enemy Celtic Picts. We must remember that during the Roman occupation period, there were no Scots in Caledonia. The "Scotti" were a Celtic Irish tribe and did not invade Caledonia until the latter days of Roman Britain. Nor were there any "English" in Britain. The first "English" were the Anglo-Saxons and would not occupy Britain until after the Roman military departure. The natives of all the British Islands were of Celtic stock. Celtic farmers provided taxes in the form of money or corn for their Roman masters. They were treated tolerably well as long as they obeyed Roman laws and paid their taxes. The Romans built a fleet of eight-hundred merchant ships to take corn exports out of Britain. Lead was probably another major export. Roman Lugdunum in Gaul had several aqueducts. Some used inverted syphons to cross valleys. To withstand the pressure of water, the various huge lead pipes of Lugdunum's aqueduct-syphons used a total of forty-thousand tons of lead.

In the Roman Empire, there was no shortage of funds from an Imperial Government with which to build forts, barracks, roads, and aqueducts. What is more important however, for an en-route supply base is that Concangis was at the tidal limit (in Roman times) of the Roman Vedra *Fluvius,* the River Wear. The tributary, the River Cone or Cong Burn was the Roman Con *Fluvius* and an artificial channel led from this stream right up to the wall of the Roman fort.

We shall discuss shortly, the huge amounts of stores which arrived at the fort by Roman merchant ship up to Hylton (Sunderland), and then by *codicaria* (general purpose barge) from there right into a barge basin under the north-eastern corner of the fort where the Public Swimming Baths now stand. Years ago, before landscaping, a mysterious pool called "Hinegan's Pond" sat in a hollow at this point, and a high-and-dry curious water channel of a size which could easily have taken boats, led away from the stagnant pool, with its water lilies and bulrushes, towards the River Wear. This channel headed in the direction of the Lumley fish-trap.

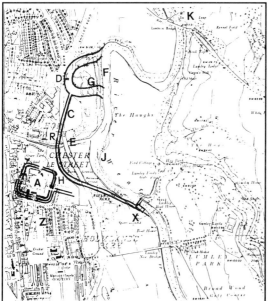

During the construction of the Swimming baths, a huge square-sectioned Roman sewer was cut into, and this led down from the north-east corner of the fort towards the site of Hinegan's Pond, the latter in the course of being infilled by landscapers and building workers.

Because of the importance of "Concangis" as a staging post of the Imperial Roman Empire, we must spend some time considering not only the river supply systems, but also the huge network of military roads which has been discovered in recent years. We shall also look at the frontier zone to the north, for which Concangis was a major supply base for troops en-route.

Roman features superimposed on modern map.

Chester-le-Street's Roman fort and its transportation features.

A = the Roman fort with Cade's Roman road (Latin name unknown) heading north, underneath our present Front Street.

H = former "Hinegan's Pond," now landscaped away and underneath modern swimming baths. This pond is thought to have been originally, a Roman barge basin.

C = the former course of the Cong Burn (Roman Con Fluvius). This small river is thought to have been canalised from an old River Wear loop "G" into Hinegan's Pond and then back to the River Wear (Vedra Fluvius) at "X."

E = modern course of Cong Burn.

F = modern course of River Wear.

D = an old dam, believed to be Roman, found when sewage works were built in 1930 in the old dry loop of the River Wear. A Roman altar was also found at this spot.

R = opus revinctum (bind-fast work dove-tailed Roman masonry) found here when the bed of the Cong Burn was cemented in 1930. It is thought that the Roman stones were part of a minor dam to carry the Roman canal across the small river, the latter being used as a "feeder."

K = present tidal limit of River Wear.

D = Roman tidal limit of River Wear.

X = further suspected Roman dam underneath Lumley Fish weir and modern Northumbria Water weir. Locks at "X" on former site of childrens' paddling pool would have allowed Roman navigation with the aid of further weirs upstream, possibly to Kepier (Durham) and beyond.

J = medieval (and possibly Roman) ford on road to Lumley.

LC = Lumley Castle, at junction of two suspected Roman roads.

Z = author's house where this is being written.

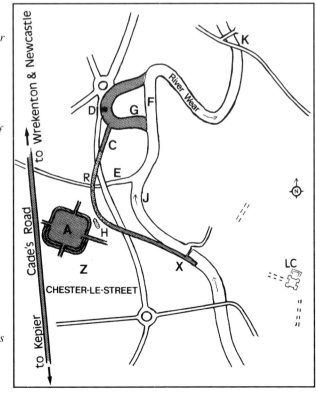

The "Deanery manor house" with church beyond, on the site of the Roman fort. The line of trees in the foreground is on the embankment of the suspected Roman canal, and Hinegan's Pond is in the dip to the right. A modern school complex is now on the site of the former "Deanery."

Underneath the later stone fort was an early turf and timber fort but this fact does not alter the strategic placing of the site. An inscribed stone, now lost, carried the name of the 2nd Legion (Legio II Augusta) so that legion must have taken part in construction work. An inscription of AD216 tells us of an unidentified auxiliary cavalry unit working on an aqueduct and a bath-house.

The northbound Roman road through Chester-le-Street, underneath our present Front Street was first noticed by Dr Cade in the 18th century; hence it is known as "Cade's Road." No Roman maps of Britain survive and there are no Roman references to Chester-le-Street or its considerable road network which is coming to light. A Roman road well to the west of Chester-le-Street, called "Dere Street" by the later Saxons, gets Roman mentions of mileages between stations, in a document called the Antonine Itinerary which tells us that a road (no name given) passed by High Rochester (Bremenium); Corbridge (Corstopitum); Ebchester

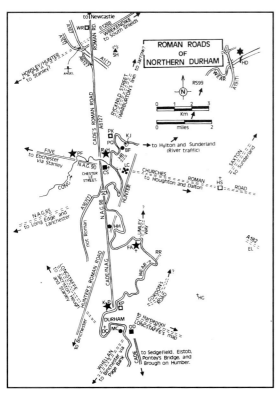

The Roman Roads of Northern Durham.

BF = Bruggeford Saxon river crossing.

CS = Concangis (Chester-le-Street) Roman fort.

DC = Durham Cathedral, Roman pottery & coins found in gardens.

EL = Easington Lane suspected Roman road under A182.

FA = Finchale Priory, Roman pottery found. Old woodcut shows dam.

HB = Suspected Roman road up Hag Bank.

HD = Hylton Roman dam, dismantled c1810, stones removed to Roker.

HG = Roman artefacts found at Hallgarth Church.

HH = Iron Age settlement at Harbour House.

HS = Houghton-le-Spring, suspected Roman site, Roman road.

KJ = Keelboat jetty consisting of huge oak tree trunk.

KP = Kepier, suspected Roman bridge site, also medieval hospital.

LC = Lumley Castle, at junction of two Roman roads.

MC = Maiden Castle, Iron Age hillfort.

OD = Old Durham, Roman site, bath-house excavated 1944.

PK = Suspected Roman site at Picktree.

PF = Roman bridge on Cong Burn, remains of.

PQ = Picktree Quay, site of keelboat jetties. Also old wagonways.

RH = Roman dam and altar found 1930, dam not preserved.

RR = Ancient rutted road from quarry to river.

SD = Southburn Dene, Cade's Roman road excavated 1998.

SH = Shedon's Hill, suspected Roman signal station.

WR = Suspected Roman fort in Ravensworth Golf Course.

The Romans had excellent cranes. The derrick could be topped or slewed by guy-wires. The lifting gear was powered by men walking inside a large treadmill. The cargo-runner which lifted the load was wound around the axle of the treadmill and if this was six feet in circumference and the treadmill's walkway sixty feet in circumference, then this would have provided a ten-to-one gear ratio, requiring little effort from the men inside the drum. On this particular crane, the lifting-tackle appears to be of the "double-luff" type which would further reduce the required effort by the drum-walkers. Walking the drum one way would lift the huge load and the opposite way, lower it.

When lifting large stones, the Romans often cut dove-tailed holes into the top surface of the stone and into this hole inserted a "forfex" which consisted of two triangular wedges and a spacer. This device replaced the crane's hook. When the stone was in place, which could be underwater as during the construction of a bridge, the spacer could be removed with a lanyard allowing the wedges to come clear for a repeat operation. This system was re-invented in the fourteenth century and was then termed "lewis device" and "lewis hole."

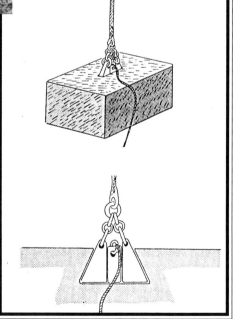

Early Saxon churches were built of timber but when the Saxons got around to building in stone, ex-Roman stones came in handy. Because of the huge size of Roman stones, the Saxons thought that the Romans had been a race of giants. This picture shows two ex-Roman lewis-holed stones built into a buttress at the front of our Chester-le-Street parish church. The reason for the positioning of Saxon churches on Roman sites stems from Pope Gregory's letter to one of his missionaries in Britain, Abbot Mellitus. This letter survives and tells the Abbot to: "instruct the converted Anglo-Saxons to build their new churches on top of the pagan sites."

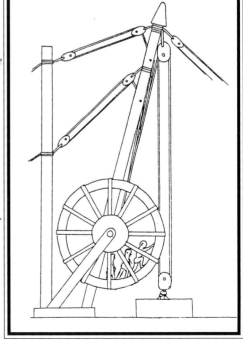

A Roman crane about to lift a huge stone, using a forfex inserted in a lewis hole.

Ex-Roman lewis-holed stones, thought to have been robbed by the Saxons from the Roman bridge at Bywell, built into the tower of St Andrew's Saxon church at Bywell. The Saxons had no knowledge of cranes so the lewis-hole of the reused Roman stone can be located on any surface, top, side or bottom.

Just downstream from the 14th Century bridge at the foot of Newbridge Bank is the Saxon river-ford at Bruggeford. The River Wear is tidal here and although part of the ford is eroded in the centre, the river can still be crossed at low tide.

North abutment of small Roman bridge on the Cong Burn (NZ 260 517) before (A) and after (B) excavation. Nine Roman coins were recovered from the stonework. The bridge is on the direct line between the Ebchester and Chester-le-Street Roman forts. Today the stream is only ten feet wide and a few inches deep but when the southern abutment was excavated, it showed that the Cong Burn in Roman times had been double the present day width.

(Vindomora); Binchester; Aldborough (Isurium); and York (Eburacum). Lanchester and Piercebridge are not mentioned although they are on the line of the road. The Roman document is not in map form; it merely gives distances between forts in Roman miles, (a Roman mile was 1,620 yards). There are several itineraries for Roman Britain and historians have to juggle the mileages to fit the known Roman sites. Sometimes they have got it horribly wrong which results in Roman forts being allocated incorrect names.

Major Roman roads such as the Devil's Causeway which runs the length of Northumberland, do not get the slightest Roman mention.

Our search for the Chester-le-Street network, which is considerable, has taken many years and we now know that six, seven, or possibly eight Roman roads lead into, or pass close by the town.

Roman technology such as the use of cranes can be detected by an inspection of large ex-Roman stones which often reveals the type of lifting-device used. This is best appreciated from the diagrams.

New information also means that our historical maps must be redrawn but that will be dealt with in detail in due course.

I must now describe this search for new evidence, the start of which (unknown to me at the time) began while I was a World War 2 schoolboy at the Chester le Street Grammar School.

Our school was right on top of the Roman fort though sadly there was no visible evidence of it except for a few inscribed stones and other odds and ends in nooks and corners of the parish church. I did not know at the time that one day, I would become an archaeological air survey pilot and be able to solve many problems about our town's history.

Before moving to the Grammar School, while still a pupil at the happy Red Rose Elementary School, I had sat in an aeroplane for the first time in my life. A *Luftwaffe* Messerschmitt Bf 109 single-seat fighter had force-landed fairly intact in the south of England during the Battle of Britain, and it was being demonstrated around the North-East. The latter was out of range of the single-engined German planes. This Messerschmitt Bf (Bayerischeflugzeugwerke) 109 had been reassembled in the south-west corner of the Chester-le-Street cricket field, beside the Ropery Lane gate. We had to pay a penny (old money) to get into the field and tuppence to sit in the cockpit. A Home Guard soldier who was guarding the aircraft nodded to me as I sat in the pilot's seat, and asked if I thought I could fly the plane. When I answered: "yes," he nudged his mate and smiled; but I did fly a Messerschmitt many years later - not a Bf 109, but one of its stable-mates, a Bf 108.

During my grammar school days, I was fascinated with the war which was going on all around us. The Battle of Britain was over but the bomber Battle of Germany was in full swing. As soon as I was old enough, I left the 2nd Chester-le-Street Boy Scout troop, and joined No.1507 Air Training Corps Squadron which had its headquarters in our school.

The physical training master, Mr Charlton, was our commanding officer, with the rank of squadron-leader, and various other teachers, businessmen and officials from the town were officers. I remember them very well: Robert Exeley, ex World War 1 aviator; William Hedley, mathematics teacher; Thomas Foster, adjutant; William Murray, radio and electrical instructor; Stephen Taylor, aircraft recognition expert; Cecil Davis, admin officer, and Jimmy Yarwood, armaments instructor, disciplinarian, and squadron warrant officer.

Most of my spare time was taken up with aeronautical training: on Monday nights, I practised morse and familiarised myself with associated radio and electrical equipment; Tuesday nights we studied air navigation; Wednesday night was shooting practise in the indoor rifle range of the Territorial Army Drill Hall; Thursday nights, we practised aircraft recognition and I am pleased to say that our squadron won the cup for the North-East, at a competition held in Durham Town Hall, defeating the experts of the Royal Observer Corps. I can still visualise the shapes of all those wartime aeroplanes, both friend and foe.

This Messerschmitt 109, shot down in the south of England during the Battle of Britain in 1940, was displayed around the North East. In Chester-le-Street cricket ground, the author, as a Red Rose schoolboy, sat in this wrecked aircraft and became hooked on flying. He later became an airline navigator/radio officer and also an air survey pilot. He completed his aviation career as an air traffic control officer at major airports all over Britain. He then took a BA (Hons) degree in archaeology at Newcastle University.

Friday night was drill night and we marched and counter-marched up and down the school tennis courts which served as our drill square. Somewhere in the same vicinity, just a few feet below the surface was the Roman parade ground where the centurions had barked at Roman auxiliaries. Our warrant officer was no less severe and he remarked that before we could become aviators, he first had to turn us into men and soldiers.

On occasional weekends, we visited RAF aerodromes and I was thrilled to receive my very first flight, at Pocklington, Yorkshire, in an "Airspeed Oxford" training aircraft (I can even remember its number, X7235). The warrant-officer pilot gave four of us a twenty-minute ride across to York, around the Minster and then back to base. From then on, I was hooked on flying and remained so for the rest of my life. Pocklington was a bomber station with four-engined Handley Page Halifaxes as its equipment. From the scars of battle damage on some of them, it was obvious that the battle over Germany was proving to be a tough one.

In addition to my ATC squadron aviation training, I was further assisted during school day-classes. Our brilliant geography master, Mr Rollason taught those of us who were interested, the basics of astro-navigation. He had an old Nelson-era marine sextant, and in order to practise the establishment of a noon latitude (when the Sun crosses the meridian as it reaches its highest point at due south), he would say: "The electric light bulb is the Sun and the window-sill your sea horizon; find your latitude." Therefore, due to this very learned master, I became able to navigate using the Sun, Moon and stars while still a mere fourth-form grammar school pupil. The tuition would not be wasted on me.

Mr Rollason was a gentleman of the old British Empire. I remember him telling me how the explorer, Dr David Livingstone, navigated across darkest Africa. He used a sailor's sextant but in order to do this, one must be able to see both the celestial body, plus a clear sea horizon, and measure the angle between the two at the meridian crossing (this angle has a direct relationship to the observer's latitude). Dr Livingstone had no sea horizon in his mountain and rain-forest surroundings, but he overcame the problem - he poured some of the expedition's golden syrup into a frying pan and measured the angle between the midday Sun in the sky and its reflection in the treacle. He then divided by two. Thus he obtained the Sun's meridian altitude from which he calculated his latitude. In order to get a cross-bearing as a second position line, he measured the temperature at which the water for his tea boiled. Water boils at 100 degrees C at sea level and at lesser temperatures the higher you rise. This is why tea tastes awful on a mountain - the water may be boiling at only ninety degrees. Dr Livingstone, in the East African mountains, using altitude/boiling-point tables, got his approximate height, and crossed this contour line with his latitude, thus establishing his position in darkest Africa.

I was extremely lucky to have been a pupil in those two excellent schools, the Chester-le-Street Red Rose School and the Chester-le-Street Grammar School.

My home in St Cuthbert Avenue was just a few yards from the Grammar School, and I am writing this in the very same house where I was a schoolboy. Winters were more severe in those days and the gentle hill on which now stand the youth centre and swimming pool, was steeper. Before landscaping reduced the gradient, the hill was ideal for sledging, and after the slightest snowfall, the area collected children from the whole area. Where the swimming baths now stand was a duck pond in "Hinegan's Field." This was a dangerous pond, noted for its lack of a firm bottom.

There were some funny "humps and bumps" in the same field and a curious high-and-dry channel ran into the pond from the east. As I sledged down the hill, I often overturned as I went through this obviously artificial gulley. It was slightly higher up the contours than the old course of the River Cone which was marked on some maps. Rivers do not climb out of their beds and run along hillsides at a height of about ten feet from the bottom. The true purpose of the channel remained a mystery for a long time.Twenty-five years later, I was back in Chester-le-Street having done a few years maritime service before changing to flying and carrying out airline duties in all parts of the world, a lot of it in Africa. In Central Africa, as well as normal aircrew duties on Dakotas, DC4s, Vikings, Herons and Bristol 170s, I also used to fly a De Havilland Dove air survey plane. On my return to England, I had a chance meeting with a university professor and in my spare time, I found myself carrying out archaeological air surveys over Northern England and Southern Scotland.

Before one flight, part of which was to be over the Chester-le-Street area, the professor and I were studying old maps in Durham University. As I scanned the old Ordnance Survey map of 1850, of the Chester-le-Street area, my eyes became transfixed to a river feature! In the depression in which the modern sewage works were built in 1930, the map marked an old and dry loop of the River Wear. In addition to that, lying across the old river course at right angles to the ancient flow was marked: "ruins of a stone pier."

With a flash of vision, although I had as yet no proof, I knew that I was looking at part of a Roman water transportation system. The dam was at the ancient tidal limit of the River Wear. A ten-foot-high dam would have ponded the River Wear's tributary, the River Cone or Cong Burn, back into the Hinegan's Pond area and beyond into the high-and-dry channel. Was this pond the remains of a Roman barge basin, right under the wall of the Roman fort? Much research was necessary but results soon came pouring in. Records told me that when the sewage works were being constructed, a Roman altar was found close by the remains of the old "pier." The altar was dedicated to the Roman prefect who was evidently a very capable water engineer.

Everything fitted together - with the Roman dam intact, the old but high-and-dry channel would have connected Hinegan's Pond along the foot of our sledging hill, back to the River Wear at yet another dam beside Boat Cottage, a hundred yards or so downstream from the site of the old "Penny Bridge."

This dam was marked as a "fish-trap" but fish-traps were not constructed with thousands of tons of masonry. Our fishermen of old were not multi-millionaires. The structure was used as a fish-trap but purpose-built fish-traps consisted merely of a line of stakes only part of the way across a river, and funnel-shaped wicker baskets were placed between the stakes.

In the west bank of the river beside the surviving but ruinous "fish-trap" dam, a childrens'

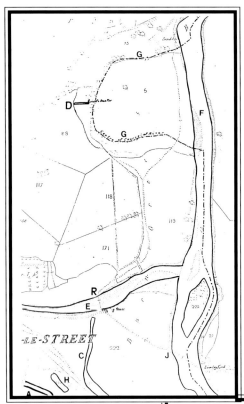

Map of 1850 showing old river features.

A = Roman fort.

H = Hinegan's Pond.

C = canalised Cong Burn.

E = present course of Cong Burn.

R = findspot of Roman "opus revinctum."

F = present course of River Wear.

G = old loop of River Wear.

D = "ruins of stone pier." This pier lies across the river and is thought to have been a Roman navigation weir at the Roman tidal limit.

J = Lumley Ford.

Plan of Chester-le-Street Roman fort. The church sits in the centre of the fort and the Parish Centre is on top of the Roman Commandant's house. There were probably two Roman forts on the same site, one built about AD80 and the other about AD120. The Roman name for the fort and town was probably "Concangis" but there is no direct evidence to prove that.

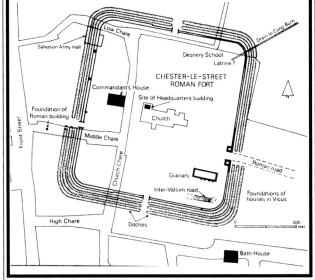

Fish-traps were simple and inexpensive devices like this one on the River Severn. This technique has been used for thousands of years. Expensive barriers such as weirs have naturally been used as fish-traps and this has confused the original purpose of the structures. Fish-traps seldom spanned the whole river. Two or three stakes with wicker-baskets between sufficed.

paddling pool had been constructed by the town council. It looked as if this depression had been the site of some kind of lock to lift barges to the higher water level above this second Chester-le-Street dam or weir. Old maps showed a "dry channel" running to this site from the Hinegan's Pond direction.

There is also an old reference to a short watercourse leaving the dam in the direction of Hinegan's Pond, but fizzling out after a short distance. Salmon were caught by driving them up this blind water-alley. It looks as if this was the remains of the upstream end of our Roman canal coming via the fort. Not only did it look as if Roman barges had plied between Sunderland and Chester-le-Street; it seemed that they had gone further upstream, to Finchale Abbey where Roman pottery has been found (an old woodcut of the priory shows a huge dam, now completely disappeared); Durham where there was a known Roman site at Old Durham and a further suspected one on the peninsula where many Roman artefacts constantly come to light in the cathedral gardens; and Binchester, near Bishop Auckland where an aerial survey has revealed a further "dry canal plus dry pond system." Roman tiles stamped "N Con" manufactured at Concangis (Ch-le-Str) by the Roman garrison, the *Numerus Concangios*, have been found at Binchester. Did these heavy cargoes get there by barge?

Before we go any further into this subject, let us compare road transport with water transport: A modern Clydesdale horse will pull a load of 1½ tons on a good level smooth road in a cart with well-oiled wheels and rubber tyres. The same horse if hitched to a river or canal barge will pull a hundred tons.

The ratio is even greater if we compare road transport with sea transport. Let us see how far a gallon of fuel or the equivalent weight of fodder, will carry a ton of cargo via various modes of transport:

Vehicle/Animal/Vessel	Fuel	Dist 1 ton can be moved with 1 gall of fuel:
Large modern cargo ship	heavy oil	4,600 miles
Modern coaster	heavy oil	600 miles
Modern freight train	diesel oil	250 miles
Modern lorry	diesel oil	50 miles
1944 Lancaster bomber	aviation gasoline	1 mile
6 camels (to carry 1 ton)	fodder	2.4 miles
Roman merchant ship	food/cooking	1,280 miles
Roman *codicaria* (10-ton barge)	food/cooking	32 miles
6 mules (to carry 1 ton)	fodder/grain	2.4 miles
2 Roman ox wagons (each with ½ ton)	fodder	0.8 miles

If you go by car down to the local supermarket to buy a bag of apples, the money you have spent on petrol would bring that bag of apples by sea, all the way from New Zealand. The efficiency of water transport was brought home to me at an early age because my ambition to fly military aircraft was shattered when World War 2 ended. The Royal Navy and RAF had a glut of highly experienced flyers and the mushrooming civil airlines could pick and choose from war-experienced crews, most of whom did not want to return to their pre-war mundane professions. An airline would not train an Air Training Corps cadet who could only fly gliders, when ex-lieutenant-commanders and squadron leaders with DSOs and DFCs were available. Rather reluctantly, I became an ordinary ship's officer with a resolve to change to flying as soon as an opportunity presented itself. However, the nautical training was to prove extremely useful because, by the time I got into the co-pilot's seat of an airliner a few years later, I was an experienced navigator, radio operator and meteorologist, all skills which help a pilot reach old age.

As an added bonus, I gained a working knowledge of the transportation of massive amounts of material around the world. Also, as an officer on a large troopship which was the captured German liner, *"Ubena,"* renamed by us *"HMT Empire Ken."* I helped move thousands of troops at a time, to the far-flung bases of the British Empire.

When I became an archaeological air survey pilot, I was looking at the ground through the eyes of a sailor, and, sparked-off by the mysterious suspected Roman canal system at Chester-le-Street, I would survey all the Roman forts in the north of England and Southern

Scotland. When opportunities arose, I would also photograph Roman sites in Southern England, France, Belgium and Italy. A pattern presented itself - most Roman sites had water transport features though most of these were extremely well camouflaged. Medieval millers had reused Roman dams (they would have been crazy not to have done so) and they placed their water-wheels in the old Roman by-pass canals. A give-away however, was that the medieval millers had to block up three-quarters of the width of Roman dam by-pass canals because they were far too big. Were the medieval millers stupid enough to build mill-leats several times too large and then infill most of the ditch? The millers did not have money to throw away like that.

I am not trying to say that the Romans dug long artificial canals in Northern England and Southern Scotland - what I am saying is that the Romans canalised the rivers which is a completely different thing. They also cut off large river bends with short-circuiting channels. When the river became too shallow for navigation, they built a dam, and to surmount this dam from the low level below to the (usually) ten feet higher level above, they dug a bypass canal which contained some kind of lock. These bypasses became ideal for later watermill sites and saved the millers an immense amount of money.

When Roman bargemen encountered really shallow water, they strapped dozens of pairs of inflated animal skins underneath their lighters thus lifting already shallow-draft craft almost out of the water. The insignia of the Roman civilian bargemen, the *Utricularii*, was such an inflated animal skin. There are records of units of the Roman military bargemen, the *Barcarii Tigrisienses* (Bargemen of the River Tigris) being stationed at Arbeia ...(South Shields) and Lancaster. The home port of the *Barcarii Tigrisienses* was Arbela in Iraq so the possible name Arbeia (not yet proven) of the South Shields Roman fort may be a mis-spelling.

The discovery of a huge unknown Roman transportation system right under our noses came as a surprise to archaeologists of the establishment. The Cambridge publisher Patrick Stephens heard a BBC broadcast I made about the subject and asked me to write a book for his company. This book was entitled *The Piercebridge Formula* (because of important evidence found in the River Tees at Piercebridge). The book sold out and it also won a Rolex International Award for Exploration which was presented

Even without artificial depth increases provided by weirs, Roman rivercraft could navigate into extremely shallow water by the strapping of dozens of pairs of inflated animal bladders under the boats, thus decreasing an already shallow-draft to just a few inches. The insignia of the Roman civilian boatmen, the Utricularii, was an inflated animal bladder.

The famous Roman ox-wagon has always been regarded as the standard Roman method of heavy goods transport but simple calculations and an inspection of the road system show that this could not have been the case. If a Clydesdale horse pulls a modern cart with well-oiled rubber-tyred wheels, on a very smooth and level tarmac road, it can pull a load of about 1½ tons. If the same horse is hitched to a barge, it can pull a hundred tons. If the cart-pulling horse encounters a gradient of one-in-thirty, two horses, are needed. For a smooth tarmac gradient of one-in-three, eleven horses are necessary. Roman roads had six times the friction of modern smooth tarmac roads and an ox-wagon with a load of half a ton (the maximum permitted) would have needed seventy oxen for a typical Roman one-in-three gradient.

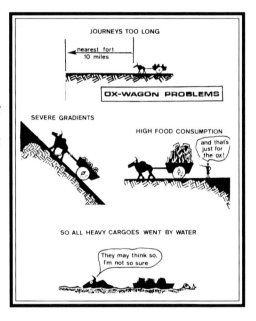

to me by the Antarctic explorer, Sir Vivian Fuchs, at the Inn on the Park, London. Subsequently, I made a television series for ITV.

Historical writers had seen mosaics of Roman ox-wagons and assumed that these vehicles, together with the thousands of miles of well-engineered Roman roads, had formed the whole Roman army logistics system. Now and then however, occasional thinkers had wondered at the severe gradients of Roman roads which would daunt a modern bulldozer, never mind a one mph (on the flat) Roman ox-wagon.

Let us have a closer look at these Roman roads:

Roman roads did not always follow a single continuous ruler-straight heading, but usually incorporated several straight lengths. Any alterations of courses of up to ten degrees were

Archaeological divers have now established that the Lumley fish trap has a Roman base to it. We have always thought that this huge construction was too elaborate for a mere fish-weir. The fishermen of old were not millionaires. It also looks as if there have been Roman locks at the west end of the dam,

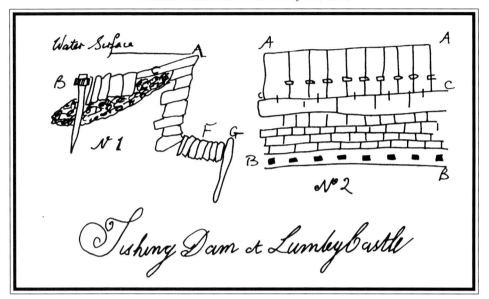

usually made at high points with sudden changes of direction.

The Roman surveyors liked to sight on distant hills and they did not use *gromas*. These instruments with four plumb-bombs suspended from a pole-mounted horizontal cross, were for getting right-angled corners of buildings correct. In the case of the roads, the Roman surveyors (*mensores*) lined-up sighting poles or smoky fires in line, to plan their intended tracks. Every legion had a number of surveyors among its ranks. Their job was to find and mark suitable routes. Engineers would follow behind and carry out the construction of the roads.

Across easy country, the straight lengths were long, and alterations of heading few. On occasion, an existing meandering native track was paved and incorporated into the system. How did the Roman surveyors achieve such accuracy? There was more to it than just keeping poles and fires in line. They had to know where they were going, and in which direction to make a start. We are told that the Romans did not have magnetic compasses. This may be true. What archaeologists should say is that they have not found one yet. Compass needles must be of iron and such delicate artefacts would easily corrode away to nothing. The Chinese had magnetic compasses in their Third Dynasty (Second Millennium BC). It was south-seeking and was called a *Tchi-Nan*. Emperor Tcheou gave one to ambassadors from Cochin China to assist them find their way home. *Yachting Monthly,* (February 1985) tells us that the Roman statesman and admiral, Pliny the Elder (23-79 AD), wrote about errors caused by the proximity of *alio* (another) "needle." The magazine claims that Pliny mistakenly spelt alio as *allio,* the latter meaning "garlic." This, according to the magazine, is why for 1,700 years, there was a superstition at sea that garlic affected compasses. I cannot find the original reference but it is certainly true that one compass does affect another one if they are placed too close together.

It is now known that the Romans traded (by sea) with China and had every opportunity to observe Chinese technology. What has all this got to do with the history of Chester-le-Street? Please bear with me for a while because most of the technical information is important to our understanding of why the Romans selected our home town for their fort.

Whether or not the Romans had magnetic compasses remains to be seen. They certainly used a type of direction-finder but it did not use the Earth's magnetism. They also knew how to find true north from simple observations, and their direction-finding instrument performed the calculation in a few seconds, with a sequence of five simple operations. This instrument is certainly a compass although it was not recognised as such by the archaeologists who found it. They refer to it and other examples found at various sites, as "portable sundials." The instrument is of course, a "sun-compass." As soon as I saw it, I knew what it was and how to operate it because I had used an instrument which performed the same task, while flying aircraft in polar regions where magnetic compasses are unreliable. Our aircraft instrument (astro compass) did not physically resemble the Roman sun-compass but the latter had the same inscribed settings on it as the aviator's navigation aid. I found that I could set up the Roman instrument with the Royal Air Force check-list. As will be seen in Chapter 12, the Vikings also possessed a sun-compass but of a totally different design from the Roman device.

The Roman architect and engineer, Vitruvius tells us how to find north without instruments:

"Describe a circle on the ground and push a stick vertically into the centre. The stick's height must be such that the end of the shadow in the early morning and late afternoon lies outside the circumference of the circle, but inside at midday. Once in the morning and again in the afternoon, the end of the shadow will just touch the circumference. Join these points thus obtaining a chord. Then from the centre of the circle draw a line which bisects the chord, and this line is true north."

The Roman sun-compass dispensed with the above lengthy procedure (see "Roman Ships," Chapter 7 for drawings and checklists).

The Vikings refer, in a *saga,* to a "sunstone" with which they used to take bearings of the Sun in overcast weather *(Raudulfs Pattr ok Sonum Hans).* There is also a Roman reference by the Roman admiral and writer, Pliny the Elder, to a similar stone which he calls *Solis Gemma.* The material is a calcite mineral called cordierite, and bearings of the obscured Sun can be taken even when it is up to seven degrees below the horizon. A modern airman's navigation aid called a "Kollsman's Sky Compass" uses the same principle. The "sun-stone" will be dealt with in greater detail in Chapter 12.

I knew an American yachtsman who often sailed from San Francisco to Hawaii and he carried no navigation aids whatsoever; he said: "I merely follow the vapour trails," (most trans-Pacific aircraft refuelled at Honolulu during that period). Ancient navigators often followed migrating birds so there is nothing new.

Useful bird-pathfinders for ancient mariners were the wild geese which flew in "V-shaped" skeins. Geese do not adopt the V-formations so that the leader can "break the air" like Good King Wenceslas treading a path through the deep snow for his poor little page following behind him. Each bird flies just outside the turbulent wash of the bird in front. When an aircraft pilot flies in formation, he does the same thing. If he flies directly behind the aircraft in front, the controls become difficult to handle and the aeroplane bucks about like a bronco.

A glider pilot being towed by a powered aircraft, flies just above or just below the wash of the tug.

We will now look further at ancient navigation and the importance of this to Chester-le-Street. This will become obvious to readers when we look closely at Roman trade and travel. For serious students of Chester-le-Street's early history, we must study evidence from elsewhere in the Roman Empire, and even further afield, in order to understand what we are finding in the rivers of our home area.

Our archaeological divers have established that the Lumley Fish Trap was originally a Roman weir. While searching the bed of the river, our two experts, for a few seconds, thought that they had found the remains of a Roman barge. Unfortunately, it turned out to be the wreck of the sea cadets' boat which was let loose by vandals some thirty years ago. The boat was swept over the weir and wrecked. While our underwater searches for more Roman evidence continue, let us look at the finds in some other British rivers:

An astonishing amount of information about Roman inland water transport is tucked away here and there:

Near the Roman fort at Netherby (Castra Exploratorum) NY 397 716, on the River Esk, north of Carlisle, an account is left for us, written c1536, by the antiquarians Leland and Bainbrigg:

"Men alyve have seen rynges and staples yn the walles, as yt had been stayes or holdes for shyppes...Ships' sides, anchors and iron rings, such as ships are tied up to, were found there, but the accummulation of sand had shut the sea out for a distance of several miles, blocking the port, and the ancient little city was now a corpse."

An aerial search showed that a stream passing the fort and joining the Esk at Scaurbank, may have been used as a canal of the same type that we had running into Hinegan's Pond at Chester-le-Street. In the vicinity of the Netherby Roman fort, a ground inspection showed that the bed of the stream is paved.

In the main river, upstream from the fort, is a broken weir and the stonework is of the "herring-bone" type so often seen in the cores of Roman buildings, take Lanchester Roman fort for example.

The Netherby dam, now ruinous, has been impressed in more recent years, to provide a head of water for an electric generator which supplied the Netherby mansion house. The latter sits right on top of the fort and obscures most of the Roman remains.

Although nothing to do with navigation, and away from the river, a curious auditorium-shaped, semicircular recess has been cut into a low hill to the north of the fort. It may turn out to be a small, hitherto unknown theatre. In 1958, the remains of two vessels of the Roman period were found in London, one in the River Thames in the mud under Blackfriars Bridge, and the other at Guy's Hospital in Bermondsey, when the foundations for a new surgical block were being excavated. The Blackfriars ship was flat-bottomed, constructed of oak with iron fastenings, and had a cargo of Kentish ragstone on board. Pottery sherds in the ship dated the vessel to the second century AD.

Only part of the Guy's Hospital vessel survived, but the construction was similar to that of the Blackfriars ship and, although both ships had been used by the Romans, they were of Celtic-type construction; Roman-built ships used planks edge-to-edge (carvel built) with mortise-and-tenon joints, whereas Celtic types used overlapping planks (clinker-built) with caulking of hazel twigs in the seams. The "clinker" type of construction was used in northern Germany and the later Saxon and Viking ships were built in a similar manner.

In 1910, a Roman ship was found at County Hall in London and this vessel was of standard Roman mortise-and-tenon construction although the species of oak used was not native to the Mediterranean. On the continent of Europe, there is more evidence:

A craft estimated to have been fifteen metres in length was found in 1899 at a depth of five metres during the excavation of the Brugge-Zeebrugge canal. This craft had a step for a mast similar to that found in the Blackfriars ship. The remains which are stored in the Musée de la Marine in Antwerp have recently been radiocarbon-dated to AD180.

The partial remains of a Roman river barge were found at Wanzenau in Alsace and this had a cargo of basalt-lava millstones. It is thought to have been a *lintre* of the third century AD.

In 1892, a craft believed to be Roman was found at Vechten near Utrecht in the Netherlands. From its description, it is similar to the County Hall ship. Another vessel similar to the County Hall ship was found in 1809 on the banks of the Somme, and was surrounded by Roman weapons and pottery.

During the period 1968-71, the *Instituut voor Prae-en Protohistorie* of the University of Amsterdam, excavated a Roman auxiliary fort called Nigrum Pullum (Black Chicken) on the south bank of the River Rhine. In 1971, a dugout boat was found, and in 1974, a series of further excavations recovered three more dugouts, three barges and a steering oar. The three dugouts are all of oak and their length and beam measurements are: 6.99m x1.05m; 5.48m x 0.76m; and 10.40m x 1.40m. These craft would have been capable of navigation into the very highest reaches of rivers, and calculations show that two of them would have carried five tons each and the third, ten tons. This last cargo is equal to that of twenty ox-wagons.

This illustration of a modern Dutch barge shows the advantage of water transport over land transport. Here, a barge carries the same cargo as eighty railway freight wagons. A Roman codicaria (general purpose barge) carried at least ten tons (equal to twenty ox-wagons) and was operated by four men. The one-mph ox wagon with a crew of two and only a half-ton load, could make five miles per day not counting gradients, some of which would have been impossible for any type of wheeled vehicle to negotiate.

A Roman general purpose codicaria which would have plied between Hylton and Chester-le-Street, and almost certainly further upsteam to suspected Roman sites at Finchale and Durham and to a known fort at Binchester. Binchester has an ancient canal system which is obvious from the air.

This painting is of a cargo canoe in Northern Canada. The heavy craft is being towed up rapids by four hauliers. Rivers like this in Britain have been incorrectly assessed as having been un-navigable to the Romans.

Modern historians often dismiss rivers as having always been un-navigable. This is far from the truth. When necessary, dreadful rivers have been navigated. Take for instance this picture of aviation fuel on its 750 mile journey up the River Tocantins to the Brazilian airfield at Carolina. This river is dangerous and riddled with rapids. Progress was slow and, time after time, the big drums had to be unloaded to make the river boats light enough to be hand-hauled through the swirling waters. On the first leg of the trip, from Belem to Maraba, five trans-shipments had to be made. Each time, the drums had to be heaved up the bank and hand-rolled around the rapids. At one spot, the job was made easier by a little wood-burning railway. At another, a truck was used. At a third spot, the undergrowth was too dense for the drums to be carried overland so they were dragged through the water. At Maraba, the drums were transferred to smaller, more agile craft, but the endless unloading-hauling-loading sequence continued. The author thinks that the Brazilian hauliers of the River Tocantins would regard minor British rivers such as our own Wear as easy transport routes. Compared with their tortuous navigation of the River Tiber into the mountains 150 miles from the sea, no doubt the Roman bargemen thought so too.

A keelboat of the 18th & 19th centuries. We can learn much about the ancient transportation use of our northern rivers from records by later navigators. Seven-hundred-and-fifty keelboats plied the River Wear and each keel carried 21 tons, 4cwt, of coals (eight chaldron [wagon] loads) from upstream pits to seagoing colliers waiting in the river mouth at Sunderland. The keels could make Biddick on every tide but Picktree Quay at Chester-le-Street only on the fortnightly Spring Tides. The Romans seem to have had a better system with a permanent high tide at Chester-le-Street as a result of their massive stone weir at Hylton. A keelboat was crewed by four men and could be rowed, towed, sailed or poled exactly as the Roman codicariae which had plied the same river one-and-a-half-thousand years earlier. There is a record of the coal-owning Lambton family operating keels in 1580. In 1829, keels transported one-million-eight-hundred-and-fifty-five-thousand tons of coal down the Wear to Sunderland.

Roman barge being loaded at Ostia for the journey up the Tiber to Rome (from an illustration in the Vatican Museum).

A Roman warship carrying a cargo of barrels on the River Moselle. This sketch was made from a stone-carving found at Neumagen, Germany (Landesmuseum, Trier.)

A 1,500 lb, 50 ft riverboat with a five-man crew being poled against fast water in the rapids of the Seneca Bypass of George Washington's Patowmack Canal. The boat is a replica built by the Virginia Canals and Navigation Society. One crewman handles the steering sweep while another stands in the bow, fending off rocks. The other three propel the boat by jamming their poles against the bottom and walking the planks that run on both sides from bow to stern. The Seneca Bypass avoids a seven-foot-high waterfall in the main river, and by lowering the gradient with a wide bend, does so without any kind of lock.

A Roman codicaria under tow. Each haulier had an independent tow-rope to the short towing-mast and each haulier used a walking-stick. Roman records tell us that the bargemen chanted as they progressed along river or canal banks.

The three barges found at the same site at Nigrum Pullum/Zwammerdam, have been dated to the second century AD. The first one is 22.75m in length with a beam of 2.80m. It has a mast-step too small for a sail-carrying mast so the mast must have been for tow-ropes. The second barge is 34m long with a beam of 4.40m. It has a step for a large mast and was therefore capable of being sailed. The third barge is 20.25m long and has a beam of 3.40m. Typical Roman mortise-and-tenon joints were used in its construction. The mast-step is a quarter of the length from the bow, and this is not on the point of balance necessary for a sailing mast, so this craft must also have been of the towed variety. The largest of the three barges would have carried over fifty tons of cargo which is equivalent to a hundred ox-wagon loads.

In 1975, a new canal was under construction near the small village of Pommeroeul in Belgium. This village is about half-way between the towns of Mons and Tournai and is close to the point where a Roman road leading from Bavai to the north crosses the small River Haine and a tributary. The modern canal constructors uncovered a completely unknown Roman settlement beside the junction of the rivers. Archaeologists found a Roman *vicus* (civil settlement) in the silted-up bed of the River Haine, and also timber quays which they were able to date to the second century AD. Five boats were also found in the silt of the river bed. One was too badly damaged to be identified, but of the remaining four craft, two were identified as dugouts and two as barges. The date of abandonment of the vessels has been estimated at either the second half of the first century AD or the first half of the second century. One barge is estimated to have been 18-20m long with a beam of 3m, and, including the gunwhale, 0.67m high. The construction was a large dugout split down the middle with extra planks inserted between the halves. On the poop was a transverse steering-platform fitted with anti-slip strips and there was a cabin 2.30m long near the stern.

Large amounts of Roman artefacts were recovered from the river silt, many of them pieces of nautical equipment. Several dozen pole-ferrules and boat-hooks were found as well as a stone sounding-weight with a groove for the string, and anchor stones. Other finds indicated

Pommeroeul, on the River Haine in Belgium, about halfway between Mons and Tournai. Modern canal constructors found a completely unexpected Roman port and civil settlement on this small river, the latter about the size of our own Cong Burn. Five Roman rivercraft were recovered; some still had their cargoes on board. In Britain, Roman river-supplied forts nearly always have strange river loops, old channels and islands close by. Chester-le-Street is no exception.

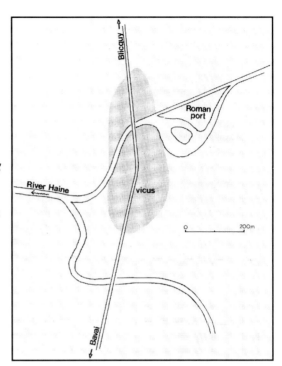

that the cargoes had been varied: leather, coal, peat, pottery and building-stone.

Pommeroeul is on a very tiny river (about the size of our own Cong Burn) and is sixty-three miles from the sea. The Roman port has a layout which will be noticed time and time again as our search progresses. A bend in the river has been short-circuited by an artificial channel and the main river has been widened to form a basin with an island in the middle. This configuration provides ideal sites for weirs and locks. For now, I will call them "funny rivers." A typical example is at St Albans (Verulamium). The River Ver divides into two branches north of the Roman town-wall and there are tell-tale signs of a possible barge basin. In the eleventh century, the biographer of Abbot Ealdred of St Albans recorded that: when the holy man had stones for his new church dug from the Roman ruins of Verulamium, his men came across oak timbers smeared with pitch and with rivets in them, half rusted anchors, and pine oars, down by the river bank. Presumably these were the remains of a Roman ship, and this is the earliest account of the digging-up of one. Just over two miles downstream at the Roman Park Street villa site, a Roman jetty was found. In 1630, the Benedictine monks at St Albans were using an old Roman "causeway" as a mill-dam.

Other ex-Roman towns and forts with "funny rivers" are: Canterbury (Durovernum); Dorchester (Durnovaria); Colchester (Camulodunum); Winchester (Venta); Lincoln (Lindum); Chester (Deva); Inchtuthil; Bertha; Glenlochar; and dozens more.

Mr J Gibbons-Partridge writing in *Popular Archaeology* Feb 1985, refers to Irchester and a possible artificial Roman canal from the River Nene. A small inlet from the Nene leads to a wide suspected harbour and then to a ten-feet-wide waterway which extends for nearly four-hundred yards and terminates below the north wall of the fort. This is very nearly the same as the Concangis set-up at Chester-le-Street except the harbour (Hinegan's Pond) has an extra water channel leading out, heading south-east for the Lumley "fish-trap."

The examples are endless and to cover them all would take up too much space in this book, so let us return to our home area of Chester-le-Street and see what other evidence there is:

A few years ago, from our aircraft, we spotted a possible Roman site at Picktree (NZ 280 530). The earthworks of one corner of a suspected Roman fort platform can be seen clearly in the field just south of Picktree House. The other corners can be seen from the air as crop marks or soil marks. The keelboatmen had a jetty in the wood below, hence the name Picktree Quay Wood.

Picktree, near Chester-le-Street. In the field at centre are earthworks (right) and soil marks (left) of a suspected early Roman fort. Maybe large Roman barges docked here with smaller codicariae making it to Hinegan's Pond and further upstream to Durham and beyond. Bottom right is Picktree Quay Wood, so named by the later keelboatmen who loaded coal here for Sunderland. When the motorway was constructed, a worker using a metal detector found a considerable number of Roman coins in the copse, centre left.

73

During the construction of the A1(M) motorway to the west of the site, a workman using a metal detector found a couple of dozen Roman coins in a small copse (NZ 281 527) on the east side of the southbound slip-road. In the next field south (NZ 283 523), a lady-potato-picker in 1945 picked up a very valuable gold Roman coin. There are some very strange large ditches in Picktree Quay Wood, and these may have something to do with Roman defences, or they could even be part of a Roman waterway.

The purpose of the strange ditches in the area could be explained as follows:

In 1796, a canal was proposed to link the City of Durham with the River Tyne; down the Wear to Picktree and then via an artificial ditch to the Tyne. This canal was never built but the proposed line of the ditch to the Tyne takes an easy route and I quote from R Dodd's Report of 1796:

"The second part of the line is from the River Wear, near Picktree, to Redheugh in the River Tyne, nearly opposite to Newcastle, containing 7 miles, 2 furlongs and 6 chains, and lies down the beautiful Vale of Team; the lower part of which, near the River Tyne if fo flat, that after locking-up from the river southwards, one lock will carry us nearly 3 miles, as may be feen by the profile of levels on the plan. Still pursuing this vale southwards for the purposes of navigation, I find it rifes to the height of 91 feet 7 inches above high water mark; but as the extreme height of this is but a few chains in length, I recommend a little deep cutting to reduce it to 80 feet, fo that 10, eight feet locks will enable us to ascend its height; with the like number to descend; the principal part of this cutting will be, in crossing the road from Durham to Newcastle, near Sir John Eden's waggon-way, the line then defcends through a deep hollow-way, part of it like a canal already cut, and abounding with springs of water; it then curves a little to the eastward, and enters the navigable part of the River Wear near Picktree. Thus two great rivers are joined by only 7 miles, 2 furlongs and 6 chains, canal navigation."

The strange ditches can still be seen. Dare I suggest that the Romans beat the 18th century planners to it, and had a canal between the Wear and the Tyne?

A rise of 90 feet would not have deterred Roman canal builders. Roman engineers planned a canal to link the Rivers Moselle and Saone. Roman general Lucius Vetus prepared to connect these rivers so that goods could route from the Mediterranean, up the Rivers Rhone and Saone, through the canal, into the River Moselle, then via the Rhine to the North Sea. When this canal was proposed, the Romans were already making full use of the above rivers for transport but a linking canal would have avoided trans-shipping cargoes to expensive pack animals for the crossing of the watershed. For political reasons, the Roman canal was not built but the modern Canal de L'Est which approximates to the Roman planned line has a climb of 450 feet in thirty miles. The modern canal uses pound-locks.

Even if the Romans used only flash-locks which they describe, the argument is academic because when single flash-lock barriers are close together, they form a ladder of pound-locks.

In a letter to Emperor Trajan which survives, Pliny the Younger, the Roman governor of Bythinia asks Emperor Trajan for permission to build a canal from an inland lake to the sea because of the high cost of road transport. He tells the emperor than he can accommodate changes of canal levels by means of "sluices" (flash-locks?).

When Emperor Claudius came to Britain in AD 43 to observe the British surrender, he travelled by ship to Gaul, and by a mixture of river and road transport across that country, and then by ship again to Britain.

Southern Britain had many Roman water routes across it, both natural and artificial. The Romans constructed long canals linking one river to another, but in the Fen country, navigation was easy.

Until about the middle of the Nineteenth Century, Fen lighters carried their own staunching tackle to overcome shallows in the River Nene between Wisbeck and Peterborough. Temporary weirs, using an empty barge, stakes and canvas sheets, were constructed. The sheets were supported by the stakes and the bottoms of the sheets trodden into the river bed. This raised the water level above the temporary weir. The author Hugh McKnight in his *Shell Book of Inland Waterways* believes that in places, the Romans negotiated the Nene in a similar manner. Roman waterways "experts" in the Fens talk about the Romans diverting rivers into catchwater-drains; surely it should have been the other way round? A complete re-think is necessary with regard to Roman logistics in the area. In the *Sunderland Echo*, Friday 6th August 1999, the Tyne & Wear County Archaeologist, David Heslop, commented on a possible Roman site in Sunderland. He said that he thought that a Roman fort or fortlet had existed under the now redundant Vaux Brewery and as this building is to be demolished, an excavation should take place. Mr Heslop also said that he thought that a unit of the *Bacarii Tigrisienses* had been stationed in Sunderland. He also spoke of the large amount of Roman finds in Sunderland and called for an intensification of investigations. Our own Society will be in the forefront of any such searches.

Earlier this month (Aug.99), the Information Officer for Tyne & Wear Museums, speaking on BBC2 said that South Shields Roman fort had been a base for Roman supply ships and that the whole eastern part of the Roman Wall had been supplied by barge from South Shields.

We know that the Romans built navigation weirs and dams all over their Empire. It is strange that none have been officially recognised in Britain. The next chapter will show that remains of Roman dams do exist here, but have been identified incorrectly as bridges and fish-traps, and also frequently disguised by later reuse as mill-dams. The Institution of Civil Engineers of Northampton greatly assisted me with the work at Piercebridge. This Roman fort and town proved to be the archetype for further investigations of Roman river supplied sites.

Opus Revinctum

In 1930, when the bed of the Chester-le-Street Cong Burn was cemented to ease the clearance of rubbish, large Roman stones with dove-tailed cut-outs for butterfly locking-cramps, were found. The Romans called this type of stonework *"opus revinctum"* (bind-fast-work), and this technique was invariably used in situations where pressure of water caused problems for structures such as bridges, dams, jetties and cisterns. The dove-tailed stones at

Chester-le-Street were not found in the vicinity of the Roman road-crossing of the Cong Burn but well downstream, just where the old dry water-course from Hinegan's Pond to the dam in the Sewage Works loop would have intercepted the stream. It looks as if the Romans carried their canal across the Cong Burn on the upstream side of a dam which would also have maintained the navigation-level into Hinegan's Pond and beyond to the Lumley fish-trap which we are now sure began life as a Roman navigation structure. Several years ago, the Northumbria water authority constructed a concrete weir on top of the ancient ruinous masonry structure and many Roman-looking stones came to light. Quite recently, our own archaeological

OPUS REVINCTUM Roman stones

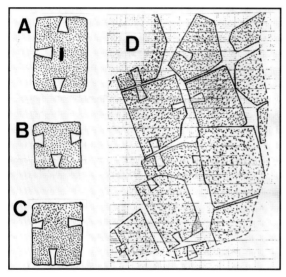

A = Roman stone from the Roman dam at Hylton (Dam dismantled in the early 1800s). Hundreds of these stones were used for harbour repairs, but dozens, surplus to requirements were merely dumped on the north side of the inner North Mole and around the inner South Mole where they still lie today. Some stones have lewis lifting holes as well as opus revinctum holes, the latter for butterfly-cramps.

Other ex-Roman stones still have quarry perforations drilled in lines by Romans using star-chisels. The quarrymen broke off these stones which separated along the perforations.

B = Ex-Roman stone from Jarrow Saxon Monastery. It is built into the south wall. We are certain that a Roman fort existed at Jarrow and this stone probably came from a Roman jetty on the River Don.

C = Stone from Roman bridge over the River Kelvin at Balmuildy. This stone is preserved in the Hunterian Museum, Glasgow.

D = Opus revinctum in the Chesterhope Burn at Habitancum (Risingham) Roman fort, West Woodburn, Northumberland. These stones are said to have been part of a Roman bridge but they may have formed part of a Roman jetty.

Opus revinctum stones were removed from Chester-le-Street's Cong Burn in 1930. The fate of these stones is unknown. Opus revinctum stones were invariably used in positions where water pressure had to be resisted: bridges, dams, jetties, locks, cisterns etc. The so-called "strong-room" in South Shields Roman fort uses "OR" in its walls but as there is a sump (for a Ctesibian pump?) in the floor, the building is more likely to have been the main cistern for the Roman fort. Bank vaults do not have sumps in their floors.

A stone in a Roman structure at Risingham (Habitancum) Roman fort. This stone is one of several in the Chesterhope Burn near its confluence with the River Rede. It may be part of a Roman bridge abutment, or a jetty.

A reused Roman opus revinctum stone built into the wall of Jarrow Saxon monastery. This stone is probably from a Roman jetty. It is highly likely that Jarrow Monastery sits on top of a Roman site.

A guillotine or portcullis-type lock gate. The author thinks that the Romans used this type of gate in their canal locks. The Latin word cataracta has two meanings; "portcullis" and also "waterfall." Both meanings are brought together in a canal or river lock.

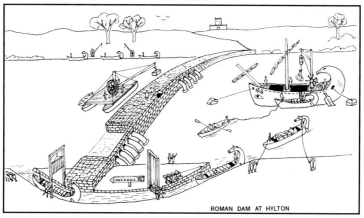

An artist's impression of the great Roman dam at Hylton. This dam, in a ruinous condition, was removed in the early 1800s at the insistence of the keelboatmen to whom it was an obstruction to navigation at low tide. Its Roman role would have been to provide a constant level of high tide all the way to Chester-le-Street. Further Roman dams at Chester-le-Street would have enabled Roman navigation to destinations upstream from Chester-le-Street.

A Norwegian PBY Catalina flying boat taxiing into the River Wear from Sunderland Harbour c1945. Behind is the old pilot-house, now demolished. Behind the aircraft, part of the pier is built of vertical timber piles and huge roughly-cut stones. This part of the pier was refurbished recently and most of the stones proved to be reused Roman ones of the "opus revinctum" type, i.e with dove-tailed holes which had been used to tie the stones together with butterfly-shaped iron cramps. All the Roman stones are thought to have come from Hylton when the great Roman dam was dismantled in the early 1800s. Many more ex-Roman stones, surplus to c1810 requirements, were dumped on the north side of the North Inner Mole and around the Inner South Mole.. They are still there for all to see.

An ex-Roman stone (broken in two near the lewis hole) dumped on the outside of the North Inner Mole at Sunderland (Roker) Harbour. This stone, along with dozens of others, according to records, was dumped here when the great Roman dam at Hylton was dismantled in the early 1800s.

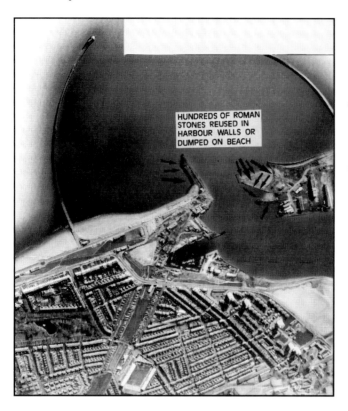

HUNDREDS OF ROMAN STONES REUSED IN HARBOUR WALLS OR DUMPED ON BEACH

The old inner moles at Sunderland Harbour. On the outside of the North Inner Mole, hundreds of dumped ex-Roman stones of the opus revinctum type can be seen at low tide. Some stones also contain "lewis holes" for the forfex lifting devices of Roman cranes. A few stones also have lines of Roman chain-drilled quarry holes, which the Romans used to break stones away from the quarry face. The Romans drilled lines of these "perforations" with "star-chisels." Just as this book is going to print, our investigators decided to look into the private dockyard beside the South Inner Mole at Sunderland to see if any Roman stones had been dumped there. They were astonished to find about two-thousand tons of them built in random fashion into dockside walls and dumped as rough sea-erosion defences. Some had both lewis holes and opus revinctum dove-tailed holes for butterfly cramps. This discovery has changed Sunderland from a town with little Roman history into the forefront for investigation. Geologists from Sunderland University have siezed on the project and very soon, our local history books will have to be scrapped. The lewis lifting device was re-invented in medieval times but the lewis-holes at Sunderland are definitely of the Roman type, most of Mark-1 style but a few of Mark-II, the latter which had just one end of the lewis cut angled. There is no record whatsoever of the medieval or later use of opus revinctum and many of the ex-Roman stones have both types of cut-outs. To the experienced and qualified Roman historian, there is no doubt whatsoever that the Sunderland stones are Roman. Experts from anywhere in the world are invited to inspect the stones.

A Roman stone with opus revinctum dove-tailed holes for butterfly-cramps. This stone has been recovered from Roker and is now on display at NAG HQ in Washington. This stone is almost identical to one of the Roman stones on display in the Hunterian Museum, Glasgow. The Hunterian stone was recovered from the Roman bridge over the River Kelvin at Balmuildy. Many dozens of similar stones still lie on the beach on the outside of Roker's North Inner Mole. Two-thousand more tons of ex-Roman stones lie in the small inlet on the south side of the South Inner Mole in the strictly private area of Sunderland docks. Some of the lewis-holed/opus revinctum stones weigh over six tons each.

divers have examined the river bed below the dam and there is a line of Roman-type oak piles, fastened to horizontal timbers which have the usual Roman mortise-and-tenon joints. The only purpose this dam or weir could have served would have been to make the River Wear navigable upstream from Chester-le-Street. This subject will be mentioned again later but shortly, we will look at the River Wear downstream towards the sea. Just before that however, there follows a list of the places in northern England and southern Scotland where examples of the Roman water civil engineering stones, *opus revinctum* can be seen, or positions known.

North Inner Mole, Roker, (stones from Hylton Roman dam).

South Inner Mole, Sunderland, (stones from Hylton Roman dam).

The Roman bridge abutment (or possiby a jetty) in the Chesterhope Burn, a tributary of the Rede, at the Roman fort of Risingham (Habitancum) near West Woodburn, Northumberland. Map ref of evidence: NY 889 862.

A large stone in the Hunterian Museum, Glasgow. This stone was taken from the Roman bridge across the River Kelvin at Balmuildy.

Hadrian's Wall Roman bridge abutment beside the River Irthing at Willowford. NY 621 663.

Hadrian's Wall River North Tyne Roman bridge near Chollerford. Pier of early bridge incorporated into later eastern abutment. NY 914 702.

Stones recovered from ruins of Carlisle Roman bridge, now lying on the river bank at the confluence of the Eden and the Caldew. NY 396 567.

Roman bridge-stone in Melrose Roman Museum.

Recently discovered ex-Roman stones built into the walls of the ruinous Saxon monastery at Jarrow, Tyne & Wear. NZ 338 653.

Stones from the Cong Burn at Chester-le-Street, fate of stones unknown; findspot (of probable dam): NZ 276 515.

Stones in the so-called "strong-room" of South Shields Roman fort. As this sunken rectangular feature has a deep well built into the west wall and a sump in the centre of the floor (for the intake-pipe of a Roman Ctesibian pump?), it is likely to have been the main water cistern of the fort. Very similar cisterns can be seen in The House of Trebius Valens in Pompeii, and The House of the Wooden Partition in Herculaneum. (see p302, *Roman Building, Materials & Techniques,* by Jean-Pierre Adam).

Roman navigation of the Vedra *Fluvius* (River Wear)

Now to return to Concangis and the River Wear: there is not much doubt that the site for Roman Concangis was chosen because it was at the tidal limit of the Vedra *Fluvius*. Due to "isostasy," the Romans had two more feet of high Spring Tide than present-day levels. Also the base-ramp of the 14th century bridge into Lambton Park, at the bottom of Newbridge Bank, is the modern limit of Spring Tides, but that bridge was not there in Roman times though there was some kind of crossing called "Bruggeford" there in the Saxon period. There was also a Saxon chapel at this point.

Thus Chester-le-Street was within easy reach of the sea by Roman barges. If we leap ahead in history to the keelboatmen of the pre-railway era, we will find that 750 keelboats (cargo 21 tons each), plied the River Wear from Sunderland to various collieries upstream.

Records tell us that the keelboats could make Biddick on every tide (seagoing ships were also built near here), but could only reach "Picktree Quay" at Chester-le-Street once per fortnight on Spring Tides. It is fairly certain that Roman engineers would have made their Vedra *Fluvius* navigable to Concangis on every tide and it just so happens that down at Hylton there was a most unusual Roman structure across the river.

The Roman dam at Hylton

Some antiquarians said it had been a Roman bridge, but it was a solid causeway, and lay at an angle of 45 degrees to the river flow. Other antiquarians said it had been a Roman paved ford but it was laid across the Pool of Hylton, the deepest part of the whole length of the River Wear. Just a couple of hundred yards downstream, the river shallowed to a depth two feet at Low Spring Tide, so surely any fords must have been in this area.

Con *Fluvius*

The River Cone (Roman "Con *Fluvius*") must have been of importance to the Romans as they included "Con" in the name of their fort: "Concangis." Also, a Roman altar dedicated to the "God of the Waters' Meet, (Condatis)" was found at the confluence of the Wear and Cone. The Romans were up to something with the waterways. We are now fairly sure what it was: the River Wear was the major Roman supply line for heavy goods. The Roman road network served an all-weather police-action function and it has been realised only recently that the Roman one-mile-per-hour (on the flat), five-miles-per-day ox-wagons would not have been able to cope with the very severe Roman road gradients, often one-in-four, occasionally one-in-three. All of a sudden, it has been admitted that Roman forts were nearly always sited on rivers because of the low cost and ease of water transport. Roman records tell us that land transport was fifty-eight times more expensive than sea-freight and sixteen times the cost of inland haulage by general purpose barges *(codicariae)*. The Roman regiment, the *Barcarii Tigrisienses* (Bargemen of the River Tigris) at South Shields, and recent research, point to a Roman riverside fort under Castle Street in Sunderland.

Now let us return to the River Wear down to the sea from Chester-le-Street:

The destruction of the Roman dam at Hylton

Early in the 1800s, the huge but mysterious Roman structure was removed from the River Wear at Hylton. It was a solid barrier of massive stone blocks and lay at an angle of 45 degrees to the river-flow. Its position was approximately from the Shipwright's Arms on the north side of the river to slightly downstream of the Golden Lion Inn on the south side. The Hylton Ferry landing reused many massive Roman stones which could be seen until the recent refurbishment and landscaping of the southern river bank.

The purpose of the structure across a very deep stretch of the river, baffled the antiquarians of the day. It was not a bridge, nor would anyone in their right mind build an artificial ford across the deepest part of the river for miles. The structure carried Roman inscriptions and decorations, now lost.

Roman ships having negotiated the river mouth shallows on sixteen-feet high tides could have sat safely in the deep "Hylton Pool" below the dam when the tide went out, ready to transfer cargo to lighters. Norman-French deeds for the Hylton area survive and these tell us that: *"In le Damflat qatuor silioes,"* (In the Damflat there are four selions [strips of rig & furrow]). We are now sure that the structure was a Roman navigation weir, to make the Vedra (Wear) navigable at all stages of the tide, all the way to Concangis (Chester-le-Street). There were further dams and civil engineering works at Chester-le-Street and beyond, to allow onward shallow-draught water transport to proceed to Durham, and also to Binchester (near Bishop Auckland).

Records of the destruction of the Roman structure survive and I will quote some of them here:

The keelboatmen who were plying between the seagoing colliers waiting to be loaded just off the mouth of the Wear at Sunderland and the many jetties from Biddick up to Picktree, relied on the flooding tide to take them upstream. As they had to begin their journeys at the turn of the tide, the ruinous Roman dam impeded their progress and the boatmen campaigned for the structure's removal. They had to manoeuvre through a gap at the southern end through which, at low and half tide, water poured in a torrent.

The structure was dismantled in the early 1800s but discussions continued by antiquarians for many years afterwards. These gentlemen were at a loss as to the purpose of the structure. They knew it could not have been a Roman bridge because Roman bridges did not consist of solid causeways at 45 degrees to the river flow and on the deepest section of the river into the bargain. Roman bridges all had independent foundations on the river bed and Roman bridge-piers were constructed inside evacuated coffer-dams. It was also against Roman law to block a river with a solid barrier unless the structure was to assist navigation.

An antiquarian, The Rev. Featherstonhaugh interviewed a local resident who had observed the destruction of the Roman barrier. The witness described it as a substantial dam which extended over the whole river and was raised many feet above the bed. At ebb tide, the water fell over the whole structure in a cascade. Initially, when the structure was first broken into between the centre and the northern shore, the stones were of massive size, of regular shape, and were tied together with iron cramps bedded in lead. The bottom layer of stones was laid on oaken piles driven into the bed of the river, and on the lower side, and outside the structure, stood piles of greater height. There was a good deal of horizontally laid timber with mortised joints between the piles.

Some of the lead plates connecting the cramps to the stones had curious markings; one circular metal plate had raised Roman letters. The letters were IM.D.AG...AVG around the margin, and S.C. or S.G. in the body of the plate.

An interesting point was raised at a meeting of antiquarians: if the structure had been a ford, then it was a dangerous one. A Mr William Maude had been drowned in 1753 when he was swept away while trying to ride over the remains of it, and Mr Rowland Burdon was so inconvenienced while trying to cross that it gave him the incentive to prospect the new Sunderland bridge. At the close of the meeting, the purpose of the structure remained a mystery.

It does not seem to have been known to antiquarians of that period that the Romans constructed dams all over their empire. Many survive to this day. The Romans dammed the Rhine, and had constructed a bridge over the Danube with nineteen piers, each 150 feet high. Roman engineers could build beautiful bridge spans and did not resort to solid crossings with three times the amount of stone necessary for a bridge.

Mr Lister, the shipyard owner at Hylton, saw hundreds of tons of stone taken out of the river bed by steam cranes, and hundred -weights of lead from the cramping-links were recovered by apprentices during dinner hours. The boys made pocket money from the sale of the lead. One of Mr Lister's lighters sprang a leak and the pile of huge rectangular blocks of stone landed on the quay reached a height of ten feet.

Much of the stone was landed on North Dock at Roker where some of it was used to construct the Inner North Mole, but many hundreds of tons surplus to requirements were merely dumped as rip-rap on the north side of the inner mole. These Roman stones still lie were they were dumped in the early 1800s. Just as this book is being completed, at least two-thousand tons of reused Roman blocks have come to light in the sea defences around the old

South Inner Mole. Some of the blocks must weigh six tons and a great many have Roman style lewis holes for Roman cranes' forfex lifting devices. Many of the stones also have *opus revinctum* - dove-tailed holes for joining butterfly cramps. The discovery removes all argument about the tremendous size of the Roman Hylton structure.

Other stones from the dismantled Roman dam at Hylton were reused for riverside repair works. There were many attempts during the 19th century to remove all the Roman "brigstones."

The Sunderland harbour engineer's report of 1881 has also come to light:

"Gentlemen, I beg to report that a cut of from 90 to 100 feet in width and from 12 to 15 feet in depth below zero level, has now by means of the dredger Hercules, been completed through the 'Brigg Stones' at Hylton, and the result is that the low water of an Ordinary Spring tide has been lowered from the level of a similar tide of 8' 4" on the Hylton tide gauge in 1870, to 3'0" on the same gauge in 1881, thus giving a vertical tide gain of 5'4" at Hylton. It is satisfactory for me to state that this is the result which I anticipated in 1870 would be accomplished by the dredging of the river when carried up to Hylton. I am not yet in a position to state definitely what the actual amount is of tidal gain at Ordinary Spring tides but I do not consider it to be less than 390,000 cubic yards. The dredger Hercules is at present engaged cutting through a sand bank above the Hylton Ferry and on completion of this cut, I propose that she shall commence to remove the projecting point of rock and sand at Parks Nook.

Your obedient servant,

(signed) Henry H Wake."

During the dredger's work of removing the "Brigg Stones" at Hylton, she broke several teeth from one of her cog wheels. If you look at the size of some of the ex-Roman stones dumped on the north side of Roker's North Inner Mole and around Sunderland's South Inner Mole, you will understand why.

Roman cranes, forfex/lewis device

As well as the dove-tailed *opus revinctum* Roman engineering stones, the Romans with their excellent man-wheel driven cranes, as previously mentioned, used a device called a *forfex* which consisted of two triangular metal wedges which fitted into a vertically-cut dove-tailed hole in the top centre of the stone to be lifted. Some of these stones were reused by Saxons after the Roman military departure from Britain. These stones reused in Saxon churches are important for the location of unknown Roman sites, but we will return to this subject in due course.

Later in this book, in the appropriate place, the coal industry, waggonways (old spelling) and coal transport will be covered in great detail by experts on the period, but just for now, let us have a quick look at keelboats in order to compare their operations with Roman barges.

As mentioned previously, keelboats could only make Chester-le-Street on Spring Tides which occur fortnightly when the Sun, Moon and Earth are approximately in line. The tidal limit of the river was now the massive stone ramp on which the 14th century bridge at New Bridge Bank is built. Old wagonways (of the horse-drawn type) can be seen running towards Picktree Quay Wood. Before the medieval bridge was built, the spot was known by the Saxon name "Bruggeford" (Bridge-ford) so there was an ancient crossing here. This can be seen at low tide about fifty yards downstream from the 14th century bridge. The Lambton end of the bridge also carries a well-worn inscription on the downstream parapet in memory of one Charles Swinburne who came down the old road (now in the wood) at New Bridge Bank. The road turned ninety degrees left at the foot of the bank to cross the old bridge. Swinburne and his horse went straight ahead over the parapet into the river and the spot is known as "Swinburne's Leap." The old medieval grass-covered road in the wood may be a reused Roman road from Sunderland to Chester-le-Street.

About a mile downstream (NZ 288 526) on the Lambton side of the river is an old keelboat jetty. This takes the form of a huge oak tree-trunk set into the bank-side for keelboats to come alongside to be loaded. Early Ordnance Survey maps mark a horse-driven gin-crane at this spot.

Coal by water, the only way to avoid bankruptcy

Coal owners of the period could not sink their pits more than five miles from navigable water because of the high cost of land transport to the river. Packhorses are recorded as carrying 2 hundred weights (102kg), and carts, 8cwt (407kg). These modes of transport were abandoned very early for the wain which carried 17cwt (864kg). The *wain* was drawn by two horses and two oxen.

In the mid-seventeenth century, horse-drawn *chaldrons* which ran on primitive wooden rails, began to replace the *wains,* and these *chaldrons* (load 2 tons), transported coal from the mines to the the keelboat staithes. Each *chaldron*, pulled by only one horse, could make 2 trips per day on a five-mile run between mine and staithe whereas a *wain*, with four draft animals could complete only one return journey.

The rule for the coal industry was that you used sea transport wherever possible, inland water where you couldn't, and land transport (prior to the development of iron rails and the invention of the steam engine) only for very short distances, otherwise the operation went bankrupt.

The Elizabethan tycoon Thomas Sutton bought up Leicestershire coal for the London market in an attempt to undercut Tyneside's product. The River Trent should have allowed him to do this but his colliery at Coleorton was eight miles from the river and this short land journey increased his costs out of proportion and defeated his plans. He sold out very quickly.

In Bath, Tyne coal coming 400 miles by sea and canal undercut Mendip coal which travelled only twelve miles by road.

During a coal shortage in Bordeaux in the eighteenth century, the Marquis de Solage sent an experimental load six miles from Carmaux by road and 200 miles by inland water. A Tyne collier beat his cargo to Bordeaux and he made a very heavy loss on the operation. These examples demonstrate the high costs of the pre-railway-era land transport. Historians often quote the "Silk Road" as an example of long distance road transport, but commercial roads of that type were used only for luxuries of the very highest value. They could not have coped with vast quantities of heavy or bulky loads. Mail, diamonds and pharmaceutics go as air-cargo today; coal, oil, grain and ore go by ship. You can air-freight cement to South Africa, or the Falkland Islands, but by the time you get it there, it will cost £150 per bag (1999 prices).

Let us get back to our River Wear and the keelboat trade: early steam engines were used to pump water out of collieries; later, stationary steam engines situated on high points on the ridge overlooking the coast, pulled strings of loaded trucks up from lower lying inland collieries. These loaded trucks descended by gravity to the coastal ports and the endless-cable pulled empty trucks the other way. When steam engines were mounted on wheeled chassis, they became mobile locomotives and pulled trucks wherever they needed to go as long as the gradient was fairly easy. Land transport became economical for the very first time; keelboats were rendered redundant and our river's transport role ended.

The following table shows why railways were able to compete with canal and river transport.

Friction: Force required to move 1 ton along level ground:

Loose, sandy soil	457 lbs per ton
Gravelled road	320 lbs per ton
Macadam road	55 lbs per ton
Railroad	8 lbs per ton

The railway still needed far more power than waterborne craft but there were fewer trans-shipments.

Roman cranes and Saxon churches show the way to the Roman sites!
We can pinpoint hitherto unknown Roman sites by the later Saxons reusing Roman building materials. We will now just borrow a little history from Chapter 11 in order to explain this point:

When the Roman army was withdrawn from Britain cAD410, for the defence of Rome, it was not long before the ill-defended and poorly organised Romanised native Celts suffered an invasion by Saxon tribes. The latter were probably encouraged by Saxon mercenary soldiers who were already serving in the Roman army of Britain. These mercenary Saxons probably deserted en-masse from the departing Roman army in order to establish homes in Britain.

The Celts were pursued into the West Country, Wales and Scotland by the new Saxon invaders. The rough new masters of England had no use for Roman aqueducts or heated bath-houses. They did however paganise the Roman temples, some of which had been Christian shrines for the last hundred years of Roman rule. It took another 150 years or so for the Saxons to be Christianised by a double-pronged religious onslaught from the Roman church and from the Celtic church in the Scottish islands. The first Saxon churches in England were rough timber structures but the positioning was important for our researches. Pope Gregory in AD601 sent a letter to his missionary in Britain, Abbot Mellitus and in this he tells him to: "instruct the Anglo-Saxons to build their new churches on the pagan sites." These churches were often placed on the ex-Roman temples inside Roman forts. These late-Roman Christian sites had been modified to accommodate the pagan images of the gods of the invading Saxons.

After the conversion of the Saxons and the subsequent building of timber churches, Flemish artisans would be employed to rebuild the churches in stone and this is where the ruinous Roman forts and temples came in handy - there was a lot of worked stone lying about. Some of these stones were so huge that the Saxons reasoned that the Romans must have been a race of giants. They did not know that the Roman civil engineers had lifted these stones with the aid of huge cranes, powered by convict or POW-driven treadmills.

Some of our early Saxon churches still survive and with a little knowledge, ex-Roman stones from the Roman temples and other buildings, can be identified because of their method of attachment to Roman cranes. For the lifting of heavy stones, the Romans dispensed with hooks, and lifted the stones with iron triangular wedges which were inserted and then locked with a spacer, in a dove tailed hole cut vertically into the top surface of the stone. This device was called a "*forfex*" and the hole it fitted into is known by its modern name: "lewis hole." In the Roman building, this "lifting-hole" was always on the top surface of the stone but as the Saxons had no knowledge of cranes, the hole which later became known as a "lewis hole" can be found on any side of the stone due to the random nature of Saxon construction.

Two ex-Roman lewis-holed stones can be seen in the buttress to the right of the main door of our Chester-le-Street parish church. The lewis-holes have been filled with cement by modern tidy minded maintenance workers.

Unfortunately, lewis holes were re-invented in the medieval period, so such a feature does not prove a Roman origin unless the stone is in a pre-thirteenth century building. Saxon churches are therefore the number-one clues in our search for unknown Roman sites.

In the past, historians have mostly missed the ex-Roman stones and when pointed out to them, they have usually dismissed the evidence as: "stone robbed from the Roman Wall" or: "washed down the river from Corbridge." The truth however is often: "The Romans were up to something right here."

The first mention of the medieval re-invented lewis devices comes in 1357 with "*ij paria lowys*" and in 1368: "*j lowys, j hamo pro codem. (Salzman, Building in England.)*" The 14th century lewis devices consisted of two crescent-shaped prongs but by the end of the 15th century, triangular wedges similar to the Roman types were back in use.

In the medieval period, by far the greatest cost in building was the transportation, not the quarrying, of stone. We are told that: "for the repairs to Tutbury Castle in 1314, the cost of transport by pack-horse over five or six miles, came to nearly twice the cost of the quarried stone." The Saxon church-builders must therefore have looked for stone very close to home.

Roman Hexham?

In addition to the many Roman lewis-holed stones reused in Hexham Abbey, a large Roman tombstone of two tons in weight was found below the floor of the Priory Church. The tombstone is of a cavalryman "Flavinus." According to Dr Bruce, (1883), local masons at the time of discovery were sure that the stone had been taken from the nearby quarry in the cliff face of the Brockley Burn. Dr Bruce rejected suggestions that the ex-Roman stones had been brought from Corbridge. He was certain that Hexham itself had been a Roman station.

The Roman bridge at Bywell

There has long been a tradition of a Roman bridge at Bywell. Two piers were blown up by gunpowder in 1836 and work commenced on the new bridge, slightly further downstream, on the same day. Many ex-Roman stones were re-cut and used in the new bridge.

Our archaeological divers have located some Roman stones, surplus to 1836 bridge requirements, on the river bed. An excavation on the cliff top successfully located the unknown Roman road which had crossed the river via the Roman bridge. In the drought of 1995, about forty Roman lewis-holed stones could be seen on the river bed. They are identical to those used in the tower of the Saxon church of St Andrew's, close by.

According to author-architect Sir Nikolaus Pevsner, Bywell Castle is also built entirely of reused Roman stones.

The Roman bridge at Page Bank

The drought of 1995 also revealed the remains of a Roman bridge at Page Bank, in County Durham. This served a Roman road (mentioned by old antiquarians Gordon and Whellan) between Sunderland and Binchester, via Houghton-le-Spring and Old Durham.

At one time, it was thought that only two Roman roads (Dere Street and Cade's Road) made the transit of County Durham and the discovery of an unknown Roman road anywhere in Britain was heralded as a major discovery. We now know that the whole of Britain was criss-crossed with hundreds of Roman military roads, and there are many more to be found. The Roman road map must have been almost as complex as our modern AA maps. Although we are constantly finding major and secondary hitherto unknown Roman roads which are easy to excavate and identify, it is unlikely that we will ever see the full picture of their minor roads, farm tracks and footpaths. The description of the very recent accidental discovery of a completely unknown Roman vicus road in the centre of Chester-le-Street follows.

A Roman *vicus* road in St Cuthbert Avenue, found 1999

In the Spring of 1999, the owner of bungalow No. 5 St Cuthbert Avenue, Chester-le-Street, David Easton and his friend Keith Balfour, were replacing a water pipe under the driveway of the house. At a depth of three feet, they hit a pavement eighteen feet wide, made of river-washed cobbles, running north-south, parallel with St Cuthbert Avenue, but offset, the western half in the front garden and the eastern half disappearing under the house.

The pavement was flanked on both sides by kerbs of very large rough stones. Dozens of pieces of Roman pottery were picked up and this ranged from 1st century samian to 4th century Crambeck ware. No coins or other metal artefacts were found.

This was a *vicus* road, part of the network of streets just to the south of the fort, in a huge but unexplored civil settlement.

The old "Penny Bridge" below Lumley Castle at Chester-le-Street. A Roman bridge is thought to have existed near the same location.

The Swing Bridge, between Newcastle and Gateshead is on the same site as the Roman and medieval bridges. This photograph taken in 1927 shows the new Tyne road bridge under construction.

upper: The recently discovered vicus road in the front garden of No.5 St Cuthbert Avenue, Chester-le-Street. Left to right: Brenda Ludvigsen, Roman road expert; Christian N. Alexander Selkirk, apprentice digger; Pauline Magee, BA(Hons), qualified archaeologist.

lower: The surface of the road comes to light. At the present time, another vicus road is being examined in the garden of the next street east - Eardulph Avenue. The report will be too late to appear in this book.

The next chapter deals with a very strange Roman "bridge" found at Piercebridge in 1972, high-and-dry in a field a long way from the river. Evidence showed that the river had neither migrated sideways nor scoured-out a deeper channel, so the structure could not have been a bridge at all - it was "A Bridge Too Far!" - it was too far away from the river and too high up the contours. Members of The Institution of Civil Engineers of Northampton agreed with me, and bridge and dam designer, Gordon Heald, produced drawings of the Roman structure which showed that it was the flood-spillway of a Roman dam or weir. This evidence was essential to the investigation of the Roman river supply system so the incorrect interpretation of the structure as a bridge had to be overturned.

A Roman mosaic from Ostia, showing the trans-shipment of amphorae from a merchant ship to a river-craft. In the case of our own River Wear, it is likely that these trans-shipments from seagoing ships to river barges would have taken place at the great Hylton Roman dam. The ship would probably have sat in the deep pool below the dam while cargoes were transferred to barges in the artificially increased water level above the barrier. Perhaps, the trans-shipment took place nearer the river mouth with the Concangis-bound codicariae negotiating the dam via a lock.

With the extra depth of water above the dam/weir, natural obstructions to navigation such as the Biddick rock ridge, would no longer cause problems.

Chapter 4
A Bridge Too Far

"When fact appears opposed to a long train of deductions, it invariably proves to be capable of bearing some other interpretation"

Sherlock Holmes, in Sir Arthur Conan Doyle's, *A Study in Scarlet.*

At Piercebridge, some very important river navigation evidence was found, hence my book of 1983 entitled *The Piercebridge Formula.*

The Roman settlement at Piercebridge sits astride the River Tees and the Roman fort is on the north side of the river, opposite the George Hotel. Two-thirds of the Roman fort lie under the medieval and modern village and one third, plus the civil settlement, lie to the east. The *vicus* fills the Tofts Field and spreads beyond.

Aerial views of the crop mark of the Roman vicus (civil settlement) (V) and the fort (F) on the north bank of the River Tees at Piercebridge. The crop mark of the Roman road "Dere Street" runs from North to South through the vicus. The site of the Roman Dere Street bridge (X) is obvious. The

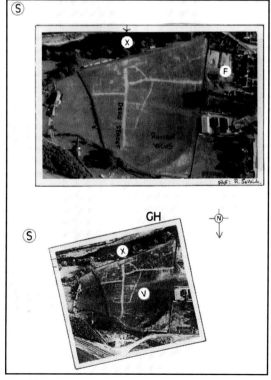

stonework found in 1972, a long way from the river and sixteen feet above the present river bed is at (S). This stonework was incorrectly identified as a "second Roman bridge" and this caused much confusion. The stonework (S) is actually the flood spillway of a Roman navigation weir. These flood spillways were usually at one extreme end of a dam and this explains the position away from the river and high up the contours. When our divers found the genuine bridge at "X" which proved that the Roman river bed and the present day river bed were one and the same, the evidence was resisted by the establishment with convoluted and preposterous arguments. "GH" is the position of the George Hotel which has been a base for all our diving operations.

The Roman road Dere Street comes down from the north and is underneath the very straight B6275 until just a few hundred yards north of the River Tees, where the modern (and medieval) road swings off to the west to cross the old stone bridge. This bridge of three arches is a rebuild of the medieval bridge which had five arches. The Roman bridge was a few hundred yards downstream and Dere Street can be seen clearly from the air across the Tofts Field. The road strikes the Tees at right-angles and this is the obvious site of the Roman bridge. Wooden piles still stuck out of the river at this point just before the Great Flood of 1771 swept them away. Witnesses tell us that this bridge was 260 paces downstream from the "modern bridge" and this agrees with our aerial photographs.

During the drought of 1933, wooden piles were seen on the bed of the Tees at this exact position and all historians and archaeologists were happy with the situation: the fort, the Roman bridge and the line of Dere Street. Pictures of these Roman piles appeared in the *Northern Echo* on 16th Sept 1933 and this demonstrated that the Roman river bed and the present river bed were one and the same.

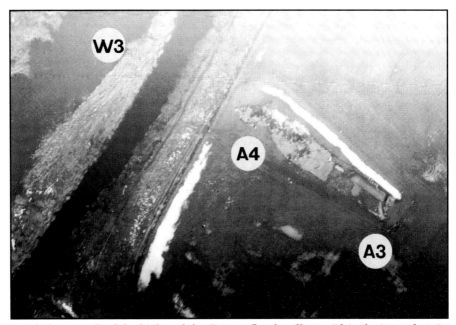

Aerial photograph of the high and dry Roman flood spillway. A3 is the intact but tiny (sixty-ton) southern abutment of the paved flood spillway. A4 is the tumbled remains of the northern abutment which can be mentally reassembled to form a mirror image of A3. W3 is the line of the Roman weir which increased the level of the river by ten feet for small-craft navigation further upstream. The white marks are snowdrifts. The position of the genuine Roman bridge is further upstream and exactly in line with the arrow-straight Roman Dere Street off this photograph. The elongated island is not a Roman feature and was formed some forty years ago by debris from a cliff-collapse half a mile upstream.

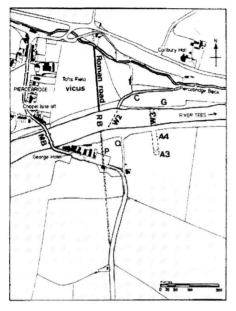

"MB" is the existing three-arched stone bridge which is a rebuild of the five-arched medieval bridge. "RB" is the findspot by divers, of the Roman bridge, exactly in line with the Roman road Dere Street. "C" is a Roman canal which linked the Tees with the Piercebridge Beck. The latter joins the Tees a kilometre further downstream. The whole complex has been reused by later watermills thus camouflaging the Roman handiwork. The canal is however about ten times too large for a simple mill-leat. "W2" is a medieval mill-dam which probably started life as a Roman "wing dam" to deflect water into the huge canal. "A3" is the intact southern abutment of the Roman weir's flood spillway. "A4" is the position of the tumbled remains of the northern abutment of the flood spillway. "W3" is the position of the Roman weir. It is not known yet if the main dam structure was straight or curved. Linear earthworks at "G" are possibly Roman riverside jetties. "P" is the position of the Roman road excavated by our team for a BBC documentary filmed in July 1999. "Q" is a Roman quarry.

This plan shows yet another suspected Roman weir at "W1." This weir has deflected water into a system of huge channels which are part of a suspected Roman barge basin ...(BB), now dry after the destruction of the W1 dam. The system has naturally been reused by medieval millers but the channels are large enough to have floated World War 2 submarines, never mind Roman river barges.

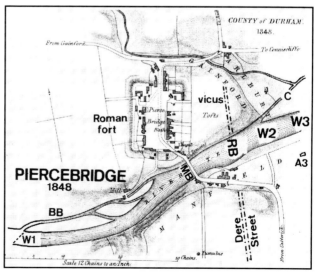

Engineer Neville Andison beside the "A3" southern abutment of the high and dry Roman flood spillway of the "W3" Roman weir. Andison points out the small holes for angled timbers of a light footbridge across the Roman flood spillway. Such a footbridge would have carried the windlasses to operate the cataractae fine-water-level control devices. "B" is the balustrade in which the cataractae would have been installed.

The high-and-dry flood spillway of the Roman weir "W3." "A3" is the southern abutment. At "A4" are the tumbled remains of the spillway's northern abutment. Roman bridges were not built on pavements; each Roman pier always had an independent foundation on the river bed. Normal thousand-ton bridge-piers would have merely sunk down through this nine-inch-deep pavement.

Plan of the southern end of the flood spillway of Roman weir "W3." The "Wall" shown in the now withdrawn official guidebook is the balustrade of the spillway.

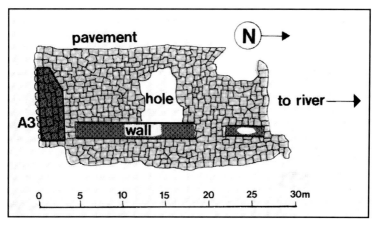

A high and dry large river bridge in the middle of a field?

In 1972, the applecart was upset completely when a gravel-digger hit some Roman stones a few hundred yards further downstream, well off the line of Dere Street, and high and dry in the middle of a field to the south of the river. A small abutment with half a cutwater, stood on a thin paved strip. Although the abutment was complete and contained only 60 tons of stone instead of a normal bridge abutment's 2,000 or more tons, the structure was immediately identified as a "second Roman bridge." "For what else can it be?" said the investigators. But why was the structure high-and-dry by some sixteen feet, and why was it 150 yards from the river? It was *"a bridge too far,"* - too far away from the river and too high up the contours.

The explanation from the archaeologists was: "Simple, old chap; the river has moved sideways since Roman times and has cut a deeper channel (through solid rock) at the same time." This did not ring true.

In our present interglacial period, rivers are depositing gravel, not scouring deeper channels. In our other northern rivers, bases of Roman bridge piers are pristine on the river beds, with not even the Roman toolmarks worn from the stones.

No piers were found on the Piercebridge Roman pavement, but as a bridge had to have piers, five were postulated and marked on the plan with great confidence, but not the slightest evidence.

Roman bridge piers for this size of river were at least a thousand tons each but the abutment was only sixty tons. Any bridge arch, timber or stone would merely have pushed this tiny abutment over.

The tiny abutment also had obvious slots for sloping timbers but these timbers were far too tiny to have been for a Roman bridge. Also they sprang from just two feet above the so-called river bed - the pavement! The explanation was that the Roman engineer had made a mistake and put the timbers in too low before realising his mistake. In addition to that, if the pavement had been the river bed in Roman times, then most of the lower Tees valley including Darlington, would have been inundated.

A guide-book was written, and although Roman bridges were not built on pavements, (each pier always had an independent foundation on the river bed), the guide-book contained a drawing showing postulated piers far bigger than the tiny abutment. This is an engineering impossibility.

In order to convince the general public that this was indeed a bridge, the guide-book contained a drawing of Trajan's bridge over the River Danube, standing on a similar pavement. This immediately brought a blast from Professor JJ Wilkes of London University who enclosed excerpts from a book by Danube bridge expert, D Tudor. This book, *Les Ponts Romains Du Bas-Danube*, clearly demonstrates that the piers of Trajan's bridge had independent foundations on the bed of the Danube and that some of the coffer-dams still surrounded the bases of the piers. The Piercebridge guide-book was immediately withdrawn.

There were more mysteries: why build a second bridge when there was a perfectly good

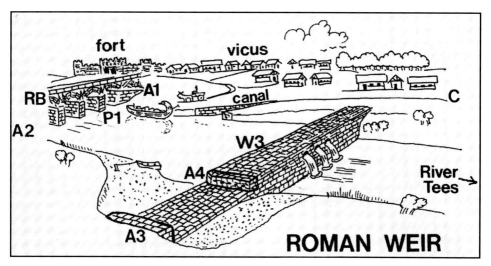

The Roman W3 weir showing its position with relation to the genuine Roman Dere Street bridge and the canal. To simplify the upper drawing, the cataractae of the flood spillway have been left off. The central summer spillway is carrying the normal river flow and the flood spillway is dry.

one a few hundred yards further upstream and exactly on the line of the Roman road into the bargain? The official answer was simply (with no evidence whatsoever): "The first bridge must have been washed away."

Also, along the downstream edge of the pavement of the so-called "second bridge," a wall had been built. You do not block a bridge with a wall. An amazing convoluted tale explained the wall: In Roman times the river moved and this necessitated a third bridge so the Romans must have robbed the stone from the piers of the second bridge in order to build this one! The archaeologists got themselves into a corner from which it was difficult to get out, but pride blinded common sense.

The postulated purpose of the wall was that it was a causeway, which connected the tiny abutment of the redundant bridge with the third bridge. As this "causeway" was only two feet wide, I asked if the Roman oxen had been trained in the ancient equivalent of Billy Smart's circus?

The so-called causeway is, according to the members of the Institution of Civil Engineers of Northampton, the balustrade of a flood spillway of a Roman weir. The balustrade would have contained *cataractae* (lifting gates) for the fine control of river levels above the dam. A light timber footbridge has spanned the flood spillway and this explains the reason for the angled holes for small timbers in the A3 spillway abutment. The most abrasive river in the world is the Colorado in USA and this has cut the mile deep Colorado Canyon. American geologists tell us that this river has taken two-thousand years to cut its bed a foot deeper. The river is also liquid sandpaper and carries ten tons of sand past any given point every second. Why is it that the Tees which is sand-free has had sixteen times the cutting action of the Colorado and why did the cutting action just commence in Roman times? Where therefore, is the Piercebridge Canyon?

The authorities could not answer any of these questions but refused to discuss the issue. Clearly what I had to do in order to prove that the Tees had neither moved sideways nor cut a deeper channel, was to find the remains of the genuine Roman bridge in line with Dere Street, and prove that the bases of the bridge piers stood on the present river bed and that the Roman river bed and the present one were the same. For this I had to have expert divers and this is where Rolfe Mitchinson of Bournemoor and Bob Middlemass of Belmont joined our team.

Photographs of a model of the Roman river complex at Piercebridge. A1 & A2 are the huge abutments needed to take the sideways pressure of a normal Roman bridge. These abutments must have used several thousand tons of stone. They have yet to be excavated. "W3" is a Roman navigation weir and "C" the bypass canal which must have contained some kind of lock to raise and lower the barges. "S" is the flood spillway of the Roman weir and "A4" the tumbled remains of the sixty-ton north abutment of the spillway.

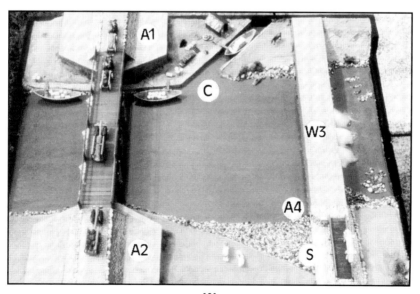

Top. Engineer Andison stands on the excavated balustrade (B) of the flood spillway of the Roman weir "W3." In the background is the "A3" abutment of the spillway. (Bottom) The official guidebook, now scrapped, described this flood spillway as a "second Roman bridge" built after the first one had washed away! The guidebook then talked about the River moving sideways in Roman times, necessitating yet a third Roman bridge and to reach this third bridge, a causeway had been built across the remains of the spurious second one. It was pointed out to the establishment that the so-called "causeway" was wide enough only for a dog, never mind an ox-wagon. "B" is of course, the balustrade of the flood spillway of weir W3.

Further views of the balustrade "B" of the flood spillway of Roman weir "W3" The lower view is to the north and the River Tees is over the hedge and down a sixteen-feet-high bank.

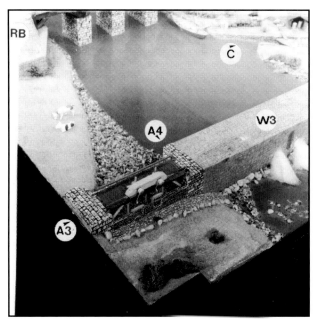

RB = *Genuine Roman Dere Street bridge, the remains of the northern two piers have been found by divers on the present river bed. The third pier lies under the silt of a recently deposited elongated island formed by a cliff collapse upstream. Remains of this southern pier were reported in the Northern Echo, Sept 16th 1933 during a drought. Many Roman piles were visible. These are now hidden under the island.*

W3 = *Roman weir.*

A3 = *Intact southern abutment of Roman flood spillway.*

A4 = *Position of tumbled remains of northern abutment of spillway.*

C = *Upper end of Roman canal to Piercebridge Beck, and subsequently back to river after bypassing yet another Roman dam,*

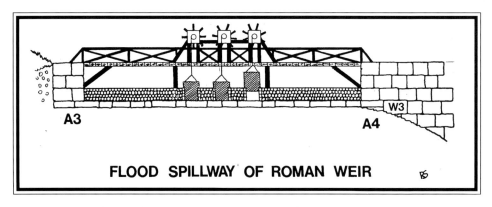

FLOOD SPILLWAY OF ROMAN WEIR

The flood spillway of Roman weir W3 at Piercebridge. The model shows two lifting cataractae gates whereas this diagram shows three. There could have been many more. The spillway of a Roman weir at Montignies St Christophe in Belgium has thirteen small arched and gated culverts.

The flood spillway of the Piercebridge W3 weir compared with the bridged spillway of a medieval dam in the West Country. Light timber bridges across flood spillways would have been necessary for access to the dam for maintenance work.

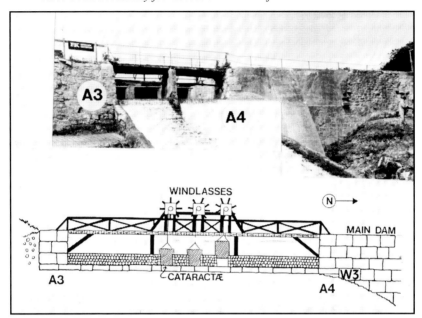

This is a sketch of a medieval painting of a Roman dam and spillway. It hangs in the Monastery of Subiaco in Italy and shows the top of a 120 feet-high-dam which once spanned the River Anio in the garden of Nero's villa. It was the middle one of a cascade of three ornamental dams. St Benedict is shown fishing from the crest of the dam. Later, the lake formed by the dam was used as a reservoir for one of Rome's aqueducts, the "Anio Novus." The medieval monks tampered with the structure and it collapsed as did the other two structures close by.

A small post-hole in the pavement of the flood spillway of weir W3 at Piercebridge shows that only a tiny timber bridge spanned the gap of the spillway. Timbers for normal Roman river bridges were huge.

Centre: The Piercebridge Roman canal at its upstream end. This end of the canal is in the centre of the Roman vicus. Bottom: With the River Tees in flood, the water level with the Roman weir intact was simulated and under these conditions the canal would still have been able to handle a barge. The channel is far too big to have been designed as a simple mill-leat.

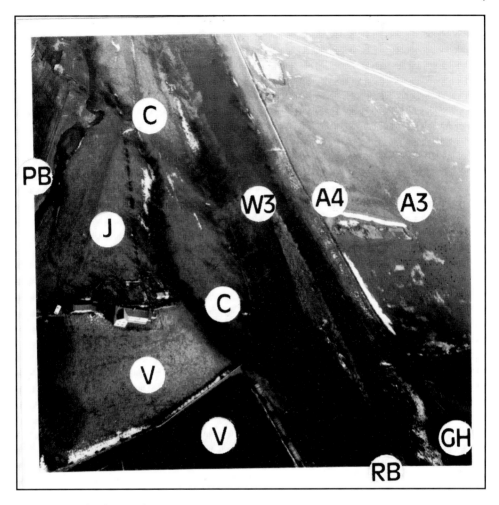

PB = Piercebridge Beck.

C = Roman canal which links River Tees to Piercebridge Beck.

V = Roman vicus.

J = Suspected Roman jetties beside Piercebridge Beck.

W3 = Line of W3 Roman weir.

A3 = Surviving southern abutment of flood spillway.

A4 = Tumbled remains of northern abutment of flood spillway.

RB = Site of Dere Street Roman bridge.

GH = Gardens of George Hotel.

(Top) Although not a Roman structure, this 18th century navigation weir at Bedale in North Yorkshire uses the same principle as Roman weirs. A tiny river has been dammed to extend navigation upstream. A canal with a lock, bypasses the dam, in this case in the field to the right (north). A spillway keeps the navigation upstream at the correct level. (Bottom) Who would think that a small town in the middle of Yorkshire would have had a harbour? The harbour was never used because the Great Flood of 1771 washed away locks in the River Swale. The Bedale Beck is a tributary of the Swale. It looks however as if the Bedale Beck was navigated by the Romans. To the north-west of the military airfield at Leeming and on the west side of the Roman road Dere Street, on the north side of the Bedale Beck, we have found a Roman triple-ditched fort at SE 293 896, partially covered by a roadside farm. I asked an RAF pilot at Leeming, Squadron Leader Moffat, to scan the area and he was successful.

(Top) The spillway of a Roman weir in Belgium on the River Hantes at Montignies St Christophe in the province of Hainaut. On the upstream face of the spillway, the thirteen small arched culverts all have recesses for lifting cataractae.

(Bottom) At the downstream side of the spillway, the excess water falls 2.5 metres (8 feet) down the face of the spillway. Upstream, the small river is ponded back and forms a lake.

The Montignies weir is a typical "Piercebridge Formula" structure. All the elements are there: spillway with narrow pedestrian bridge across it, main dam, and bypass canal, later reused as a mill-leat. As with the Piercebridge weir W3, there was a Roman road in the vicinity but did not cross the weir. This puzzled Belgian historians into first of all twisting the Roman road to cross the spillway footbridge but when a horse and cart tried to cross, it fell into the river. The historians then concocted a Roman ford in line with the Roman road. As at Piercebridge, there was probably a genuine Roman bridge at this spot. Only recently, with the discovery of intense Roman navigation of even the smaller rivers, have archaeologists admitted that the mysterious structure is a Roman navigation weir.

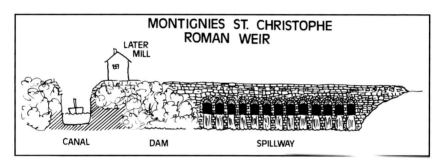

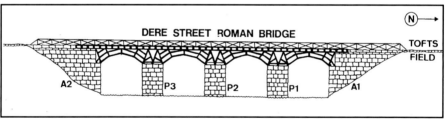

The Dere Street Roman bridge at Piercebridge. In order to prove that the high and dry flood spillway (A3/A4) of the Roman weir was not a second Roman bridge over a river bed which had migrated sideways and dropped sixteen feet, the remains of the genuine Roman bridge had to be found on the present bed of the River Tees and directly in line with the Roman road Dere Street. Not only did our divers find the remains of two piers (P1 & P2) of the Roman bridge, but also thousands of artefacts thrown by the Romans into the river. Dozens of kilos of broken pottery were recovered from between boulders on the river bed. The types of pottery spanned the whole four-hundred-year occupation period. As well as junk, the Romans threw votive offerings to the River gods. Hundreds of coins also spanned all the emperors of the occupation period with no gaps. There had been one, and only one Dere Street bridge. A total of some three-thousand artefacts has been found to date along the line of the bridge, and this includes: figurines, jewellery, Roman boots and a leather swimsuit and all manner of lucky charms, nick-nacks, insignia, weapons and armour.

With the help of Professor Dennis Harding's aerial photographs of Dere Street approaching the north river bank, I was able to put the divers onto the exact line of the genuine Roman bridge. It did not take long for an answer. Rolfe and Bob quickly located the bases of two Roman piers. Oak piles, some of twelve inches square section and others ten inches diameter circular section, had been driven vertically into the river bed and sawn-off level with the present (and Roman) bed. On top of these piles were fixed huge horizontal timbers which had formed base-rafts for the piers. Calculations showed where a third pier should lie but the south part of the river has silted-up into a linear island. This was formed many years ago when a cliff upstream fell into the river and the debris were swept downstream. It will take mechanical equipment to uncover this third Roman pier. The position of the huge southern abutment of the Roman bridge was clear and some very large stones peep out of the bankside right underneath the gardens of the George Hotel.

There were bonuses in store for the divers. Right across the river on the line of the bridge, Rolfe and Bob probed in the hardened mud between the river-bed boulders and found thousands of Roman artefacts. Broken pottery abounded but a large amount of valuable items were recovered - hundreds of coins, rings, figurines, pieces of weapons, segments of armoured mail-shirts, lucky charms etc etc.

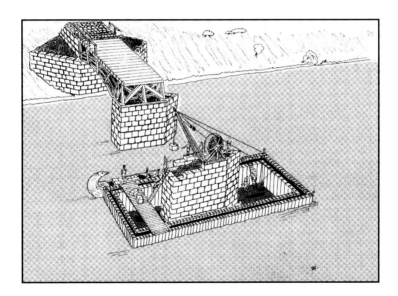

Roman bridges were not built on pavements: each pier had an independent foundation on the river bed and where necessary, these foundations were constructed inside coffer dams as on Trajan's Bridge over the Danube and Roman bridge No.2 at Trier, Germany. The Romans were skilled bridge-builders. They had excellent cranes, pile-drivers, pumps, architects, engineers, surveyors and divers. They also knew that cement would harden underwater if the mix contained volcanic ash.

Unless there was solid river bed-rock, the foundations of Roman bridge piers were built on wooden rafts which were nailed to the tops of dozens of piles driven deep into the river bed. On these rafts, either stone piers or timber pylons were built. This illustration is of a pier-base of the Roman bridge at Mayence, France, and was drawn in 1906 and subsequently published by Professor Albert Grenier of Paris. The bases of the piers of the Roman Dere Street Roman bridge at Piercebridge were constructed in this same standard manner.

A thousand ton Roman bridge pier for a river the size of the Tees, compared with the tiny Roman A3 spillway abutment said by some to have been the abutment of a second Roman bridge. The sideways stresses of a normal-type Roman bridge would have pushed this tiny sixty-ton abutment over.

(Top) A model of the Piercebridge Dere Street Roman bridge showing local wagon traffic between jetties and vicus. A codicaria has just arrived at the upstream end of the Roman canal. This small general purpose Roman barge would have carried the same cargo as twenty ox-wagons. (Bottom)When the Swing Bridge at Newcastle upon Tyne was constructed on the site of the Roman bridge, parts of the timbers of a Roman pier-base-raft were found. These timbers are almost identical to the raft-timbers of the Dere Street Roman bridge at Piercebridge.

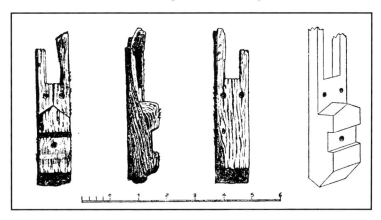

(Above) Early samian pottery and Crambeck ware (below) found by divers on the river bed at Piercebridge on the line of the Dere Street Roman bridge.These pottery finds span the whole four-hundred-year occupation period.

This samian bowl, found on the river bed on the line of the Piercebridge Roman bridge, is stamped with the potter's name, ATILIANI. From this stamp, we know that the bowl was made in Gaul at the Lezoux Pottery.

Roman boots and a leather swimsuit found on the line of the Dere Street Roman bridge (RB) at Piercebridge. The studded boots are equivalent to modern Size 8 shoes. The Roman leather swimsuit is almost identical to the one found in the Thames on the line of the London Roman bridge.

Roman rings, some inscribed, and a brooch (central stone missing) picked up from the river bed on the line of the Piercebridge Dere Street Roman bridge (RB). At eleven-o'-clock is a gold ring with an inset ruby. At two-o'-clock this ring has an inset intaglio. At six-o'-clock this ring is inscribed DM/ ART (for deo Marti, "to the god Mars"). At nine-o'-clock, this ring is inscribed "AVE AMA" (Greetings, Love Me).

An enlarged view of the Roman ring inscribed "AVE AMA."

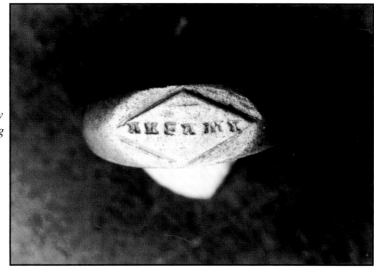

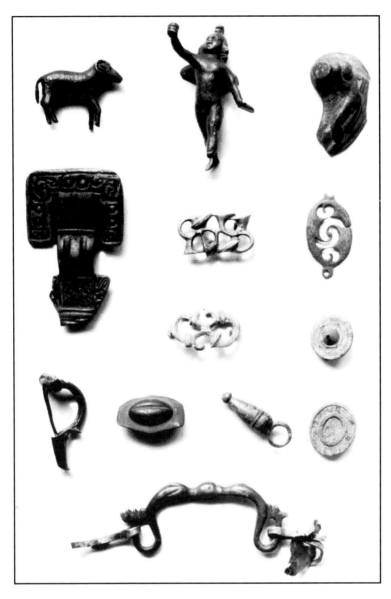

Various artefacts found on the line of the Dere Street Roman bridge (RB). Centre top: bronze figurine of Harpocrates. Top right: Atys expiring under a tree. Top left: the ram of Mercury. Bottom: The hanging handle from a Roman helmet. It depicts two dolphins holding a sphere between their mouths. The Romans knew that the world was round. This helmet-strap is almost identical to the modern Royal Navy submariners' insignia.

Enlarged view of some of the Piercebridge bridge (RB) artefacts.

Top left: the intaglio showing a Roman lady milking a goat.

Top right: the bronze figurine of Mercury's ram.

Bottom: a seventh century Saxon buckle. This Saxon artefact suggests that not only was the Roman Dere Street bridge (RB) not washed away early in the occupation period, but was actually still in operation well into the Saxon period. Why should we be surprised at this? - the Roman bridge at Newcastle upon Tyne lasted a thousand years.

The pottery spanned the whole Roman four-hundred year occupation period as did the coins. In Bishop Auckland on 14th March 1990, a coroner's inquest was held to determine the reason for the deposit of Roman artefacts across the river bed. Dr John Casey, a numismatist, gave evidence and, as reported in the *Darlington and Stockton Times* on 17th March 1990, he said:

"A hundred of the coins contain silver...they date from the First Century AD to the end of the Fourth Century. They were probably thrown into the river deliberately as offerings to the river gods.

We don't know the name of the deity of the River Tees, but most rivers had them at that time. Some of the coins were bent, folded or pierced to take them into the next world."

The jury took only three minutes to decide that the artefacts were votive offerings thrown from the bridge during the entire period of Roman occupation. The coins which were the subject of the inquest were identified by Dr John Casey who prepared a report entitled *"A Votive Deposit from the River Tees at Piercebridge, County Durham."*

Thus we had one Doctor of Durham University telling us that votive offerings had been thrown from the bridge into the river for the whole of the Roman four-hundred year occupation, while another senior archaeologist tried to tell us that the same bridge had been washed away in the First Century AD, thus necessitating a second bridge ("the bridge too far") up in the middle of a field with a postulated river bed some sixteen feet higher than the proven Roman river bed.

There had been no second bridge, so what was the mysterious structure downstream? Civil engineers soon had the answer - it was the flood spillway of a Roman dam or weir. The spillway had been 70 metres wide, and as is usual for a flood spillway, was placed at one end of the dam, in solid ground, hence its position in the middle of a field. The main dam structure had been a solid structure right across the river. A few piles survive in the north bank of the river so there has been no river movement. Across the rock bed of the river where the dam had existed, the divers found no Roman artefacts, but hundreds of pieces of lead as if huge stones had once been tied down in the usual Roman manner with iron cramps seated in lead.

As most of the houses in Piercebridge are built of Roman stones and the river is very shallow in summer, it is easy to figure out where all the stones have gone.

In the north bankside opposite the dam is a massive canal, now dry. This has been the by-pass canal for Roman barges and must have contained some kind of lock.

While our search was in progress, Mrs Elizabeth Waller of Piercebridge told me that there was a line of strange holes cut into the rock river bed some 500 yards further downstream. This single line of square holes angled across the river at thirty degrees. From hole No 9, the divers recovered two coins of Hadrian. They were welded by age to the bottom of the hole and had to be prised-off with a diver's knife. In holes 10 and 11, wooden stubs remain and these can be dendro-dated whenever it can be arranged. There had been a cascade of four Roman dams at Piercebridge but this can best be appreciated from diagrams.

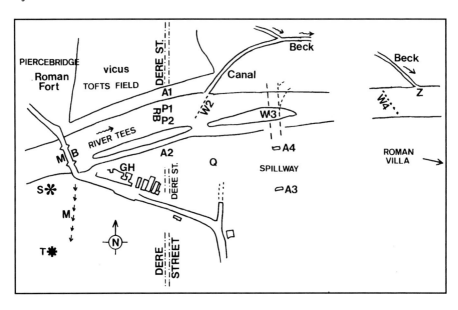

T	=	Tumulus, reused by Cromwell's troops as a cannon emplacement.
S	=	Site of suspected Roman signal station.
MB	=	Medieval bridge.
M	=	Medieval track possibly on top of early Roman road.
GH	=	George Hotel.
A1/A2	=	Sites of abutments of Dere Street Roman bridge.
P1/P2	=	Remains of two of three piers of Dere Street Roman bridge.
W2	=	Medieval mill-dam, possibly ex-Roman canal wing-dam.
Q	=	Roman quarry.
W3	=	Line of Roman navigation weir.
A3/A4	=	Flood spillway of Roman weir, W3.
W4	=	Post holes of Roman weir W4. Roman coins found in holes.
Z	=	Confluence of Piercebridge Beck and River Tees. There is another suspected length of Roman canal to the East of High Coniscliffe and the remains of more suspected Roman dams/weirs further downstream as well as upstream from Piercebridge.

Early in the twentieth century, Mr Wooler of Darlington said that all the huge mill-channels at Piercebridge must have been constructed with Roman slave labour. He was half-right. The channels were indeed Roman but the mills came later, reusing the massive leats. One of the canals, right inside the Roman vicus, was lined with perfect Roman ashlar, but the local museum took no action and a farmer salvaged the stone and built himself a garage with it! As the canal has four or five feet of silt in it, all is not lost as the lower levels of stonework will have survived.

Our divers recovered some three-thousand artefacts from the river bed on the line of the genuine Roman bridge. One bitter archaeologist said that these were merely washed out of the river banks and trapped by the timbers of the Roman bridge pier-bases. In that case, the ruinous medieval mill-dam slightly downstream should have trapped millions of artefacts of all periods. After a complete day's search the divers recovered only two artefacts from the dam - an inkpot of the 1920s and the radiator badge from a bull-nozed Morris. The latter went into a local motor-car museum.

The Piercebridge site forms an archetypal water-supplied site, and other suspected Roman navigations can be compared with it. Our findings were not popular with the establishment at the time but The Rolex Company of Switzerland awarded my book *The Piercebridge Formula*, an international prize for exploration. The rapidly increasing amount of evidence is now recognised world-wide and it gives me great pleasure to know that the whole search was sparked off at Hinegan's Pond in my native Chester-le-Street.

Belgium has a whole host of Roman river navigation evidence but the most important structure is at Montignies Sainte Christophe in the province of Hainaut. Like the Piercebridge structure, the Montignies structure was labelled as a "bridge" even though it had thirteen tiny culverts instead of two normal-size arches which the Romans would have used for a river of this size. The thirteen arches stood on a solid dam, and Roman bridges were not built in this manner. On the upstream face, the surviving arched culverts have slots for lifting gates and on the downstream side, the river falls in a vertical waterfall down the air-face of the dam.

The Belgian authorities, who like their British opposite numbers, at first labelled the structure as a "bridge" but were puzzled because it lay several hundred metres upstream from the Roman road. Also, the thirteen-culvert bridge which straddled the dam was only four feet wide on the top, and an attempt to cross it with a cart resulted in the latter falling into the river. It was then decided that the bridge was for pedestrians only, while the road traffic splashed through an unlocated ford a considerable distance downstream!

The spillway becomes a solid dam half way across the river and as at Piercebridge, there is a canal at one end which has been later utilised as a mill-leat. This huge leat was obviously the original bypass canal for Roman barges.

The Roman dam-spillway has ponded the river back into a large lake which some historians said was a fish-lake. The true purpose of the structure has now been realised when archaeologists have assessed the meaning of the five intact Roman rivercraft which were found at Pommeroeul only a few miles away. The great Hylton Roman dam and the two

Chester-le-Street Roman dams may have been of similar designs to either the Montignies or the Piercebridge structures.

All over the former Roman Empire, unidentified structures and many hitherto somewhat doubtfully labelled "fish-traps" or "paved fords" are now being reclassified into river navigational features.

We are now well into the mysteries of that subject most neglected by civilians who write about history. That subject is "military logistics." While amateur military "experts" spend all their time talking about strategy, generals speak mostly about logistics. Without massive supply lines, armies cannot move, nor can they even remain static, as the next chapter will show.

Belgium's Piercebridge

Our society sent archaeological investigator Terry Shaw to examine and photograph the Roman "pont-barrage" (bridge-weir) at Montignies St Christophe on the River Hantes in the province of Hainaut (see pages 109, 110 & 121). The thirteen culverts which sit on a Piercebridge-type spillway all have recesses for lifting water level control cataractae. At the far end of this picture, the spillway changes to a high solid dam and beyond is a canal which has been converted in medieval times into a mill-leat for a watermill. The Montignies structure is a surviving example of a Roman inland navigation weir and is located on a river much smaller than either our River Wear (Roman Vedra) or the Tees (Roman Tisa).

Chapter 5
Military Logistics

"The threat of starvation is a far greater worry to a soldier than a fierce enemy"

Vegitius (Roman military writer)

The Search Intensifies; a new look at Roman choices of fort sites

We must now look more closely at the evidence for the Roman choice of the Chester-le-Street site. It is commonly held that Roman fort sites were chosen for their defensive positions but this is not so. Except in circumstances like defensive lines such as Hadrian's Wall and the Antonine Wall, the Roman forts were not built on strategic positions. The favourite fort site was a riverside one, usually where a tributary joined the main stream. Let us take a closer look at the Chester-le-Street Roman site, the headquarters-building of which was under our parish church. Apart from the slope up from the Cong Burn on the north side of the fort, the ground to the south and west, approaches downhill to the fort from Chester Moor and Waldridge. From the east side of the fort, a gentle slope runs down to the River Wear.

Another postulated reason for the choice of a Roman fort site is: "to guard the bridge." Does this make sense? There was a Roman bridge across the Cong Burn but was the fort built to prevent Picts getting across this stream? During the Shrove Tuesday football matches of the 19th and early twentieth centuries, the horde of players and spectators rushed backwards and forwards through this water without even noticing it. Would such a bridge over an easy-to-ford stream have necessitated a huge fort to defend it?

During the Nazi occupation of the Low Countries in World War 2, the Germans did not consider a fort necessary to protect a bridge - a couple of sentries was deemed sufficient. If saboteurs damaged a German bridge, many hostages were executed in retaliation. I am sure that likewise, the Roman army would not have shown leniency towards those who had dared damage military property.

Daniel Defoe, author of *Robinson Crusoe*, made a journey through England and Wales in the early 18th century in the course of which, he visited Chester-le-Street. His description reads:

"From Durham we came by the common road to Chester in the Street, an old dirty thoroughfare-town empty of all the greatness which antiquaries say it once had when it was a Roman colony. Here is a stone bridge but instead of passing over it, we rode under it, and riding up the stream passed under one of the arches, not being over the horse hoofs in water."

Severe gradients and ox-wagons do not mix

At long last, archaeologists and historians are beginning to realise that the Roman roads in Britain, due to their impossible gradients and other factors, were for the fast movement of police-action troops, and that all long distance heavy cargoes were transported by sea, rivers, canalised rivers, canals, lakes and even minor streams.

Gliding on ice!

If you carry out a ground archaeological search in a county like Northumberland, with its rough terrain which includes thorn-thickets, gullies, swamps and rough moorland; after an hour, every muscle in your body is aching, and an occasional cart-track is sheer bliss. If a modern tarmac road is encountered, it is like gliding on ice. One then understands the purpose of the Roman roads which was to deploy troops to any distant trouble spot, in any kind of weather, and still allow the troops to retain enough energy with which to fight at the end of the forced march.

With regard to the severe gradients of Roman roads, take the long straight stretch of Dere Street in Northumberland. This road switchbacks up and down without the slightest attempt to ease the gradient. At one spot, it goes right over the peak of a hill which would have halved the already tiny cargo of an ox-wagon. When the medieval people tried to reuse the Roman roads, they had to put in easy-gradient deviations at the Roman climbs and descents of valleys. These medieval deviations from the Roman line, form recognition features in the search for unknown Roman roads. A search along a direct line which short-cuts the medieval deviation will usually reveal the original line of the Roman road.

The marked *agger* (cambered paved surface) of a Roman road also meant that if a wagon moved from the crown to make way for opposite-direction traffic, it would probably have overturned. The rammed-gravel convex surface of Roman roads in Britain was however ideal for good drainage and soldiers' marching feet.

Roman cavalry also moved along the roads but the horses were not normally shod. If they had to move on hard surfaces, temporary shoes called *hipposandals* were fitted to the animals. The antiquarians of the 18th century said that the Roman roads in Durham and Northumberland were of the three-lane type, with a central paved *agger*, the latter flanked by kerbstones and deep drainage ditches. Outside these ditches were grass tracks for unshod animals. Most of these outer tracks have been ploughed-away but recently, we have found some excellent surviving examples, the most important being at NZ 090 890, one mile south-west of Netherwitton, Northumberland. This newly-discovered Roman road branches off north from the Devil's Causeway and has been christened by the finders, the Northern Archaeology Group, as: "The Devil's Highway." Other three-lane Roman roads have also been found in the area. The deep drainage ditches between the central *agger* and the outer tracks would have prevented the latter from being used as overtaking lanes.

Roman records tell us that an ox-wagon *(clabularia)* was pulled by eight oxen in summer and ten in winter and that its speed was one mph. It worked only five hours per day. The ox (neutered bull) needed sixteen hours per day for rest and digestion and like other working animals, you could graze it or work it but not both. If it worked, it had to be fed with fodder, so after just one day's toil, the ox-team would have eaten most of its own cargo, which was limited by law for the protection of the road surfaces, to 1,500 Roman pounds (1,000 Imp lbs,

North of Corbridge, and beyond the line of Hadrian's Wall, the modern A68 follows the Roman road Dere Steet on its way northwards. All motorists must have wondered at the switchbacks on this very straight road with its severe dives, harsh climbs and dangerous blind summits. Not the slightest attempt has been made by the Romans to ease gradients with angled deviations although medieval and subsequent modern engineers have been forced to leave the Roman line here and there. How about those poor Roman ox-wagon drivers with their cumbersome one-mph (on the flat) clabularia?

The only way an ox-wagon could have negotiated Dere Street, would have been to load all the oxen and crew onto the wagon and attempt to achieve 100 mph on the dive, hoping to reach the crest on the other side! At one point, the Roman road goes right over the peak of a hill and then down the other side. This would have reduced the load of a wagon to nil and possibly oxen would not have made it even with an empty cart.

The answer is of course that the heavy cargoes would be waiting for the Roman soldiers at Risingham (Habitancum) on the River Rede, near West Woodburn, the Roman barges having negotiated the Tyne, North Tyne and Rede. The Roman road was for marching troops and the odd pack-animal. The severe gradients of Dere Street would have been tiring for soldiers causing them to curse, and would have reduced the range of their pack-animals loaded with tents and weapons for en-route use. At each river where the road crossed, would be the safe haven of a Roman fort and waterborne supplies in plenty.

455 kg). This is not the way to supply a distant army.

German general learns a harsh lesson in logistics

Roman chroniclers mention soldiers "foraging" for food and like any other army, the Romans stole what they could, but to rely on this type of supply is fatal. Let us look at the disaster which befell the German General von Kluck in 1916. In his "First Army" alone, he had 84,000 horses and these consumed two-million pounds of fodder per day. To carry this, 924 standard fodder-wagons were required. Because of the tremendous transport problem, von Kluck decided that during his great advance, his horses would have to live off the country. Even though the season was favourable for this, by the time they crossed the French frontier, the cavalry horses were exhausted and almost useless, and the heavy artillery had fallen great distances behind the main army.

Supply problems launch Robert E Lee into a disastrous battle

Another disaster due to a failure of logistics happened to the American Confederate Army at Gettysburg on July 1-3, 1863. The army consisted of 75,000 troops, mostly infantry, and was under the command of General Robert E Lee. He advanced into southern Pennsylvania in late June which was the harvest date for the winter wheat grown in that region. His army secured an area of three-hundred square miles in one of the most productive agricultural regions of the United States. Efficient transport in the area included a railroad and a network of roads which the well-organised army horse and mule drawn wagons utilised.

In spite of all these advantages, after only two days, the food began to run low. The same rules are valid for all armies of all periods and the main logistical lesson is that when an army remains stationary in a position remote from water transport, either sea, river or canal, it will quickly eat all the supplies from the entire area no matter how many wagons and pack-animals are available.

Because of this, General Lee could not conduct a long defensive against the Federal troops and was forced to initiate the disastrous attacks of July 2nd and 3rd, 1863.

The supply problems of Alexander the Great's army

When Alexander the Great moved off with his army of 65,000 for the conquest of India c332BC, his first order was: "Burn all wagons." This was because they could not keep up with the army's pace of two mph. Pack-animals were the load carriers.

For Alexander's army, for every 50 men, one pack-animal would have been needed to carry tents, blankets, fuel, personal possessions and other non-eatables.

If the army travelled through terrain from which water and forage were available for its 6,100 cavalry horses, then it would have been necessary to carry only grain, and the weight of this grain for one day would have been 269,000 pounds, i.e. about 120 tons. This would have needed 1,121 grain-carrying animals. If two days' supply of grain had to be carried, then 2,340 grain-carriers would have been needed. Theoretically, 40,350 grain-carriers would have been necessary to move the army for fifteen days, and 107,600 for twenty days. Clearly, such numbers of animals were not available in the entire country of transit.

In practice, Alexander's army could not feed itself for more than a few days, so his army had to route between towns which had either seaports or navigable rivers. Where the rivers were not navigable, he made them so. His supply ships were waiting for him at these points. The itinerary included the coastal towns of Amphipolis, Abdera, Maroneia and probably Aenos and Sestos.

Alexander's army averaged nineteen miles per day. Researchers comment that on many of his stages, the local populations did not have enough food for themselves, let alone a passing army of 65,000 men, plus thousands of animals. Two-thousand ships formed a supply chain for Alexander's campaigns.

Agricola's logistical problems

When Roman general Agricola invaded Caledonia with 25,000 troops in AD 83, it has been calculated that his (undefendable) supply lines must have been fifty miles long! Surely if that had been the case, the Picts who inhabited the most hostile territory the Romans had ever encountered, would have thought that all their birthdays had come at once! The Roman army covered ten to fifteen miles in a day's march. These ridiculous estimates of lengths of wagon trains would mean that the head of the column was arriving in the early fort of Concangis while the tail-end was just leaving the Legionary headquarters at York! Sedgefield to Chester-le-Street, (via Cade's Road) or from Binchester via a branch of Dere Street would have been more like the correct distances. If a legion of 5,000 soldiers was on such a march north, 5,000 suppers and 5,000 breakfasts plus 25 tons of fodder and grain for about a thousand cavalry horses would have been necessary at Concangis for the night-stopping legion. Where did such quantities come from? The answer is not ox-wagons which carried only half-a-ton by law. The oxen themselves would have consumed most of their load after a one-mph daily five-mile journey even if they could have managed the impossible gradients like the one at Ragpath Wood (NZ 204 422) near Esh Winning, or the recently excavated one-in-three gradient of Cade's Road in Southburn Dene (NZ 275 497), Chester-le-Street. The medieval road south of Chester-le-Street negotiated the same Southburn Dene three-hundred yards west of the Roman crossing, via a long gentle gradient down through the wood to the west of the A167(T), and crossed the stream via a stone bridge which survives underneath the modern railway viaduct (NZ 272 498). Even so, in medieval and later times, a team of cattle was kept at Chester Moor Farm to assist vehicles up the gentle inclines. There is no evidence whatsoever for extra Roman animal teams at the numerous severe gradients of Roman roads.

The answer of course is that the supplies for Concangis came in thousands of tons by Roman ships to Hylton, and then onwards to Concangis by ten-ton (or possibly much bigger) barges. A ten-tonner was equal to twenty ox-wagons. The barge was operated by one steersman and four hauliers and could have made Chester-le-Street from Sunderland in a few hours. The twenty ox-wagons would have needed 160 oxen in summer, 200 in winter, with 20 drivers, 20 cursors (bridle-leaders) and the trip would have taken two days, with the oxen consuming all of their own cargo. This is why there is no reference whatsoever in any Roman records to long-distance heavy wagon transport. The wagons which have left the rut-marks in fort gateways travelled only between the fort and *vicus* and down to the jetties, where strangely for Roman roads, these jetty-to-fort roads do take easy gradients, as at Binchester and many other locations.

The Romans themselves give evidence

Agricola's son-in-law, the Roman chronicler, Tacitus, tells us how his father-in-law's Caledonian expedition was supplied: He records that as the Roman army moved north, so did the Roman navy keep pace with it. The ships had regular contacts with the shore because Tacitus goes on to tell us that every night, the land soldiers and marine troops exchanged yarns; the infantry telling of battles against fierce enemies, and the sailors and marines countering with tales of dreadful storms at sea. There follows a quote from Tacitus in his *Commentary*, p159:

> *"...in his (Agricola's) plan of campaign. This year, he advances by Stirling into central Scotland, keeping as far as possible in touch with his fleet by camping at points on navigable rivers."*

On page 159 of the same account, he refers to the fact that the fleet was used entirely to

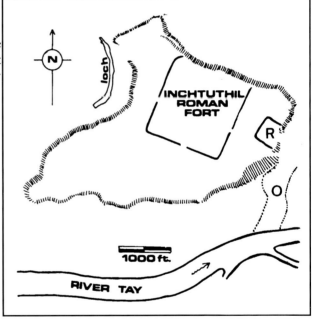

The Roman legionary fortress on the River Tay at Inchtuthil has obviously been surrounded by water at one time. The linear loch to the west (Delvine Loch) resembles a canal, and there is a three sided (ship beaching site?) at "R.". Clearly visible at "O" is an old (artificial) course of the river Tay. Downstream, at the Roman fort of Bertha and the Roman tidal limit of the River Tay and its confluence with the Almond, is a ruinous curved weir which is thought to have had a Roman navigation origin. A suspected Roman canal, now called the Pow Burn, links the rivers Almond and Earn north of the Roman Gask Ridge frontier line. "Pow" is the Scottish vernacular for "artificial ditch." The name also occurs on some man-made-looking ditches which may have linked rivers in the north of England. A very suspicious one, (the "Pow Charney Burn") now dry, may have joined a headwater tributary (the Tipalt Burn) of the South Tyne via the Gilsland Gap to the Irthing and thence to the Eden and the Irish Sea.

The Binchester Roman fort was entirely surrounded by water at one time, with the loop of the River Wear to the north, west and south, and a narrow artificial-looking channel (now dry) to the east. This channel is too high up the contours to have been an old channel of the River Gaunless. The dry channel is a suspected Roman canal. A map of 1772 drawn by Jeremiah Dixon (who also marked the USA/Canada boundary, the Mason-Dixon Line) can be seen in the Bishop's Palace at Bishop Auckland. The canal has been surveyed in typically Roman straight lengths and there is a suspected barge basin in "Stone Horse Field" and "Low Car."

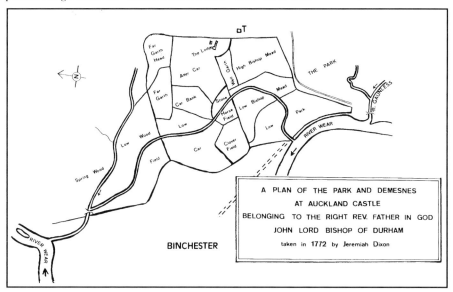

A PLAN OF THE PARK AND DEMESNES AT AUCKLAND CASTLE BELONGING TO THE RIGHT REV. FATHER IN GOD JOHN LORD BISHOP OF DURHAM taken in 1772 by Jeremiah Dixon

support the army, and on page 162, he states that a single ship carried 200 troops.

Tacitus described Roman ships of the period: No doubt these were the types used for the supply of Agricola's army in Caledonia:

"...some were of shallow draught, pointed bow and stern, and broad-beamed to withstand heavy seas. Others were flat-bottomed to allow grounding. Most of them were equipped with steering-oars at both ends to allow quick movement forward and backwards. Many had decks for the transport of artillery, horses and supplies. They were easy to sail..."

The same writer also had this to say about British rivers:

"I would only add one remark, that nowhere else does the sea make its power more felt: the tide causes long stretches of the rivers alternately to ebb and flow, nor does it simply rise and sink upon the shore, but it runs far inland, and winds about and makes its way into the very heart of the hills and mountain chains, as if the sea were the Lord of all."

Military Logistics

The Romans bypassed the Iron Gates rapids on the Danube with a canal. This canal must have used some form of lock. Flash locks (single opening barriers) close together would have acted as a flight of pound locks (double barriers). There was a fort at each end of the canal and an inscription tells us that Trajan built the navigation to avoid the perils of the waterfall. The canal was fed from the side by streams in a similar manner to which we think Chester-le-Street's Roman canal was fed by the Cong Burn.

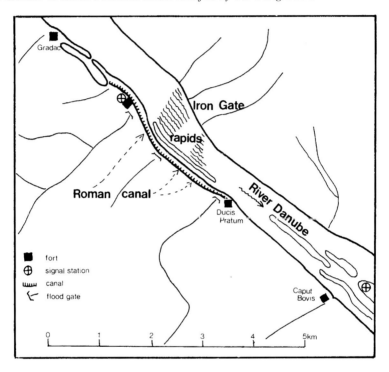

In order to navigate the Danube's Orsova Gorge, Trajan cut a tow-path along the base of the cliffs, just above the water. The ledge was widened by cantilevered planks supported on timbers. The timbers were probably removed in winter when huge ice floes came down the flooded river.

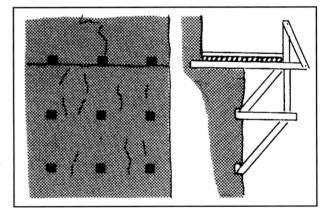

No doubt, the Roman regiment *Barcarii Tigrisienses* (bargemen of the River Tigris) accompanied Agricola's army for the deep penetration of rivers beyond the points to which seagoing ships could navigate. The civilian boatmen, the *Utricularii* also were probably impressed. Both organisations used ten-ton barges called *codicariae*. They were general-purpose lighters which could be rowed, sailed, towed, or poled.

The Romans canalised their rivers, cutting-off bends and bypassing shallows. The River Nene has many such Roman canals short-circuiting meandering loops and wide river bends. Where necessary the Romans deepened shallow stretches with dams.

On the Danube, Trajan bypassed the dangerous Iron Gate rapids, a drop of 200 feet, with a canal. There must have been locks in this canal. Flash-locks (single barriers) would have been close together thus forming a ladder of pound locks (chambers with gates at each end). An inscription attests the building of this canal to Emperor Trajan:

"Ob periculum cataractarum derivato flumine tutam Danuvi navigationem fecit."

(On account of the danger of the waterfall, he diverted the river and made a safe passage of the Danube.)

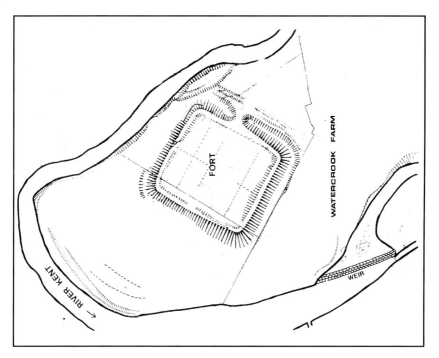

The Roman fort at Watercrook, Kendal, is a typical example of a riverside Roman fort. The expected mill-dam is there. Visit any Roman fort and look for the medieval water-mill which has reused a Roman bypass channel. Also the mill-dam probably has a Roman base to it.

A huge Roman navigation dam (*moles*) across a branch of the Rhine got a mention in Roman records (Tacitus) only because it became newsworthy by being destroyed in an uprising. This dam ponded-back water into a military canal which led away from the river. Roman seagoing ships negotiated this canal into extensive Dutch lakes.

Nero had a cascade of three dams on the River Anio, just to make his garden look pretty. One of the dams was 120 feet high. This dam was later used as a source for one of Rome's aqueducts.

The Roman poet Horace tells us of a long journey by canal-barge. The craft contained 300 passengers and was pulled by one mule. Horace tells of mosquitoes and the horrible stench of water but this was evidently preferable to the expense of road transport.

In Britain, an archaeologist has claimed that the Car Dyke Roman canal was not used for navigation because uncut baulks of earth lie across it in a couple of places. Pliny the Younger, the Roman governor of Bithynia (northern Turkey) in a series of letters to Emperor Trajan, asks permission to construct a canal from a lake to the sea because of the high cost of road transport. Trajan warns him not to drain the lake accidentally with his canal but Pliny's next letter assures the emperor that a safety-device of an uncut dyke between lake and canal will take care of this. The Romans were not short of manpower with which to trans-ship cargoes over such obstacles.

Pliny also tells the Emperor that he can accommodate the canal's anticipated level-changes by means of "sluices."

This photograph of an unidentified creek, possibly in Lincolnshire, shows the amount of traffic handled by even tiny rivers.

This strange structure in the River Eden was used as a fish-trap by the monks of Wetheral Priory. It looks however, as if it was designed originally as a flash lock for navigation. Three stone piers span a channel between the river bank and an artificial stone island of considerable length. Beyond the island, the river tumbles down a series of rapids. To operate as a flash lock, an opening gate would have been provided in the widest gap of the lock, and there is a winch pit in the central pier. This winch would have been used to pull barges through the gap against the current. Winch pits in the other piers may have housed winches for operating movable weirs which could have been planks, gates or a system of movable timbers called rimers and paddles. When movable weirs are lowered or opened, the level of the river above the flash lock drops. When the level decreases sufficiently, the navigation gate is opened and a barge is winched upstream. A downstream-bound craft can shoot the fast flow. The upstream-bound craft has the gate closed behind it so that a depth of water builds up for navigation to the next barrier. The types of barriers were many and varied and had different names from place to place, but the principle was always the same: open the weir, let most of the water out; open the gate; pull a barge up through the gap or let one ride down it; then shut the gate and raise or close the weir.

The Romans mention the use of flash locks on the upper reaches of the Tiber, over a hundred miles from the sea. At Ebchester, on our local River Derwent, there is a dam and an old dry canal right under the Roman fort. Also, in the main river is an artificial linear island. It looks as if the Romans have got as far as Ebchester with their rivercraft.

The subject of Constable's painting entitled "Boat-building near Flatford Mill," is a barge under construction in a simple riverside dry-dock. The Romans describe exactly the same method of construction. Constable's dry-dock has a gate through which water will enter when the barge is completed. The dry-dock would become a pound lock if it were situated in a river-loop, and had gates at both ends. The Romans called dry-docks "navalia" and had a guild of dry-dock builders.

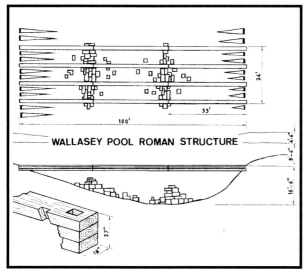

There have been Roman dams at many places in Britain but their remains have always been misidentified as bridges or fish-traps. A typical example is the Wallasey Pool structure which was discovered in 1850 and immediately labelled "Roman bridge" although it was entirely covered by water at high tide. In order to accommodate this theory, a massive sinking of the land was postulated, but engineer David Armstrong, B.Eng, C.Eng, points out that the land there has actually risen since Roman times.

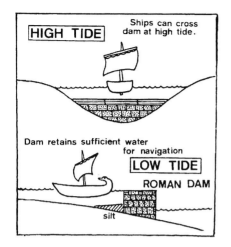

Engineer David Armstrong's drawing of the Wallasey Pool Roman structure.

Ancient timbers on the bed of the River Tyne at Ovingham at NZ 084 634. These may be the remains of a Roman navigation weir. It looks as if the structure has been timber boxes filled with rocks. It lies at an angle of thirty degrees to the river flow. Ovingham Saxon Church close by uses ex-Roman stones in its tower.

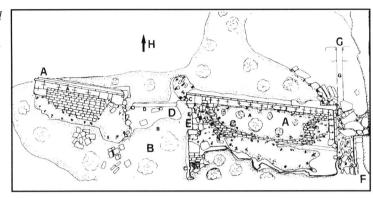

The ruinous Bywell dam is mentioned as early as 1200. It has been used by various watermills and other industries but it may have started life as a Roman navigation weir. Most of the dam was dismantled in 1862 and Roman-type square post-holes can be seen cut into the rock river bed. The

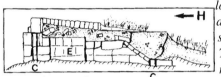

lower courses of the surviving part of the dam appear to be Roman. An aperture in the structure may be the remains of a pound lock. There are slots for cataractae and also a recess for a possible counterweight of a lifting bridge. There was a Roman road bridge a few hundred yards downstream and a network of Roman roads has been excavated in the immediate vicinity. In front of St Peter's Church is a "V-cut" thought to have been a Roman canal. This rejoins the river upstream at NZ 045 613 where the remains of yet another dam, possibly Roman, lie on the river bed.

Bywell's second church, the Saxon St Andrew's, has its tower built almost completely of reused Roman stones. In St Peter's churchyard, during a burial in 1902, part of a Roman altar was dug up from a depth of six feet. In 1750, a Roman silver cup inscribed "Desidera Vivas" was found by an angler close to St Peter's church. The authorities, without any evidence whatsoever, say that this cup was washed down from Corbridge but we think there is a major Roman site at Bywell. The "washing-down the river theory" is used by many "experts" when they do not know, or more commonly "do not want to know" about new evidence.

> *A = Remains of main structure of dam.*
> *B = Lock, possibly a pound lock.*
> *C = Slots for cataractae (lifting gates).*
> *D = Bottom of lock; Roman-type holes cut into rock bed.*
> *E = Recess for lifting-bridge?*
> *F = Spillway cut through solid rock.*
> *G = Drain from spillway cut through rock bed of river.*
> *H = Direction of flow of River Tyne.*

There have been many modifications and alterations over hundreds of years but the essential structure of the dam has a stepped air face and sloping water face, typical of Roman dam structures in other parts of the empire.

John Fryer's map of 1779 shows that Corbridge once had an unusual river loop and island beside the Roman town. It is reminiscent of Pommeroeul Roman barge basin in Belgium. Intrigued by the canal, now landscaped away, our divers searched the river just opposite where an associated dam should be. There it was, almost intact: a solid barrier of lewis-holed and cramped Roman stones, right across the river. It is only some fifty metres upstream from the site of the Roman bridge.

In the north shore, downstream from the bridge is a Roman jetty, which has produced scores of pieces of Roman pottery, coins and other artefacts. For unknown reasons, the structure has been listed by the authorities as a "Saxon watermill." It is no such thing.

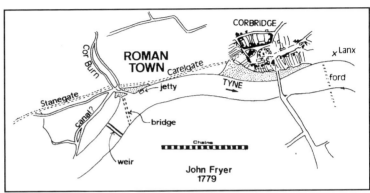

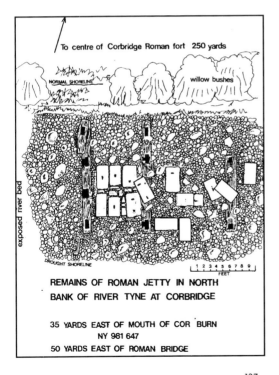

The Corbridge Jetty high and dry during a drought. The jetty is rich in Roman artefacts and is a magnet for illegal metal detectorists. It looks as if a Roman barge has overturned offshore as there is a scattering of Iron Pyrites on the bed of the river. The Romans used this material (fools' gold) in the manufacture of sulphuric acid.

REMAINS OF ROMAN JETTY IN NORTH
BANK OF RIVER TYNE AT CORBRIDGE

35 YARDS EAST OF MOUTH OF COR BURN
NY 981 647
50 YARDS EAST OF ROMAN BRIDGE

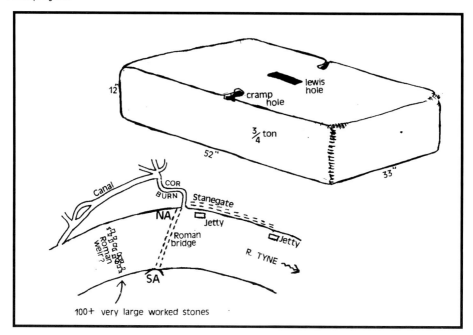

Details of the Roman structures at Corbridge showing the Corbridge weir and an example of one of the worked Roman stones. A Roman "bronze cat" (possibly a puma) was found among the huge stones of the Roman weir.

NA = the position of the North Abutment of the Roman bridge.

SA = the remains of the South Abutment of the Roman bridge.

There is much talk by "experts" of the river having moved sideways south since Roman times but that would have placed the southern abutment of the Roman bridge in the middle of a field and the jetty in mid river. It seems that the Roman bridge had only five piers (the bases of four survive on the river bed with the centre one missing) and not eleven as hitherto postulated.

A second Roman jetty has been found further downstream and this is being investigated.

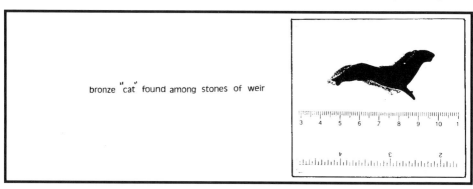

bronze "cat" found among stones of weir

A Roman jetty on the coast of Cyprus. Note the opus revinctum dove-tailed holes for butterfly cramps. The use of opus revinctum was almost always in structures which had to resist water pressure.

The eastern abutment of the Roman bridge at Chollerford, Northumberland.
W = Hadrian's Wall arriving at the bridge abutment.
M = Mill built onto the rear of the Wall.
L = Water leat to mill from a dam somewhere upstream.
C = Position of small crane on south wing of bridge abutment.
J = South wing of abutment is longer than the north to serve as a jetty. A dam downstream of which only the cobbled spillway survives, has ponded back the river to lift barges to this jetty.
An earlier and smaller Roman bridge predated the larger bridge. One of the piers of the early bridge is encapsulated in the later abutment. The stones of the early pier have been held together with opus revinctum. The later bridge used iron tie-bars.

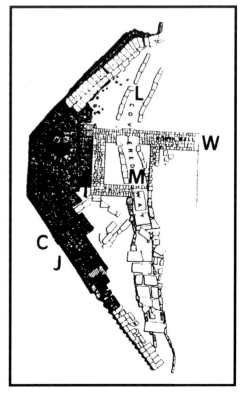

The hole for the crane-post in the southern wing of the bridge abutment. This crane was placed in a prepared mounting on the finished bridge and therefore could not have been used for the construction of the bridge. You do not erect a crane on a completed bridge. In any case, the crane would have been too small to handle the huge blocks (each 12 cwt) of stone. The mast of the crane sits in a prepared hole cut into huge lewis-holed blocks which themselves have been lifted into place by a much larger Roman treadmill-operated construction crane. The small crane would have been used to lift cargoes of grain from barges into the watermill.

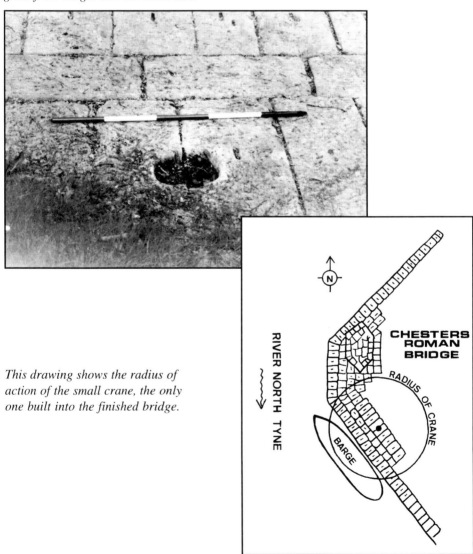

This drawing shows the radius of action of the small crane, the only one built into the finished bridge.

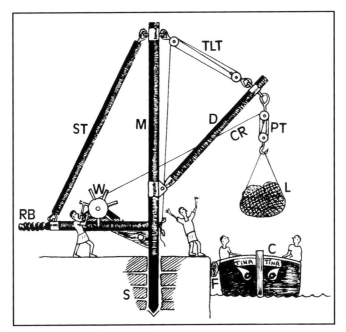

The small Roman derrick-crane on Chesters Roman bridge abutment.

M = *Mast.*

D = *Derrick.*

ST = *Strain-taking boom.*

S = *Seating for rotating mast in finished bridge.*

RB = *Rotation boom which swung the whole crane around. The bottom of the mast was probably seated in a grease-filled metal liner.*

PT = *Purchase tackle. This would have quartered the load already halved by the winch ratio.*

TLT = *Topping lift tackle (to luff derrick).*

CR = *Cargo runner.*

C = *Codicaria discharging cargo.*

F = *Fender.*

L = *Load.*

W = *Windlass. This example has a light timber drum. No counterweight would have been necessary for a light crane of this type. This windlass will give an advantage of 2:1 if the circumference of the ends of the bars is twice that of the drum. The Purchase tackle will further half or quarter the load depending on the number of sheaves in the Purchase Tackle Blocks. Thus a moderate load can be lifted by one man or even a boy. The large stone, obviously a windlass-drum ,found on the bridge abutment and now preserved in the Chesters Museum, was far too heavy for this crane and was probably a vertical capstan for warping barges alongside the jetty.*

Evidence from France and Belgium

In the 1930's Professor Albert Grenier wrote that he thought the Romans had navigated all the lesser rivers and even small streams of Gaul. Grenier had this to say:

"In addition to the large rivers and principal streams, many moderate water-courses, which today seem unsuited to navigation, had been used by Gallo-Roman traffic. Here again the works of the Middle Ages have provided useful indications to ancient archaeology. As with the study of the roads, where we must place the greatest regard on documents of the Middle Ages and place names, so also with research into water communications. The existence of navigation, until quite recent times, must lead us to research the documents and any remains in order to establish that waterways had been used by the Gauls and Romans. It must be conceded that river traffic in the Gallo-Roman era had been extremely developed and that the smallest waterways had played the same part as the innumerate local roads of which traces have been found."

Our Chester-le-Street River Cone or Cong Burn fits into Professor Grenier's category of lesser Roman streams capable of being navigated.

Professor Grenier's great volumes show Roman river navigation features at Arles, Basle, Bayonne, Beauvais, Bescancon, Bordeaux, Chalons-sur-Saone, Cologne, Dax, Evreux, Frejus, Geneva, Grenoble, Metz, Naix, Nantes, Narbonne, Neuchatel, Orleans, Paris, Poitiers, Rennes, Rouen, St Martory, Scarponne, Sens, Soissons, Strassbourg, Tournus, Treves and Vienne.

He also shows a very peculiar Roman bridge at Montignies-Saint-Christophe (Hainaut) on the River Hantes in Belgium, which has thirteen tiny culverts instead of two arches normal for this length of bridge. The structure looks like a navigation barrage. It has pounded a lake behind it and there seems to be an ex-Roman bypass canal around the end of the structure, which has naturally provided an ideal home for a later medieval water-mill.

Evidence from Germany

Recently, Dr Martin Eckholdt in Germany has discovered that ditches, hitherto thought to be mere farm drains, had once been Roman canals.

Space here does not allow a full copy of Dr Eckholdt's findings but some of his observations about Roman inland water transport follows:

"In a shallow gravel-bottomed river, the current could be concentrated by rows of oars, driven into the bottom, to form a narrow channel, thus generating a strong rush of water in its course which would remove the gravel."

"Who would have carried out such maintenance work? The Romans set conscripts and tribal groups, often prisoners of war, to carry out such tasks to maintain communications, both by road and by river..."

"In some rivers, navigation would have been restricted to special flat-bottomed ships at times of full flow, or in conditions of particularly careful river bed conservancy."

"In a few cases, it indicates a waterflow too slight for navigation and where the cargo would have had to be lightened by dividing up the blocks of stone to be transported, or by making shallow rivers navigable with the aid of barrages."

"The simplest artificial method of making shallow waters navigable is by means of constructing a reservoir upstream which would be filled when water was high, which could be released as required. Such places were well known in antiquity; Pliny for example, mentions in his Natural History, Book 3, such ponds (piscinas) on the upper Tiber."

"Pliny says that in the summer, navigation was difficult on the upper Tiber and barges often had to wait two weeks for water to collect between the sluices."
"In some cases, it is clear that navigation can only have been accomplished through artificial means, possibly with the aid of dams..."

"Archaeologists and historians must appreciate that in finds from river beds, and documents, there is evidence, hitherto disregarded, which should be investigated to see whether it may be connected with navigation..."

That is precisely what we have been searching for at Chester-le-Street and numerous other locations all over Britain.

There was much more water about in Roman times and recently we have found that County Durham had an ancient "lake district." These lakes are now completely dry but dozens of Roman artefacts have been found on a knoll with the name "Island Farm." Another slight rise above the level of one of the former lakes, is called "Great Isle Farm." A suspected Roman barge basin has been found at Mordon, NZ 327 266. It also looks as if the Romans have connected the Rivers Tees and Wear via these lakes and the Ferryhill Gap. The latter is an Ice Age spillway and also contains a Roman road. Before the railway was built through the gorge, it contained a string of lakes.

The now dry "Lake Pickering" also seems to have been used by Roman barges, as hundreds of Roman ships' rivets have been found by metal detectorists along the 23 metre contour line.

Professor Hoskins tells us of the surprisingly high heads of river navigation in the medieval period. At most of these locations today, there is insufficient water for a duck to paddle, but it comes as no surprise to find that at all of the old navigation limits he mentions, there was once a Roman fort or town.

This is borne out by the recent excavation, as mentioned in *The Daily Telegraph* 25.4.97, of a huge Roman villa complex in Wiltshire, beside the now dry River Og, a few miles north of the Roman town of Cunetio on the River Kennet. The villa, at 600 ft above sea-level has jetties. A boat-hook was also found.

Until recently, archaeologists and historians have largely ignored ancient inland water transport because in an age of motorways, they have been blinded by the Roman roads. Time and time again, impractical and landlubberly "experts" have identified remains of Roman dams as "medieval fish-traps." A fish-trap consisted of a few stakes with wicker baskets between, and seldom spanned the full width of the river. The Roman barrages, often reused by medieval millers, contained thousands of tons of stone and would have cost the ancient equivalent of the cost of a modern airport runway.

Hollywood has not helped the history of transport, with films of (empty) covered wagons speeding at 40 mph away from hordes of hostile Indians. In fact, one mph was more like the true speed and few American wagons made it across North America. The settlers started off with loaded wagons but the trails soon became littered with discarded pianos and furniture. The draught-animals were then killed for food, and the surviving settlers usually arrived in the West, months or years later, with their only possessions the clothes they stood up in.

South African oxen problems

Let us look at a country which did use ox-wagons for long distance transport - South Africa in the 18th & 19th centuries: The Afrikaaner ox-wagons were pulled by teams of 16 oxen and had a crew of two, driver and *voorloper* (bridle-leader). The wagons were small and narrow and a full load was three hogsheads of wine or the equivalent.

Traces of the old *trekpads* (wagon tracks) can still be seen in many parts of the country as they sweep from side to side in search of easy gradients, usually 1:100. How did the Roman ox-wagons manage without such deviations? The comparison is highlighted by the facts that the Afrikaaner ox-teams contained twice the number of animals as the Roman. Furthermore, the South African oxen were far bigger beasts and one of them, which plied from Capetown, is recorded as having a horn-spread of 11ft 5ins (3.5 metres).

Lord Baden-Powell's Boer War records tell us that captive balloons were used for reconnaissance and artillery spotting but they were restricted in use because the only method of transporting the heavy cylinders of hydrogen, when away from the railway, was by ox-wagons, and the latter just could not cope.

The logistics of the Roman army and comparisons with others

In order to understand the selection of the site for the Roman fort at Chester-le-Street and most other Roman forts, we have to appreciate the most important military subject of all - LOGISTICS. One cannot carry out any activity whatsoever without fuel, food, weapons, clothing and transport. This subject, especially when dealing with the Romans, is the most neglected by historians and archaeologists.

Although I am a professional archaeologist, I have spent many years with ships and aeroplanes, moving masses of military equipment and personnel around the world. This gave me an insight into similar problems which must have been experienced by ancient armies.

The advantages of water transport. This unusual sketch is of the keelmen's strike of 1822. William Hedley's early locomotive, the Wylam Dilly, was mounted on a Tyne keelboat and with its railway wheels replaced with paddles, it became one of the river's first steam tugs. After the strike, the locomotive was returned to colliery railway service. It is now preserved in the Royal Scottish Museum, Edinburgh.

A further sketch of the Wylam Dilly steam keelboat. The loaded keel is carrying more coal than the entire trainload in the background.

Comparison with Hitler's proposed invasion of Britain

Like Adolf Hitler, who contemplated an invasion of Britain after the fall of France in 1940, it may have seemed to Julius Caesar that the island which was often in clear view from the French coast, was ill-defended and within grasp. Hitler never made it and the same unpredictable narrow sea turned both Caesar's attacks, in 55 and 54BC, from full-scale invasions into little more than commando-raids. Another hundred years was to elapse before the Romans, in AD43, came, and stayed.

Unlike Hitler, Julius Caesar did not have to gain air superiority before his seaborne assault. Also, unlike Hitler, he did not have a British navy to face in "Fretvm Gallicvm." Many of the problems however were the same for Julius Caesar and Adolf Hitler. One was logistics, and the other, the sailors' number one enemy in war and peacetime too - the weather.

The swift fall of France in 1940 left Hitler wondering how to transport the necessary thirty divisions across *der* Kanal once he had gained mastery of the air (in modern warfare, to land troops on a shore still dominated by an enemy air force is to invite disaster). Hitler's answer was to collect thousands of canal barges from all over Europe and the idea was to use captured Dutch tugs to tow strings of them across the Channel. Half of the German army transport was still horse-drawn, and the German admirals were horrified at the thought of trying to escort this totally unsuitable armada, with a very much smaller navy than the opposing Royal Navy. The RN had available in or near the Channel: five capital ships, eleven cruisers, seventy-six destroyers and hundreds of torpedo-boats and armed trawlers. For the escort of the motley armada, the *Kreigsmarine* had only seven destroyers, twenty torpedo-boats plus some fast gun-boats. Hitler needed a flat calm for his sea-crossing with the low-freeboard canal barges. His admirals warned that British destroyers would race at thirty knots (35 mph) across the crawling strings of scows and swamp them without the need of gunfire. The German generals suggested laying two minefield barriers across the Channel to protect the corridor, but the German admirals replied: *"The Channel has thirty-foot tides; do we set the tethered mines for high tide or low tide? If we set them for high tide, they will flop around on the surface at low tide and the British will destroy them with gunfire. If we set them for low tide, the British destroyers will pass safely over the top of them at high tide. As for magnetic mines, which lie on the sea-bed, the British ships are each protected by a generator and a large coil of wire which neutralises the ship's magnetic field."*

In the event, Hitler never obtained the necessary air superiority although it was a close-run thing. He was also extremely short of fuel and decided to go for the Caspian oilfields which involved an attack on Russia. All the German *Luftwaffe* fuel used in the Battle of Britain and the later blitz, had been supplied by the Soviet Union which hoped to see the capitalistic British and Germans fight each other to a standstill.

Another planned invasion

One-hundred-and-thirty-six years earlier, in 1804, Napoleon Bonaparte had stared with frustration across *la* Manche towards the hated English. Everything was ready for his invasion. Unlike Hitler, he was fully equipped for the assault. His *Grande Armée* comprised

200,000 crack veterans, and the host of sea transports and assault barges were to have been escorted by a fleet of warships. For months, Napoleon paced the beach at Boulogne trying to make up his mind, and then he turned around and moved his army into the heart of Europe. The deterrent had been the Royal Navy. The rest is well known history.

German logistical problems, 1940

In 1940, the brilliant British war leader, Winston Churchill, realised the German logistical problems but fostered the threat of a German invasion in order to rally a spirit of unity in defence, into a previously largely indifferent British public, now bewildered at the swift fall of France. The threat produced a determination to fight to the bitter end, and unified the whole population with an excitement spurred by a common purpose.

Two-thousand years earlier, there had been no uniting leader among the mutually hostile Celtic tribes of Iron Age Britain, who faced the Romans; nor was there a British navy waiting to intercept the Roman invasion fleets.

Fall of France, 1940

As France fell in 1940, Churchill had been fortunate to have had a spell of excellent flat-calm conditions in the English Channel, and 364,000 troops were rescued from Dunkirk instead of the expected 45,000. An armada of small craft which included yachts, fishing boats, lifeboats, and even a Thames fire-fighting float, greatly assisted destroyers, tugs and ferries, with the evacuation. The Royal Navy used thirty-nine destoyers of which only four were sunk. The English Channel had chosen to be kind to the British.

Unknown to the British people, Churchill was so confident that the Germans had immense logistical problems, that, at the height of his "invasion scare," he sent three regiments of tanks, and enough 25-pounder guns to equip a field regiment, out of Britain, to the North African theatre, where he knew that sooner or later, the Axis powers would attempt to take the Suez Canal, thus cutting the British Empire in two.

Churchill was also reading the top secret German radio messages with the help of decrypted *Enigma* codes plus a brilliant team of code-breaking academics.

The Germans had a method of assault unknown to the Romans, i.e. parachutists. Churchill knew that Hitler had only 357 Junkers 52, trimotored troop transports, which flew at 140 mph, and each of these could carry only twelve paratroops, or eighteen soldiers if the aircraft landed. Alternatively, an empty Ju 52 could tow a glider, but the standard German DFS 230 glider carried twelve soldiers so there was no advantage except the short landing-run of the glider and its ability to do so on unprepared terrain. Without German mastery of the air, both sides knew what would happen to the bumbling Junkers transports or gliders if the 300+ mph Spitfires and Hurricanes got among them.

The Chester-le-Street Golf Course sprouted anti-glider landing telegraph poles and other huge timbers. Someone had overestimated the range of German Ju 52s towing gliders, but it all helped Churchill's invasion propaganda. The warning for invasion was to have been the ringing of church bells and those of our beautiful parish church remained silent for several years.

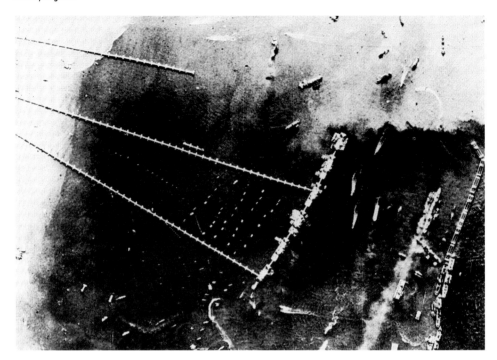

An aerial view of the temporary harbour at Arromanches, Normandy, shortly after D-day, June 1944. By the end of June, 875,000 Allied troops had been landed in Normandy as well as thousands of vehicles. The Allied military command required to disembark 3,000 tons of stores per day by D-day plus four; 7,000 tons of stores by D-day plus eight, and thereafter 12,000 tons of stores per day and 2,500 vehicles per day. This is logistics, a subject which has been almost totally ignored by academics when they discuss ancient warfare.

When the Allied supreme commander, General Eisenhower, while summing up the operation, declared that as well as fighting vehicles, the success had relied on logistics equipment, (usually ignored by historians) - these were the bulldozer, the jeep, the 2½ ton truck and the C47 "Dakota" transport aircraft. None of these items had been designed for combat. Also indispensable to the operation were the DUKWs, (amphibious trucks, which could load from ships offshore and then run up the beaches). It was based on the 2½ ton US Army truck and had been designed by Engineer Hartley Rowe of the United Fruit Company who had experience in landing cargoes onto difficult shores in South America. General Motors had the first prototype ready for testing in thirty-eight days. All wars centre on logistics.

All summer of 1940, the Germans practised invasions on the Dutch coast, trying to coax reluctant mules down improvised gang-planks from unpowered or underpowered canal barges. During all these rehearsals, they never managed to land successfully, a single armoured fighting vehicle even though the barges had been modified with concrete floors and removable bow-doors. Caesar's ship-borne horse-slings were much superior to the 1940 German methods. Why is it that many of our historians refer to the Romans as "landlubbers"? In Britain alone, they managed three times, what Napoleon and Hitler never even attempted. It is true that a high proportion of the seamen of the Roman ships were from seafaring nations conquered by Rome but that does not make the attack any less Roman. In the Battle of Britain of 1940, five-hundred of the three-thousand Royal Air Force pilots were from the British Commonwealth and Empire, Poland, Belgium, Czechoslovakia, France, Holland, Norway, Palestine, Ireland and America. It was still a British battle.

Allied Invasion of Normandy, 1944

In 1944, when the turn came for the Anglo-American and allied armies to invade Hitler's Europe, it had taken three years for the combined might of the United States, the British Empire and allies, to prepare for the Normandy landings. Thousands of special landing craft with bow-ramps, had been constructed, and two complete floating harbours were towed in sections across the Channel and assembled under the enemy cliffs. The floating harbours took Hitler by surprise as he had assumed that the allies would have to capture a port very early in the invasion for the tremendous amount of supplies that would be needed. The logistical problems were enormous and shortly before the allied armada sailed, the grass verges of major roads at suitable points, all the way from the south coast of England to the Scottish border, were crammed with military vehicles, awaiting their turn to move south to embark. The road north of Chester-le-Street, later to become the A1M, had trucks and other vehicles, all marked with the allied "white star" insignia, side by side on the grass verges most of the way to where the Angel now stands.

The combined Anglo-American invasion fleet contained ninety-three destroyers, and 4,024 special landing craft which could discharge tanks, vehicles, guns and infantry directly onto the beaches and then return to southern England for more. Hundreds of merchant ships carried supplies and the cargoes were transported to the beaches by 2,583 amphibious trucks (DUKWS). Several capital ships were also in attendance including the British cruiser *Ajax*, which had damaged the German battleship, *Admiral Graf Spee* off Montevideo, and the American *Nevada*, once again in service after being raised from the mud of Pearl Harbor.

The Roman landing of 55BC

It is not certain whether Julius Caesar's expedition of 55BC was intended as a full-scale invasion, or a reconnaissance-in-force. If the intention had been invasion, then his bad luck with the weather downgraded it to a trial run. Caesar's loss of ships in a storm has been used by some historians to label the Roman navy as incompetent. As any modern sailor knows, the English Channel can be a hostile place, and modern quarter-million-ton supertankers are still lost, even though they are equipped with radar, satellite-navigators, echo-sounders, facsimile-weather-chart-read-outs and international voice and telex radio communications.

In 55BC, a single Roman spy-ship had been sent to scan the British shore and this returned with details of possible landing sites. For the crossing, Caesar needed a wind with a southerly component, and, at midnight on 11th August, he departed from Portus Itius (Boulogne). He arrived below the chalk cliffs in the Dover area and selected the best available beach for a landing. The Celtic Britons were waiting on the shore. The draught of the ships prevented a dry landing for the troops who didn't like the idea of the deep water. The story of the Eagle-bearer of the Tenth Legion leading the disembarkation by leaping into the water is well known. To preserve the honour of the Legion, the rest of the soldiers had to follow the Eagle. The ensuing battle in the breakers and on the beach was fierce but after a difficult start, the Romans managed to put the enemy to flight, and the Britons sued for peace.

Later, eighteen transport vessels bringing the Roman cavalry were sighted but the wind backed to easterly and increased to gale-force, driving the ships down-channel. Many of the ships of the main force were driven ashore and some totally wrecked.

On seeing the difficulties, the British reneged on their peace treaty and attacked again. Under difficult circumstances, Caesar repaired all but twelve of his ships, and still without his cavalry, he decided to call it a day and return to Gaul. The English Channel had been unkind to Julius Caesar.

The synoptic situation which caused such havoc was not unusual for the time of year. A deep depression had moved east-north-east along the coast of Gaul. In June 1944, the floating "Mulberry Harbours" of the Allied invasion of Normandy experienced a similar storm. The American harbour was wrecked and the British one severely damaged yet nobody referred to the British or Americans as "landlubbers." Parts of the American harbour were salvaged to repair the British one.

The Roman Invasion of 54BC

Caesar was still determined to invade so he rebuilt his fleet. This time his ships which numbered over eight-hundred, were of a more suitable type with shallow-draught. He was ready by June of 54BC, with five legions (25,000 men), two-thousand Gaulish cavalry, plus their horses, stores, baggage, artillery, missiles and building material for forts. Persistent northerly winds delayed his departure, but on 20th he left with a gentle south-westerly breeze. About midnight, the wind dropped away but the flooding tide carried the ships on, and a landing was made on a shelving beach at Deal.

Faced with such a formidable armada, the Britons did not oppose the landing. Caesar marched his troops twelve miles inland and the Britons retired to a fortified position, probably the hillfort at Bigberry, near Canterbury. This hillfort was successfully stormed and taken, but once again the English Channel was unkind to Caesar. He received news that a storm had wrecked many of his ships which had been riding at anchor. Instead of pursuing the demoralised Britons, his army worked non-stop for ten days to repair the damaged vessels. They were dragged up the beach into a fortified encampment. The channel weather had cost Caesar an excellent chance of a resounding victory.

The Britons managed to forget their tribal conflicts and had formed a temporary alliance under Cassivellaunus but all they managed to do was fight delaying actions. The British were saved by trouble in Gaul. When Caesar received this news, he ordered a return to Gaul but a fleet of ships expected for the evacuation did not materialise. He packed his men into what ships remained from the storm damage, and calm seas allowed a safe crossing. The British had not defeated the Roman army; on two occasions, the North Atlantic low-pressure systems sweeping up the Channel had done the job for them. Julius Caesar managed to claim his second expedition as a victory but another hundred years were to elapse before the Romans experienced genuine military successes in Britain.

Soldiers and supplies

By now, it should be appreciated by readers, from the accounts of Julius Caesar (and Adolf Hitler) that an invasion is not merely a question of loading troops into ships and setting sail. The same problems apply to land campaigns and military occupations, and the main difficulty is that of *logistics.*

The supply of an army is often glossed-over by the phrase: "The Romans foraged for their food." After a day's march is over, you do not feed an army of thirty-five-thousand men and thousands of horses, by turning them loose into the fields which barely supported the natives. We are now looking at the forgotten Roman supply lines, the discovery of which will furnish us with a mass of new information about the specific sitings of Roman forts including our own at Chester-le-Street, plus the discovery of an unknown communications network and the implications of these on the strategy of the Roman army.

Julius Caesar and Adolf Hitler had two obvious enemies, the inhabitants of the British Isles and the capricious weather of the English Channel. The third enemy, which does not go away with good weather or an enemy retreat, is the hunger of one's armies. This is summed-up very neatly by the Roman military writer, Vegetius, who said: *"The threat of starvation is a far greater worry to a soldier than a fierce enemy."*

We can now move on to the third and successful invasion of Britain.

The Roman Invasion of AD43

In AD43, during the reign of the Emperor Claudius, a carefully planned assault was made on Britain, under the command of Roman general Aulus Plautius Silvanus. The reasons were once again economic, and a quest for political success. The lessons from Julius Caesar's attacks were remembered. A hundred years of trading since Julius Caesar's campaigns had also acquainted the Romans with the British shores just as in the 1930s, the peacetime German airline *"Lufthansa,"* operating in and out of London's Croydon Airport, had photographed most of the military installations in southern England.

The problems were threefold: first, get the army across the Channel; second, defeat the opposition; and third, keep the army supplied and fed while it followed up its initial attacks and occupied the territory of the enemy.

From historical snippets and estimates by military experts, it seems that the invasion force contained about 45,000 men. The breakdown of this figure is:

Four legions (4 x 5,000)	=	20,000 Roman citizens
Ten regiments of cavalry,	=	5,000 horsemen
and auxiliary cohorts, all		
non-citizens from countries		
within the Empire	=	15,000 infantry
Mule handlers and		
transport workers	=	5,000 supply troops
Estimated total number		
of men in landing force,		
not counting ships' crews.	=	45,000

As well as the 5,000 horses of the cavalry, some 10,000 transport animals would have been required for the movement of tents and baggage, but rations for only two days' march from the beach-head. Longer marches would require an ever increasing number of pack-animals. The following estimate of shipping space allows for only a modest two weeks' rations for 45,000 men at the landing-site supply base. The Roman norm was to have a year's supply in hand.

Using the size of Caesar's ships of the 54BC invasion for the calculation, the total number of similar ships required would have been about one-thousand.

Paved roads would not have been available for the army advancing from the beach-head area. As the army moved forward, it may have been necessary to prepare temporary tactical roads, clearing scrub and bushes where necessary. Many authors at the stroke of a pen tell us that as the Roman army advanced, so did the engineers build a network of roads behind them (or even in front of them!) The latter would have been very unpleasant for engineers, working undefended ahead of the army in enemy territory! Words are quickly written but the work of the army engineers and prisoners of war took much longer. An average permanent Roman road contains up to 20,000 tons of stone per mile, and each mile took many weeks to complete.

British army roads compared with Roman roads

Shortly after the Argentine surrender in the Falkland Islands, I found myself doing a spell of temporary duty as a ship's officer in Port Stanley and while driving our ship's jeep on various errands ashore, I noticed that the Royal Engineers were building a network of military roads. There were hardly any roads at all in the Falklands and farmers operated old motor-bikes along sheep tracks. The only half-decent roads were from Stanley to the old Stanley Aerodrome, and from Stanley to Moody Brook, and even those were fit only for four-wheel-drive vehicles.

The Argentine occupation forces had settled into two main defended areas, Stanley and Goose Green, and surrounded themselves with minefields. If the Romans had occupied similar islands, they would have set to work immediately building roads in all directions so that they could meet military threats from any direction. The Argentine forces made no such efforts during the seventy-four days of occupation. The British landing was unopposed by the Argentine navy after the loss of its capital ship, the *General Belgrano.* This modernised cruiser, armed with the deadly *Exocet* (flying-fish) missiles, was the ex-USS *Phoenix,* which had survived the Japanese attack on Pearl Harbor.

Only the Argentine Air Force opposed the British landings at San Carlos, and this had been made possible by the scrapping, before the conflict, of the angled-deck aircraft carrier *Ark Royal* and the inability of the new-type aircraft carrier *Invincible* and the old *Hermes,* to operate Gannet radar picket aircraft which would have given early warning of air attacks.

The Argentine forces did not expect the British to land forty miles from the capital and walk to Stanley. The ten helicopters which should have relayed the troops across the horrible peat moors, were lost when the logistics ship *Atlantic Conveyor* was sunk.

British army boats in the Falklands in 1983 not long after the Argentinian surrender. There were few roads in the Falkland Islands and farmers before the war had used old motor-bikes along sheep tracks. Until the Royal Engineers built roads, everything went by helicopter or boat. The army had more boats than the navy and these British waterborne soldiers were the modern equivalent of the Roman Barcarii Tigrisienses.

The greatest loss was three Chinook helicopters which could each transport underslung loads of 12 tons. Among other items, tents for 4,000 troops were lost.

The campaign is history now, but the large British garrison was still faced with transportation problems after the Argentine surrender. It was too expensive to continue routine supply with Chinook helicopters and caterpillar-tracked vehicles. A network of roads had to be constructed for day-to-day needs and in case Argentina made another attack.

During this period, most army transportation was carried out by water. The army had more boats than the navy and the harbour and surrounding waters were criss-crossed with the wakes of army speedboats, assault boats and powered pontoons, all manned by khaki-clad soldiers. I wondered if I was witnessing the modern equivalent of the *Barcarii Tigrisienses*. Meanwhile, the Royal Engineers were busy constructing their network of army roads.

The similarity of these British army roads to Roman ones was astonishing. Even the method of construction was the same. The Royal Engineers cut a deep trench across country and filled this with large boulders gathered locally or blown-up by explosives from rocky outcrops which abounded. Deep drainage ditches ran alongside the roads, following the Roman pattern. Where necessary, drainage culverts, also of the Roman type, ran underneath the British roads. The Romans crossed boggy land by laying bundles of faggots in the bottom of the excavated trench; the Royal Engineers used special rolls of reinforced plastic.

Our historians have told us that, as the Roman army advanced, so the Roman engineers kept pace with them with newly constructed roads. I very much doubted this.

I was given permission to inspect the Royal Engineers' road construction works. The soldiers wondered why a sailor was taking so much interest in mundane road-building, but were intrigued to learn that their work was being compared with that of the Roman legions. Major Bradbury, RE, gave me the specifications of the roads:

Roadway width, single carriageway	6 metres
Roadway width, double carriageway	10 metres
Average thickness	600 millimetres

Therefore quantities for 1 kilometre of road

$= 1000 \times 0.6 \times 6 = 3,600$ cubic metres (single lane)

or $1000 \times 0.6 \times 10 = 6,000$ cubic metres (double lane)

The conversion factor for cubic metres to tonnes = 1.6 therefore 5,760 tonnes are needed for 1 kilometre of single-lane road and 9,600 tonnes for 1 km of double lane. The engineers were using six-wheel-drive Hydromatic dump trucks which carried 6 to 7 tonnes at a time, which was 823 truck-loads for a kilometre of single-lane road and 1,372 truck-loads for a kilometre of double-lane. Forty loads per day was the average achieved in the Falklands, and it took 21 days to lay a kilometre of single-lane and 35 days for a double. In addition, the Royal Engineers had a Chinook helicopter to move heavy equipment about.

Average Roman roads were the same width as single-lane Falklands roads but usually the Roman roads had deeper foundations than those built by the Royal Engineers.

Roman engineers would have needed 12,902 ox-wagon loads of stone per kilometre of road of the same dimensions as single-lane Falklands type. For a single-lane Roman road (18 feet wide) from Richborough to London, over a million ox-wagon loads of stone would have been needed.

When I told the RE major that according to some of our historians, the Romans could build roads ten times quicker than the British army, his reply was unprintable.

Roman supply problems

How long was it before Roman roads could have been used to supply an advancing army? Even when they were finished, their severe gradients still presented formidable obstacles to wheeled traffic.

From the beachhead at Richborough, a single small Roman supply ship with enough stores for the whole army could have arrived daily at any point in the Thames using no energy at all except the sailors trimming sails. It is obvious how the Romans did it. We will look at this seaborne answer to logistical problems shortly.

It will be appreciated that as the Roman army moved forward, not only did mules carry supplies for the soldiers, they also needed to feed themselves so that a situation presented itself where extra fodder-mules were necessary to carry food for their ration-carrying kin, and themselves. The longer the supply lines, the more fodder-carriers were needed in a mathematical progression which was a nightmare for ancient quartermasters. At the end of a day's work, animals cannot revitalise themselves wholly by grazing. You either graze them or work them but not both. The animals do of course browse in their off-duty hours but this is not sufficient in itself to keep them in a fit working condition. Horses, mules and camels will eat properly only during the day. If they work, they must be fed. Unlike men, the physical condition of cavalry horses and transport animals cannot be restored by periods of rest and good diet after they have been worked excessively with insufficient food. Such treatment renders them permanently unfit.

Many comparisons will be made as we consider the problems which faced the Romans. Most of our history books continue to talk of the Romans "supplying themselves" as they went along but clearly this was impossible. When Hitler attacked Russia in 1941, the Russian army retreated burning everything that would have been of use to the Germans. The Russians also pulled up the railway tracks (which were of a different gauge to the rest of Europe in any case) as they fell back. The rivers in Russia run south to north and were useless for German water transport, so the German supply lines grew longer. Finally the Russian winter caught the Germans clad in summer uniforms, at the gates of Moscow. We all know the rest of the story.

In southern England in AD43, the British tribes took their herds of animals with them as they retreated, thus denying them to the advancing Romans. Perhaps they also burned what crops they had even though May and June were early months for a harvest in Britain.

As Aulus Plautius moved out of Richborough, fighting his skirmishes and heading for the Medway and the Thames, probably with about thirty-thousand men and thousands of cavalry horses and pack-animals, one of his main worries would have been the provision of supplies for his army. The frightening (for planners and quartermasters) exponential escalation of numbers of supply animals against time and distance has already been stressed. Was there an alternative? Of course there was: what happened to the thousand vessels of the invasion fleet? There were warships equipped with heavy artillery (catapults etc), which carried a complement of marines in addition to the operating crew. The fleet also used transports of many types and sizes. Roman merchantmen of 1,000 tons or more were not uncommon. Even a 250 tonner which would be about the size of a very small modern coaster, or a trawler, would carry the same amount of cargo as 2,500 mules or 500 ox-wagons. Thus just two small supply ships, suitably escorted, would dispense with the expedition's impediment of several thousand pack-animals. One small ship arriving every day at some pre-arranged rendezvous would have fed and refurbished the whole invasion force, and Plautius had several hundred ships to choose from.

Comparisons with modern history

We can learn about military logistics from modern history. Let us look at World War 2 when things were going badly for Britain. Germany had occupied most of Europe and although Britain had gained breathing space after defeating the *Luftwaffe* during the Battle of Britain in the skies over southern England, Britain's lifelines were under threat.

In North Africa the German *Afrika Korps* under the command of the able and successful Field Marshall Rommel was moving towards the Suez Canal in an attempt to cut the British Empire in two.

Previously, British and Commonwealth troops had lost Crete after a German airborne invasion. However the German parachute regiment's casualties were so high that Hitler never used the Regiment in its parachute role again. This was to prove fatal for Rommel because the British island of Malta held out in spite of a German and Italian blockade and intensive air attacks. Hitler should have used the rest of his parachute regiment on Malta because British RAF and Royal Naval torpedo-bombers, based on the island were sinking Italian tankers and other ships carrying essential supplies for the *Afrika Korps*.

Rommel ran out of diesel fuel and petrol and was held at El Alamein at the battle of which, the British Eighth Army, now well stocked, turned the tables and drove the *Afrika Korps* back along the Libyan coast.

Also, although the Battle of Britain had been a close-run thing, the German U-boat campaign in the North Atlantic in 1942 brought Britain much closer to defeat. The convoys from USA and Canada were being decimated and Britain was down to a few weeks supplies. The day a country runs out of fuel is the day that country loses the war.

It was well known that a convoy of merchant ships was fairly safe if it was escorted by anti-submarine bombers, but Britain had few aircraft carriers and those were spread thinly around the world. Churchill had some eccentric but successful ideas. His first one was to mount catapults on selected merchant ships and each ship so equipped carried a Hurricane single-seat landplane fighter. When the U-boats' spy in the sky, a Focke Wulf 200 "Condor" reconnaissance bomber arrived on the scene, a Hurricane was catapulted off and more often than not, shot the enemy aircraft down. The pilot then baled-out and was picked-up by the nearest ship.

Shortly afterwards, Churchill ordered that suitable merchant ships would have their upper works removed and replaced by flight-decks. These "Woolworth carriers" carried only two or three old "Swordfish" aircraft, but these outdated single-engined biplanes carried depth charges and kept the U-boats away from the convoys.

Even though USA was neutral, the US Navy escorted British convoys halfway across the Atlantic, using patrol bombers and also "Blimp-type" airships. The latter bomb-carrying dirigibles could remain airborne for a week or more, and no convoy so escorted ever lost a ship.

German U-boats of that period used diesel engines on the surface and electric motors while submerged. They had to surface at night to charge their batteries using the diesel engines to turn the DC electric motors which so driven, performed as generators. Improved allied airborne radars caught the U-boats on the surface and so the Battle of the Atlantic, which could have been called "The Battle of Logistical Survival" was won.

Flying ox-wagons

Aeroplanes are magnificent amalgamations of engineering and science and I have been mixed up with transport aircraft for a large part of my life so I understand their shortcomings. They have the same problem as the Roman ox-wagons - they use a terrific amount of fuel for a relatively small payload. A typical example is the ubiquitous and highly successful Lockheed Hercules which can carry a cargo of 9 tons, 4,100 miles but it uses 29 tons of fuel to do so. That is why we had to resort to air-to-air refuelling on the Ascension Island - Falklands "Air Bridge" after the Argentinian surrender in 1982. The cargo of the Hercules was increased to the maximum payload of 20 tons and the aircraft was refuelled by a flying tanker halfway down the four-thousand mile flight; an expensive logistical exercise for urgent essentials, but mundane heavy stuff such as fuel, flour, building materials and even drinking water, had to go by ship.

The Berlin Airlift is often quoted as an example of successful airborne logistical supply, but the Russians did not shoot at the transport aircraft. There was no war situation. The Russians had merely shut off surface access to Berlin which was a western enclave inside the Soviet occupation zone. The aircraft did not deliver military supplies, only food, fuel and medical supplies.

A better example of an attempt to supply an army completely by air was at Stalingrad in January 1943, when the Red Army surrounded a German army of 300,000 men. In spite of using 500 transport aircraft, the *Luftwaffe* delivered only 20 per cent of the required stores. The starving German army surrendered to the Russians after a siege of three weeks. The transport aircraft were merely flying ox-wagons and could supply only a fraction of the trapped army's requirements.

Camel Calculus

From the Falkland Islands, where strangely, we have found out by comparisons with modern figures how long it would have taken to build a length of Roman road, we must now look at Afghanistan in the year 1905 so that we can compare the pack-animal logistics of Agricola's invasion of Caledonia c83AD with known figures for a similar invasion planned from northern India by the British Army.

It came to the notice of the British Government in 1905, that Imperial Russia was planning an invasion of Afghanistan and a contingency plan for a British counter-invasion was drawn up. An Indian division of 16,000 men was to march to Kabul and as the Afghans preferred the British and Indians to the Russians, the Indian division would be treated as a friendly force. Therefore no extra troops would be needed to protect the flanks of the supply lines. A memo by Sir G S Clarke, with suggestions for the calculation of the required transport for the expeditionary force, dated 7.7.1905, is explained as briefly as possible as follows:

The railway could be used to get supplies to within 70 miles of Kabul. After that it was to be pack-animals only, and no grain or forage was available on the line of march. The most suitable animal was the camel which could manage ten miles per day. The 70 miles would therefore be divided into 7 stages with relays of animals operating on each of the 7 stages of 10 miles.

For every 10 Indian soldiers at Kabul, one three-hundred weight camel-load had to arrive each day, which amounted to 1,600 military loads per day. As no fodder was available over the 70 miles, all requirements had to be met from base camp, so for every 10 camels with military loads, one fodder-carrying camel was necessary, plus food for the drivers who each controlled 3 camels. Therefore 1,600 military load-carriers plus 160 fodder-carriers = 1,760 were needed to carry loads daily between Camp Six and Kabul, moving outwards on one day and returning unloaded the next. Therefore 2 x 1,760 = 3,520 camels were needed to operate the stage. As the 1,760 loaded camels were en-route each day between Camp Six and Kabul, they passed about halfway, 1,760 unloaded camels coming in the opposite direction on their return from Kabul to Camp Six.

There was no food at Camp Six except that brought up by camel, therefore between Camps Five and Six, 2,112 loaded camels had to make the daily outward journey with military loads, fodder loads for the military load-carriers, and further fodder-loads for the original fodder-carriers, and so on. These were passed by 2,112 unloaded camels returning from Camp Six to Camp Five. The calculation for the number of camels required on each stage and for the total operation, was worked out by the following formula:

Let n = number of camel loads required daily at Kabul, and r = number of stages.

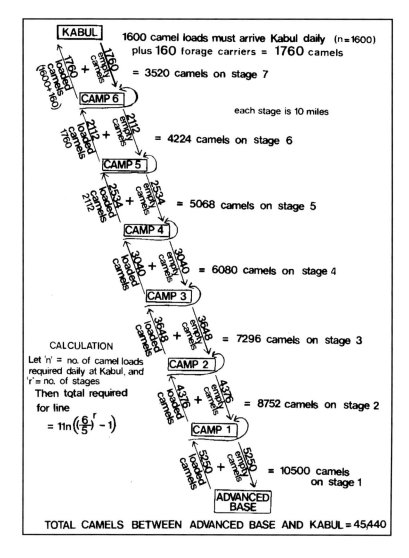

The calculation by the Royal Engineers to establish the number of pack-animals necessary for an invasion of friendly territory in Afghanistan. Even though the supply lines did not need to be defended, 45,440 camels would have been required, which was an impossible number. Agricola's invasion of Pictish Caledonia used over twenty-thousand troops in the territory of the most fierce enemy the Romans had ever encountered. The Roman invasion force had to be supplied by sea and this is borne out by Roman chronicler, Tacitus.

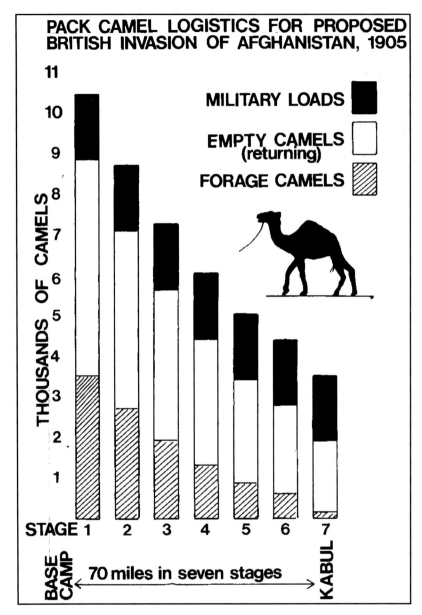

Graphical illustration of number of camels required for the proposed British invasion of Afghanistan. For obvious reasons the invasion could not take place. In any case, it became unnecessary because the Russians could not invade because of similar logistical problems.

Then total number of camels required for the line will be as follows:

Stages of 10 miles.	Calculation.	No. of Camels
Kabul - 6	2 x 1,760	= 3,520
Camp 6 - 5	2 x 1,760 x 1.2	= 4,224
Camp 5 - 4	2 x 2,112 x 1.2	= 5,068
Camp 4 - 3	2 x 2,534 x 1.2	= 6,080
Camp 3 - 2	2 x 3,040 x 1.2	= 7,296
Camp 2 - 1	2 x 3,648 x 1.2	= 8,752
Camp 1 - Base	2 x 4,376 x 1.2	= 10,500

Therefore total camels required on any one day = 45,440

This does not include the transport of fuel for cooking, and it should be noted that the Indian division will require 20 tons of this per day, but it is assumed that this will be available locally.

As the operation is through friendly territory, neither has any provision been made for escorting troops nor troops guarding the camps or flanks.

Allowing 20% for camels resting, and 100% per annum for casualties, the total number required for the line for one year is: **109,956 camels.**

It was realised that the Russians could not mount their operation because of similar logistical problems, therefore the British/Indian invasion was not necessary. The Russians made it seventy-four years later with heavy transport aircraft, helicopters, and military vehicles. Bulldozers and explosives were used for building and improving roads.

Agricola's supply system

If Agricola had used pack-animals for his expedition into Caledonia, how many would he have needed, taking into consideration the problems of operating in the most hostile territory the Romans had ever encountered? There just wouldn't have been enough animals or escorting troops in the whole of Britain.

We now know of course that Agricola's expedition was totally sea and river supplied.

Summary of evidence

In this chapter, not only have we looked at the Chester-le-Street area, but have crossed the wide world in search of evidence which will help us understand the choice of our town as a Roman site. A new picture emerges: the Romans in command of the seas with several warfleets, and a huge merchant marine linking the Roman Empire together. We can now see large Roman merchant ships entering the River Wear at high tide to negotiate the river mouth shallows and then anchoring in the deep pool at Hylton. Barges would have plied between Concangis and Hylton, supplies coming in, and corn and lead exports going out.

The purposes of the Roman roads and their limitations should now be perfectly clear, and it is exciting to know that our Roman fort, was linked direct to other parts of the Roman Empire by water. The initial investigation of possible Roman river navigation up to our Hinegan's Pond has resulted in a Europe-wide search and the overturning of many long-held, but seriously flawed theories. However the archaeological search is really just beginning.

Mathematics upset history again

We must now study a mathematical solution to the question of the inability of the Roman military roads in northern Britain to handle heavy wheeled-traffic on severe inclines.

Let me introduce information from the book *"Victorian Britain, The North East"* written by that great local authority on industrial and engineering matters, Dr Frank Atkinson OBE, who was the founder and director of our Beamish Open Air Museum, the winner of "The Museum of Europe competition":

With reference to these Roman roads, which have gradients of often one-in-three, how much longer do we have to listen to establishment and university archaeologists talking about long-distance Roman ox-wagon transport? Let us look at the mathematics of Dr Frank Atkinson.

He quotes that a large horse pulling a wagon with well-oiled rubber-tyred wheels on a perfectly level road in good condition, will have to exert a horizontal traction of equivalent to one-thirtieth of its load to overcome friction. If the load is thirty hundredweights (1½ tons), which is about the limit for a powerful horse on the level; one hundredweight will be required to move the wagon horizontally.

The formula for required traction is the total wagon-load divided by the gradient.

If a gentle gradient of one-in-thirty is encountered, an extra one-thirtieth of the load will be added to the traction necessary as the horse is now partially lifting the load as well as overcoming friction. As 1½ tons is about the limit for one large horse, an extra animal must be added.

If the single horse encounters a one-in-three gradient, extra traction of one third of the load will be needed which means an extra ten horses, making the total eleven, i.e. a thousand per cent increase of traction for a gradient of 1:3.

A Roman *clabularia* (heavy wagon) was pulled by eight oxen in summer and ten in winter. A Roman gravel-and-cobbled road had about six times the friction of a modern tarmac road, hence the large animal team. We must assume that the eight or ten-oxen Roman team could have coped with gentle gradients, but how about those dreadful one-in-three narrow tracks which are encountered very frequently on Roman roads. We can work out, that to overcome friction, six oxen would have been necessary on a level Roman road and the eight or ten quoted by the Romans must have been to take care of gentle gradients. Using Dr Atkinson's figures however, for a one-in-three gradient, an extra sixty oxen would have been needed for the severe climb.

Roman records tell us that a ten-ton *codicaria* general purpose barge, towed by four men and steered by one, operated at only one-sixteenth the cost of land transport. Compared with sea transport, the Romans tell us that land transport was fifty-eight times more expensive. It seems that the ox-wagons operated only around the farms and *vici*. There are no references whatsoever to ancient long-distance wagon transport.

With reference to Roman transport, our historians and archaeologists have seen a mosaic of a Roman ox-wagon and assumed that this was the long range logistics vehicle. The truth is that these vehicles operated only on short local trips and that all heavy cargoes went by water, hence almost every Roman fort (except defence lines like Hadrian's Wall) is situated on a river, not to protect the bridge, but for access to cheap water transport.

Cade's Road was a major north-south Roman road running through Chester-le-Street, and excavations have shown that once away from the town, the road became a narrow track with a marked agger and a rough surface, plus impossible gradients. If this was the main road, what were the secondary ones like?

Before this chapter ends let us have a quick look at what military logisticians have to say about the Roman army:

"Roman troops marched from a very early breakfast to midday and the rest of the day was spent on camp-building and other chores. In spite of their magnificent all-weather road system, movements were slow. Ox-wagons held up an army as an ox needed sixteen hours per day for rest and digestion and could make little more than one mph on the flat. It has been calculated that a Roman legion needed 170 tonnes of wheat per month and a quinquenary ala needed 53 tonnes of barley for its horses."

Successful Roman campaigns were often the result of confrontations between well-fed Roman soldiers and starving natives or invaders who did not have the organisation to establish a military logistical system. Even with their front line bases with well-stocked granaries however, the Romans still had problems as their cavalry could advance at fifty miles per day but no logistics transport vehicle could keep up with them. Even in the case of infantry marching on good roads, supply from the rear would have been difficult. The Romans knew that terminal resupply was infinitely better than base-line supply and this is where the Roman navy, merchant marine and lightermen proved their value. To a Roman legion marching northwards towards Pictish enemy Caledonia, the tidal navigation limit of the River Wear at Chester-le-Street would have been as useful to the Roman army as a modern day para-drop by a formation of fifty Lockheed Hercules transport aircraft. This is why the Roman fort of Concangis was situated on the site of our future town. One twenty-ton Roman barge could carry the same payload as a modern 'Hercules.'

Conclusion:

The Roman road network was not the grid of high-class ancient "motorways" as some of our ill-researched history books would have us believe. The Roman mosaics of ox-wagons which our historians have taken as blueprints for Roman transport, merely depict farm wagons moving between forts and jetties and around the farmyards.

Details of specific Roman roads in the north of England will be given later.

The next chapter concentrates on Roman skills with water engineering and water supplies. The importance of clean fresh drinking water to both an army and a civil population will become apparent. It will also be seen that the Romans used hitherto unknown stretches of water for inland navigation and these routes have not been noticed before because they have almost disappeared - but a few clues remain!

An American army truck transports troops c1944

Chapter 6
Splashing About With The Romans

Aqueducts

In the days of the British Empire, the Royal Engineers of the British Imperial Army built almost identical bridges in Scotland, India and Africa. Two-thousand years earlier, the Roman legions also built their own brand of civil engineering structures right across the Roman Empire. An exception to the standard pattern was in the case of aqueducts.

The Pont du Gard aqueduct bridge (arcade) consists of three tiers of arches and was built entirely without lime or cement. In earthquake zones, mortared constructions tend to crack whereas dry stone merely jiggles around (up to a certain point).

The aqueduct which was carried across the River Gardon by the Pont du Gard, en route from the "Fountain of Eure" near Uzés, to the city of Nimes, delivered four-million gallons of pure water daily.

The Romans knew nothing about microbiology, but they had observed that the consumption of contaminated water caused plagues. The reason the Romans had long life expectancies compared with later peoples was because of their meticulous sanitation and clean water supplies.

"The aqueducts are amongst the most striking examples of the greatness of the Roman Empire."

These words were spoken in AD98 by Frontinus, the curator of the waterworks in the city of Rome. He goes on to tell us how important huge supplies of pure running water were to the Romans for drinking, baths, toilets and fountains.

In the dryer climates of Italy, Spain, southern France, the Middle East and north Africa, the *specus* (water channel) of an aqueduct could be up to seventy miles long. Valleys and low-lying plains were spanned by *arcades* (aqueduct bridges), and hills pierced by aqueduct-tunnels. In the wetter climate of Britain however, the average length of an aqueduct was about four miles and simple contour-following leats usually sufficed. As a result of this, most Roman-British aqueducts remain to be discovered.

The Lakes of the Roman Wall

In the central sector of the Roman Wall across Northumberland, there is a group of little-known lakes to the north of Chesterholm (Vindolanda) and Housesteads (Vercovicium). Only Crag Lough, right below the Wall, is easily seen by walkers. Broomlee Lough can be seen from the high ground west of Housesteads but Greenlee Lough is almost totally hidden in a valley.

Rather surprisingly, in the so-called "No-man's land" to the north of the Wall, a six-mile contour-following leat was discovered, running from Greenlee Lough to the Wall-fort of Great Chesters (Aesica). A precedent had been set - the Romans had used one of the lakes as a reservoir - why not the others? An investigation was called for.

Guides to Roman sites will point out a well as having been a water-source for a fort and/or town/*vicus* but they have not calculated the amount of water needed for constant-flow-operated bath-houses, latrines, forges, water wheels and ornamental fountains. This amounts to several million gallons per day. Therefore *all* forts and towns must have had aqueducts. A simple aqueduct one foot wide, six inches deep and flowing at the walking speed of three mph will deliver one-and-a-quarter million gallons per day. Most Roman sites had more than one aqueduct to allow for accidents and planned maintenance.

Our investigation showed that there had been much more water around in Roman times. Two unknown aqueducts were found leading to Vindolanda, one from Crag Lough and another from a long-gone Peel Lough, now just a swamp. Armstrong's map of 1769 shows another lake, "Caw Lough" of which there is no sign today. This fed Greenlee Lough and so augmented the water supply to Aesica.

Crag Lough is only half of its Roman size and the suspected rough boulder dam to the east is now high and dry and almost invisible under grass.

Peel Lough filled a defile immediately north of the Wall and the latter served as a dam. Aqueduct channels can still be seen through the Wall about a third of the way up the courses (so they could not have been drainage culverts). A mysterious spurious tower attached to the Wall at this point, between Milecastles 39 and 40 and turrets 39A and 39B was probably

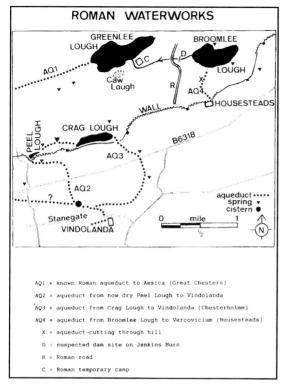

ROMAN WATERWORKS

The Roman Waterworks of Hadrian's Wall

AQ1 = known Roman aqueduct to Aesica (Great Chesters).

AQ2 = aqueduct from now dry Peel Lough to Vindolanda.

AQ3 = aqueduct from Crag Lough to Vindolanda (Chesterholm).

AQ4 = aqueduct from Broomlee Lough to Vercovicium (Housesteads).

X = aqueduct-cutting through hill.

D = suspected dam site on Jenkins Burn.

R = Roman road.

C = Roman temporary camp.

```
AQ1 = known Roman aqueduct to Aesica (Great Chesters)
AQ2 = aqueduct from now dry Peel Lough to Vindolanda
AQ3 = aqueduct from Crag Lough to Vindolanda (Chesterholme)
AQ4 = aqueduct from Broomlee Lough to Vercovicium (Housesteads)
  X = aqueduct-cutting through hill
  D = suspected dam site on Jenkins Burn
  R = Roman road
  C = Roman temporary camp
```

an aqueduct control post.

Down in the valley to the south of the Wall, the low-lying Grindon Lough has no visible outlet. It drains away through porous rock. It looks as if this lough was the Roman sump for the waste-water from the Housesteads complex.

The Housesteads aqueduct

Many archaeologists including myself have searched long and hard for the water supply to the Housesteads fort which sits on a crag on the natural line of defence of the Whinstone Sill. Until now, all searches have ended in failure. Below the fort, in a defile through which runs the Knag Burn is the fort's bath-house, a few yards south of the Wall. During the summer of 1994, no water flowed down the Knag Burn for over two months and a Roman Wall "expert" said: "Maybe the Romans didn't wash in the summer."

Broomlee Lough to the north had always been ignored because there was a hill between it and the Knag Burn defile and no suitable valley for a contour-following aqueduct broke the high ground.

My team wondered if the Romans had resorted to an aqueduct-tunnel, and calculated the spot which would entail the shortest possible bore.

Close by the Roman fort of High Rochester (Bremenium) five miles north-west of Otterburn in Northumberland, an old school building by the side of the A68(T) is built almost entirely of reused Roman aqueduct-channel stones. The Roman fort must have had an extensive waterworks system.

Chester-le-Street's Roman aqueduct after its four mile run from Broomhouse Farm near Sacriston, terminated at a very large bath-house at the top end of Roman Avenue.

The Romans were capable of driving tunnels through mountains and we have records that the Romans used thirty-thousand workmen for eleven years to drain "Lacus Fucinas" to create farmland. The tunnel ran from the lake to the River Garigliano (then called the "Liris").

At Broomlee Lough, we were astonished to find a huge cutting through the hill. It was mostly filled-in with farm rubbish but its purpose was obvious - the Romans had tapped Broomlee Lough for their water supply to the Knag Burn.

The work was tiny compared with the drainage of Lake Fucinas but the principle was the same, except that the Romans had dug a cutting at Broomlee Lough rather than a tunnel.

Old shorelines show that Broomlee Lough had been larger at one time and this drying process continues as a two-hundred year old boat-house and stone jetty are now high and dry by about four feet. Also, the Romans may have artificially increased the level of the lake as there is a possible rough dam site in the gorge via which the Jenkins Burn drains the lake to the lower Greenlee Lough. A Roman road (part of the "Pennine Way") has been identified crossing the gorge and a stub-road leaves the main road and terminates at the possible dam site (NY 783 696). The Pennine Way track crosses the Wall at the Rapishaw Gap and antiquarians of the 18th and 19th centuries said it was Roman. They were correct.

Although the source of the water to the Knag Burn bath-house has now been discovered, how did the Romans get the water from the Knag Burn defile up to the fort on the crag above? The answer is probably a water-wheel which drove a Ctesibian double-acting Roman pump (*Pneumatikon Organon*), of which several examples have been found in Roman ships' bilges and in Roman wells. An example can be seen in the British Museum. When one looks at this pump, one realises how close the Romans were to developing a steam engine. Only the sliding valve-gear is missing. The Roman pumps are very similar to emergency hand-operated fuel transfer pumps used in American aircraft during World War 2.

In the Knag Burn defile, a few yards above the remains of the bath-house, there is a waterfall eminently suitable as the site for a water-wheel, and a masonry-lined pit close-by is labelled as a "Roman well." Why have a well right next to a sparkling silver stream? The well was probably the sump for a Roman pump which supplied water to the latrines and services in the fort some fifty feet above. Perhaps we will hear no more talk of the Romans flushing constant-flow toilets with hundreds of soldiers carrying rainwater in buckets from wells.

The following story illustrates how the Romans could have lifted water about fifty feet in height to the Housesteads bath and toilets, from the Knag Burn below.

The use of a Roman-type pump driven by a water-wheel was effectively demonstrated in 1582 by a Dutch engineer, Peter Morice. London's water supply system was crude, ineffective, and contaminated and the engineer was given charge of large-scale improvements. Construction of a new waterworks at London bridge incorporated water-wheels installed under the arches. These wheels drove Roman-type Ctesibian pumps. In his demonstration, Morice squirted a jet of water over the top of a nearby church steeple. He was given financial

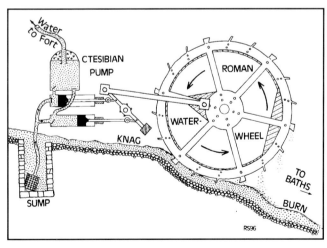

At long last we have found the Roman aqueduct to the Housesteads Knag Burn bath-house. The fort sits on a crag above the bath-house and evidence points to a water-wheel having driven a Roman Ctesibian pump which supplied a constant water-flow to the soldiers latrines and the commandant's private bath-house in the fort perched above the Knag Burn defile. The Romans went to great lengths to ensure a constant flow of pure water.

What were the Romans growing on these cultivation terraces at Housesteads? The suggestion that they resembled the rice terraces of China was rejected by the establishment but fairly recently, rice pollen has been identified in the Roman Lunt fort

at Coventry. It has also been pointed out to the authorities that the rice-fields of Northern China have a much worse climate than that of Britain. Vineyards have been suggested by "experts." However, the steep banks of the Rhine have ancient terraces cut into them but the modern Germans ignore these terraces and cultivate their vines on wires stetched straight up the hillsides.

support to install several more water-wheels and pumps. The system remained in use until 1822. Even so, as late as 1866, there were still 14,000 deaths from cholera in Britain and 5,500 of these were in London.

It is obvious that there was much more water around in Roman times. Armstrong's map of 1769 shows lakes in the depression to the south of Great Chesters (Aesica). They would have formed excellent extra rear defences to the south of the south-facing *Vallum* but they may have also served a secondary purpose as paddy fields. The Romans mention rice *(oryza)* as being twice the price of wheat. At Housesteads, the cultivation terraces resemble the rice terraces of Burma, but rice is also grown in northern China which has a worse climate than Britain. Recently, the Queckett Microscope Club have detected rice pollen near the Roman fort at Coventry (The Lunt) and samples of the acid soil at Housesteads show that it would have been suitable for rice cultivation.

There was also more water in the rivers in Roman times and this has implications for Roman transportation.

Aqueducts in enemy territory?

Why were the Roman Wall aqueducts in so-called semi-hostile territory? A recently-discovered grid of patrol roads *north* of the Wall, suggest that a *limes* (defensive grid) was policed by allied or mercenary native tribes, but that is another story which we will come to anon.

Now that we know for certain that the water levels were higher in Roman times, we can look at former suspected Roman lakes with more confidence....

The Roman aqueduct to Chester-le-Street had its source on Broomhouse Farm near
Sacriston. The Long Edge farm road sits on top of a Roman road and another suspected
Roman road joins it from the south from Flass Hall, and the westerly turn of Dere Street
at Ragpath Wood. The joining road has been used as a boundary between two different
areas of medieval rig and furrow strip-fields.

The Ancient Lakes of County Durham

A few years ago, while working as an archaeologist and air survey pilot, I found a hitherto unknown Roman road to the south of Sedgefield, in County Durham. This road, mostly camouflaged by a later cart-track called "Peter's Lane," ran in a south-westerly direction, and I lost it when it arrived at the edge of a mile-wide former swamp, now drained and in use as farmland. Ground inspections showed that the Roman metalling had ceased suddenly at the 75m contour at the former swamp edge, and I assumed that the road's stonework beyond this had sunk into the one-time morass. I did however find a Roman fortification on the road, at the edge of the former carr in the hamlet of Mordon. There were also some strange unidentified earthworks at the very edge of the one-time swamp (NZ 327 265). The evidence was filed for future reference but the information on the shelf was almost forgotten.

When it was realised from evidence elsewhere that there had been much more water around in Roman times, I wondered if the ancient swamp had actually been a *lake* in Roman times and that the reason the Roman road stopped suddenly was because a *ferry* service had taken over from that point (Mordon). Air and ground searches were restarted with a greater

The spring at the source of the Chester-le-Street Roman aqueduct (NZ 217 478). The channelled stones are identical to those in the soldiers' latrine in the Housesteads Roman fort.

vigour than before and the new insight sparked-off new discoveries. The ancient shoreline was traced with reference to the contours and the edges of medieval rig & furrow cultivation patterns. On the opposite side of the suspected lake, the Roman road recommenced suddenly at the 75m contour and was found to be lined-up on the distant town of Staindrop where it met another Roman road, the latter well known. The ancient lake was named by us "The Mordon Lake" and it was confirmed that traces of the old shoreline followed the 75m contour. The small River Skerne which had at one time fed the lake at one end and drained it at the other now meandered along the dry lake-bed. A medieval field-name at Mordon was "Maldesmyre."

Further investigations showed that there had been a *series* of lakes, and a narrow defile at the north end of the Mordon Lake actually led to another lake which had flooded to the 80m contour. There must have been some kind of ancient lock or barrage at this point in the hamlet of Bradbury. This pointed to artificial water control by the Romans. There are unidentified earthworks at Bradbury and the medieval name of the hamlet was "Bradmere."

It looked as if the earthworks at Mordon constituted a rectangular barge basin, complete with grass-covered breakwaters and a gap for small vessels to enter. Perhaps I may be excused for not realising this earlier as there was not a drop of standing water in sight for miles.

In the former Mordon Lake, it was also noticed that two areas of ground rose above the 75m contour line, and on these "bumps" were two farms with the peculiar names, "Great Isle Farm" and "Little Isle Farm." Clearly these farms had continued to be surrounded by water at a much later date than the Roman period.

An aerial survey located a suspected Roman barge basin on Great Isle Farm. That was not the end of the search however - far from it; indeed, the quest was just beginning. The old and dry bed of the Bradbury Lake was examined and followed to the north where the River Skerne entered from the north-east. The lake bed however continued northwards and ended at a natural-looking embankment. A scrutiny of this much-eroded earthen bank revealed that it was actually an ancient dam with its stone flood-spillway filled-in with rubble by modern farmers. Beyond the dam was yet another dry lake, this one with its former shoreline around the 82m contour. This smaller dry lake-bed continued towards the ruins of Bishop Middleham medieval castle. Below the castle, an earthwork spanned what looked like a dry river bed. This was thought to have been a medieval defensive moat crossed by a causeway. The "dry river" was far too large for a moat and a closer inspection of the earthwork showed that at one time it had been reinforced with stepped stonework on the downstream side, and sloped paving on the upstream face, in the manner of Roman dams. There are the remains of an almost identical Roman structure in a tributary of the Euphrates.

The old causeway (former dam) joined the medieval castle to a farm on a hill, around which the artificial-looking "river bed" completely encircled.

One would have thought that the "defensive watercourse" should have surrounded the medieval castle instead of a mere farmstead but a glance at the map told us that the name of the farm was "Island Farm."

The medieval castle is a protected historical site and no archaeological searches were permitted, but the farmer agreed to a metal detector search of his "Island Farm" and this search produced 200+ Roman coins and ten Roman brooches.

The initial investigation was still not complete. From the 82m Lower Bishop Middleham Lake, an arm swung off to the north-west and this entered the "Ferryhill Gap" through which the main London to Edinburgh railway line runs. The "gap" is a break in the hills and was formed c10,000 years ago when the great ice sheets melted and the floodwater cut a huge natural spillway. The railway runs on a causeway through a string of small loughs and swamps which follow this natural defile. A known Roman road crosses the north-south gorge at right angles, descending from the west to its lowest level of 85m at the bottom of the valley before climbing away to the east. The finger of the lake, now thought to be a Roman canal, extended underneath a long-gone Roman bridge and beyond, into the flat lands to the north. In this direction lay the River Wear, the ancient Roman "Vedra *Fluvius*." On this medium-sized River were several Roman forts. If our canal continued northwards, then the evidence would point to the Romans having linked the large River Tees to the south, via the small River Skerne and the "lost" lakes, the Ferryhill post-Ice-Age spillway, and the Tudhoe and Croxdale Becks, to the River Wear.

In the Ferryhill Gap, at the point where the suspected Roman canal passed under the Roman road, at the highest point of the valley floor, an old document tells us that a spring rose at this location and the water flowed in two directions, both north and south, one to the River Wear and the other to the Skerne. It looks therefore as if the Romans made excellent use of the natural topography of Durham's "disappeared Lake District."

To the north of the Ferryhill Gap, the valley of the Tudhoe Beck which becomes the Croxdale Beck, was a great surprise. For almost the whole length, the stream had at one time been canalised into leats for a series of watermills. These leats were obviously repairs of a much older and vast system. The mill-races were far bigger than ordinary mill-leats and although now dry and much damaged by time, had once been large enough to accommodate ten or twenty-ton barges. At one point, a length of Roman road was discovered alongside the leat.

The antiquarian Dr Cade writing in c1770, told us of a Roman fortification above the Croxdale Beck. This was found from our aircraft as a shadow mark in the high pasture at NZ 275 383.

Underneath the north end of the railway viaduct over the River Wear at NZ 262 376, clearly visible from an aircraft, is the filled-in loop of a canal. Upstream from the viaduct in the south bank of the river is a stonework abutment of an unidentified structure of unknown date.

Intensive searches must be carried out and selected sites excavated here and there.

Inland water-link, Durham to Cambridge?

We are close to finding a water link all the way from the River Wear and possibly the Tyne, to Cambridge. The route is from Chester-le-Street; River Wear; Croxdale Burn; Tudhoe Beck;

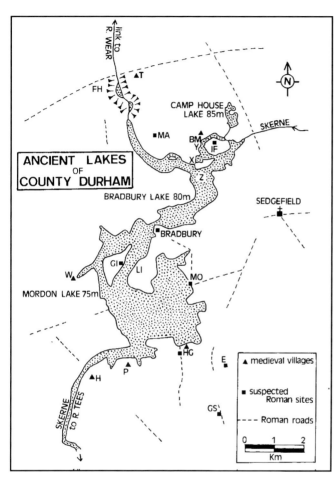

ANCIENT LAKES
OF
COUNTY DURHAM

The Lost Ancient Lakes of County Durham.

FH = Ferryhill Gap, ancient spillway from melting of ice sheets.

T = Thrislington Deserted Medieval Village (now destroyed).

MA = Mainsforth, suspected Roman site.

BM = Bishop Middleham.

IF = Island Farm, many Roman artefacts found.

Y = Suspected Roman earth dam at Bishop Middleham.

X = Further suspected Roman dam.

Z = Modern pumping station to keep ancient lakes dry.

W = Woodham Deserted Medieval Village.

GI = Great Isle Farm.

LI = Little Isle Farm.

MO = Mordon, suspected Roman temporary camp and possible barge basin (now completely dry).

H = Heworth Deserted Medieval Village.

HG = High Grindon

P = Preston Deserted Medieval Village.

E = Elstob: suspected Roman double-ditched fort shows as cropmark.

GS = Great Stainton, Roman remains found.

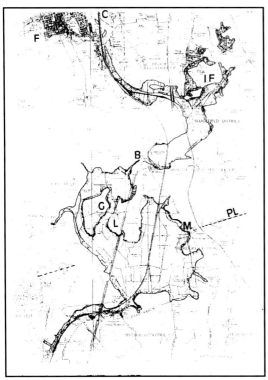

The Lost Ancient lakes superimposed on a modern map.
F = Ferryhill.
C = Suspected Roman canal through Ferryhill Gap.
IF = Island Farm, suspected Roman site.
B = Bradbury, suspected Roman remains.
G = Great Isle.
L = Little Isle.
M = Mordon. Roman road Peter's Lane terminates at camp and barge basin?
PL = Peter's Lane, suspected Roman road.

Unidentified earthworks on Great Isle
These earthworks are on the edge of the former Mordon Lake and would have been partially flooded in ancient times. They look remarkably like jetties but only an excavation will reveal the secrets.

Ferryhill Gap; Durham Lakes; River Skerne; River Tees; River Wiske; River Swale; River Ouse; River Humber; River Trent; Roman Foss Dyke (canal); and the Roman Car Dyke (canal). During the winter when the Romans tell us sea navigation was restricted, this would have been an excellent and relatively economical route. A Roman punt which could float on a few inches of water, could carry a ton, the equivalent of two ox-wagons, or seven pack-mules. The punt didn't eat anything.

The Ancient Lake of Yorkshire

Once I knew that ancient lakes had existed in Northumberland and Durham, my search temporarily switched to Yorkshire to see if there were similar features in that region. At once, my attention was drawn to the low-lying area of the Vale of Pickering. Vast areas called "carrs" told me that this whole valley had been a swamp at one time. It was known that a very large stretch of water had filled the area in Mesolithic times because hunter-gatherer settlements have been located, the most famous of these being at Star Carr, where bone harpoons and other Middle Stone Age implements were recovered.

While giving a lecture to a Yorkshire Historical Society, metal detectorists in the audience gave me the astonishing information that all around the 23m contour line of the Vale of Pickering, hundreds of Roman copper boat-rivets had been picked up! The Mesolithic lake had continued into the Roman occupation period. Furthermore, it looks as if the lake still existed in the Viking era as there is a village with the Old Danish name of "Flotmanby." This can be translated as: "The place of the ferryman, or boatman."

At the end of the Ice Age, the River Derwent avoided the Vale of Pickering and followed its ancient short-cut to the North Sea, to the north of Scarborough. Deposited debris from the melting ice blocked this old outlet to the sea and the river turned westwards and flooded the Vale of Pickering for several thousand years until it broke through a ridge and drained to the south becoming a tributary of the Yorkshire Ouse and then the Humber.

Early in the 19th century, Sir George Cayley, cut a canal (called the Sea Cut) down the ancient and debris-blocked river channel in order to avoid periodic floodings of the Vale of Pickering. Perhaps Sir George had been beaten to it by 1700 years as metal detectorists have now discovered hundreds of Roman artefacts in the vicinity of Scalby Mills, where the 19th century Sea Cut (and ancient Derwent channel) meets the coast. This may have been the Roman entrance from the sea to Lake Pickering, the other route being the long way round up the Rivers Humber, Ouse and Derwent all of which are easily navigable.

The Roman fort of Malton lies at the gap in the ridge through which the ancient lake had cut a drainage overspill. A Roman dam at this position could have controlled the level of the lake and indeed, records tell us that an ancient dam of unknown date was removed at Malton in 1820 as it constituted an obstruction to proposed navigation to Yedingham further upstream.

Between the eastern end of the ancient Lake Pickering and the sea is a mile-wide high bank of ice-deposited debris and it is possible that the Romans surmounted this with canals and locks, as a stream in which Roman artefacts have been found, climbs from the sea, up "Primrose Valley." On the inside of the wide sea-bank, the River Hertford rises and heads inland whereas once it had flowed into the sea. From its source on the sea-bank above Hunmanby, the infant Hertford is known as "The Dams" for over a mile. Perhaps these dams were for Roman navigation across the sea-bank.

A suspected Roman harbour at Filey Brigg

On the outside of the sea-bank is "Filey Bay" and "Filey Brigg." The latter is a rocky peninsula which juts out into the North Sea and forms an excellent shelter for small vessels during north-east gales. The ruins of a Roman signal station sit on the Brigg. In 1922, the famous archaeologist, F. Gerald Simpson found an artificial-looking pier, jutting out from the Brigg in a southerly direction. He thought that it was of Roman construction but his thesis was not given support by the establishment.

Simpson's pier can be seen only twice per year during the lowest equinoctial tides. Professor Simpson's daughter, Dr Grace Simpson, was a lecturer in archaeology at Oxford University and she has given me copies of her father's papers. They are very convincing.

In 1995, severe storms removed about four feet (1½m) of sand from the outer end of Filey Brigg, and metal detectorists found dozens of *denarii* of Emperor Hadrian.

Whilst we are looking at the importance of Yorkshire in our Roman supply system which includes deep-sea navigation into Sunderland and barge navigation almost definitely upstream to our town, and also possibly southwards via the Ferryhill Gap and the Durham Lakes, we must also have a quick glance at Whitby and the surrounding area:

Roman Whitby?

At the Synod of Whitby in the year 664, Oswy, King of Northumbria, decided in favour of the Roman form of Christianity in preference to the Irish, a momentous decision for British Christianity.

The monastery which was the meeting place of the Synod, and which was founded in 657 by St Hilda of Hartlepool, was destroyed two centuries later (867) by the Danes, and not refounded until the coming of the Normans. The present abbey-church was probably started in the very same year as Salisbury Cathedral, 1220, and although so far apart, they have stylistically, a good deal in common.

The monks belonged to the Benedictine order, and never numbered more than sixty. In 1539 they departed, and their Abbey was abandoned to the wind and the rain and the pillagers of stone. The central tower lasted well, and fell only in 1840.

Further evidence is coming to light about a Roman presence at Whitby. The abbey was funded by King Oswy of Northumbria, (AD642-71). Deiran princess, Hilda (AD614-80) became its abbess. It was called "Streonaeshalch" which the Saxon historian Bede, writing about AD731 quotes as meaning: "The harbour of the watch tower." Also, the 12th century chronicler, the monk Simeon of Durham tells us that there was a *"Pharos"* (lighthouse) at Whitby. This has been incorrectly translated by later historians as a "signal station." These historians possibly thought that because there was a known string of Roman signal stations up the Yorkshire coast, the Whitby site must have been one of them.

There have been hundreds of Roman finds at Whitby and a Roman dam was removed from the Esk in 1910. It had probably held a head of water in the non-tidal basin of an inner harbour but like many other Roman river structures, it was labelled "paved ford" or "fish-trap" by historians who had little knowledge of ancient civil engineering.

Whitby may have been the long lost Roman town of "Praetorio." This site has never been located.

A Roman road-book called *The Antonine Itinerary* tells us that from Eburacum (York), it was seven Roman miles to Derventio, (A Roman mile was 1620 yards). It was also thirteen Roman miles from Derventio to Delgovicia and twenty-five miles from Delgovicia to Praetorio. Modern historians have placed Derventio at Malton but it is twenty Roman miles from York to Malton, not seven. The same historians have quoted Millington as Delgovicia but this involves a hundred degree southward twist of the Roman road. The same historians then cite Brough on Humber as Praetorio but it has been found from modern excavations that the true name of Brough on Humber was "Petuaria."

However, if we place Roman Derventio at Stamford Bridge, where four, or possibly five Roman roads converge, (and where metal detectorists have recently found over five-thousand Roman coins); Delgovicia at Malton, and Praetorio at Whitby; then all Roman quoted distances (7, 13, & 25) agree exactly and there is no need to twist the Roman road backwards on itself.

With Whitby as the Roman road's final destination, a ferry would have been necessary across Lake Pickering but water crossings have been included in other distances quoted in the *Antonine Itinerary*.

Another possible location for Praetorio is Bridlington, in the direction of which a Roman road strikes out from Malton. Bridlington is also twenty-five miles from Malton and this should be taken into account by modern historians. Unfortunately, there has been much coastal erosion at Bridlington and a Roman port there may have been lost to the sea.

A Roman lighthouse is suspected on Flamborough Head but as yet has not been located. There is much scope for amateur searchers.

Other factors also tell us that the Roman occupation of Yorkshire was far more intense than hitherto thought and now we must add an unknown massive lake, several times the size of England's famous Derwentwater. This has implications for the history of Roman inland water transport which appears to have been on a vast scale. It looks as if the waterways were even more important than the roads.

Water, water everywhere

It seems that in the later Saxon times, much of the English landscape was marsh, and the biographer of St Guthlac of Crowland, writing shortly after AD700, told of a fen of "immense size" that stretched from Cambridge northwards to the sea. It was overhung by fog and was characterised by wooded islands and tortuous streams.

Bede tells us that the Isle of Ely received its name from the great quantity of eels to be found around; and pre-Doomsday Fenland charters refer to fishermen, nets and boats.

Britain drying out

Research on this project has therefore confirmed that Britain has been "drying out" for the last two-thousand years and I am sure that the implications of this will not be lost on our climatologists and planners of future water supplies in a country which has been increasingly suffering from droughts and water shortages, (until the floods of 2000).

In the next chapter we must look at another much neglected subject - Roman and other ancient ships. Many landlubbers have written at length about the Roman navy and merchant marine, and we read about Roman ships being unable to tack into wind and that they hugged the coasts because they could not navigate out of sight of land; utter nonsense as Roman references and recent discoveries will show.

In 1978, at Chester-le-Street, a Roman sewer was cut into during the construction of the squash courts and swimming baths. The sewer ran from the fort's north-eastern corner in the direction of the former course of the canal which ran into Hinegan's Pond.

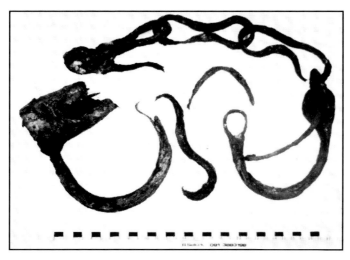

While our divers were investigating the remains of the Roman bridge piers on the bed of the River Tyne at Corbridge, they picked up a pair of ankle shackles and part of a Roman slave-chain. One of the shackles has a bronze barrel lock. At the request of Mr Thompson, who is the expert on Roman and Celtic slaves-chains, and who excavated the Iron Age hillfort at Bigberry, near Canterbury, our shackles went on display for six months in the Piccadilly headquarters of the London Society of Antiquarians. A good identification feature of Roman slave chains is that the figure-of-eight links do not join in the middle.

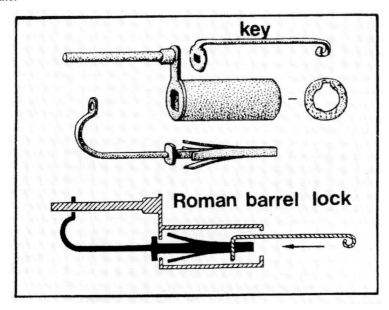

Remains of a Roman river-craft found in the bank of the River Rhine while preparing the foundations of the Hilton Hotel at Mainz.

Roman bridge of boats from a relief on a monument in Rome.

Chapter 7
Roman Ships

*So many are the merchant vessels that arrive here that Rome
has practically become a common workshop for the whole world...
There are always ships putting into or sailing out of the harbour*

Aristides

A close look at sailing ships

One of the most interesting jobs I have ever undertaken was as navigator on the replica of the sixteenth-century *Golden Hind(e)* (both spellings used in Drake's time). My old shipmate Dennis Ord was the captain and I joined the ship in Bangor, Northern Ireland.

Captain Dennis Ord of South Shields (right) and Seaman Neville Andison of Chester-le-Street on board the replica "Golden Hinde" en route from the Forth to the Tyne. Bass Rock is in the background. The modern compass was fitted at the insistence of the insurers, Lloyds of London.

The ship had been to North America three times, circumnavigated the world and had starred in the film *Shogun*.

I was delighted to be invited to join the crew even if it was only for a short period of duty in European waters.

The replica *Golden Hinde* was built by the Hinks Shipyard in Appledore.

The sail-plan allows for two square sails on both the foremast and mainmast and a lateen on the mizzen-mast. The bowsprit on this type of ship is really an angled mast and carries a sprit-sail or artemon below it.

GOLDEN HINDE

sailed the world 1577 - 1580

Side view of Golden Hinde showing its sail plan. Note its Roman style "artemon" sail on the bowsprit. The holes in the lower corners of this sail are for drainage when the ship dips her bows.
Average-sized Roman merchant ships were about the same size as the Golden Hinde (about 500 tons).Some Roman ships were many times larger.

Underneath the bowsprit and just aft of the artemon sail is the triangular space known as the ship's beak or head, and as Sir Francis Drake was the only crew member with toilet facilities, the original crew's lavatory was this head, the grid of which flushed itself every time the ship dipped her bows. The deer's head figurehead was carried on the apex of the beak. Toilets on modern warships are still known as "heads."

The power of sails is not fully appreciated so let me quote an example from which we have accurate figures: The Tea Clipper *Cutty Sark*, launched in 1869 could set a maximum of 32,000 square feet of canvas. This was equal to a 3,000 horsepower engine, which gave the ship a top speed of 17½ knots. The speed of the tubby *Golden Hinde* with her sail area of 4,150 sq ft was nearer four knots.

The replica *Golden Hinde* was fitted with a small auxiliary diesel engine to simplify harbour manoeuvring and to comply with insurance regulations. If the engine was being used during filming, the exhaust could be switched to either side of the ship to conceal tell-tale plumes of smoke.

During my period of service, our crew consisted of twenty-five girls who were extremely efficient and also looked very smart in their uniforms of red windcheaters and blue trousers. In bad weather, a favourite clothes-line for wet garments was a wire which ran above the hot exhaust of the diesel engine. This wire was part of the steering system and linked wheel to rudder.When a large alteration of course was made on one occasion, many feminine garments moved into the pulleys and necessitated some fiendish hacking with knives.

During our voyage, we entered Southampton Water and I was given the wheel for the passage of the busy waterway. During my troopship service out of this port, I never visualised that one day, I would be at the wheel of a galleon in the same fairway. The troopers were long

A Roman merchant ship about the same size as the Golden Hinde.
Note the ship's "artemon" sail at the bow and its square-rig mainsail. Roman records tell us that these ships could tack into the wind. As with later square-rigged sailing ships, this would have been done by easing the trusses which hold the yard to the mast and swinging the yard round as in the top diagram.

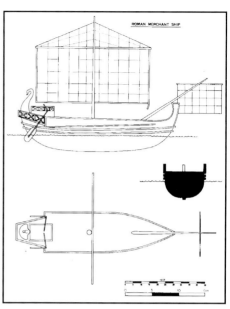

ROMAN MERCHANT SHIP

The "Golden Hinde" alongside the quay at Newcastle upon Tyne. Note the bowsprit which is really a Roman-type angled mast and is rigged as such. The author sailed as navigator on this ship.

gone, but the *Queen Elizabeth 2*, outward bound, saluted us with her siren and we replied with a blank round from a cannon. Saluting with cannon had to be restricted to open water as on a previous voyage, detonations had broken windows in a large waterfront hotel and also set off hundreds of car alarms.

In the Solent, other nostalgic memories flooded back as Tiger Moth, G-APLU flew over the ship. I had done some of my pilot-training on this type of aircraft, along this south coast of England. We passed the famous Calshot Spit where the Vickers Supermarine S6B racing seaplane in 1931 had won fame for Britain by winning outright the Schneider Trophy. A direct descendant of the S6B, the Spitfire, in conjunction with Hawker Hurricanes, had saved our nation from Nazi slavery by defeating the *Luftwaffe* in the Battle of Britain. As we passed

A Roman bireme warship of the Classis Britannica *(Roman British Fleet). Like modern super-powers, the Romans had several fleets throughout their empire. The ships of the Classis Britannica were camouflaged with blue paint. The sails and ropes were dyed blue; the sailors had blue uniforms and their faces were dyed blue. Because of their blue-painted faces, the sailors were nicknamed "Picts."*

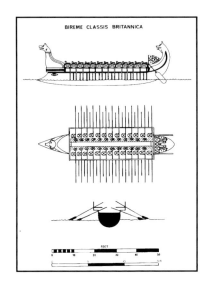

BIREME CLASSIS BRITANNICA

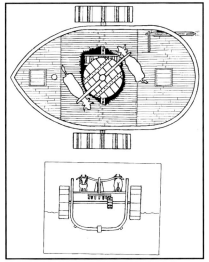

An ox-driven boat as described at the end of the fourth century AD by an anonymous author writing about warfare. Some modern historians argue that such a ship would not work but they are wrong: In the "Penny Magazine" of 1840, there is a story about a similar vessel, powered by two horses, working as a ferry-boat on the River Niagara between Canada and USA. (On the Trail of the Legions, Selkirk,R. p336-338).

Many supposed learned historians get their facts completely wrong when they write about ships and the sea. Here an ancient ship is proceeding backwards - the sail is driving the ship to the right but the high curved end is the ship's stern. The historian has been unsure what the steering-oar was so he has lifted it out of the water into a horizontal position. Numerous books show Roman merchant ships proceeding astern.

close by the old seaplane base, on the slipway there was a Sunderland flying boat in civil markings. This famous maritime patrol-bomber which had escorted WW2 North Atlantic convoys, was now being refurbished and was destined for a museum in the United States.

Running parallel to my occasional seagoing duties was my career as an archaeologist. It was natural for me to specialise in Roman maritime affairs. Roman warships (called "long-ships" by the Romans) were sleek, much resembling giant versions of Oxford and Cambridge "eights." Roman merchant ships were tubby and were called "basket-ships" or "round-ships" by the Romans. The insignia for a merchant ship was a basket at the mast-head or on top of a pole. The usual small-to-medium Roman merchant ship closely resembled our replica warship *Golden Hinde*. By Tudor times, warships had lost their sleek lines possibly because of the large volume needed for stores for increasingly long voyages plus stowage space for treasure taken from enemy prizes.

A Roman merchant ship coming alongside the quay presumably at Ostia. This relief depicts an accident - the ship has broken its angled bowsprit-type foremast. There is a "wedding-cake-type" lighthouse in the background surrounded by various deities. The ship's workboat which was towed astern while at sea is now under the steering oar while a sailor carries out some task.

Land-based historians get it all wrong

When many historians discuss ancient ships, they immediately betray themselves to ex-navy men as hopeless landlubbers. Our "experts" tell us that seamen of the Classical Period hugged the shores because of a lack of expertise in navigation. What rubbish! Ancient oared-warships *could* hug the coasts because they had the ability to manoeuvre against wind and tide but to stay near the coast in a sailing ship is suicidal. Most of the dangers of the sea are related to the coastlines and a deep-sea sailor breathes a sigh of relief when the land is left far behind and a routine can be established. If a sailing ship tried to hug the coast, all hands would have had to be called to the deck to re-trim the sails every time the ship altered course. Maybe the large crews of oared warships liked to wine and dine ashore whenever possible, but then as now, merchant ships relied on the delivery of cargoes for their upkeep, and ploughed-on for weeks on end. The Greek poet Aratus tells us about seamens' knowledge of astro-navigation.

Due to a gyroscopic wobble of the Earth's axis which takes 25,600 years to describe one circle in the heavens, the pole star in Roman times was Kochab in the constellation of the Little Bear. In ancient Egyption times, the pole star was Thuban. Our own period pole star, "Polaris" will appear to drift away from our elevated North Pole, but will once again become the pole star in 25,600 years time.

Aratus had this to say in 275 BC, about Kochab, the pole star of that period:

"By her (the little bear's) guidance, the men of Sidon (Phoenicians) steer the straightest course."

The Roman poet Lucan (AD 39-65) mentions the Pole Star (Kochab) and the circumpolar stars which appeared to revolve around it:

"We do not follow any of the restless stars which move in the sky, for they deceive poor sailors. We follow no stars but one, that does not dip into the waves, the never-setting Axis, brightest star in the Twin Bears. This it is that guides our ships."

Other references to guidance from the stars can be found in Ovid. Met. iii. 592, Lucan viii.167, and Virgil. Aen. v. 161.176.

Some ancient sailing directions survive for the Mediterranean.

There follows just a few of them: Pliny the Elder tells us that precisely on the summer solstice, the shadow of Mount Athos' peak, fell upon a village market-place on the island of Lemnos, forty miles away.

From the highest peak on the island of Rhodes, which was a holy spot associated with the god Zeus, we are told it is possible to see Mount Ida in Crete, the god's own reputed birthplace, a hundred miles away.

All navigators can read the stars at a glance and no doubt ancient navigators could do the same. The RAF taught aircrew cadets the positions of all the stars in the constellation of Orion by starting in the centre and chanting:

"Better Belong to the Royal Society for Pupil Pilots who Cannot Cope with Aviation."

"Betelgeuse, Bellatrix, Rigel, Sirius, Procyon, Pollux, Castor, Capella, Aldebaran."

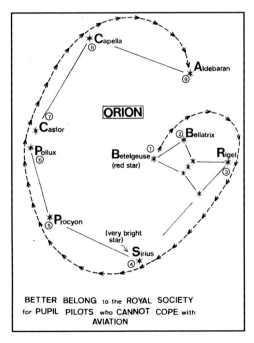

BETTER BELONG to the ROYAL SOCIETY for PUPIL PILOTS who CANNOT COPE with AVIATION

RAF
ASTRO COMPASS

The RAF Astro Compass. This is not a sextant. The sextant measures altitudes and other angles. The astro compass measures directions but uses heavenly bodies instead of the Earth's magnetism. The device is particularly useful in polar regions where magnetic compasses are sluggish and have huge errors.

ROYAL AIR FORCE CHECKLIST FOR ASTRO COMPASS.

Before operation, check that instrument is fixed securely to its mounting with the lubber-line on the aircraft's centre-line and facing the nose of the aircraft.

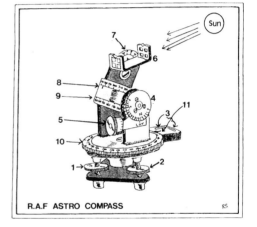

R.A.F ASTRO COMPASS

1,2.   *Set levelling screws and observe spirit levels (3).*
4.   *Set latitude on scale via knob (5).*
6.   *Set gnomon at Sun's declination on scale (7).*
8.   *Obtain Greenwich Hour Angle from tables. Adjust this for observer's approximate longitude. This gives Local Hour Angle which is an angular measurement of local time. (Scale 9 is for use in southern hemisphere).*
10.   *Twist body of instrument until shadow-cross of gnomon falls on etched cross on gnomon's screen.*
11.   *Read off aircraft's true heading against lubber-line.*

It will be shown shortly that a Roman sun-compass can be set-up with the Royal Air Force Astro Compass check-list.

(Top) Cockpit of Piper Aztec G-BAVL in which Bob Fox (pilot) of South Shields and the author (co-pilot/navigator) flew in the Paris to New York Air Race of 1981. An RAF Astro compass is mounted on top of the instrument panel. G-BAVL came fifth out of 120 aircraft. Sadly, a French crew: an airline pilot and a flying instructor, was lost without trace.

(Bottom) At Paris, Le Bourget before the race, the author asked one of the French organisers why a penguin had been chosen for the Race's insignia. "Because Monsieur, you will be flying over the Arctic," replied the official. When the author informed the French gentleman that all penguins are in the Antarctic and that there are none in the Arctic, the officials second answer was "Please Monsieur, make no mention of this to the press!"

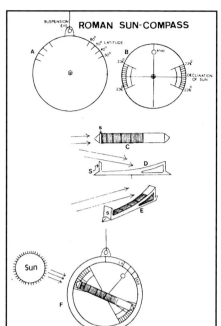

ROMAN SUN-COMPASS

Several examples of the strange Roman instrument have been found around the former Roman Empire. The authorities were unsure of its purpose and classed it as some kind of sundial. Because of its settings, the author knew it was a sun-compass and demonstrated that it could be set-up with the RAF checklist. The parts of the Roman instrument are:

A = Brass disc with latitude scale.
B = Smaller brass disc with declination-of-Sun scale.
C = Double-ended gnomon.
D = Side view of gnomon showing shadow-bar (S).
E = Oblique view of gnomon.
F = The assembled Sun Compass.

POSSIBLE ROMAN ARMY/NAVY CHECKLIST FOR SUN COMPASS

1,2,3. As instrument is suspended, no levelling is needed.

4.   Set approximate latitude on outer scale (4) against knob (5) on inner disc.

6.   Set gnomon to declination of Sun (7). This is marked as a date on the Roman instrument.

8.   Note the local time from hour glass or other device.

10.   Twist the body of the instrument on its suspension string until the shadow of the gnomon's shadow-bar coincides with the gnomon's correct local time hour-line as noted from an hour-glass.

11.   The instrument is now lined-up exactly north-south i.e. on the meridian.

The RAF instrument can be set up with stars, planets and the Moon as well as the Sun, so it is more complex. The Roman instrument used only the Sun. Nevertheless, the Roman Sun Compass can be set-up with the RAF checklist.

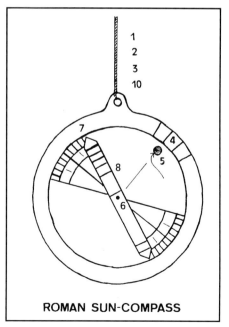

ROMAN SUN-COMPASS

The relationship of the altitude (angle above horizon) of
Polaris (Pole Star) to the observer's latitude. The unique
position of Polaris gives our latitude as well as an
indication of true north. Polaris is a rather dim star merely
because of its distance from Earth. It is actually 6,000 times
brighter than our own Sun but it is 680 light years away.
This means that light from Polaris arriving at Earth in AD
2,000 actually left the star six years after the Battle of
Bannockburn (1314).

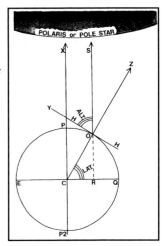

P   =   North Pole
P2   =   South Pole
EQ   =   Equator
C   =   Centre of Earth
X   =   Direction of Polaris
O   =   Observer
Z   =   Observer's zenith (overhead point)
YH   =   Observer's horizon
OCQ =   Observer's latitude
YOS =   Altitude of Polaris
OCQ =   YOS (with a slight correction due to Polaris being almost one degree [58
          minutes] off the true elevated pole)

THE PRECESSION OF THE EQUINOXES

The Earth's axis makes a gyroscopic wobble in space but this takes almost twenty-six-
thousand years to complete one cycle. Over long periods, this causes the "pole star" to
change. "P" is "Polaris," our present day pole star, but our Earth's extended northern
axis is drifting slowly away from it in an anticlockwise
circle. However, Polaris will be our Pole Star again in
26,000 years time. "V" = Vega which will be the Pole Star in
AD 12,000. "T" is "Thuban" and was the Pole Star in
Ancient Egyptian times, and "K" is "Kochab" which was the
Pole Star in Roman times. Roman writers mention the north-
finding navigation value of this star in "The Constellation of
the Lesser Bear."

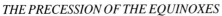

The Greek astronomer Hipparchus discovered the Earth's
precessional "wobble" about 140 BC. Hipparchus also used
a grid of lines of latitude and longitude. They are still in use
today. In ancient times however, the prime meridian passed
through Alexandria and later was switched to the Canary
Islands which the Mediterranean peoples thought was the
most westerly land in the world. The Phoenicians, Greeks
and Romans knew that the world was round but they did not
suspect a huge continent westwards from Europe/West Africa
and eastwards from Japan/China.

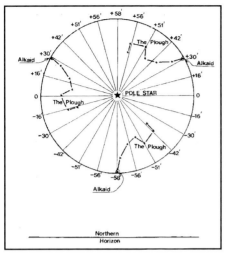

THE FISHERMAN'S CLOCK

The present North Pole Star (Polaris) is not exactly above the North Pole - it is 58 minutes (almost one degree) offset. This subtends a distance on the Earth's surface of 58 nautical miles. The observer's latitude is equal to the angular distance (altitude) of Polaris above the horizon, plus or minus a correction found in tables. This correction varies from zero to 58 minutes (zero to 58 nautical miles on the Earth's surface) depending on the local hour angle of the First Point of Aries (a fixed reference point in the sky).

A quick method of finding one's latitude without tables is to measure the altitude of Polaris and then note the position of Alkaid, the leading star in the constellation of "Ursa Major" (the latter is also known as the Plough, the Dipper, Charlie's Wagon etc). This correction, shown in the diagram, is added to, or subtracted from the altitude of Polaris and the answer is the exact observer's latitude. In Roman times, Kochab was the nearest star to the Celestial North Pole and no doubt the Romans knew how to correct for True North (for steering) and altitude (to find latitude). In 300 BC, the famous Greek navigator Pytheas sailed to "Thule" (probably Iceland) which he said was six days sail (about 600 nautical miles at 4 knots) north of the British mainland's most northerly point. He reached fringes of the "Great Frozen Sea where the Sun went to sleep for only very short periods." One of his tasks was to find the correction-angle between the Pole Star (Kochab in his day) and the true elevated North Pole. The ancient peoples were far more competent navigators and astronomers than portrayed by some of our modern historians.

The relationship of observer's latitude to the altitude of the Sun at its meridian crossing. With zero declination (at the equinoxes), the Noon Zenith Distance (90 degrees minus the Sun's meridian altitude) is equal to the observer's latitude. At other times, to obtain latitude from the meridian altitude of the Sun, the Sun's declination must be taken from tables and added to, or subtracted from the Noon Zenith Distance, depending upon whether the declination is North or South. A sextant measures altitudes but ancient navigators had cruder but still effective instruments.

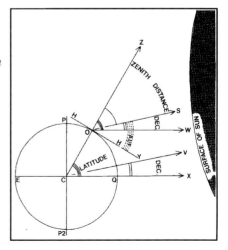

The Taurus Mountains in Turkey can be seen from Cyprus on a clear day and on a similar day, Africa can be seen from the peaks of Sicily.

The island of Pantellaria is an excellent site for modern aeronautical radiobeacons. In ancient times, the flocks of migrating birds which rested there (and still do) made excellent pathfinders for ships of antiquity.

Ancient signalling was carried out from various high points:

The poet Aeschylus describes news of the fall of Troy being flashed from island to island along the Mediterranean, from the Hellespont in Asia Minor, across the Aegean to Greece and onwards to the Greek colonies in southern Italy.

Old records tell us that the clouds which formed over Mount Vesuvius, near Naples, were visible for over 120 miles. Sometimes the volcano's plume of smoke and flashes of fire extended the range.

The flat and featureless coastline of Egypt was a danger to ancient mariners. This is the reason why a chain of lighthouses was constructed, the most famous being: "The Pharos of Alexandria" which took its name from the small island on which it stood, the Isle of Pharos. A smaller lighthouse stood thirty miles to the west at Abusir and served the port of Taposiris which was also the entrance to lake Mareotis and a network of inland navigation systems.

The light from the Alexandria Pharos could be seen fifty miles away, and a Roman writer said of the light that it resembled: "a planet or star low over the horizon." Roman lighthouse designers copied the tiered shape of the Alexandrian structure and evidence of this can be seen in Roman mosaics and on Roman coins.

The Pharos of Alexandria, built by King Ptolemy, and designed by architect Sostratus of Cnidos, was destroyed by an earthquake in AD1375. A century later, Burji Mameluk Sultan Qaitbay built a fortress on its foundations. In the heart of the Mameluk fort, in the ancient foundations of the lighthouse, is a mosque. This is not orientated on Mecca as is normal, but on the four points of the compass as per the ground-plan of the ancient lighthouse.

If ancient ships had hugged the shores as some of our historians would have us believe, lighthouses fifty feet high and not five-hundred would have sufficed.

During my own service as a mate on a sailing ship, I shudder to think what the crew's reactions would have been if we had hugged the coast and called all hands on deck every few minutes, to ease the trusses and adjust the yards, as we altered course around every headland, dreading a shift in the wind which would put us on the rocks. We always got away from the coast and its associated dangers as quickly as possible.

This brings me to a related subject - many lubberly historians claim that square-rigged ships such as Roman merchantmen could run only before the wind - absolute nonsense. With a wind on the beam or even afore the beam, the trusses (which connect the yards to the mast) are eased and the yards swung round. Thus the angled sails deflect a beam-wind rearwards and the reaction, with suction on the front of the sail and high pressure behind, (similar to that of an aircraft's wing), drives the ship forward. This is essential for the zig-zag progress to windward known as "tacking." A sailing ship with its yards swung almost fore and aft can proceed into wind up to that point where the pressure of air behind the sail is lost. This results also in the loss of suction on the front of the sail and the sail stalls. Having said that, fore-and-aft rigged ships such as yachts and schooners can sail closer to the wind than square-riggers.

When the replica of Captain Cook's ship, "*Endeavour*," sailed to Whitby from Australia in 1997, John Hedges of NAG, visited the ship and asked the captain if he could "tack" and how close to the wind could he get? The captain replied that of course he could tack, and the lumbering replica of Cook's square-rigged collier, transformed into a survey ship, could get to within 70 degrees of the wind.

Now let us look at a few nautical words and phrases which can be found in Roman literature:

(Top) The Roman lighthouse at Boulogne built by Caligula cAD40. It was repaired by Charlemagne and fell to pieces c1644. It was 200 feet high and had twelve stepped stages. The diameter of the base was 64 ft. It was built of white and yellow stone and red brick. This sketch is based on one drawn by Chatillon, cartographer to Henry IV.

(Lower) Lighthouses as depicted on Roman mosaics.

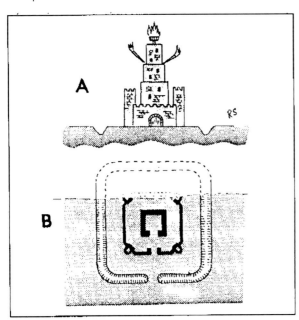

(A). The Romans had lighthouses and signal stations but some served a dual purpose. The Roman structure on Castle Hill, Scarborough (TA 052 892) may have served such a dual purpose.
(B). A third of the Roman structure has fallen down the sea cliff. Aerial photography reveals a possible later lighthouse/signal station slightly further back from the cliff and a little to the north. Investigations continue.

This Roman illustration on Trajan's Column shows a pure signal station on the Danube frontier. A torch on a semaphore arm sticks out of an upper window and close-by are two prepared fires ready to be ignited as an emergency signal.

Facere pedem "to trim the foot-ropes" (of the sails) [Virgil, Aen. v. 830].

Obliquat laevo pede carbasca = "he turns the sails so as to catch the wind blowing from the right" [Lucan, v.428].

Currere utroque pede = "to sail with a wind right astern"   [Catull.iv.21].

In contrarium navigare prolatis pedibus = "by tacking" [Pliny,ii.57].

Cymbulae onerariis adhoerescebant = "each ship towed a work-boat".

The vast number of different types of Roman ships also tell us that contrary to popular opinion, the Romans were certainly not landlubbers. The various Roman regional war-fleets did however use many seamen from occupied countries such as Greece and Egypt and because of this, the Roman navy was organised as "*auxiliaries*" in a similar manner to "non Roman citizens" who served in the Roman army.

Navis longa , warship[Caes.B.G.iv.25]

Liburna fast, light galley, [Horat.Epod.i.1]

Navis praetoria flagship

Naves onerariae ships of burden[Caes.B.G.iv.20]

Navis mercatorius merchant ship [Livy.xxiii.1]

Navis corbita (basket ship)merchant ship (a basket at the masthead was the Roman insignia for a merchantman [Festus.Cic.Att.xvi.6]

Naves frumentaiae corn ships[Livy.xxiii.1]

Naves vinariae wine ships

Naves oleariae oil ships

Naves piscatoriae fishing boats

Naves speculatoriae spy ships[Livy.xxx.10]

Naves exploratoriae survey ships

Naves piraticae or *praedatoriae* pirate ships [Livy.xxxiv.32.36]

Naves hippagogae horse transports[Livy.xliv.28]

Naves tabellariae courier ships[Senec.Epist.77]

Naves vectoriae gravesque heavy transport ships [Caes.B.Gv.7]

We have a description of one of the larger Roman merchant ships, the *Isis*, which was on the grain run from Alexandria to Ostia, but was blown off course and ended up at Piraeus, the port of Athens. The homeward journey from Egypt, which involved tacking against contrary winds, always took longer than the outward journey. The *Isis* had encountered some of these adverse winds. The description is by one "Lucian" who travelled from Athens down to Piraeus to view the vessel:

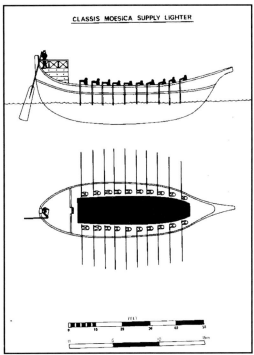

CLASSIS MOESICA SUPPLY LIGHTER

Classis Moesica (Lower River Danube Fleet) supply lighter.

A Roman merchant ship as depicted on a First Century graffita in Pompeii. The name of the ship is "Europa". Note the angled mast at the bow (left). At the stern (right) one of the steering oars has been raised to the horizontal position, presumably either for repair by the crew of the towed workboat (extreme right) or because the ship is getting ready to come alongside the quay. This type of ship could carry 10,000 large amphorae. This relatively small ship is about the same size as the Tudor Golden Hinde.

A Roman warship being manoeuvred. Note corvus (raven) in raised position. The corvus was an assault-gangway which was dropped onto the deck of an enemy ship. A beak-like spike on the underside of the corvus held it in place and Roman marine troops swarmed onto the enemy deck.

Three Roman altars which indicate the possibility that the Second and Sixth Legions were marine regiments. We know that these legions were recruited mainly from merchant seamen. Altars (A) and (B) were dredged from the River Tyne at the site of the Pons Aelius (Newcastle upon Tyne) Roman bridge. Altar (A) depicts a sea creature curled around the staff of a trident. Altar (B) has an anchor motif. Altar (C) belonged to the Second Legion. Does the "capricorn" (fish-tailed goat) indicate that the legion spent half of its time at sea and half on land? Also does the winged horse imply the ability of the Legion to strike behind enemy lines (by ship)? Pegasus was used as a badge by the British Airborne Regiments of World War 2 to indicate their ability to attack without fighting through fortified front lines.

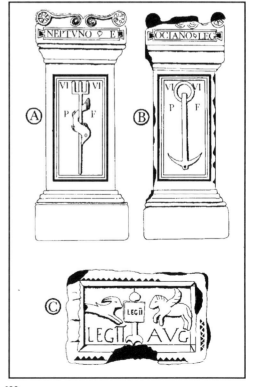

Caligula's giant ship, which was purpose-built to bring an obelisk from Egypt, was later filled with rocks and concrete and sunk to form a foundation for a breakwater at the harbour of Portus, just north of Ostia. Pliny, the Roman admiral and writer had described the tremendous size of the ship but he was not believed by later historians. An ancient ship of such dimensions seemed impossible, but excavations by O.Testaguzza have established that the dimensions of the ship were: length 300 ft, beam 70 ft and it had a cubic capacity of 7,400 tons.

While carrying the obelisk to the Tiber, the ship had carried 1,200 tons of lentils as a combined ballast (saburra) and a soft bed for the giant monument.

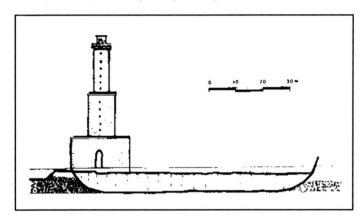

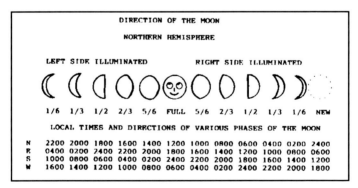

A practised navigator can establish the direction of the Moon with the Moon's phase and the local time. This is most useful during thin overcast when the stars are obscured but the Moon still visible. With thicker cloud, a quick glimpse of the Moon through a gap in the clouds will suffice. To within a few degrees, (in the Northern Hemisphere) the Full Moon is due south at midnight, the left half due east at midnight and the right half due west at midnight, and all points in between for other phases. The practised navigator can tell them all at a glance. The ancient peoples too were excellent astronomical observers.

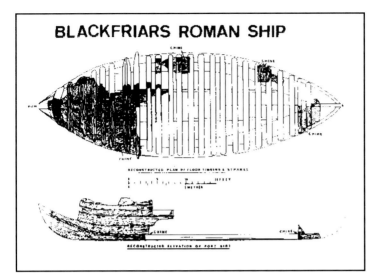

BLACKFRIARS ROMAN SHIP

The remains of the Roman ship found in the Thames at Blackfriars London. There must be remains of Roman ships and barges in all our other rivers including the Tees, Wear and Tyne. There was much more water around in Roman times: even on the tiny dried-up River Og in Wiltshire, Roman jetties have been found at a recently excavated Roman villa. A boathook is listed among the artefacts found.

Roman Ship *Isis*

"What a size the ship was! 180 ft in length, the ship's carpenter told me, the beam more than a quarter of that, and 44 ft from the deck to the lowest point in the hold,and the height of the mast, and what a yard it carried, and what a forestay held it up; and the way the stern rose up in a gradual curve ending in a gilded goose head, matched at the other end by the forward more flattened sweep of the prow with its figure of Isis, the goddess the ship was named after, on each side. Everything was incredible; the rest of the decorations, the paintings, the red topsail, even more,the anchors with their capstans and winches, the cabins aft.

The crew was like an army. They told me she carried enough grain to feed every mouth in Athens for a year, and it all depended for its safety on one little old man who turns the great steering oars with a tiller that is no more than a stick! They pointed him out to me; woolly-haired little fellow, half bald. Heron was his name, I think."

This ship was of unusual size, but the description clearly demonstrates the ability of the Romans to construct and operate very large seagoing ships. The Romans themselves tell us that 600 ships were built specially to take corn exports away from Britain. The Romans had a direct sea-service between the Tyne and the Rhine.

Various historians have estimated the cargo capacity of the *Isis*. Let us use the figures given by Lucian:

If the depth of the hold was 44 ft from deck level, a safe draught would be about 30 ft, which would give the ship a freeboard of 14 ft, that is, the distance from the deck down to the water, with the ship fully loaded. This gives the figures of: waterline length (about 20 ft less than overall length) 160 ft, beam 45 ft, draught 30 ft. Convert these figures into English feet and use the standard naval formula to find the capacity of a boat or ship, which is *length* x *beam* x *draught* x 0.6 (the 0.6 takes care of the pointed and rounded ends of the vessel):

155 x 43.6 x 29 x 0.6 = 117,589 cubic feet = vol of water displaced by loaded ship.

By Archimedes' Principle, a floating object displaces a weight of water equal to its own weight, and this volume of water weighs 7,349,325 lb = 3,281 tons. This is the total weight of the ship plus cargo. If one third of this is the weight of the empty ship, then the weight of cargo is 2,187 tons.

On Lucian's figures, on arrival at Ostia, the onward journey of the cargo up the Tiber to Rome would have needed 109 twenty- ton barges or 218 ten-ton barges. If the cargo had been moved by road, it would have taken 4,896 ox-carts, between 20,000 and 50,000 oxen, and 9,792 drivers and bridle-leaders. The wagon train would have been 83 miles long. If pack-mules had been used, 18,135 animals would have been needed. If hundred-ton barges were available, only twenty-two would have been necessary. The port handled half-a-million tons of grain per year.

If a Roman ship of only half the size of the *Isis* had arrived in Sunderland with a cargo for Chester-le-Street, then to move the cargo inland, nine-thousand pack-animals would have been needed, or two-and-a-half-thousand ox-wagons. The River Wear would not have been ignored and 100 x ten-ton barges, 50 x twenty-tonners or 10 x hundred-tonners would have performed the task with relative ease.

Only a few days ago, the *Times* newspaper, on 21st April 1999, published details of a tremendous archaeological discovery at Pisa in northern Italy. Just half-a-mile from the famous Leaning Tower, an inland Roman harbour has been found during the construction of a railway communications centre. The harbour, an inland lake at the confluence of the Rivers Arno and Auser, is thought to contain about forty intact Roman ships. Eight have been excavated so far. Andrew Wallace-Hardrill, director of the British School in Rome, said that the ships were tremendously impressive, extremely well-preserved, and in pristine condition.

Giovanna Melandri, the Minister of Culture, said that the find was of exceptional importance and that the ancient port of Pisa was emerging from the mud after two-thousand years. The ships are of intermediate size (about 500 tons) and it is thought that they plied the coast and also brought cargo up the river to Pisa after taking cargo from very large ships anchored off the mouth of the river. One ship is carrying sand as ballast and this sand has been identified as coming from the Bay of Naples. Thousands of amphorae constitute part of the cargoes of the ships. The contents are being examined.

On 16th May 99, the *Daily Telegraph* carried a full-page report on the Pisa Roman ships and harbour but quoted the number of intact Roman ships excavated as TEN. It is thought that many more Roman ships lie in the vicinity.

Similar Roman ships must have plied in and out of our north-eastern rivers. For comparison of ship sizes, the replica Tudor Golden Hinde is about 500 tons.

Here are some typical average times taken for voyages by Roman merchant ships:

Byzantium	- Alcxandria	9 days
Byzantium	- Rhodes	5 days
Gibraltar	- Carthage	7 days
Ostia	- Alexandria	10 days
(this journey by road took two months)		
Ostia	- Cadiz	7 days
Ostia	- Corinth	5 days
Ostia	- Narbonne	3 days
Ostia	- NE Spain	4 days
(this journey by road took one month)		
Straits of Messina	- Alexandria	7 days

The Roman victories at sea over the great naval power of Carthage were secured by the use of a "secret weapon." Up to that time, the main tactic used by warships was to ram each other. Then the Romans invented the *corvus* (raven). This was a gangway suspended from the Roman ship's mast in an upright position. A large spike protruded from the underside of the outer end of the gangway. The technique was to go alongside an enemy ship and drop the gangway onto the enemy ship so that the spike stuck into the victim's deck. Dozens of Roman marines then boarded the enemy ship and cut the crew to pieces. The Romans had introduced land warfare to the high seas.

Roman marines served both at sea and on land. The Second and Sixth Legions, sometimes used in naval actions, were also no newcomers to the sea as they were recruited from merchant seamen. Insignia used by these legions were: anchors, capricorns (goats with fish-tails) and "Pegasus" (the winged horse which indicates the ability to strike behind enemy lines).

Roman sources tell us about huge ships. One built by Ptolemy was said to have been 420 feet long with a tonnage of 7182. Another was 300 feet, tonnage 3197. According to Pliny (xvi.40 & 76), the ship which brought from Egypt the great obelisk that stood in the Circus of the Vatican in the time of Caligula, in addition to the obelisk itself, had 120,000 *modii* of lentils (about 1,138 tons) as ballast (*saburra*). This probably also served as a bed for the giant stone in a similar manner to those horrible modern plastic packaging chips which blow all over the garden when a large postal parcel is opened.

The giant ship was later filled with rocks and concrete and purposely sunk to form part of the 2,500 feet-long southern breakwater of the harbour of Portus, just north of Ostia. A lighthouse was built on top of the sunken ship. Modern historians have pooh-poohed Pliny's account but the silted-up harbour (now inland) was excavated by Italian archaeologist, O. Testaguzza in 1963. The ship had six decks and was 600 feet long and its cubic capacity has been calculated at an amazing 7,400 tons, ("Port of Rome" in *Archaeology* Vol 17, No. 3 Sept 1964). Pliny was telling the truth when he said: "it took four men linking arms to encircle the ship's mainmast."

Roman trade with India and China and an ancient Suez Canal

We now know that the Romans traded with India and China but how did they get through the Suez Isthmus?

Ferdinand de Lesseps finished his 85 mile-long sea-level ditch between the Mediterranean and Red Sea in 1869. The Khedive of Egypt commissioned the composer, Verdi, to write the opera, *"Aida"* for the occasion.

The French lost the controlling interest in the canal company when the bankrupt Khedive sold his shares. British Prime Minister, Disraeli, snapped them up.

I had been amazed to learn from my geography master at school that: thousands of years before de Lesseps cut his canal, ships sailed between the two seas. This ancient route was first up the River Nile and then along a canal between the Nile and the Red Sea. The canal is reputed to have been built by Pharaoh Sesostris of the Twelfth Dynasty. It fell into disuse but was repaired by various later rulers; by Necho in 600 BC, Darius in 521 BC, Ptolemy Philadelphus in the third century BC, and finally by the Roman Emperor Trajan in AD 98. From then it remained navigable until the third century AD. The canal length was over sixty miles and it was evidently large enough to take the biggest sea-going vessels of the period.

De Lesseps' canal had no problems with level changes as the Mediterranean and the Red Seas are the same height although the usual prophets of doom had argued otherwise. There was however, a difference of level between the River Nile and the Red Sea. Two ancient writers, Strabo and Diodorus both refer to a device which overcame this problem. Strabo says:

"The Ptolemaic kings cut their canal and made it so that it could be closed so that, when desired, they could sail into the sea without difficulty and also sail back."

Diodorus Siculus also refers to the device in the canal:

"At a later time, the Second Ptolemy completed it, and in the most suitable spot, constructed an ingenious kind of lock. This he opened whenever he wished to pass through, and quickly closed again, a contrivance whose usage proved to be highly successful."

This device must have been a pound-lock and I see no reason for surprise as the Romans had a guild of dry-dock constructors and a dry-dock is a very close relative of the pound-lock. If a dry-dock is situated in a river bend and has gates at both ends, it also becomes a pound-lock. Due to the small tides in the Mediterranean, Roman ships were often built in dry-docks and in the Mediterranean, they used these devices for repairs to the underwater parts of a ship.

Strabo tells us of another canal, this one between the Nile and Lake Moaris. Strabo refers to the difference in levels between the river and the lake and says:

"While these conditions are the work of nature, yet locks have been placed at both mouths of the canal, by which the engineers regulate both the inflow and outflow of water."

Clearly, the ancient engineers could accommodate changes of levels of canal and river waters and it is time our historians changed their ideas about who invented the pound-lock. Some say it was the Dutch in 1373 at Vreeswijk; others say it was the Chinese at Huai-yin in AD 983. It seems that both schools of thought are wrong.

From May to September, in the Gulf of Aden and the Arabian Sea, the monsoon blows from the south-west, and a sailing ship can proceed direct from the Red Sea to India without tacking, keeping clear of the coast and its pirates. Between November and March, the wind shifts 180 degrees, blowing from the north-east thus enabling a sailing ship to make the return journey quite easily.

Before the ancient Greeks obtained this information, Arab ships had carried cargoes in the Red Sea, and Indian ships the rest of the way to India.

In 120 BC, Eudoxus, a native of Cyzicus, was working as a ship's captain for Ptolemy VIII. Eudoxus was in Alexandria when a half-drowned Indian sailor was brought to the court. The sailor was nursed back to health and given lessons in Greek. He was taken home by Eudoxus who learned the secrets of the monsoons. This information subsequently became available to the Romans when they took over Egypt and its merchant marine.

The Moon as a Navaid

If one knows the local time, (by sandglass or other device) the Moon becomes a very useful direction-indicator. Julius Caesar refers to Celtic sailors' skills using the Moon thus. The magnetic compass is useful for navigation, but not essential; the sky is full of compasses. Even when no celestial navigation is available, a course can be held for several hours merely by reference to the directions of the wind, seas or swell.

Orographic uplifted clouds and thermal-generated *cumuli* mark the presence of coastlines and islands well beyond visible horizons.

As will be seen shortly, new information is constantly being revealed about ancient sea trade.

New technology rediscovers ancient major Roman harbour

Just as the text of this book is being completed, news of an astonishing rediscovery by modern technology, of an ancient Roman port in Italy, has been given headlines in the International Section of *The Guardian* newspaper on Tuesday November 30th 1999.

The headline is:

FORGOTTEN SEAPORT FED ROMAN EMPIRE, by Rory Carroll in Rome

A precis of the article follows: " *Beneath Fiumicino Airport lies a gargantuan seaport that saved imperial Rome from starvation and enabled it to build a mighty empire, so British archaeologists revealed yesterday*

Revolutionary survey techniques have stunned historians by detecting canals, jetties, warehouses, arches, bridges and roads, through which supplies were transported nonstop to a huge expanding population.

The scale of the intensity of the logistics activity at Portus, twelve miles from Rome has solved the mystery of how the Roman emperors managed to feed a city with more than a million inhabitants.

Ships from Egypt, Turkey, Greece, the whole Mediterranean, and Britain too, unloaded supplies that were transferred to barges which plied a 130 feet-wide canal which led into the River Tiber. Mules hauled a continuous procession of barges to Rome with hourly deliveries of corn, wheat and lead without which, the metropolis would have collapsed centuries earlier, historians reported.

A team from the University of Southampton, the British School at Rome, and Italy's Soprintendenza Archeologica di Ostia has mapped 67 acres (28 hectares) beneath the airfield surface at Rome's Fiumicino, 'Leonardo da Vinci' Airport.

The presence of the harbour has been known since the 16th century but few major excavations have taken place. With the information supplied by modern ground-probing electronic equipment, archaeologists said that it would take decades to put together a picture of the huge complex below the surface of the airport."

Experts now admit that to have transferred supplies to Rome by ox-wagon from Naples' port of Puteoli 120 miles to the south was a slow, expensive and near impossible task. Therefore in AD50, Emperor Claudius ordered a giant port to be built at the mouth of the River Tiber. Claudius' successor, Trajan, built a smaller inner harbour of hexagonal shape, two-thousand feet wide, inside the perimeter of the larger port. "Trajan's port was crammed with cranes, jetties, warehouses and shipyards," said Andrew Wallace-Hadrill, director of the British School. He continued: "Rome was the most populated city in antiquity. What we see at Portus is an extraordinary feat: a permanent procession of barges seven days a week."

The canal linking Trajan's harbour to the Tiber was lined with buildings into which the ships discharged marble, wine and all manner of cargoes.

The modern equipment which is being operated in the exploration is a geophysics technique which uses radar-type impulses on X-Ray frequencies, to penetrate the soil. Computers compare echoes from solid structures, soil, and wet areas. At this stage, excavations are not necessary and archaeological scientists can work at an extremely fast rate.

"The results are revolutionising our understanding of Rome's complex trading structures," said Simon Keay, professor of archaeology at the University of Southampton.

Yet it is not long ago, that most British archaeologists called the Romans "landlubbers" and denied their ability to operate a huge merchant marine and an inland barge-logistics network. They still believed that the whole of the Roman Empire had been supplied by the slow, expensive one-mile-per-hour ox-wagons. Simple mathematics clearly demonstrate the impossibility of such a system. The ox-wagons plied just around the town and jetties, and the mules hauled the huge barges along the canals and up the rivers.

When I wrote my book *"The Piercebridge Formula"* in 1983, which expressed the opinion that 95% of Roman logistics was carried out on water, I was howled down by many members of the British archaeological establishment. Now the old "ox-wagon brigade" of UK has been completely defeated. Fortunately, some foreign archaeologists and historians were not as blinkered as our own, and my 1983 book was awarded in Switzerland in 1984, a Rolex International Award for Exploration.

It will be shown shortly that the information provided by the team now exploring Portus is not new, and the whole layout of the Roman port was known one hundred years ago as described in H. Stuart Jones' book, *"Companion to Roman History."* What is new is that the modern archaeologists have realised that all the onward transportation of cargoes from Portus/Ostia to Rome was carried out by river barge and not by ox-wagons. I suggest that the change of heart came not from radar read-outs but from the logistical mathematics described in *" The Piercebridge Formula"* (PSL 1983) and *"On the Trail of the Legions"* (Anglia 1995). The geophysics survey has merely given our experts an excuse to put their history of Roman logistics in order.

The distance by the River Tiber from Portus to Rome was about the same as the distance up the River Wear from Sunderland to Chester-le-Street. The huge Roman dam at Hylton would have increased the depth of the Wear and compensated for the fact that our River Wear is smaller than the Tiber. In the much later coal industry era, keelboats plying from Sunderland to Chester-le-Street could make it only fortnightly on high Spring tides due to shallows in the River Wear such as the Biddick ford which utilised a rocky shelf. The great Roman dam at Hylton ponded-back enough water to form a state equal to permanent Spring tide all the way to Concangis, providing ample depth of water over the top of all shallows and other obstructions. Below the Roman dam, the incoming high tides allowed Roman merchant ships to cross the river mouth shallows and gain the safety of the the deep pool of Hylton just below the Roman dam.

In the 18th and 19th centuries, a shipbuilding slipway on the south side of the River Wear would launch new ships into the Hylton Pool. With regard to river navigation, what the Romans did in one part of their Empire, they did in all parts, as did the Royal Engineers, the Royal Navy and the Merchant Marine of the later British Empire. The recent rediscovery of the Roman harbour at Portus and the realisation that the whole of the Roman Empire relied on water transport should not have come as such a shock to the establishment, because, as mentioned earlier, details of most of the great Roman Italian harbours have been well recorded in the past:

The earliest port of Rome, outside the Porta Trigemina, was constructed in 199BC and in 174BC, it was paved and enclosed. Rome also possessed its *Navalia,* naval arsenal and docks. These were hard by the Forum Boarium.

Warships with their light draft could navigate the Tiber up to Rome but deep draft loaded merchant vessels were forced to discharge cargoes into lighters at the river mouth under adverse conditions.

The Naples port of Puetoli was a long way from Rome and it was obvious that the building of a port at the mouth of the Tiber to serve Rome was a high priority task. The Romans had the technology to do this. Let us look again at Naples. In addition to the civil port of Puetoli, there were bases for warships. In 37BC, Agrippa constructed the "Portus Iulius" as a base for the Western Mediterranean Fleet. Lake Avernus, an extinct crater of about one kilometre in diameter, was connected by a canal with the Lucrine Lake, a shallow lagoon separated from the sea by a sand-dune, along which ran a causeway known as the *"Via Herculanea."* Agrippa constructed entrances to the lake at both ends of this causeway as well as a mole in front of the eastermost channel. Because of the shallow depth of the Lucrine Lake, the naval base was superseded by the more spacious harbour at the western extremety of the Gulf of Pozzuoli

Under the Imperial regime, more than one effort was made to provide Rome with an adequate harbour at the mouth of the Tiber. The remains of Ostia show that the town enjoyed great prosperity in the Imperial period, and the warehouses on the banks of the Tiber prove that this prosperity was due to commerce and not to the local market-gardening industry. Howeveÿÿr, the harbour was never safe, because siltation prevented large vessels from entering and these huge ships had to anchor offshore and to discharge cargoes into lighters, a dangerous technique in bad weather

Claudius, undeterred by the objections and difficulties raised by his engineers, caused an entirely fresh port to be constructed. A basin was dug about two miles to the north of Ostia, and connected with the Tiber by a new cut.

The outlines of the harbour were described by H Stuart Jones, MA, of Trinity College Oxford, in 1912:

"It was protected from the sea by two jetties which curved inwards, and were separated by entrances 120 yards wide from an artificial island. To form this island, the ship which had conveyed the obelisk from Alexandria to Rome and then set-up by Caligula in his Circus (now in the Piazza of St Peter's), was filled with concrete and sunk in the mouth of the harbour. Masses of further concrete were than heaped upon it. A lighthouse, after the model of the Pharos of Alexandria was built upon the island. The works were begun in the second year of Claudius' reign, and are mentioned in an inscription of the year AD46, but Nero seems to have either completed the harbour, or claimed credit for it, as we find it represented on his coins.

In stormy weather, although the corn-fleet was inside the large harbour, ships were still wrecked, and to avert this danger, Trajan added an inner basin, hexagonal in shape, around which grew up the city of Portus, the remains of which have yielded statues and other works of art, but which still await scientific excavation. Temples, baths and a theatre have been discovered, and on the spit which separated the Harbour of Trajan from the outer basin dug by Claudius, was a richly decorated palace, possibly an Imperial residence. Trajan's attention was not confined to the mouth of the Tiber. Some miles to the north, he created the port of Centumcellae in an open bay upon the shores of which stood an Imperial villa. The 'hundred docks' designed for warships, were protected in the same manner as the harbour of Claudius, by two convergent moles and an artificial island, the construction of which was similar to that of the harbour of Claudius at the mouth of the Tiber.

On the Adriatic coast, Trajan also built the port of Ancona which is represented on his Column. We see in the background the vaulted docks in which the Imperial galleys were harboured, and in the foreground, the jetty with its triumphal arch, which still stands, although the statues which surmounted it have long since been destroyed."

Early Chinese compass. The Chinese had magnetic compasses as far back as the Third Dynasty (Second Millennium BC) As the Romans traded with China, it is strange that our archaeological establishment denies the possibility that the Romans possessed similar instruments. Chinese magnetic compasses (Tchi-nan) were south-seeking (see pages 63 & 64)

A modern sun-compass. These instruments are extremely useful for desert navigation as there are no magnetic elements to be influenced and distorted by the metal body and fittings of a vehicle. They were used extensively by the British "Long Range Desert Group" in North Africa in World War 2.

Headlines in Nov 99 national and international newspapers tell us about the rediscovery using electronic methods, of the Great Roman harbour of Portus, just north of Ostia, and now under Rome's modern Fiumicino airport. Details of this massive harbour complex should not have come as a surprise because detailed plans were drawn a hundred years ago from visible remains and random excavations. This illustration appeared in H Stuart Jones' book "Companion to Roman History," written in Oxford in 1912. The most important information the international newspapers have published recently is that at long last, our historians and archaeologists have realised that the Roman Empire relied on sea and river transport and not on thousands of impractial lumbering ox-wagons.

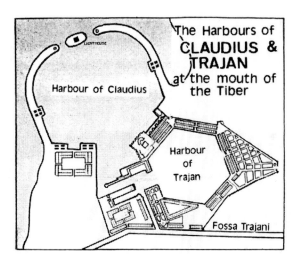

This is a sketch by an unknown artist of what the great Roman harbour of Portus may have looked like.

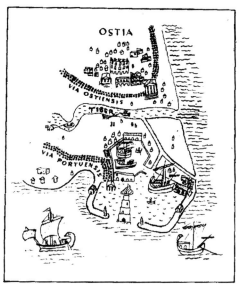

It is now time to leave the sea, ships and barges, and take a closer look at those military roads in north-eastern England.

Chapter 8
The Lost Roman Roads of County Durham

The Lost Roman Road by Bernard Berry

Some luck is needed
You may walk that way a hundred times
And then
In a certain light
And at the right season Say, when the smallest shoots
Best show the shaping of the soil
Like some close-fitting coat
Then you may see the line
Across that lonely field
And looking where their road once went
You see the Roman might
Just like a blaze of distant light
And brighter still for all the dark between

County Durham's Lost Roman Roads

The chapters on the lost Roman roads of County Durham and Northumberland are included in this work to give Chester-le-Street historians a better understanding of the Roman north-east.

In addition to that, it is hoped that readers will realise that a vast amount of evidence remains to be found and that one must not sit back thinking that the "experts" know all that needs to be known. There is room for the work of hundreds of archaeologists, amateur and professional, in our northern counties.

County Durham was certainly not a Roman backwater and many of the "lost Roman roads" which are now coming to light were actually mentioned by eighteenth and nineteenth century antiquarians such as Cade, Gale, Gordon, Horsley, Hunter, Longstaffe, Stukeley Warburton, Whellan, and others.

Most historians today rely on surviving information from a Roman road book called the *Itinerarium Provinciarum Antonini Augusti* known to most of us as the *"Antonine Itinerary."* Routes are given throughout the Roman Empire with distances between Roman stations. The *Itinerary* mentions only one road through the County Durham area. No map survives and only distances are given between Cataractonium - Vinovia (XXII Roman miles); Vinovia - Vindomora(XVIIII Roman miles) and Vindomora - Corstopitum (VIII Roman miles). [Catterick - Binchester? - Ebchester - Corbridge]. This road has been known from Saxon times as "Dere Street," probably Deira (South Northumbria) Street, but its Roman name is not known. Nor are the Latin names known for any other Roman roads in Britain. This lack of information has led some historians to declare that County Durham must have been a sparsely populated "desert" during the Roman period. Clearly that is nonsense. Neither Cade's Roman road nor a Roman fort at Chester-le-Street are mentioned in any surviving Roman material. In Northumberland, there is not the slightest mention of the Roman major road, "The Devil's Causeway" which runs from Corbridge to Scotland. This unmentioned Roman road has branches, discovered from the air, running to all parts of Northumberland. Excavating them will take my society several years, and more suspected Roman roads are constantly being found.

This chapter with its maps shows that the North of England had a huge network of unknown and unmentioned Roman roads, and we still have nowhere near the full picture.

Cade's Road

The north-south Roman road (Cade's Road) which passes through Chester-le-Street on its way from Newcastle to Brough-on-Humber (Petuaria) has already been mentioned previously but a more comprehensive description follows:

We know that there was a Hadrian's Wall fort called "Pons Aelius" at Newcastle upon Tyne and that the Roman bridge across the Tyne was on the site of the modern Swing Bridge. The Roman bridge lasted over a thousand years and pieces of it were recovered when the Swing Bridge was built.

During recent demolition work behind Bottle Bank on the south bank of the Tyne in Gateshead in line with the Swing Bridge, a hitherto unknown Roman fortification has been found.

The Roman road, called Cade's Road after the antiquarian, Dr. Cade, who first noticed it, ran from the south end of the Roman Tyne bridge up to Wrekenton where, a few years ago, we spotted, from the air, the shape of an unknown suspected Roman fort in the Ravensworth Golf Course. Cade's road altered course here and its new arrow-straight southerly heading took it through Birtley and Barley Mow to "Concangis" (unconfirmed Roman name for Chester-le-Street). At Wrekenton another straight road arrived from the South Shields (Arbeia) direction. Old antiquarians from the 18th and 19th centuries said that this road crossed Cade's road at Wrekenton and continued to Kibblesworth, Stanley and points further west. We will look at the evidence for this in due course. We do not have any direct evidence for the Roman name "Concangis" but we do know that a unit of the "Numerus Concangios" was stationed at the Chester-le-Street fort, so the name is not certain, but it is a strong possibility. There are two forts on the same site, one on top of the other; the first one probably built about the time of the Roman Governor Agricola cAD 80, and the second c122, about the time of the building of Hadrian's Wall.

Cade's road crossed the Cong Burn (Roman Con *Fluvius)* at the bridge end of Chester-le-Street and is under the Front Street southwards up past the Lambton Arms and beyond. The Ordnance Survey maps mark the Roman road swinging slightly to the west at the foot of

NZ 269 591. Suspected Roman fort in the Ravensworth (Wrekenton) Golf Course at the junction of Cade's Roman road and the Wrekendyke Roman road. Only the eastern end of the fort platform has survived the urban sprawl. This view is to the west over Low Fell. When the wagonway (top left to bottom centre), now dismantled, was constructed, a hoard of gold and silver coins was found.

Clifford Terrace and following the modern A167(T) to Plawsworth and Pity Me. Recent excavations have shown that the Ordnance Survey map is incorrect: the Roman road passed slightly to the west of Concangis fort, the centre and headquarters of which is under our parish church.

Opposite the foot of Clifford Terrace at the site of the old Red Rose Hall (NZ 275 505), the Roman road continued straight ahead on the same alignment as through Birtley and Barley Mow, and passed just to the west of the Red Rose School, underneath Coronation Street, Jolliffe Street and Dean Villas. It passed under the present bypass [A167(T)] about a hundred yards south of the former Red Rose Garage, at present a derelict Shell site. The Roman road maintained its arrow-straight southerly course across the fields to the east of the [A167(T)] bypass. It intercepted the Southburn Dene at map ref NZ 275 497 where the paved Roman surface went down a hollow-way with a gradient of one-in-three. The excavated cobbled pavement of the road was only eight feet wide. Troops on the march would have had to reduce to double or even single file, and the road (a supposed major Roman highway) would have been impossible for wagons of any kind although pack-animals may have been able to manage the gradient.

Remains of a Roman ford were found in the South Burn. From the ford, the Roman road made a very steep zig-zag up the southern bankside to the crest of Holm Hill. Here again, the Roman surface was excavated (at NZ 275 495), and Roman samian pottery was recovered. On Holm Hill, the Roman road resumed its heading of due south and a ruler placed on the map through Birtley, Barley Mow, and central Chester-le-Street will show that the Roman road surveyors have continued the same straight line south of the town.

N.A.G.
EXCAVATION
IN
PROGRESS

RS99

↑
SOUTH

NZ 275 497
CADE'S ROAD
SOUTHBURN DENE
CHESTER-LE-STREET.

Cade's Roman road excavated in Southburn Dene, one mile south of Chester-le-Street. The Roman road south of Chester-le-Street runs in a perfectly straight line to Kepier, Durham, where a Roman site is suspected. It was previously thought that the Roman road lay under the modern A167(T) through Chester Moor and Pity Me. The genuine Roman road runs down a very steep incline, has a cobbled surface set on heavy foundation stones and is only eight feet wide. A subsidiary unpaved track, possibly for pack animals leaves the paved road at the top of the hill and takes an easy zig-zag gradient.

On the south side of the South Burn, the paved Roman road resorted to a zig-zag climb of the steep Holm Hill.

The unpaved track possibly for pack-animals, takes an easy gradient down to the South Burn.

Many Roman roads had unpaved outer tracks for unshod animals. The centre hard surface was for marching troops. Perhaps the Southburn Dene dirt road is a variation of the three-lane Roman road pattern.

To the south of Southburn Dene, Cade's Roman road runs across Holm Hill due south to an isolated tree at four-o-clock to a trapezium-shaped wood. Many years ago, a hedge was grubbed out from the Roman road. Excavation showed the surface of the Roman road to be rammed gravel. First century samian pottery was taken from the excavation.

The hamlet of Chester Moor is at the top of the photograph; the main railway line to Durham crosses the A167(T) at top right and the River Wear flows from left to right towards Chester-le-Street. The Roman road is lined-up precisely on Kepier to the south (left) and Chester-le-Street church spire to the north (right). The Roman road is also exactly on the same alignment as the section through Barley Mow, Birtley and Wrekenton.

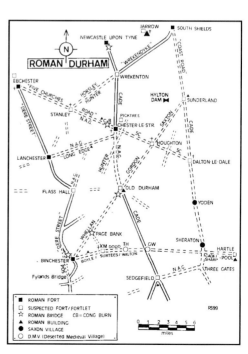

Roman Durham. A huge network of Roman roads is emerging and we do not have the complete picture yet. Much more work is needed.

NAG = Northern Archaeology Group.
CB = Cong Burn.
5C = Five Churches Roman road.
PDS = Proto Dere Street.
KM = Kirk Merrington Church.
TH = Thrislington DMV.
GW = Garmondsway DMV.

A suspected Romano-British settlement was found from the air, many years ago, by Professor Dennis Harding and myself, to the west of Harbour House at map ref NZ 278 480. Cade's Roman road passes right by this site. The Iron Age village had no defensive ditches or ramparts, suggesting that *Pax Romana* was in force. Cade's Road and another Roman road, "Hunter's Road," which will be mentioned shortly, cross near this location although the actual intersection has not yet been located.

The projected line of Cade's road runs straight to the west bank of the River Wear opposite the medieval hospital at Kepier, Durham (NZ 282 433). There is obviously some kind of Roman site under Kepier Farm. Old antiquarians reported the remains of a Roman bridge at Kepier, but a medieval watermill on the site has confused the issue.

Cade mentioned the Roman bridge at Kepier as follows:

"A gentleman with whom I am acquainted has carefully surveyed the old road from this place (Old Durham) by Kepyre Hospital (the medieval hospital) and he assures me that, in the dry season, the piers of a Roman bridge are obvious in the bed of the river, seemingly of Roman construction."

The word *"kep"* is Saxon for "catch" so the Saxons probably used the wreckage of some Roman structure to build a ramshackle fish-trap.

Cade's road continued to Old Durham and Shincliffe. Old Durham Farm looks as if it is standing on a typical Roman fort platform, Roman coins have been found there (Cade, *Archaeologia vii,* 1785). He gives a further mention of Old Durham.

"This station I imagine, was formerly thought of great consequence, but at length suffered the fate of many others in northern parts, when William the Conqueror made that horrible devastation between York and this place, and erected his castrum in the new city; the fortifications were then partly levelled, but enough is left to point out its former magnitude and importance; it being in my opinion much larger than Dr Stukeley has described; and the rivulet Pidding had with great labour and ingenuity, been diverted from its original channel, where it ran into the Wear, near Shinkley Bridge, to answer the purpose of the Fosse along the southern and western sides of it".

To the south of Old Durham, a bath-house was excavated in 1944. This was a rescue operation when gravel quarrying hit Roman walls. The findings were that the bath-house was of the domestic type and a villa was suggested but the great earthwork under Old Durham Farm was not investigated. Surtees, also in Archaeologia vii, 1785, mentions another Roman bridge apart from the one at Kepier, this time a timber one at Old Durham.

"During the late dry summer, the wooden piers of a bridge over the Wear, leading exactly to the station at Old Durham, were not only visible, but those very piers, left high and dry, were taken up, consisting of long trunks of trees, squared and bored, and mortized together so as to form a strong foundation on each side of the river. At the same time, from the same side of the river, piers of solid masonry were discovered on

Cade's Roman road crossed the River Tees via Pontey's Bridge (Pont Tisa) at Middleton-One-Row. It was thought that the bridge had been completely lost, but NAG divers found the remains of the southern abutment (marked here with roadworks tape) and one pier- base further out in the stream.

the north side of the Wear below Kepyer Hospital, confirming, it would seem, the old tradition, that a great road passed this way across the Race-ground, and so by Kepyer northwards...."

Surtees also reported in the same summer, there were:

"vestiges of a mill-dam across the Wear, formed by stakes and large stones, a little below Old Durham."

Thus there was a dam *and* a bridge at Old Durham. The inference is that there was a considerable Roman settlement at Durham.

At Shincliffe, Cade's road is prominent under the public footpath at the west end of a wood (NZ 292 410) due north of the church. A Roman signal station is suspected on the hilltop on the same site as the former "Spion Kop Farm," now just a clump of trees (NZ 296 408). Another Roman road coming in from the north-east appears to join Cade's Road in this vicinity.

South of Shincliffe, Cade's Road passes through Bowburn and Coxhoe en-route to the River Tees at Middleton-One-Row where our archaeological divers found the long-lost remains of the Roman "Pontey's Bridge" (Pont Tisa, NZ 347 121). Some two miles south of Pont Tisa, there is a little known Roman fortlet at NZ 368 096, just north of Castle Hill Farm. Half of the Roman structure has fallen down the cliff into the river.

The final destination of Cade's road was the Roman fort at Brough on Humber which is now known by excavation to have been "Petuaria" although some Ordnance Survey maps still mark it incorrectly as "Praetorio."

Shincliffe to Ferryhill

I thought that Cade's Road seemed to divide at Shincliffe and it looked as if a footpath which leaves the bend of the A177 in Shincliffe at NZ 293 401 and heads south was a Roman road. This footpath joins the bend of a minor road which has a crossroads with South Grange Farm to the east and High Butterby to the west. The road straight ahead, "Strawberry Lane," is thought to be Roman and heads for Tursdale House, Hett Moor and joins the Kirk Merrington to Hartlepool Roman road at Ferryhill. It may have continued south of Ferryhill via Little Chilton and Great Chilton. That is as far as I got with my survey but I was unaware that Robin Walton of Coxhoe was working up the other way, having found that Cade's Road forked near Great Stainton on its way north. Robin's search was more comprehensive than mine and is printed later in this chapter under the sub-title, "Robin Walton's Cade's Road West Branch".

Ordnance Survey maps: mistakes and omissions

How about our Ordnance Survey maps showing incorrect information? My enquiries to OS produced the explanation: "We are not archaeologists; we only publish the information we are given".

The Ordnance Survey people do attempt to get things right but they have a long way to go. When I wrote my last book on archaeology, *"On the Trail of the Legions,"* OS gave my publisher £2,000 to help towards the cost of air surveys etc. Now the Heritage Lottery Fund has given me £8,000 for further research and the printing of this book. These researches show that Chester-le-Street was at the junction of six, possibly more, Roman roads, arriving from Wrekenton, Jarrow, Sunderland, Dalton-le-Dale, Kepier, Binchester, Lanchester and Ebchester. These will be discussed in due course as we go along.

The Five Churches Roman Road, Ebchester to Dalton-le-Dale

A totally unknown Roman road has been found between Ebchester Roman fort and Dalton-le-Dale, and is a perfectly straight line which transits five existing churches, Ebchester, Stanley (another St Andrew's), Chester-le-Street, Houghton-le-Spring and Dalton-le-Dale (St Andrew's). Modern churches are usually on medieval church sites which in turn were often on Saxon church locations. As has also been mentioned previously, these Saxon churches are invariably on Roman sites. Pope Gregory's instructions to one of his missionaries in Britain, Abott Mellitus, was to tell the Saxons to build their churches on the pagan sites which were mostly ex-Roman forts, and which had contained Christian churches for the last hundred years or so of Roman rule. These shrines had been re-paganised by the incoming Saxon invaders in the fifth century.

Pope Gregory's Roman shaven-headed invaders who trudged along grass-covered military roads built by their great-great grandfathers, carried not swords, but Christian messages to the pagan Saxons.

Five Churches Road in the Chester-le-Street area

To the west of Chester-le-Street, just to the south of the Pelton Fell road and to the south

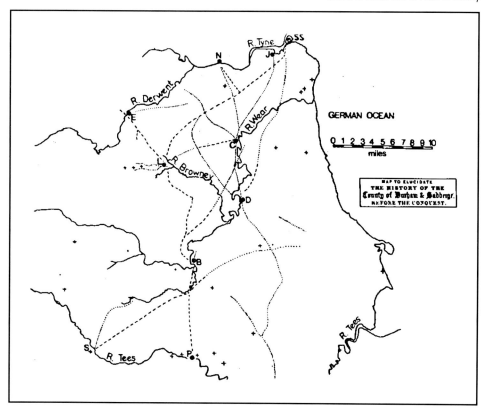

A simplified version of Longstaffe's "Map to Elucidate the History of the County of Durham & Sadberge Before the Conquest." A Roman road is shown from Chester-le-Street to Jarrow. This may be "Rycknild Street" mentioned by Warburton.

E   =   *Ebchester Roman fort (Vindomora).*

N   =   *Newcastle upon Tyne Roman fort (Pons Aelius).*

J   =   *Jarrow, suspected Roman site under Saxon monastery.*

SS   =   *South Shields Roman fort and harbour. Note that South Shields stands on an island.*

L   =   *Lanchester Roman fort (Longovicium).*

C   =   *Chester-le-Street Roman fort (Concangis?)*

D   =   *Durham: Roman site suspected under cathedral, and there is a known Roman site at Old Durham.*

B   =   *Binchester Roman fort. Due to recently discovered Roman road "Proto Dere Street," the name "Vinovia" has had doubt cast upon it .*

S   =   *Startforth, suspected Roman site at Barnard Castle.*

P   =   *Piercebridge, Roman fort on Dere Street.*

of a garage, a small Roman bridge abutment was located in the north bank of the Cong Burn (NZ 260 517) exactly on the predicted line of "The Five Churches Road." A further search exposed the southern abutment in the south bank of the stream. Excavations revealed details of the bridge, and nine Roman coins were recovered during the work. The surface of the road which crossed the bridge contained much iron slag and it is known that the Romans mined iron ore further up the valley. A Roman building which resembled a barrack-block was found in the paddock just to the north of the small Roman bridge and south of the garage.

To the east of Chester-le-Street, this Roman road probably crossed the River Wear just upstream from the Lumley fish-trap (now known to have had an origin as a Roman weir) by a bridge approximately on the site of the old "Penny Bridge." Lumley Castle is on the line of the "Five Churches Roman Road", and also very close to another Roman road: Dr Hunter's Road which came up from the south-south-west and will be mentioned next.

Dr Hunter's Road

In addition to Cade's Roman road which ran to Chester-le-Street from Durham via Kepier, another Roman road, according to Dr Hunter, came from the Crossgates Moor area of Durham, and bypassed Chester-le-Street to the east, on a heading for South Shields. This road ran past Hag House, across Harbrass (Harbour House) Moor and behind Lumley Castle. It has been observed from the air across Chester-le-Street Golf Course and the line just misses Lumley Castle to the east. Reused Roman stones have been found in the bottom course of the north wall of the north-east tower of Lumley Castle. The site of Lumley Castle would have been ideal for a Roman signal station.

Roman signalling in and out of Concangis and other valley forts

Concangis, due to its valley location was out of sight of a suspected Roman signal station on Sacriston Heugh (NZ 234 485). However, a repeater station on the knoll where Lumley Castle would be built later, would fill the gap. Lumley Castle is in clear view of Sacriston Heugh and Concangis. Repeater stations on knolls in sight of both valley forts and high-ground signal towers are common. Corbridge is one example and Greta Bridge another. Aerial surveys have located the missing links in both places. Greta Bridge's repeater is to the south east at NZ 088 127 and Corbridge has two satellites, one to the north at NY 974 667 (a house called Mount Pleasant which sits on a prominent mound) and to the south-east at NY 983 630 in the paddock of a bungalow with a red roof. Both suspected satellite signal stations are in full view of the Roman Wall complex. Corbridge fort and town are not. There are many more, too numerous to be mentioned here. Look for a Roman fort in a valley and then search nearby high points for repeater signal stations.

On the hill to the south-west of Risingham (Habitancum) near West Woodburn, not only is there a Roman aqueduct on the hill at NY 887 852, (many aqueduct channel-stones are built into a dry-stone quarry wall behind a shepherd's hut), but a prehistoric burial mound looks as if it has been reused as a Roman repeater signal station, (NY 887 851).

Rycknild (Ricknild) Street

To the north-east of Chester-le-Street, the historian Warburton marked the line of a Roman

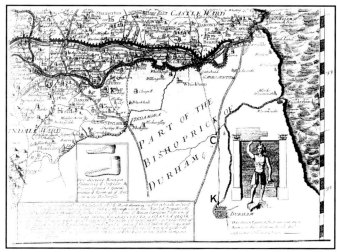

Warburton's map shows Cade's Road from Kepier (K), Durham, to Chester-le-Street (C), Gateshead, Newcastle upon Tyne and beyond. Another Roman road approaches Chester-le-Street from the south-west and passes between our Roman fort and the River Wear. It then runs to Jarrow via Hedworth. Dere Street is marked through Ebchester to Corbridge and splits at Portgate on the Wall with the Devil's Causeway heading north-east. Another Roman road (Forster's Road) leaves Corbridge and passes just south of Hexham then turns south-west. Hexham is given the Roman name of "Axleodunum." At the south-west corner of the map, a hitherto unknown Roman road passes by Shorngate Cross near Allenheads.

Part of Longstaffe's Map which shows Gordon's Roman road from Durham to South Shields; Warburton's Rycknild Street from Chester-le-Street to Jarrow; the Wrekendyke extending westwards to Kibblesworth and beyond, and a Roman road from Chester-le-Street (here marked as "Epeiakon") to Lanchester. Note that Jarrow is marked as

"Portus Egfridi Regis" (King Egfrid's Port) and that Boldon is marked as "the Bilton to which Leland extends Egfrid's Port." Clearly the now tiny River Don was navigable in ancient times; Boldon church contains reused Roman stones.

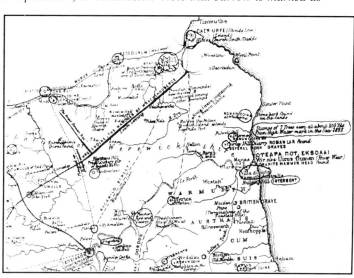

road "Rycknild Street" passing near Picktree and then heading north-north-east. We are still searching for evidence of this road. It sounds as if it went through Rickleton, and "Green Lane" (NZ 277 526) between Junction 63 of the A1(M) at Picktree, and Pelaw House, is a possibility. Warburton's map shows the road passing very close to the River Wear at Picktree and then heading for Jarrow. There is a suspected Roman site at Picktree.

Hag Bank road

About six hundred yards to the north-west of Lumley Castle is the relatively modern "Hag Bridge"over Lumley Park Burn. The footpath continues from the bridge north-east up the hill and as it passes through a gate at the top edge of the wood (NZ 285 515), it can be seen to be a Roman road. Large boulders which have been used as kerbs peep out of the ground here and there and the cobbled surface which also appears to be Roman is in good condition. Its position and alignment fit neither Hunter's Road, nor Warburton's Rycknild Street. It seems to have originated beside Boat Cottage where the "Five Churches Road" is thought to have crossed the River Wear at NZ 283 512. "Hag Bank road" heads for the top of Newbridge Bank and may have joined a Sunderland to Chester-le-Street Roman road at this point, or crossed it on a heading for South Shields, crossing the River Wear in the vicinity of the Lamb Bridge in the grounds of Lambton Castle. From our aircraft, we can see stonework in the river a couple of hundred yards downstream from the Lamb Bridge, but this seems to be the remains of an old weir, date unknown. Permission has not been obtained to enter this area for a ground search.

Lumley Way

We are fairly sure that some kind of Roman site existed underneath the later Finchale Priory. Some old maps mark a possible Roman road heading from the top of the Finchale Priory cliff steps towards Lumley. Do not dismiss a formidable staircase as part of a Roman road - at several points in their Empire, Roman main roads went down steps; Carthage for example (see p 150 *Roman Roads of Europe* by NHH Sitwell). This is yet further evidence that Roman military roads were built primarily for marching troops.

The Wrekendyke

The known Roman road "Wrekendyke" runs perfectly straight from near South Shields to the south-west and was thought to have terminated at its junction with the Chester-le-Street to Newcastle Roman road (Cade's Road), at Wrekenton. The shape of a suspected Roman fort has been seen from the air in the Ravensworth Golf Course (situated in Wrekenton) close to this junction. A hoard of coins, said to have been Roman, was found here when the wagon-way to the east was constructed.

Old antiquarians said that the "Wrekendyke" continued across Cade's Road to the south-west, past Lamesley and Kibblesworth, and it just so happens that the postulated extended Wrekendyke is lined up precisely on the church at Stanley which is also on the "Five Churches Road" from Ebchester to Dalton-le-Dale via Chester-le-Street and Houghton-le-Spring. The curious little steeple of Stanley's St Andrew's Church makes a good surveyor's marker for searchers of Roman roads. Several native Romano-British farmsteads have been located from

This old woodcut of 1728 by Nathaniel Buck shows the ruins of Finchale Priory. Roman pottery has been found here. This woodcut shows a huge dam across the river just upstream from the priory. The hillside is now completely covered with trees but the ravine to the right may be the suspected route of a Roman road from Ryhope and Houghton to Finchale.

the air in the Stanley area but any military installation is likely to have been underneath the church, especially if the modern church is on top of an earlier Saxon structure.

Perhaps part of the extended Wrekendyke is underneath the "Elders Path" in Pockerley Wood, north of the Beamish Museum. This was known as the "Old Road" in AD 1280. There is however, part of a suspected Roman road exactly on the Wrekendyke extended line, just to the east of the eastern perimeter of the Beamish Museum, at NZ 223 548.

Gordon's Road

Dr Gordon mentioned a Roman road which ran from Sunderland to Old Durham. At Old Durham, a Roman bath-house was excavated in 1944 and a Roman fort is suspected in the vicinity of Old Durham Farm. On Longstaffe's *"Map to Elucidate the History of the County of Durham & Sadberge Before the Conquest"* Gordon's Road is marked as a sinuous line from Old Durham to South Shields. A more definite line is shown from Old Durham through Houghton-le-Spring to Sunderland on Saxton's map of 1576 with amendments by P Lea in 1686.

Whellan's Road

Francis Whellan mentioned a Roman road from Binchester, through Byers Green and

Whitworth, heading for Old Durham. This line crosses the River Wear at Page Bank, and Ian Johnson of Shincliffe, a former lecturer at the Houghall Agricultural College, spotted the remains of a Roman bridge on the river bed there during the drought of 1995. The now dismantled single-track road bridge at Page Bank which utilised an old railway bridge, lay on top of the ruinous Roman structure. The rail/road bridge was demolished recently and replaced by a new structure slightly further downstream. Divers reported that most of the Roman stones were just a few feet upstream from the condemned bridge. When the new bridge was finished, the old bridge was removed. Little interest was shown by the authorities but the Roman remains, it is hoped, still lie on the river bed.

This road possibly arrived at Binchester from the north crossing the Bell Burn at NZ 211 320, and then climbing up to the fort. This road seems to have had a branch which deviated around the crest of the plateau to the east of the fort, and then joined Dere Street at NZ 213 312. Another Roman road is suspected coming in from the south-east, from Petty's Nook (NZ 339 190), Cobbler's Hall (NZ 264 265), Old Eldon and Coundongate.

Roman Sunderland and the Roman Coast Road

Roman remains were found in Castle Street, Sunderland but these are now under the Vaux Brewery. A Roman kiln was also found in the docks and a Roman road was exposed c1902 in Low Row in the vicinity of the Hat & Feather public house. John Robinson in Vol V 1904 of Antiquities of Sunderland said that he thought that this road connected with a stretch found near Seaham c1900.

In "Sharp's *History of Hartlepool*," we read:

"Mr Cade considered Hartlepool, or The Port of Hart, at Hartness, an artificial Roman harbour, and that a Roman road once passed in that direction."

According to V Nicholl's *Literary Anecdotes* vol 8:

"A road, I should conjecture, from the map of Drake's Roman roads in Yorkshire, came directly from Dumus (Whitby) to the trajectus at the estuary of the Tees, opposite Bellasis, which has certainly been a castrum, and continued along the shore to Hartlepool and Wearmouth."

Sharpe, in his *History of Hartlepool* written in 1816, says:

"Within the last three years, several drains have been formed at the north-west extremety of the Slake at Hartlepool where square holes have been discovered, filled with human bones; these are found about five feet below the surface in graves nearly eight feet square."

Hartlepool stands on a hook-shaped promontory which juts out into the North Sea and forms a natural harbour, protected from north-easterly gales. This safe haven was probably used from very early times.

A religious house for men and women was established here cAD640 and was destroyed by the Danes cAD 800. When the Conqueror avenged the murder of Comyn, "he entered

Heorteness, wasting and warring with fire and sword." In 1189, Hugh Pudsey, Bishop of Durham, here fitted out a magnificent ship in which he meant to accompany Richard Coeur de Lion on his Crusade. As late as 1614, Hartlepool is mentioned as the only Port Town in the County of Durham. There are strong grounds for a Roman site at Hartlepool. Is it a mere coincidence that monastic settlements are located on former Roman sites? Jarrow is a typical example and both Monkwearmouth and Finchale Priory have yielded Roman pottery.

Old Trade Roads

This is probably an appropriate place to get rid of much confusion caused by historians who mention Roman roads, Saxon roads, Medieval roads, Drove roads, Salters' roads, Lead roads etc as if they were all separate categories. In the main, all roads in use in the medieval period were former Roman roads, in a very poor state of repair, with fords replacing the lost Roman bridges. Later, monastic influence and expertise would replace some of the lost Roman bridges. However, there were few, if any, purpose-built medieval roads. A medieval road not following a Roman line was usually more a "right of way" than a specially constructed road. This is obvious from the air when we observe the multiple confused tracks where medieval travellers attempted to find better ground around patches of the route which had become deeply rutted or had degenerated into quagmires. The "right of way" allowed medieval travellers to diverge if necessary from the unpaved right of way into surrounding fields and crops.

Also the terms, "Salters' road, Lead roads and Drove roads," give readers the impression that these roads were made for specific purposes in later history. The truth is usually that these names are only derived from the usage to which medieval and later peoples, gave the former Roman, and even pre-Roman roads. Certain types of trade led to ancient roads being given new names such as: Maltway, Oxdrove, Sheepdrove and Saltway. Salt roads leading from salt towns; *wiches* such as Nantwich, Droitwich, Middlewich and Northwich etc, can be traced by "salt" place-names like Saltersgate and Saltersford. Portway is another specialised name for a usually ancient road being used as a market road.

A road which has been used by an army may have the name "herepath" (using the Old English word for army, "*here*"). Many place-names can give us clues to ancient roads, for example: "*way, stretton, street, stane, heol, sarn, fford, gate,*" etc; names derived from Latin, Old English, Celtic, and Norse.

Drovers' roads were often given the name "Drift" such as the "Driftway" cattle road north-west from Elsdon in Northumberland. We are sure that this old drovers' road is a reused Roman route.

Research into the often well-recorded journeys by medieval kings and bishops shows that in the main, the VIPs were struggling along ex-Roman roads which had not been repaired for several hundred years.

A Roman road from Binchester to Hartlepool

Roman pottery has been found at Seaton Carew and Catcotes, both within the neighbourhood of the port. During the excavation of the medieval village of Thrislington,

1973-74, a piece of Roman mortarium was found.

The *Newcastle Weekly Chronicle,* August 9th 1890, said:

> *"A number of antiquarian relics and a handsomely paved Roman bath were discovered at Westerton Folly (NZ 239 310), near Bishop Auckland."*

Westerton would have been a most promising site for a Roman signal station. It can be seen from both Hartlepool and Binchester. A circular stone observatory, Westerton Folly, was built by Thomas Wright, a distinguished mathematician and astronomer, who was born at Byers Green. On its wall is a tablet erected in 1950 by Durham University to commemorate his treatise on *The Theory of the Universe,* which was published in 1750. Perhaps this tower occupies the site of a signal station.

Robin Walton's investigation of the Binchester - Hartlepool road

The line of this Roman road is: Binchester - Kirk Merrington - Stob Cross - Trimdon - Hartlepool.

During the summer of 1983, Robin Walton, a retired colliery administrator and an amateur historian, of Coxhoe, County Durham with the help of Mr Wittering, did some exploratory work in the low swampy area between Ferryhill and the Thrislington Deserted Medieval Village. This natural gap in the high ground is an Ice Age spillway and is followed by the Edinburgh to London railway line. Walton and Wittering discovered a fifteen-feet-wide *agger* of a double-ditched causeway. In the summer of 1984, the whole length of the suspected road from Binchester to Hartlepool was explored. Trial trenches here and there revealed the Roman metalling. At a stream crossing, the bed was paved.

Little interest was shown by the establishment, but the magazine *Anglia Archaeology* gave the amateur archaeologists full credit for their excellent work.

In *The History of the Urban District of Spennymoor* by James Dodd, an account of the Battle of Neville's Cross mentions:

> *"The English from Merrington moved forward along the old Roman road on top of the ridge to Ferryhill."*

Surtees, in his *History of Durham*, 1822, mentions a "causey way and paved road between Ferryhill Wood and Thrislington Wood." This is shown on the map of *Distribution of Roman remains in Durham County,* by Rev R E Hoopell and J W Taylor.

Robin Walton has spent many years investigating Roman roads in southern Durham and he has shown me some of his results. Here are some of them:

Shincliffe to Binchester

Robin Walton has traced a suspected Roman road from the crossroads of minor roads south-west of Shincliffe (NZ 294 387), in a direct line to the old church at Croxdale Hall, NZ 274 379. [author's note; we have found from the air, a Roman temporary camp in the field a short distance to the north of this Croxdale old church] then down the hill to cross Croxdale Beck close to the present bridge. From there, the road climbs the hill where the *agger* is visible as far as the Sunderland Bridge village. The route from there is to the "Nicky Nack pub" and behind the pub to Tudhoe village. On to Tudhoe Grange, the road crosses a stream close by Burton Beck Farm, arriving at the back entrance to Whitworth Hall. From here it goes over the Spenny Moor to Page Bank and then over the fields (the latter have been open-cast mined), to Byers Green. At this village, it joins a straight stretch of road which crosses the Tod Hills to Binchester Blocks road. After that it makes a large curve before coming into Binchester from the north.

Robin Walton's Cade's Road West Branch;

Cade's Road divides at Great Stainton and reunites at Shincliffe [author's note: Cade's road from Brough on Humber has already been mentioned.] The line I know is from Pont Tisa (Pontey's Bridge), through Great Stainton, Shincliffe and Old Durham. From my aircraft, I found an unknown double-ditched Roman fort on it on Elstob Farm, map ref, (NZ 338 239), ref: *The Piercebridge Formula,* p 13 (R. Selkirk, PSL, 1983).

I said earlier that I had surveyed a suspected Roman road which seemed to branch off Cade's Road at Shincliffe and proceed down Strawberry Lane. [Unknown to me, Robin Walton was surveying up the other way and the following is his information:].....A branch of Cade's Road leaves the known Roman road on the Great Stainton Sedgefield section at the Elstob Lane dismantled railway level-crossing (NZ 334 242). It proceeds to Howe Hills Plantation (NZ 331 251) and follows the west side of the plantation. From there it joins an old overgrown lane which leads into the village of Mordon (NZ 328 264). [author's note: I am quite willing to accept Robin Walton's findings as I have also found a Roman road which comes into Mordon from the East-North-East. This road is under Peter's Lane, and Mordon has a suspected high and dry Roman barge basin on the east side of the former ancient lake (NZ 327 266).Peter's Lane connects Robin Walton's road with the known Cade's Road at NZ 344 269.]

From Mordon, the west branch follows the modern road on the west side until it arrives at the main railway line where it leaves the modern road, crosses over the fields and enters the village of Bradbury at High Farm, NZ 315 283. After crossing the village street, it follows a hedgerow, heading towards the River Skerne. North-west of Bradbury, the road crosses another Roman road, a west to east one from Binchester to Coundon, Rushyford, Nunstainton Farm and Sedgefield. A branch of the latter road may have ended up at South Shields.

"Cade's Road West Branch," follows Gypsy Lane, and a few yards south of the Gypsy Lane dismantled railway crossing the Roman road leaves the grass verge of the modern Gypsy Lane and runs parallel to the latter. It then passes close to Chilton East House Farm (NZ 305 306). One field north of this farm the road has been obliterated by limestone, sand and gravel extraction, and further north, by a council estate.

At Wood Lane (NZ 295 333) it crosses another Roman road, the Binchester - Hartlepool road, (via Kirk Merrington, Ferryhill and Stob Cross).

Passing a few yards to the west of a reservoir, it descends a hill, into an old quarry where traces of the road were found at NZ 293 336. Continuing northwards through the fields, it then crosses Thinford Lane at NZ 289 347 and follows a modern road to Hett Mill. The Roman road is on the east side of the modern one at first and then crosses to the west. Just south of the main railway-line level crossing, kerbstones are visible on the west side of the modern road. A ford was used to cross the Tursdale Beck and then the road makes a sharp turn up the hillside through a cutting which is paved (NZ 29 370). The Roman road is then followed by the medieval "Strawberry Lane" and then proceeds to East Grange Farm, NZ 294 398, and from there to High Shincliffe, where it meets Cade's Roman Road and the reunited roads cross the Old Durham Beck at NZ 291 414 and follow the line of Cade's road, as described earlier, to Chester-le-Street and Newcastle upon Tyne. [author's note: what a coincidence that Robin found this northbound road when I was following it south. Fortunately, I didn't search beyond Chilton, so further duplicating Robin's work. I am very pleased though to see that my own "Roman road tracking" is confirmed by an expert such as Robin Walton.]

Robin Walton's road from Piercebridge to Lanchester

One mile north of Piercebridge on Dere Street, the road branches across the fields to Denton and then under the modern road to Houghton-le-Side. It crosses the West Auckland to Darlington (A68) at Houghton Bank and the railway at Shildon between East and West Thickley. It then passes Old Eldon where Roman coins have been found, and then on to Leasingthorne and Kirk Merrington.

The route is then from Kirk Merrington (which is at a Roman crossroad) to Whitworth Hall, and Page Bank where there is a known Roman crossing of the River Wear. The route is then over Brancepeth Golf Course passing between Brancepeth Castle and the church. At Pithouse Plantation 330 yards west of the Trig point, it crosses the modern road and another half mile on, it crosses the Roman road, Dere Street. It runs through Holburn Wood and crosses the River Deerness by a ford close to the present bridge; going through Esh Winning, it passes close to a redundant chapel and at a place marked "Heugh," it joins up with Dere Street. [author's note: Robin's searches continue and we wish him the best of luck].

Sedgefield - Three Gates road

A hitherto unknown Roman road has been traced from Sedgefield to Three Gates, where it meets a branch from the Roman coast road. The "Sedgefield East" road lies under the modern A689 for a couple of miles, passing Beacon Hill Farm, and then crosses open country towards Embleton. A Roman site is suspected underneath Sedgefield church.

Proto Dere Street

Roman road Dere Street runs due north from Piercebridge and across the top of Brusselton Hill, NZ 206 249, where a Roman signal station is suspected. From this high point, the road follows the eastern edge of Brusselton Wood which is a very steep gradient. A mile north of the highest point of Brusselton Wood, the Roman road does a peculiar thing. It alters course at the bottom of a valley. Alterations of headings of Roman roads are usually at high points. This alteration occurs at Fylands Bridge, NZ 205 268, where the Roman road makes a right turn of ten degrees from a heading of 360 degrees to 010 degrees, and then proceeds up the full length of Bishop Auckland Main Street. The Roman road then follows around the outside of the large bend of the River Wear below the Bishop's Palace, and crosses the River Gaunless, close to its mouth just a few yards to the west of the Gaunless bridge, NZ 214 307. The Roman road then climbs the wood to the south-east of Binchester Roman fort, past the Roman well at the top of the wood, NZ 212 308, through the centre of the Roman fort and then on a north-westerly heading down towards the sewage works where a Roman bridge (or ford) crossed the River Wear at NZ 204 318. On the west side of the River Wear, the Roman road continues north-westerly for a few hundred yards following a line of trees, and crosses first a dismantled railway line, and then a gill via an embankment (NZ 198 322) just to the south-east of the Hunwick Equestrian Centre. The Roman road continues under the equestrian centre and just north of this centre, alters course right to north-north-west. This turn is a junction with a hitherto unknown Roman road coming up from the south. A few hundred yards further north, the combined Roman roads cross the Hunwick Gill, NZ 194 326, where the earth embankment of a Roman bridge still exists on the southern side of the gill.

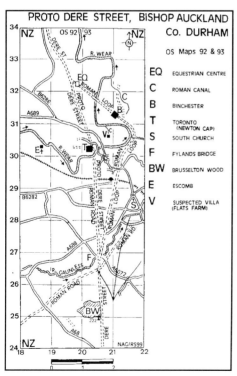

A hitherto unknown but quite easy to identify Roman road has been found running direct from Fylands bridge to the Hunwick Equestrian Centre. This is "Proto Dere Street" and the Roman loop road which turns right at Fylands bridge and passes via Bishop Auckland High Street is a deviation and possibly an afterthought. Proto Dere Street is marked on some maps as "Mitchell's Causeway." Proto Dere Street crossed the River Wear via a Roman bridge on the same site as the medieval "Newton Cap Bridge." The now demolished Newton Cap Hall has camouflaged suspected Roman ramparts in the field to the south of Newton Cap Farm at Toronto. A further suspected Roman road runs towards Escomb Saxon church where another Roman riverside site is suspected. As Binchester's identification as "Vinovia" depends on its position on Dere Street, it means that a Roman site at Newton Cap may be the true Vinovia. This new evidence will be unwelcome to many historians but the evidence is there for all to see if they so wish.

The deviation of the Roman road at Fylands Bridge and subsequently up Bishop Auckland High Street and into Binchester is not Dere Street; it is a by-road and a loop which rejoins the TRUE DERE STREET just to the north of the Hunwick Equestrian Centre. From Fylands Bridge, the True Dere Street, named by us Proto Dere Street, continues north without any alteration of heading, and has crossed the River Wear in the vicinity of Toronto, upstream from the refurbished Newton Cap railway viaduct (now a road bridge). The old stone bridge just upstream from this viaduct seems to be on the same site as the Roman bridge. Surrounding Newton Cap Farm on the hill to the WNW of the old stone bridge are Roman-looking earthworks (NZ 203 303). There are reused Roman stones in the farm buildings. This farm is at the south end of Toronto village and it is highly likely that here lies a hitherto undiscovered major Roman fort. The earthworks were thought to have been left by the demolition of Newton Cap Hall, but the mounds are of Roman shape and are far too extensive. The newly discovered Roman road, Proto Dere Street, passes a few yards to the east of these earthworks on its way down the hill to the Newton Cap Roman bridge which was on the same site as the medieval bridge.

To the north of the Newton Cap/Toronto site, Proto Dere Street can be picked-up along a hedge line and this runs all the way to the Equestrian Centre at Hunwick where it is joined by the Roman road coming in from the south-east, from Binchester Roman fort. Binchester Roman fort is therefore not on Dere Street, but on a Roman branch-loop which leaves Dere Street at Fylands Bridge and rejoins it just north of the Hunwick Equestrian Centre. Binchester Roman fort therefore may not be "Vinovia," because the identification of Binchester as Vinovia depends upon its mention in the *Antonine Itinerary*.

In the large loop of the River Wear to the south of Binchester is Flatts Farm, and from the air, this appears to be standing on a Roman-type earthwork. Also, a crop mark of an infilled waterway can be seen leaving the river and proceeding south to this possible Roman villa.

There is also a Roman canal at Binchester. This is now a mainly-dry waterway and consists of typical Roman angled straight lengths. It is too high up the contours to be an old course of the River Gaunless, an excuse which has been used in the past to get rid of unwelcome evidence. A full map of the waterway, drawn by Jeremiah Dixon in 1772 can be seen in the Bishop's Palace, or on p247 of *On the Trail of the Legions* (R Selkirk) 1995. Jeremiah Dixon was one of the surveyors of the Mason-Dixon boundary between USA and Canada.

An aerial photograph taken by an unknown RAF pilot c1930 shows the Roman (loop) road leaving Binchester fort to the south-east and following the hedge-line around the large bend of the river. This defeats all the previous arguments about this Roman road crossing the River Wear twice, or the other school of thought about the whole bend of the river migrating eastwards.

Roman tiles found at Binchester are stamped "N CON" *(Numerus Concangios)*, a Roman unit stationed at Chester-le-Street. It is likely that these heavy cargoes of tiles arrived at Binchester by barge.

As previously mentioned, north from Toronto, the newly discovered Roman road, Proto

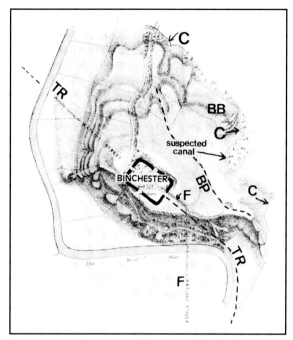

This old map of Binchester shows "Watling Street" crossing the River Wear to the north-west of the fort. That is correct and I have marked this as "TR"(True Road). The old map then shows the Roman Watling Street (Dere Street) turning and crossing the River Wear to the south-east of the fort. This is incorrect (F = False Road). The True Road follows the bend of the river and then passes down Bishop Auckland High Street to Fylands Bridge. Another school of thought said that the Roman road ran south from the fort and that in Roman times the river loop was further west. This school of thought is also wrong. The river has hardly moved a yard since Roman times. Another Roman road "BP" bypasses the fort around the top of the high ground and then heads north. A suspected Roman canal "C," now dry except at the north-west end, survives, and there is a suspected barge basin (also dry) at "BB." This canal is shown on Jeremiah Dixon's map which hangs in Auckland Castle.

This aerial photograph taken about 1928 by an unknown RAF pilot has lain unrecognised in a museum file for seventy years. It took another pilot to recognise the target. This AP shows the true course of the Roman road without any shadow of doubt. This view is to the south-east.

The black barn at Binchester Farm (7 o-clock from centre) is still there and is a good marker for the Roman road.

The scrub on the hillside at 2 o-clock to the fort is now a mature wood. A Roman well survives just inside the wood where the Roman road leaves the flat field and begins its descent of the hill.

This photograph taken from a modern aircraft shows the true Roman road east of Binchester Roman fort, showing as a parch mark in the field. The "false road" which has caused so much confusion to modern historians is marked by the line of three trees. This false

line does not match up with the excavated Roman road in the centre of the fort. The "true line" of the parch mark does.

At bottom left, a Roman road which has bypassed the fort is followed by a hedge line around the edge of the escarpment.

At top left, further crop marks may indicate Roman activity on the south side of the River Wear in the Flatts Farm loop.

Even if the old RAF photograph had not come to light, it should have been known to

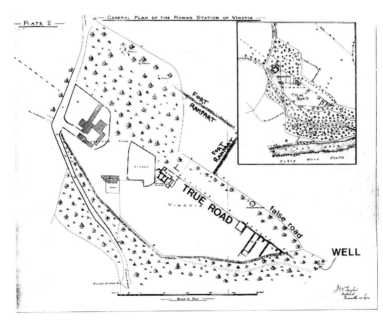

modern archaeologists that the "three bridge theory" and the "river movement theory" were wrong because the plan drawn c1870 by JW Taylor of the Rev Hooppell's excavation clearly shows the true course of the Roman road. Why has this information been ignored by the modern establishment?

Dere Street is followed by a hedge line and a public footpath all the way to the Hunwick Equestrian Centre. At NZ 197 322, Proto Dere Street has crossed a gill and there are scores of tons of stones, some of them worked, obviously Roman, lying in the gill. It looks as if there has been some kind of fortification as well as a bridge at this point. Just a few yards further north, at NZ 197 324, in a strip wood, the public footpath just to the west of the equestrian centre, is right on top of Proto Dere Street. An excavation is not necessary: flood-water has washed the soil off the road and a perfect Roman road surface lies exposed.

We have now renamed the Roman road through Bishop Auckland, and Binchester Roman fort, "the Binchester Loop." Once again our history books will have to be altered.

Stukeley's map of 1755, simplified for clarity. Scholars have suggested that this map is a result of forged evidence but until recently, Brough on Humber was marked on modern maps as "Praetorio."

Recent excavations have proved that the correct name was Petuaria. Stukeley's map showed the correct name. There may be other valuable evidence on this map. A through-waterway is marked across the West Country. Did the Romans connect the rivers Parrett and Stour with a canal? Stukeley also marks a through-waterway down the Great Glen in Scotland. There have been Roman finds at Fort Augustus. Although the Roman road north from a junction at Ragpath Wood, south of Flass Hall, near Esh Winning, was only found in recent years by our aerial surveys, Stukeley marked it in 1755.

The Barnard Castle to Fylands Bridge road extends to South Church

The Roman road which comes in to the south of Fylands Bridge from the Barnard Castle direction was thought to have terminated at its junction with Dere Street. Directly opposite, a farm track which heads for South Church is now known to be a Roman road too. Where it goes after South Church is possibly Trimdon and Hartlepool.

Escomb Church stands on a Roman site

It is also interesting to note that the Saxon church at Escomb seems to be standing on a Roman-type earthwork. Roman pottery and coins are constantly found at Escomb. Did the Saxon monks who were supposed to have robbed the stone from Binchester also remove broken pottery and coins out of date by several hundred years? Were the Saxon monks the "binmen of Binchester?" I have never believed that the reused Roman stones in Escomb Church came from Binchester. The argument is further defeated by the presence of a possible Toronto fort being much closer. A suspected Roman road leaves Toronto and heads for Escomb. Investigations continue.

Dere Street and its branches

The known Roman road "Dere Street" which heads north from Binchester Roman fort, makes a sharp 75 degree turn to the west at Ragpath Wood (NZ 205 422), near Esh Winning. An unknown, but long-suspected Roman road has been identified straight ahead from the corner, and a Roman site is thought to lie under Flass Hall, just north of the alteration of heading. The northbound hitherto unknown road, meets another Roman road (NZ 214 477) which lay hidden under the farm road called "Long Edge" to the north of Broomhouse Farm. The Roman origin of "Long Edge" was discovered in 1982 when a drain from an open-cast mining site was cut through it. In the same field where the northbound road joins Long Edge, the source of the Roman four-mile aqueduct to Chester-le-Street was also found (NZ 217 478).

On its way to the Newcastle upon Tyne area, the Flass Hall northbound road passes Esh and descends "Groove Bank" (NZ 214 444) at Langley Park. Before going down the bank, it crosses an east-west ridge-road which may have Roman origins. This road heads from Esh towards Durham via Vffhaw (Ushaw) and is shown on Saxton & Lea's map of 1686.

Intercepting the north-west 75 degree turn of Dere Street in Ragpath Wood, an east-west woodland track runs along the ridge at the southern side of the wood. This track is not only a suspected Roman road but also a possible Roman defence line. Just inside the wood to the north of the track is a huge *fosse*. As will be seen shortly, there was a network of defensive patrol roads across Northumberland, all on headings of about 250 degrees. The Ragpath Wood track is also on this alignment. More suspected patrol roads are being investigated.

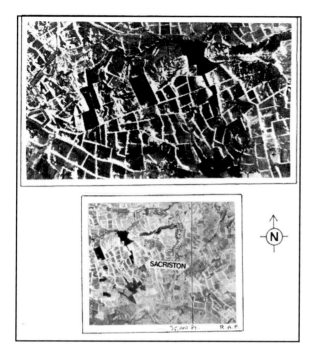

(two aerial photographs) The "Long Edge" Roman road can be seen on this high level vertical aerial photograph as a straight snow-line from near bottom left to near top right. Open-cast mining has removed the Roman road at the eastern (right) end of this photograph. The smaller picture shows the position of the Roman road (left centre) with relation to Sacriston.

The open-cast workings west of Sacriston Heugh cut through several pre-historic bell pits. Iron-stone has been removed from this particular bell pit. Photograph by kind permission of Hutchinson Mining.

A low level oblique aerial photograph of Sacriston Heugh looking west towards the Long Edge Roman road which can be seen crossing a strip wood at top left. The fields above centre, left of the gorse patches and with parallel field drains, have been open-cast mined.

Sacriston Heugh road

On the *Map to Elucidate the History of the County of Durham & Sadberge before the Conquest,* dated 18th June, 1857, drawn by W Hylton Dyer Longstaffe and published by Bell & Daldy, a supposed ancient road is shown to the east of Holmside Hall. This road runs north-west from Durham, passing Findon Hill and Sacriston Heugh on its way to Kip Hill, Stanley. A comment beside the line of the old road states: "paving recently removed." An aerial search failed to locate any trace of the line.

Sacriston Heugh was built between the 13th and 15th centuries and was originally allocated to the Sacristan of Durham Cathedral by Bishop Pudsey for the upkeep of his office, and from its revenues, he was duty bound to feed two-hundred people on St Catherine's Day, each person receiving one loafe and two herrings. The buildings were demolished in the 1930s and aerial surveys show only a patch of rough grass.

The ancient road which passed Sacriston Heugh may have been used as a pack-horse trail as there is a reference to pack-horses carrying wool from the Yorkshire dales to the Newcastle wool market, resting at "Lingey Close" (now Lingey House Farm.)

The old road also passes Findon Hill and was perhaps used by soldiers at the Battle of Neville's Cross, 17th Oct, 1346. The closing stages of the battle were fought on this hill.

Fulforth, Sacriston Heugh, Edmondsley, Plawsworth, Kimblesworth, Holemyers (now known as Nettlesworth) and Broadmyers are all mentioned in Bishop Pudsey's list of his possessions (*Boldon Book* 1183). Most of the place-names in the area are of Saxon origin.

The ancient road passes to the east of Wheatley Green Farm, and about a mile to the east of Holmside Hall.

Salters' Road

On Longstaffe's "Before the Conquest" map, Salters' road is marked from Sunderland to Sedgefield. This is probably a Roman road reused by the salters. We thought we could see it from the air to the east of the large suspected tree-covered burial mounds at Warden Law but our excavation failed to locate it. This was one of our very few failures. We now think that the Salters' road may be underneath the modern road which passes between the two burial mounds just before it crosses the B1404.

Steerable axles on Roman wagons

I was staggered to hear a lecturer once claim that Roman roads were straight because the front wheels of a Roman wagon couldn't pivot. That old wives' tale is dead forever because a complete Roman wagon has been excavated from a swamp in the Balkans, and its front axle was mounted on a turntable which swivelled through forty degrees (Venedikov 1960, *Trakijskate Kolesniza Sofia, Thracian Vehicle)*. We all (except a few members of the establishment), knew of steerable Roman front wheels because in Diocletian's price edict, a spare part of a wagon labelled *columella* (vertical pillar) is mentioned. There is only one place on a wagon for such a part and that is on a swivelling front axle. We must remember of course that these wagons could not take the severe gradients of Roman roads and it seems that the wagons plied only around the forts, farms and *vici*. There is no Roman reference anywhere to long-distance Roman wagon transport.

A Roman wagon mascot

Incidentally, on the same wagon, a pair of small bronze horses about two inches high, decorated the sides above the front wheels. A similar horse, found at Vindolanda, has been on display in a Newcastle museum for many years, labelled: "Legionary standard." We always thought it was a bit small, rather like having a Union Jack the size of a pocket handkerchief on the flag-pole of the House of Commons. The Newcastle horse disappeared suddenly when details of the Roman wagon were published.

Vindolanda Letter mentions Roman roads unfit for wagons

Vindolanda letter of cAD115, written by one Octavius of unknown status, and recovered from boggy ground at Vindolanda, speaks of the poor state of Roman roads which are unfit for wheeled traffic, and how the writer will go bankrupt if he does not receive goods from Catterick, for which he has already paid.

The Blackstone Edge Roman road is not in Durham but has been mentioned here because of an unusual feature: it has a peculiar trough down the centre of its steeply inclined surface, and the usual marked camber of a Roman road is missing.

All kinds of weird and wonderful purposes have been attributed to this groove but the most likely explanation is that it was a rainwater gutter. When a cambered road passes a critical angle of descent (try tilting a beer can under a running tap), water does not flow down the sides of the camber; it flows down the centre. The Romans must have known this and dispensed with the usual camber and substituted a central gutter.

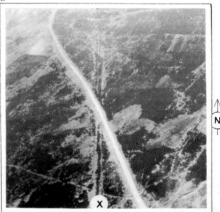

X = NY **987 328**

Right Top: Aerial view of the Stanhope-Eggleston Roman road (top centre to bottom centre). The Roman road has attacked the hill head on whereas the modern road has had to deviate to ease the gradient.

Right, lower: The very marked agger (cambered surface) of the Roman road would have rendered the road useless for wheeled vehicles of any kind. The road was obviously intended for men and pack-animals. It seems that the road was used as a pack-horse trail for the transportation of lead in the heydays of fairly recent lead mining, but the road has all the signs of being built originally by the Romans. Many Roman-type culverts pass underneath the road.

NZ 095 133　　GRETA BRIDGE ROMAN FORT　　Pilot: R. Selkirk RS

Greta Bridge Roman fort from the air. The fort lies on the Roman road from Scotch Corner to Bowes and the Stainmore Pass. The A66(T) modern road follows the Roman road except for occasional deviations. In this photograph the Roman road was thought to have been under the medieval and modern road (M) but that is not the case. This photograph shows the Roman road (R) tracking over the field to the south of the farms and hump-backed bridge. There are slight remains of a possible bridge abutment at (A) and an unidentified earthwork at (E). The Morritt Arms Hotel sits on the north end of the Roman fort.

The Roman road network in the Barnard Castle area. "S" is Startforth, a suspected Roman site. The A688 (on top of a medieval road) swings to the south to zig-zag down to the River Tees. The Roman road swung the other way and crossed the river at (B), the site of the Roman bridge. The Roman road was encountered during the 1930s in the gasworks (G). Dent Gate Lane, and the minor road (ZZZ), are lined-up on the site of the Roman crossing and are therefore believed to be on top of Roman roads. Egglestone Abbey also probably hides some kind of Roman site.

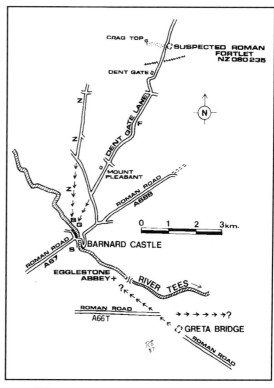

A Roman paved ford at NZ 219 379, in a stream to the north of Brancepeth Castle. This is on a branch of the Dere Street Roman road which leads from Willington towards Durham but is lost in the Brandon area.

NY 995 123. A suspected Roman road running south-south-east from the Bowes Roman fort (Lavatrae) towards Scargill Moor. The modern road bottom right is from Gilmonby to Sleightholme. This view is to the SSE.

AK Orlandos' drawing of a Roman glissage in the Roman quarry at Pentelikon. A huge dressed stone, complete with lewis-hole is sliding down the ramp on a sledge. As well as the suspected glissage at West Rainton, there is another in Salters' Nick (NZ 053 824) in Shaftoe Crags, Northumberland. A recently discovered (and excavated) Roman road leads to the west from the bottom of the Salters' Nick glissage.

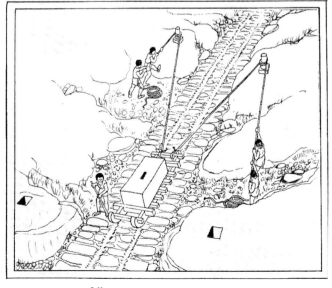

The possible Roman glissage (quarry-slide) down Malley Gill (NZ 307 460) near West Rainton. The upper picture shows the rutted road down the ravine and the lower drawing is of a similar Roman road in France.

RS

Close-up views of the ruts of the glissage which leads down to the east bank of the River Wear about a mile upstream from Finchale Priory.
Access is via a footpath from Woodside, over a farm bridge which crosses the A1(M).
After crossing this bridge, turn left to a wood and follow the path in the wood to the river. It is possible that the glissage has a Norman origin (or reuse) as the Normans transported stone from this area upriver for part of the construction of Durham Cathedral. The black marble in Durham Cathedral was rafted down the River Wear from Frosterley.

The upper sketch is from a tomb in Rome and shows Roman stone-masons using a belt-driven drill.

The Lower picture shows a Roman stone which has been separated from the quarry face by a row of holes. These holes were drilled with star-chisels. The large chisel had a cross-shaped cutting blade and it was hit repeatedly, rotating the chisel slightly after each blow of the hammer. This stone is lying on Roker beach, Sunderland along with hundreds of other Roman stones, dumped here when the great Roman dam at Hylton was dismantled in the early 1800s.

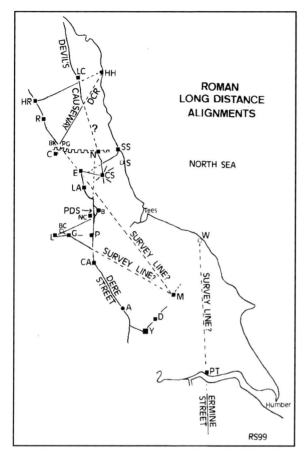

ROMAN LONG DISTANCE ALIGNMENTS

NORTH SEA

RS99

It is known that the Romans were excellent navigators and surveyors and this is reflected in their road system. It looks as if they had some kind of triangulation survey and this can be very useful when it comes to looking for hitherto unknown Roman roads. In Northumberland, the Devil's Causeway makes a most unusual turn to the north (the Devil's Corner) at NZ 122 923, and a search revealed an unknown Roman (DCR = Devil's Coast Road) road running to a suspected Roman harbour at Howick Haven (HH). Also, the known Roman road east from High Rochester (HR) passing Learchild (LC) was thought to have terminated at the Devil's Causeway, but it seems that an extension has also gone to Howick Haven.

Many Roman artefacts have been found at Howick Haven and we must look at the possibility that the native hillfort there was manned by frontier tribesmen in the pay of the Romans.

The long straight Roman Dere Street, running down Northumberland towards Beukley, if extended, is lined-up precisely on the Malton Roman fort (M), seventy miles away. No known Roman road follows this line. Perhaps it is just a survey line.

From Greta Bridge (G) the Roman road under the A66(T) is also lined-up on the distant Malton Roman fort, with no known Roman road south-east of Scotch Corner. Ermine Street, north from Lincoln is lined-up on Brough-on-Humber (PT = Petuaria). An extension of this line north strikes Whitby (W) where a major Roman fort and a lighthouse too, have long been suspected in the vicinity of the abbey.

The Wrekendyke from South Shields (SS) was thought to have terminated at Cade's Road between Chester-le-Street (CS) and Newcastle (N), but old documents tell us that it continued to Kibblesworth and probably onward to Stanley. The Wrekendyke is lined-up exactly on Stanley Church which has the significant name of St Andrew's.

PDS = Proto Dere Street and this was found by ignoring the Roman loop of Dere Street north-east from Fylands Bridge and thence up Bishop Auckland Front street towards Binchester (B). The direct line straight ahead from the bend at Fylands Bridge towards Newton Cap (Toronto) and beyond was explored.

The result is that we suspect that Vinovia may not be located at Binchester but at Newton Cap (NC) which is on Proto Dere Street!

HR	=	*High Rochester (Bremenium)*
LC	=	*Learchild*
HH	=	*Howick Haven*
R	=	*Risingham (Habitancum)*
DCR	=	*Devil's Coast Road*
C	=	*Corbridge (Corstopitum)*
BK	=	*Beukley*
PG	=	*Portgate*
N	=	*Newcastle upon Tyne (Pons Aelius)*
SS	=	*South Shields (Arbeia? or Arbela?)*
E	=	*Ebchester (Vindomora)*
CS	=	*Chester-le-Street (Concangis?)*
S	=	*Sunderland*
LA	=	*Lanchester (Longovicium)*
PDS	=	*Proto Dere Street*
NC	=	*Newton Cap (Toronto)*
B	=	*Binchester*
L	=	*Bowes (Lavatris)*
BC	=	*Barnard Castle*
G	=	*Greta Bridge*
P	=	*Piercebridge*
CA	=	*Catterick (Cataractonium)*
M	=	*Malton (Delgovicia?)*
A	=	*Aldborough (Isurium)*
D	=	*Stamford Bridge (Derventio?)*
Y	=	*York (Eburacum)*
PT	=	*Brough-on-Humber (Petuaria)*
W	=	*Whitby (Praetorio?)*

Chester-le-Street is in the centre of the whole network but for the sake of clarity of survey lines, several Roman roads radiating from Chester-le-Street have been omitted.

We must now move on to our great neighbouring county of Northumberland, which contains not only several Roman frontiers but also a vast amount of hitherto unknown or little understood evidence. The more we know of our whole north-eastern area, the better we will understand our own local Chester-le-Street history and the town's place in history.

Chapter 9
The Lost Roman Roads of Northumberland

Great roads the
Romans built that men might meet
And Walls to keep strong men apart, secure.
Now centuries are gone, and in defeat, The walls are fallen, but the roads endure.

Ethelyn Miller Hartwich

This story begins in the closing stages of World War 2 when, in 1945, I was an Air Training Corps cadet, eagerly awaiting a flight at the RAF aerodrome Ouston, near Heddon on the Wall, Northumberland. I did not foresee that after many years of airline flying and other aviation duties, I would become an archaeologist and return to this very same area, searching for traces of the handiwork of the Roman legions and auxiliaries.

My introduction to the Roman Wall was in an old Avro Anson aircraft. I was allowed to sit in the co-pilot's seat, and immediately after take-off, it was my job to wind up the undercarriage with 160 turns of a hand crank. The pilot flew low along the Roman Wall, over Housesteads and Crag Lough and I realised what a wonderful tool the aeroplane was for observing the history of our countryside.

On another occasion at the same airfield, a Free-French pilot took me up in a De Havilland Dragon Rapide, a twin engined biplane. There was no co-pilot's seat, but I sat in the radio operator's position just behind the pilot. He pointed out, in a plantation, the result of a German air-raid. A row of bomb craters was just a bit wide of the aerodrome. Thirty years later, while looking for a Roman road in this same plantation, by this time a mature wood, I came across these craters. One of the bombs had scored a direct hit on the Roman road, saving me the trouble of an excavation.

My entry into archaeology came late in life when I was home on leave from my professional aviation duties, and became involved as a part-time air survey pilot for a university professor. My interest in the subject led me to become a fully qualified archaeologist and my favourite pursuit was, and still is, the search for long-lost Roman roads.

The Rothley Road

The Roman road which the German aircraft had inadvertently bombed was not initially found by aerial reconnaissance. I happened to be driving down the long straight stretch of road south from Grangemoor Farm (NY 046 866) near Scots Gap, to the River Wansbeck crossing at the deserted medieval village (DMV) of South Middleton (NY 053 841) when I noticed in my driving mirror that the road behind me was lined-up exactly on the folly on the top of Rothley Crags (NY 044 887). As explained previously, this was a typical Roman surveyor's trick so a full-scale search was initiated.

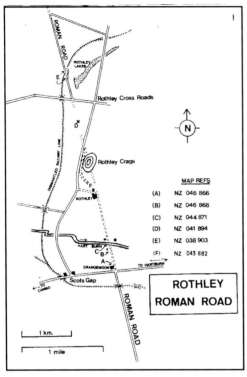

ROTHLEY
ROMAN ROAD

MAP REFS

(A)	NZ 046 866
(B)	NZ 046 868
(C)	NZ 044 871
(D)	NZ 041 894
(E)	NZ 038 903
(F)	NZ 043 882

The Rothley Road in the vicinity of Rothley Crag (once called Roadley Crag), Northumberland. This section is easy to follow.

A = Suspected Roman columns in barn of Grangemoor Farm.

B = Cross section of Roman road in N bank of small stream.

C = Post holes in rock bed of Hart Burn.

D = Paved Roman ford, Roman coins found.

E = Roman agger visible where modern road on top of Roman road has deviated to cross railway bridge.

F = Suspected Roman fort or fortlet in gardens of farm cottages.

The Roman surveyors have lined-up their road on a suspected signal station, now under a folly, but the Roman road builders have deviated their road around the base of the crag, to the west, before picking up the original alignment.

Just north of East Shaftoe Hall (NZ 059 823), the Romans have made a road cutting through a small cliff.

ROTHLEY
ROMAN ROAD

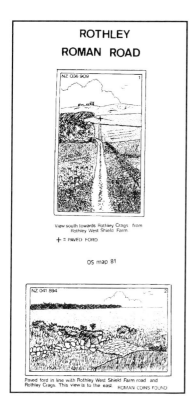

View south towards Rothley Crags from Rothley West Shield Farm
+ = PAVED FORD

OS map 81

Paved ford in line with Rothley West Shield Farm road and Rothley Crags. This view is to the east. ROMAN COINS FOUND

In the Simonside Hills, the Romans have cut imitation paving into solid rock (NZ 023 994). A niche for an altar was found here in the cliff below the ledge along which the road runs. This was a holy spot.

Roman road visible in north bank of small stream north of Grangemoor Farm and just to west of farm road (NZ 046 868).

The road was indeed Roman. The survey line had gone right across the top of Rothley Crags, but the Roman road constructors who were allowed to bypass obstructions, had laid their road around the western base of the precipitous outcrop before regaining the original line. Just to the north of Rothley Crag a Roman paved ford was found in the bed of a small stream (NY 041 896) and fourth century coins of Constantine the Great and Valentinian 1, were found by the field-walker who operated the expedition's metal detector. Combined aerial and ground searches located the Roman road all the way from the Iron Age fort at Great Tosson (NU 023 005) in the Coquet valley to Whitchester (NZ 099 683) a mile north-west of the Roman Wall fort of Rudchester.

Points of interest on the Rothley Road

General alignment: 165/345 degrees

NU 024 004	Square earthwork (possible Roman fortlet or signal station) just to south of Great Tosson Iron Age hillfort on north side of Simonside Hills.
NZ 023 993	Imitation paving cut into solid rock. Possible niche for altar cut into cliff to west. Apart from this spot, road very rough, reused by public footpath.
NZ 022 975	Prominent *agger* across heather to west of Selby's Cove. Ruined shieling between road and cove contains reused stones.
NZ 025 965	Coquet Cairn: suspected Roman survey point.
NZ 033 922	Spot height, 284 metres: suspected Roman survey point.
NZ 035 909	Rothley West Shield Farm. Many small roadside quarries. Roman road under cart track.
NZ 038 902	*Agger* cut by old railway line.
NZ 039 900	Old culvert removed by farmer and rebuilt.
NZ 041 894	Roman coins found in paved ford: Constantine the Great (AD 307-337) and Valentinian 1 (AD 364-375).
NZ 042 885	Suspected Roman road around west base of crag.
NZ 043 888	Folly probably hides remains of Roman signal station.
NZ 043 881	Rothley DMV on south side of road. Possible fortlet in garden of old farm on north side of east-west farm road.
NZ 045 875	Roman road suspected underneath straight north-south cart track from Rothley to Hart Burn.
NZ 045 871	Remains of Roman bridge abutment a few yards upstream from modern ford. Wade up river edge to observe stone. Just upstream from bridge, natural rock sill has post-hole cut into stone at south end.
NZ 045 869	Cross-section of Roman road visible in north bank of small stream just to west of farm road, 300 yards north of Grangemoor Farm.
NZ 046 866	Possible Roman columns reused in farm buildings of Grangemoor Farm. Farm on top of Roman road.
NZ 052 844	*Tumulus* in field to west of public road.

NZ 054 841   Crossing of River Wansbeck: South Middleton DMV. Suspected Roman fort under western part of DMV. Suspected Roman aqueduct coming in from west.

NZ 059 822   Artificial cutting through small cliff near east end of reservoir. Two large burial mounds further east.

NZ 061 813   Crossing point with Devil's Causeway known Roman road.

NZ 062 810   Ford or bridge across small stream 150 yards east of Devil's Causeway crossing of same stream. Public footpath uses Devil's Causeway crossing.

NZ 064 802   Crossing point with modern A696(T) road.

NZ 064 798   *Agger* in strip wood to east of, and parallel to farm road.

NZ 066 796   Square earthwork of Roman shape inside South Bradford DMV.

NZ 069 786   Circular earthwork in Cuddy's View Plantation.

NZ 070 785   Prominent road-paving in pasture down east side of Cuddy's View Plantation.

NZ 075 773   Square earthwork, suspected Roman fortlet, at south edge of wood, ("Cut Plantation") 300 yards north of isolated circular copse.

NZ 074 768   Circular copse: *tumulus* just to east.

NZ 077 751   Known Roman remains marked on OS map. Reason for presence not under-stood until discovery of Rothley Road.

NZ 079 751   Stony ford in Blackheddon Burn.

NZ 083 732   Heugh: quarry and unidentified earthworks.

NZ 089 716   Crossing of River Pont. Old mill-dam probably reused stones of Roman bridge.

NZ 092 708   Street Houses. Much stone behind copse 400 yards north of village, west side of road.

NZ 092 704   Hilltop Plantation, much stone.

NZ 097 695   Ford across Med Burn.

NZ 099 690   Loudside: large stones to west of farm.

NZ 099 683   Suspected pre-Wall Roman fort under Whitchester farm.

Horsley's "Blakehope east" road

It is obvious that Rothley Crag was an important Roman survey point; and likely that the folly on the top hides the remains of a Roman signal station. In addition to the Great Tosson to Whitchester road, the modern road past Winter's Gibbet at Steng Cross (NY 963 908) is also lined up on Rothley Crag (to the east) and the Blakehope Roman fort (NY 859 946) on the known Roman road "Dere Street," to the west. It is possible that the Steng Cross road is on top of an unknown Roman road. Horsley in his *Britannia Romana* (1731) tells us of such a Roman road leaving the Blakehope fort area and heading east:

> "A branch of a military way seems to have gone from Elsdon through Greenchesters to Watling Street passing by Elishaw and falling near Blaikhope on Watling Street, at a large angle, not much short of a right one."

This road remains to be identified but at Hillhead (NY 940 918) to the west of Steng Cross, where the main road turns northwards to Elsdon, an *agger* continues straight ahead towards Greenchesters (NY 870 941) and Blakehope. There is a small unidentified square site seen from the air on the same line at NY 923 921 on the south side of a public bridleway.

Roman remains at Elsdon (NY 937 935) were reported by Hodgson in his *History of Northumberland*, Vol 2: "Strong Roman masonry, an urn, boar tusks and two Roman tablets were found here."

The Driftway

Although its name suggests a drove road, "The Driftway" which runs north-west from Elsdon should be checked to see if it obeys some of the rules for Roman roads. Extreme care should be taken as it runs through a military firing-range. This has also delayed attempts to investigate it from the air.

A lost Roman road network in the Central Tyne Valley

Before our surveys, only three Roman roads were known in Northumberland - Dere Street, the Devil's Causeway and the High Rochester to Learchild road. The most significant new evidence has been the discovery of a complete network in the Central Tyne Valley, an area which has seen more archaeologists at work than even the Valley of the Kings in Egypt. Nevertheless, until now, that major complex had remained undiscovered, so how many more miles lie hidden?

The first clue to its presence was the tradition, long ignored by archaeologists, that there had been a Roman bridge at Bywell. Old woodcuts show the remains of two ancient piers sticking out of the river there. On August 10th, 1836, these piers were blown up by gunpowder and work started on a new bridge further downstream on the same day. Reused Roman stones can be identified here and there in the new bridge, and about thirty, complete with lewis-holes, presumably surplus to requirements, lie on the river bed and are visible in low water conditions.

Experts denied any Roman presence whatsoever at Bywell but a little research showed that in 1750, a Roman silver cup was recovered from the Tyne there by an angler. It was inscribed *Desideri Vivas*. Surprisingly, for such a small hamlet, Bywell has two churches, very close to each other. St Andrew's is the older of the two and the tower and west wall of the nave are Saxon. The nearby St Peter's used to stand on a prominent platform before the levels of the surrounding fields were raised during landscaping. In January 1902, in St Peter's churchyard, part of a Roman altar was found at a depth of six feet. An inspection of the tower of St Andrew's revealed many ex-Roman lewis-holed stones identical in size and appearance to those lying on the river bed under the 1836 bridge. The bell-sounding holes at the top of St Andrew's tower looked peculiar: the holes were not always in the centre of the stones and these had obviously served another purpose in some other building. The pear-shaped holes looked remarkably like Roman lavatory seats. Clearly, in spite of official disinterest, a major investigation was called for at Bywell.

First of all, we had to find the position of the two suspected Roman bridge piers in order to give us a line on a possible Roman road. Our two expert divers, Rolfe Mitchinson and Bob Middlemass very quickly found the remains of the 1836 gunpowder explosions. Roman stones and large pieces of typical Roman concrete with its oversize aggregate, lay scattered on the river bed about a hundred yards upstream from the 1836 bridge. On the spacing, there should

THE LOST ROMAN ROADS OF THE TYNE VALLEY

A whole network has been found in the central Tyne Valley and some of these roads were quite easy to predict. Others have received vague mentions in old documents. The most important clue was the tradition, ignored by modern historians, that there had been a Roman bridge at Bywell.

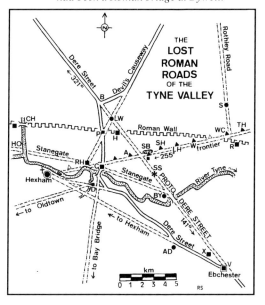

Proto Dere Street

V = Ebchester (Vindomora) Roman fort.
X = Suspected early Roman fort (NZ 083 571).
BY = Bywell, Roman bridge, Saxon church.
SS = Suspected signal station (NZ 032 647).
SB = Shildon Bog, lake in Roman times.
H = Halton Chesters (Onnum) Roman Wall fort.
LW = Little Whittington DMV, at least two Roman roads cross here.
B = Beukley, junction of Dere Street, Proto Dere Street and later Devil's Causeway.

Stanegate

BY = Bywell, Stanegate excavated here.
C = Corbridge, (Corstopitum). Roman town.
RH = Red House, early Roman fort lost under A69(T).
HO = Howford, ford across North Tyne to east of Warden Saxon church.

Original Devil's Causeway.

LW = Little Whittington.
P = Portgate.
RH = Red House.

Ebchester-Hexham Road

V = Ebchester.
AD = Apperley Dene.

Dilston network

D = Dilston, Roman crossroads, bridge, and suspected fortlet.

Frontier Road

TH = Turpin's Hill. Roman early frontier road, Roman fortlet, Roman well. Treasure found in fortlet 18th century.
WC = Whitchester, suspected early frontier fort on 255 line.
W = Welton Hall and Welton DMV, early frontier milefortlet?
LH = Laker Hall, early frontier milefortlet.
SH = Shildon Hill Celtic Hillfort, early frontier milefortlet?
SB = Shildon Bog (Roman lake), reservoir to Corstopitum? Roman frontier road deviates to south of lake, earthworks of milefortlet visible on Roman road to south of former lake.
A = Aydon, frontier milefortlet.

Rothley Road

S = Street Houses, much Roman stone lying in fields.

Roman Wall forts

CH = Chesters (Cilurnum).
H = Halton (Onnum).
R = Rudchester (Vindovala).

The tower of St Andrew's Saxon church at Bywell is built mostly of reused Roman stones. The latter seem to have been robbed from the Roman bridge as identical lewis-holed stones still lie on the river bed.

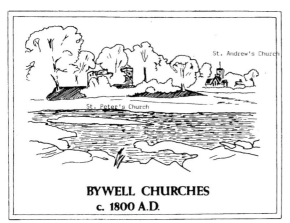

BYWELL CHURCHES
c. 1800 A.D.

Left: The Bywell Saxon Churches, St Andrew's in background, St Peter's in foreground.

Before extensive landscaping, St Peter's stood on a very Roman-looking platform. The fields around have been raised in height. Old records tell us that in 1750, an angler found a Roman silver cup in the Tyne near St Peter's; it was inscribed

"Desideri Vivas."

Officials say that this cup must have been washed down from Corbridge. The truth is more likely to be that there was a Roman fort right here in Bywell.

Right: During a burial in St Peter's churchyard in 1901, this fragment of a Roman altar was found six feet down in the graveyard which is situated on the suspected Roman fort platform. This stone was certainly not "washed down from Corbridge."Right alongside St Peter's church, an artificial-looking "canal" leaves the river and returns to it further upstream. At the upper confluence, the last remains of piles of a second Bywell dam lie in the river bed.

Left: An old woodcut of Bywell in 1834. This print shows the old Roman bridge-piers, front left, which were blown-up by gunpowder in 1836. Work started on the new Bywell bridge on the same day. Many ex-Roman stones are reused in the 1836 Bywell bridge. St Andrew's Saxon church is in the background. Below Bywell Castle is a mill-dam thought to have started life as a Roman navigation weir.

The modern Bywell Bridge. The Roman bridge was beyond this bridge, slightly further upstream. During low river levels many ex-Roman stones, surplus to the requirements for the new bridge, can be seen on the river bed downstream from piers "A" and "D". This view is upstream.

An old painting of the Roman piers at Bywell. This view is downstream.

A pier of the 1836 Bywell Bridge. The circular holes were drilled in 1940 when a German invasion was feared. The holes were for explosives and many bridges had one pier prepared for demolition to delay a German army. Chester-le-Street's 14th century bridge at the foot of Newbridge Bank also had the pier nearest Chester-le-Street prepared to take explosive charges. The holes can still be seen.

Lower.
Ex-Roman stones, complete with lewis holes, from the Bywell Roman bridge piers, blown-up by gunpowder in 1836, lie on the river bed below the 1836 "new" Bywell Bridge.

Once our divers had located the site of the Bywell Roman bridge, work started on the search for the Roman road system which had used the bridge. In this photograph, the unknown Roman road "Proto Dere Street" emerges from the ground in the Bywell Woods (NZ 048 623). The road is 6 metres wide, 1½ metres thick, heavily cambered, with deep side ditches and heavy rough kerbstones. Cobble sizes increase with depth.

Roman coins and pottery were taken from the excavated side-ditches.

After fallen trees and undergrowth were removed, a small Roman bridge for "Proto Dere Street" was excavated in the Bywell Woods. The "long lost Stanegate" Roman road to Corbridge was also found branching-off from this point.

have been a third pier near the north bank. This would have placed it on a rock shelf and easily accessible to stone robbers. The third Roman pier was probably the source of the Roman stones in St Andrew's Church.

While the divers were in the water, a peculiar incident occurred. It has been widely claimed that the Tyne is un-navigable above the Tidal limit at Wylam but up the centre of the river walked a gentleman in waders, towing a fairly large rowing boat across some shallows. He introduced himself as an eel-man and enquired of the divers, the state of his eel-traps in the deep pools. He had several hundredweight of eels on board his boat and he informed us that he was bound for Hexham to inspect more traps before returning to Wylam where a road tanker would take his cargo to a destination in Germany. The eel-man had never heard of the "experts" who said the upper Tyne was un-navigable, so he proceeded on his way and manned his oars when he regained deeper water. Had we just witnessed how the Romans transported their heavy cargoes?

From the Ordnance Survey map, it is obvious that the very straight stretch of Roman Dere Street which heads south-east across southern Northumberland towards Beukley (NY 983 707) on a heading of 141 degrees is bound for a destination other than Corbridge. The known Roman road however bends off towards Corbridge at Beukley but a projection of the 141 degree line crosses the Tyne exactly at our Roman bridge position at Bywell. Furthermore, a continuation of the same line goes right in through the front gate of the Ebchester Roman fort (NZ 104 555). These surprising observations could not be discarded as coincidences. Permission to investigate at Bywell was kindly given by the landowners and a trial trench was opened along the top of the cliff on the north bank of the river in line with the river-bed ruins of the Roman piers. The bridge must have crossed the river at a slight angle because we could find no trace of a road. It was obvious that we were close, because our two expert metal detectorists, Dr Irene Robinson, and Liz Robinson (of the BBC) scanned all the spoil coming out of the trench, and many Roman coins, missed by trowellers, were recovered. Without this detector-derived information, we may have lost heart and given up. As it happened, our failure to find the road on the cliff top was fortunate because I moved away from the river into the woods to a point where I thought the line of the road must have crossed a small stream. In thick scrub, a large fir tree had fallen and its up-ended roots grasped large stones. The disc of surface soil removed by the fallen tree revealed a cobbled surface. A new excavation commenced and this involved heavy work removing jungle-type undergrowth and fallen trees but it was well worth the effort. A junction of three Roman roads was uncovered. One was the expected 141 degree line; a second was the long lost "Stanegate," postulated east of Corbridge but never found until now, and a third road headed off towards the Bywell churches. The excavation produced dozens of Roman coins and sherds of Roman pottery and a bonus-find was an excellent culvert-type bridge which had crossed the tiny stream just to the east of the road junction (NZ 048 623). Archaeologists made the journey from Oxford to view the evidence and went away very excited with this new piece for the jig-saw puzzle.

The second road which proved to be part of the missing "Stanegate" left the junction on a heading of 287 degrees, exactly on track for Roman Corbridge. A compass course was followed on the 287 heading and the Clockey Burn was intercepted 900 yards to the west-north-west. Massive stone blocks lay in-situ in the bed of the burn at NZ 042 625. The detectorist was summoned and within minutes, found a Roman disc brooch between two of the stones. The same burn runs down to join the River Tyne just to the east of Bywell Castle. Before it reaches the river, it disappears into an underground channel and emerges from the Bywell cliffs via an arch which looks just like a miniature version of the discharge tunnel of Rome's main sewer, the *Cloaca Maxima*. *Cloaca* is Latin for "sewer." Is it a coincidence that Bywell's *cloaca* is called the "Clockey" Burn?

An aerial search of the newly-discovered Stanegate-line revealed a legionary-size temporary Roman camp straddling the road at NZ 001 639 in the parkland to the south of the Howden Dene country house. The Roman line subsequently joined Spoutwell Lane which heads exactly for the known section of Stanegate in the Corbridge Roman site.

The third road which left the Bywell excavation headed towards the churches where St Andrew's tower is built largely of Roman stones. The mound (now camouflaged by landscaping) on which St Peter's stands may well turn out to be the platform of a missing Roman fort.

Once we had an exact line on the Roman 141/321 degree road, now called "Proto Dere Street," we moved back to the cliff top and dug another trench some twenty yards to the west of our earlier failure. The cobbled surface and heavy foundation stones of a typical Roman road were exposed very quickly.

Proto Dere Street was followed both to the north and the south and a vast amount of information obtained. Further strange evidence was found in the river which seem to indicate that a possible Roman fort at Bywell may have been river-supplied by the ancestors of our eel-man.

Points of interest on Proto Dere Street

Alignment: 321/141 degrees

NZ 103 555	Ebchester Roman fort.
NZ 083 569	Suspected early Roman fort in angle between Dere Street and newly discovered Proto Dere Street.
NZ 083 579	Terraceway down hillside to south-east of Spring House.
NZ 078 585	Green road runs down hill from Hedley Grange.
NZ 068 597	Prominent *agger* in hedge line.
NZ 054 618	*Agger* through grounds of Stocksfield Hall.
NZ 051 619	Site of Bywell Roman bridge. Piers blown up 1836.
NZ 048 623	Junction of three Roman roads excavated, coins and pottery found.
NZ 032 648	Suspected Roman signal station in east corner of wood at spot height of 163 metres. Earthworks visible.
NZ 030 650	Causeway across linear quarry in strip wood.
NZ 020 658	Crop mark of Roman fortlet seen from air. Roman coins and pottery found while inspecting site on ground.
NZ 020 662	Crossing with suspected Roman frontier road (more of this later). Shildon Bog was a lake in Roman times and thought to have been a reservoir for Corbridge.
NZ 016 667	Roman road visible for 300 yards. Then passes along west edge of Fox Covert Plantation.
NZ 009 674	Suspected Roman culvert conducts stream under road.
NZ 003 683	Corner of fortlet projects from underneath field wall, directly below high tension power lines.
NY 999 684	Map of 1779 shows a road lined-up north-west/south-east, just clipping north east corner of Halton Chesters Roman Wall fort.
NY 991 695	Little Whittington DMV. Crossing with early line of Devil's Causeway. Stanegate at Vindolanda is also lined-up on this DMV. What else does it hide?
NY 983 707	Proto Dere Street joins known Dere Street at Beukley near Stagshaw BBC radio mast.

Ebchester to Hexham Roman road

The known Roman road "Dere Street" leaves Ebchester for Corbridge and for the first 3.7 miles (6 km), except for a very slight dog-leg is straight and approaches Apperley Dene on a heading of 297 degrees. At Apperley Dene there is a native British farm, at one time thought to be a Roman fortlet until its excavation some years ago. Just to the north-west of this Romano-British site, the Roman road leaves its 297 degree direction and makes a turn to the north after which it follows a winding and most un-Roman course to Corbridge. If one ignores this turn and places a ruler on the map on the 297 degree line, it will be seen that the extended line goes right through Hexham Abbey. Old antiquarians thought that Hexham had been a Roman town and there are hundreds of tons of re-used Roman stones in the abbey and other buildings but current archaeological opinions, without the slightest proof, declare these stones to have originated from the Roman fort at Corbridge.

In his Comprehensive Guide to Northumberland, W W Tomlinson reports on Hexham:

> *"Dr Bruce ascribed a Roman origin to Hexham. There is a large number of tooled stones that comprise the crypt beneath the Abbey Church with many others that have been found with inscriptions upon them built into old houses.*
>
> *A Mr Fairless discovered a connected chain of earthenware pipes, of manifest Roman workmanship, lying in-situ, and intended to all appearance for the conveyance of water.....two Roman altars of large size, of which only one bears an inscription; a sculptured slab, of Roman workmanship, discovered on 19th Sept. 1881 by Mr Charles Clement Hodges, when making an excavation under the floor of the slype, with a view to finding a crypt which was said to exist there. It represents a well armed cavalry soldier, with a standard in his hand and plumes on his helmet, riding over the crouching rude body of a repulsive-looking barbarian.*
>
> *In a sunken panel below is an inscription, rendered as follows by Dr Bruce: 'To the Gods the shades Flavinus, a horse soldier of the cavalry regiment of Petriana, standard-bearer of the troop of Candidus, twenty-five years of age, having served seven years in the army, is laid here."*

In Hodgson's *History of Northumberland*, Vol 4, he says: *"Below the floors of St Wilfrid's Church, a chapel was discovered built out of the ruins of a Roman town, Severus and Caracalla."*

The Ordnance Survey map of 1862 shows the graveyard in the north-west quadrant of Hexham Abbey grounds, named "Campey Hill." This is very suggestive of a Roman fort.

Now let us return to Apperley Dene (NZ 055 581) where the Roman road swings off towards Corbridge, obviously following a native track. Another road has continued straight ahead on a heading of 297 degrees and at NZ 051 584, a zig-zag containing hundreds of tons of stone descends to the Stocksfield Burn where a modern bridge carries a private road to Wheelbirks Farm. Older stone-cut abutments on a slightly different line can be seen under this bridge. On the north side, the farm road makes a zig-zag up the steep slope but the suspected Roman road short-circuits this zig-zag as a grass-covered angled terraceway.

Points of interest on the Ebchester to Hexham Roman road

Alignment: 297/117 degrees

NZ 104 555	Ebchester Roman fort.
NZ 085 564	Slight alteration of heading of Dere Street.
NZ 085 569	Suspected early Roman fort. Complete perimeter visible from air. Ditches visible at ground level. Two prominent gateways visible. Infilled Roman well intact, incorrectly labelled "coal-shaft" on 1850 OS map. Tithe Map calls this "Water Pit Field." Stream just to north-west of Wood House farm cottage has been used as Roman drain. Follow this to south-east corner of fort. Site is under threat from open-cast mining.
NZ 055 580	Apperley Dene native farmstead. Roman road junction here. Newly found road goes straight on to Hexham, known Dere Street bends away to Corbridge.
NZ 051 584	Zig-zag down to Stocksfield Burn. Hundreds of tons of stone visible.
NZ 049 584	Angled terrace-way short-cuts farm road hairpin bend.
NZ 037 590	A small stream is crossed by a ford just upstream from overhead high-tension cables and a buried gas pipeline. This pipeline is marked by the usual orange markers to assist helicopter inspections.
NZ 035 593	A small stream flows through a culvert but no modern track, road or path use this bridge.
NZ 029 595	In a small pasture just to the south of Gallaw Hill Farm, suspected Roman road foundation stones seem to have been dragged out of the ground by the farmer, who has then given up and left them.
NY 999 609	An angled terrace-way climbs up a steep slope in wood on north side of March Burn.
NY 968 627	Remains of a modern timber footbridge on same spot as an old stone abutment at crossing of Devil's Water.
NY 959 632	Cottage named "Five Gates." Other Roman roads in vicinity; crossing with "Forster's Roman road," (more of this later).
NY 935 642	Hexham Abbey on site of suspected Roman town, possibly lost Roman town of "Epiacum." Other contender for this identity is Bywell.

There are more Roman roads arriving at Hexham from other directions and these are under investigation.

New Discoveries By NAG At Hartburn And Bolam

Further discoveries which increasingly render our history books of the Roman period obsolete, are being uncovered by our active field-teams.

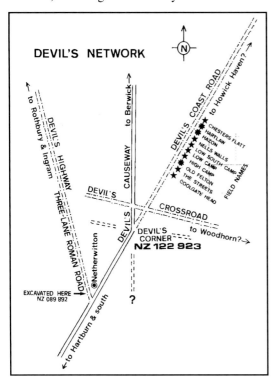

The newly discovered network of Roman roads in the Netherwitton area of Northumberland. Our society has called this Roman road system: "The Devil's Network." The so-called "bend" of the Devil's Causeway is now known to have been a junction of six Roman roads.

The three-lane hitherto unknown Roman road,The Devil's Highway, at Netherwitton. Famous historians such as Hodgson and Horsley reported such three-lane Roman roads in Northumberland and Durham. Jessie Mothersole also repeated their reports early in the 20th century. The central agger was for marching troops and the grass outer tracks for unshod animals. Roman cavalry horses and pack animals were seldom shod and if they had to move on hard surfaces, temporary shoes called hipposandals were fitted.

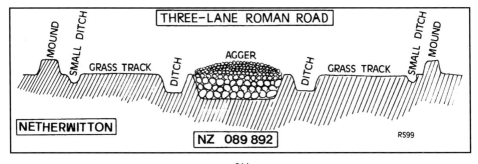

We have discovered that the so-called "bend of the Devil's Causeway" Roman road to the south-west of Longhorsley at map ref NZ 122 923, is not a bend at all but a junction of at least five, probably six or even more, Roman roads. The original Devil's Causeway carried on north-east to a suspected Roman harbour at Howick Haven. The road was traced initially by the field names along it: "Coolgate Head, The Streets, Old Felton DMV, High Camp, Low Camp, Low South Camp, Nell's Walls, Hazon DMV, Hartlaw DMV and Chesters Flatt." Fieldwork soon located most of the road.

Last year, once and for all, we have established the true line of the Devil's Causeway Roman road at Hartburn. This Roman road crossed the Hart Burn where the post-holes of the Roman bridge survive in the rock bed for all to see. The famous historian, the Rev J Hodgson who is buried in Hartburn churchyard, described these holes. His information was ignored by later historians.

Teams from our society dug four trenches on both sides of the river across the suspected line of the true road, about 250 metres downstream from the line marked on the OS maps. They uncovered the Devil's Causeway in all of them. The Ordnance Survey maps will have to be amended.

Until two weeks ago (early June 1999) the "missing" Roman fort or fortlet at Hartburn had not been located, but since that date we have found it. It is underneath the post-Saxon Hartburn St Andrew's Church.

A heavy tractor which was descending the public footpath to the south of Hartburn Church and the B6343 modern road, got stuck. Another tractor pulled it out and in doing so, stripped the turf from an immaculate length of hitherto unknown Roman road. This road is not part of the Devil's Causeway though there may be a link road for which we are searching.

Our teams just happened to be on hand working in Hartburn village when the tractor had its incident. As well as being efficient, archaeologists must be lucky! The newly-discovered Roman road negotiates the severe incline with a one-in-three gradient which angles down the steep hill to a minor stream. At the top, the road swings into the B6434 exactly opposite the south gate of the Hartburn Church. The road is only eight feet wide and would have been impossible for wheeled traffic. The surface is rammed gravel mixed with cobbles which are set on top of a bedding of huge river-polished stones. The kerbs survive in pristine condition on the down-slope side of the road but the uphill side has had a low retaining wall which has collapsed into the drainage ditch.

As well as the Roman-type kerbs, there are heavy foundations, and a cobble-plus-gravel surface. Another identification feature is the "mirror image" descent and climb to negotiate a ravine (to lessen the gradient from a suicidal one-in-two to a difficult one-in-three). The Roman surveyors pegged-out the directions for the Roman roads but the engineers seem to have been allowed to make deviations as long as they got back to the surveyed line. These deviations to cross ravines always went in the upstream direction. Henry Maclauchlan noticed this c1840 when he was inspecting the Fosse Way between Bath and Cirencester.

Incidentally, Maclauchlan also mentioned that Dere Street at Ebchester was a "three-

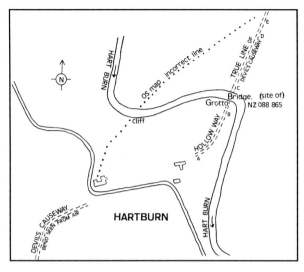

It was seen from our aircraft that the line of the Devil's Causeway as shown on the Ordnance Survey maps was incorrect. To the west of Hartburn village, the Roman road turned eastwards and lined up with the hollow-way down to the Grotto. The Rev Hodgson who was the rector at Hartburn from 1833 until his death in 1845 said that the Roman road crossed the Hart Burn at the rocky sill a few yards downstream from the Grotto, where post-holes for bridge timbers could be seen in the rock river bed. They are still there. The true line of the Devil's Causeway was excavated at five places, A,B,C,D, and E and an immaculate Roman road found in all five trenches. Our divers excavated the post-holes and took a Roman bronze votive pin from every hole. The Romans had placed these offerings in the holes before inserting the bridge timbers. The Rev Hodgson who is buried at the east end of Hartburn Churchyard was right.

The Grotto at Hartburn appears to be a natural cave which was converted into a chapel by Dr Sharpe who was the rector at Hartburn Church from 1749 to 1796. The archdeacon's hobby was folly building and his works can be seen at various places in the woods around Hartburn. However, because of the proximity of the cave to the Roman bridge, a Roman origin was suspected by us. Archdeacon Sharpe built an internal wall with a Gothic arch inside the cave and added a fireplace. The natural stone of the jambs of the entrance to the cave however are carved into imitation Roman-style huge ashlar blocks, along with Roman-style toolmarks. The niches above the cave's entrance once held statues of Adam and Eve, but it is more likely that they were cut for Cautes and Cautopates, the guardians of Roman Mithraic temples. These Roman Mithraic temples were all originally caves and only later became artificial buildings which simulated a dark cave. An underground passage leads from the cave entrance to the river and this probably served some function in the rites of the Roman army's secret Mithraic society which involved ordeals by fire and water. Similar niches for statues can be seen in other Roman locations.

upper: The square post-holes cut into the Hart Burn at Hartburn on the proven line of the Devil's Causeway Roman road.

lower; A close-up of the post-holes. In the summer, the water over the rock sill is only about one foot deep.

A drawing of the Hartburn Grotto. The circle of light in the cave's entrance represents a torch beam shining on the archdeacon's internal chapel wall.

THE GROTTO AT HARTBURN

THE CIRCLE IN THE CAVE ENTRANCE REPRESENTS A TORCH BEAM
SHINING ON ARCHDEACON SHARP'S INTERNAL WALL AND ARCH.   RS99

NZ 088 865

lane" type Roman road just as we found on our hitherto unknown road at Netherwitton which we have christened "The Devil's Highway." Maclauchlan said the Ebchester road had four ditches: a central paved *agger* flanked by deep drainage ditches and two grass tracks for unshod animals. These grass tracks had minor ditches on the outside, once again, just as we found at Netherwitton not to mention the upstream-pointing "mirror-images" to boot.

The "new" Hartburn Roman road can be followed visually in places and with probes elsewhere, all the way south to the Bolam Saxon Church of St Andrew's. We have long thought that this church stood on a Roman site and now we are sure. The church sits on a very good defensive east-west ridge and three suspected Roman roads arrive from the north-east, north (our Hartburn road) and the north-west. A prominent suspected Roman road running south from the church can be seen as a "bump" in the east-west cart-track to the south of the church, and in the meadow beyond, further to the south.

Investigations continue; it is amazing how all the St Andrew's churches seem to be on Roman sites - for example, Corbridge, also Bywell (where our society excavated a Roman road network; (see " *On the Trail of the Legions*"), and Hexham Abbey where part of Wifrid's first (Saxon) St Andrew's church survives as the crypt. This crypt is built entirely of reused Roman stones. We are sure that Hexham Abbey hides a Roman site and resistivity and other electronic methods seem to confirm this. We have yet to excavate several suspected Roman roads which converge on Hexham Abbey. An obvious one leaves the Roman Wall bridge at Chollerford and proceeds through Wall Village bound for "Old Bridge End" at Hexham. This road can be seen clearly in a paddock (NY 916 693) to the north-west of Wall Village. Roman bridges were seldom built for single roads and the French archaeologist Raymond Chevalier says: "Roman bridges usually had 'bird's foot patterns' of roads from both sides."

As a pilot, I was intrigued to hear from local residents how Bolam Church was almost destroyed by a German bomber in World War 2 during the night of 5th May 1942. This *Luftwaffe* aircraft was being pursued by a British fighter and was flying on a north-easterly heading. In an attempt to escape, the German pilot jettisoned four bombs. One landed and exploded in the front garden of Bolam rectory where the crater now forms a bowl-shaped depression in the lawn beside a walnut tree. The second bomb went through the lower wall of the Hedley Dent Chapel on the south side of Bolam Church but failed to explode. The third and fourth bombs landed north-east of the church in Windmill Field and the explosions formed craters one of which is now a duck pond. This pool is only a few yards from one of our suspected Roman roads. The bomb which had hit the church and was embedded in the floor was not noticed for 24 hours. St Andrew must have been looking after his church on that occasion.

The German bomber crashed at Longhorsley.

The Stanegate: further evidence

The Roman "Stanegate" has been mentioned several times so far, so this will be the next Roman road to be dealt with in detail. It has been widely held that this road was the Roman frontier across Britain prior to Hadrian's Wall being built. Excavations show however, that the Stanegate, unlike frontier roads in Germany and elsewhere, had neither a palisade nor a defensive ditch. The line of the road has been known for many years between Carlisle and Chollerford on the North Tyne; also an isolated piece in the vicinity of the Corbridge Roman fort. Many attempts have been made over the years to trace the missing section between the North Tyne and Corbridge. An extension east of Corbridge had been widely postulated but never discovered until recently. The speculated routes of this missing road went to all kinds of weird and wonderful places.

The first solid evidence was our lucky excavation at Bywell and the subsequent discovery of the line all the way to Corbridge. The following table covers this length after which we will progress to further hitherto unknown sections:

Points of interest on the Stanegate between Bywell and Corbridge, and beyond

Alignment: 287/107 degrees

NZ 048 623	Roman road junction in the Bywell Woods.
NZ 042 624	Paved ford in Clockey Burn, extremely large stones still *in situ*. Roman disc brooch found between stones.
NZ 029 629	Crossing of Stoneyverge Burn east side of A68. Very large stones in stream bank. Roman crossbow brooch and scatter of Roman coins found.
NZ 023 631	Roman road crosses narrow neck of wood east of High Barnes Farm.
NZ 001 639	Legionary-size temporary camp seen from aircraft in park to south of Howden Dene country house. This camp straddles Stanegate. Gallow Hill is contained inside rounded corner of prominent earthwork. Further earthworks just to west. Roman brooch found. Cultivation terraces in steep wood to south of camp.
NY 997 640	Stanegate joins modern private road.
NY 994 641	Stanegate under private road joins Spoutwell Lane which is lined up exactly on Corbridge Roman site.
NY 993 640	Findspot of famous "Corbridge Lanx" (large silver plate).
NY 979 648	Known crossing of Stanegate over Cor Burn just to west of Corbridge Roman town.
NY 970 651	Last known position (until now) of Stanegate as it passed early Roman fort of Red House which predated Corstopitum.
NY 964 649	Suspected remains of early Roman bridge south-west of Red House site and west of Prior Thorns. Branch *agger* runs from prominent Stanegate at foot of slope, down to River Tyne. Main Stanegate, easy to see, continues west and climbs slope towards A69(T). Route is then to Anick, St John Lee and Howford.

Before the search is described, just a few more words in general about the Stanegate: observations from aircraft show that it differs from most Roman roads in that it does actually select easy gradients in places. At Boothby, a kilometre south of Lanercost Priory and just to the north-west of Naworth Castle, at NY 553 627, the road bends back on itself as it runs south up a gully into West Park. What unusual behaviour for a supposed Roman frontier! About a mile south of Roman Wall Turret 52A, it does the same thing again at NY 575 633, this time deviating to the north. The Roman Military Way, the service road immediately behind Hadrian's Wall, was not built until many years after the Wall's completion, so I am inclined to believe that the Stanegate served as the supply road for the Wall and was one of the very few Roman roads which the famous ox-wagons could actually have negotiated. The very straight length of Stanegate to the west of Vindolanda at NY 765 663 is lined up on the spot height of 279 metres on the crag to the east of the fort and also on Little Whittington DMV, thirteen miles

The "long lost" Stanegate Roman road, now found, runs along the hillside (NY 904 665) to the north of the Fourstones paper mill.

to the east at NY 991 695, north-east of Portgate. The actual road does not follow the sighting line until it gets back to Newbrough (NY 873 678) and Fourstones (NY 893 680).

An obvious Roman road leaves Fourstones and routes to the north of Warden Hill which overlooks the junction of the two Tynes and is capped by a large Iron Age hillfort (NY 903 678). The road divides and the northern branch goes to the Roman fort and bridge at Chesters (Cilurnum) near Chollerford and the other branch was shown by E Sockett to transit the north side of Warden Hill and then turn south parallel to the North Tyne.

A little research however tells us more. At Fourstones, according to Hodgson in his *History of Northumberland*, Vol 4, "Carel Street" (Carlisle Street), [another name for the Roman road in this area] divided even before the fork on Warden Hill. Thus we have two divisions of the road very close together. At Fourstones, the first division took place. Hodgson was convinced that the southern branch went around the south of Warden Hill bound for Howford on the North Tyne very close to the confluence of the two rivers. Hodgson was absolutely correct. The Roman road is in perfect condition at NY 902 668 where it is a terraceway along the hillside north of Warden paper mill and some hundred yards east of the railway line and the public road. Park your car at the level-crossing beside the paper mill and the Roman road will be seen on the hillside. A couple of hundred yards further south, the Roman road is visible again but ends abruptly where the farmer has taken it out leaving about 250 tons of stone in a pile in the field. Past generations of farmers have also dumped stone into the railway cutting. The road heads for the Saxon church at Warden. As has been mentioned previously, this church contains reused Roman stones and although the usual excuses have been used to explain the stones away (they were "stolen from Chollerford," or were "washed down the river"), it is most likely that they came from a Roman building which was associated with the river crossing at Howford. In the west bank of the River North Tyne at NY 917 663, the Roman road surface is perfectly preserved and runs right down to the water's edge. Very large stones lie in the river and the rapids thus formed are an easy marker for the Roman ford which continued in use right through the medieval period and later.

According to the *Newcastle Journal* of May 25th, 1927, an interesting Roman stone was found here:

> "A well-known local gentleman who was angling on the north side of the river, immediately opposite the Saxon Church of St Michael and All Angels, observed a stone some 3 feet long, which had long been lying there, but which has recently been turned over. On examination it was found that this stone had been a Roman altar...
>
> The find gives added interest to this historic part of Northumberland, for it was made close to the adjoining Saxon village of Warden, which has now disappeared, but which stood in the fork of the meeting of the rivers, and where many Roman stones have already been discovered."

The Saxon village of Warden was probably placed on the promontory between the two Tynes because in addition to the ex-Roman ford over the North Tyne at Howford, the South Tyne was also easily fordable at the confluence of the rivers. The North Tyne is the dominant river and when it floods, it retards the South Tyne which has dropped a shingle bar over its mouth. This ridge of stones is easily fordable thus the Saxons and the Romans before them, had fords in close proximity over both the River Tynes.

On the east side of the River North Tyne, exactly in line with the Roman ford, during the construction of the North British Railway, several cists (burials) of Bronze Age date were discovered but according to a letter published in the *Hexham Herald* in 1877, a *"patera"* was found and this was: "exactly similar in shape and size to those found in the *sarcophagus* discovered at Harpenden in Hertfordshire in 1844." (the Harpenden *patera* was samian DR33).

In the 1960's, Professor St Joseph of Cambridge University took aerial photographs (Numbers D001, D002 and D003) which indicated a Roman marching camp at the same position on the east side of the river at Howford.

Once again, I refer to Hodgson in his *History of Northumberland* Vol 4, where he continues with his prediction of the route of Carel Street (Carlisle Street, also known as the "Stanegate"), towards Corbridge and Newcastle.

> "...and that it passed from Howford by Acomb and Anick to Corbridge, and thence by the Ald-he-way to Newcastle. It is still used each way from Howford as a drift-way for the fairs of Stagshaw-bank, and partly as a cart-way; and at Wardon is still known by the name of the Warded-road. I have also heard it said, or rather conjectured, that it went from Howford, under Earn's-how banks, by Hermitage to Corbridge."

If we stand on the old North British Railway embankment at Howford and look east in the direction indicated by Hodgson, a prominent feature straight ahead is the spire of the Church of St John Lee (NY 933 656) on the escarpment known as Eagle's Mount, one mile distant.

A very straight road leaves the church and is lined up exactly on Corbridge and Anick, as mentioned by Hodgson. Although the church is not Saxon, it had a Saxon predecessor, and just inside the door of the church is a Roman altar which was used as a font in the Saxon church. There is another Roman altar in the garden of the rectory.

A close inspection of the whole site shows that the graveyard and adjacent field are on a square promontory with rounded corners. It is a possible Roman site and adjacent to an almost certain Roman road.

The straight road carries on east-south-east for two thirds of a mile and passes a significant place-name, Peasley Gates on the way, and after West Oakwood continues in the same direction as a prominent stone-filled hedge-line. At Anick, a public footpath crosses this line and the construction of the Roman road can easily be identified at NY 953 653, just south of Anick Grange Farm. A typical Roman culvert passes under the Roman road which is a hedge-line at this point. Here, the observer is in sight of Red House and Corbridge and the Roman road is on the correct alignment. We now have the "long lost Stanegate" all the way from Carlisle to Bywell.

Most of the Roman roads in Northumberland and Durham are constructed in a similar manner to this Roman road across Wheeldale Moor. The surface layer of rammed gravel has eroded away leaving a layer of larger stones uncovered. The next layer down is usually, but not always, of very heavy boulders. Note that this Roman road, like many others, is not perfectly straight.

Checklist on Stanegate between Fourstones and Corbridge

Alignment between Fourstones and Howford: various

NY	884 679	Fork of Roman roads at Fourstones. Northern branch further divides at NY 894 683 with one branch going to Chesters Roman fort and the other across the north of Warden Hill before turning south near river.
NY	900 673	Southern branch passes springs at this position.
NY	902 668	*Agger* very prominent as hedge-line along hillside to east of railway line and public road.
NY	904 666	*Agger* very prominent over field. Farmer busy removing road at time of writing. Pile of several hundred tons of stone in field above railway cutting.
NY	906 664	Junction with another possible Roman road coming down from Warden Hill.
NY	900 665	Unrecorded suspected Neolithic long barrow to west of Warden's massive earthwork *motte* (NY 912 665).
NY	914 665	Warden Saxon church contains many reused Roman stones. Saxon village (Howford) used to occupy promontory to south-east of church. Saxon word *ho/hoh,* (pronounced "how") means "promontory."
NY	917 664	Surface of Roman road descends west bank of North Tyne to ford. Many large stones in river. Roman altar found by angler, 1927.
NY	917 660	Although not on the "Stanegate" a shingle bar over the mouth of the South Tyne should be taken into consideration in the study of Roman roads in the area.
NY	921 665	Roman *patera* found, 1877. Marching camp found by Cambridge University, c1960.
NY	933 656	St John Lee Church on site of Saxon church. Roman altar in church. Possible Roman fort earthworks
NY	936 656	Place-name "Peasley Gates" on straight road from St John Lee church aligned 100 degrees on Corbridge Roman site. Stone-filled hedge-lines continue on same alignment.
NY	953 653	Culvert under suspected Roman road beside public footpath south of Anick Grange Farm
NY	970 651	Site of Red House Roman fort (pre-dated Corstopitum).
NY	979 648	Known crossing of Stanegate over Cor Burn.

The Stanegate is now known all the way from Carlisle to Bywell. In river flood conditions, the Romans have travelled via the bridge across the North Tyne at Chesters and at low water levels they have taken the short-cut across the ford at Howford.

Stanegate: The last missing section

The only major unknown section of the Stanegate is now between Bywell and Newcastle upon Tyne. It would be good practice for readers to use the search for this as an archaeological exercise and put the last piece of information into place.

To the east of Bywell, it looks as if the Stanegate runs east along the hillside above the north bank of the River Tyne, and heads for Ovingham (NZ 085 637) where there is yet another Saxon church with reused Roman stones in its tower. Between Bywell and Ovingham, the suspected Stanegate can be seen as an *agger* at NZ 053 623, a public footpath at NZ 060 627 and a possible Roman culvert-type bridge over a small stream at the south-east end of a strip wood at NZ 066 634, south of Ovington village.

To the east of Ovingham, a Roman period farmstead is visible from the air at NZ 095 646 in a field aptly called "Camp Hill." There are ancient bell-pits in Horsley Wood (NZ 104 650) and in the 1750s General Wade had trouble dragging his cannons along an old riverside road to the east of Wylam where later the famous George Stephenson was born. The significant name "Street Houses" occurs on this line. These clues may assist with the positive identification of the last missing piece of the elusive Stanegate.

The 255 degree suspected Frontier Road

Let us return to Turpin's Hill (NZ 108 685) just north of the Wall, where the hoard of Roman coins was found in 1766. JC Hodgson said that six *castella* were placed equally apart in a line along the Heddon ridge. I managed to locate four of these sites from the air, and when I came to plot them on the map, I was astonished to find that they were all 1,620 yards apart - a Roman mile. Not only was this a Roman road - it was some sort of defence line, or even part of a frontier system.

Before Hadrian built the Roman Wall in AD 122-26, there must have been an earlier frontier and until now it was thought that this was the Stanegate Roman road. Because of the road's lack of a palisade and defensive ditch, its meandering character and poor selection of a military line, this is unlikely. Hodgson's *castella* are on a line which if extended, would intercept the east coast at St Mary's Island and the west coast at Maryport. The line crosses the Roman Wall at NZ 086 681, just south of Albemarle Barracks, the former RAF Ouston aerodrome.

I plotted search areas across Northumberland at Roman mile intervals. Most of the sites appeared within a few yards of the predicted positions. Quite a few were located at significant places, the names of which crop up time and time again in our searches for the Romans. One was the Red House Roman fort (NY 970 651) which pre-dated Corstopitum. Another is the site of Hexham Abbey and a third, the Roman fort of Wreay .

The suspected early defence line will be discussed in greater detail in Chapter 10.

The network south of Corbridge

The main Roman road from Edinburgh to York is known by its Saxon name "Dere Street" because its Latin name is lost. The places it passed however are recorded in the *Antonine Itinerary* so its course is fairly certain.

On its way south, it crossed the Roman bridge at Corbridge, and then headed south-east to Broomhaugh (NZ 018 615), Ebchester, Lanchester, Binchester, Piercebridge, Catterick, Aldborough, and York.

Forster's Road

What is not so well known is that another Roman road left the southern end of the Roman bridge at Corbridge and headed 1 mile due south to Dilston where it made a turn to the west. Robert Forster says in his *History of Corbridge*, (1881):

> *"Another Roman road commenced at the south end of the bridge, and proceeded in a straight line direct south, passing near the east side of the old toll bar at Dilston, continuing further south for about three hundred yards, then at right angles westward and onward through Hexhamshire, passing Alston on the north and still westward towards Penrith. When the new road was made in 1829, betwix Corbridge bridge and Dilston, this ancient road was unexpectedly come upon and cut through, and was found to consist mostly of paving stones firmly bedded and united together; the discovery attracted at the time considerable attention."*

Forster makes a further reference to the road:

> *"Besides the grand Roman way which proceeds from Dover in Kent and crossed the Tyne here (Corbridge), there was another military road which passed from this place south-west through Dilston Park, over Hexham Fell to Old Town in Allendale, and meets with the Maiden Way at Whitley Castle."*

Eric Birley in his *Corbridge Roman Station*, has this to say:

> *"Down Dere Street from the north came many a Scottish army, such as that of King David 1, which stayed at Corbridge for a time in 1138; and it was the Roman road system, still in use for all its ruinous state, that led the army of Henry VI's Queen Margaret to its disastrous defeat at Hexham, by the side of the branch-road to Whitley Castle, in 1464."*

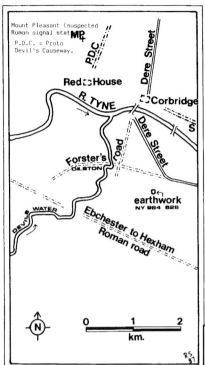

The Roman road network around Corbridge.

Corbridge and Dilston Roman road network.

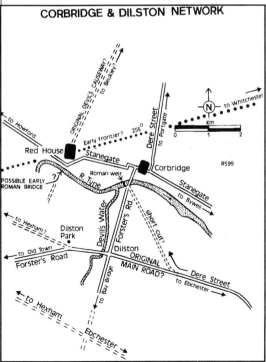

Forster's Roman road at Dilston Park.

The Roman road network around Corbridge as described by Horsley in his Britannia Romana of 1753.

Note that the Roman road south from the Roman bridge at Corstopitum makes a right-angled turn from south-west to south-east at Dilston. This is not the way modern maps mark it. Horsley was right but he missed the other two arms of the Dilston crossroads, one of which went west by Hexham and then to Alione, and the other south to Bay Bridge.

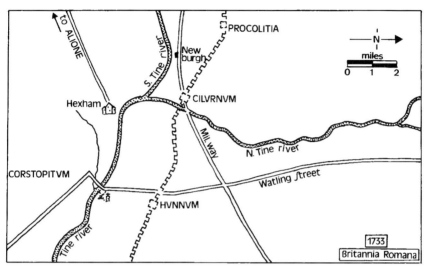

A temporary bridge built by Boy Scouts at Dilston. The construction of this bridge closely resembles the techniques used by the Roman army for campaign assault bridges. The Roman bridges were of course much larger.

An eagle carved into a stone in the north face of the tower of St Andrew's Church, Corbridge. Corbridge was a huge Roman town and a Roman fort is likely to be underneath St Andrew's Church. When the author, looking for reused Roman stones in the Saxon church, spotted this eagle, local historians said that the rain had washed the stone into this shape. Professor Richard Bailey, using builders' ladders, inspected the stone and declared the eagle to be of Saxon origin and on the strength of this, re-dated the church.

Corstopitum is a huge Roman settlement. It is far larger than our establishment anticipated. A legionary-sized temporary camp was found from our aircraft on Gallows Hill to the south of Howden Dene House which is well to the east of modern Corbridge. The long-lost Stanegate Roman road also passes this camp before following the line of Spoutwell Lane into modern Corbridge. A possible early Roman fort is often visible as parch marks on the flat-topped north-eastern corner of the English Heritage Roman site to the west of the town. The early Roman fort and bath-house at Red House one mile west of the town predate Corstopitum. We suspect the remains of an early Roman bridge south-west of Red House one mile upstream from the known Corstopitum Roman bridge. There is also a recently discovered fairly intact Roman weir about fifty yards upstream from the site of the known Roman bridge at Corstopitum. Fryer's map shows an old canal by-passing this dam. This was the clue that led our divers to the discovery of the weir which is a solid structure right across the river and in no way can be classified as a bridge. It is also too expensive to have been a "fish-trap." The stonework of the weir is most definitely Roman, some of the stones having both lewis holes and opus revinctum cramp holes.

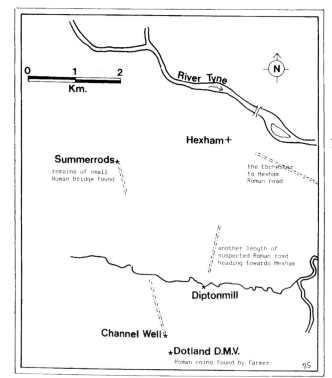

The Roman road network to the south of Hexham.

Dilston (NY 975 635) is a small hamlet on the modern A695 road between Corbridge and Hexham but it is a complex little place. A hall is built on the site of a medieval castle and a later castle survives in a ruinous state close by. There is also a medieval chapel with a Roman gravestone built into the east wall and a stone with a lewis-hole in the top of the tower, a watermill, two farms, the site of an old toll-bar and a disused medieval road. This hamlet presented several problems which had to be solved before we could concentrate on the search for Roman roads. There were obvious reused Roman stones in the Dilston watermill but records show that these were taken from the ruins of the Corbridge Roman bridge c1810 and used in the construction of the new mill-race.

The main problem was to find the Roman crossing point of the Devil's Water. About two hundred yards upstream from the A695 modern bridge, a ruinous medieval bridge pier stands close to the water-mill. Hodgson in his *History of Northumberland* says: "the bridge had ribbed arches." The springers of these can be seen on the ruined pier. The situation was confused by Frank Graham's *Bridges of Northumberland and Durham* (1975), which shows a drawing by Carmichael c1820. In this drawing, the artist depicts a bridge with vertical piers and a flat wooden superstructure. Graham took this to mean that the same bridge had been reconstructed but a little research solved the problem. The six inch OS first edition map shows that the flat-topped bridge was several yards further upstream from the medieval bridge . Hodgson tells us that it was an aqueduct which carried water from the water-mill to an hydraulic threshing machine at the farm on the opposite bank. A close inspection of old woodcuts of this aqueduct show water dripping from the horizontal superstructure.

We still had to find the Roman crossing, but suspected Roman bridge-stones were found in the bed of the river downstream from the medieval pier. One stone had a channel for a tie-bar, very similar to the stones in the Chollerford Roman bridge abutment. An aerial search located shadow marks of an earthwork on the hillock just to the south of Dilston Farm (NY 976 634) and this looks like a Roman fortlet. The aerial search also showed that a branch of Dere Street had continued due west to Dilston from the bend where the known road turned towards the Corbridge Roman bridge. Another unidentified suspected fortlet or signal station was observed close by this link-road at NY 985 629, in the field above a bungalow with a red roof. The earthwork has a single gate in the north side whereas native RB sites had their gates on the east. This site is in full view of the Corbridge Roman fort and could be a repeater signal station to relay messages to the Wall system which is out of sight of the Corbridge fort.

We now have an unknown Roman road heading for Dilston from the east. It is likely that Forster's right-angled turn of a Roman road at Dilston was actually a Roman crossroads with two arms not visible in Forster's day. The link with Dere Street is the third arm. A fourth arm went due south and I quote from the *Proceedings of the Society of Antiquaries of Newcastle upon Tyne*, Vol 6, c1839:

> *"They would travel along the ancient Roman road from Corbridge to Stanhope still partly in use which is mentioned in ancient documents and which crosses the valley of the Derwent at Bay Bridge, a mile west from Blanchland."*

This leaves only the westbound arm of the Roman crossroads on the west side of the Devil's Water at Dilston Mill. Forster already mentioned it passing Dilston Park (NY 968 635), and a very straight farm track runs from Dilston Mill to this position. The suspected Roman road gets a mention by Henry Maclauchlan in his *Survey of the Watling Street*, 1852, when he quotes the evidence of Thomas Harle, a drainer, for the existence of an ancient road which ran south-westwards from Corstopitum crossing the Devil's Water at Dilston Mill and running onwards for about sixty yards on the south side of Park South Farm, and thence by a bend towards the wood.

There is a double hedge-line in exactly this position and a central *agger* is crammed with large stones. The bend is still there and the road heads for "Five Gates Cottage," mentioned previously in connection with the Roman road from Ebchester direct to Hexham.

The road from Dilston to the west is surely the long lost Roman road to Old Town in Allendale, mentioned by all the old antiquarians but ignored by present-day students.

Checklist for network south of Corbridge

North to South road from Corbridge Roman bridge

NY 980 647	South end of Corbridge Roman bridge (abutment can be seen in river at low water conditions).
NY 977 635	Site of Dilston toll-bar.
NY 976 634	Suspected Roman crossroads beside possible fortlet on hillock to south of Dilston Farm.
NY 974 628	Suspected Roman road joins modern B6307.
NY 955 555	Suspected Roman road through Slaley Forest.
NY 950 518	Pennypie House, on line of suspected Roman road.
NY 959 499	Bay Bridge. Reports of remains of old bridge.

Westward extension of Dere Street

NY 987 633	Dere Street forks. One branch goes to Corbridge Roman bridge. The other continues westwards to Dilston.
NY 976634	Crossroads (invisible at ground level) beside hillock and suspected fortlet.
NY 975635	Suspected site of Roman bridge across Devil's Water.
NY 970 635	Roman road under straight cart track to Dilston Park.
NY 968 635	Dilston Park Farm. Roman road just to south.
NY 965 633	*Agger* up strip wood. Many large stones.
NY 959 632	Five Gates Cottage.
NY 930 610	Diptonmill. Natural rock ford 150 yards upstream of public house and modern road bridge.
NY 814 582	Supposed site of Roman fort at Old Town reported by many antiquarians but now mostly disregarded. Searches should continue.
NY 745 515	Suspected Roman road underneath modern A688.
NY 699 493	Roman bridge abutment, now high and dry in west bank of South Tyne, directly opposite Underbank Farm. To east of Underbank Farm, Roman road can be seen zig-zagging up steep slope. Inscribed Roman stones in byres of Underbank Farm. Whitley Castle Roman fort just to west.

The Roman glissage in Salters' Nick on Shaftoe Crags.

There is a Roman quarry at the top of the glissage on the north side of the road. There are further Roman roads in the area. Just north-west of Bolam West Houses, on the west side of the main road, down the west side of the triangular "North Plantation" is an excellent example of a three-lane Roman road. Further north, (NZ 059 832), another

Roman road crosses the modern B road proceeding from Bickerton, crossing the Devil's Causeway (NZ 073 835), and heads towards our above-mentioned possible "Hecate signpost," NZ 047 828.

A branch of the Devil's Causeway Roman road led to Brinkburn Priory. Old records report the remains of a Roman bridge. Modern archaeologists chose to challenge these reports and an expedition hoping to find nothing succeeded. Our own team however found the Roman road angling down the steep cliff-like river bank below Brinkheugh Farm. We successfully excavated the Roman road in two places. We also found the remains of the base of a central bridge-pier in the middle of the Coquet. We also located the northern abutment of the Roman bridge. The Roman road up the north bank of the Coquet forms a mirror-image of the angled descent down the south bank - a typical Roman surveyors' trick. On the high ground to the east of Brinkburn Priory, the agger of the Roman road can be seen heading north. Over the Coquet to the west of the Priory, our aerial photograph shows a mound right centre, believed to be a Roman fort platform, later covered with medieval rig and furrow strip farming. Across the loop of the river is a suspected Roman canal. This is said to have been a monastic fish trap but thousands of tons of soil have been removed and obviously used to construct the mound right centre.Up and downstream other loops of the Coquet have similarly been short-circuited. It looks as if Roman rivercraft were navigating the Coquet at least as far as Holystone.

In Chapter 8, a Roman *glissage* (quarry-slide) in County Durham near Finchale Priory was described. We have another one in Northumberland at Salters' Nick on the Shaftoe Crags. Many more hitherto undiscovered ones are likely. Several are suspected in the Lake District and information has been passed to the local societies there.

There has been a long tradition of a Roman road branching-off the Devil's Causeway to the south of Brinkheugh, crossing the Coquet by a bridge below Brinkheugh Farm to the area just east of Brinkburn Abbey and Brinkburn Mill. For some reason, in 1989, a university Ph.D student decided to prove that there was no such Roman road in the vicinity of Brinkburn. Hoping to find nothing, he succeeded. His trenches must have been in the wrong place.

The rocky outcrop to the west of Bolam West Houses in Northumberland has long been known to have had Celtic settlements on its higher points. Now we have found that it is criss-crossed with hitherto unknown Roman roads in addition to the known Devil's Causeway which passes by the Neolithic burial mounds just to the west of Bolam West Houses. A curious ravine called "Salters' Nick" at the west end of the Crag is now known to have been a Roman quarry glissage, and from the base of this ramp, a grass track, after excavation in several places, was shown to be a Roman road in first class condition. In this photograph, the author is walking along the Roman road away from the camera in a north-westerly direction. Another Roman road coming from the direction of the South Middleton DMV, passing Middleton South Farm, joins the above Roman road just to the south of a square standing stone, which has been carved on three sides. Quite often, Roman crossroads consisted of two staggered T-junctions rather than an "X-type." It is thought that this may have been because the Roman goddess of crossroads, "Hecate" had three faces and could watch three lanes but not four. Perhaps the standing stone on its three well-worn carved surfaces, carried the three faces of this goddess.

A section across a Roman road angled down the steep southern bank of the Coquet below Brinkheugh Farm. Excavated at NZ 118 984.

The remains of the Roman bridge abutment in the north bank of the Coquet a short distance downstream from Brinkburn Priory. This feature has since been covered over with spoil dumped from a farm track.

At the Roman Wall fort and town of Chesters (Cilurnum) near Chollerford, the Roman vicus lies mostly to the south of the fort. South of the Vallum which ran into the south ditch of the fort from the river bank is a Roman graveyard. The Vallum must have been infilled by the Romans themselves as there are several graves along the line of the Vallum ditch. These show as circles of random rubble (crazy paving). Further south at a bend of the river are two larger graves. These once held gravestones which are now in the Newcastle University Museum after being rescued from Alnwick Castle. The original findspot had been forgotten. The author recognised the bend of the river from this old woodcut and was therefore able to inform the university of the original location of the grave markers.

Upper: A Roman road from Whitley Castle heads east and climbs the hill to the east of Underbank Farm via a zig-zag.

Lower: West of Underbank Farm, the ruins of a Roman bridge lie on the west side of an old and now dry former course of the River South Tyne.

It is now time to leave the unfinished work of the discovery of lost Roman roads and look closely at the northern Roman frontier system which fortunately for us in Chester-le-Street is within easy reach. The frontier *limes* is of far greater extent than hitherto imagined. Some of the new evidence is a grid of parallel patrol roads which extend all the way north from central County Durham to beyond the modern Scottish border. Some of the east-west defence-in-depth frontier patrol roads are actually south of Chester-le-Street. The Frontier *Limes* will be discussed in greater detail in the next chapter.

Chapter 10
Roman Frontiers

"Britaniam petit in qua multa correxit, muramque per octoginta milia passuum primus duxit, qui barbaros Romanosque divideret." "He went to Britain where he set many things right and was the first to build an eighty mile wall to separate the Romans and barbarians."

Spartianus *(from his Biography of Hadrian).*

Because Chester-le-Street was a staging post on the approaches to the various military frontiers across Northumberland, students should have an understanding of the Roman defence zone. Much Roman military activity has been misunderstood by scholars for many years but new evidence (found by our Chester-le-Street based team) is clarifying the picture.

The conception of a scientific frontier was foreign to the government of the Roman Republic which preceded the Roman Empire. The Republic constantly extended its territory and sphere of influence and it got a bit out of hand.

With the advent of Augustus to power, all was changed. For the first time, it was recognised that a consistent frontier policy must be followed, and Tacitus tells us that one of Augustus' greatest achievements was that of confining the Empire within the limits of sea, ocean and distant rivers. To this could be added deserts. In his final conception, the Rhine and Danube formed the northern frontier (more or less) and it is here that we first meet with the earliest use of the term *"limes,"* which was in time, to describe a frontier, after a gradual change from the original meaning of a "military road" such as those the Romans constructed into newly conquered territories. These roads were intended to render the communications of an occupation force easy and secure.

In the later Trajanic period, we find the word *"limes"* used in the sense of "frontier." Thus a grid of frontier tracks developed into a clearly defined barrier with a network of roads behind it and a few more extending into "no-man's-land."

Claudius had withdrawn three legions from the right bank of the Rhine for his conquest of Britain, but a strip of land was still held on the "enemy" side of the river and no encroachment on this was permitted to the German tribes.

In Britain thirty-five years later, the beginnings of frontier defences were seen. Agricola, the Governor of Britain, reduced to submission a number of tribes hitherto independent of Rome. Tacitus tells us that at the close of Agricola's second campaign, he secured the conquered districts by a line of *praesidia* and *castella*. This line may have approximated to the line of the later Wall which would be built between the Tyne and Solway some forty years on.

Roman frontiers in the late Third Century. The Roman frontiers in Britain were quite short compared to others in the Roman Empire. This diagram shows a Roman frontier which stretched all the way from the North Sea to the Black Sea. It was however, mostly a multiple timber fence behind a ditch, and where possible, ran along the south bank of the major rivers, Rhine and Danube. Other defence lines which, in the absence of rivers, used deserts as natural barriers, ran down through Syria, and another stretched all the way from the Atlantic to Egypt.

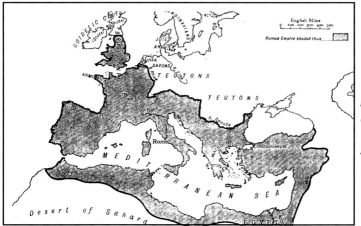

In AD81, Agricola reached the estuaries of the Forth and Clyde and here again, a line of *praesidia* was established. After Agricola's armies were withdrawn from Caledonia to provide reinforcements for a war in the Balkans, some of his strategic positions would be used again sixty years later when Antoninus Pius erected a rampart between the Forth and Clyde cAD143.

Agricola had depended on seaborne supplies, so his fortified bases must have been located on waterways. The Rivers Carron and Kelvin were probably his supply routes from the Forth and the Clyde. During his advance north, he also established the first of four forts at Newstead on the Tweed, and no doubt this was river supplied. During excavations, the steering-oar of a Roman barge and a boathook were found here.

Trajan reverted to a policy of expansion, but he lavished time and money on roads along the frontier lines. The most famous of these was that which connected the Rhine frontier with that of the Danube. He also constructed a network of military roads in North Africa.

With the reign of Hadrian, there was a distinct change of policy with regard to frontiers. Not only was expansion halted; a systematic policy of erecting barriers around the Empire's boundaries was adopted. Palisades of split oak trunks, nine feet high plus deep ditches were his favourite boundary markers.

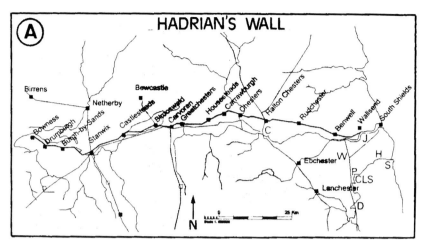

A. Map of Hadrian's Wall and approaches.

S   =   Sunderland, suspected Roman port.

H   =   Hylton (dam), remains found recently.

CLS =   Chester-le-Street, Roman supply base.

P   =   Picktree, (Roman site seen from the air).

W   =   Wrekenton, (Roman site seen from the air).

D   =   Durham, various Roman sites.

J   =   Jarrow, suspected Roman port.

C   =   Corbridge,(Roman jetty and navigation weir found).Author Nick Higham of Manchester Univeristy in his latest book has marked Corbridge as an inland Roman port. Chester-le-Street Roman site is now receiving similar recognition.

B. Hadrian's Wall was not the first Roman frontier across Britain but it was the most complex and least understood one. It faced both north and south and this has caused utter confusion among non-military archaeologists. The north-facing Wall and

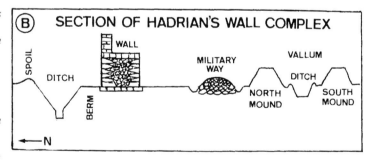

south-facing Vallum (Latin for "Wall") were built about the same time.The proof of this is that the Vallum makes deviations around some Wall-forts, but other late additional forts, obviously afterthoughts or changes of plan, sit on top of levelled Vallum mounds and an infilled Vallum ditch.

The Romans said that a wall less than seventy feet high could not be defended properly. It was therefore expected that the fifteen-feet-high Hadrian's Wall could be breached. Hundreds of Picts piling their bodies against the Wall would have made a human mound over which thousands of tribesmen could have surmounted the barrier.

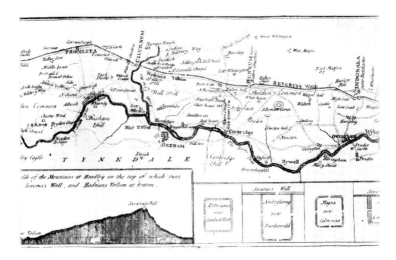

The central sector of Hadrian's Wall as it was seen in the antiquarian John Horsley's time (1733). It was thought in those days that Emperor Severus had built the Wall and Hadrian the Vallum. Although Severus later rebuilt the Wall, we now know that Hadrian built the whole complex of Wall and Vallum.

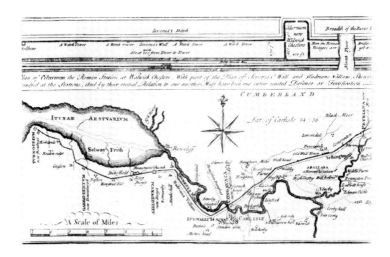

The western sector of the Roman Wall as seen by antiquarians of the 18th century. In some cases these old antiquarians were right while modern scholars have misread the ground and made mistakes. A glaring example is at Chesters (Cilurnum) near Chollerford.

This old map shows the Vallum running into the south ditches of Chesters fort. Professor Haverfield also reported this after his excavations in 1904. He was ignored and modern scholars declared that the Vallum deviated around Chesters fort. It did not. The situation is clearly visible from the air and the Romans themselves filled in the Vallum ditch, the proof of which is that the infilled ditch contains dozens of recently discovered Roman burials. You cannot bury people in the thin air of an open ditch.

After modifying and strengthening his German frontier in AD121, Hadrian visited Britain and ordered the construction of the Tyne to Solway Wall. It is widely held that the predecessor to Hadrian's Wall-frontier was the Stanegate (Saxon *stane* + Norse *gata* = stone-road) Roman road on a poorly defensible line to the south of the Wall. It is not known if this road was constructed by Agricola or Trajan, but excavations have shown that this road had neither palisade nor ditch. The road also bends back on itself in several places to the west of Nether Denton, most peculiar for a frontier but ideal for a pack-horse trail seeking easy gradients.

Next, let us consider the mysterious *Vallum* to the rear of Hadrian's Wall. How much longer do we have to put up with explanations that this south-facing tremendously expensive *Vallum* was;

a) a customs barrier,

b) a cattle fence, or

c) marked a no-go area for local civilians:

all of which would have cost a trifling sum compared with the construction of the *Vallum* which can be financially equated with the whole complex of Hitler's "West Wall" of the Normandy coast.

The *Vallum* earthworks must have cost the ancient equivalent of billions of pounds. It was no "stripey-pole" customs check-point nor a cattle compound for which a wattle fence would have sufficed. Also, civilians would not have needed a "Maginot Line-type construction" to remind them of the dire consequences of trespassing on Roman army property; a few notices would have been sufficient.

What a modern general fears most is that an enemy armoured spearhead will break through his line, fan out behind and attack his undefended rear. A present-day general therefore positions many guns facing backwards in case enemy tanks do just this and attempt to destroy his soft-skinned logistics vehicles from behind. As will be seen very shortly, the Roman Wall plus *Vallum*- system could contain a breakthrough intended to mount an attack from the rear.

When the Japanese army swarmed down the Malayan peninsula in 1941, the British military authorities were severely criticised because the large guns of Singapore Island pointed seawards and it was said that they could not turn towards the north to face the Japanese threat. This was not entirely true as some of the guns *could* turn through 360 degrees but only anti-ship armour-piercing ammunition was available and this was useless against infantry. At a later stage in the war, these guns *were* taken in the rear - the Japanese moved them to the Aleutians where American Marines came over the back of the island instead of the expected frontal beach landing. The Japanese had not learnt the lesson that they had taught the British.

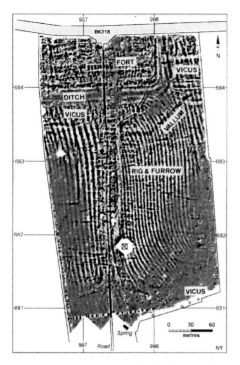

A geophysical plan of magnetic read-outs of the Hadrian's Wall fort of Halton Chesters (Onnum) (NY 998 684). The southern half of the fort is at the top and the infilled Vallum which has deviated around the fort can be seen as a black line. The field to the east and south of the fort is covered with medieval rig & furrow agriculture which has largely destroyed the Roman vicus. The square with a cross in it is a modern electricity pylon. Bottom right is a row of Roman houses which seems to have been avoided by the medieval agriculture.

Grey Scale magnetometry plot. The reversed-S shape of extant medieval ridge and furrow overlies some of the anomalies; this effect is particularly evident south of the *Vallum.*

The read-out in plan form of the magnetic anomalies of Halton Chesters Roman Wall fort and vicus.

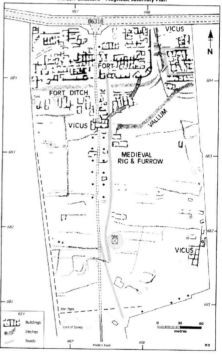

Interpretative plan of magnetic anomalies.

Aerial photograph of the medieval rig & furrow agriculture which overlies most of the Halton Chesters vicus. The structure bottom right casting a shadow is an electricity pylon. At centre is the row of Roman houses which has narrowly escaped being obliterated by the later rig & furrow. This picture faces south.

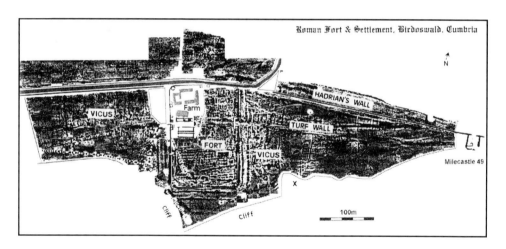

Magnetic anomaly plan of Hadrian's Wall fort and vicus at Birdoswald, Cumbria (NY 615 663). The modern farmhouse, (the outbuildings of which have been converted into a visitor centre and tearoom) sits on top of the north-west corner of the fort. A few Roman buildings including two granaries have been excavated and left open just south of the farmhouse. The River Irthing is in the gorge to the south of the fort. Position 'X' is a suspected but hitherto unknown Roman road leading down the steep slope. There is a whole network of further suspected Roman roads in the area. Also there must be an as yet unlocated aqueduct somewhere along the high ground to the west of the fort.

Roman records tell us that a wall less than seventy feet high was bound to be breached from time to time, therefore they must have expected the fifteen-foot Hadrian's Wall to be crossed occasionally. The tremendously expensive rearward-facing *Vallum* would have been of great use at these times as the Wall plus *Vallum* would form an elongated fort, defendable from both north and south. There are precedents for Roman two-way-facing systems. We have a full Roman description of one of them: at the seige of Alesia, an encircling Roman inward-facing inner *vallum* prevented an enemy escape while a concentric outward-facing outer *vallum* prevented reinforcements or supplies getting to the beseiged city. The multiple ditches of both inward and outward facing *valli* contained fearsome obstacles such as poisoned, sharpened stakes and tangles of thorn branches.

The Romans attack a well-fortified enemy city. Bottom right is a stone-throwing
'ballista.' Another version of this weapon fired dart-shaped bolts.Bottom Centre is an
'onager' (wild ass). This is about to hurl a heavy stone into the crumbling enemy wall.
Centre: Wall-scalers emerge from the protection of a 'testudo' (tortoise), formed by
soldiers' shields.Centre-left: a battering-ram is operated from inside a mobile building
which has been moved into position on rollers.Top left: A siege-tower discharges troops
onto an enemy wall-tower. The lower floors of the siege-towers were often equipped with
'ballistae.'

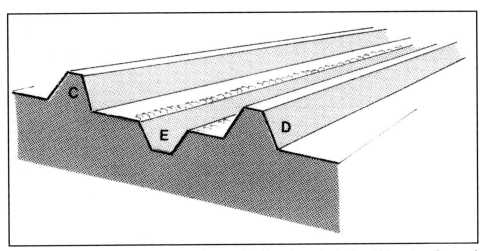

The construction of the much misunderstood Vallum, but why it should be misunderstood is the great mystery. The well-known Roman siege works at Alesia explain the whole complex as will be seen later. With the Vallum, the Romans were merely protecting their rear in the manner of any professional general, in case of a successful breakthrough from the north fanning out behind the Wall line and attacking an undefended rear.

C =   *North mound of Vallum.*

D =   *South mound of Vallum.*

E =   *Vallum ditch. There are slight mounds on the lips of the ditch as a result of the Romans cleaning out the ditch periodically.*

A typical Roman defence line. The Romans used many combinations of ditches, mounds, palisades and occasionally, stone walls.

The deviation of the Vallum as it passes to the south of Downs Hill which is on the line of Hadrian's Wall and the modern B6318 road which overlies it for many miles. Note the double mounds of the Vallum and the central ditch with two marginal mounds (cleaning out debris) and not just one as hitherto believed. The breaks in the Vallum mounds centre right were multiple Roman crossings for reasons as yet unknown. Note also the Roman quarries on both sides of the Vallum. At left centre, the Roman Military Way can be seen between the wood and the Vallum.

In the wood on the highest point of Downs Hill is a hitherto unknown suspected Roman signal station. Roman signal stations were not always built at precise intervals, but where the lie of the land provided good lines of sight. This one is between Turret 20B and Milecastle 21. There is also a suspected early Roman fortlet to the south-west of this area at NZ 003 682 on the east side of a field wall and exactly underneath the electricity high tension grid cables. This fortlet lies on "Proto Dere Street" which has been described in Chapter 9, and which passed this way on its route from Bywell to Little Whittington and Beukley. There are also many Roman aqueducts in the area, most of them unlisted. At least two served Corbridge. One of the Roman reservoirs for Corbridge is the former Shildon Lough, now just a swamp. From Shildon Lough, the aqueduct passed through "The Wood of the Seven Wells" (NZ 008 653). Another Roman reservoir can be seen in the gully to the north-west of Halton Castle. The ruinous Roman dam (NY 994 680) has been reused and repaired many times for various functions such as a millpond. The stone Roman spillway survives with its typical stepped air face. The reservoir has now silted up to the level of the former water surface and this takes a very long time. The Chester-le-Street based archaeological team which discovered all this got its expertise by searching for and discovering the Roman aqueduct to Chester-le-Street which is described in Chapter 6. There is exploration work for hundreds of archaeologists, qualified or not.

The Roman use of two-way-facing fortified lines is well described by Roman military writers and it is surprising that the Roman Wall complex is so poorly understood by modern civilian historians. Military men have few problems in appreciating Roman methods.

When the Romans besieged an enemy city which was situated in territory from which a relieving enemy force could materialise, the Romans used *"Bicircumvallation."* Caesar's description of the siege of Alesia in central Gaul in 52 BC allows us to appreciate the strategy:

Alesia was situated on a plateau about a mile long, a kilometre wide, and 500 feet high. Vercingetorix's army of 80,000 men occupied this apparently impregnable position. Caesar decided on a double line of concentric and continuous temporary barriers. One faced inwards towards the enemy plateau at a distance of about a mile, and the outer line, some 200 metres distant faced outwards to intercept any relief attempt by the allies of Vercingetorix. The

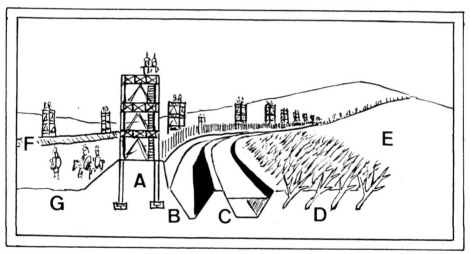

The siege system described by Caesar at Alesia is known as 'Bicircumvallation.' An inward facing palisaded mound with interval towers was fronted by several obstructions which included two ditches, one of which was filled with water when terrain allowed. In front of the ditches were several belts of anti-personnel and anti-cavalry obstructions. This inward-facing 'vallum' prevented the besieged enemy escaping. A similar concentric outward-facing outer-Vallum prevented a relieving force gaining access to the besieged city, or any guerrilla activity interfering with the inward-facing line.

A = Earth mound with palisade and towers.
B = Dry ditch, probably filled with thorn branches.
C = Water-filled ditch.
D = Sharpened branches set in ground.
E = Area filled with man-traps (lilia) and anti-cavalry devices.
F = Concentric rearward facing Vallum system.
G = Safe area between inner and outer Valli.

Hadrian's Wall plus Vallum is merely a linear form of Roman bicircumvallation. Guerrilla forces cannot attack from behind, nor can an ememy breach a weak point and attack an undefended rear. The bicircumvallation is a linear fortified area defended from both sides. It is surprising why this system has caused so much confusion among historians when Caesar has described it so simply.

distance between the inward and outward perimeters varied so that the outer line could take advantage of the lie of the land would also deny water and grazing to enemies from inside or outside the besieged city. Our Hadrian's Wall *Vallum* also deviates like this, in places for obvious reasons, at others, not yet fully understood.

At Alesia, Caesar first established 23 forts as refuges for his soldier-workers while the two continuous lines of ditches, ramparts and barriers were being constructed. The 23 standard forts were inside what would become the *intervalli* military zone. Around the outer *vallum* would be placed four infantry camps and four cavalry camps. The legionaires first dug a vertical-sided trench about six metres wide, across the plain at the foot of the plateau. This was to contain any enemy sallies while the Romans were busy with the main works around the plains. Four-hundred metres behind this trench, the legionaires dug two ditches five metres wide, and where possible, filled the inner one with water.

These two trenches extended all the way around the enemy city and formed a closed circuit 16km long. The earth from these ditches was piled up behind the outer trench to form a rampart on which was built a continuous timber palisade with towers at intervals of 25 metres. Pointed stakes projected horizontally from the top of the rampart to deter would-be scalers. On the inward side of the double-ditch line, booby-traps were set in the form of lines of hedges of spikes and in front of these, the famous Roman *lilia,* which were circular holes covered with brushwood and other camouflage, but which each contained a sharpened vertically mounted, pointed stake which impaled an unsuspecting attacker who fell in. Finally, in front of the "lilies," anti-personnel or anti-horse metal spikes protruded from the ground. Multi-pronged metal *"calthrops"* were also scattered as an anti-cavalry measure. The outward-facing lines were similarly constructed and formed a continuous circuit-barrier at varying distances from the inner line. The outer perimeter was 28km in length. The whole complex looked rather like Hadrian's Wall/*Vallum* system twisted round a large piece of enemy territory. Therefore, it should be seen by readers that the "bivallated" Hadrian's Wall system is merely an adaptation of the siege *"bicircumvallation."* Hadrian's Wall *bivallation* prevents movements of enemy personnel from the expected enemy side, but also strays, or incursions from the rear. Let us hope that we will hear no more talk of "multi-million *denarii* customs barriers!"

When modern assault troops have to cross obstacles such as a barbed-wire entanglement, the first troops who arrive throw themselves into prostrate positions on top of the wire, thus flattening the obstruction and so form a human causeway over which the remainder of the troops cross the barrier. Needless to say, the troops wear well padded combat jackets.

To surmount the fifteen-feet high Hadrian's Wall, a few hundred Picts could easily have embanked their own human bodies into a living ramp up which their colleagues swarmed across the barrier. They then had to cross a narrow strip of land between the Wall and the triple-obstruction *Vallum.* The Roman defenders could easily have thrown lines across this enclosed strip thus containing the enemy. If the Picts had succeeded in crossing the two mounds and central ditch of the *Vallum,* they could have spread out, but to gain access to the Wall Zone, would once again have had to mount an attack on a defended line, this time from the south.

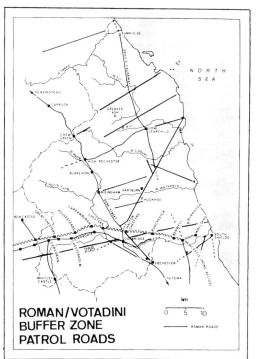

**ROMAN/VOTADINI
BUFFER ZONE
PATROL ROADS**

Some of the Roman patrol roads which have been found across north-eastern England at regular intervals. They are approximately parallel to the newly-discovered 255 degree frontier line which runs from St Mary's Island, through Hexham to Langley Castle, Staward Manor and Cold Fell to Wreay and Maryport. On occasion, the patrol roads run through Roman forts such as Bremenium (High Rochester) and Habitancum (Risingham), but mostly they transit Celtic Iron Age circular forts. It looks as if the latter were built by mercenary Votadini. The Romans describe such a native-policed buffer state and it was newsworthy only because the Votadini were in the habit of defecting to the enemy Picts. Many more patrol roads remain to be discovered. They are easy to find.

The Roman outpost Auxiliary fort and Annexe at Birrens near Ecclefechan in south-west Scotland. The fort has multiple ditches, likewise the annexe. The annexe is showing as a crop mark in corn and is not usually visible whereas the fort is a standing earthwork.

True purpose of Hadrian's Wall

Now let us consider the purpose of Hadrian's Wall; why are all the aqueducts and waterworks situated to the north of the Wall in supposed semi-hostile territory? During the trench warfare of the 1914-18 War, British and French troops dare not drink water from a stream which originated in German-held territory. Likewise, the Germans would have been foolish to drink water from a source which originated behind allied lines.

Roman patrol roads north of the Wall

Recently discovered evidence shows a whole network of Roman military roads across Northumberland and southern Scotland. These roads are all parallel and are lined up on 250 degrees in Northumberland and 240 degrees further north. They occasionally transit a Roman outpost fort but in the main, they cross native Celtic-type hillforts but strangely, the hillforts are not very often on hills! It looks as if the area between the Tyne and Forth was policed by mercenary native tribesmen in the pay of the Romans. If so, the Wall was not a front line but a rear stop-line in case of a Caledonian victory over the Romans' frontier zone defence force of mercenary allied Celtic tribesmen. The latter are mentioned at length in Dr David Breeze's various publications. The Romans wrote about a "buffer zone" patrolled by the Votadini tribe. These "frontier scouts" were newsworthy because they were unreliable and went over to the enemy Picts.

On such occasions, the higher class Roman auxiliaries were safe between the "backstop Wall" and the rear-facing *Vallum*.

When the dispensable Votadini irregulars performed their correct lower-echelon function as buffer-zone Pict-fodder, the Roman troops were still safe and comfortable between their parallel double-facing "Siegfried Line." If the buffer-zone tribesmen were totally defeated, then the Roman army could issue forth, fresh and rested and deal with the enemy, at the same time defending their vulnerable aqueducts and reservoirs to the north of the Wall.

The parallel lines of Roman patrol roads in northern Northumberland and Southern Scotland are being found very quickly now that we know where they should be. A long-known Roman road between High Rochester (Bremenium) on Dere Street, and Learchild on the Devil's Causeway is a 250-degree road, and has been shown to continue all the way to the coast at Howick Haven where a native hillfort appears to have guarded a Roman harbour. Many Roman artefacts have been recovered from the vicinity of this native site. One native circular hillfort in central Northumberland on a Roman 250-degree patrol road, can be seen from the air to contain rectangular buildings instead of the usual native rondavels.

Rock too hard for the Romans?!

At Limestone Corner on Hadrian's Wall, a section of the north ditch is unfinished and the Ordnance Survey map of the Wall remarks: "ditch unfinished due to hardness of rock." A few yards to the south, the Romans have sliced the equally large ditch for the *Vallum* complex through the same outcrop of rock, as if the so-called "hard stone" had been warm butter.

It looks as if the Romans may have had a change of mind during the cutting of the fighting ditch. Perhaps the general had decided that Limestone Corner was an ideal spot to position a fort, and ordered rock-cutting to cease. Then maybe there was another change of plan, as frequently happened elsewhere during the construction of the Wall defences. A fortlet was placed at Limestone Corner and this may mean that a proposed fort was decided against and by this time the rock-cutting work gangs were elsewhere and the job forgotten or relegated to a lower priority. This is a far more plausible explanation than that given by the authorities about the Roman engineers' inability to cut the same hard rock through which they had just sliced their *vallum*.

A Newly Discovered Roman Frontier

The 255 Line: A pre-Hadrianic frontier across Northumberland and Cumbria

Now let us return to some time before Hadrian, when there must have been an earlier *limes* even though we didn't quite know where it was. We do now...

The evidence, for and against the Stanegate has already been mentioned.

The first clue in the chain of research which led to new evidence, was the reference in JC Hodgson's *History of Northumberland*:

"*Heddon Law, Dewley Law, Turpin's Hill are all capped with tumuli cairns and other ancient works. Between these stations in 1728, there were six castella, in a series without interruption, measuring exactly 1,485 yards. In the nearest to Vindolanda on the east in 1766, an urn was found full of gold and silver coins.*"

When asked about their views on this reference, most Roman period experts said that: "the old antiquarians must have mistaken Romano-British settlements (native farmsteads) for Roman fortlets." This did not ring true, as groups of RB sites were not sited in straight lines, nor at equally spaced intervals. An investigation was called for:

A survey flight was undertaken with a full crew of archaeological observers and photographers. I was the pilot. The runway at Newcastle airport is lined-up on 250 degrees and it just so happened that this runway pointed straight at our search area of Heddon Law, Turpin's Hill etc. It was therefore no problem for air traffic control to allow me to continue on runway-heading for several miles after take-off. Within minutes, we had located all the supposed fortlets mentioned by JC Hodgson. After the flight, we plotted the positions.

Ordnance Survey 1:50,000 maps, numbers 88,87,86 & 85 were cellotaped together and a navigator's parallel ruler used to see if the sites mentioned by Hodgson formed part of a greater alignment. There was an extremely surprising result - with the rulers positioned on Turpin's Hill and Heddon Law, the extended line, when drawn between the North Sea and Irish Sea coasts, traversed several well known Roman sites, other suspected Roman sites and several findspots of Roman artefacts. The sites formed a near-perfect straight line from coast to coast on an alignment of 075/255 degrees True. Here and there, modern roads or cart tracks followed the line.

Navigator's dividers were then set to the distance mentioned by Hodgson - 1,485 yards, to see if this was the correct interval between the various sites. There was a discrepancy, and I noticed with further astonishment that the distance between the sites was 1,620 yards - a Roman mile. With the dividers still set to 1,620 yards, I marked Roman mile intervals on the maps all the way from coast to coast. Most of the following significant sites were exactly at Roman mile intervals. Exceptions were suspected signal stations, major forts and river crossings:

St Mary's Island (NZ 352 755), Roman coins often found.

Backworth (NZ 301 720), Roman treasure found many years ago.

Newcastle Airport, line passes past crop mark to south of runway.

Callerton DMV (NZ 165 704), apparently unknown until this survey.

Heddon Law (NZ 141 693), reuse of *tumulus* as signal station?

West Heddon DMV (NZ 125 688), earthworks.

Turpin's Hill (NZ 108 685), gold & silver Roman coins found 1766.

Whitchester Farm (NZ 099 683), suspected Roman fort under farm.

Earthworks (NZ 094 683), suspected milefortlet in strip wood.

Crossing of Hadrian's Wall (NZ 086 681).

Welton DMV (NZ 063 676), pele tower built of Roman stones.

Laker Hall (NZ 050 673), early Roman coins found.

Shildon Hill IA hillfort (NZ 023 662), Square earthwork N end.

Shildon Bog suspected fortlet (NZ 023 662), standing earthwork.

Shildon Bog suspected fort (NZ 022 658), crop mark seen from air.

Aydon (NZ 016 660), mound in field at correct interval.

Red House Roman fort (NY 968 652), destroyed by A69(T).

Hexham Abbey (NY 935 642), Roman town long suspected under abbey.

Causey Hill (NY 925 637), long tradition of Roman road.

Langley suspected Roman site (NY 837 622), seen from air.

Staward Pele (NY 802 607), much reused Roman stone.

Cypress Linn (NY 801 606), natural rock abutments, iron cramps.

Beacon Hill (NY 764 594), possible signal station.

Spot height 409m (NY 698 573), site of old currick (watch-tower).

Tows Bank Farm (NY 687 572), Roman-type ditches, coins found.

Cold Fell (NY 605 557), probable Roman survey point.

Longdyke Farm (NY 538 536), significant name.

Wreay Roman fort (NY 44 49). Name is Old Norse for "frontier."

Old Carlisle Roman fort (NY 25 46).

Heather Bank Roman fortlet (NY 07 41).

Not only was this line a Roman road, but it was also some kind of frontier.

The survey of the suspected frontier has hardly started, and any new information will be welcome especially from the western half of the country. There follows a summary of what is known so far and may make a starting point for interested field-walkers. All the sites mentioned lie on the 255 degree line from St Mary's Island to Maryport. The sites are mostly suspected fortlets at Roman mile intervals, and I often refer to them as "milefortlets" to distinguish them from the "milecastles" of Hadrian's Wall.

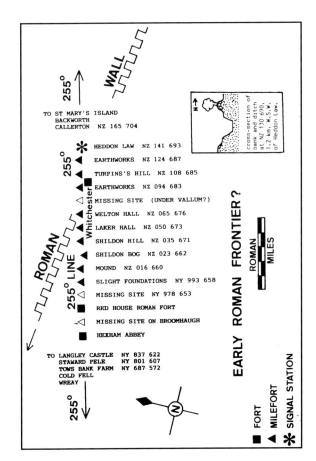

A suspected pre-Hadrianic frontier has been found from St Mary's Island near Whitley Bay, to Hexham, Langley Castle, Staward Manor, Cold Fell, Wreay and Maryport. There were milefortlets at every Roman mile and major forts at approximately ten mile intervals.

St Mary's Island is an islet just off the Northumberland coast, four miles north of the entrance to the River Tyne. Navigators of various ages have erected markers and lighthouses on it and Roman coins have been found there. The island is connected to the mainland via a causeway which dries out at low tide. It would have made an excellent eastern terminus for a frontier.

Four miles inland is the village of Backworth, and the findspot of a famous hoard. Historians have often doubted the discoverer's findspot because they could not conceive anything of Roman importance in the area. The finder of the hoard may have been telling the truth after all.

The 255 line runs across Newcastle Airport south of Runway 25/07 and converges on it towards the western end. Pilots landing and taking off have seen crop marks in fields on the south side of the eastern end of the runway.

Just after take-off from Newcastle's Runway 25 [252 degrees Magnetic which is 245 degrees True], if a climb is continued on runway heading for a minute or so, the aircraft passes over a line of low hills. The suspected frontier lies along the top of these. The excellent choice of line is obvious from the air and Tacitus mentions that Agricola had a keen eye for selecting the optimum military use of the lie of land. Maybe this is an example of his skill.

The first hilltop with a visible earthwork on it is at NZ 165 704, just to the south of the Callerton DMV. This DMV seems to have been unknown until our survey. A ground inspection shows a low rectangular earthwork, 40 yards x 30 yards.

Two miles further on is the prominent 500 ft high Heddon Law although it has also been known as "Penny Hill." There is an obvious *tumulus* on the top but it may also have been used by the Romans as a signal station. It is not at an exact Roman mile interval, but its unique outlook would determine its use. The whole of southern Northumberland is visible from this point. Two trial trenches dug in 1925 revealed a four feet thick dry-stone wall around the peak at a depth of 18 inches. Penny Hill is probably derived from the Middle English *Pen-y-gwel* which means "Rampart on the Hill." The suspected Roman road runs along the line of hills under a farm track just below the crest to the south. This is known as a "military horizon" ie, out of sight of an enemy to the north.

At NZ 132 690, this farm track has become a tarmac road and turns a right angle from 255 degrees to south-south-east. A feature continues straight ahead on 255 degrees (NZ 130 689) and this is a deep *fosse*, far too large to be a drainage ditch. The ditch is lost at the bottom of a small valley, and the next items of interest are the earthworks of the West Heddon DMV at NZ 125 688. Another farm-track has now materialised on our suspected Roman line and can be followed to the junction with a north-south public road at NZ 114 686. This public road continues south to Hadrian's Wall and Rudchester Wall fort, a thousand yards distant. The 255 line is lost to sight across the fields to the south of Turpin's Hill Farm, but the site where the urn of gold and silver coins was found is marked at the time of writing by a lone hawthorn tree in the middle of a field at NZ 108 685. There is a possible Roman well in the field boundary just to the south of the tree.

A public footpath is picked up at NZ 105 685 and this leads to, and is aligned with, the Whitchester Farm road. This farm road is on top of the suspected Roman frontier road and Whitchester Farm sits on a prominent earthwork and may conceal a major fort. It is too large for a milefortlet and it is not situated at a Roman mile interval.

Some six hundred yards further down the farm road to the west is a strip wood on the north side of the road. There are slight earthworks in this wood very close to the road. At the end of this farm road is the crossing point with Hadrian's Wall. The latter is hidden under the B6318 road. If there was a 255 degree-line milefortlet at the next Roman mile, it has been lost under the later *Vallum* of Hadrian's Wall which crosses at exactly this point. Our 255 line is now to the south of Hadrian's Wall and *Vallum*.

Across to the west of the Whittle Dean reservoirs is Welton Hall and the Welton DMV. The B6309 coming south from Hadrian's Wall makes a right-angled turn to the west at the gates of the hall. After this turn, the B6309 is parallel to the central street of the DMV and just a few yards to the north. This DMV green track is on the suspected Roman frontier road. The pele tower incorporated into the buildings of Welton Hall is built of Roman stones previously thought to have been robbed out of the Wall to the north. They may have come from a 255 line milefortlet right on the same site.

Shildon Bog sector of 255 Line Frontier. The Roman frontier road has made a deviation around Shildon Bog which was a lake in Roman times. Proto Dere Street also crosses this area on its way north from Bywell to Beukley.

A   =   Aydon suspected milefortlet.
SB =   Shildon Bog milefortlet (earthworks exist).
SH =   Shildon Hill Iron Age Celtic hillfort. Roman milefortlet at north end.
F   =   crop mark of suspected Roman fort on Proto Dere Street.
PDS =   Proto Dere Street.
AQ1 =   Roman aqueduct from Shildon Lake to Corbridge.
AQ2 =   Suspected Roman aqueduct from Shildon Lake to Bywell. Shildon Lake was finally drained via the same route.
7W =   Wood of the Seven Wells.

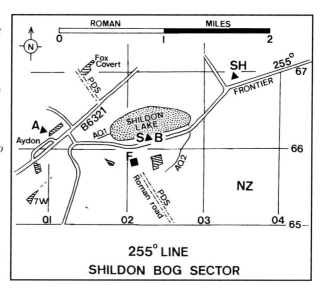

255° LINE
SHILDON BOG SECTOR

Five hundred yards west of Welton Hall, the B6309 sidesteps slightly to the south and then continues on its previous heading, but now right on top of the frontier road. The B6309 turns south at Welton Farm but a minor road continues straight ahead on top of our 255 line.

Laker Hall is one Roman mile west of Welton Hall and, just to the east of Laker Hall, exactly at the 1,620 yard interval is a pile of stones in the field beside an electricity pylon. Early Roman coins have been found here.

Another Roman mile ahead along the same road is the Iron Age hillfort on Shildon Hill. On the north end of this, and just north of a brick reservoir, is a square earthwork believed to be a 255 milefortlet. The road on top of the 255 line divides just west of Shildon Hall. The southern fork which heads south-west is our Roman frontier road, and this sudden and typical Roman deviation was necessary because, straight ahead on the 255 alignment, is Shildon Bog which was a lake in Roman times. The Roman road has skirted the lake with several angled straights.

On the north side of the road, at NZ 023 662, are suspected Roman earthworks with two prominent rounded corners. The road has bisected a suspected milefortlet. The half to the south of the road has been ploughed out. This is exactly one Roman mile (as the crow flies) from the Shildon Hill earthwork.

Just to the south-west, and halfway between two woods at NZ 022 658, the crop mark of a suspected Roman fort was seen from the air. Samian pottery and Roman coins have been picked up from this field. This crop mark was seen several years ago but its position not understood until now. The Roman road "Proto Dere Street" (from Ebchester and Bywell to Beukley) is now known to have crossed the suspected 255 frontier at this point. The small wood to the west of the crop mark contains a quarry. It is extremely likely that Shildon Lake was used by the Romans as the source of one of their aqueducts to Corbridge. A wood at NZ 007 653 is known as "The Wood of the Seven Wells" and this lies on the line of the suspected aqueduct (Corbridge seems to have had several aqueducts). Mackenzie's *Northumberland and Durham* of 1825 tells us about the draining of Shildon Lough:

"A great quantity of rain fell about a century ago, at the commencement of harvest time, when the lough overflowed and burst like a deluge to the westward, sweeping away not only the crops but also the fences.
At Corbridge East Field, the water turned into the Tyne, leaving immense numbers of pike in every standing pool - when Sheldon Common was improved, the lough was drained."

The lough may have also been used by the Romans as a source for an aqueduct to Bywell. The Brock Hole Burn has its source at the east end of the lake and this stream runs all the way to Bywell.

There is still an artificial cut at the east end of the lake but that may date from the final draining.

The Romans were not the first to use Shildon Lake. Dug-out canoes and stone axe-hammers have been found. Near Fox Covert plantation to the north of the lake, a cinerary urn was discovered, but this is likely to have been Roman as Proto Dere Street runs up the west side of this wood. This recently discovered Roman road must have crossed the western tip of the lake on piles as the *agger* can be seen just to the north of the swamp and is lined up exactly on Little Whittington and Beukley. The BBC radio mast at Beukley is an excellent marker for the road's heading, and no doubt the Roman surveyors used smoke signals at the same high point now occupied by the twentieth century signal station.

One Roman mile west of the Shildon Lake suspected Roman milefortlet is a mound in a field at NZ 016 660. Do not confuse this rounded mound with a mining spoil-heap not far away. The farmer has removed a great deal of stone from the mound and has managed to plant his crops over the top of it. The stone lies at the field boundary to the west. A little further west at NZ 005 662 are unexplained channels which may be yet another one of the aqueducts to Corbridge. It has been estimated that the baths, latrines and dozens of fountains in the Roman town would have consumed two million gallons of water per day. When you think that a two-inch petrol pipe puts twenty gallons of fuel into a car in half a minute, it does not take long to calculate the amount of water flowing through a 3 ft wide x 1 ft deep aqueduct, and there were several such channels supplying the site.

A further Roman mile west of the Aydon "bump" are some earthworks on top of a hill at NY 994 659 just to the north of the Cor Burn and a gap in a wood.

A mile further on, the A69(T) may have removed evidence, just as it destroyed the Red House Roman fort which is on the line two miles to the west. As the latter was a major fort, it may not have been at an exact Roman mile interval. The 255 line crosses the Roman Stanegate here. Which one was the genuine frontier? Maybe both were and formed part of a greater *limes* system. Only fieldwork will provide the answers.

There is a missing site on Broom Haugh to the north-east of Hexham, and a suggested search area is NY 953 647.

The next site is Hexham Abbey which has already been mentioned at great length as a probable Roman town and fort with a network of roads, some of which have been discovered only recently. The site would have been river supplied and would have formed the lynchpin of the whole system.

To the south-west of Hexham is Causey Hill, and tradition has long held that a Roman road passed here. If so, up to now, it has eluded survey pilots and field-walkers.

There is no doubt that the survey line of the suspected frontier continued on 255 degrees because we pick up more Roman sites on this alignment further to the west. There may have been a salient west of Hexham which approximated to the large northward bend of the River South Tyne. A suspected Roman road runs through Highwood Farm and the paving sticks out of the ground at NY 905 650. It can be seen again at Coastley at NY 895 656.

Back on the 255 line, there are earthworks at Blossom Hill farm (NY 903 633).

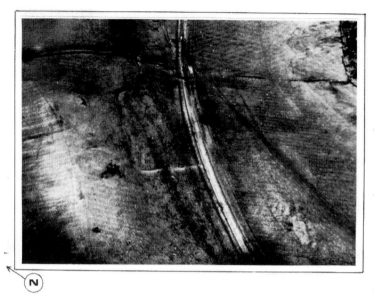

255 Line milefortlet on the ridge to the south of Langley Castle at map ref NY 837 622. The railway line, now dismantled has cut right through the Roman site. The public footpath to Humbleton crosses the old railway line at the milefortlet site. This Roman site was discovered many years ago by our Chester-le-Street based air survey team but its function was not understood until the fairly recent discovery of the rest of the 255 Frontier Line.

Reused Roman stones in gatehouse of Staward Pele, NY 802 607. The source of these Roman stones was a mystery until the discovery of the 255 Frontier Line, especially the recently discovered fort on the sloping field to the south-east of the Gingle Pot ruined cottage.

Roman altar which fell down the cliff into the Harsondale Burn from its reused position in the wall of the gatehouse of Staward Pele. It was recovered and is now in the front garden of Staward Manor. Other reused Roman stones have fallen into the Harsondale Burn where they still lie. One has a typical Roman lewis hole in it.

If there has been a salient to the north, the Roman line was back on the 255 degree line to the south of Langley Castle, where a suspected Roman fortlet was observed from the air at NY 622 837, on the north side of the dismantled railway line, and exactly on the public footpath which leads from Langley Castle, past Humbledon Cottage to the modern B6305 road. The railway has cut right through the ancient rectangular site, but one complete side and two rounded corners can still be traced at ground level. The site is in clear view of Barcombe Hill, the position of the known Roman signal station to the east of the Stanegate fort of Vindolanda. This is five miles to the north-west.

The next visible evidence is at Staward Pele (NY 801 607) where the gatehouse contains many reused Roman stones. Professor Eric Birley, in his lecture read on 16.4.1950, said that he did not think the Roman stones had been transported very far in view of the wild terrain with its deep ravines and numerous streams (it is more reminiscent of Canadian British Columbia than northern England). A Roman altar had been used as a quoin in the gatehouse but this altar fell down the sheer cliff into the Harsondale Burn in 1947. It has since been recovered and now stands in the garden of Staward Manor. The altar has an inscription which reads:

I   O   M

OH IIII GALL

I.PraEst.L.ll

GIVS PVDEN

.PRaEFECT

RAM pOSVIT   V V S.

The altar is attributed to the Fourth Cohort of Gauls and the inscription restored and expanded reads:

" *Iovi Optimo Maximo cohors IIII Gallorum cui praest Lucius....gius Pudens praefectus aram posuit ut voverat solvens libenter*".

[*To Jupiter Best and Greatest, the fourth cohort of Gauls, in command of which is Lucius gius Pudens, prefect, set up this altar, as it had vowed to do, willingly fulfilling its vow.*]

The Fourth Cohort of Gauls served at Vindolanda during the third century, but had been at Templeborough in the first century and at Risingham at the time of Antonius Pius. (E Birley in "A Roman Altar from Staward Pele and Roman Remains in Allendale" in *Archaeologia Aeliana* 1950).

A short while ago, Colonel Bell of Staward Manor contacted me to inform me that he had read in *"On the Trail of the Legions"* about the "255 Frontier" and that he thought he had a section of it through his back garden and on into the adjoining fields. A quick inspection showed that it looked as if the Colonel was absolutely right and an excavation was planned. Other tasks prevented me from taking part but I sent a first class and highly experienced team to do the job.

The 255 Line Frontier Roman Road was successfully excavated in 1999 in the field to the west of Staward Manor. Half a mile further west, a Roman long-term work camp, or a turf-and-timber fort has been found just to the north of the old Staward railway station.

Trenches were cut across the suspected road in two places and it proved to be Roman and on the exact 255 degree line. Further towards the River Allen, fieldwalkers searching the extended line of the road to the south-west think that they may have located a hitherto unknown Roman fort. Time will tell.

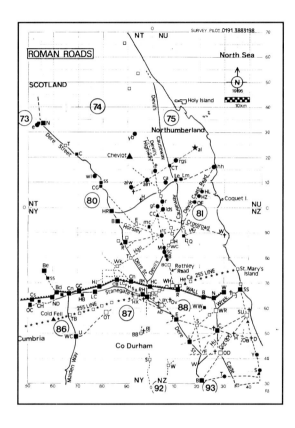

This map shows scores of miles of hitherto unknown Roman roads, and newly discovered archaeological sites, found by aerial surveys, excavations, fieldwalking and geophysics. Work is still in progress and the caption would be impossibly long for this book. A forthcoming book entitled "The Lost Roman Roads of Northern England" will cover the subject. The half-completed map is printed here to show readers how much more information remains to be found. There is enough work for dozens of archaeologists, amateur or professional, to last for many years.

It seems that the Romans have made the most of the topography of Northumberland. The later Hadrian's Wall makes use of the magnificent Whin Sill but there are many lesser ridges to the north, all of which seems to have been used as defence-in-depth patrol roads. The latest one to be found passes along a natural ridge on which Bolam Saxon church stands. The patrol road then continues to the west over Shaftoe Crags. The cleft in the rocks called "Salters' Nick" is a Roman quarry *glissage* (ramp for sledges loaded with stones to slide down). This *glissage* then becomes a Roman road which we have excavated.

We also now know that there was a Roman town at Hartburn and a hitherto unknown Roman road to the north from Bolam church has been excavated at intervals all the way from

Bolam to Hartburn. This road has nothing to do with the Devil's Causeway although there is a connecting link from just south-west of Hartburn Church across to the hollow-way which leads down to the Roman crossing of the Hart Burn where the post-holes for the timbers of the Roman bridge can still be seen in the stream's rock bed.

We think that the Roman defence-in-depth system also existed south of the Wall, probably built prior to the Wall. The natural ridges of Durham also lie on a 250 degree alignment and as has already been mentioned, the east-west ridge road at Ragpath Wood looks as if it has been fortified.

Another possible patrol road is "Long Edge" to the west of Sacriston.

Shortly, we must leave the Romans, their frontiers, towns, forts, aqueducts and roads, but before we move on to other periods of history, we must remember that no roads were built in England for well over a thousand years after the Roman departure. Nevertheless, medieval armies followed these ruinous Roman roads which were totally unsuitable for wheeled traffic and which had lost almost every bridge. A glance at an atlas of historic battles will show that most of them took place on or near Roman roads.

We will pick up the history of later roads in due course when we look at the first decent roads since the Romans - the "Turnpikes" which were built after 1750. The first modern roads would be the work of Telford (1757-1834) and McAdam (1756-1836) but first we must consider what happened to our country and town after the Roman military departure and the subsequent invasions and conquest by the Germanic Anglo-Saxons.

This is usually termed the "Dark Age" because of the scarcity of written evidence. There is much scope for amateur historians and archaeologists; you do not have to go to the South American jungles to discover lost civilisations - there are several just two or three feet below our feet in our North-Eastern countryside. We can all become explorers in our own land.

An explorer in his own land.

Facts and figures of the various Roman frontiers in Britain

A Roman mile = 1481 metres, 1620 yards.

The Wall was constructed from Wallsend to Bowness-on-Solway which is 73 miles, 118 kilometres.

Ten miles of Wall are visible.

Many forts are visible except those which have been built over.

Forts were spaced at intervals of about six to eight miles.

A few milecastles and turrets are also visible.

Long stretches of the *Vallum* are almost perfect.

There was a Roman military road (the Military Way) between the Wall and the *Vallum*.

The *Vallum* was always to the south of the Wall but at varying distances.

The *Vallum* was not constructed east of Pons Aelius (Newcastle upon Tyne) or west of Bowness.

The Wall ended at Bowness but a chain of watch-towers continued down the Irish Sea coast probably as far as St Bees' Head.

Roman bridge remains can be seen at Chesters on the east bank of the River North Tyne.

Both lewis holes and *opus revinctum* can be seen in the stones.

A peculiar structure can be seen at Willowford on the east side of the River Irthing. Notices tell us it is a bridge, but it may be the spillway of a dam which has utilised the Wall as a water barrier. Expert dowsers have sensed a possible bridge abutment much closer to the River Irthing.

A few stones of the River Eden bridge can be seen at Carlisle close to the confluence of the Eden and Caldew. Most of these stones contain *opus revinctum*.

During the construction of Hadrian's Wall, there were several changes of plan. The first plan was to place the forts behind (to the south of) the Wall on the Stanegate military road, but this was changed to the forts being built integral with the Wall. This second plan allowed for forts to be built every half-dozen miles or so, with milecastles at every Roman mile and two turrets at third of a mile intervals between each milecastle.

Dates

55BC	Julius Caesar attempted an invasion of Britain. Bad weather wrecked his ships.
54BC	Julius Caesar tried again but once more had problems with storms.
AD43	Claudius ordered Conquest of Britain. He sent four legions plus auxiliaries: possibly up to 40,000 men.
AD78-84	Agricola, Governor of Britain. Stanegate Roman road linked Newcastle via Bywell and Corbridge to Carlisle.
AD117	Hadrian became Emperor. Aulus Plautius Nepos, Governor of Britain.
AD121	Hadrian strengthened Roman German frontier.
AD122	Hadrian visited Britain and supervised plans for Wall.
AD138	Hadrian's Wall decommissioned. Antonine Wall built of turf (with stone forts), between Forth and Clyde.
AD 190	Antonine Wall abandoned, Hadrian's Wall reoccupied.
3rd C.	Emperor Severus rebuilt large sections of Hadrian's Wall in the early Third Century AD.

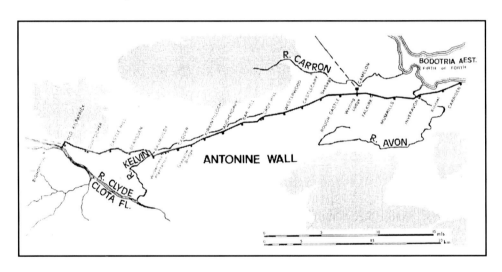

The Antonine Roman Wall which stretches from the Firth of Forth to the Clyde. It is extremely likely that this Wall was supplied via the Rivers Carron, Avon and Kelvin. At Balmuildy there was a Roman bridge and stones from this structure are now preserved in the Hunterian Museum, Glasgow, They are of the 'opus revinctum' type with dove-tailed cut-outs for butterfly joining-cramps. They are identical to Roman stones found recently at Sunderland, Jarrow, and at Chester-le-Street in 1930 when the bed of the Cong Burn was cemented. The Antonine Wall was made of turf on a stone foundation. The interval forts were built of stone. There was no rearward-facing Vallum.

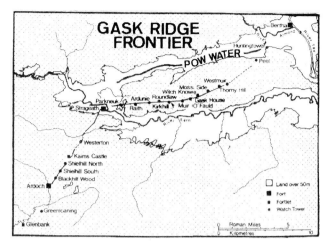

The Gask Ridge Frontier is a line of Roman watch-towers in Perthshire. It was thought at one time to have been a very short-lived feature but recent investigations by Manchester University have discovered several periods of reconstruction. In the valley to the north is the "Pow Water" which runs from the River Almond to the River Earn. Streams do not flow like this from one river to another. The Pow

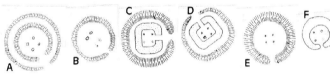

Water looks man-made and indeed, here and there it cuts the same contour twice, a sure sign of the artificial. Previous suggestions that the Pow Water was a Roman supply canal were rejected but not any more. The Roman fort of Bertha is at the Roman period tidal limit of the River Tay which is also at the confluence of the Tay and Almond. An ancient weir called 'Derder's Ford' could have started life as a Roman navigation dam. Slightly further up the Tay is the site of a Roman timber bridge. Cross-country military logistics transport would have been quite possible via the Pow Water between Bertha on the Tay and Strageath on the Earn. The "Statistical Account of Scotland" refers to a supposed 'Roman canal' in the Huntingtower area.

Without doubt, the Romans have continued navigation up the River Tay to the legionary fort of Inchtuthil, which has a three-sided rivercraft beaching site on an old dry loop of the Tay. This partially-dry river loop has at one time encircled the whole plateau on which the fort sits. Binchester Roman fort, near Bishop Auckland, on our own River Wear had a similar water-loop around it.

The shapes of some of the Gask Ridge watch-towers are shown below the map:

A = Blackhill Wood.
B = Westerton.
C = Parkneuk.
D = Gask House.
E = Witch Knowe.
F = Moss Side.

Records and literature relating to the Wall

The first reference is AD270 by Spartianus who wrote a biography of Hadrian which referred to "a wall 80 miles long to separate the Romans from the Barbarians."

731 Bede gives the Wall's dimensions and refers to St Cuthbert's visit in AD685, to Carlisle where he was taken to see the Roman walls.

1599 William Camden described the Wall in His *" Britannia"* but said: "he could not with safety take the full survey for the rank robbers (border reivers) thereabouts."

1732 The Rev John Horsley, Presbyterian minister and master of a private school in Morpeth, included a description of the Wall in his book, *"Britannia Romana."*

1802 William Hutton, a 78 year-old shopkeeper from Birmingham, walked to the Wall, along it, and home again, a total of 601 miles, and kept a diary. He wore a black suit and carried an umbrella, a bag, and an inkhorn. He wore the same socks for the whole journey and they suffered no holes. The journey cost him 40 guineas and he lost a stone in weight.

1839 The Rev John Hodgson of Jarrow devoted the whole of his last volume of *"The History of Northumberland,"* to the Wall.

1863 Collingwood Bruce's famous, standard work on the Wall was published.

The building of the Wall was managed by the Roman Legions (all Roman citizens) but on completion, it was manned by auxiliaries who were from Roman occupied territories and who were serving 25 years in the Roman army in order to gain Roman citizenship. When the Wall was finished, the Roman Legions retired to their Legionary bases, the 2nd Augusta returning to Isca (Caerleon) in South Wales, the 20th Valeria Victrix to Deva (Chester, on the Dee) and the 6th Victrix to Eburacum (York).

The Roman army was organised as follows:

8 soldiers = 1 *Contubernium,*

10 *Contubernia* = 1 *Century,*

10 *Centuries* = 1 *Cohort,*

10 *Cohorts* = 1 *Legion.*

The ranks of the senior officers were:

Governor, *Legate* and *Tribune*: politicians and other civilians serving in the army before returning to civil administrative duties.

Centurion, professional soldier in charge of 80 men. He was of higher rank than a modern sergeant major, probably about the same as a modern captain. However, he carried out sergeant major's duties as well as those of an officer. He was a strict disciplinarian as well as an exec.

The senior *centurion*, the *primus pilus* was the most important man on the battlefield.

Britain had been conquered by four legions but after the Wall was built, three were left to police Britain. Spain, which had taken 200 years to conquer, needed only one legion to ensure *"Pax Romana."*

Altogether, Rome had 25-30 legions. Each cohort of 500 men had an *onager*, a huge sling, and one *ballista* , per century. Also, *cheiroballistae*, huge very powerful crossbows, could be used by individual soldiers. The flanks of the highly organised infantry were protected by auxiliary cavalry.

In the early fifth century, the Roman Empire was under threat from enemies from all directions. The Roman army was withdrawn from Britain even though the latter was under attack by Saxon sea pirates, Caledonian Picts and Scotti Irish raiders. Having been deserted by their Roman masters, the Christian Romanised Celtic natives of the former Roman Britain were left to defend themselves against pagan Saxon invaders. These Angles, Saxons and Jutes would be the first "English," and the native Celts would be driven to the fringes of their former British homeland.

The Rhine frontier (restored). This frontier stretched all the way from the North Sea to the Black Sea and followed the Rhine and Danube. In places there was a stone wall; but mostly it was a ditched double timber fence. A zone containing defensive roads (limes) backed the frontier

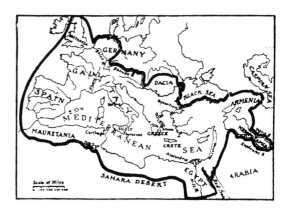

The Roman Empire at its greatest extent

King Athelstan delivers the book, Bede's Life of St Cuthbert, to the shrine at Conceastre (Ch-le-Str) in AD937. The picture shows St Cuthbert in spiritual form accepting the gift.

The peninsula at Durham on which the Saxon monks after fleeing from Conceastre built a succession of churches.

The Normans later destroyed a Saxon cathedral and replaced it with their own massive building. A Saxon castle was also replaced by a Norman structure.

Old Durham Farm is at top left and Maiden Castle is the tree-covered hill top centre.

Chapter 11
Saxons

'Tis the tramp of Saxon foemen,
Saxon spearmen, Saxon bowmen,
Be they knights or hinds or yeomen,
They shall bite the ground.'

from *"Men of Harlech."*

A Romanised Celtic Briton called Patricius Sucat was born about AD 400. He would become St Patrick and his teachings and those of his successors would have a profound effect on the establishment of Christianity in Celtic Hibernia (Ireland), Celtic Caledonia (Scotland) and the future Northumbria (combined Bernicia and Deira) of the Angles. Events at Cuneceastre or Conceastre (Chester-le-Steet) would be influenced by this trail of Christianity around these remote northern regions.

It is thought that St Patrick was born in or near Birdoswald which is towards the western end of Hadrian's Wall. He had been educated as a Christian in the troubled days following the departure from Britain of the Roman army, but before the invasions of the pagan Anglo-Saxons (*Adventus Saxonum* - the coming of the "English").

About 416, at the age of sixteen, Patrick was captured by Irish sea-raiders. These pirates of the " Scotti" tribe were natives of Ireland and were in the process of invading Caledonia, the land of the Picti. They made the sea-crossings in hide-covered *curraghs*. Although they sound flimsy, these craft were extremely seaworthy.

It all sounds very confusing for readers to learn that at this period, there were no English in what would eventually become England, and hardly any Scots in Pictish Caledonia which would become "Scotland" after the invasion of the Scotti Irish.

The future Saint Patrick worked in Ireland as a slave-swineherd/shepherd for six years before escaping to Gaul (the future "France"). For a time, he lived in Gaul and became a monk. Later he returned to Britain and dreamed one night of Irish voices calling: "We pray thee, holy youth, to come and walk again amongst us as before." This, Patrick decided was a missionary call to Ireland. He returned to Gaul and spent fourteen years preparing for his work. He was consecrated bishop, and landed at Strangford Lough as a missionary, and there founded his first church. His first mission settlement was built near Armagh and he sanctified the shamrock by using it as an illustration of the Trinity. Patrick's subsequent conversion of Ireland (432-461) started Christianity on the circuitous northern route by which it returned to Northern England and managed to pick up the pieces after the disintegration due to strife and wars, of the good work carried out by Paulinus from the Kentish Roman Christian mission, but more of that shortly in the appropriate place.

Christianity had been boosted in the west of the British Islands just before the invading pagan Anglo-Saxons destroyed it in the east to make way for the worship of Woden and Thor. The pagan invaders began their campaigns of terror against the Celts, now on their own, along the eastern and southern coasts of what was to become in the distant future, "England."

After the departure of the Roman army from Britannia, the Romanised Celtic Britons continued to suffer from attacks by Saxon pirates from across the North Sea; by Celtic Picts (the "Painted Ones") who swarmed from Caledonia across the now disused Roman Wall, and by Celtic Irish (Scotti) seaborne attacks on the west coasts. During the final years of military rule in Britain, the Romans had hired Saxon mercenary troops to help defend the northern frontier and coastlines against the three-pronged raids. This was fine as long as there was Roman gold in the pay-chests. Some of the Saxon mercenaries were protecting the coasts of Roman Britain against their own kinsmen and the Romans referred to "friendly" mercenary Saxons as *"Germani"* and enemy Saxon raiders as *"Saxones."*.

After the Roman military departure, the Romanised Celtic Britons also decided to recruit Saxon mercenaries just as their Roman masters had done. This worked for a short time but the "hired troops" changed sides and eventually became masters of the despairing Celts. The latter were pushed out to the west and found themselves between the Ocean and the *Volkwanderung* (the great migration of German peoples).

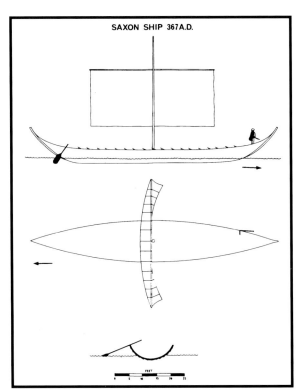

SAXON SHIP 367A.D.

A Saxon ship of AD367. Saxon ships closely resembled the later Viking ships. Saxons were close kinsmen of Vikings, though bitter enemies. Saxon ships were "clinker-built" in the manner of Viking ships. They could be propelled by oars or sails or both. The fact that the Sutton Hoo burial ship was a rowing boat has led some historians to claim that Saxon ships could not sail. This is not so. The Sutton Hoo ship may have been specially built as a burial ship.

These invading Germanic tribes were a mixture of three peoples: Angles, Saxons and Jutes. The Angles came from "Angulus" or "Angeln" in southern Denmark, and the Saxons from the Eider -Ems-Weser coastlands. The differences between them in language and customs were slight. The Jutes were a smaller tribe, kindred but distinct, and it is thought that they came to Britain from northern Denmark and also from Frisia. The vacant lands left by the departure of the three tribes would be taken up by Norsemen from Norway who will figure in further invasions of Britain at a later period. The Swedish Vikings would turn east and inflict their raids on the lands which would become Russia. They managed to negotiate the Russian rivers all the way from the Baltic to Constantinople, using smaller ships in the upper reaches and dragging these mini-longships manually on rollers, sometimes on wheels, over the watersheds.

The ships of the Saxon invaders of Britain closely resembled those of the later Vikings. We hear about the great Saxon chief Ida, who, with a fleet of fifty ships made a landfall on the Yorkshire coast at Flamborough after a four-hundred mile voyage across the North Sea. Ida then proceeded northwards and founded the kingdom of Bernicia which extended from the Firth of Forth to Teesside. He selected the rock of Bamburgh for his seat of power and built a fortification of logs protected at first by a thick thorny hedge. Increasing numbers of Angles appeared in Bernicia and the places which would become, Alnwick, Whittingham, Warkworth, and Berwick became Anglian settlements. There was probably a temple to Woden on what would later be called "Church Hill" at Alnmouth.

After Ida's death in 559, a rival Anglian chieftain established another kingdom called Deira on the southern boundary of Bernicia and it extended from the Tees to the Humber, with its capital at Eoforwic (York), on the old Roman legionary fortress of Eboracum, where the Minster now stands.

Bernicia came under attack from Celtic tribes to the west and at one point, Bamburgh became the target, and the king was forced to flee to Medcaut (Holy Island) for three days.

Later the Angles massacred the Celtic Britons killing the Celtic chief, Urien and his son.

An even more bloodthirsty Anglian chief followed - "Ethelfrith the Destroyer," and he united Bernicia and Deira into the huge new kingdom of Northumbria. Under Ethelfrith, Northumbria increased its territorial influence and it became one of the most powerful states in the British Islands.

By this time, the Celtic-Irish Scotti tribes had occupied much of Caledonia, and the Irish-Scotti King Aedan of Dalriada marched eastwards to make war on Ethelfrith. They met in 603 at the Battle of Daegsastan. Ethelfrith's brother,Theobald and a large number of Angles were killed, but the Angles rallied and cut the enemy to pieces. Aedan fled with a handful of followers leaving a battlefield full of corpses.

Bede, writing in 731 tells us that: "From that day to the present, no king of the Scots (Irish), in Britain has dared to make war on the English." (By this time the Angles and also their cousins, the Saxons and Jutes, had become known as the "English").

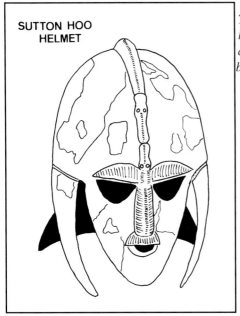

SUTTON HOO HELMET

The Sutton Hoo helmet. An excavation of a burial mound at Sutton Hoo on the Suffolk coast in 1938 uncovered a rich Saxon ship burial. Although the timbers of the large 27 metre-long rowing boat had rotted away, the clear imprint of the clinker-built planking remained. The central burial chamber contained a collection of outstanding objects of 4th to 7th century date, from all over Europe. Although no body was found and it was thought at one time that the ship may have been a cenotaph, it is now known that the acid sand consumed all the human remains. Lesser burials around the site have been forensically examined and the sand has been found to contain human acids. The helmet is thought to have been an import from Sweden. The artwork on this gilt-bronze helmet is remarkable. The eyebrows are the wings of a goose; the nose is the bird's body and the moustache, the tail feathers. Another goose is coming over the top of the helmet and meets the first bird, beak to beak on the helmet's forehead. The whole treasure is now in the British Museum. Many more mounds and lesser burials remain to be excavated.

The Angles and Saxons had settled the greater part of Britain from the Forth to the borders of Cornwall, and the Jutes occupied Kent and the Isle of Wight. All three tribes are referred to collectively by both ancient and modern historians as: "Anglo-Saxons" who were the first "English."

While the Saxon occupation of Britain south of the Forth was taking place, the progress of Irish Christianity was remarkable, with monks travelling in skin-covered *curraghs* to remote northern British islands. They also definitely made it to Iceland and there is a possibility that they got as far as Newfoundland and North America three-hundred years before the Vikings. A leading seagoing explorer-monk was "Brendan the Voyager" born near Tralee. He would become St Brendan after his death in 578.

A medieval text entitled *"Navigato"* describes Brendan's most famous journey. This story is part fiction, but has remarkably accurate descriptions of places visited.

It tells of volcanic fires of Iceland, the great ice sheets (of Greenland?) and the delights of the "Promised Land" (North America?) long before any Norse references to the subject.

Saint Columba (Colum Cille) was born of noble birth in County Donegal, and spent fifteen years preaching to his native Irish, and founding monasteries - the greatest of which were at Derry, Durrow and Kells.

Columba carried Christianity from Ireland to western Scotland in 563 and Aidan would extend its influence to Northumbria a generation after the landing of the Augustine mission in Kent in 597. Thus there was a circuitous double-pronged advance of Christianity on mainland Britain. It was not the intention of the Irish Church to become a rival to the Roman mission but differences of procedures between the two branches of Christianity would cause rifts until the Synod of Whitby brought agreement in 664.

Shortly before his death in AD597, Columba, the Irish missionary, looked out across the small Hebridean island of Iona where he had established a monastery, and uttered a memorable prophecy:

"Unto this place, albeit so small and poor, great homage shall be paid, not only by kings and peoples of the Scots, but by the rulers of barbarous and distant nations, with their people also."

This island with an area of only five square miles, became, through the work of St Columba and his disciples, the most famous centre of Celtic Christianity. Of Columba's monastery, built in 563, probably of wattle and daub, nothing remains. After the saint's death, the island was raided several times by the Vikings and its community massacred, some of them on the beach still known as "Traigh Ban nam Monach." (the White Strand of the Monks).

One of the Christian outposts of Iona would be Lindisfarne, the future Holy Island, off the Northumberland coast, but that is looking ahead a little. Meanwhile, the various pagan tribes of Anglo-Saxon invaders had been busy with their warlike pursuits, fighting each other, the Picts of Caledonia, the Irish Scotti invaders of Scotland, and the Celtic tribes who had been pressed into the West Country and Wales from the southern two-thirds of Britain.

The Celts who had taken refuge in the West Country surrendered and became slaves. Wales held out and became a Celtic stronghold. The Celtic language, a type of Gaelic, also known as Welsh, was ignored by the conquering Anglo-Saxons who absorbed very few Celtic words into their Germanic language. Those Celtic words they did adopt were usually names of rivers or other geographical features. Even so, the Saxons didn't bother to try to understand their meanings. We get the Saxon "River Avon" which merely means: "River River." Also "Cheetwood" in Lancashire which means: "Wood Wood."

Our own River Wear merely means: "River Water." The Saxon word "Welsh" means slaves, so this shows us the attitude of the Saxons towards the Celts.

Our main source of information for the "Dark Age" of the *"Adventus Saxonum"* (The arrival of the English) is from the Celtic monk, Gildas who died in AD570. In his *Excidio Britanniae et Conquestu* ("Concerning the Ruin and Conquest of Britain"), probably written in Wales during the 530s, he criticises the Celtic British warlord (possibly Vortigern) for inviting the hordes of *Saxones* into the land. He gives few names and no precise dates and is extremely vague. He describes Britain being left defenceless by the departing Roman legions and the attacks by the Caledonian Picts, the Irish Scots and the hordes of invading Anglo-Saxons as mentioned above.

The large numbers of Saxon would-be settlers came up the tiny rivers as well as the Thames and Humber. The Saxon shallow-draft undecked ships, powered by twenty-eight oars, could penetrate far inland. These ships closely resembled the Viking ships which would figure in later invasions of the British Isles.

The later chronicler, the Saxon Venerable Bede, uses Gildas as his main source of information.

Another contribution to the great silence of the Saxon "Dark Age" is the fact that the Anglo-Saxon invaders were using a Runic alphabet which was totally unsuitable for recording accounts of events. It was not until after the Christian mission's arrival to convert the pagan Anglo-Saxons, that the Germanic language of the invaders began to appear in texts using the Latin alphabet.

Most of the Romanised British Celts had been Christians, but the invading Saxons had persecuted them and they sought refuge in the mountains, so Augustine was certainly not setting foot in an entirely pagan land. There are traditions of his contact with former Celtic British bishops. Unfortunately these wisps of information reach us only through the dark mists of that time.

DARK AGE NORTH

Next we get a small influx of Romans into Britain, this time not a military invading force but a group of missionaries sent by Pope Gregory in an attempt to Christianise the pagan Anglo-Saxons. These Roman monks feared the land which they had entered, treading cautiously along the now grass-grown military roads which had been laid down by their forefathers in the four-hundred year occupation period. This had ended over a hundred-and-fifty years previously.

Northern Britain in the Dark Age Saxon period. The Celts have been pushed out to the west by the incoming Saxons. The Saxons have set up several kingdoms, and the Irish Scotti Celts are invading Caledonia of the Celtic Picts.

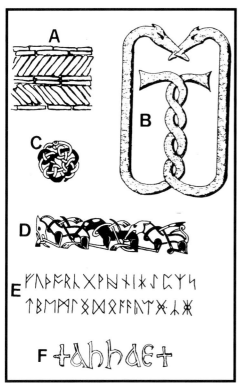

A. Herringbone masonry often seen in Saxon buildings. The Romans also used this technique. Examples of the latter can be seen in the outside wall of Lanchester Roman fort. Herringbone decorated reused Roman stones can be seen in Seaham St Mary's Saxon Church, the gatehouse of Staward Pele, in several old buildings in Hexham and dozens of other locations.

B. Intertwined serpents carved on the 7th century portal stones of the Monkwearmouth Saxon church.

C. A typical Saxon motif of intertwined snakes.

D. Another typical Saxon motif pattern of strange beasts.

E. Saxon Runic alphabet.

F. Saxon inscription in Latin from Whitby Abbey.

The mission which landed on the Isle of Thanet in AD597 was lead by Augustine, who would become the first Archbishop of Canterbury. He was accompanied by forty monks. The work of conversion of the pagan Anglo-Saxons was made easier because the wife of King Ethelbert of Saxon Kent, Bertha, was a Christian from a Gallic Royal family. As a wedding present, the King had refurbished a ruinous Roman church (St Martins) for the Queen's personal use. Therefore Augustine started his mission with an unexpected bonus - an operational Christian church in Canterbury. Augustine was allowed to preach, and succeeded in converting the king to his cause.

Paulinus, a Roman, was sent to Britain by Pope Gregory in AD601 to assist Augustine and remained with him in Kent until 625 when he was ordained bishop, and accompanied Princess Ethelburga (daughter of Ethelbert, Saxon King of Kent and Christian Queen Bertha) to her marriage with Edwin, the Anglian King of Northumbria. The Anglian Northumbrians would hear about Christianity for the first time, from Paulinus.

Edwin came slowly out of his old pagan ways. He was the powerful king who had founded Edinburgh (Edwin's Burgh). King Edwin, together with all the noblemen of his race and a vast number of the common people, finally became Christians in 627, about 180 years after the arrival of the Saxon "English" invaders in Britain.

A speech which seemed to have swung Edwin's Northumbrians to Christianity was made by a Saxon noble, possibly at Bamburgh:

"This is how the present life of man on Earth, O King, appears to me in comparison with that time which is unknown to us. You are sitting feasting with your ealdormen and thegns in winter time; the fire is burning on the hearth in the middle of the hall and all inside is warm, while outside, the wintry storms of rain and snow are raging; and a sparrow flies swiftly through the hall. It enters at one door and quickly flies out through the other. For the few moments it is inside, the storm and wintry tempest cannot touch it, and after the briefest moment of calm, it flits from your sight, back into the storm. So this life of man appears but for a moment; what follows or indeed what went before, we know not at all."

When Edwin finally decided for Christianity, it was his pagan chief priest, Coifi, who denounced the old religion. On a stallion and armed with a spear, both previously forbidden to a chief priest, he set off to destroy the pagan temple at Goodmanham (near Market Weighton). He thrust the spear into the temple door and burned the building down with all it contained. As no calamity befell them, Edwin and his chiefs went to York and were baptised on Easter Day, 627. This took place in a humble wooden church inside the old Roman fort, where now the minster stands.

Paulinus continued to preach the gospel throughout Northumbria until Edwin's death in 632. Thus we have had successful missions from the Church of Rome operating in Northumbria. At that time, it was said that Edwin's kingdom enjoyed a peace during which a woman with a new-born child could cross the whole land in safety from sea to sea.

Mass baptisms took place in Northumbria but the achievements of Paulinus had a setback in 626, when, according to the *Anglo-Saxon Chronicle*, the pagan Saxon Penda became King of Mercia (central England). At the Battle of Haethfield in 632, some seven miles north-east of Doncaster, King Edwin and his sons were killed and his army scattered by a combined army from Mercia and Wales under Celtic Cadwallon of Gwynedd (a Christian in name but with the temperament of a barbarian). Defenceless Northumbria was occupied, and Christians including women and children slaughtered by the combined occupation force of Christian Britons (Celts) and Mercians (pagan Saxons). This strange combination of allies does however show that at last, Saxons and Celts were beginning to overcome racial differences.

One of Edwin's sons had been killed in battle and the other murdered by Penda while a prisoner. Eanfrith, the first-born son of Aethelfrith, was drawn out of his exile in the land of the Picts to claim Bernicia, the northern part of Northumbria.

Paulinus, with Queen Ethelburga, her daughter Eanfled, her infant son, and her retinue, fled to Kent by sea which was the only safe route. Northumbria reverted to paganism.

Safely back in Kent, Paulinus accepted the see of Rochester in 633 and held that position until his death in 644.

The nearest surviving claimant to Deira, the southern section of Northumbria, was Edwin's Christian cousin, Osric.

Early Saxon churches (and later temporary churches) were of timber but with the help of artisans from the continent, stone churches were built. Glass-making was also learnt again making this product available for the first time since the departure of the Romans.

A. *Typical "long and short" quoinwork in a Saxon church.*

B. *The principle of "long and short" Saxon work.*

C. *The chancel arch in Escomb Saxon church.*

D. *Window in Tichborne Saxon church.*

E. *Later church quoinwork incorporating a reused Roman stone complete with Roman lewis hole for Roman crane's forfex lifting device. The lewis hole would have been on the top surface of the stone in the Roman building, but the Saxons had no knowlege of cranes and the stones were reused in a random fashion. Examples can be seen at Chester-le-Street, Bywell,Corbridge, Warden and Hexham.*

F. *Window in Worth Saxon church.*

G. *Window in Hardham Saxon church.*

H. *Window in Thursley Saxon church.*

J. *Saxon church window constructed of reused Roman tiles.*

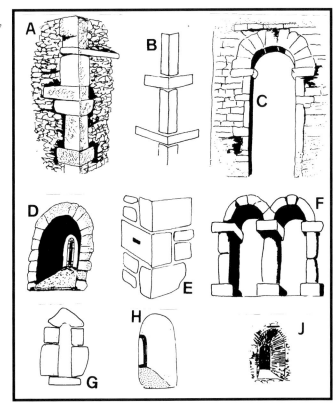

Much of our information on the Saxon period comes from the writings of the Venerable Bede. A great man of Northumbria, Benedict Biscop (born 628), a Saxon prince, was to give up his title to become a monk. He built two churches, one at Monkwearmouth and the other at Jarrow. During this period most churches were built of wood but these two were exceptions - they were built of stone with help of masons from the continent. Further technical assistance arrived from the same area when glaziers arrived to make and insert windows. The art of glassmaking had been lost to Britain after the departure of the Romans.

To accommodate the monks, each church had a monastery attached. The usual pattern was to add a square garden, called a cloister-garth, at the south end of the church. Round it was a covered cloister-walk where the monks could sit. They also had a meeting room, kitchen, library and sleeping quarters.

At Jarrow in 686, there was a terrible plague. Nearly all the monks were dead or dying. At last only Abbot Ceolfrid and one boy were left to sing the praise of God. The boy was Bede. He had been brought to the monastery when he was seven years old, to be trained as a monk, and he was now fourteen.

When Bede grew up, he spent much of his time in the library which he loved. Benedict Biscop had placed there Latin bibles and books by Christian saints, together with learned material from Greece and Rome.

Bede studied Latin and Greek and then wrote books himself. He wrote the whole history of the English Church and told the stories of St Augustine, St Aidan and St Hilda. When a priest went to visit Rome, Bede asked him to bring copies of Pope Gregory's letters written to St Augustine more than a hundred years before. These were incorporated into his book.

In all he wrote seventy-nine books and translated the bible into the Germanic language of the Saxon English. His books were very advanced for those days and he wrote about the Moon causing the tides, astronomy, the workings of the calendar, volcanoes, thunder and lightning, why the sea is salt, and a host of other subjects. He tells of Holy Island becoming an island twice per day.

Irish-born St Aidan who, with a company of Irish monks established a Christian mission on Lindisfarne in 635. Aidan died at Bamburgh in 651, having prepared twelve English disciples to continue his work. He was buried beside the high altar at Lindisfarne.

As Bede grew old, a boy assisted him with his writing while Bede dictated from a hard bed in his little cell. Bede declared: "There is yet one more sentence to be written down," and as the boy finished, he cried: "It is finished!" That night Bede died.

In the 12th century, Bede's remains would be taken to Durham Cathedral but that is leaping ahead; let us return to Lindisfarne in AD635 and examine the Christian mission which arrived from Iona thus forming a second front of Christian conversion in addition to the south-based Roman church operations. (see Appx "A", AD633, 635).

Irish-born Aidan and a company of Irish monks arrived at Lindisfarne in 635 where they established a collection of huts and an oratory which would become a wooden monastery. In this year, a boy who would be called Cuthbert was born in the hills of Northern Northumbria.

Aidan was utterly indifferent to his dignity as first bishop of Lindisfarne, yet intimate with kings and nobles. By his humility and devotion, he influenced men of all ranks and his astonishing achievements were due to the popular veneration in which he was held. Aidan died at Bamburgh in 651, having prepared twelve English disciples to continue his work, and he was buried beside the high altar at Lindisfarne. Legend tells how on the night of his death, the young Cuthbert was tending his sheep on a Scottish hillside when he saw shooting stars, and that later, when he heard the news of Aidan's death, he realised that he had seen angels descending to carry the saint to Heaven. Then it was that Cuthbert put his sheep in the fold, and turned his steps towards the monastery at Melrose, there to begin his life of devotion to Christianity.

St Aidan was succeeded as bishop-abbot by Finan, also from Iona, and his episcopate was marked by a notable extension of Christianity south of the Humber through bishops of his creation. In 653, he baptised Peada, son of Penda, the pagan king of Mercia who at Makerfield in 642 had desecrated the dead body of Oswald, the founder of Lindisfarne Priory, setting his head up on a pole. The head was recovered and carried to Lindisfarne, and when the monks were forced to flee from Holy Island before the Danish onslaught in 875, they placed Oswald's head inside Cuthbert's coffin, in the dead saint's arms.

Finan was succeeded by Colman, the last of Lindisfarne's Celtic bishops from Iona, but he and many of his monks retired to Iona and after the Synod of Whitby in 663, the huge Diocese of Northumbria was divided.

The year 664 saw the coming of Cuthbert to Lindisfarne. This simple shepherd boy was to become the sixth and most famous of all the sixteen bishops at Lindisfarne. He had been born about 635, the same time as Aidan's arrival on Holy Island to found the priory. Cuthbert was probably of Saxon stock but some schools of thought say that he may have been the son of the Irish princess, Sabina. When Cuthbert was eight years old, he was handed over to a Christian foster-mother called Kenswith in the unidentified village of Hruringaham. Cuthbert often visited his foster-mother in later life.

As mentioned above, Cuthbert entered the monastery of Melrose in 651, later becoming prior under its first abbot, Eata, one of the twelve English disciples of Aidan.

Saxons

Anglo-Saxon Durham. *For reasons not yet fully understood, Anglo-Saxon churches with the significant name "St Andrew's" invariably stand on Roman sites or Roman roads. This helps with our search for the Romans.*

TM = Tynemouth. King Edwin between AD617 and 633 erected a wooden religious residence on the headland. In 634, Oswald replaced the wooden structure with a stone one. (see "Appx A").

SS = South Shields. Bede said monastery existed here.

JW = Jarrow. Anglo-Saxon monastic site c682. King Egfrid gave the land to the monks. The King anchored his fleet in the mouth of the River Don (Jarrow Slake). Egfrid's coins carry the King's head and an Arabic legend. Saxon monastic ships were trading with North Africa. (See "Appx A" AD671, also AD672, 673, 674, 680, 682, 685. 735, and "Appx A" AD794, 875, 1022, 1069 & 1073.

GH = Gateshead. Bede said monastery existed here.

BD = Boldon. The Bilton to which Leyland ascribes Egfrid's port. The Don was navigable in Saxon and Norman times. There are reused Roman stones in West Boldon church. When Boldon Colliery railway viaduct was built, the skeleton of a ship was found in the mud bed of the Don.

WM = Wearmouth. Anglo-Saxon monastic site c674.

EB = Ebchester. Monastery founded c660. On 5C Roman road.

5C = Five Churches Roman road.

SL = Stanley. St Andrew's Church, significant name. 5C Roman road. (see "Appx A").

CS = Chester-le-Street. Anglo-Saxon wooden cathedral 883. Network of unknown Roman roads found including 5C road. Tradition of Lambton Worm. (A-S "wurm" = dragon), probably Viking "dragon ship." Another "wurm" (Laidler Worm) at Bamburgh in Northumberland. See "Appx A," AD 883, 1045.

HS = Houghton-le-Spring. church on line of 5C Roman road.

DN = Dalton-le-Dale. St Andrew's Church, significant name, also on junction of 5C Roman road and Roman coast road.

SH = Seaham. Anglo-Saxon Church, once St Andrew's, now St Mary's.

DU – Durham. Saxon wooden church, Saxon White Church, Saxon Cathedral (dismantled by Normans), Saxon fortifications, Norman cathedral and castle. See "Appx A" AD 995, 998, 1017 1092 & 1093.

EL = Elvet. Early Christian establishment. Bishop of Whithorn ordained here long before St Cuthbert's refugee monks arrived from Chester-le-Street.

YO = Yoden. Anglo-Saxon village.

CE = Castle Eden. Saxon burial, green-blue glass beaker found. Many recent metal detector finds of Saxon grave goods in nearby coastal denes.

HT = Hart. Anglo-Saxon stone church with some sculpture.

HL = Hartlepool. 7th century buildings and Christian Anglo-Saxon monastic burial ground. Monastery founded c640. (see Appx "A", 1833.

HY = Hamsterley. Unidentified rectangular earthworks; possibly Dark Age rough copy of Roman fort.

ES = Escomb. Christian Anglo-Saxon stone church built of reused Roman stones. Roman stone not robbed from elsewhere, Escomb sits on top of Roman earthwork clearly visible from the air. Roman road found recently at Newton Cap, heading north for Hunwick, underneath "Mitchell's Causeway." Easy to find.

BA = Bishop Auckland. A-S free-standing cross, 8/9th century, at St Andrew's Church, South Church. Roman road found here recently (extension of the one coming from Barnard Castle).

TH = Thrislington. DMV and A-S burial ground. On Roman road from Binchester to Hartlepool via Cleve's Cross and Stob Cross.

SD = Staindrop. Christian Anglo-Saxon stone church.

GF = Gainford. Christian A-S monastic site. Grave cover and many stone crosses found. (see Appx "A" AD 801).

AY = Aycliffe. AD 789, Synod at Aycliffe. St Andrew's Church, significant name.

DT = Darlington. grave covers and crosses from a pagan A-S burial ground. See Appx "A", 1865."

HW = Hurworth. Free standing cross.

DD = Dinsdale. A-S grave cover.

SB = Sockburn. Christian A-S stone church, Viking cemetery, tradition of A-S "wurm" (dragon) ("Sockburn Worm"), possibly Viking dragon ship. Roman road to east lined up on Girsby, High Worsall, High Leven, Maltby, Stainton, and Eston Nab. AD 781, Bishop of Lindisfarne ordained at Sockburn (Appx "A").

NO = Norton. tower of late A-S period.

BL = Billingham. early cemetery, inscribed stone, A-S tower.

GR = Greatham. fragments of early church.

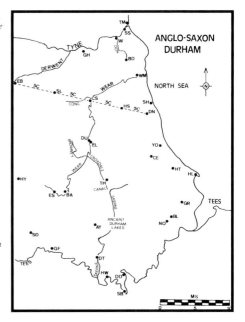

ANGLO-SAXON DURHAM

NORTH SEA

Cuthbert followed Eata to Ripon and then to Lindisfarne. In 676, Cuthbert lived on the Islet of Hobthrush and then retired to a cell on the Farne Island. In 684, he became unwillingly, the Bishop of Hexham but exchanged that seat for Lindisfarne the following year. Soon afterwards he returned to the solitude of his cell on the Inner Farne and died in the early hours of the morning of March 20th, 687, prematurely aged and worn out from his self-imposed austerities. His body was taken to Lindisfarne and placed in a stone *sarcophagus* which was buried under the floor of the church to the right side of the altar.

Eleven years to the day after Cuthbert's death, his *sarcophagus* was ceremoniously opened on March 20th 698, so that his bones could be recovered and "elevated" into a coffin-reliquary in the same place, but above the floor, for greater ease of veneration.

Eadberht, the Bishop of Lindisfarne had given his permission for the "elevation" but was not present at the exhumation. He had retired to St Cuthbert's Isle for prayer and meditation during Lent. His quiet contemplation was rudely interrupted when a group of monks burst in with the exciting news that they had found the body of St Cuthbert completely undecayed.

It is thought that at this "elevation," the coffin already contained the pectoral cross, the double-sided ivory comb and the silver-cased altar which are now on display, along with various other Cuthbert relics, in the Treasury of Durham Cathedral.

Though Cuthbert's term of office was short, his persuasive oratory converted large numbers from heathenism. He moved over the country at the head of a large retinue, preaching to the people in the hills, ordaining priests in Carlisle, and visiting noblemen on their isolated estates. At home he persuaded his monks to wear simple clothes of undyed wool, and established a common way of life for them so that by the end of the seventh century, they had accepted the Benedictine rule as a supplement to his precepts.

Soon after St Cuthbert's death, the lovely *Lindisfarne Gospels* were produced. A masterpiece of seventh century art, probably influenced by some manuscript brought from Italy by Benedict Biscop, they were illuminated by Eadfrith, a monk who became Bishop of Lindisfarne eleven years after Cuthbert's death. Carried off with St Cuthbert's body, they fell into the sea off the coast of Scotland during the wanderings of the monks, but were recovered at low tide and eventually ended up at Durham. They are now in the British Museum.

When the Venerable Bede visited the community early in the eighth century, his name was inscribed on another famous manuscript preserved in the British Museum, the *Liber Vitae,* and before leaving, he read the draft of his *Life of St Cuthbert* to the senior monks and had it approved by them.

In AD793, Lindisfarne Priory was sacked by the Vikings and most of the monks were slain. *The Anglo-Saxon Chronicle* records the event in dramatic fashion:

"Terrible portents came over the land of the Northumbrians and miserably frightened the people. There were immense sheets of light rushing through the air, and whirlwinds, and fiery dragons flying across the firmament. These tremendous tokens were soon followed by a great famine, and a little after that in the same year on the sixth of the Ides of June, the harrying of heathen men miserably destroyed God's church in Lindisfarne through rapine and slaughter."

Viking dragon-ships arriving at the coast of Northumbria. The shields which were stowed away at sea are now in the defensive position for entry into rivers and bays. The early fortress of Bebbanburgh (later Bamburgh) is on the horizon. The birds in the foreground are Eider Ducks, which St Cuthbert protected and cherished and are still known as "Cuddy's Ducks" along the north Northumberland coast.

Ninth century gravestone from Lindisfarne, Northumberland showing a band of Viking warriors on one side and a symbolic representation of the Day of Judgement on the reverse. This stone is in the Lindisfarne Priory Museum.

Chapter 12
The Coming Of The Vikings

Come; and strong within us
Stir the Vikings' blood;
Bracing brain and sinew;
Blow, thou wind of God!

Charles Kingsley

The raid on Lindisfarne was followed in the next year, 794, by a raid on Jarrow, Bede's old monastery. This time the Vikings didn't have it all their own way. One of their leaders was slain and several Viking ships were wrecked by a storm and the survivors were killed as they struggled ashore. Also in 794, the Irish Island, Reachrainnn (Rathlin) and the Hebridean Isle of Skye, were attacked. In 795, St Columba's monastery on Iona was assaulted, and again in 802 and 806.

Also in 795, the Irish west coastal island monasteries of Inisbofin and Inismurray were plundered and damaged, and the church on Lambey Island near Dublin was burned down.

In 799 the Abbey of St Philibert on the island of Noirmoutier, near the Loire Estuary was looted for the first time. The Viking pirates had really unleashed themsleves.

Viking Runic alphabet. As well as letters of the alphabet, each rune had its own meaning.

The Mystical Norse Runes

THE RUNIC ALPHABET

HJALTASTEYN
Whiteness, Shetland

	Runic	Name	Meaning		Runic	Name	Meaning
				M	Y	mannar	mankind
A	ᚠ	asur	god	N	ᚼ	naudir	need, necessity
B	ᛒ	berkana	fertility	O	ᛜ	opala	property
C	ᚲ	kauna	fire, torch	P	ᚴ	perpru	no known meaning
D	ᛗ	dagar	day, prosperity	Q	ᛏ	cweorp	meaning
E	ᛖ	ehwar	yew tree	R	ᚱ	raidu	journey
F	ᚡ	fehu	cattle	S	ᛌ	sowelu	sun
G	ᚷ	gebu	gift, sacrifice	T	ᛏ	tiwar	the god Tyr
H	ᚼ	hagla	hail	U	ᚢ	urur	strength, fame
I	ᛁ	isar	ice	V	ᛨ	no name	
J	ᛃ	jara	harvest	W	ᚹ	wunjo	joy, peace
K	ᚴ		same derivation as "C"	Y	ᛉ	yr	yew bow
L	ᛚ	lagur	water	Z	ᛊ	algir	defence

Saxon Monks bearing St Cuthbert's coffin away from Lindisfarne. This painting hangs in Chester-le-Street Parish Church.

In spite of these disasters, the monastic tradition continued at Lindisfarne. In the Autumn of 874 however, the Vikings returned and entered the Tyne. The Viking fleet was under the command of Halfdan who decided that as it was late in the year, they would anchor for the winter in the River Tyne, off the mouth of the River Team, (upstream from the modern Gateshead). In the Spring of 875, the church of St Andrew at Hexham, built by Bishop Wilfrid of York, was left blazing. The monasteries at Monkwearmouth and Jarrow were plundered and wrecked and Whitby had already been attacked during the previous year.

At Tynemouth, where two of Northumbria's kings, Oswin and Osric were buried, the seventh-century monastery on the headland called Penbal Crag, overlooking Prior's Haven, was left as a smoking ruin.

The Vikings then sailed north but word had gone ahead to Bishop Eardulph and the monks on Lindisfarne. The Bishop knew of the plea which had been made by St Cuthbert in 687, which was that if ever the monks were forced to leave Holy Island in the face of a heathen invasion, they should dig up his bones and carry them away with them to rest in Christian surroundings.

St Cuthbert's coffin was lifted and the monks placed inside, alongside the body of the Saint, the bones of St Aidan and three other priests, the skull of Oswald, Cuthbert's portable altar, and the *Lindisfarne Gospels*. These had been written by Bishop Eadfrith and formed the finest book of the early Saxon period and the earliest fully illuminated English book known. It has 258 folio pages of vellum which contain 22,800 lines of half-uncial script and magnificent coloured illustrations. A solitary monk was left as an observer while Bishop Eardulph and his flock made their way across to the mainland. The monastery was left to be destroyed.

Reconstruction of the lid of St Cuthbert's coffin showing the image of Christ and the four Evangelists.

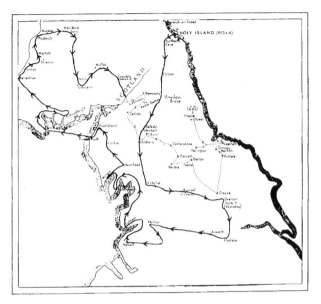

Howard Pease's map of 1927 showing the route of the flight of the monks from Lindisfarne to Conceastre leaving Holy Island in AD875 and arriving at the future Chester-le-Street in AD883.

The Vikings arrived and the lone monk hid. From the mainland, Bishop Eardulph watched the flames rise over Holy Island. The great bishopric of Lindisfarne was finished and the monks were homeless.

The journey into exile was to last seven weary years. The monks tramped with their precious relics across the length of Northumbria, Cumberland, Lancashire and Yorkshire, The chronicler, Simeon of Durham, tells us that the monks were showered with gifts. Eventually they found a suitable home, in 883, at Conceastre, on the site of the old Roman fort of Concangis, the future Chester-le-Street.

Halfdan had shared out land belonging to Northumbrians and his Vikings began ploughing, but it seems that the Danish settlement took place almost entirely south of the Tees. This explains why there are few Scandinavian place names in Northumberland (as apart from *Northumbria*). It is also likely that if the monks had encountered Viking settlers, the latter, who were now colonists were probably attempting to begin a peaceful life. Viking pirates however, still sailed the North Sea.

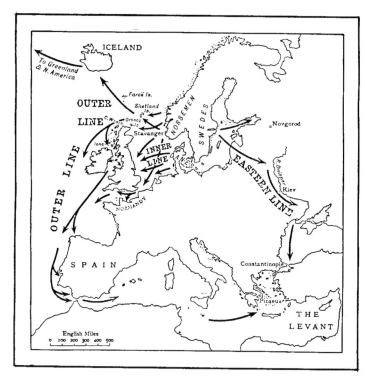

Map showing the routes taken during the Viking expansion. The Danes and Norwegians followed the Inner and Outer lines and the Swedes the Eastern line.

At Conceastre the monks built a wooden cathedral-church and as it contained the bishop's seat (*cathedra* = chair), Conceastre became a cathedral city even though the church was merely a humble timber structure. A piece of wood in the anchorage of the Chester-le-Street Parish Church of St Mary and St Cuthbert may be part of the original cathedral.

By the time they arrived, peace had been restored to Northumbria through agreement between Alfred the Great who was the Saxon monarch of Wessex, and Guthrum, the second Viking ruler of York. The Bishop of Conceastre was granted a see which extended from the Tees to the Firth of Forth and from the North Sea to the Irish Sea, including the towns which would become Edinburgh, Carlisle, Newcastle and Durham. From Conceastre, the whole northern diocese of England was governed. England was divided between the Danes, who occupied "The Danelaw" and the Anglo-Saxons, who retained Northumberland and Wessex. As mentioned previously, the Danes occupied the southern half of the old "Northumbria" which was south of the Tees.

King Alfred confirmed the grants of power to the Bishop of Conceastre and bestowed upon the Saint the other extensive privileges and immunities which eventually converted the patrimony of St Cuthbert into a county palatine.

The Viking invasion routes and Viking settlements. Most of Northern Northumbria remained in the hands of the Anglo-Saxons (English) with the Viking settlements to the south of the Tees.

The peace would be shattered from time to time between the Anglo-Saxons and the Vikings. Viking settlers increasingly wished to live at peace with their Saxon neighbours but wandering Viking pirates continued to make raids here and there.

"Danelaw" extended from the Tees, south to the Thames and westwards to the old Roman road, "Watling Street." The Danelaw was established between 878 and 886 and by 1016, the good Danish King Canute, loved and respected by both Saxon and Viking, ruled most of England.

Viking pirates however still roamed the seas and in 993, Bamburgh was sacked by the crews of longships, and it lay desolate until the time of William the Conqueror who is thought to have built a strong wooden castle there.

Also in 993, the Saxon King Athelstane visited Conceastre and bestowed gifts. King Edmund, Athelstane's brother and successor, also visited with more presents. About this time, the *Lindisfarne Gospels* were translated at Conceastre by Bishop Aldred into the Saxon language. This must have been between 947 and 968, during which time Aldred served at Conceastre, and it is known that the gospels were here during all that period. An Anglo-Saxon " *gloss,* "or word-for-word translation was written in red ink between the lines of the Latin text of all the four gospels contained in the book. Aldred also wrote a tailpiece which states that:

> *"Eadfrith Bishop of the Lindisfarne Church he this book wrote, at first for God and St Cuthbert and all the saints in common who in the island are, and Ethilwold, the Lindisfarne islanders Bishop, pressed it outside and bound it as well as he could..."*

Here in Chester-le-Street, only a few hundred yards from where this is being written, Cuthbert's body remained until 995, when further raids by Viking pirates caused the monks to seek a safer refuge. They had thought themselves safe from the raiders at a distance of fourteen miles from the sea, but the River Wear was an easy route for the Viking ships which could sail on only two feet of water. Even if rivers had un-navigable stretches, the Vikings could portage their ships past rapids on log rollers, often using stolen oxen as motive power.

At fortnightly intervals, when the Sun, Full Moon and Earth were in line, High Spring Tides made the River Wear easily navigable as far as Conceastre. There were no hindrances to navigation between the sea and Conceastre except the great Roman dam at Hylton which was ruinous.

The 14th-century medieval bridge at the foot of Newbridge Bank which is constructed on a solid foundation-ramp right across the river, had not yet been built.

The Swedish Vikings (the *"Rus"*) who unlike their Norwegian and Danish cousins, turned East instead of West, crossed the whole of Russia, south to Constantinople, using major and minor rivers, and negotiated watersheds by the method mentioned above.

During the period from 883 until the Norman Conquest, Lindisfarne was desolate and ceased to be mentioned in documents. No archaeological remains have as yet been found from that period but it is extremely likely that Lindisfarne's Saxon timber cathedral was on the same site as the later Norman priory. The possible remains of an early chapel have still to be excavated on the Heugh. St Coomb's Farm, near the modern water tower may hide another. On St Cuthbert's Islet of Hobthrush, there is both documentary and archaeological evidence for Cuthbert's cell and a chapel.

Before we move on to a closer study of the Vikings, perhaps the names of the Saxon months may give readers an appreciation of the everyday life of the Saxon inhabitants of Conceastre:

Names of Saxon Months

January	**Wolf-monath:** Hungry wolves preyed on villages.
	or Aefta-Yula: After Christmas.
February	**Sprout-kele:** Broth making month (using *"kelewurt"*).
March	**Hyldmonath:** Windy/stormy month.
	or Rhede-monath: after the English goddess,"Rhoeda". After the introduction of Christianity, March was held in great reverence, as the month in which Lent began.
April	**Oster-monath:** Month of the East winds, also Heathen festival of the Rising Sun.
May	**Trimilci:** Cows can be milked three times per day.
June	**Weyd-monath:** Cattle began to feed in the meadows, on *"weyd."* The meadows were usually marshy. The English also commenced their long voyages in this month. Much woodcutting was done for the fitting-out of ships.
July	**Heu-monath:** Foliage month,
	or Hey-monath: Hay-month,
	or Lida-aftera: The second month after the Sun's descent.
August	**Arn-monath**, **Barn-monath:** Harvest month.
September	**Gerst-monath:** Barley month, so called after the liquor *"beerlegh,"* hence "barley."
October	**Cold-monath:** Cold month
	or Wyn-monath: Wine-making month. The vine was extensively cultivated in Saxon England.
November	**Wint-monath**, **Wind-monath:** Windy month. These storms were expected to last until March.
December	**Aerra Geola:** The Sun turns his glorious course.
	or Heilig-monath: Holy month (after the introduction of Christianity). Before Saxon Christianity, it was the festival of Thor. During the Roman period, Dec 25th had been: *"Saturnalia"* when masters waited upon their slaves.

Names of days of the week

The names of days of the week developed as follows: The Babylonians decided that a market should be held every seventh day. They also held religious meetings on that day. The Jews followed their example but used the day for religious purposes only.

When the Egyptians adopted the seven-day week, they named the days after the Sun, Moon, Mars, Mercury, Jupiter, Venus and Saturn.

We get our modern days' names from the Saxons, who copied a couple of Roman gods' names but substituted a few of their own. *Sunnandaeg*(Sunday), *Monandaeg* (Moonday), *Tiwesdaeg* (Tiw = Mars), *Wodensdaeg* (Wodensday), *Thorsdaeg* (Thorsday), *Friggdaeg* (Frigg = wife of Odin) and *Saeternsdaeg* (copied from Roman *Saturnalia*).

Now for a closer look at the Vikings who caused the Lindisfarne monks to flee and wander for seven years before settling, first in Conceastre for 112 years. In 995 these Vikings would cause the monks to flee again to a safer refuge on the high peninsula-rock of Dunholme (Durham).

Not all of the Scandinavians were Vikings: most were farmers or fishermen, scratching for a humble existence in harsh Norwegian surroundings. In the medieval Scandinavian languages, the word *vikingr* means a pirate who seeks wealth by ship-borne raids on foreign coasts or by attacking peaceful seafarers in home waters.

This existence was attractive to such people as the sons of farmers who were faced with an ever decreasing size of an already tiny smallholding. This was also coupled with the ability of the Scandinavians as excellent shipwrights and their superb products, manned by first class seamen. The shape of the Viking "longships" or "dragon-ships" cannot be improved upon by modern computers.

As the Vikings wandered far and wide in search of booty, the undefended coastal monasteries of lands to the south became easy targets. The Vikings, unlike most seamen, were excellent horsemen, and could range far and wide on mounts stolen from farms near landing sites.

After the first raids, it became increasingly obvious to these Vikings that the lands to the south and west were ill-defended. The answer to their problems of money and an increasing shortage of farmland at home was to seize and settle foreign territory.

By the end of the ninth century, the Vikings had conquered large areas of the British Isles and established Norse and Danish kingdoms with capitals at Dublin and York.

A Viking king who claimed all the Islands of Caledonia proved his ownership by sailing round them. Certain peninsulas had only a narrow strip of land joining them to the mainland. The king ordered his ship to be dragged out of the water and pulled on rollers over the neck of land, thus proving that he has sailed his ship all round the peninsula and therefore as an island, it was rightly his. These necks of land are usually called "Tarbert" or "Tarbet" (isthmus).

A Viking ship under sail could proceed to windward by "tacking" if necessary. As the ship could be rowed as well as sailed, the ship was "powered" which was especially useful while making an entry into bays and rivers in adverse weather and tidal conditions and where a narrow winding channel had to be negotiated.

The Kingdom of Northumbria suffered particularly badly from Viking attacks but only those more southerly parts of England, now known as Yorkshire, Lancashire and Cumbria were settled in large numbers by the invaders. Most of Northumbria north of the Tees remained in the hands of the Angles.

In the past, landlubberly historians have claimed that the square-rigged Viking ships could, while under sail, run only before the wind. The same has been said about the Romans but as has been seen earlier, the Romans *could* "tack." Likewise, as mentioned above, so could the Vikings. A replica Viking ship has shown its ability that while close-hauled and zig-zagging to windward, it could hold a course with sail only, at 60 degrees to the direction of the wind. The yard, about 33 feet long could be swung round once the trusses were eased, to catch a beam wind or even one from 60 degrees on the bow. Ornate weather vanes have been found while excavating Viking ships and these would have been most useful for the helmsman to judge the angle of the sail to the wind in the critical conditions of trying to make headway to windward. The most likely position for the vane was the top of the mast but a Viking-period wood-carving from Bergen shows forty-one longships moored side-by-side to a jetty. Three have wind-vanes in place of the more usual dragon's head, One is also flying a windsock-type flag.

Circular shields, almost always shown on drawings of Viking ships, did not adorn the ships' sides at sea: they were stowed away. Only when the ships entered rivers or bays were the overlapping multi-coloured shields deployed, each one covering a single rower. It was in the rivers where the shields were necessary to provide protection against arrows and other missiles fired by unseen defenders who were hidden behind riverside foliage.

Nor were the Vikings' helmets adorned with animal horns - only the helmet of the medicine-man or witch-doctor, who was probably also the ship's navigator, was so decorated. Forensic evidence shows that some of the Viking raiders were girls!

The Vikings were excellent navigators although it is said by most "experts" that they did not have magnetic compasses. A magnetic compass is not necessary for navigation - the sky is full of compasses!

The Chinese had possessed magnetic compasses since the Third Dynasty, (second millenium BC) and this Chinese navigation aid was called a *Tchi Nan* and was south-pointing. It is now known that the Romans traded with China, and the Vikings got as far as the Middle East. It is therefore possible that both Roman and Viking ships were similarly equipped.

The Coming of the Vikings

The Vikings also had a sun-stone which was a polarised crystal of cordierite which allowed the navigators to take bearings of the Sun in overcast conditions. Tourmaline, which can be found in the Oslo Fjord area, is another stone with the same property. Pieces of it, and also of cordierite, have been found in Viking ship-burials. Experiments have shown that in overcast conditions or fog, the light coming through the crystal when aligned on the unseen Sun, changes from yellow or pink to blue. Bearings could even be taken with the Sun up to seven degrees below the horizon so the Viking navigators continued to take Sun-bearings after sunset. A reference to the use of the sunstone is made in *Raudúlfa Páttr ok Sonum Hans*:

> *"the weather was thick and stormy. The King (St Olaf d1030)looked about and saw no blue sky;....then the King took the sunstone and held it up, and then saw where (the Sun) beamed from the stone....."*

An airman's navigation aid called a "Kollsman's Sky Compass" uses the same principle.

A wooden *pelorus* which is a kind of dummy compass for plotting bearings, was found in 1948 on a Viking site in Greenland. It was also very likely to have been used as a sun-compass. It is notched with 32 points which correspond to the markings of medieval and later magnetic compasses. A few of these antique 32-point compasses are still in use today on old-fashioned and "replica" ships.

The surviving part of the Viking sun-compass disc has some of its 32 divisions emphasised by certain scratches; these seem to relate to the cardinal points.

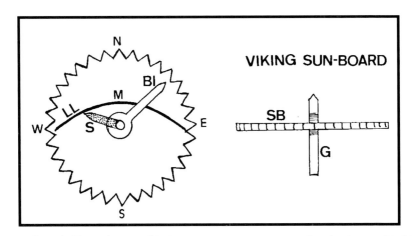

Viking sun-board. Not only was this instrument a sun-compass but it also enabled Viking navigators to sail their ships accurately along predetermined lines of latitude when sailing east or west. When sailing north or south, the ship's distance made good could be checked with the establishment at noon (when the Sun crosses the meridian) of the line of latitude being crossed. SB = circular disc with 32 points of the compass. G = Gnomon pin, adjustable for the time of year. BI = rotatable bearing indicator. S = shadow of central Gnomon pin. LL = mathematical curve depicting line of latitude. M = length of Gnomon's shadow at noon. This gives an accurate reading of the ship's latitude.

The Viking navigators' language "Old Norse" contains names for eight points of the compass; those for NE and SE are "landnorth" and "landsouth," and those for NW and SW are "outnorth" and "outsouth." These names were obviously devised by seamen on routes where most land masses lay to the east and open seas to the west.

The Viking pelorus-sun-compass is a circular rotatable wooden disc with a central vertical handle underneath. On the top side is a central hole, obviously for a vertical gnomon. There is also an offset arc of a mathematical curve, cut into the disc. It is fairly obvious how the Viking long range sea navigators used this device. Before departure, if the navigator adjusted the height of the vertical gnomon so that the shadow of the tip just touched the etched elliptical arc, they could steer due west, for example, along a line of latitude to a destination of which the latitude was known. As the altitude of the Sun altered during the year, different lengths of gnomon must have been inserted or a long one adjusted by pushing it up or down through the central hole of the disc; but as described below, the Viking navigators had a good knowledge of these techniques. Magnetic compasses have to be compensated for "Variation" which is the angle between True North (the direction of the Earth's Geographical North Pole) and Magnetic North, which wanders all over the place and is at the moment in Arctic Canada. The sun-compass has no corrections and points to the northern end of the Earth's axis which is Latitude 90 degrees North. This axis runs from the Geographic North Pole through the Earth's centre to the South Geographic Pole (which is Latitude 90 degrees South) and the Earth spins once in 24 hours around this axis in an anticlockwise direction if viewed from above the North Pole.

The Viking sun-compass could also be used at night by lining up the north point on the dial with the North Pole Star, therefore to be accurate, the device should be called an "Astro-compass" and not merely a "Sun-compass."

Another function of the Viking Astro-Sun-compass could have been that while sailing north, or south and thus changing latitude, the new latitude being traversed could be estimated by the length of the gnomon's shadow at midday. The shadow will decrease on consecutive middays if the ship moves south and increase if the distance made good is to the north.

It is possible that the Viking Sun-compass had several mathematically etched arcs on the disc, concentric to the carved one, and the extra curves would then indicate specific parallels of latitude as demarked by the tip of the shadow of the gnomon.

Before the satellite-electronic navigation era, long range aircraft flying over the Arctic and Antarctic regions (where magnetic compasses have huge errors and are unreliable), carried astro-compasses which look quite complex but performed the same functions as the Viking device.

As has been mentioned earlier, any modern ship's officer or airline pilot knows that the sky is full of compasses. As well as the Sun, stars and planets, the Moon is an excellent aid to navigation if one knows how to use it. Navigation by the stars has been carried out for several thousand years, and as mentioned previously, the Pole Star, as well as indicating True North can also be used to find one's latitude in the Northern Hemisphere because the altitude (angle above the horizon) of the Pole Star is equal to the observer's latitude (to within one degree in the present epoch).

It was known to Viking navigators that as well as the altitude of the Pole Star being equal to the observer's latitude, the altitude of the midday Sun at its highest point as it crossed the meridian, bore a relationship to the ship's latitude. Altitudes are best measured by modern sextants but the ancient navigators had "rule of thumb" methods:

An Icelandic Viking set of tables survives and gives the Sun's midday altitude for every week of the year, as observed from northern Iceland. These tables are ascribed to a man known as Star-Oddi, and date to the eleventh-century. The extremely accurate calculations are expressed in units called "half wheels" which are half the apparent diameter of the Sun, i.e. 16 minutes of angle.

A navigator holding at arm's length, a stick marked-off in these units, could record the Sun's meridian altitude and thus derive his latitude.

An Icelander on a pilgrimage to the Holy Land about 1150, reported that the latitude of his position on the bank of the River Jordan was such that as he lay on his back and raised one knee, then placed his fist on the knee, with the thumb pointing upwards, the Pole Star appeared exactly on the tip of his thumb.

Vikings, who knew the latitudes of various places could find their way back to them by sailing along known latitudes of destinations.

The Vikings navigated successfully to Iceland, Greenland, Newfoundland, and almost certainly North America, five-hundred years before Columbus was supposed to have "discovered" the New World. Eric the Red settled at Brattahlid in Southern Greenland in 985 and a Viking settlement at L'Anse-Aux-Meadows has been excavated in Newfoundland.

A Viking map which marks Viking "Vinland" on the American mainland, survives in Yale's library. This map is a 15th century German copy of a Viking map of c1000. It seems that the Vikings in North America came into armed conflict with the North American Indians, and therefore withdrew to Newfoundland and Greenland.

The Vikings settled Iceland by 930 and a Norwegian Viking sailing direction says: "From Hernar (in Norway) set sail due west for Greenland."

A crude form of Radar (in this case more accurately called "sonar") was used by the Vikings. When the navigator, in foggy weather, estimated that he was closing the coast, he had a horn-blower blast his instrument at frequent intervals and echoes from unseen cliffs would give the navigator his distance from the danger.

In clear weather, distant mountain tops provided Vikings with navigational information. An example of this follows:

"From Hernar in Norway, set sail due west for Hvarf in Greenland. You are to sail north of Shetland in such a way that you can just sight it in clear weather; but to the south of the Faeroes, in such a way that the sea seems to be half-way up the mountain

slopes; and steer south of Iceland, in such a way that you can sight birds and whales which frequent the waters there."

Long before the Viking era, early navigators followed flocks of migrating birds. The Viking navigators could also obtain approximate positions by the observation of bird types. When nearing an expected destination for example Iceland, good evidence would be the appearance of a darker version of the well known white fulmar petrel of Norwegian waters. An increase in the number of puffins would have indicated the proximity of the Faeroes. One of the *sagas* tells of a ship's crew who knew of the proximity of the Irish coast by observing "Irish birds" after getting near destination by following a known line of latitude, for example.

It is interesting to note that not only the human race improves its technology and knowledge from generation to generation; the animal kingdom also learns from experience, and from humans too. Our small birds migrating south from northern Europe had to climb over the high Alps. Now lots of them are going through the St Bernard Tunnel and other tunnels!

When the Vikings approached Greenland, they could see the brilliant white reflection of the ice-cap on the cloud base. Modern North Atlantic aircraft ferry pilots, the author included, are well aware of this phenomenon.

The last Scandinavian Viking attack on Britain came in 1066 when Norwegian King Harald Hardradi attacked Yorkshire. The English Saxon King Harold Godwinson with an army of allied Viking settlers defeated this Norwegian army at Stamford Bridge but three days later, the Normans under William the Conqueror invaded the south coast of England. The Normans were merely Norsemen who had settled in France and adopted the French language. Duke William of Normandy (William the Conqueror), was the great-great-great grandson of Rollo, the Viking Chief, and the Norman-Vikings had established their own "Danelaw" in northern France.

After a forced march south, the Saxon and Viking settlers were extremely tired and the rest is well known history. The "English" Anglo-Saxon-Viking settler-army lost to William the Conqueror and the Normans became the masters of England.

The Bayeux Tapestry is a pictorial representation of the Norman invasion and it shows Viking-type longships, some with cavalry horses and armoured knights on board.

We will come back to the Normans shortly but for now, let us return to the Scandinavian Vikings. (Readers who wish to know more about Viking dates should consult Appx "A").

*Part of the Bayeux Tapestry showing Norman
knights fighting a combined army of Saxons
and Vikings at Hastings.*

*Portage of a river boat by Swedish
Vikings in Russia*

*A weather-vane from a Swedish church,
believed to have originally belonged to a
Viking ship.*

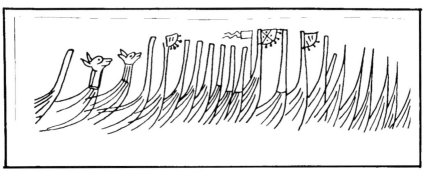

*The prows of Viking ships. Some carry wind-indicators in place of the more usual
figureheads.*

*The most common place for a wind-vane was the top of the ship's mast. This illustration is
from a wood carving found in Bergen.*

Chapter 13
English, Norsemen And Normans

The Saxon is not like us Normans. His manners are not so polite. But he never means anything serious till he talks about justice and right, then he stands like an ox in the furrow with his sullen set eyes on your own, And grumbles, 'This isn't fair dealing, my son, leave the Saxon alone.'

Rudyard Kipling

The Vikings could also obtain bearings on land below the horizon by releasing ravens. If the ravens climbed to height and then returned to the ship, no distant land was in sight. If however the ravens disappeared on a straight course, land was visible from aloft, and the Vikings could follow the birds or merely use the direction as a navigational bearing in the same way as modern navigators use a bearing from a radio-beacon off to one side of course, to measure progress along the desired track.

Locked in the Viking navigator's mind or written down in sailing directions, were the latitudes of important positions such as river estuaries or natural harbours. Our Saxon monks in Conceastre were therefore living in a fools' paradise if they had assumed that the Vikings could not find the mouth of the River Wear. The latter would lead the Viking ships to the monks' supposedly safe refuge.

The floorboards of Viking ships, if fitted, were not permanently fastened down in order to facilitate bailing, and while at sea, tent-shaped awnings, rigged on frames, gave some protection to the crew and cargo. Small boats which could be used as harbour tugs, lifeboats, or ship-to-shore runabouts, were either towed behind Viking ships or stowed aboard.

The steering-oar (*steerboard*) of a Viking ship was always on the starboard (right hand) side and while alongside a jetty, the opposite side, (the larboard side), later called the "port side" could rub against the harbour structure (with suitable fenders). Thus the steering gear would not be damaged. Steering oars are extremely efficient and can be easily replaced at sea. To install a spare modern stern-rudder while at sea is a very difficult and almost impossible task. The stern-rudder is also heavy to operate and on a sailing ship, often needs two or three men to handle the wheel in bad weather. The steering oar, rotating around its central shaft presents a surface to the water both ahead and behind the pivoting axis and is therefore balanced like the rudder of an aircraft. Thus the helmsman can steer the ship with one hand even in bad weather.

The Vikings during their attacks on the habitations of their victims had a secret weapon: suicidal attacks were made by warriors who were known as " *berserks*". These gentlemen worked themselves up into a frenzy and swung their battle-axes killing all around them, even their friends, the latter of course keeping well clear of them in battle.

Once the Vikings settled in Britain, it was only a question of time before they made peace and intermingled with the Saxons (English) and Celts and they became part of the modern British nation which probably had a lot to do with Britain's future lead as a world maritime power.

Vikings settlements in Britain are often revealed by place-names. These invariably end with "*by*," such as Whitby etc.

It appears that when the Vikings settled in Britain, they adopted the "open field" cultivation system which is thought to have originated with the Saxons, though it is difficult to get the archaeological establishment to agree to a date on this.

The Lambton *Wurm*: pure fiction or a grain of truth?

The legend of "The Lambton Worm" is well known in north-eastern England. The so-called "Worm" is supposed to have been a giant reptile which terrorised the population of Wearside by killing riverside dwellers and devouring their livestock.

Lots of fables spring from just a grain of truth and that may well be the case here. Was it possible that a Loch Ness Monster-type animal lived in the River Wear? It is very unlikely but the name gives us a clue. Is the word "worm" which describes a small soil-dwelling invertebrate appropriate to an amphibious giant which could consume a herd of cattle? Surely, "sea serpent", "sea monster", or "dragon" would be more suitable. It just so happens that the Saxon word "*wurm*" means "*dragon.*" Could our "Worm" have been one or more of the dreaded Viking "Dragon Ships"?

As explained previously, late in the eighth century, the Vikings began to raid the British shores. These fierce sea raiders attacked coastal monasteries and villages and sailed up the rivers in their "*dragon-ships*". The Norwegian and Danish longships with dragon figure-heads on their bows, and sterns carved like serpents' tails, did bring slaughter and pillage to the Saxon inhabitants of Northumbria. These Vikings attacked the eastern coasts of Britain while other Norsemen went for the western coasts and islands and also Ireland. The Swedes moved the other way and penetrated Russia to Kiev. From there, they sailed down the Dnieper and crossed the Black Sea to Constantinople.

In north-eastern England, the next river to the south of the Wear is the Tees, and this river also has its sea-monster legend. Here it is known as the "Sockburn Worm" (once again the word "worm" is used rather than "monster"). Both the Lambton area on the River Wear and the Sockburn district on the Tees are beside stretches of water which were easily navigable to the shallow-draught Viking ships.

At Sockburn there are the remains of an Anglo-Saxon church and there is also a Viking graveyard complete with "hog-back" gravestones. A suspected Roman road also approaches from the east-north-east, and this may have also been used by the Vikings, as it passes through Normanby, Ormesby, Tollesby, Ingleby and Girsby, all names of Norse origin.

 The Durham historian Hutchinson was of the opinion that the legend of the Sockburn Worm is a reference to some long forgotten Viking rover who sacked and plundered this part of the Tees valley. Today, Sockburn is little more than a farm but in Anglo-Saxon times it was an important place as it was here that Eanbald, Archbishop of York, and Highbald, Bishop of Lindisfarne, were consecrated in the eighth century.

The author and poet, Lewis Carroll was inspired by the Sockburn Worm story to write about the "Jabberwock" in *Alice through the Looking Glass.*

Worm legends are a feature of both Anglo-Saxon and Viking mythology, where "worms" are usually ferocious serpents or dragons. There are more "worm legends" associated with Northumbria, such as the "Laidley Worm" of Bamburgh, which was another Anglo-Saxon establishment attacked by Vikings.

In north-eastern England there is a tradition that the longships reached Hexham, 30 miles up the River Tyne from the sea, a small feat compared with the Swedish Vikings' marathon crossing of all Russia. As we have seen in Chapter 3, during the 19th century the keelboatmen (lightermen) who supplied the seagoing colliers at Sunderland with their cargoes of coal, made tremendous use of the tides up the River Wear to Picktree. This ease of navigation of the River Wear is important to our story.

With reference to our "Worm;" over the centuries, the size of this beast has increased with the telling, and in the Old Tyne Theatre in 1867, the now famous song was sung about the monster.

This ballad tells about the Worm lapping itself ten times round "Pensher" (Penshaw) Hill. On this hilltop today, there stands a monument which is a near replica of the ancient Greek temple of Theseus in Athens. Some locals will tell you that it was built to commemorate the "Worm" but it was actually erected in 1844 in honour of John George Lambton, Earl of Durham and the first Governor-general of Canada. The helical path to the top of the hill is not the mark left by a giant serpent but the track which had to take an easy gradient to enable the horse-drawn stone-laden builders' wagons to get to the summit.

The huge Doric-style temple can be seen for miles around and was especially useful as a marker for the pilots of the nearby Usworth aerodrome before a new monster, the Nissan car factory, swallowed up the airfield and the surrounding woodlands.

Quite near to Penshaw Hill is the village of Fatfield and on its riverside, there is a much smaller hill called "Worm Hill." This is the traditional lair of the "Lambton Worm." From the air, this hill looks artificial and could be an ancient burial mound though it is neither the shape of a Neolithic "long barrow" nor a Bronze Age "round barrow." It may be of Saxon origin but Fatfield has a long maritime history and the mound could turn out to be a humble ballast hill or the remnants of ancient mining. There was an active shipyard at Fatfield in medieval and post-medieval times, once again highlighting the extensive navigation in the past of the fairly small River Wear.

So, when next you stand beside a quiet stretch of the River Wear, perhaps waiting patiently for a trout to take a fly, or hoping to catch a glimpse of the speeding kingfisher, try to penetrate the mists of time and listen for the chant of the Roman *barcarii*, singing in unison as they trudged upstream, dragging their "*codicaria*" (a general purpose barge which could be rowed, towed, poled or sailed); or peer through the years of haze to visualise the Saxon *cyuls* (keels?). If you sense the passage of a Viking dragon-ship, where now only a mallard and a moorhen paddle the waters, you may even smell the smoke of a burning village and probably understand how the tale of a ferocious sea-monster has survived the dark centuries.

Short summary

It seems odd that the Saxons were afraid of the Vikings as they themselves had first arrived in Britain as sea raiders during the last phases of the Roman occupation and as settlers after the Roman military withdrawal about AD410. The warlike Saxon seaborne invaders had driven the disorganised Romanised native Celts out to the west of England but during the following four centuries of pastoral life, the former masters of the *Oceanus* Germanicus (North Sea) had lost much (but not all) of their former appetite for seafaring.

Although the Romans in Britain had tolerated the Christian religion for the last hundred years or so of their occupation, and Emperor Constantine had made it the official creed of the Empire, the new Saxon invaders were pagans. It took many years for the double-pronged campaign, beginning in the 6th century, with missionaries from Rome in the south and slightly later, from Iona in the west, to convert them to Christianity.

As time went on, with Viking attacks and Viking settlers, the country was divided into Saxon and Scandinavian sectors. In the course of time, the races intermingled and it was the Christian Saxons who converted the Vikings to Christianity. Another ingredient to complete the mix of races would be the Normans who would invade and conquer in 1066. The present day English race would then be complete although there would be a close call in 1940 when another Nordic attack looked imminent.

A few Scandinavian names in our home area

On the north end of the Cleveland Hills is an isolated pinnacle which resembles a miniature "Matterhorn." Its present name is "Roseberry Topping." It was once however known as "Odinsburg" which is Norse for "Odin's Mount" and "Topping" is also derived from the Danish *toppen* which means "summit."

Not far to the north is Sadberge which is a name of Viking origin (Setberg) meaning "flat topped hill." There is a place called "Setburg" in both Norway and Iceland, and "Sedburgh" near Kendal. All have the same meaning.

The Saxon monks in Durham

On the high peninsula-rock at Durham (Dunholme = rock-island)the monks felt secure with the loop of the river almost encircling their new refuge. There they built a temporary rough shelter of boughs in which to house their holy relics. A further timber church, the *Alba Ecclesia* (White Church) was built and this was replaced in 998/99 by a stone church, the *Ecclesia Major* (Great Church). The church would not be completed until 1017 but Cuthbert's body was moved into the unfinished church in 999.

This new Saxon cathedral must have been an impressive building and had two towers, both topped with brass pinnacles, one over the choir and the other over the west end. To this

Saxon cathedral came the converted Canute on barefooted pilgrimage from Garmondsway, near Trimdon, bringing with him deeds concerning gifts of land. Great stores of valuables also found their way here when it was proved that the city was able to withstand siege. Ancient relics were also collected from other shrines. Among these were the bones of the Venerable Bede, stolen from Jarrow.

The Saxons' fortifications of the peninsula were built against attacks by both Scots and Danes. Records tell us that during the early eleventh century, the Scots twice besieged the city and both times suffered defeat and incurred large numbers of casualties.

Norman Norsemen

The Normans (the word is derived from "Norsemen") consisted of a large colony of Vikings who had invaded and settled in Normandy, picking up the French language in the process. Their land was an area of Danelaw similar to that in Britain and was constantly in confrontation with the Frankish tribes around Paris. These Normans had retained their skill as seafarers and were also excellent horsemen. Both skills were essential to their forthcoming invasion of England and the subsequent successful conquest of Britain.

Disunited England had long been plagued by battles between Saxons, Danes and Norwegians but William of Normandy brought the lesser conflicts to an end with his victorious conquest in 1066.

After reducing the south of England, William sent Robert Cumin with 700 men to occupy the north-east. On 30th January 1069, they arrived in Durham. The local Saxon population plotted resistance and during the night surrounded *en masse*, and broke into the city at dawn, burning Cumin's lodgings and slaughtering every Norman in sight. It was reported that only one Norman escaped. The fire from Cumin's house almost spread to the western tower of the nearby Anglo-Saxon cathedral.

It was about this time that the navigability of our River Wear gets another mention. Surtees tells us that the harbour at the mouth of the River Wear, "Wiranmuthe," or "Ostium Vedrae," was well known in the Saxon Ages; and it was here that, soon after the Conquest, Malcolm, King of Scotland, during a ruinous inroad along the eastern coast, found Edgar Atheling, the heir of England, his sister Margaret, the future Queen of Scotland, and a train of Saxon exiles, lying in the haven, waiting wind and tide to escape from their Norman conquerors into Scotland. It is later however, in the charter of Hugh Pudsey, towards the close of the twelfth century, that we get more detailed evidence of the existence of the Port or Borough of Southern Wearmouth as a place of maritime commerce.

To return to our story of the time just after the Conquest: two great earls, Edwin and Morcar who rebelled against William, were forgiven but rebelled again with the help of Danes. William himself therefore came north in 1069 and devastated the area. Every human being the Norman soldiers could catch was slaughtered and the land was laid waste. The bishop and the congregation of St Cuthbert were caught up in the panic and hurriedly withdrew to Lindisfarne, taking the body of their Saint with them.

When things quietened down, the monks returned to Durham in the spring of 1070, there to remain. William himself arrived there on his way back from Scotland. William was curious about the reports of the saint's uncorrupt body and wished to see it for himself. On the morning when the shrine and coffin were to be opened, William was taken with a violent fever which was put down to the wrath of the saint. In fright, William took off and never drew rein until he had crossed the Tees. Sometime during his stay in Durham however, he had made sure that the Norman regime would never be challenged again, by ordering a great castle to be built on an earlier Saxon fortification.

The River loop at Durham

There may have been another Saxon defensive element of the Durham peninsula: the loop of the River Wear at Durham provided a good strategic position for the various churches, castle and cathedral but there was a weak spot. Although the name Durham means "island rock," it is not quite an island. As it is now fairly certain that the Romans navigated the River Wear up to and well beyond Durham, perhaps the Romans had made a cut short-circuiting the river loop as they have done in other parts of their empire. Several examples of these cuts can be seen across the bends of the River Nene. Medieval references to a water ditch across the low neck of land at Durham tell us that the ditch could be flooded in times of danger by opening a water gate. This gate was called the *Cleur Port* and this name survives in the modern name of the road which crosses the area - "Clay Path."

Local political problems between Saxons and Normans

At the time of the Conquest, a noble Saxon called Liulph (an ancestor of the Lumley family) lived in Lumley village. He was a trusted counsellor of the first Norman Bishop of Durham, Walcher. Liulph complained to the bishop about the extortions that two of the bishop's officers were exacting. Leobwin, the bishop's chaplain, and Gilbert, his chamberlain, hired assassins to kill Liulph and some of his family at their hall in Lumley. The Saxons, including men from Conceastre (now called "Chester"), demanded that the bishop should meet them at St Mary's Church, Gateshead, and explain why Liulph had been murdered.

The bishop met the angry Saxons and things got out of hand. The bishop and his men had to take refuge in the church which the Saxons burnt to the ground.

The Normans took vengeance on the area and most of the Saxons' huts in Chester were burnt and many inhabitants slain. This occurred in 1080.

The Durham area, except for calling it "St Cuthbert's Land," is not included in the *Domesday Book* (a Norman survey of land ownership in England). After the two devastations, there was little left to record. Also the Bishop of Durham had become a Count-palatine and had secular as well as religious power over the people of Durham (known as the *haliwerfolc,* the people of the holy man, St Cuthbert). What the king did elsewhere, the bishop did in Durham. He had his own army, created his own knights and had his own law court. He had his own mint, mineral rights and owned several manors, including Chester (Ch-le-Str).

The *Ecclesia Major* of Durham (Saxon cathedral) was regarded by the Normans as not good enough a repository for St Cuthbert's remains and its demolition was ordered in 1092.

On the 11th August 1093, the foundations of the new Norman monastic church were laid by Bishop William de St Calais (known as Carileph to the Saxons). In 1099, Ralph Flambard became the Bishop of Durham by which time the nave had been built.

On 4th September 1104, St Cuthbert's coffin was opened for inspection and then the remains were transferred from their temporary cloister home and placed with great ceremony in a sepulchre in the new Norman cathedral-church. Cuthbert's coffin would be opened again four times: 1104, 1537, 1827 and 1899. The last occasion was the only time a proper medical study was carried out and this was under the direction of Dr Selby Plummer who came to the conclusion that Cuthbert had been a muscular man, about 5 ft 8ins tall, and that he probably died of tuberculosis.

During the examination, Cuthbert's bones, and other contents of the coffin, were recovered. These consisted of some seventh-century cloth, the famous pectoral cross (a cross worn on the chest) as well as other items of jewellery, and a bible, now known as the *Stoneyhurst Bible*.

The discovery of these artefacts, especially the pectoral cross which had been concealed in Cuthbert's robes, seems to discredit the theory put about in medieval times that for safe-keeping, St Cuthbert's body had been re-buried in a secret location and the body of another monk substituted.

St Cuthbert's body lay in a wooden, carved coffin, which was inside two other coffins, and stood on a marble base. It was to this shrine that pilgrims came throughout the Middle Ages, seeking spiritual contact with the saint and his healing powers. The pilgrims often left precious gifts.

At the reformation in 1539, as part of the reformers' zeal to focus people's prayers on God rather than saints, this elaborate shrine was broken up. St Cuthbert's coffin was buried below where the shrine had stood. The stones around the grave slab are all that now remain of the shrine.

But now we will return to Bishop Flambard's time: after some political trouble, Flambard continued the building of the walls of the cathedral-church and integral monastery to roof height. During this period, he founded Kepier Hospital and gave Finchale Hermitage to the monks. He also ordered the building of Framwellgate Bridge.

Bishop Geoffrey Rufus built the great north and south doorways of the nave and constructed for the monastery a wonderful chapter house, later rebuilt by the Victorians in 1895.

Bishop Hugh Pudsey was elected in 1153 and provided for Finchale to become a priory. He also built a hospital for 65 lepers at Sherburn. Two more were built, at Witton Gilbert and Northallerton. Elvet Bridge was also ordered to be constructed and the castle improved. Pudsey also built the Galilee Chapel on the western end of the cathedral. The main entrance had been on this end but Pudsey transferred it to the north side.

The house of Lindisfarne was refounded as a dependent priory of Durham. It is the splendid ruin of this Norman monastery that still stands on Holy Island. Even though we have searched hard for the site of the original wooden structure, we have not found any traces so it may be underneath the later Norman stone structure. This ruinous but beautiful monastery is much visited by tourists to Holy Island. The statue of Aidan faces the ruin which looks as if it has been a smaller version of Durham Cathedral. Stone from the ruinous Lindisfarne Priory was used to build Holy Island Castle on Beblowe Crag as a defence against Scotland. Building began in 1549 and the work was completed in 1550.

It was not the Vikings who turned the Norman Lindisfarne Monastery into a ruin, but Henry the Eighth and his dissolution of monasteries.

A formidable force to fight the Scots was concentrated here in 1543 and most of the monastery was pulled down to provide building-stone for the new castle. The priory church itself was converted into a military store-house. In 1613, Lord Walden took off all the roofs but the lead was sunk at sea on its way south. When Turner painted the priory in 1830, it was already the romantic ruin we see today. Enough remains to show visitors the superb craftsmanship of the stonemasons of the period. The museum on the site has many carved stones on display.

For those who wish to consult a table of dates for the Norman period and later, see Appendix/A.

We will now move on to the recognition of the various words and names which make up our modern English language, with particular reference to our landscape.

Recognition of ancient names
The Celts:
Celtic river names have survived from antiquity but few other Celtic words have made it into modern English.

The Anglo-Saxons;
England is the land of enclosures. This is denoted by the character of Anglo-Saxon names which end in *"-bury," "-fold," "-ham," "-hay," "-ton," "-yard"* and *"-worth."* Saxon settlement began in the 5th century in what was later to become "England".

An examination of Saxon names shows the love of privacy, and the seclusive character of the early "English" who imposed names upon what would become the "English" countryside.

The family bond was important to the Anglo-Saxon race and the suffix *"-ing"* to persons' names had very much the same significance as the prefix "Mac" in Scotland, "O" in Ireland and "Ap" in Wales. A whole clan or tribe, or body of adventurers attached themselves to the standard of some chief, and were thus distinguished by a common patronymic or "clan" name. Saxon colonisation was an invasion by families. The head bought or built a ship and embarked in it with his children, his freedmen, and his neighbours, and established a family colony identified by a name with the suffix *"-ing,"* on any shore to which winds carried them(forget about the myth that Saxon ships had no sails).

Note: The Anglo-Saxon *"wic"* (wick) = dairy farm, is not to be confused with the Viking *"wick"* which means "bay."

The Anglo-Saxon colonisation period is often referred to as the "Dark Age" because the few snippets of history we have were not written down until later. The heathen Saxon invaders used a Runic alphabet and it was fine for a charm on a sword or a name on a stone, but it was not used to take down annals, or to transcribe the long-lost epics sung by the gleemen in hall, of which more than one must have told the deeds of some hero who came seeking Britain over deep water.

The historian has two points of light, and even those are dim. He sees an orderly Romano-Celtic world late in the Fourth Century, beginning to fall into chaos. Two-hundred years later, he sees a Saxon-Celtic barbarism emerging confusedly into the renewed twilight of history, and he hears the marching chant of Augustine and his monks bringing back with them the Latin alphabet and thus the ability to make written records. Between these points stretches the darkness. The most important page in our national history is a blank - the chief names of this missing period: Hengist, Vortigern, Cerdic, Arthur, may be those of real or imaginary men. All that archaeology and history can do is to indicate, not the dates, leaders and campaigns, but only the general character of the warfare that destroyed Roman Britain and gave the land to the "English." Thus the new "English," still pagans, took over from the Roman Christianised Celts. It would take over two-hundred years and Christian missions from both Rome and Iona to convert the new pagan owners of the land, to Christianity.

From the "*History and Antiquities of Sunderland*," we get references to the siting of the later Saxon Christian settlements in our local area:

"The Saxons had the most lasting, general, and deep-rooted possession of the island. They very commonly settled in Roman towns, and especially chose them on account of their materials for the sites of their churches and monastical institutions. York, Newcastle, Hexham, Jarrow and Chester-le-Street are well-known instances of ecclesiastical edifices having been erected upon the ashes of Roman foundations; and doubtless too, when Benedict Biscop brought over workmen from Gaul to build his celebrated monastery at Wearmouth, which was constructed in stone after the Roman manner, he found abundance of materials in the long deserted Roman station "Ad Ostium Vedra."

This Roman site in Sunderland may have also been known as "Dictis" which is a missing Roman site in the north-east and is listed in a surviving Roman document.

The Vikings

The Scandinavian method of colonisation of parts of Britain was quite different to that of the Anglo-Saxons. It was effected by soldiers of fortune who abandoned domestic ties at home, and after a few years of piracy, settled down with women, captured from all parts of Europe.

Topographical names in ancient and later languages:
Mountains and hills

Ard,	Celtic;	a height, e.g. Ardrossan.
Ben,	Gadhelic;	mountain, e.g. Ben Nevis.
Bryn,	Welsh;	brow, ridge, e.g. Brandon.
Cenn,	Gadhelic;	mountain, e.g. Kenmore.
Drum,	Erse;	ridge, e.g. Dundrum.
Dun,	Celto-Saxon;	a hill-fort.
Fjeld,	Norse;	hill-side (fell).
Gebel,	Arabic;	mountain, e.g. Gibraltar (Gebeltariq).
Haugr,(how)	Norse;	a mound, hence Northumbrian "haugh."
Hlaw,	Anglo-Saxon;	a mound, rising ground.
Ho,(Hoo)	Anglo-Saxon;	a spit of land running into the sea.
Holl,	Norse;	hill.
Hyl,	Anglo-Saxon;	hill.
Pen,	Welsh;	mountain, e.g. Pennigant.
Ness,	Norse;	a headland, e.g. Sheerness.
Ross,	Celtic;	a promontory, e.g. Kinross.
Scar,	Norse;	a cliff, e.g. Scarborough.
Stan,	Anglo-Saxon;	stone, e.g. Stanley.
Stain,	Old German;	stone, e.g. Stainmore.
Tarbert,	Gaelic;	an isthmus.
Tell,	Arabic;	a small hill.
Tor,	Celtic;	a tower-like rock, e.g. Mam Tor.

Plains

Achadh,	Erse;	a field, e.g. Ardagh.
Blair,	Gadhelic;	a plain clear of wood.
Gwent,	Celtic;	a plain.
-ing	Anglo-Saxon;	a meadow, or a family link.
Maes,	Welsh;	a field.
Man,	Celtic;	a district.
Tir,	Welsh;	land.

Forests and fields

Feld,	German;	a forest clearing (trees felled).
Field,	English;	an enclosure for agriculture.
Fold,	Anglo-Saxon;	an enclosure made of felled trees.
Hay,	Anglo-Saxon;	a place surrounded by a hedge.
Holt,	Anglo-Saxon;	a copse.
Hyrst,	Anglo-Saxon;	a thick wood, e.g. Lyndhurst.
Leah,	Anglo-Saxon;	a wood.
Ley,	English;	an open place in a wood.
Lund,	Norse;	a sacred grove.
Sceaga,	Anglo-Saxon;	a shady place in a wood.
Thwaite,	Norse;	a forest clearing.
Toft,	Norse;	an enclosure of turf.
Worth,	Anglo-Saxon;	an enclosure, homestead.
Wudu,	Anglo-Saxon;	a wood.

Valleys

Combe,	Celto-Saxon;	a bowl-shaped valley.
Denu (dene),	Celto-Saxon;	a deep-wooded valley.
Gil ,	Norse;	a ravine.
Glen,	Gaelic;	a narrow valley.
Strath,	Gaelic;	a broad valley.

Rivers and waters

A,	Norse;	water.
Afon,	Celtic;	a river, e.g. River Avon.
Burn,	Anglo-Saxon;	a stream.
Broc,	Anglo-Saxon;	a brook.
Don/dan,	Celtic;	water/river.
Dwr,	Celtic;	water, e.g. part of River Wear.
Ea,	Anglo-Saxon;	water, e.g. part of River Wear.
Flet,	Anglo-Saxon;	a flowing stream.
Foss,	Norse;	a waterfall.
Hithe,	Anglo-Saxon;	a wharf.

Linn,	Celtic;	a deep pool.
Mere,	Anglo-Saxon;	a lake, a marsh.
Ofer,	Anglo-Saxon;	a shore.
Rhe/rhin,	Celtic;	water/river.
Tarbet,	Gaelic;	an isthmus.
Wick,	Norse;	a bay.(do not confuse with A/S *wic*).
Wysk/esk,	Celtic;	water/river.

Islands

Ea, (ey),	Anglo-Saxon;	an island.
Oe,	Norse;	an island in the sea.
Holm,	Norse;	an island in a river.

Roads, bridges and fords

Bab,	Arabic;	a gate, e.g. Bab-el-Mandeb.
Briva,	Old Celtic;	a bridge.
Brücke,	German;	a bridge.
Brugge,	Anglo-Saxon;	a bridge.
Gata (gate),	Norse;	a road or street.
Pons,	Latin;	a bridge.
Pont,	Welsh/French;	a bridge.
Sarn,	Welsh;	a road, e.g. Sarn Helen.
Stan, stain,	A-Saxon/Norse;	stone.
Stanweg,	Anglo-Saxon;	stone-way.
Strata,	Latin;	a road or street.

Habitations and enclosures

Burgh,	Anglo-Saxon;	walled defended enclosure.
-by,	Norse;	village, town.
Caer,	Welsh;	a castle.
Caster,	Anglian;	a castle.
Castra,	Latin;	a fort or castle.
Ceastre,	Anglo-Saxon;	a castle.
Cester,	Mercian;	a castle.
Chester,	Norman;	a castle.

Church,	Southumbrian;	a church.
Ecclesia,	Latin;	a church, e.g. Ecclesfield.
Eggles/Eccles,	English;	corruption of "ecclesia."
Cote,	Anglo-Saxon;	a mud cottage, plural = *"coton."*
Garth,	Norse;	a guarded fenced area, e.g. garden.
-ham,	Anglo-Saxon;	a home.
Heim,	German;	a home.
-ley,	English;	a clearing in a wood.
Kirk,	Northumbrian;	a church, e.g. Kirk Merrington.
Peel,	Celtic;	a stronghold.
Rath,	Erse;	an earthen fort or mound.
Scale,	Norse;	a shepherd's hut.
Sell,	Anglo-Saxon;	a better cottage than a *"cote."*
Seta,	Anglo-Saxon;	a settlement, e.g. Dorset.
Stede(stead),	Anglo-Saxon;	a place.
Stoc (stoke),	Anglo-Saxon;	a stockaded place.
Thorpe,	Norse;	a village.
Tun (-ton),	Anglo-Saxon;	an enclosure, hence: a village.
Vic (wick),	Anglo-Saxon;	an abode, related to Latin *vicus.*
Yard,	English;	an enclosed area (with a fence).
Yerde,	Anglo-Saxon;	a switch or rod, (part of a fence).

Meanings of place names in County Durham

Key   **C = Celtic and Pre-Celtic.**

E = English.

S = Scandinavian.

N = Norman.

L = Latin.

Aislaby (Aslac's village). E.

Barnard Castle (the castle of Bernard Baliol). N.

Beamish (beautiful mansion). N.

Bearpark (the fair retreat). N.

Billingham (Billa's peoples' homestead). E.

Binchester (the Roman fort used as a cattle shelter). E.

Birtley (bright clearing). E.

Bishopwearmouth (the Bishop's waters' mouth). E/C/E.

Blaydon (black hill). S/E.

Bolam (round hill). E.

Boldon (homestead hill). E.

Burnhope (stream valley). E.

Chester-le-Street (Roman fort on the road). E/N/L.

Coniscliffe (king's cliff). E.

Consett (hilly hill). E.

Dalton-le-Dale (valley farm). E.

Darlington (Deornoth's peoples' village). E.

Dere Street (Deira Street) or (Yorkshiremen's road). E.

Durham (hill island). C/E/N.

Easington (the village of Easa's people). E.

Ebchester (the Roman fort where St Ebba settled). E.

Eden Burn (gushing water). C.

Edmundbyers (Eadmund's byres).

Egglescliffe (church cliff). C/E.

Escomb (at the park). E.

Esh (ash tree). E.

Ferryhill (wooded hill). E.

Finchale (finch valley). E.

Gaunless River (useless river). S.

Greatham (gravelly homestead). E.

Gyrwe (Jarrow) (marsh dwellers). E.

Haliwerfolk (Holy People). E.

Hardwick (herd farm). E.

Hartlepool (stag island by the pool). E.

Hetton-le-Hole (hip-covered hill by the hollow). E/N.

Houghton-le-Spring (hill-settlement by the copse). E/N.

Ireshope (Irish valley). S/E.

Kirk Merrington (the village of Maera's people with a church).S/E.

Lanchester (long fort), E. also: Longovicium (ship fighters). L.

Muggleswick (Mucel's farm). E.

Penshaw (hill wood). E.

Piercebridge (osier bridge). E.

Quarrington (millstone hill). E.

Raby (boundary homestead). S.

Rookhope (rook valley). E.

Ryhope (rough valley). E.

Ryton (rye-growing farm). E.

Seaham (homestead by the sea). E.

Seaton Carew (seaside village of the Carews'). E.

Shincliffe (haunted cliff). E.

Sockburn (Socca's strong place). E.

South Shields (fishermens' huts). E.

Spennymoor (enclosed moor). E.

Staindrop (stony valley). E.

Stanhope (stony valley). E.

Stanley (stony clearing). E.

Stockton (homestead built of logs). E.

Sunderland (separate land). E.

Tees River (boiling waters). C.

Thorpe Thewles (naughty hamlet). E.

Tow Law (tower hill). E.

Trimdon (wooden monument hill). E.

Tudhoe (Tudda's hill). E.

Tyne River (flowing water). C.

Urpeth (bisons' path). E.

Ushaw (wolf wood). E.

Walworth (enclosure of the Britons). E.

Wear River (waters). C.

Westoe (women's place). E.

Whickham (homestead with a quickset hedge). E.

Wingate (windy pass). E/S.

Wolsingham (Wulfsige's peoples' homestead). E.

Wolviston (Wulf's farmstead). E.

and an interesting one in North Yorkshire:

Ainderby Quernhow (Eindrithi's village, by the mill hill). S.

The great monster which according to fable, terrorised Wearside inhabitants, may have been one or more Viking dragon ships as the Saxon word "wurm" means "dragon." There was also a fearsome "worm" on the River Tees at Sockburn and it just so happens that there is a Saxon church at Sockburn and also a Viking cemetery. Another monster called the "Laidley Worm" raided the Bamburgh area of Northumberland.

A Viking "wurm" (dragon ship) at sea.

A Norman "Motte and Bailey" (mound and enclosure) castle. Later, when the earthern mounds had consolidated, selected castles would be rebuilt in stone. A good example is Durham castle.

The keep of Durham Castle built on the "motte."

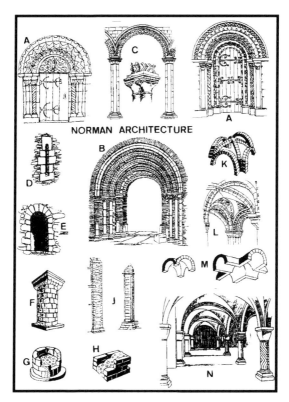

Norman architecture.

A = doorways with recessed orders of chevron decoration.

B = entrance with deeply recessed orders of chevrons.

C = Galilee Chapel, Durham Cathedral, c.1170.

D = slit opening in wall.

E = round-headed opening in wall.

F = rubble-infilled piers had to be huge to acquire strength.

G = method of construction using rubble-infill.

H = rubble-infilled wall.

J = buttresses were used where necessary to strengthen walls.

K = diagonal-arched supports for vaulting.

L = ribbed quadripartite vaulting.

M = intersecting barrel vaults becomes groined cross-vault.

N = groined vaulting.

The central tower of Durham Cathedral from the SW corner of the cloister quadrangle.

It is now time to leave the time of the amalgamation of Celts, Saxons, Vikings and Normans and look at the resultant English nation in the medieval period.

Chapter 14
A Brief Guide To The Middle Ages

'Beautiful city! so venerable, so lovely, so unravaged by the fierce intellectual life of our century, so serene!...whispering from her towers the last enchantments of the Middle Age.....Home of lost causes, and forsaken beliefs, and unpopular names, and impossible loyalties!

Matthew Arnold

This diagram shows how the development of the City of Gloucester can be traced from the Roman walls, through the Saxon settlement and into the medieval period. Note the importance of the docks. Seventy miles further up the River Severn from Gloucester is the Roman town of Viroconium at Wroxeter. Archaeologists digging at Wroxeter have recently found a huge Roman inland harbour. Thus it is now known that the Roman navigation of the River Severn was far more developed than hitherto thought. This has implications for the rest of Britain and the whole of the Roman Empire. Also, on 22/2/ 2000 the Daily Telegraph reported the discovery of a huge inland port on the River Tiber in the middle of the City of Rome. The Roman seaport of Portus north of Ostia has been mentioned at length earlier in this book but now we know the location of the capital's inland harbour in the Trastevere area of

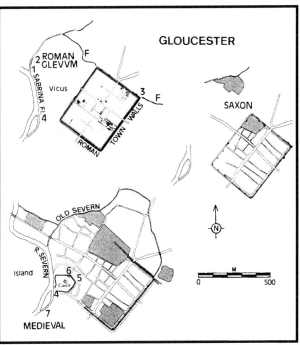

the city. We must remember with some pride, that the discoveries which unleashed the realisation of the importance of Roman inland river transport began here in Chester-le-Street in 1983 with the publication of the then revolutionary book, The Piercebridge Formula. This was followed in 1995 with much more evidence in On the Trail of the Legions. Now the whole of the Roman period archaeologists are scrambling in on the act. With regard to Gloucester of the Roman period, 1,2,3,& 4 are findspots of Roman jetties. "F" is the "Full Brook," which is the lower reach of the canalised River Twyver. The River Twyver is thought by some historians to have been used by the Romans to float down stone from Cotswold quarries for the building of Glevvm, and for supplying water to the ditch of their town wall. In medieval Gloucester, "5" is the findspot of a medieval barge. "6" is where rigging of a ship was found, and "4" are Roman docks. "7" is the position of modern docks.

The medieval period may be said to have begun about the time of the First Crusade, that startling outward thrust of the new Europe which had been reorganised by the feudal system. Feudalism is the characteristic institution of the Middle Ages. It means a fixed and legal social order to which the various classes of society must adhere. It rose in the dark days of the 8th Century when central governments were too weak to defend populations. The king granted lands ("*fiefs*") to his vassals and the latter swore oaths of homage to the king and promised to provide a quota of armed knights to serve in the king's army in time of war. The word "*fief*" comes from the Latin word "*feudum*". The king's vassal in turn took under his protection, serfs who could not defend themselves, and provided them with parcels of land and rough accommodation. The serfs worked the lord's lands as well as their own. This system, which grew up in different parts of Europe, was introduced into England by William the Conqueror after the Battle of Hastings (1066). Odo of Bayeux received the Earldom of Kent as his *fief* from William, and for it, he owed the services of fifty knights.

Knighthood first began amongst the pagan Germanic tribes. After a young warrior had shown his prowess in war, he was presented by his chieftain at a special ceremony, with a sword and shield. The Old English word "*cniht*" is the equivalent of "knight." There are references to "knighting" of Saxon kings, e.g. Athelstan. The equivalent Latin word for a knight was "*eques*" (horse-soldier).

Hand to hand conflicts between heavily armoured mounted knights flourished in the age of chivalry before the use of firearms and gunpowder-revolutionised warfare.

In times of danger, the ordinary peasants fled into the castles to receive the protection of their overlords.

A would-be knight began his training at the early age of seven when he was taken to the castle of a nobleman. Until he was 14, he served the lord and his lady as a page. He also received religious instruction from the chaplain and arms training from the squires. During this period, he also became an expert horseman. The lady of the manor and her attendants taught him to honour all women.

When he was 14, he was promoted to "squire" and learned how to bear the weight of heavy armour, use the sword, shield, lance, axe and mace, and handle his horse expertly at the same time. He had to accompany his knight to war and look after his master's equipment. If the knight became wounded or was killed, the squire would carry him off the field.

The young man would be made a knight at the age of 21 if he had acquitted himself well. After a bath of purification, and the taking of solemn vows, the candidate knelt or stood alone all night in prayer in front of an altar. On this altar lay the sword which he would don at a ceremony on the morrow.

In the courtyard, in front of the assembled knights and ladies, the candidate, wearing full armour, sword and spurs, knelt before the officiating lord or knight, and was touched lightly on the shoulder by the lord's fist or more usually with the flat of his sword. At the same time, the lord said: "In the name of God and St Michael and St George, I dub thee knight; be brave and loyal." Extravagant festivities and entertainment followed.

Feudal society took the surplus products of the serfs and divided it among barons, knights, bishops and abbots. This enabled wealth to accumulate in the hands of lords and prelates.

An aspect of feudalism was that military, political and judicial power was organised on a local basis. The barony, or the manor was the unit of power. Over this decentralised society of feudal barons and knights, stood the mighty Roman Church. As most of the learning and clerkship was in the hands of the clergy, the control of the Church over the state was very great in the Middle Ages.

Thus Medieval society had its beginnings with a makeshift arrangement between knights, the clergy, and frightened, superstitious, hungry peasants, for the mutual protection of poverty-striken unsophisticated country villages against rogues, unwelcome visitors and evil spirits.

Slowly however, out of these primitive arrangements, would come the England of Chaucer, cathedrals, universities, and parliament.

Early Norman castles usually consisted of a wooden stockade on the top of a man-made flat-topped conical mound (*motte*) of earth. This was surrounded by a water-filled ditch which later became known as a "moat" possibly because of its association with the "*motte.*" A wooden stairway ran down the steep slope of the *motte* to a drawbridge which spanned the moat and led into a fenced compound at one side of the foot of the *motte*. This was called the "*bailey*" in which houses, stables etc were situated. Entry to the *bailey* was via a gate in the fence and an ordinary bridge if the *bailey* was moated.

Some Norman castles were later rebuilt in stone. If the earth *motte* could not take the weight of a stone "keep" the latter was built inside the *bailey*, the perimeter fence of which was usually replaced by a stone wall.

A very good example of the remains of a Norman *Motte & Bailey* can be seen at Elsdon, Northumberland. These earthworks are known today as the "Mote Hills" and are located at the north end of the village on the east side of the B6341 road to Rothbury. Medieval rig & furrow "strips" also survive in the surrounding fields. Another example of a Norman *Motte & Bailey* earthwork can be seen in County Durham at the south end of Bishopton village which is about 3½ miles west of Stockton on Tees at NZ 366 209. There are many more examples in our north-eastern England.

Throughout the Middle Ages, our British islands were still on the north-west periphery of all things. Only in the remote fiords of Iceland and Norway did tales linger of "Vinland;" a land on the other side of the great Western Ocean which Viking navigators had reached a thousand years after Christ. However, Western civilisation was no longer centred on the Mediterranean but further north with the cultural leadership divided between France and Italy, and political and military power centred on the French and German states. The Norman Conquest had also brought southern England into closer contact with Normandy, Paris and Flanders in the fields of politics, commerce and literature.

Unlike the Roman Empire, medieval Europe was not a single state and the only collective name was "Christendom" with its capital of Papal Rome.

After the Norman Conquest, Britain became strong enough to defend her coastline and the seas no longer presented an easy pathway for enemies. Also, the French influence of the Norman conquerors would begin to be absorbed by the atmosphere of England. At the Battle of Hastings, the Norman victors had scorned everything English, but by the time of Henry II, the successors of those victorious knights were saying: *"Nolumus leges Angliae mutari"* ("We don't want the customs of old England changed").

Foreign chivalry and foreign clericalism greatly influenced the scene under Norman and early Plantagenet Kings. High above the humble wattle-and-daub huts and thatched roofs of the Saxon villeins, towered a stone castle and sometimes a great stone church or cathedral. Nevertheless, it was the despised English and not their foreign masters who would prevail in the end. Under the protection of Norman kings from further foreign attacks, a national unity emerged with a single system of native law for the whole kingdom. The long-bows of English yeomen would make their presence felt in the front lines of armies of the Kings of England. The English long-bows brought down the enemy feudal knights and the king's cannon breached castle walls. England was no longer on the fringe of international activity and with the blood of seafaring Saxons and Vikings in the veins of her peoples, she would become an oceanic power.

How English became the leading international language

Why do all the ships and aircraft of the world use the English language? How has the mother tongue of the small group of Europe's offshore islands become the international language? One factor is that the early English navigators were great explorers and brought a large part of the world into a British Empire. The second factor is that English is a very simple language with lots of short words. Also the grammar is fairly basic but it was not always so. The answer lies in the Medieval period when the Norman knights spoke Norman-French and the clergy, Latin, while English was left to lose its complex grammar in the voices of illiterate Saxon peasants. As the clergy spoke Latin, this was also the language for all official documents of Medieval England. The clergy could also travel all over Europe using only the Latin language as all state documents and scholarly works were written in Latin. The Latin of western Europe also developed about AD800 into several European languages, all having a strong resemblance. Italian was established about 850, Spanish and Portuguese some fifty years later. Ancient French became a separate tongue based on Latin about the same time.

Many English authors wrote in Latin to make their books available to a wider public and Bede in the 8th Century wrote his famous history in Latin.

About a quarter of our English is borrowed from Latin and we can hardly speak a sentence without using Latin words such as "mile, army, justice, religion, impediment (baggage), ambulance, omnibus (for all)," etc.

Before the Saxons who were the first "English," came to Britain, Celtic tribes and others before them, had owned most of northern Europe until the Romans took it from them.

Unfortunately, the Celtic language was not written down in those early days.

After the Roman military withdrawal from Britain, the invading Saxons pushed the Celts out to Cornwall, Wales and western Scotland and very few Celtic words entered the English language. When the Viking invasions came, their language was absorbed into English. When the Norman French conquerors arrived, they tried to impose Norman-French onto the Saxon inhabitants but gave up and started speaking the crude English of the uneducated peasants. Monks, who spoke Latin amongst themselves had tried to preserve the proper Old English of the early Saxons as a language for the serfs. This old Saxon language had a complex grammar, which was now mutilated by the natives whilst their educated masters tried to stick to Latin and Norman-French. In the meanwhile, the crude communications of the English peasants became by accident and ignorance, the simplest language in the world.

Because of the mixture of Latin, Saxon, Viking and French languages, simple modern English has double the vocabulary of either French or German, but because a language has a simple structure, this does not mean that a writer need have difficulty expressing himself.

Shakespeare, with all his varied writings used only about 15,000 different words. Milton needed only 8,000 words for *Paradise Lost,* and the *Old Testament* contains fewer than 6,000 words. Most of the British population use no more than one or two-thousand words.

The beauty of writing and speaking lies not in the number of different words, but in the choice and placing of them. Simple language is the most beautiful. The finest English can be found in the *Bible, The Pilgrim's Progress,* and *Robinson Crusoe*. In each of these books, the language is so simple that a child can understand it, while learned men find equal pleasure in reading it.

Many academics who use little-known words and vast appendices, merely scare potential readers away and their books remain unsold.

About a thousand-million people in the world have some ability in English and the 350 million people whose mother tongue is English are outnumbered by more than two-to-one by speakers who use English as a second language.

The *Oxford Dictionary* lists about half a million words and about 1,500 new ones are added every year. Unlike French, English is greedy for foreign words and the language soon absorbs them. English words borrowed from Southern Asia are: bungalow, verandah, dinghy, thug and cash.

Many of our nautical words also originated in the old seafaring nations:

During the Crusades, a Saracen Chief was an *Amir* and if he served at sea, he was an *Amir-al-bahr* (commander-at-sea). This became the French *Amiral* and passed into English as Admyrall which developed into "Admiral."

Caput was the Saxon word for head or chief, and *thane* was a title of honour. *Caput thane* became "Captain."

Scandinavia provided the word *schiffe* and the Dutch word for a captain was *schipper* which became the Anglicised "Skipper."

Batsuen was an old naval rank. *Bat* was Saxon for boat and *swein* meant a boy. This became "boatswain."

The word "pilot" is derived from the pilot's depth-finder, the *peil loth* (lead line).

The side of a Viking ship with the steering oar was the *steorbord* (steering paddle) [starboard], and the loading side, was *ladebord* (larbord). To avoid confusion, the latter was later changed to "port."

Lubber is derived from the Saxon word *lobbe* which means a slow clumsy person and land-lubber describes a person who is awkward and out of place on board ship.

The Saxon word *gang* means "to go" and from that we get "gangway."

Mess is related to the Latin *mensa* (table), Spanish *mesa* (table) and Gothic *mes* (dish). The Latin *patene* (two arms stretched) became the Saxon *faehom* and the modern "fathom" (six feet).

The list is endless and although the international language of the sea is English, it is really a mixture of all the languages of all the ancient seafarers.

English is just as widely spread in aviation. In the following phrases, words of one syllable only are used:

"You are clear to take off."

"You are clear to land."

Most of the parts of an aircraft use single-syllable words: "bolt, deck, door, fin, flap, floor, frame, knob, nut, pin, pump, screw, seat, stick, strut, tail, tank, wheel, wing, wire, etc," and two-syllable words cover most of the rest - "bracket, check-list, engine, fillet, lever, rudder," etc. French words used in aviation are longer - "*aileron, empennage, fuselage,*" etc.

Air traffic control towers and communications centres all over the world speak English to all aircraft including those of their own nationality. A German pilot landing at a German airport will usually be speaking English to a German controller and a Japanese pilot landing at San Francisco will be speaking the self-same aeronautical English language to an American radar-man.

We must now return to the medieval period and discuss "Monks and Monasticism," and the agriculture of the Middle Ages.

Monks and Monasticism

The word "monk" is from the Greek word "*monos*" which means "alone" but in the course of time this word was used to describe a member of a religious community. Similarly, the word "monastery" originally meant a hut or a cell, but later was used to describe a building to accommodate a number of men who lived according to strict sets of rules and who were devoted to the service of God.

In the Egyptian desert in the early days of Christianity there lived a number of religious hermits and these got their name from the Greek word "*erimites*" which means: "a dweller of the desert." The most celebrated of these was Paul of Thebes, who lived about the middle of the 3rd Century. These hermits were noted for their harsh self-denial, abstinence and austerity.

The first known monastic organisation was that of St Anthony, established about AD305 near the Nile city of Memphis. The monastery was merely a collection of huts and although the monks were under St Anthony's direction, they did not have any special rules. The earliest community of monks living under a common roof, was established by Pachomius in AD340 on an island in the Nile called Tabennisi. Pachomius compiled monastic rules. The monks of St Anthony had spent all their time reading the Scriptures, praying and fasting; while Pachomius' followers led an active life in which religious studies alternated with practical agricultural work.

From Egypt, monasticism spread northwards and about the year 360, St Basil established a monastery at Pontus on the southern shore of the Black Sea. St Basil is regarded as the founder of Eastern Monasticism. The famous monastery on Mount Athos is a later representative.

St Basil's teachings were that a monk must not just live for himself, but attend to the welfare of his fellow men. This was put into practice by building hospitals, orphanages and hospices in the vicinity of his monasteries. He also provided schools for boys. The education was general and not confined to turning the pupils into monks. St Basil believed that work was more important than self-imposed hardships or punishments, thus the routine was divided between prayers and reading and hard work.

Monasticism went from Egypt direct to Italy, and nunneries as well as monasteries sprung up along the entire Italian peninsula, especially in the Rome area. From the land which would one day become Italy, monasticism spread into Gaul where St Martin of Tours founded Lingugé near Poitiers, in 360. The island monastery of Lérins near Cannes produced many famous bishops and saints. St Patrick, the Apostle of Ireland, was trained there. This would lead to many monasteries being founded in Wales and Ireland with a resultant effect on Britain in the turbulent years which were to follow. Celtic missionaries would spread across Britain and convert pagan peoples to Christianity.

The best known name in the history of Western Monasticism, is that of St Benedict of Nursia, (in Italy), who was born about 480. He founded the Monastery of Monte Cassino in 529 and this became the prototype for most of the religious houses in western Europe. Benedict's method of achieving goodness in and around his establishments was via hard work at agriculture, the teaching of trades, and the encouragement of the arts. The Benedictine Order became famous for its promotion of education and many of the older universities developed from Benedictine schools. The Benedictine monks were formerly known as "Black Monks" because of their black habit.

Nearly all the medieval monastic orders were founded on Benedictine lines. There were the Carthusians established by St Bruno in 1086 at Chatreuse, and the Cistercians, or White

Monks, founded by St Robert of Molesme, at Citreaux, in 1098.

Monasteries were self-contained communities and the abbey-church was their home, place of worship, a centre for book-writing and copying; all kinds of learning, and a base for organised tasks in workshops, forges, bakehouses, barns, gardens and the fields of the surrounding countryside. Hospitals were provided and there was usually a shelter for travellers. Alms were given to the poor, and underpriviledged boys received free eduction.

Near the monks' cloisters was a "calefactory" (warming room) and the fire was lit on Novemember 1st, The Feast of All Saints, and was kept burning until Easter.

The head of an abbey was an "abbot," and the head of a priory which was usually smaller than an abbey, was a "prior." An abbot's deputy was however, also called a prior. The prior was responsible for discipline. The head of a convent was an abbess, (now known as a "mother superior").

The daily life of a monastery was carefully arranged. Church services took precedence over other work and the church formed the greatest social force in medieval life.

A distinction must be made between monks and friars (the latter name comes from the French " *frere*" (brother). Both monks and friars are members of religious orders and are known as Regular clergy as distinct from the diocesan and parish (Secular) clergy. Seculars are not bound by rules of poverty, and may own property.

Friars and friaries are usually found within or close to cities, as friars engage in work which brings them into close contact with the outside world. The chief orders for friars are Dominicans (Black Friars), Franciscans (Grey Friars), Carmelites (White Friars) and Augustinians.

Friars originally depended on offerings from the people and were called "medicants" (from the Latin word "*medicare*" to beg).

The dissolution of the Monasteries

Monasticism suffered a serious setback in England during the reign of King Henry VIII (1509-47). Henry was married to the widow of his brother, Arthur. She was Catherine of Aragon. Henry was an intelligent, jovial and handsome youth and was skilled in outdoor activities though later in life he became obese, ungainly and coarse. For almost forty years, he ruled England with a strong hand.

Early in Henry's reign, he joined a league organised by Pope Julius II against France, and won the "Battle of the Spurs" at Guinegatte in Normandy. Just a few days later, James IV at the head of a Scottish army invaded northern England and was met at Flodden on September 9th, 1513, by the Earl of Surrey in command of an English army. The Scottish army was almost completely destroyed.

During his first twenty years of reign, Henry left the government of England mostly in the hands of Cardinal Wolsey. Henry wished to divorce Catherine of Aragon because he had tired of her and she had not provided him with a male heir. He had also fallen in love with a young lady of the court, Anne Boleyn.

The Pope however refused to annul Henry's marriage and Henry was furious at Cardinal Wolsey's failure to persuade the Pope to fall in with his plans. Wolsey was arrested for treason and Henry appointed Thomas Cranmer as Archbishop of Canterbury. Cranmer granted Henry a divorce and Henry married Anne Boleyn. The Pope had been defied and ties between the English Church and Rome were severed. All payments to Rome were stopped and the Pope's authority in England was abolished.

Henry was declared Supreme head of the Church of England by an Act of Parliament and to deny this title was made an act of treason. The Bible was translated into English and copies were placed in the churches. Some changes were also made to the Church services.

The monasteries throughout England were dissolved (1544) and their vast tracts of land, funds and goods turned over to Henry. The King in turn, granted the former monastic estates to noblemen and gentlemen upon whose support he could rely. A rebellion in northern England on behalf of the monks was supressed with relentless force.

The revenues of our Collegiate Church in Chester-le-Street were siezed by the Crown and the property which supported the clergy was sold by Henry VIII. The establishments at Lanchester, Bishop Auckland, Darlington and other places were also dissolved and the property appropriated by the King.

Henry had his second wife, Anne Boleyn executed, and Jane Seymour, his third wife, died just over a year later. She had however provided him with an heir who succeeded him as Edward VI. Henry quickly divorced his fourth wife, Anne of Cleves, and his next wife Catherine Howard was executed. Catherine Parr however, survived Henry. Two of Henry's daughters, successively became queens: Mary I, daughter of Catherine of Aragon, and Elizabeth I, daughter of Anne Boleyn.

Medieval agriculture

Let us now examine the feudal system of the manor. In Chester-le-Street, this was owned by the Prince-Bishop and administered by his officers.

In the Twelfth Century, the number of freeholders in an English manor was very small. The lord and his villeins shared most of the land and its produce between them but not in fair proportions.

The serf or villein was bound to the soil by birth and inheritance. He and his family were sold with an estate when it went to a new owner. He could not give his daughter in marriage without the lord's consent and the payment of a fee. When a serf died, his best animal, sometimes his only cow, was taken as "heriot" by the lord. The villein could not move away from the manor, withdraw his services or go on strike. He was forced to work on his lord's domain so many days of the year without pay. The lord's bailiff supervised the villeins at work on the lord's fields in case they slackened their rate of toil.

The lowly villein however had lands of his own allocated to him by the lord. This land took the form of "strips" which lay in three huge open fields. These strips were not fenced and were ploughed by a team of oxen owned and operated commonly. Each strip was separated from the next by a baulk of grass which served as a footpath. The strips were banked into elongated mounds for drainage, and many thousands of acres of them are still visible in our modern countryside. Chester-le-Street Golf Course has some excellent examples of this surviving medieval "rig and furrow" strip-field agriculture. Each serf had about thirty strip fields spread across the whole manor so that every man got a share of the good land as well as the bad. The lord had more strips than the serfs and his land was worked, as previously mentioned, by the villeins. The villein also had access to the village meadow (the common hayfield), the village pasture and the woodland and waste where his swine could be turned loose to forage.

The dammed waters of the local stream would have provided the power to drive a watermill which was owned by the lord.

The three huge fields were divided into open strips, the latter called "furlongs." This word is used in modern times to define a length of 220 yards, or an eighth of a statute mile. In the Saxon period however, it meant: "*furlang*" from "*furh*" (furrow) and "*lang*" (lang) = "*long furrow*." This indicates that the "rig and furrow" system existed in Saxon times. The Norman-French word for a "strip" was a "*selion*" as evidenced by Norman-French deeds of the Hylton area of Sunderland, which tell us of two "selions" next to the "Damflatt" (Roman dam) area.

Around each group of "rig and furrow strips," was a headland, or grass road. This is where the ox-teams turned but as the headlands are narrow, the plough must have been uncoupled and the team turned on the spot. Some of the strips take the form of a "reversed S" and this was probably to get the agreed area into a strip.

We now know that there were far more Roman roads in northern England than hitherto realised and several of these roads cross areas of medieval rig and furrow. It has been noted that the medieval rig and furrow strips in the vicinity of the Roman roads, lie parallel to the ancient roads, thus saving huge amount of labour by removing the thousands of tons of stone in a typical Roman road. In these cases, the medieval farmers have used the Roman roads for access to the fields and also as headlands for turning the oxen plough teams.

With regard to the necessity for keeping the land fertile, one large common field was each in turn left fallow for one year in order to revitalise itself by cattle grazing over it. This method of putting life back into the land with animal manure was in full use. Of the two remaining large fields which were cultivated in rotation each year, one was planted with wheat or rye, and the other with oats or barley. While under crops, the large field and all its component strips would have been protected by hurdles of temporary fences in order to keep stray cattle out.

The English weather was then as now, unpredictable, and if a crop failed after a wet summer, there was famine in the village. Wild animal food was harder to come by than in Saxon times because the Norman Kings and vassals claimed huge tracts of forest which were protected by cruel laws.

The medieval village, isolated by poor communications along pot-holed mud tracks, and

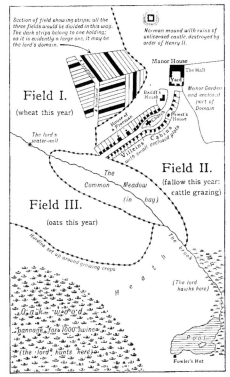

Section of field showing strips; all the three fields would be divided in this way. The dark strips belong to one holding; as it is evidently a large one, it may be the lord's domain.

Norman mound with ruins of unlicensed castle, destroyed by order of Henry II.

Manor House
The Hall
Yard
Bailiff's House
Manor Garden and enclosed part of Domain
House of Freeman
Church
Priest's House
Villeins' Cabins with small enclosed plots

Field I.
(wheat this year)

The lord's water-mill

The Common
Meadow (in hay)

Field II.
(fallow this year: cattle grazing)

Field III.
(oats this year)

Hurdles set up around growing crops

The brook

Oak and wood

pannage for 1000 swine

(the lord hunts here)

(The lord hawks here)

Pool

Fowler's Hut

An imaginary English village under the medieval Manorial System.

its peasants who were bound for life not to stray, had to manufacture essentials for itself and among the villeins were carpenters, thatchers, blacksmiths etc. The womenfolk were all "spinsters" and wove coarse cloth as well as tanning hides for leather-ware. Only the family and officers of the lord's house were likely to visit traders' establishments in nearby towns.

The original well-constructed Roman roads were now in a dreadful state of repair and even as late as the 16th century, medieval roads were no more than inconvenient paths between villages. They were almost unusable in winter, and when spring came, the accumulated mud had to be cleared away by teams of horses hitched to road-ploughs.

All this was in spite of the fact that in 1555, parliament had ordered that parishes were to maintain existing roads. Every able-bodied man was supposed to work on the roads for six days in the year. The system failed to work.

Up to the 18th Century, most merchandise had to be carried by pack-horse, making their slow way across country on narrow tracks. It is recorded by Macaulay that when stage-coaches were introduced in the mid 17th Century, they often became stuck fast in mud until a team of cattle could be procured from a neighbouring farm to pull them out. At Chester-le-Street, a team of cattle was always on hand at Chester Moor Farm, to assist the stage-coach up the relatively gentle incline of the medieval road which can still be traced as a holloway just to the south-west of the Chester Moor railway viaduct.

In 1770, the great British traveller, Arthur Young, complained of a Lancashire road that its ruts measured four feet deep. He also mentioned that the "mending" of this road was merely the tipping into holes of loose stones; the surface of this "repair" jolted the carriage in a most intolerable manner. Salt was a necessity for medieval life, for the preservation of meats and fish. Locally produced wool would often be exchanged for salt.

How about the villein's rights? The *"Magna Carta* (1215)" did not apply to him as he was not a "free man" and he could not sue the Lord in the King's courts. He had however, a double protection against ill-usage; he had the security of village tradition expressed in "the custom of the manor," enforced in the Manor Court, which was held sometimes in the lord's hall, or locations such as underneath an oak tree in the centre of the village.

It was in the lord's interest to give the villein willing work rather than enforced labour because if the serf ran away, he was difficult to replace. The Manor court was the lord's court and not the king's but at least it had an open court and the villeins shared with the freemen, the duty of acting as judges.

When the system worked properly, a villein knew what work he must do for his lord, and he knew that he could not be evicted from his hovel, nor could the lord raise his rent or amount of work due. During the centuries, the system flourished in England and the population increased except in instances of plagues such as the "Black Death" of 1349.

Life on the manor was hard and it took the villeins a long time to develop into the jovial English yeomen of later days. The feudal system reached its peak between the 11th and 13th Centuries but long before the end of the Middle Ages, the life had passed out of it. It became easier for the king to hire mercenary troops and the pride and independence of the feudal barons were broken. With the advent of gunpowder, it became easy for the king to blow to pieces, the castle of any dissenter. In England, land tenure by Knight-service was not finally abolished until 1660, and the last relics of feudal land law were removed by an Act of Parliament in 1925.

The parish of Chester-le-Street contained 18 townships and chapelries: Beamish with Tanfield, Birtley, Edmondsley, Harraton, Hedley, Kibblesworth, Lambton, Lamesley, Lintz Green, Great Lumley, Little Lumley, Pelton, Plawsworth, Ravensworth, Urpeth and Ouston, and Waldridge.

In Durham County, the four great wards of Chester, Darlington, Easington, and Stockton, all of which were under the jurisdiction of the Bishop of Durham, who, as Count Palatine and Earl of Sadberge, was lord of all the county with power in civil government for the preservation of peace and with licence to mint money as required by law or by convenience. The Bishop raised his own army, called his own parliament, and administered the law courts. He received all revenues and rents together with fines and forfeitures.

The Bishop's Manor House in Chester-le-Street was in Mains Park (where this book is being written) and appears to have been on the site of the later Deanery. In 1280, Bishop Bek rebuilt the Parish Church as a collegiate establishment. This collegiate church lasted until the dissolution of 1544. In all 25 Deans were appointed. The duties of the Deans included looking after the fishery on the Wear (an old Roman structure reused as a fish weir); the collection of rents of tenant holdings belonging to the church at Chester and Waldridge, and the demesne at Harraton.

After the Dissolution, the Deanery became the property of the Hedworth family, for in 1614, we read that: "John Hedworth had the Decanal House of the Collegiate Church of Chester-le-Street, with barns, buildings and *'girnales'* (granaries) now waste and ruinous, and a garden."

Much of it was clearly rebuilt for in 1830 the Deanery is described as a "handsome brick house in a pleasant situation near the east side of the town, and commands a fine prospect of rich cultivated grounds and a pleasing view of Lumley Park and Castle". Collegiate churches are few in this diocese and comprise St Andrew's Auckland, Darlington, Norton, Chester-le-Street, Staindrop and Barnard Castle. Various structural alterations with additions to, and the reversal of the priests' stalls usually marked the change of status when an older church became collegiate. So we find the history of Chester-le-Street as with other townships, inextricably bound up with the history of its parish church.

How our church looks in the year 2000

The weather-vane of our parish church was replaced in 1957. Below the tail of the vane is the Lambton Arms. Under the point of the vane is High Chare. The stonemasons in the photograph are: Left, John Loughlin and right, Ray Lines.

At Chester-le-Street, the Bishop's Halmote Court appears to have been held only twice a year, spring and autumn.

The books of the Bishop's Court (The Halmote Court) go back to the year 1520, but the court rolls to 1345 (Edward III).

After the feudal period, people held land largely on a service basis whereby occupants were obliged to provide the Bishop with produce from the lands they occupied, and also to work on the Bishop's demesne lands on fixed days of various seasons. Later on, such services could be commuted for money payments.

In addition to formulating the by-laws as to division of lands, pasturage, right of access to the common lands, admission to holdings in the arable lands, upkeep of highways or the King's street, upkeep of hedges etc, the grieve and jury of the various Halmote courts dealt with many nuisances and complaints of which the following are most commonly found:

Pains (fines) were inflicted for: rescuing ye cattle from ye pinfold; trespassing on the Bishop's demesne lands; not baking at the township's bakery; not brewing at the local brewery; cutting down ye trees without licence; refusing to grind at a Bishop's mill; refusing to plough or reap the Bishop's lands; marrying without the Bishop's consent; poaching on the Bishop's warren, refusing to scour the watercourses; refusing to repair the mill-dam; non-ringing of ye swine, etc.

The Halmote Court met in later years at the Deanery Manor House, the Queen's Head, and the Lambton Arms. The last two mentioned establishments were coaching inns and were set back so that coaches could pull in off the main road.

The Queen's Head in 1616 also supplied communion wine for the church and records tell us that a quart of sack and a quart of claret were bought for the preacher, Mr Cole, for the price of 1s 7d (19 old pence = 7.9 new pence).

In 1616, The Halmote Court, which was the Prince Bishop's Law Court in Chester-le-Street, met three times a year in the Queen's Head, before transferring to the Lambton Arms. The insignia of the Queen's Head Inn was originally the head of Queen Elizabeth I. It was not until 1925, that the Halmote Court had its final meeting, its feudal function by then defunct.

As late as 1855, the stage coaches, "True Briton" and "Omnibus" stopped in Chester-le-Street en route from Newcastle to Durham, at 5pm and 5.30am. The coaches returned at 7.30am and 6.30pm. Opposite the Queen's Head slightly further upstreet was the old Crown Inn (not the High Crown which is much further south). The site of the Crown, which was rebuilt in 1924, is now occupied by modern shops, but a crown insignia can still be seen near the roof. A mile-post, 3 feet high, stood in front of the Crown Inn. The Crown Inn did not sit back from the main road so it is assumed that coaches used the pull-ins of the Queen's Head and the Lambton Arms.

The Lambton Arms was a coaching house with the "Telegraph" calling there. As a posting house, letters could be left for despatch by coach or to be collected; the recipient paid the fee. Likewise, the Queen's Head, collected mail, and there, horses could be changed and accommodation provided for travellers.

The *Chester Volunteers* was the name for a local reserve regiment which was a kind of Napoleonic period "Dad's army." It was never called to front line service, but its manoeuvres in the local area caused mayhem from time to time. On one occasion, a false invasion alert caused the 'Volunteers' to attempt to evacuate the population of Chester-le-Street to Waldridge Fell. The French army never left the beaches at Boulogne, but more of this later.

The Bishop's Manor house stood on the site of the later Deanery which in turn was replaced by the Grammar School, later to become the Park View School. Underneath the Park View School, Deanery and church is the lost Chester-le-Street Roman fort of Concangis which was on the intersection of a Roman road network and also at the Roman period tidal limit of the River Wear (The Roman Vedra *Fluvius*).

In 1547 when Chester-le-Street church ceased to be collegiate, the Dean and prebends were dismissed and one curate with a stipend of £10 a year now had charge of the parish and one curate each was appointed for Lamesley and Tanfield.

In 1862 the church was restored. The low-pitched one-span roof (probably built in Tudor times) was removed and the roof and walls raised to the original height.

CASTLES and other old buildings in our area
Lumley Castle

Lumley Castle from the air. In the foreground is the golf course and behind the castle is the A183 and Lambton Park.

The south-western tower of Lumley Castle. The flag of England is flying in a stiff breeze and in the foreground is the helicopter landing area. The "H" was designed by the author and the parallel sides of the letter indicate to the pilot the direction of approach with the least obstacles.

Robert de Lumley built a manor house and this was transformed by his son, Sir Ralph Lumley into a castle in 1392 after a licence to fortify and crenellate had been granted by King Richard II. A considerable portion of the original manor house can be detected in the buildings on the west side of the quadrangle.

Further alterations were made by John, Lord Lumley, about 1580, and by Richard, the Second Earl of Scarbrough, about 1721. In spite of the alterations, Lumley Castle is still just as impressive a building as it was when it was built over 600 years ago.

The original gate of the manor house faces east into the courtyard and above the entrance, John, Lord Lumley, who died in 1609, placed a series of nineteen shields which still survive today, although in a deteriorating condition. Sixteen of them represent John's ancestors, while the final three give the family arms - *argent, a fess gules between three popinjays vert* - flanked by the arms of his two wives, Jane Fitzalan, daughter of the Earl of Arundal, and Elizabeth, daughter of John, Lord Darcy of Chick. The sixteen shields which are supposed to represent the Lumley ancestors tell us that the Lumleys are descended from the Saxon noble, Liulph, who had fled from the south of England after the Norman invasion. He married the daughter of Earl Aeldred of Northumbria. Their son, Uchtred was said to have been a baron and an important man in the Palatinate of Durham. Uchtred's son William, is supposed to have assumed the name Lumley. The insignia on many of the shields are thought to be fictitious.

The effigies known as the "Lumley Warriors" in Chester-le-Street Parish Church are just as suspect as some of the Lumley early heraldry above the original gateway. Of the fourteen effigies, only three are genuine. One of these has an unknown provenance and two were removed from the graveyard of Durham Cathedral in 1594 in the belief that they were of the Lumley family. The other eleven were made to order.

At Lumley Castle, we have a chance to compare medieval sanitation with that of the Romans. Roman longevity was mainly due to clean drinking water supplies via aqueducts from distant springs, and good hygiene with flushing toilets and bath-houses.

King James' room in the north-east corner tower of Lumley Castle seems to have had one of the few lavatories in the whole building. The efflux of this toilet is via a circular hole in the castle wall just to the west side of the great northern window of the visiting King's bedroom. This can be seen in the south-eastern corner of the outer (northern) courtyard. Similar toilet discharges can be seen in the walls of Dilston Castle, near Corbridge.

Ravensworth Castle

In 1728, S & N Buck produced a sketch of the old fort which preceded the later Ravensworth Castle. This building consisted of four oblong-shaped towers connected by a curtain wall enclosing the Lord's mansion. Before this date however, the outer wall and towers had enclosed a central tower or keep. The Mansion House and outer walls lasted until 1808 when the whole castle (except two of the towers which were incorporated into the new building) was demolished. After this demolition, the erection of the new castle commenced. The original castle evidently dated back to pre-Norman times. There were traces of an ancient moat in

1728.

The "Butter Cross" in the middle of the grounds may be evidence of an ancient road.

The new castle did not last long and the ravages of time and neglect caused damage. Mining subsidence also resulted in huge cracks in the walls. Therefore the 7th Baron, Robert Arthur Liddell, in 1936, decided to pull the castle down and erect a model village from its timber and stone. Although the castle was demolished, Lord Ravensworth was not to see his dreams come true because he died in 1950 in Hexham General Hospital at the age of 48, as the result of a road accident.

Throughout its long history, Ravensworth had seen many distinguished visitors - the Duke of Wellington stayed there in 1827 when a fellow guest was Sir Walter Scott.

The choir of Lamesley Church sang various anthems at Henry George Liddell's 21st birthday party in the castle when the Duchess of Gloucester, the Duke of Cambridge, Arch-Duke Frederick Ferdinand of Austria, the Marquis of Normanby, the Earl of Scarbrough, and most of the leading aristocrats of Northumberland and Durham attended.

Lambton Castle

This castle is not a fortress-castle. It is a large mansion in the form of a castle of the type built by rich landowners and industrialists as a place of residence large enough to display statues, paintings and family portraits etc. Lambton Castle stands on the site of Harraton Hall, an Elizabethan mansion which was the seat of the D'Arcy and Hedworth families in succession. Lambton House, the old family home of the Lambtons stands half a mile to the south-west of the castle and in the 19th century was transformed into two cottages.

Harraton Hall came to the Lambtons via a marriage with a Hedworth heiress and the Hall was dismantled in 1797 by William Henry Lambton, the father of the first earl. Harraton Hall was replaced by Lambton Hall, the latter designed by a Durham architect called Bonomi who had also designed Durham Prison.

In 1833, Lambton Hall was enlarged and the mock castellations added and has since been called "Lambton Castle."

In 1854, subsidence caused by old colliery workings endangered the castle. Coal had been mined since 1600 but the pillars of coal left by the miners in the underground galleries to support the roof, were not large enough for the weight of the castle above. A Newcastle architect was engaged to design the rectifications.

The colliery workings were filled with brickwork and the walls of the castle were stabilised with iron ties.

The single-span "Lamb Bridge" near the castle was designed by Bonomi in 1819. Downstream from the bridge is a curved weir of unknown date, and upstream there is at least one intact keelboat jetty. In 1999, permission was refused for archaeologists to search the park for further evidence.

Alterations were made to the castle in 1875 and part of it was dismantled in 1929 after the

Although Lambton Castle is not a medieval castle, it is included here for interest. Lambton Castle is at the present normal tidal point of the River Wear, the present (fortnightly) Spring tidal limit being the 14th Century bridge at the foot of Newbridge Bank.

family suffered two deaths and two lots of death duties in a single year.

The Hermitage

This large Georgian stone house is just to the south of Chester-le-Street on the west side of the main London to Edinburgh railway line which runs north-south through the grounds. The house gets its name from the hermit's cell in the wood to the west of the railway viaduct, to the south of the hall, and on the north side of a footpath which leads down to the South Burn. One wall of the cell could still be seen a few years ago in a recess cut into the steep wooded bankside.

The mansion house was probably built by the industrialist, Thomas Cookson who lived there in 1827. It was Cookson who refused permission for the railway to cross his land and only an Act of Parliament forced him to give way.

The railway was opened for passenger traffic in 1872. The estate was sold to the N.E. Railway Co., and later to a Mr Featherstonehaugh who sold it in turn two years later to the Rev H Shepperdson, a retired rector of Warkworth. Shepperdson's granddaughter inherited it but later sold it to mining engineer Lindsey, later created a baronet. His successor, Sir

Arthur Lindsey Wood died in 1939 and his heir sold the house and part of the estate to the Durham Miners' Association who turned the building into a rehabilitation centre for injured and sick miners. The huge park is now being whittled away by ever expanding housing estates.

The Napoleonic battery at Sunderland

Around the southern coasts of Britain and also at strategic points throughout the British Empire, small circular forts with very thick walls, were built to counter Napoleonic attacks. The flat roof had a built-in turntable so that a large cannon could be trained quickly in any direction. I know of no such towers on our north-east coast but there were isolated batteries such as the one on the cliff just north of Alnmouth. At Sunderland, the old south inner mole of the harbour has a battery built into it. A circular railway track carried the rear end of a large cannon so that the gun could be trained over a wide seawards arc. Also on this south inner mole, there are the remains of a pulley system which raised and lowered a boom-defence cable for the prevention of enemy ships sneaking into the mouth of the River Wear. Many ex-Roman stones from the great Roman dam at Hylton are built into the south inner mole and at least two-thousand tons of huge ex-Roman stones have been dumped onto the beach south of the south inner mole, to prevent sea erosion. Napoleon's ships never came.

Sir John Duck and Lumley's Duck Hospital

A young chap called John Duck arrived in Durham during the reign of Charles I, and became a butcher's apprentice. He didn't like the work and couldn't put his heart and soul into it. One day, he was given the task of taking a cow to a sale in Houghton-le-Spring. During his trudge, in a melancholy frame of mind, he stopped for a rest by the wayside in Rennington (Rainton). As he sat there in despondency, he felt a sharp blow on the top of his head, and looking up with a start, saw a raven hovering above him. At his feet lay a gold coin, a "jacobus" or "unite". John had never possessed such wealth before. He continued to Houghton-le-Spring and sold the cow on behalf of his master, Mr Heslop, and then refreshed himself with meat and drink in one of the old inns, possibly the White Lion. While in conversation with some drovers in the inn, he purchased a cow with his gold piece and sold it for a considerable profit. Overjoyed with his success, he walked back to Durham, paid off his master, and went into business on his own. His enterprises were a great success and soon he had hundreds of gold pieces. John became rich and invested his money in land leases and collieries in the Rainton area.

The bird which dropped the gold coin on his head was more likely to have been a jackdaw than a raven. Jackdaws are noted for their habit of collecting bright objects such as fragments of silver paper. The poem, *The Jackdaw of Rheims,* describes such a bird stealing a diamond ring from the Cardinal's quarters. A few years ago, a jackdaw's nest at Guisborough was found to contain some silver Roman coins, so in that area, this bird had found a Roman site, which has so far, escaped the notice of archaeologists and historians.

Before 1680, John Duck owned the manor of Haswell and by 1688, he possessed lands at West Rainton and Lumley. His next step was to become leasee of the mines under the Dean and Chapter of Durham where he mined the valuable seam still known today as "Old Duck's Main."

Besides the hall he built at Rainton, he owned a town house in Durham City near Framwellgate Bridge. In later years, this house became the Black Lion Inn, and then the premises of Mr Caldcleugh, the ironmonger.

In one of the upper rooms, a painted panel shows John dressed as a butcher's boy, in cap and jacket, and towards him is flying a raven with an enormous piece of money in its bill. On the right of the picture is a building which is most probably the hospital built and endowed by Sir John at Lumley.

John Duck became Mayor of Durham in 1680 and was made a Commissioner of the Peace by Lord Crewe. He was an ardent Tory and Royalist, and in 1686 his loyalty to that cause resulted in a baronetcy whereby he became Sir John Duck, Baronet, of Haswell-on-the-Hill.

He died in 1691 aged 59, leaving no heir so the title became extinct. He was buried in St Margaret's Church, Durham and by his side lies his wife, Anne who died in 1695.

On the floor of the nave, the marble tombstone is inscribed in Latin. It tells us of his generosity and how he built a poorhouse in Lumley for twelve people. The poorhouse contained twelve apartments and a chapel.

This Lumley poorhouse was known as "The Duck Hospital" and just a few years ago, the remains of it could still be seen at map ref NZ 289 493. At the time of writing, the site is grassed over.

We must now step back a little and look at the history of wagonways and our coal industry which is of significant importance to our town, area and nation.

A "whim gin" (horse operated hoist) being used to raise coals at a pit-head.

On the OS map of 1850, such a gin-crane is marked beside the surviving keel-boat jetty on the south side of the River Wear about a mile below the medieval bridge at New Bridge.

A horse-operated waggonway may have terminated at this point.

A horse-operated waggonway supplying a Tyne keelboat staithe. A loaded chaldron is descending the inclined track with the horse trailing behind. An empty chaldron is being returned uphill by a horse.

If horse-drawn loaded chaldrons had to ascend inclines, the gradient did not exceed one degree

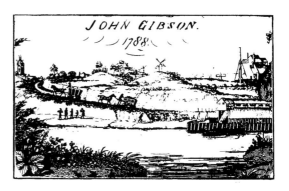

The Causey Arch, near Stanley, County Durham, built in 1727 by stonemason Ralph Wood. It was designed to carry horse-drawn coal wagons and is claimed to be the oldest railway bridge in the world.

Chapter 15
Coal and waggonways — Chester-le-Street from 1650 to 1850

Introduction

This chapter tells the story of how the coal industry became a significant part of life in Chester-le-Street. It covers a long period from the end of the Civil War to the beginning of Queen Victoria's reign. In those two centuries the coal industry grew in national importance and fuelled the world's first industrial revolution. Chester-le-Street, like many other towns in Britain, grew with the coal industry. The town and its surrounding villages did not, perhaps, grow in comparative national significance but played a national role by virtue of the achievements of the miners and coalowners who lived there. The following account attempts, as best can be done given the limitations of time and historical records, to chart those achievements and bring together for the first time some of the facts about Chester-le-Street's early coalmining heritage.

Six factors[1] played an important role in Chester-le-Street's development as a colliery district – geography, the River Wear, the development of waggonways, advances in colliery drainage, the static nature of mining techniques and the willingness of both local landowners and "outsiders" to invest in new collieries. In terms of geography, the area is on the eastern edge of the exposed coalfield and close to the inland tidal limit of the River Wear. Furthermore, the Great North Road dissects the area south to north parallel to the river and the coalfield. This geography was advantageous for those wanting to work coal, both the local landowners and the outsiders who leased land and collieries.

The River Wear was, of course, a particularly important factor in the growth of Chester-le-Street's coal trade for, during most of these two centuries, the district depended on the 'seasales' – the coal export trade with London and other east coast centres. Although the Wear trade followed on from what had been developed on the Tyne, during these two hundred years it grew to have an important trade of its own and a great rivalry between the two river trades developed. It is significant that, despite the Tyne and Newcastle being first in the field, there were staithes on the River Wear before 1650 and, by 1800, although Chester-le-Street was still only a small town, or a "considerable village" as described in the *Universal British Directory* of 1790[2], it was an important meeting point for coalowners and their agents. However, because Chester-le-Street and its district was a supplier of the Wear export trade, growth was relatively little in comparison to the growth of Sunderland, which was the focus of the exports.

Coal transport in the early days was provided by coal wains, carts drawn by oxen along primitive roads. This method of carriage of coal over land was difficult and expensive; the pithead price of coal could double by a journey of ten miles. As the easily accessible coal outcrops nearest the rivers became worked out, transport over greater distances was necessary and it was essential that efficient land transport was developed. Waggonways, special roads or ways were built wherever possible, with wooden rails laid to reduce friction on the wheels of horse-drawn carts. The development of waggonways in Chester-le-Street district in the eighteenth century redefined the structure of the area and was a key factor in the expansion of the district. As an improved means of getting coal to market they created prosperity for the landowners and colliery lessees who constructed them. Wooden waggonways were the predecessors of steam railways, which, of course, by 1850 were changing the face of Britain as well as Chester-le-Street district.

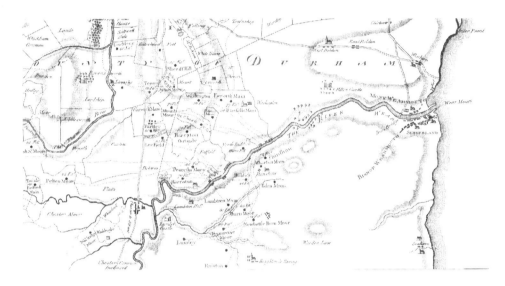

Extract from Casson's Map of 1801

In turn, the geography of the district influenced the economy of the coal industry. Waggonways would generally take the shortest and most convenient route to the river but frequently had to negotiate difficult topography and the colliery operators needed to agree wayleaves with the owners of land through which a waggonway was to pass. Wherever possible the waggonways followed or dropped down the land contours, but, even where a colliery was considerably higher than sea level, the route to the nearest place of water transport or port of shipment could involve horses pulling chaldron waggons of coal up lengthy inclines. [3]

An excellent early interpretation of a waggonway was given in a Council's opinion upon a conveyance dated 1672.

... a new method was invented for carrying Coals to the River in large machines called Waggons made to run on Frames of Timber fixt in the Ground for that purpose and since called a Waggon Way which frames must of necessity lye very near, if not altogether upon a level from the Colliery to the River and therefore when there are any Hills or Vales between the Colliery and the River and the same cannot be avoided, it is necessary in order to the laying such waggon ways, then to make cutts through the Hill or level the same, and to raise or fill up the Vales so that such Waggon Ways may lye upon a level as near as possible[4].

Similarly, Dr Stukeley, a visitor to the North East in 1725, recorded :

The manner of conveying the coals down to the river side from the pits is very ingenious; a cart-way is made by a frame of timber, on which the wheels of the carts run without horses, with great celerity; so that they are forced to moderate their descent by a piece of wood like a lever applied to one of the wheels.

Stukeley also visited "Colonel Lyddel's" waggonway at Tanfield, a few miles west of Chester-le-Street, where the embankment and magnificent arch had then only recently been completed. The visitor noted that :

..... he carries the road over valleys filled up with earth, 100 foot high, 300 foot broad at bottom: other valleys as large have a stone bridge laid across: in other places hills are cut through half a mile together; and in this manner a road is made, and frames of timber laid, for five miles to the river side.[5]

In the 1770's coal from a pit at Ouston was hauled south along the 150 feet contour and then east to Rickleton before the waggonman could take advantage of the fall to the River Wear and ride the waggon brake trailing the horse behind. Some lines were heavily engineered with immense cuttings, "batteries" (earth embankments) and stone or timber bridges being used to overcome hills or valleys across the route of the waggonway and to reduce the work of the horses. Passing places were constructed and double "ways" provided on busy routes to allow full waggons to proceed for shipment unhindered by the returning empty waggons. By the end of the eighteenth century the use of iron plates to protect the vulnerable timber rails was seen, to be later superseded by flanged iron tramplates and edge rails, first of cast iron and then of wrought iron, but horse transport was still the order of the day.

Due to the limited technology available, coal workings below ground could not extend far from the pit shaft, and therefore the life of an individual pit was often short. New pits were sunk nearby to continue extraction and the waggonway on the surface would be moved to suit. Not surprisingly, different maps of an area over quite a short time period can show a variety of waggonway routes. Therefore, as has been clearly demonstrated in Levine and Wrightson's study of Whickham[6], the ability to secure wayleaves was a very significant factor in the cost of transporting coals to the river. Lord Justice North aptly summarised the significance of wayleaves during his visit to Newcastle about 1676:

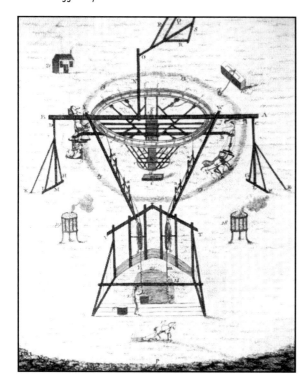

A representation of a coal pit when working by E Sarrat of Chester-le-Street courtesy of the North of England Institute of Mining and Mechanical Engineers.

Another thing that is remarkable is their wayleaves; for when men have pieces of ground between the colliery and the river, they sell leave to lead coals over their ground; and so dear that the owner of a rood (quarter of an acre) of ground will expect £20 per annum for this leave.[7]

As important as investing in wayleaves was investment in colliery drainage. Proximity to the tributaries of the River Wear such as the Team and Chester and Lumley Park burns allowed the development of water driven pumps in the seventeenth century. The introduction of Newcomen engines enabled steam power to gradually replace water power during the eighteenth century. Lord Harley, on his visit to Chester-le-Street in 1725, noted a large steam pumping engine working alongside water gins. Despite these innovations, the way the collieries were worked changed very little over the two centuries. It was not until the end of our period that working methods and conditions began to improve. John Hedworth's account of the dangers of the pit, written in 1708, stands for much of our period :

… I must acquaint you with the nature of Coalmines, which are in general subject to Stithe or Sulphur. Stithe as vulgarly called by the Pitmen, I think corruptly from stench or stink, is a bank of air or rather such foulness in the Air that overcomes the Spirit of the men and so suffocated them as well as extinguishes the candles.

Sulphur differs in this, that as the other suffers not the candles to burn, this makes them burn too fast: and the flame by the impulsive quantity of the Air or attracted by the Sulphur, extends itself upwards into a prodigious length & as a match lighted for the discharge of a cannon, as speedily sets on fire, that vapour equally destructive. [8]

Ultimately, of course, the control of land and the willingness to invest in collieries was probably the single most important factor in the development of Chester-le-Street's coal industry. Long established families like the Lumleys and the Lambtons prospered with the development of their collieries but the industry also needed "incomers" to invest as George Grey did in the seventeenth century, Thomas Allan did in the eighteenth century and Benjamin Thompson and his partners did in the nineteenth century. This was particularly important at the beginning of the period when the landowners had little expertise in managing their land to win coal and when Bishopric royalties, later largely worked out, were on offer. The rivalry between coalowners was also a factor, as it was elsewhere in the region. It is hard to forget Charles Montague's opinion at the end of the seventeenth century when he came from London into the Whickham coal trade - "few are to be believed, much less relyed on in colliery". [9]

Coal working before the Civil War

Coal was, of course, being worked in Chester-le-Street in the Middle Ages, but it is in the seventeenth century that the first strong evidence of the importance of coal mining comes. In the period before the Civil War there were three groups of collieries operating near Chester-le-Street. Firstly, workings on the moors and wastes to the north, west and south of the town, within the Parish or Ward of Chester-le-Street. Secondly, workings south east of the River Wear in the Lumley and Lambton estates. Thirdly, workings on the north bank of the Wear, including Harraton Colliery. [10]

Prior to the seventeenth century most of the coal mined in Chester-le-Street had been for local consumption (landsale) and, although the Lambtons had sent coal by river to supply salt pans in Sunderland from the late fourteenth century, the seasale trade had been small. This remained the case until an increase in demand for coal from the salt and alum industries in the late sixteenth century led to the development of collieries downstream of Chester-le-Street, such as Offerton, Penshaw and Herrington Wood. After this, exporting coal by river from Chester-le-Street seems to have taken off. In the second decade of the seventeenth century a number of new staithes were built along the south bank of the Wear east of Newbridge, the furthest navigable part of the river. In the 1620s coal under the Lumley estates and adjacent freehold areas around Great Lumley was leased by a number of complex business partnerships. Among these was the partnership of George Lilburne of Sunderland and George Grey of Southwick who figure significantly in the early years of the development of the coal industry in Chester-le-Street. [11]

The increase in demand for coal also seems to have led to more investment in collieries west of Chester-le-Street prior to the Civil War. The moors and wastes of Chester-le-Street ward were spread over a wide area and went beyond the bounds of the current Chester-le-

Street District. The Bishop of Durham owned most of the royalties and much activity at the beginning of the century seems to have been north of the River Team, particularly on Black Burn Moor between Lamesley and Sunniside.

There were three sets of leases, although the arrangements were complex. Firstly, the Black Burn leases, secondly the Chester Moor/Urpeth leases which extended from Chester Dene north-westwards as far as Beamish Park Burn and also included Chester South Moor and, thirdly, the "Chesterburne" leases, which included the demesne and copyhold land in and around the town of Chester-le-Street. [12]

Also important in the pre-Civil War Wear coal trade were the Lambton family who leased salt pans from the Bishop at Sunderland and sent coal mined on their estate downriver to fuel these. Building on this, Sir William Lambton (c.1589-1644), ensured that the coal under his estates was exploited by the development of two collieries – High and Low Lambton. High Lambton was probably located on what later became the Racecourse field linking to staithes on the southern bank of the river downstream of Newbridge. The Low Lambton colliery was possibly near Scorer's Wood in the centre of the Lambton estate. [13]

Further work is needed to establish the importance of all these early collieries around Chester-le-Street. However, preliminary research by Mr. Chris Goldsmith suggests that their operation embodied three factors discussed above that were crucial to the development of Chester-le-Street's coal industry. That is : staithes to allow river transport, a waggonway to allow easier access from the colliery to the staithes and improved drainage of the colliery, using water-powered "coalmills", to allow greater coal production.

The Civil War – high and covetous spirits

The Civil War had a significant effect on the organisation of Chester-le-Street's developing coal industry. All the main colliery estates were affected in one way or another. The Bishop's estates were first taken over by the Scots and then sequestered by Parliament, as were the Hedworths' Harraton estates. As royalists, both the Lambton and Lumley families had to cope with damage and occupation of their estates and sequestration fines. Sir William Lambton was killed in the King's service at Marston Moor in 1644 and this led to sequestration fines and other tribulations.[14] However, Henry Lambton (c.1614-93), Sir William's son, ensured the further development of the Lambton estates during the later part of the Commonwealth and after the Restoration.[15] Lumley Castle was garrisoned and Richard, Viscount Lumley and his son were fined and threatened with sequestration for their service to the King. Nevertheless, in 1649, Viscount Lumley was able to lease the rights to work coal in Stub Close and North and East Lumley Park for a combined rent of £300 plus 55 chaldrons of coal.[16]

The early part of the Civil War appears to have given an impetus to the Wear coal trade as, briefly, a Parliamentary blockade stopped the Tyne trade. After Marston Moor in 1644, Parliament's control in North East England was established and Sir Arthur Hazelrigg became Governor of Newcastle. Hazelrigg seems to have had a malign influence on the coal trade, which he sought to control for his own and his cronies' gain. John Hedworth II, whose Harraton estate was sequestered by Parliament, wrote of Hazelrigg :

... it was my unhappy fate to live in the age when Sir Arthur Haslerigge became Governor of Newcastle, a man of high and covetous spirit, the whole County of Durham being too little in revenue to content his greedy appetite, a man that will admit of no rule but to walk by his own crooked and perverse will of the sword.[17]

It is, perhaps, not surprising that Harraton colliery was the target of Hazelrigg's "greedy appetite". In 1644, the colliery was valued at £3,000 per annum and it was claimed that the lessee was making £15 a day through operating it. However, the manner of sequestration is, perhaps, surprising and illustrates the complexities of the colliery business even at that early date.

In 1642, the year civil war broke out, Sir John Hedworth, who had held estates at Harraton, Rickleton and Urpeth as well as further afield in County Durham, died leaving the management of his estates in turmoil. A contemporary thought Hedworth "a careless man in managing of his estate, and one very easily persuaded with for very small and inconsiderable sums to lease or grant away his lands".[18] The Harraton estate was leased to Sir William Wray of Beamish. Like many of the early Wear coalowners[19], Wray was a Roman Catholic and had been convicted as a recusant. Therefore, in 1644, when Parliamentary control was fully established in the North East after the Battle of Marston Moor, his collieries were sequestered.

Parliament did not hand the collieries back to Hedworth's heir (also John Hedworth) but leased them to George Lilburne of Sunderland and George Grey of Southwick, a partnership, which also had interests in Lumley and Lambton collieries. George Grey was John Hedworth II's father-in-law and George Lilburne, a well-known opponent of the monarchy and established church, was related to Colonel John Lilburne, the Leveller. In 1649 the partnership broke up and Sir Arthur Haslerigg "turned out the Lilburnes" and let the whole estate to Colonel John Jackson and other Army officers. However, John Hedworth II continued to be excluded from his estate being "forced to hire his own ground of those who occupied it, to put some cowes to give a little milke to feed his poor young babes". In 1651, Hedworth petitioned Sir Henry Vane and the Parliamentary Committee of the Militia for County Durham for the return of his lands claiming that his loss was £6,703 and that of Grey and Lilburne £10,950. He also claimed in a separate petition to Parliament that the collieries had lain "drowned and lost" from 1642 to 1647 and that Grey and Lilburne had spent £2,000 to restore production. Hedworth was not successful in his case, which, as might be expected, generated claims and counter-claims of great complexity. These were reported in such Commonwealth pamphlets as *Lilburne tried and cast* and *Musgrave muzzled*.

John Hedworth II died in 1655, leaving his heir, also John Hedworth, a minor without possession of the estates. Furthermore, Hedworth's widow, married Colonel John Jackson, one of the occupiers of the Harraton estate. Jackson became lessee of two parts of Harraton, which were seized by Cromwell's Protectorate. In 1659 the Hedworth estates were recorded as broken up as follows[20]:

Harraton (two parts)	Sequestered by Parliament and leased to Colonel John Jackson.
Harraton (remaining third)	Dower of Dame Dorothy Hedworth (widow of Sir John Hedworth)
Burninghill (worth £40 pa)	Occupied by Alderman Cropley of London
Herrington (worth £120 pa)	Sold to Henry Smith
Picktree (worth £20 pa)	Sold to Robert Marley
Rickleton (worth £40 pa)	Sold to Robert, Ralph and Thomas Marley
Urpeth (worth £220 pa)	Purchased by Robert Bewick of Newcastle in 1640.

The Harraton collieries came back to the Hedworths after the Restoration in 1660 and eventually passed to the Lambton family. In 1696 John Hedworth III's daughter, Dorothy (1675-1757), married Ralph Lambton (c1652-1717) having inherited half the estate on her father's death in 1688. The other half (moiety) was inherited by Dorothy's sister, Elizabeth who married Sir William Williamson of Monkwearmouth. Ralph Lambton bought out the Williamson moiety in 1714. It is worth noting that another branch of the Hedworths also married into the Lambton family at this time. In 1676 Ralph Hedworth of Chester Deanery (1654-1705) married Eleanor Lambton, Ralph's sister. Their son, another John Hedworth (1683-1747), became the Member of Parliament for County Durham and a leading figure in the Wear coal trade of the first part of the eighteenth century.[21]

Restoration and the rise of Lumley

Up to the Civil War, North East landowners, generally, saw the coal under their estates as something for others to deal with. For example, Viscount Lumley, cannot be described as "coalowner" in the sense that his successors were. He, in common with Sir William Lambton, was more concerned with the intense political and religious conflicts of the day. Nevertheless, by the time of the Restoration in 1660, the coal resources under Chester-le-Street's estates were, with rising demand for coals in London, becoming of more significance to landowners. As well as obtaining rent, landowners began to negotiate royalties – 6d for every 20 corves (or baskets) of coal was negotiated at Lumley after 1662 – and to view (inspect) the operations of lessees to see that they were complying with the terms of the lease.[22]

By the end of Charles II's reign the Lumley Collieries were beginning to come to national prominence because of the quality of the coal exported to London. Beastall estimates that by the end of the seventeenth century the Lumley estate covered about 600 hectares (1500 acres).[23] A description of the collieries during Lord Chief Justice North's visit in the late 1670's demonstrates both the area's national significance and the importance of drainage to the enterprise :

His lordship was curious to visit the coal-mines in Lumly Park, which are the greatest in the North, and produce the best coal, and, being exported at Sunderland, are distinguished as of that place. These collieries had but one drain of water drawn by two engines, one of three stories, the other of two. All the pits, for two or three miles together, were drained into these drains. The engines are placed at the lowest places that there may be the less way for the water to rise; and if there be a running stream to work the engines it is happy. Coal lies under the stone; and they are twelve months sinking a pit …. When they are by the side of a hill they drain by a level carried a mile underground and cut through the rock to the value of £5,000 or £6,000, and where there is no rock it is supported by timber.[24]

At that time Viscount Lumley's successor, his grandson, Richard, was becoming prominent at the court of Charles II, being Master of Queen Catherine of Braganza's Horse in the 1670s and early 1680s. However, in 1683, he quit his post and allied himself to the anti-Catholic cause becoming, in 1688, one of the signatories of the invitation to William of Orange to 'secure the liberties of England'. This put Lumley on the right side in the Glorious Revolution and it is said that his influence in the London coal trade was an important factor in giving William III and Mary II the control of the capital which they needed to take the crown from James II. Lumley was created Earl of Scarbrough in 1690, fought at the Battle of the Boyne and was Lord Lieutenant of both Northumberland and Durham. Supported by valuable estates in both County Durham and Sussex, Lord Scarbrough remained in government under Queen Anne and George I until his death in 1721.[25]

The most significant lasting development in Chester-le-Street from the Lumleys' heyday at the beginning of the eighteenth century is, of course, the remodelled Lumley Castle. Celia Fiennes' description during a visit in the early 1690s implied the need for improvement.

Thence I proceeded a most pleasant gravel road on the ridge of a hill and had the whole country in view, which seems much on a flatt to this place tho' there be a few little steep up hills and descents; but the whole country looks like a fruitful woody place and seems to equal most countys in England; 7 mile to Chester streete which is a small Market town and I rode neare Lumley Castle which gave title and name to the Lord Lumley, the building looks very nobly its in a 4 square tower running up to the top, with three round towers at the top, between the windows lookes well it's a front the four ways, its not finely furnished.[26]

Major improvements waited the accession of the second Earl, also Richard, second son of the first Earl. Soon after his father's death in 1721, the second Earl commissioned Sir John Vanbrugh, who was then in the north building Seaton Delaval Hall, to make the improvements. Vanbrugh's verdict was as follows :

Lumley Castle is a noble thing and well deserves the favours Lord Lumley designs to bestow upon it; in order to which I stayed there near a week to form a general design the whole, which consists in altering the house, both for state beauty and convenience and making the courts, gardens and offices suitable to it; all of which I believe may be done for a sum that can never lie heavy on the family.[27]

Buck's illustration of 1728 showing Lumley Castle with Vanbrugh's alterations complete suggests little of the growth of coal mining along the River Wear in the early years of the eighteenth century. This is probably because the River Wear bordering the Lumley Estate on its western side was not navigable for keelboats. This meant that the coal mined from the estate had, in order to be taken by keelboat to Sunderland, to be transported over part of the

Buck's Engraving of Lumley Castle 1728

Lambton estate to the staithes downstream of Newbridge. An agreement of 1695 demonstrates the co-operation between Lord Scarbrough, William Lambton MP (1640-1724) and the owners of the keelboats. The agreement sought to tie 18 keel owners to taking only Lumley and Lambton coals and ensure that this was delivered as speedily as possible to colliers in Sunderland harbour for transshipment to London.[28]

The Wear trade in the early eighteenth century

The Lumley/Lambton agreement of 1695 demonstrates that the River Wear was an essential artery for the transport of coal to the lucrative London market. By the early decades of the eighteenth century, the River Wear was well served by an extensive network of wooden waggonways, which connected the collieries of Chester-le-Street, Birtley, Beamish and Washington to the staithes. Waggonways were constructed on both the Lambton and Lumley estates and, more ambitiously, southwards to Rainton and westwards towards Pelton.[29] In 1737 there were seventeen staithes between Chester New Bridge and Cox Green.[30]

These developments contributed significantly to the growth of the port of Sunderland. By 1710 its coastwise trade had grown to nearly half that of Newcastle. Furthermore Sunderland's overseas shipments of coal were equal to those of Newcastle. As a result, by 1712 Sunderland's population was "computed to amount to 4000 souls or upwards". So

A coal staithe in the early eighteenth century - courtesy of Beamish Museum

aware of the growth of the Wear trade were the Tyne colliery proprietors, led by William Cotesworth, that in March 1711 they agreed "that Mr. Cotesworth propose to Mr. Hedworth a meeting of the coal owners of both rivers in order to consider of what may be proper at this juncture to be done for the common good of the Coal Trade".

In 1717, in order to ensure further growth in the Wear trade, John Hedworth, who was MP for County Durham, supported by his fellow MP, Thomas Conyers, who represented Durham City, and by other coalowners, including Lord Scarbrough, the Lambtons and the Allans, promoted an Act of Parliament enabling works to improve Sunderland harbour and the navigability of the River Wear to Chester-le-Street and Durham City. The 'Wearmen', as the promoters were called, met stiff opposition from the Tyneside owners, notably Cotesworth, who orchestrated opposition to the Bill in its passage through Parliament.[31] In addition to the Tyneside opposition there was some opposition from local coalowners. The owners of South Biddick and Urpeth Collieries argued that the Bill was intended to benefit only a clique of coalowners controlling access to the Wear. Thomas Bewick argued that if he were allowed to freely take his Urpeth coal to the Wear he could produce and supply 50,000 chaldrons a year to the London market. Despite these arguments the Bill establishing a River Wear improvement commission was passed, and, although Cotesworth and other opponents of the Wear coal trade through Sunderland were rewarded with places on the Commission, they had lost the battle to stop the improvement of the Wear navigation.[32]

The improvement of the Wear navigation in the first half of the eighteenth century seems to have been a spur to further colliery development in the area. In the 1720s the Lumley collieries were producing coal to a value of nearly £5,000 annually. A new working at Newbottle started in that period cost nearly £6,000, including sinking the shaft, installing a steam pumping engine, building a new wagon way and buying timber from another of Lord Scarbrough's estates at Stansted. The pump was purchased on licence for £200 over six years from the London "proprietors of the Invention for raising water by fire". The engine had a cylinder of 30 inches in diameter and a length of nine feet. Its use appears to have had the potential to benefit the drainage of nearby collieries since the licence agreement allowed for 6s 8d per 'ten' (approximately 50 tonnes) to be paid in addition to wayleave charges by those benefiting from the investment.

This investment was coupled with agreements on limiting coal production in order to keep up the price of coal in London, mirroring the control exercised by the Newcastle "Hostmen" in the previous century and the influence being exercised at that time by the "Grand Allies" in the Tyneside trade.[33] In 1727, the year after the Grand Allies was formed, an agreement on Wear production was made between Lord Scarbrough, Henry Lambton, John Hedworth, Thomas Allan, James Wharton and Thomas Smith. In 1731 a further agreement was made which included nine owners in all. The major coalowners were, of course, involved in distributing the coal as well as mining it. They were linked to specific keel boat operators and also were part owners of many ships. Lord Scarbrough had a share in 64 ships, 25 being based at Sunderland and 19 at Scarborough, Thomas Allan had a share in 69 ships and John Hedworth 113.[34]

Allan's waggonway

The Allan family can be described as one of the "incomers" to Chester-le-Street, who came to exploit the coal there. The family were originally from Staffordshire and settled in County Durham in the middle of the seventeenth century when George Allan became established at Blackwell Grange, near Darlington. His eldest son, Thomas (1651-1717), acquired the Flatts estate near Chester-le-Street and made a fortune from combining the coal and cattle trades. He traded in cattle in partnership with Edward Colville, a Newcastle butcher whose large fortune enabled him to retire to Whitehouse on Gateshead Fell. Thomas's fourth son, also named Thomas (c1688-1740), continued the family's coal interests on the River Wear.[35] He was buried near the pulpit in Chester-le-Street church. His epitaph states:

> *He was a gentleman whose integrity and worth placed him in the highest estimation, and whose good nature and generosity endeared him to all his acquaintance. He was earnest in promoting the good of his country, and particularly that great support of it, its trade; in the cause of which he embarked his fortune, and applied a most laudable industry; manifesting in his affairs an uncommon elegance and propriety; and as his life was adorned with every virtue that dignifies human nature, so his death is universally a most melancholy occasion for sorrow.*[36]

One means by which the Thomas Allans promoted the good of their "country" – by which, of course, was meant the good of Chester-le-Street and district – was by developing and using a waggonway from Flatts Colliery to the north bank of the River Wear. This was an important route, long known as 'Allan's waggonway', connecting to staithes at Fatfield (Chartershaugh) and, despite being dated as 1693 by previous historians[37], may have been constructed after a wayleave agreement negotiated in 1701 by Thomas Allan I and his partners with Henry Peareth of Usworth[38]. Allan's waggonway was extended to Pelton Common by 1746, giving it a total distance of 7.1 kilometres.[39] The Shafto family controlled the Allan's waggonway in the 1770's,[40] and General Lambton had inherited it by 1789.[41]

Travelling northwards from Chester-le-Street in May 1725, Lord Harley noted not only Allan's waggonway but also one constructed about the same time by John Hedworth. Importantly he also described the use of a Newcomen steam pump in tandem with a water wheel system. The new technology in harness with the old!

From Chester [-le-Street] we go about half a mile to the left where is a very large fire engine for draining the coal pits there.
The boiler holds eighty hogsheads. The fire stove consumes five fothers, or sixty bushels of coals in twenty four hours.
The brass barrel or cylinder is nine feet long. Its diameter two feet four inches. Thickness of the brass – one inch and a half. From the surface of the ground to the bottom of the water is twenty-four fathoms or forty-eight yards. The water in the pit is two yards deep. From the surface of the water to the drift or level where the water forces it out is twelve fathoms. It discharges two hundred and fifty hogsheads in one hour; it strikes (as they term it) or makes discharge fourteen times in one minute.
In the same place are two other engines for draining, called Bob-gins, and are moved by water turning a wheel. They belong to Mr. Headworth, Dean of the church, and Mr. Allan. The weekly expense of these engines is 5l. paid by the owners of the colliery to Mr. Potter the undertaker of the fire engine the owners allowing whatever coals are expended.[42]

Harley described John Hedworth's waggonway as a "double road", with a one way system in operation, crossing the Great North Road close to and slightly to the north of Allan's waggonway. Early maps show the two waggonways as more or less parallel throughout their length. By 1776, Hedworth's waggonway had a branch north to Ouston. Later the waggonway continued to Beamish South Moor and became commonly known as "Beamish Waggonway".[43]

Bewick and Urpeth

The Bewick estates at Urpeth lay north of the Allan and Hedworth colliery estates and the geography was such that coal had, with great difficulty, to be brought up on to Birtley Fell for conveyance to the River Wear. Nevertheless, about 1711 both John Hedworth and the Liddells of Ravensworth believed that the lease of Urpeth could give them advantage in the coal trade and competed for it in negotiation with Thomas Bewick. Urpeth was about the same distance from possible staithes on the Tyne as from the Wear. John Hedworth had the advantage of controlling much of the access to the Wear and owning a convenient waggonway from Pelton to Fatfield. The Liddells needed to resolve difficult and expensive wayleaves if they were to connect Urpeth to their Team waggonway northwards to the Tyne. However, there was an added complication that the estate was "entailed", which required that it passed down only through male heirs. Thomas Bewick (1648-1721) had only a daughter living when he inherited the estate in January 1703/4 and therefore without a male heir the estate would pass to his younger brother Calverley (1661-1729).[44]

Perhaps, because of this family difficulty Thomas Bewick obstructed the negotiations, playing one party off against the other, and allowing them to drag on for many years. It was, therefore, some years after his death that agreement was reached with Calverley Bewick.[45] By that time the Liddell family were part of the "Grand Allies", which a contemporary pamphleteer criticised as :

...certain monopolizers, commonly distinguished in the north by the name of the Grand Allies ... who have engrossed into their hands great numbers of collieries, which they take on lease and work, reserving great parts of those on their own estates for futurity .... To the owners of a number of other coal mines, from whence much more that half the usual vend would be supplied, did not their practices prevent, they pay annual considerations for letting their mines lie unwrought ... [46]

"The nature of Coalmines"

Whatever the deviousness and complexity applied to organising the industry by the coalowners, it is clear that eighteenth century Chester-le-Street was a dangerous place to work for ordinary people. Unfortunately, those ordinary people have left little record that is specific to the Chester-le-Street of 1700. However, John Hedworth's account of an explosion at Fatfield colliery in 1708 graphically demonstrates the dangers associated with coalmining.

On Wednesday the 18th Day of August last at Fatfield in the Parish of Chester-le-Street about three a clock in the morning,...by the sudden eruption of a violent fire, which dischar'd itself at the mouths of three pits with a great noise as the firing of a cannon, or the loudest claps of thunder, threescore & nine persons were destroyed in one instant. Three of them viz., two men and a woman were blown quite up from the bottom of the shaft fifty seven fathom deep, into the air at a considerable distance from the mouth of the Pit, One of the men with head almost off & ....the woman with her bowels hanging about her heels.
The Engine by which the coals are drawn up, & is a great height,, was removed & cast aside by the force of the blast what is more wonderful, the Fish which were in a Rivulet, that runs twenty yards under the level and at a great Distance from the mouth of one of the Pits were in great numbers taken up dead floating upon the water by several of the inhabitants...for several days a very strong & noisome smell continued to come out of the Pits.

Hedworth was reporting the accident for the benefit of the members of the Royal Society and went on to try to explain how the explosion was caused based on the accounts of the colliery manager (viewer).

The Viewer of the works takes the best care he can to preserve a free communication of air through all the works & as the Air goes down one Pit it should ascend another: but it hapn'd in this colliery that there was a Pit which stood in an eddy where the Air had not always a free passage, and which in hot & sultry weather was very much subject to sulphur; and it being then the middle of August & some danger apprehended from the closeness & heat of the season, the men were with the greatest care & caution withdrawn from the work in the Pit and turned into another, but an overman some days after this charge & upon some notion of his own being induced as is supposed by a fresh frosty breeze of wind which blew the unlucky morning & which always clears the works of all sulphur had gone too near this Pit & had met the sulphur just as it was purging & dispersing itself, upon which the sulphur immediately catched fire at his candle & so he proved the occasion of the loss of himself & so many men & of the greatest fire ever was known in these parts.[47]

The Fatfield explosion came to the attention of Daniel Defoe who recorded the event in his *Tour through the whole island of Great Britain*.[48]   However, the great journalist's interpretation was different to Hedworth's. Publishing nearly twenty years after the event, Defoe wrote :

A new coal pit being dug or digging, the workmen worked on in the vein of coal til they came to a cavity, which as was supposed had formerly been dug from some other pit; but be it what it will, as soon as upon breaking into the hollow part, the pent up air got vent, it blew up like a mine of a thousand barrels of powder and getting vent at the shaft of the pit, burst out with such terrible noise, as made the very earth tremble for some miles round and terrified the whole country.

Pits around Chester-le-Street had a reputation for being "fiery" and suffered from the presence of explosive mine gas or "fire damp". Furthermore, Wear collieries were slower to adopt the improved ventilation techniques being used on Tyneside by the mid eighteenth century.[49] Explosions appear to have been common but detailed statistics of deaths and injuries were not maintained and those available probably grossly underestimates the true situation. However, in the century after the Fatfield explosion, 300 deaths from explosion are recorded in fifteen accidents within the Chester-le-Street area (or one death every 17 weeks). [50]

1708 also saw the publication, by a Wearside miner, J.C. (Loudon), of a detailed description of mining operations – *The Compleat Collier*.[51]   J.C. described how, from the shaft, headings or roadways perhaps 200 yards long and one and a quarter yards wide were driven through the coal seam and coal was worked in a regular pattern from each side. Bords of three yards wide were wrought from the coal by each hewer at right angles to the heading and separated from the next hewer's bord by a pillar of coal four yards wide. As extraction of the coal progressed, headings were driven from the shaft to all four points of the compass such that coal was wrought by bord and pillar over an area of about 400 metres square. A new pit was then sunk on the same principle to link with the first. This led to multiple pits being sunk close to each other. A plan of 1746 shows six shafts in Mrs Allan's estate at Flatts and 16 shafts in Pelton Common adjacent to Stanley Burn whilst a plan of Lambton estate near Houghton Gate in 1763 shows two or three pits in each field.[52]

The size of the pillar of coal left standing was dependant upon the quality of the coal or its "softness" together with the soundness of the floor and roof of the seam. "Creep" occurred was when the floor in the excavations of a seam rose up due to its weakness and the pillars being insufficient in size. From JC's description of bord and pillar working in 1708 over half the coal was left underground.

The depth of the workings and their extent from the shaft increased as the technology for draining and ventilating mines improved. Water in the pits was a major problem from earliest times and the lack of outlet or technology to drain the water could seriously limit the extent of working. Driving a "water-level" or adit to adjacent lower ground might drain shallow workings but pumps were necessary where this was not possible. As early as 1676 Lumley Colliery had chain pumps, a succession of buckets or troughs on a continuous chain, worked by water wheels.[53] Deep pits required the total depth to be divided into several stages; each with its own machinery as described above by Lord Chief Justice North on his visit to Chester-le-Street in the 1670's.

It was not until the second quarter of the eighteenth century that steam engines became available for pumping. John Potter of Chester-le-Street maintained the Newcomen pumping engines at Allan Flatts about 1725 and Newbottle about 1733. Engines are recorded at Lambton in 1757, a second in 1766 and at Fatfield in 1772.[54] A plan of 1763 shows an underground "water level" leading from workings south of New Bridge Lane (now the road A183) across the Lambton estate to the "Crow Bank" beam engine near the River Wear.[55] The deepest pit shown on Gibson's map of the coalfield in 1787 is Harraton at 70 fathoms (128m) whilst Lambton Main is 60 fathoms (110m) and Pelton Moor 40 fathoms (73m).[56]

The thickness of the different coal seams varied greatly within a colliery and across the region. The Hutton seam is typically 1.5 m thick within the current Chester-le-Street District, the Low Main 0.9 – 1.4 m thick, the Maudlin 1.4 m (but only 0.4 m at Urpeth) and the Main Coal from 0.3 to 1.7 m. Seams as thin as 0.75m required the hewer to spend his entire working day on his "hunkers" or lying on his side.[57]

Pitmen, therefore, often had an arduous task working in wet conditions or thin seams and they were always vulnerable to injury or death by explosions and Loudon described these men and their wages. The "sinker" undertook the skilled and often dangerous work of digging the shaft for pay of 12d or 14d per day. The "hewer" won the coal by pick, shovel, maul and wedge for 10d to 12d per score (20) of corves whilst the "barrow-man" or "putter" filled the corves and moved the coal from the face to the shaft bottom at 20d to 22d per day with perhaps an additional 2d if working up hill. Corves were the hazel baskets of 15 peck capacity (about 0.3 cubic metre) used for conveying coal. The "chief banksman" was paid 16d per day to keep count of the coal raised, set aside the token, or small stick, by which each hewer marked his corves and to monitor the coal quality. The "over-man" was in charge of the pit and placed the men at work for a salary of 8s per week but technical decisions were taken by the "viewer" who might manage several pits for the owner and be paid 15s to 29s per week.[58] By comparison, agricultural wages at the time might be 8d a day.[59]

Furthermore, pitmen often benefited from being provided with housing built close to the pit by the owner, although these properties could be very small. In the 1770's the 4th Earl of Scarbrough built pitmens' houses at Lumley, which were single storey dwellings costing about £15 each, 3 metres (10 feet) high and 7 square metres (72 square feet) in area, built of local stone and pantiles with brick floors. These were perhaps one room 2.7 metres by 2.5 metres with a mezzanine above for sleeping.[60] Pitmens' houses were noted however for being clean and containing comparatively expensive furniture including four poster beds, tall chests of drawers and chairs in mahogany.[61]

From as early as 1700 it was customary to hire pitmen by a "bond", a written agreement for a whole year's service.[62] Pitmen were paid "binding money" upon signing or making their mark on the bond but were tied to the owner's terms for the entire period. A Bond of 1767 at Charlaw Colliery, four miles south west of Chester-le-Street, paid hewers 13d per score of corves (eight pecks to the corfe). However, it required that for every corfe delivered to bank not properly filled, the hewer had to fill another for no pay and for any corves deemed "foul" with stone or splint the hewer was deducted one penny from his pay. Barrowmen were paid sixpence for transporting the coal up to 100 yards east or 60 yards west of the shaft and one penny more for every twenty yards further.[63]

The pitmen suffered physical hardship, control by the coal owner through the bond and were affected by the fortunes of the coal trade as a whole. Bad weather could prevent the colliers from sailing, forcing them to stay in harbour and stopping the trade. The cartels amongst coal owners and the defections by some provoked the "fighting trade" and could force major fluctuations in required output at individual collieries. Learning was discouraged amongst the lower ranks of society and, in the eighteenth century, the educated miner was the exception. Indeed, at the beginning of the nineteenth century, it was still common for boys as young as six to work up to eighteen hours a day as trappers opening and closing the ventilation doors below ground.

Pitmen who protested about their conditions risked losing their livelihood, their homes and even imprisonment. When feelings ran strong, pitmen did protest, either locally or on occasions across wider areas of the coalfield. Early power of union is noted in 1662 when miners attempted to petition the King to improve the ventilation of the pits. Wear pitmen were renowned for the violent nature of their protests. In 1731 several Wear owners decided to stop supply of coal for a month to drive up prices and some announced they were to increase the size of the corves without any increase in pay to the pitmen. On 25 October 1731 pitmen gathered at the Earl of Scarbrough's Newbottle colliery and "broke several lead pipes by which the engine was hindered from working". Threats were made to the Earl's steward and

Pit Head from J.Holland <u>Fossil Fuel, the Colleries and the Coal Trade (1835)</u>

Coal Staithes from T.J. Taylor "The Archaeology of the Coal Trade" <u>Proc. Archaeological Institute</u> (1852)

OLD COAL STAITH—LOADING OF KEELS.

after three weeks stoppage, the demands of the pitmen were met, for fear that the pit would be drowned. Protest continued elsewhere and at the beginning of November Moaborn (Meaburn) Smith's "fire engine" at Murton (Morton) pit and Henry Lambton's engine at Bowes Biddick pit were attacked and stopped from drawing water. "Ale, wine and victuals" were plundered from the storehouses of the staithmen at Fatfield and the men forced stoppages further west at Causey, Beckley, Crooks Field and Bucksnook. Agreement was reached that a delegation of two pitmen belonging to each colliery should present their grievances to the owners at Ravensworth Castle, seat of the Liddells.

The delegation did not attend on the allotted day, but on the 15th November a group of two hundred pitmen descended on Ravensworth Castle and raised such alarm that the riot act was read out. On the 17th almost one thousand men from Tyne and Wear gathered at Chester-le-Street and marched off with the intent "to throw down all Ginns and Corves wherever they found them standing and to resist in case of opposition", a plan attributed to the Wear men. The pitmen were met at Urpeth by a strong force raised by the magistrates and they dispersed. Four days later troops arrived at Newcastle from Berwick "to quell our mutinous pitmen" and their presence in the area was sufficient to subdue the pitmen. It was another thirty-four years before any significant mass protest occurred again.[64]

In the 1740s a factor which influenced subsequent coalmining protests was established in Chester-le-Street. This was Methodism. John Wesley preached at Pelton in 1743 and by the 1780s Chester-le-Street was part of the new Sunderland Methodist circuit. With Methodism came an improvement in education for pitmen and this was particularly so from the 1820s when Primitive Methodism took hold in the area. Thomas Hepburn, the famous miners' leader a century after the Wear colliers' protest discussed above, was a Primitive Methodist.[65]

Coal and iron : Chester-le-Street in the mid eighteenth century

The second half of the eighteenth century was a less buoyant period for the coal trade than the first half. However, by mid-century, Chester-le-Street was slowly becoming a focus for other industries as well as the coal trade. These developments were the foundations for the area's growth in the next hundred years. Significant for this growth was the development of the Whitehill estate between Chester-le-Street and Pelton Fell by John Cookson (c1712-1783). Cookson had wide business interests on Tyneside and in Cumbria including iron founding, glass-making and salt manufacture. He purchased Whitehill with part of his marriage settlement to Elizabeth, daughter of Thomas Lutwidge of Whitehaven, in 1743. The estate and house had belonged to the Millot family since the fifteenth century.

Surtees, County Durham's great historian, writing at the beginning of the nineteenth century describes the position of the house :

The present house of Whithill, which includes part of the old mansion of the Millots stands almost on the very brink of Chester Burn overlooking a shivery cliff covered with native copsewood; the East view extends over quiet green home grounds, commanding a beautiful prospect of Chester spire and Lumley castle.[66]

Cookson's lifestyle seems to have reflected his new landed status. A later family chronicler

(Joseph Cookson writing in the 1860's) hints at the ostentation displayed when the Cooksons moved to Chester-le-Street :

> When John Cookson my Grandfather took possession of his Ho. situate at Whitehill in 1745 he took Mrs. Cookson with him in his carriage and four, properly attired from his mansion in Newcastle. He wore as usual his Gold laced Cocked Hat and the two outriders with the Carriage had each pistols in their holsters.[67]

However, John Cookson made sure that his Whitehill estate also contributed to his industrial ambitions. About 1745, possibly even before he purchased the estate,[68] Cookson constructed a blast furnace at Whitehill in partnership with John Button, a partner in running an iron furnace in Gateshead. As a blast furnace the Whitehill project appears to have been unsuccessful,[69] but the associated iron founding works carried on production into the first decade of the nineteenth century making "brewing vessels, soap pans, engine pumps, cylinders, cannons of all sizes".[70] Local coal from Whitehill estate was used to make coke and it has been suggested that Cookson used iron-ore from ironstone seams in the local coal measures, supplemented by ore imported from Whitby (where it was gathered on the beach and shipped via the Wear to Chester-le-Street).[71] Cookson had other business interests at Whitby, being involved in the alum trade there.[72] It is, also possible that Cookson was shipping coal from the Wear to use in alum manufacture at Whitby. This was an established trade; from the early sixteenth century Wear coal had been used for this purpose.[73]

The Whitehill foundry made cannon for Woolwich Arsenal[74] and pumping engines for local collieries[75] but these do not seem to have been particularly successful ventures in the context of John Cookson's overall business 'empire'. In addition to his interests in glass, salt, coal and iron, Cookson was a partner in the region's first bank in Newcastle established in 1755. He died a very wealthy man in 1783 and left his children substantial legacies.[76] Of these, the fourth son, Joseph, is notable for squandering his legacy with a short life as a Captain of the Lifeguards, membership of what might be called the 'County-set' and gambling on horse races.[77] However, in general, the Cooksons flourished and went on to improve Whitehill Hall and build the Hermitage in the early decades of the nineteenth century.

Colliery ownership at the end of the eighteenth century

In the 1790s a number of coalowning families dominated Chester-le-Street, which was described in the *Universal British Directory* as "a very considerable village, through which runs the great post-road from London to Edinburgh".[78] Table 1 sets out the colliery ownership as defined in the Directory and, where known, the residence of coalowners.

There is no reference in the Directory to the Hedworths and Allans, who had been such an important part of Chester-le-Street's history earlier in the century. In both cases the male line had died out and the properties inherited through marriage of the female line. When the last Thomas Allan died unmarried in 1745, his mother Margaret and his four sisters succeeded to the collieries and estates. As co-heiresses the sisters all married into wealthy families and fourth daughter Camilla married Robert Shafto of Benwell, who appears to have operated the Allan collieries for a period. Upon her death, in 1782, the bulk of the Allan estates passed to her only child Camilla who married Hugh, alias William, Adair.[79] By the 1790s the estates had passed to the Lambton family.[80]

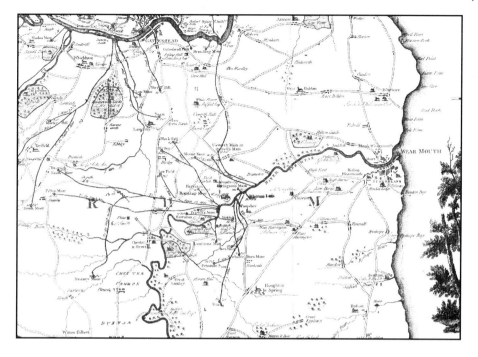

Gibson's Map of 1787

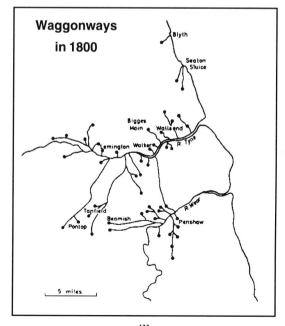

TABLE 1 : COLLIERIES AND COALOWNERS ROUND CHESTER-LE-STREET AS SHOWN IN THE UNIVERSAL BRITISH DIRECTORY c.1790.

Coalowner	Colliery	Residence
Lord Scarbrough	Lumley-park	Lumley Castle
General Lambton	Lambton, Harraton, Burnt Moor Flatts, Pelton Fells	Harraton Hall
Miss Lambton	South Biddick	South Biddick Hall
Sir John Eden	Beamish	Outside Chester-le-Street (Windlestone)
John Tempest Esq.	Penshaw	Not known
Heirs of John Neasham Esq.	Burnt Moor	Not known
William Peareth	Chartershaugh	Usworth Hall
William Peareth and Richard Humble Esqs.	Birtley	
Lord Strathmore, Lord Bute and the heirs of Sir H.G. Liddell, Bart.	Birtley Fell	Outside Chester-le-Street
John Hudson, Esq.	Ox Close	North Biddick Hall
Messrs. Russell and Wade	New Washington	Outside Chester-le-Street (Sunderland)
Messrs Wade, Biss and Allen	North Biddick	Outside Chester-le-Street (Sunderland)
Ralph Milbanke, Esq.	Harraton Outside	Outside Chester-le-Street
Messrs. Johnson & Co	Twizell	Not known

The Hedworth estates were jointly inherited on the death of the last John Hedworth in 1747 by his two daughters from separate marriages. The elder line resulted in a share of the Hedworth estates passing to William Jolliffe, MP for Petersfield in Hampshire, who opened a colliery at Deanery Moor or Waldridge Fell in 1779 and laid a new waggonway, which used Hedworth's old way for part of the route to the staithes at Fatfield.[81] The other part of the Hedworth inheritance came to the Milbanke family of North Yorkshire. Sir Ralph Milbanke (1747-1825) became a Member of Parliament for County Durham in 1790 having bought the Seaham estate, where his daughter was to marry Lord Byron in 1815. Milbanke was only a visitor to Chester-le-Street, whereas Jolliffe appears to have lived at Chester Deanery for a period, although neither he nor his colliery is mentioned in the *Universal British Directory*. The Milbanke's wife, Judith the daughter of the Earl of Wentworth, clearly thought that the colliery business did not suit her husband. In 1782 she wrote to her brother :

I hope Milbanke's stay in the North will not be longer than the fortnight you mention. I allmost wish you could have gone with him, for I fear he is not a Match for ye Jolliffes &c &cc he probably has to deal with.[82]

Milbanke and Jolliffe later had joint colliery interests at Ouston.[83] The estate lay between Rowletch Burn in the east and Bewick's Urpeth estate in the west and coal had been worked from numerous pits in both Ouston royalty and the adjacent Pelaw royalty to the south. The coal was led eastwards through Rickleton along Sir John Eden's "Beamish" waggonway for shipment from staithes at Fatfield.[84] Milbanke and Jolliffe let Ouston Colliery to Thomas Wade of Hylton Castle until about 1815[85] and Ouston 'A' Pit was sunk to "60 fathoms" (110 metres) prior to 1807.[86] A valuation of the estate by the viewers William Stobart and John Watson in 1815 confirms that a wayleave and staithroom at Fatfield had been granted to the owners of Ouston Colliery.[87]

Trade and Manufacture

As might be expected, the *Universal British Directory* says nothing of the lives of the coalminers and servants and their families whose labours ensured that this community of coalowning families flourished. However, the Directory does have some information about the "middling sort" of people many of whom benefited from the wealth generated by the growth of coalmining and other industries. In 1790, Chester-le-Street had ten victuallers (sellers of food and drink), eight shoemakers (or cordwainers as they were then called), seven butchers, five weavers and five blacksmiths, four innkeepers and four surgeon/apothecaries, three schoolmasters and three masons, two bakers and two flour dealers and a wide range of other trades and professions. In total 96 individuals are named of whom only five were women, including Mrs. Croudace, a tea dealer. The town also had a wine merchant and a Brewery, with a manager and clerk.

However, despite these references, the Directory does not appear accurate in respect of manufacturing in Chester-le-Street. There is no mention of Cookson's Whitehill Forge or of the establishment of Murray's Engine Works, which was a key industry in the town in the early nineteenth century. Two manufacturers are mentioned : Hurry &Co., salt manufacturers and Hawks &Co., iron forgers and salmon fishers. Hurry & Co. were lessees of the salt works in Birtley where salt was obtained from a natural spring in a coal pit located south of Birtley Lane. The first salt works was said to have belonged to Sir William Lambton but appears to have been totally destroyed by the Scots in the Civil War.[88] The works seems to have been revived about 1785, since Bailey, writing in 1810, states that the salt spring was :

discovered about 25 years since, in making the colliery drift, at a depth of 140 yards. It is conveyed from the place where it issues, to the bottom of the pit (about 250 yards) from whence is raised in pumps by the colliery steam engine: the spring is very regular, as the quantity of water has never been known to vary, and it is as strong now as when the salt works first began, which was soon after its discovery. The quantity of salt made is about 1,000 tons, for which £30 per ton duty is paid; and the salt is now sold at £35 per ton; of which a considerable quantity is sent to London, and the remainder sold in the adjoining counties.[89]

The salt spring occurred only in one drift and its discovery was said to be purely by chance :

its mixing with fresh water in the pit would have occasioned it to remain totally unnoticed but for an accident, which happened to the boiler of an engine room soon after its erection. One morning the bottom of the boiler dropped out; the engineer, amazed thereat, informed the undertakers, who upon examination found it encrusted with a vast quantity of strong salt and the iron wholly corroded. Upon tasting the water, though incorporated with immense quantities of fresh, it was found exceedingly brackish and salt, on which the workings were explored and the above mentioned very valuable salt spring was discovered to arise in such drifts only, and has for these nine years produced 20,000 gallons a day, four times stronger than any sea water whatever. In consequence of this discovery, a large and extensive manufactury of salt has been established by a company of gentlemen, who after encountering many difficulties, have brought it to a very great perfection, the quality being most excellent.[90]

South Shields, the other major north east supplier, consumed 100,000 chaldrons of coal annually to convert seawater into salt but in 1834 it was said that the "salt spring at Birtley has nearly annihilated the manufacture of salt at South Shields".[91]

The Hurry family who operated the works[92] were also involved in shipbuilding on the Tyne. Francis Hurry was a ship owner from Great Yarmouth, who, with his son Thomas, owned a large shipyard at Howdon Panns on the Tyne between 1758 and 1806. The yard was one of the best known in England at the close of the eighteenth century but due to a rundown in the industry went into liquidation in 1806.[93] The assignees had difficulty in winding up the business due to its size and on 1st August 1812 an advertisement in the *Newcastle Courant* offered for sale the Howdon Dock and the leasehold of the Salt Works at Birtley including a steam engine and land. However, Hurry & Co. appear to have continued the Birtley Salt Works. In 1817, a one third share of Birtley Salt Works was offered for sale, whilst in 1826 the "valuable SALT SPRING, situate at Birtley" together with buildings, land and a steam engine were offered to let.[94]

The Hawks & Co forge mentioned in the *Universal British Directory* was part of the Hawks' metal-working empire founded about 1747 at New Greenwich alongside the Tyne in Gateshead by William Hawks (1708-1755), a foreman smith at Crowley's Swalwell works.[95] Under the management of his son William II (1730-1810) in partnership with Thomas Longridge (1751-1803), the son of a Sunderland merchant, the business expanded rapidly in the 1780's. Facilities were greatly increased at Gateshead and four separate metal working sites were established along the narrow valley of the Beamish Burn where shovels and ladles were made.[96] A major iron-working complex was established at Bedlington[97] and Hawks & Longridge also built the forge at Lumley on a site leased from the Earl of Scarbrough about 1784.[98] The Hawks' empire became famous for its contracts with the Admiralty producing chains and thousands of anchors. In the nineteenth century it grew to employ over 2,000 men and to build many structures at home and abroad, perhaps the most famous of which is the ironwork for the High Level Bridge, Newcastle in 1849.[99]

The idea of having an iron works on the Lumley estate using local coal had been investigated in the late 1770's by Lord Scarbrough. Advice was sought from the Walkers of Rotherham, a leading family of iron and steel manufacturers, but nothing came of these discussions due to the high cost of building a new dam on the River Wear replacing the existing fishery dam.[100] However, the Hawks' site, which covered 4.5 hectares (11 acres), lay on the south side of the deeply incised valley of Lumley Park Burn about one kilometre above the Castle (now lying under the shadow of the A1(M) viaduct).

The Lumley Forge Co. manufactured anvils, bar iron, shovels, nails and chains from both brass and iron.[101] It comprised a forge (later a rolling mill worked by water and steam) together with nine cottages at Breckon Hill for the workmen.[102] Mr John Wight, a clerk from the Gateshead works, was manager until the forge was dismantled in the 1830's on account, it is said, of the noise of the forge hammer being considered a nuisance at Lumley Castle.[103] John Wight and his family also ran the public house and grocer's shop in this small community.[104]

The strange combination of the forge site on Lumley Park Burn and salmon fishing on the Wear offered in the lease from Lord Scarbrough predates the Hawks interest. The fishery lost money and in 1792 the company refused to pay the rent. In 1808 Hawks' solicitor confirmed:

the very considerable loss my employers have sustained by Lumley Fishery; I shall only say that they are now losing £200 yearly and that they have sustained a loss of £4,000 …[105]

New technology and old families

The second half of the eighteenth century was one of expansion for the Tyne and Wear coal owners; exports increased but so did competition for trade and labour. Upon advice of his viewer Edward Smith, the fourth Earl of Scarbrough found it necessary to invest heavily in new colliery winnings on the Lumley estate from the mid 1770's. Works were commenced to sink pits, lay a waggonway to a new staithe on the Wear on a site previously occupied by Meaburn Smith and provide whim gins, horses, wagons, smith's and wright's shops and houses. Messrs Cookson & Co. cast a 50-inch diameter cylinder for the pumping engine and large oak beams were supplied from Sandbeck in Yorkshire and Rufford in Nottinghamshire.

The colliery started to produce coal in spring 1779 but in the September there were stoppages when few ships were in the river due to the on-shore wind and the activities of the American privateer Paul Jones off the coast. Regrettably the pumping engine proved inadequate to drain the collieries in 1780 and a second had to be built. There was unrest amongst the pitmen and the lease of the collieries to John Cole of Chester-le-Street in 1781 failed before the end of 1782. It was a time of high expense and minimal income and when the 4th Earl died in 1782 he left debts of over £70,000. By that time the Lumley family had become largely absentee landlords, preferring to reside at Glentworth in Lincolnshire and, later, Sandbeck in Yorkshire, estates inherited in 1739. The 5th Earl relied on agents to run the Lumley Estate such as Luke Collings, the farm agent, and William Stobart of Pelaw House the colliery agent or viewer.[106]

In 1782 General Lambton took the lease of the six pits forming Lumley colliery for a term of 31 years and by the turn of the century had sunk new pits at Houghton Gate and near Floaters Mill. Income to the 5th Earl of Scarbrough improved under the Lambton lease but relationships were not always smooth between the parties. In 1796 Lambton's agent and viewer threatened to flood the workings of the Lumley colliery unless they were allowed to make an outstroke from the Lumley workings to reach an area of coal under Lambton's adjacent land. This dispute dragged on for some time although it did not jeopardise renewal of the lease to Lambton. In 1813, towards the end of the turbulent years of the Napoleonic Wars, the 6th Earl, who succeeded to the title in 1807, wrote:

… how great a difference to the coal trade a peace would make, and endeavour, that I as well as the Lambtons should reap the fair benefit of it.[107]

By the end of the wars, the Lambtons were certainly reaping a bigger share of the benefits of the coal trade than the Lumleys. Their rise had been steady throughout the previous century. Two of Ralph Lambton and Dorothy Hedworth's sons – Henry (1697-1761) and John (1710-94) – represented the City of Durham in Parliament successively for over fifty years. Before becoming an MP, the latter had a distinguished military career and was Colonel of the 68th Regiment, the predecessors of the Durham Light Infantry. General John Lambton MP married Susan Lyon daughter of the Earl of Strathmore in 1763. They had two sons – William Henry (1764-1797) and Ralph John (1767-1844). Both continued the family tradition and became the Member of Parliament for Durham City; the former on his father's retirement in 1787 and the latter on his brother's early death in 1797 until 1813, when his nephew was elected one of the MPs for County Durham.[108] That nephew, John George (1792-1840) went into Parliament as soon as he came of age and with a century of family tradition behind him. That tradition was very much a radical and reforming one. General Lambton supported Pitt's early attempts at parliamentary reform. W.H.Lambton was described by his contemporaries as a "Jacobin" for following Fox in opposing the Government's suspension of the Habeas Corpus Act in 1795 as the effects of the French Revolution began to take effect in England.[109]

J.G.Lambton's inheritance was, of course, not only Parliamentary. His family owned five collieries around Chester-le-Street and their estates were in a key location to ensure profitable wayleaves for access to the River Wear. During Lambton's minority, between 1797 and 1813, the estates were controlled largely by his uncle, R.J.Lambton. As with the Lumley estates, management of the Lambton estates lay with agents and colliery viewers, one of whom, Thomas Croudace, leased Lumley Grange Farm from Lord Scarbrough.[110]

However, the decade after J.G.Lambton came of age saw great changes in the Wear coal trade. The coalfield was shifting eastwards with the development of the Vane Tempest (later Londonderry) collieries at Rainton and Penshaw and, later, the Hetton Collieries. Steam locomotion was starting to reduce the costs of moving coal and, most importantly, demand for coal was growing as the industrial revolution took hold. Despite this the Wear coalowners, in co-operation with those on the Tyne, sought to limit the production of coal by what was called the 'annual vend'. Chester-le-Street was often the venue for the meetings of the Wear coalowners and J.G.Lambton was heavily involved in the arguments in 1823 and 1824 when the Hetton Coal Company sought to substantially increase the vend. Lambton had previously bought Nesham's Newbottle colliery and waggonway to ensure that he had a share in this eastern coalfield with direct access to staithes at Sunderland. At first Lambton opposed the Hetton proposals and the machinations of their leader, Arthur Mowbray, but later changed his position becoming friendly with Archibald Cochrane, the company's largest shareholder. John Buddle, Lord Londonderry's superintendent viewer at Penshaw, writing to his employer in January 1824, describes this in a way which clearly demonstrates the complex coal trade politics played out in Chester-le-Street at that time :

It is now whispered that the acquaintance between Mr. Lambton and Capt. Cochrane, which seems at last to have grown into friendship, was brought about in a rather unusual way. After the Chester meeting (8th Augt.) at which Lambton handled the Hetton Co. and old Arthur so severely, Capt. Cochrane called on him to demand an explanation of his conduct on that occasion, when he made such an apology as was quite satisfactory to Cochrane and they have been intimate friends ever since!!! At present he seems to be seeking shelter under Cochrane's wing, as I am told he dined with the Capt. the day before yesterday. Oh think of this high spirited Whig putting his legs under the same table as old Arthur after what passed at the Chester meeting!!! But we live to see strange things come to pass now a days. The next thing we shall hear of most likely will be a treaty offensive and defensive between Mr. L and the Hetton Co. He laid it down as an axiom at the Chester meeting that whatever Hetton might be placed at upon the Basis [of the Vend] he would have the same for Newbottle. If Hetton should stand out for 80-100,000 ch[aldrons] in any future Regulation [of the Vend] will Mr. L do the same for Newbottle? There is no knowing what may grow out of this friendship between the "Squire" & Cochrane and it therefore behoves us especially to have all our wits about us.[111]

Thus the shifting fortunes of the coal trade were played out in smoke-filled rooms of

Chester-le-Street's inns. Joseph Cookson, who lived in the town as a boy at the end of the eighteenth century, recounts a further tale of business practice, which also demonstrates the Chester-le-Street's importance as a meeting point on the Great North Road :

A ruse was practiced with much success many years ago in the North of England by some shrewd men of business, who had an establishment at Newcastle and also at Howdon on the Tyne. Early information as to prices and sales is all important in business; in fact to know what is doing, whilst others do not. The London Mail arrived at the Post Office Chester le St. each day about 11 o'clock a.m. there were very few letters at that time and sorting and delivery at the office was accomplished in a few minutes, but not so at N'castle where the Bags were heavy & much time required at the office before the letters could be obtained.

Well, on a smart active horse, rode forward our friend with the letters addressed to Chester le St. & reached Gateshead with them before the mail arrived at N'castle office when sorting was to commence. The hour and half on the Quay or on the Exchange was every thing, in favor of the early arrival of such information as was conveyed by these letters, via the Chester office - & the practice was continued for some time & not known or discovered till much good business had been done. I well remember the messenger, who was ordered to stop in Gateshead & proceed on foot into the Lower town of N'castle that no one should notice or understand the scheme.[112]

Urpeth and the move to the Tyne

The link with Newcastle and the Tyne was also concerning those involved with the Urpeth estate at the turn of the nineteenth century. In 1804, a new Urpeth colliery was sunk, which was destined to become part of a system linking Chester-le-Street with the Tyne rather than the Wear and, as a result, significantly changed the area's coal industry. This new colliery was developed by William Peareth (1734-1810) of Usworth who had taken out a lease in May 1803 for a period of 40 years.[113] The new pit was probably sunk to the Low Main seam north east of the Portobello Dyke, a major obstacle to coal working in the area.[114]

Waggons from this new working were horse drawn to the bank of the Urpeth Burn which provided a relatively level route north east to Rowletch Burn. Crossing the burn they climbed eastwards up the side of the valley to cross the Durham Turnpike road near the Three Tuns Inn before continuing up to the heights of Birtley Fell, near a point later noted on Ordnance Survey plans as "Old Engine". From Birtley Fell the waggonway descended via Oxclose to the Wear at Cox Green, a total distance from Urpeth of approximately eleven kilometres (seven miles). According to the viewer Matthias Dunn, writing in 1844, the project included improving the waggonway to the River Wear by adding a fixed engine, "under the direction of Mr Curr about the year 1805", to haul waggons up the incline.[115] Bailey writing in 1810 commented that waggonways :

have generally been so contrived, that the ascents were not greater than a single horse could draw a waggon up them but that recently, where this was not possible, steam engines had been substituted and at Urpeth waggonway, five or six waggons are drawn at once up an ascent, by a steam engine placed at the top.[116]

However, Peareth's waggonway from Urpeth Colliery to the Wear attracted new investment from outside the region by Harrison, Cooke & Co. to convey coals from Urpeth a distance of nine miles over Eighton Banks to the Tyne by a succession of inclined planes.[117] This investment was probably justified because the mouth of the River Wear was very dangerous for shipping at this time, with numerous shifting sand banks. Ships could not navigate very far up river and coals from the Birtley, Beamish and Washington area were transported in keels from staithes at Fatfield, Chartershaugh and Coxgreen to near the mouth of the river where they were transferred to the sailing fleet. The Tyne was deeper, seagoing vessels could load further up river, and by building a waggonway to Moody's Quay at Pelaw Main, the new owners of Urpeth Colliery could avoid using keels and load directly into ships.

The project was instigated in 1808, shortly before the death of William Peareth,[118] when a Mr Samuel Cooke of Deptford, induced Messrs Harrison, Gorst & Co. of London, to take a lease of Urpeth Colliery and make him a partner in the enterprise.[119] As a result Peareth let a sub-lease of Urpeth Colliery to "William Harrison & Co." from 7th July 1808 for 14 years at a rent of £1,500 per year for the first seven years and £2,000 per year for the remainder.[120] Although Cooke was not familiar with colliery management he was made manager of the project and immediately set about building a waggonway to the Tyne. The new system required three steam powered ascending planes a total of nearly 1,830 metres long and five self-acting planes, although two of the latter were employed on the old route to the Wear at Cox Green.[121]

The new waggonway opened on 17th May 1809 amid much public interest. According to the *Newcastle Courant* of 20th May 1809, 10,000 people assembled to witness the inauguration and there was great admiration of the style with which the fixed steam engines moved the waggons up the inclined plane. This "was beyond description grand, and fully proved the wonderful power of the machinery, though some little delay was occasioned by the breaking of one of the way-plates." The *Courant's* reporter goes on to describe the celebrations :

As soon as the waggons reached the summit of the second and highest plane, up which they went with surprising velocity and regularity, the British flag was hoisted at Ayton Cottage, and announced by a discharge of six pieces of cannon, which were answered by an equal number from the Ann and Isabella, his majesty's armed ship on the Tyne, and from Deptford-House, the residence of Mr. Cooke. Immediately on the waggons reaching the first plane, about four hundred gentlemen sat down to dinner in a tent fitted up for the occasion, and spent the afternoon with the greatest possible hilarity. An excellent military band attended on the occasion; many loyal and appropriate toasts were given, and the company separated no less pleased with the polite attentions of the donors of the feast, than with the brilliance of the whole spectacle, which has seldom been equalled in this country. In the evening, in order to prove the excellency of the level railway, six men, without horses, took with the greatest ease, four laden waggons, with each ten men on the top, from Ayton Cottage to the Tyne, and the first coals being put on board the Ann and Isabella, the same was announced by discharges of artillery as before.

Clearly, the new waggonway was launched with great expectations and after describing in detail the technical prowess of the project the *Courant* reporter concluded that "the enterprizing proprietors will soon be amply remunerated". However, it would appear that the proprietors were not for, on 24th July 1810 Martin Morrison, a "provisional assignee of the Estate of Harrison Cooke & Co., Bankrupts", wrote to the distinguished viewers Thomas Fenwick and John Buddle requesting that they provide an opinion of the collieries wrought by the lessees at Urpeth for presentation before the creditors in August.[122] The assignees chose to advertise Urpeth Colliery for sale by public auction in 1811, placing several notices in local newspapers between June and September which claimed that the Bewick Main colliery was capable of producing at least 40,000 chaldrons of coal per annum from nearly 1,000 acres.[123] Buddle was engaged by the end of 1811 to value and arbitrate between the assignees of Harrison Cooke & Co. and those of Hunt Noble & Co, a firm who paid the assignees £18,000 to take the remaining ten and a half years lease of Urpeth Colliery.[124]

The partners in the new venture appear to have been instrumental in bringing a Benjamin Thompson (1779-1867) from Sheffield at the end of 1811 to act as General Manager of Urpeth Collieries. Thompson, probably supported by London interests, believed that he could operate an efficient business if he could control both Ouston and Urpeth royalties.[125] This would benefit operations underground and take advantage of a common route to the River Tyne. Thompson began working Ouston Colliery again on 1st May 1815[126] with a plan for rationalising the operations and building a new waggonway link north east from Ouston Colliery ('A' Pit) across the Newcastle to Durham turnpike adjacent to the present William IV public house and up to Birtley Fell at a point almost one mile south of the earlier fixed engine. The Harrison/Cooke waggonway along Urpeth Burn and up to Birtley Fell via the Three Tuns was closed and coals were drawn up the new line by two steam-powered inclined planes for the first time on 17th November 1815. The journey to the Tyne at Pelaw Main staithes was completed by the original route via Eighton Banks and Heworth.[127]

Benjamin Thompson was one of a new breed of colliery managers, who transformed the area's coal industry and made major improvements to the operation and profitability of the collieries under their control. Thompson improved storage of the coal at the staithe and arrangements for coal screening at the pithead. He managed the iron works at Birtley, set up other works elsewhere, was later to be a Director of the Newcastle & Carlisle Railway and build the Brunton to Shields Railway a distance of over nine miles from collieries at Fawdon and Brunton to the Tyne near Whitehill Point. He perfected the coal drop to reduce the breakage of coal at a time when large coal fetched the highest prices and introduced this successfully at Bewick Main Staithe in 1812.[128]

A contemporary writer euphorically described the action of 'drops':

But what is your amazement when you come into sight of the River Tyne and see these waggons still careering on to the very brink of the water. To see a railway carried from the high bank and supported on tall piles, horizontally above the surface of the river, and to some distance into it, as if to allow those vagabond trains of waggons to run right off, and dash themselves down into the river. There they go, all mad together! Another moment, and they will shoot over the end of the lofty railway, and go headlong into the Tyne, helter-skelter! But behold! These creatures are not so mad as you imagine. They are instinct with sense! They have a principle of self-preservation as well as of speed in them. See, as they draw near the river, they pause! They stop! One by one they detach themselves, and as one devoted waggon runs on, like a victim given up for the salvation of the rest, to perform a wild summerset into the water below - what do we see? It is caught. A pair of gigantic arms separate themselves from the end of the railway! They catch the waggon! They hold it suspended in the air! They let it softly and gently descend, ay, softly and gently as an angel dropping to earth on some heavenly message, and wither? Into the water? No; we see now that a ship already lies below the end of the railway. The waggon descends to it ; a man standing there strikes a bolt - the bottom falls, and the coals which it contains are nicely deposited in the hold of the vessel! Up again soars the empty waggon in that pair of gigantic arms. It reaches the railway; it glides like a black swan into the native lake, upon it, and away it goes of its own accord, to a distance to await its brethren, who successively perform the same exploit, and then joining it, all scamper back over the plain to the distant pit again.[129]

Thompson connected pits in Bewick's Urpeth royalty by waggonway to Ouston 'A' Pit. From there they were led almost one mile to sidings on the north side of Birtley Iron Works (now Komatsu), which later became a focal point of transport for the "Pelaw Main Collieries" and familiar to many as "Birtley Tail" with branches running to several pits. From the Tail waggons were hauled up the eastern side of the valley, an average gradient of 1 in 16, by two stationary engines, one near St John's Church and the other at Black Fell. Horses initially worked a portion of the waggonway across Birtley Fell. This was 1,820 metres in length, lying between the head of the Blackhouse plane and the foot of the Eighton Bank plane. In 1821 Thompson converted this section to mechanical operation by utilising the reciprocal action of the two stationary engines following the principles laid down in his patent registered in that year for a "Method of Facilitating the Conveyance of Carriages along Iron and Wood Rail-ways, Tram Roads and other Roads".

By such initiatives as Benjamin Thompson's, the 1820s saw the northern coalfield, which had previously been concentrated round the rivers Tyne and Wear, expanding significantly.[130] In the next quarter of a century much of County Durham, south, east and west of Chester-le-Street began mining coal to fuel growing demands from the region's "great age of industry".[131] The town was no longer at the southern edge of the coalfield but one of a number of small County Durham towns serving the growing coal industry. As such it was part of the most significant social change of that century – the struggle for better working conditions.

Working Conditions – the great cause of the nineteenth century

Sharp as one had to be in practising the coal trade, it did not, at the end of the eighteenth century, hold the same dangers as actually winning the coal, although men such as Lambton and Buddle were soon to lend their influence to improving safety in the area's pits. The new century was heralded by another disaster in the area, when on 11th October 1799 an explosion at one of the Lumley pits killed 39 men and boys.[132] Such deaths seemed commonplace. The first great miners' leader, Thomas Hepburn (1796-1864) who was born at Pelton, was the son of a miner shortly to be killed in a colliery accident. Hepburn started work at the new Urpeth Colliery at the age of eight.[133]

The issue for miners was not so much pay as their working conditions exemplified in the annual bond. For example at Ouston Colliery, the bond listed the names and "mark" of 131 pitmen who were hired for the year 6th April 1830 to 5th April 1831 to "hew, work, fill, drive and put coals". The owners paid binding money of 1s 0d on signing and agreed to pay each of the 76 hewers;

for every score of corves (a score being 21!) of coals wrought - 3s 3d and in addition;
for double working with two hewers working in one "board" - 4d per score
for wet working - 4d per score
for 'ramble' or working seams where a thin stratum of shale lying above the coal
could easily fall and mix with the coal - 4d per score
to each putter they agreed to pay 1s 2d per score for putting a 20 peck corf for the
first 80 yards and 1d per score for every 20 yards further.

Each pitman for whom the owners provided a dwelling house was supplied with a reasonable quantity of coal for which he paid 3d per week. No payment was made for hewing and putting any corfe found to be short of a standard measure. A hewer forfeit 3d per quart of "foul coal, splint, or stone" found in corves brought to bank and if the quantity exceeded four quarts he forfeit 5s 0d or was liable to penalties at law. Owners were at liberty to lay pits off work at any time for a period not exceeding ten days and although the men were still considered 'hired' they need not be paid. If the pit could not be worked for more than three consecutive days due to an engine fault or similar occurrence then the men were paid thereafter at daily rates provided they worked at any labour offered them. Except when prevented by sickness, the men hired were expected to do a full day's work or forfeit 2s 6d for each breach. Hewers were to provide their own candles and picks. Drivers were to do a "fair day's work" of not less than 14 hours. The men must not keep "galloway, ass or dog" and where a dwelling house was provided they were responsible for repairing any broken glass in the windows.

Any man disobeying orders or committing a breach of the agreement could have up to 2s 6d deducted from his wages. The owner's permission was required before a man was allowed to work for any other colliery and if he left employment he must immediately quit the house provided by the owner who had the power to turn out men, their families, furniture and effects without having to undertake any legal proceedings.

The 1842 *Report to the Commissioners on the Employment of Children* provides a valuable insight into the earnings and expenditure of a sample of households at Urpeth Colliery in 1841 (see Table 2).[134] Housing and coal were provided free by the colliery owner apart from a charge of three pence per week for the conveyance of coal. According to a pamphlet written in 1844 by William Mitchell, a pitman at Ouston Colliery, the average earnings of William Knaggs a hewer at Urpeth Colliery were 12s 7¾d per week, although these may be understated since the figures were prepared for the miners union in support of increased wages.[135]

TABLE 2 : EARNINGS & OUTLAY FOR MINERS AT URPETH COLLIERY - 3rd MAY 1841

Earnings per Fortnight

	£	s	d
Father, 2 weeks	2	4	0
Putter, 1 boy 17yrs old	1	16	8
Driver, 1 boy 12yrs old	0	13	9
Trapper, 1 boy 8yrs old	0	9	2
	£5	3	7
	£	s	d
Total earnings per fortnight	5	3	7

Outlay per Fortnight

	s	d			
Mutton, 14 lbs at 7½d per lb	8	9			
Flour, 5 stone at 2s 8d per stone	13	4			
Maslin, a mixture of grain, 3 stone at 2s 6d per stone	7	6			
Bacon, 14 lbs at 8d per lb	9	4			
Potatoes, ½ boll at 4s 6d per boll	2	3			
Oatmeal	0	6			
Butter, 2 lbs at 1s 3d per lb	2	6			
Milk, at 3d per day	3	6			
Coffee, 1¼ lbs at 2s 4d per lb	3	0			
Tea, ¼ lb at 6s per lb	1	6			
Sugar, 3 lbs at 8d per lb	2	0			
Candles, 1 lb (of 16 to a lb)	0	6½			
Soap, ¼ stone at 6s 8d per stone	1	8			
Pepper, salt, mustard, etc.	0	6			
Tobacco & "allowance" (beer)	4	0			
			3	0	10½
Shoes, making & repairing, 9s per month	4	6			
Clothes, shirts, flannels, etc., 5 at 3s 6d	17	6			
Stockings, per fortnight	2	6			
Sundries, say	2	6			
			1	7	0
Total Outlay for a Fortnight			£4	7	10½

Contributions to benefit funds generally 1s 3d per month

The local public house was often the scene of "Pay-night" for the pitmen and a poet of the early nineteenth century aptly described the event:

See hewers, putters, drivers too,
With pleasure hail this happy day –
All, clean washed up, their way pursue
To drink, and crack, and get their pay.

The Buck, the Black Horse, and the Keys,
Have witness'd many a comic scene,
Where's yel to cheer, and mirth to please,
And drollery that would cure the splean.

With parched tongues, and geyzen'd throats,
They reach the place where barleycorn
Soon down the dusty cavern floats,
From pewter pot or homely horn.

The dust wash'd down, then comes the care
To find that all is rightly bill'd,
And each to get his hard earned share,
From some one in division skill'd.

The money matters thus decided,
They push the pot more briskly round:
With hearts elate, and hobbies strided,
Their cares are in the nappy drown'd.[136]

In the nineteenth century there were stoppages in 1810 when the owners attempted to change the binding day but it was the 1830's before a concerted effort was made to form a union. This will be forever known as "Hepburn's Union" after Thomas Hepburn of Pelton. Based on the activities of the United Colliers, who met in the Cock Inn in Newcastle throughout the 1820s, the union was formed in 1830 at Hetton Colliery where Hepburn worked. Hepburn was deeply influenced by Primitive Methodism and was known at Hetton as a "ranter" and his demands included the reduction of working hours for boys (they could be made to work 12-14 hours a day) and the end of arbitrary fines and evictions without process of law.

On 12th March 1831, under Hepburn's leadership, an "immense number of pitmen" assembled on Black Fell. The story is told that the Marquis of Londonderry rode up accompanied by a military escort and inquired "where is this great man of yours, your leader Hepburn?" The miners feared that the Marquis meant to take their leader prisoner and there could have been serious disorder if Hepburn had reacted aggressively. However, with great presence of mind, he coolly held up his handkerchief as a signal for order. It was obeyed instantly "as if he had been the general of a perfectly disciplined force". Londonderry, who had been Adjutant General under Wellington in the Peninsula War, is said to have remarked, "I never saw one man have so much influence over a body of men as this fellow has."[137]

On the 21st March nearly 20,000 pitmen assembled on the Newcastle Town Moor to discuss their grievances. When the yearly binding expired on 5 April 1831 the miners refused to enter fresh arrangements and would not return to work. Regrettably, large bands of lawless men traversed the countryside damaging property, threatening "blacklegs" and committing violent acts. The authorities and owners were sufficiently worried by these activities and the large meetings held on Black Fell in April and May that year, that the militia were roused. In June however the pitmen were victorious in getting a twelve-hour working day for boys although the dispute had succeeded in bringing out the worst passions of both men and masters. The masters had used their influence and wealth to pursue the men and the men had resorted to lawless reprisals.

Meetings of the pitmen continued, some linked to political demonstrations in favour of the Reform Act, which, ironically, was then being drafted by Lord Durham, as the coalowner, J.G.Lambton, had become. However, on Christmas Eve 1831, violent demonstrations came to Chester-le-Street, when upwards of 1,000 men assembled at Waldridge Colliery, where 20-30 men were working below ground. Unfortunately, much to the disgust of Thomas Hepburn and other union leaders, the gathering stopped the pumping engine and threw large iron tubs, wooden cisterns, corves and other articles down the shaft thus placing the workmen in danger. At Durham Assizes on 2nd March 1832 seven men were put on trial and six found guilty, being sentenced to between six and fifteen months imprisonment.

At the time of the binding in March 1832 the men withdrew their labour. The owners forcibly ejected many men and their families from their homes but the union leaders urged the men to stay within the law and keep the peace. The strike dragged on for some months interspersed with acts of violence such as the attack by a group of miners on Nicholas Fairless, a South Shields magistrate. William Jobling was later tried and executed at Durham for Fairless's murder. After the execution his body was taken by a troop of Hussars through Chester-le-Street, Picktree and White Mare Pool to Jarrow Slake where it was hung in irons on a gibbet.

The Union began to break up in September 1832 and an anonymous account published 50 years later records how Hepburn fared.

The last delegate meeting that was held was at the Cock Inn in the fore part of September, when Thomas Hepburn had the offer of £300 to set him up in business, as we all knew he would have to suffer. He refused it saying we would all have to suffer as well as him. We all did so, for shortly afterwards we got our leave from the coal trade and work was refused us at all the collieries.[138]

Despite his setbacks Hepburn maintained his dignity and in one of his last speeches for the Union stated :

If we have not been successful, at least we, as a body of miners, have been able to bring our grievances before the public; and the time will come when the golden chain that binds tyrants together will be snapped, when men will be properly organised, when coalowners will only be like ordinary men, and will have to sign for the days gone by. It only needs time to bring this about.

Thomas Hepburn lived another 32 years and, although he was active in politics this was not sufficient time to bring his vision about. He is buried in Heworth Churchyard and his monument reads :

SHORTER HOURS AND BETTER EDUCATION FOR MINERS

This stone was erected by the miners of the North and other friends, to the memory of Thomas Hepburn who died December 9th 1864, aged 69. He initiated the first great union of northern miners in 1831, and conducted the strike of 1832 with great forbearance and ability. His life was spent in advocating shorter hours and extended education for miners.

The great age of industry

By the time of Thomas Hepburn's death in the 1860s, North East England had diversified from coal into the industries for which it was also famous until recent times - iron and steel manufacture, engineering, shipbuilding. Chester-le-Street shared in this diversification, the most famous example of its industry being Murray's engine works. In 1851, Murray's was the largest engine-making works in the northern counties and, in terms of its employment of 180 men, was in the top 5% of such enterprises nationally. The firm had been founded in 1793 by William Murray I and, perhaps building on Chester-le-Street's tradition for engineering started by the Cookson and Hawks' works, made paper, lead and water mills and agricultural machines, sending them throughout England and Scotland and exporting some abroad. In 1826, Murray's two sons William II and Thomas, set up as engine builders and cast iron founders. In the late 1820s Murrays made winding engines for the Hetton Coal Company's Eppleton Jane and Elemore Isabella pits. Thomas Murray took sole control of the business after the deaths of both his father and brother in the mid 1830s and added boiler making and underground haulage engines to the firm's operations. In 1863 it was estimated that since the firm started it had built 350 stationary engines, 500 boilers and 400 mills, water wheels and other agricultural machines.[139] Perhaps the most famous of the Murray engines was the Warden Law haulage engine made in 1836 and still in use in 1955. This machine, the remains of which are at Beamish Museum, could haul five twelve tonne wagons for some 750 metres up an incline of 1 in 19.

Chester-le-Street Township was still a fairly small place at the time of the 1851 Census. It had a population of 2,580, which had doubled in size from the "considerable village" of 1790 (the Township had a population of 1,662 at the 1801 Census). However, as the coalfield grew, over the next forty years the township more than tripled in size to a population of 8,623 in 1891. The story of the growth of the coal industry to its peak in 1913 is well told in Beamish Museum and is not the subject of this chapter. By the mid nineteenth century all the ingredients for a more successful coal industry were in place in Chester-le-Street. Collieries with modern engines to drain and ventilate them. Railways with modern locomotives to deliver the coal to industry and home. By the 1860s Chester-le-Street was not only on the Great North Road but was also astride the London to Edinburgh railway. Its viaduct across the Chester Burn completed in 1868 is perhaps the most fitting monument to the progress of coal and waggonways over two and a half centuries in this location and the surrounding parts.[140]

Postscript

There is much known about Chester-le-Street's colliery history that has not been told here and more that is still to discover. The theme has been clear but the objective to celebrate Chester-le-Street as an important place for the development of the coal industry and of the waggonways, which were the forerunners of our railways, is sometimes lost through incomplete records, uncertain interpretations and an inability to find the connections and coincidences that illuminate our heritage. However, what is clear from the writing of this history at the end of Chester-le-Street's second Millennium is that the struggle to win and transport coal in this ancient place in the two centuries from 1650 to 1850 is a story worth pursuing.

John Banham & Don Bowman.
Chester-le-Street © 2000

Footnotes to Chapter 15

1   We are grateful to Dr. Winifred Stokes, Chairman of Durham County Local History Society, for this interpretation and for other valuable advice on the structure of this chapter.

2   P.Barfoot & J.Wilkes. *The universal British directory, of trade, commerce and manufacture .... together with an historical detail of the antiquities, curiosities, trade, polity and manufactures of each city, town and village, the whole comprising a most interesting and instructive history of Great Britain* (2nd edition, 5 vols., 1793).

3   The statistics relating to using horses to pull loaded chaldrons up inclines was and is subject to debate, but there were clearly limits to what could be achieved.   M.J.T. Lewis, *Early Wooden Railways* (1970) p.146 quotes a George Chalmers writing to Lord Elgin about Newcastle waggonways in the mid eighteenth century : "thirteen inches ascent in twenty yards with a loaded waggon is enough for a single waggon and they do not use more about Newcastle" (Elgin Papers). This is a relatively shallow gradient of 1 in 55; steeper gradients were tackled round Chester-le-Street but it seems likely that more than one horse would be needed making such practice uneconomic in the long term.

4   Quoted in C.F.Dendy Marshall, *A history of British railways down to the year 1830* (1938) p.7.

5   William Stukeley, *Itinerarium curiosum, centuria ii* (1776) pp. 68-9.

6   D.Levine and K.Wrightson *The making of an industrial society, Whickham 1560-1765* (Oxford 1991).

7   R. North, *Lives of the Norths* (first published 1740; ed. A.Jessop 1890, 3 vols., reprinted 1972) i, p.176.

8   British Library, Sloane MSS, 4025, Item 45, f141.   Letter from John Hedworth to Mr. Sloane MD, 13 October 1708.

9   Levine and Wrightson, *The making of an industrial society,* 67, quoting Newcastle University Library, Misc MSS 85.

10   W.A.Moyes, *Contracting Coalfield* (Newcastle 1969).

11   T.W.Beastall, *A North Country Estate – the Lumleys and the Saundersons as landowners, 1600-1900* (1975) p.13.

12   Based on information from an unpublished paper by Chris Goldsmith.

13   Northumberland County Record Office (hereafter NCRO). Burleigh and Thompson's, "A Plan of the River Wear from Newbridge to Sunderland Barr as it appeared at low water" (1737) reprinted in S.Miller, *The River Wear Commissioners – extracts from their papers, 1717-1846* (Durham 1980) shows High and Low Lambton Staithes, however these are both substantially further down river than suggested by the High & Low Lambton of the early seventeenth century. We are grateful for the assistance provided by NCRO and the North of England Institute of Mining and Mechanical Engineers.

14   R.Surtees, *The history and antiquities of the County Palatinate of Durham; compiled from original records, preserved in public repositories and private collections* (4 vols. 1820, reprinted 1972) i, pp. xcvi & ciii and ii, p.175.

15 Based on information from an unpublished paper by Chris Goldsmith.

16 Beastall, *A North Country Estate,* 14. One Newcastle chaldron was approximately equal to 42cwt (2.13 tonne) in 1600 but gradually increased to a more standardised figure of 53 cwt (2.69 tonne) by 1700.

17 Surtees, ii, 178-185.

18 ibid.

19 E.Clavering, 'Catholics and coal', *Bulletin of the Durham County Local History Society,* (1993) 51, pp. 3-26.

20 Surtees, ii, 191-2.

21 ibid., ii, 151. This branch of the Hedworth family bought Chester Deanery in 1629.

22 ibid, 15-16.

23 Beastall, *A North Country Estate,* 26.

24 North *The lives of the Norths* i, 173-4.

25 Beastall, *A North Country Estate,* 1-3.

26 C.Morris (ed.) *The Journeys of Celia Fiennes* (1959).

27 K.Downs, *Sir John Vanbrugh* (1987).

28 Beastall, *A North Country Estate,* 15-16.

29 T.Corfe, D.Wilcock, B.K.Roberts, J.Smith & D.Butler (eds), *An historical atlas of County Durham* (Durham, 1992) pp.34-5.

30 NCRO. Burleigh & Thompson, *Map of the River Wear 1737* ; John Gibson, *Plan of the Collieries on the Rivers Tyne & Wear, also Blyth, Bedlington, Hartley, ...,* (1787); William Casson, *Plan Shewing the Collieries on the Rivers Tyne & Wear* (March 1801).

31 E.Hughes, *North country life in the eighteenth century : the North East, 1700-1750* (Oxford 1952), pp.12-13, 159, 176 & 293-8.

32 S.T.Miller, 'The establishment of the River Wear Commissioners', *Bulletin of the Durham County Local History Society,* (1981) 26, pp.11-25. See also Miller, *The River Wear Commissioners – extracts from their papers, 1717-1846* "3 Geo.R, An Act for the preservation and improvement of the River Wear, and Port and Haven of Sunderland, in the County of Durham".

33 Beastall, A *North Country Estate*, 17-18; Levine and Wrightson, *The making of an industrial society,*

34 Beastall, *A North Country Estate*, 16-18.

35 W.H.D.Longstaffe, *Lineage and alliories of the Allans of Staffordshire and Blackwell, Co. Durham etc.* (1852); W.Whellan, *History, Topography and Directory of the County Palatine of Durham* (1856) p.354; Mackenzie & Ross, *View of the County Palatine of Durham* (2 vols.1834), i, p.123; W.Fordyce *History & Antiquities of the County Palatine of Durham* (2 vols. Newcastle 1857) i, Dedication, Preface, Introduction, pp.15 & 494-7; Surtees, ii, 191.

36   W.Hutchinson, *The history and antiquities of the County Palatine of Durham* (3 vols. (Newcastle, 1785-1794) ii, p.401.

37   ibid., see also John Sykes *Local Records* (Newcastle 1833, 2 vols.) i, p.125, 1693.

38   Based on information from an unpublished paper by Chris Goldsmith and information from John Elliott.

39   NCRO, ZAN M17/197c nos. 54,43 & 48, William Brown Plans.

40   John Brand *History and Antiquities of Newcastle upon Tyne* (1789 2 vols.) ii, p.125.

41   Sykes *Local Records,* i, 350.

42   Historical Manuscripts Commission, *Report on the MSS of the Duke of Portland* (1901) vi.104 in *English Historical Documents* Vol.10, p.476. Harley describes the two waggonways as follows :

"Coming from this engine towards Newcastle we pass over two wayleaves which cross the great road. These wayleaves are an artificial road made for the conveyance of coal from the Pit to the Steaths on the riverside; whereby one horse shall carry a greater burden than a whole team on a common way, and as they generally pass through the grounds of several proprietors, are very expensive to the coalowners, who pay very high prices for their tresspass on that occasion. The nearest to Chester is a single one and belongs to Mr. Allan's colliery, the other about half a mile further is a double one, and belongs to Dean Headworth; the loaded cart goes upon one, and the empty one returns upon the other. The whole length of these two way leaves from the coal pits to the place from whence the coals are loaded into the lighters or keels at Sunderland is five miles".

43   Newcastle University Library, Misc. MSS 10, 59, quoted in Lewis *Early Wooden Railways,* 124; NCRO, Watson Collection 33/18, Map of Ouston, Pelaw, Pelton and Birtley estates, c1776 (which does not mark the Beamish extension); ZAN M17/197c, Map 43.

44   J.M.Ellis, (Ed) "The Letters of Henry Liddell to William Cotesworth", *Surtees Society,* Vol.197 (1987), pp.23-125 and note regarding "entail", p.65.

45   NCRO, Grand Allies Minute Book 1726 GA/1, p1.

46   Sweezy, *Monopoly and Competition,* 27-8, quoting an unspecified pamphlet parts of which were reprinted by 'Anti-Monopolist' in *Remarks on the Present State of the Coal Trade, with a Retrospective Glance at its History* (1843) pp. 9-11.

47   Sloane MSS, Letter from John Hedworth to Mr. Sloane MD, 13 October 1708.

48   D.Defoe, *A Tour Through the Whole Island of Great Britain* (3 vols. 1724-26) ii, p.658.

49   M.Dunn, *View of the Coal Trade,* (1844), pp. 42-4.

50   Numerous lists of accident records analysed by D.Bowman.

51   "J.C" *The Compleat Collier : or the Whole Art of Sinking, Getting, and Working, Coal Mines,* (1708) pp.42-5.

52   NCRO, ZAN M17/197c, Plan 54, 51.

53   Dunn, *View*, 40.

54   Historical Manuscripts Commission, "Report on the MSS of the Duke of Portland" (1901) vi.104 in
     English Historical Documents Vol.10, p.476; L.T.C. Rolt & J.S. Allen, *The Steam Engine of Thomas
     Newcomen* (1997), pp.149, 152, 154; Dunn, *View*, 40-1. For Newbottle c1731 see Levine and
     Wrightson, *The making of an industrial society*, 400-1).

55   NCRO, ZAN M17/197c, Plan 51.

56   NCRO. Gibson, *Plan of the Collieries on the Rivers Tyne & Wear etc.*

57   *An Account of the Strata of Northumberland & Durham as Proved by Borings & Sinkings*, (1885), F-
     K p.13, L-R pp.1-2, 43, 45, 233-4, U-Z p.8.

58   *The Compleat Collier*, 22, 35, 39, 44.

59   J. Hatcher, *The History of the British Coal Industry, Volume 1; Before 1700*, (1993) p.400 quoting Dr
     Keith Wrightson.

60   Beastall, *A North Country Estate*, 28.

61   John Holland, *History & Description of Fossil Fuel, the Collieries and Coal Trade of Great Britain*,
     (1835), p. 292.

62   H. Scott, "The Miners' Bond in Northumberland & Durham", *Proc. Society of Antiquaries of Newcastle*,
     4th Series Vol.XI (1951).

63   J.S Ashton and J. Sykes, *The Coal Industry in the Eighteenth Century*, (1929, 2nd Edition Manchester
     1964), Appendix B, p.242, Bond of Charlaw Colliery in the Parish of Witton Gilbert 1767, in the
     possession of Colonel Blackett.

64   This summary of the 1731 protest is based on the fuller account in Levine and Wrightson, *The making
     of an industrial society*, 398-405, which includes as source, PRO, SP 36/25, fos.71, 79-86; Dr. R W
     Malcolmson for newspaper sources in the *Ipswich Journal*, 6 Feb. & 6 Mar. 1731, the *Gloucester
     Journal*, 9, 24 Feb. 2 Mar. & 16 Nov. 1731and the *Northampton Mercury*, 13 Dec. 1731, and NCRO,
     Armstrong Papers, 725 F49. See also, R.Colls, *The pitmen of the northern coalfield, work, culture and
     protest, 1790-1850* (Manchester, 1987) pp. 204-6.

65   Colls, *The pitmen of the northern coalfield*, 89.

66   Surtees ii, 152-3.

67   NCRO, Cookson (Meldon) Mss, ZCK/17.

68   Tyne and Wear Archives (hereafter TWA). John Cookson's Letter Book 1738-1742 shows that, in
     March 1740, Cookson wrote to the local Chester-le-Street landowners, Ralph Lambton and John
     Neasham, asking if their brickworks could supply bricks suitable for building a furnace.

69   A.E.Smailes, *North England* (1960) p.142; P.Riden 'Some unsuccessful blast furnaces of the early
     coke era,' *Historical Metallurgy* (26, 1992) pp.39-40 and C.Evans 'Manufacturing Iron in the North
     East during the Eighteenth Century the case of Bedlington,' *Northern History* (28, 1992) pp.192-3.

70 Hutchinson, *History of the County Palatinate*, ii, 398 and W.Page (ed.), *The Victoria history of the Counties of England – Durham* (1907 - reprinted 1968 in 2 vols), ii, p.290. Joseph Cookson III (1782-1865) gave details of the Whitehill furnace to Isaac Lowthian Bell, who was preparing for the British Association meeting in Newcastle in 1863. See, I.L.Bell, 'On the manufacture of iron in connection with the Northumberland and Durham coalfield' in W.G.Armstrong et al. (eds.), *The industrial resources of the three northern rivers, the Tyne, Wear and Tees, including the reports on local manufactures, read before the British Association in 1863*, (London and Newcastle-upon-Tyne, 1864).

71 Corfe et al. *Historical atlas of County Durham*, 50-51.

72 TWA, 1512/5571, John Cookson's Letter Book 1747-1769, letter dated 11 June 1763 to Robert Ellison of Newcastle.

73 J.Hatcher, *The history of the British coal industry, Volume 1 - before 1700 : towards the age of coal* (Oxford 1993) p.255.

74 Page *Victoria County History of Durham* ii, 290-1. The reference to the manufacture of cannons for Woolwich derives from Mr. Smith, agent to the Whitehill works giving the information to William Hutchinson, County Durham's first historian, prior to him completing his History in 1787. See Hutchinson, *History of of the County Palatinate,* ii, 398. This is to a degree corroborated by P.Riden, *A gazetteer of charcoal-fired blast furnaces in Great Britain in use since 1660* (2nd edition, Cardiff, 1993) pp.126-8.   This demonstrates that Cookson was a contractor for cannon from 1777 and in 1780/1 produced about 10% of the cannon bought by the Board of Ordnance – see R.R. Brown, 'The Woolwich proof registers 1780-1781', *International Journal of Nautical Archaeology & Underwater Exploration,* 17 (1988), pp.105-111.

75 Beastall, *North Country Estate*, 29.   In 1777, Cookson was supplying castings for a pumping engine for a new colliery on the Lumley estate.

76 NCRO, Cookson (Meldon) Mss, ZCK/2/6 - copy will of John Cookson.

77 ibid., ZCK/17.   Joseph Cookson was ruined when, at Newmarket in 1799, his *Diamond* lost to Sir Henry Vane-Tempest's *Hambletonian* in a 3,000 guineas match over 4 miles 1 furlong 138 yards. R.Mortimer, R.Onslow & P.Willett, *Bibliographical encyclopaedia of British flat racing* (1978) p.258.

78 Barfoot & Wilkes, *The universal British directory, of trade, commerce and manufacture*, ii, 553.

79 Longstaffe, *Lineage of the Allans.*

80 J.Sykes, *Local Records* (Newcastle 1833, 3 vols.) i, p.350, 30th March 1789.

81 ibid., i, 317, 20th September 1779.

82 M.Elwin *The Noels and the Milbankes – their letters for twenty-five years, 1767-1792* (1967) p.198.

83 J.Bailey, *General view of the agriculture of County Durham with observations on the means of improvement drawn up for the consideration of the Board of Agriculture and Internal Improvement,* 1810, pp.17,18 & 26.   William Jolliffe, appears to have died before 1810 and his interests were inherited by his son, Hylton Jolliffe.

84 NCRO Wat/33/Map 18; Bud/21 p.68.

85 NCRO Wat/3/83, Ouston Colliery; Bud/14 p.104.

86 Akenhead *Picture of Newcastle upon Tyne ... and an illustrated map of the coal district,* (1807) R.Galloway *Annals of Coal Mining and the Coal Trade,* (1898) Vol i p.374.

87 NCRO Wat/3/39 28 September 1815.

88 Surtees, i, 190.

89 Bailey, *A General View of the Agriculture of Northumberland and Durham,* 47-8.

90 G.A.Cooke, *Topographical & Statistical Description of the County of Durham,* (1805), pp.33-4, ascribed to Sir. W. Appleby; also quoted in M.A. Richardson, *Local Historian's Table Book* (1841-6), Vol.ii, p.302.

91 Mackenzie & Ross, *View of the County Palatine of Durham,* (1834), lxxiv.

92 Richardson, *Local Historian's Table Book,.*i, 305. TWA, T215/17, Birtley Parish Highway Surveyors Accounts 1791-1823; Gateshead Public Library., Birtley Parish Poor Law Account 1798-1824; NCRO For/1/13, p.9, Matthias Dunn's View Book.

93 W. Richardson, *History of the Parish of Wallsend,* (1923) pp.199-202.

94 *Newcastle Courant,* January 1817 and April 1818; *Tyne Mercury* 1 August 1826.

95 William Bourne, *Annals of the Parish of Whickham,* (1902) pp.64-5; Information on Hawks in general is from; R. E. C. Waters, *Genealogical Notes of Longridge, Fletcher and Hawks,* (c.1875); C.Evans, "The Hawks Family of Gateshead & the Tyneside Mode of Metal Production." *North East Labour History, Bulletin,* 30, 1996 pp.22-8.

96 Evans, *"Hawks Family",* p.24 quoting University of Durham Library Special Collection Shafto (Beamish) papers, 364, 365/1 367, 377, leases dated 8 Feb 1779, 30 April 1785 and 4 July 1794 and a research file by Mark Roland Jones for the Beamish Open Air Museum, courtesy of John Gall, Director of Museum Services.

97 C. Evans, *"Manufacturing iron in the North East during the eighteenth century: the case for Bedlington,"* Northern History, *XXVIII (1992), pp*178-196.

98 Evans, *"Hawks Family", p.25* quoting Sandbeck Park MSS, MTD/A27/2, lease dated 20 September 1784 (courtesy of Lord Scarbrough); *Newcastle Chronicle,* 4 November 1786.

99 Tyneside Industries, 170-1.

100 Beastall, A *North Country Estate,* 29-30.

101 Parsons and White, *History, Directory & Gazeteer of the Counties of Durham & Northumberland* (2 vols. 1828) ii, p.155.

102 ibid., 140; Tyneside Industries; *An Epitome of Results and Manual of Commerce, (1889) pp.170-1.*

103 *Monthly Chronicle of Lore and Legend* (March 1887) pp.28-9.

104 Parsons & White, *History, Directory and Gazetteer* ii,155.

105 Lumley MSS EMC/75 & EMC/1/5 quoted in D. Kirby, "Lumley Lock – An Historical Note of an Ancient fishery", *Archaeologia Aeliana,* Vol. 47, p.130.

106 Beastall, 23-37;42;108.

107 ibid, 39-47.

108 S.J.Reid, *Life and letters of the first Earl of Durham, 1792-1840* (2 vols. 1906) 12-15.

109 C.W.New, *Lord Durham A biography of John George Lambton, First Earl of Durham* (1929, 2nd edition 1968) pp.3-4.

110 Beastall, *North Country Estate,* 50.

111 Durham County Record Office (hereafter DCRO), Londonderry Papers, D/Lo/C142, Buddle to Londonderry 22nd January 1824. See also J.D.Banham, 'Business development and banking in North East England 1755 1839' (University of Sunderland, Ph.D. thesis, 1997) and J.D.Banham, 'Arthur Mowbray - adventurer or entrepreneur? A North East businessman in the industrial revolution, part 1, 1755-1819, part 2, 1820-1840', *Bulletin of the Durham County Local History Society,* 48 & 49 (1992).

112 NCRO, Cookson (Meldon) Mss, ZCK/17.

113 NCRO For/1/13, Matthias Dunn's View Book; Bud/51/109/Item 109, letter from Mr.James to John Buddle dated 26th December 1810.

114 NCRO Bud/21 1795-1809, 64.

115 Dunn, *View,* 52.

116 Bailey, *General View of the Agriculture of the County of Durham,* 34-5.

117 Dunn, *View,* 52.

118 Surtees, ii, p.45; NCRO Bud/51/Item 107.

119 NCRO For/1/8 p.36; *Newcastle Courant,* 20th July 1811, p.3, col.4: NCRO Wat/2/2 p.292.

120 NCRO Bud/3 1808-1811 p.209-210.

121 NCRO For/1/13 pp.1-7,. The existing route along Urpeth Burn and up to Durham Road south of the Three Tuns was retained, but a 640 metres long self-acting plane was introduced together with a steam powered incline 370 metres long. Horses drew waggons to the foot of a 1,100 metres long inclined plane north of the Three Tuns Inn and a fixed engine raised waggons to Birtley Fell. From this point the coals could be taken south to reach the Wear at Cox Green or north to the foot of the next incline up to Eighton Banks and thence to the Tyne.

122 NCRO. Bud/3 1808-1811 pp.137-142.

123 NCRO. Newspaper Cuttings in Bell/9 p.523. June 29th, July 27th, Aug 17th and Sep 14th 1811.

124 NCRO. East/3 pp.4-5; Bud/3 1808-1811 pp.209-210; DCRO NCB1/JB/1473-4 Buddle Atkinson Papers.

125 B. Thompson, *Inventions Improvements & Practice of a Colliery Engineer,* (Newcastle 1847) p.1.

126 NCRO Joint Coal Owners Association Minute Book 1805-15, p.261.

127 Benjamin Thompson, *Journal,* Vol.i, quoted in Tomlinson. *History of the North Eastern Railway,* 18; TWA T215/17, Highway Surveyors Accounts 1791-1823, Thompson & Co.'s wayleave, rated at £120-0-0, through Warwick's estate at South Birtley commenced in 1815.

128 ibid., Journal 2-3, 5, & 17-24. The principle of the drop had been patented in 1807 by William Chapman (1749 -1832) and tried unsuccessfully at Benwell Staithe, proving too complex and vulnerable to the wind.

129 W. Howitt, *Visits to Remarkable Places,* (1842), pp.290-1 and quoted in W.Fordyce, *History of Coal, Coke, Coal Fields, Iron, Its Ores & Processes of Manufacture,* (1860) pp. 59-60.

130 A.E.Smailes, *North England* (1960), pp.164-5.

131 R.W.Sturgess 'Factors affecting the expansion of coalmining 1700-1914', in Sturgess (ed) *The great age of industry in the North East* (Durham, 1981).

132 Sykes, *Local Records,* i, 395.

133 Colls, *The pitmen of the northern coalfield,* 89.

134 J.R.Leifchild, *Royal Commission on Employment of Children,*(1842) British Parliamentary Papers; Industrial Revolution 7, p.536.

135 W.Mitchell, "The Question Answered: What do the Pitmen Want?" (4th Edition 1844), reprinted in *British Labour Struggles - Contemporary Pamphlets 1727-1850 - Labour Disputes in Mines,* (New York 1972)

136 T.Wilson *"The Pitman's Pay"* First published 1826 (1843)

137 F.Graham, *Northumberland and Durham : a social and political miscellany* (Newcastle upon Tyne 1979) p.66 (quoting the *Newcastle Weekly Chronicle,*1882).

138 Graham, *Northumberland and Durham,* 67.

139 J.Crosby & H.J.Smith (eds) *Chester-le-Street in 1851* (Durham, no date) pp.7, 23, 34-5.

140 Tomlinson, *North Eastern Railway,* 634.

After my retirement from aviation duties, I returned to my former profession as a ship's officer on an occasional free-lance basis. I found myself on an expedition with the Royal Research Ship "Shackleton" and one of the scientists on board for the voyage was an eminent professor of a Copenhagen university. The professor had been a schoolboy in German occupied Denmark during World War 2 and he told me some of his experiences.

Morale was low in the occupied countries and although everyone looked to Britain for their salvation, it looked as if Nazi-Germany would win the war.

Like other British towns, Chester-le-Street had a high dead, wounded and POW rate. Britain was fighting for her life but although most of Europe had been defeated, she was still in the war.

The professor told me that in 1942, the Germans shot down a British aircraft over Copenhagen and the pilot landed by parachute in the zoological gardens. The RAF officer was immediately captured and escorted by German soldiers to the railway station where he would board a train to take him to a prison camp in Germany. The prisoner and escort were followed at a safe distance by Danish schoolboys, among them the future professor.

On the station platform, while awaiting the arrival of the train, the RAF pilot was allowed to smoke his pipe. On the approach of the train, a German trooper gave the order "No Smoking" upon which the British pilot knocked his pipe out on the German's steel helmet. The professor said that from that day on, he knew that Britain would win the war. For the first time, he had seen someone who was not afraid of Nazis.

Chapter 16

Important Events, 1800 — 2000

Oh, it's Tommy this, and Tommy that, and 'Tommy, go away';
But it's 'Thank you Mister Atkins,'
when the band begins to play. It's Tommy this and Tommy that, and
'Chuck him out the brute!'
But it's 'Saviour of his country' when the guns begin to shoot.

Rudyard Kipling

All Britain's wars have affected Chester-le-Street. We will shortly look at the threatened Napoleonic invasion of Britain, in 1805. From earlier conflicts, French prisoners of war spent many years in England and they contributed to some of our local history. The road through the Houghton Cut was built by French prisoners, who probably expanded a natural defile which had originally been used by a Roman road which extended from Houghton to Sunderland via Stony Gate. French prisoners also built and manned a brickworks, the major building of which can still be seen to the north of Kepier Hospital at Durham. A French POW of Scottish nationality established a school in Chester-le-Street, and recent evidence shows that the military firing range across the River Wear into Target Wood, which was once thought to have been first used in the Boer War, was actually in use in the mid-19th century. This will be mentioned in detail shortly.

A relic from the Napoleonic wars. French prisoners of war working on roads and buildings in England built this brickworks just north of Kepier Hospital at Durham.

Chester Lads For Ever; The Volunteer Movement

The second half of the 18th century was a troublesome time for Europe. Since the end of the French Revolution, a dictator had risen to power, and soon Napoleon led his armies successfully throughout Europe. No wonder the people of these islands were worried. This fear caused the formation of the Volunteer Movement. The Corps had been raised when the French declared war against England in 1793, but when peace followed, it was disbanded, only to be revived in 1802 when negotiations fell through and Napoleon was made Consul of France for life (more info in Appx/A).

Chester-le-Street was not backward to rally to the defence of the country, and was the first to raise a corps of volunteers. At first there was rivalry between the "Upstreeters" and the "Downstreeters." The officers were the local gentry and the soldiers were selected by ballot. Two corps were formed, Artillery and Infantry, but it is the latter which is best recorded in the diary of an officer. This mentions that the *Chester Volunteers* appeared in their uniforms at church on Nov 6th, 1802 for the first time, when an excellent sermon was preached by the Rev William Nesfield. The Infantry were under the command of Major Richard Bell.

The fear of invasion was so great that the Earl of Scarbrough provided them with two field-pieces which the government commandeered, so the men had to content themselves with small firearms. Colours were provided for each branch of the Corps by the Earl, and R J Lambton Esq, and were presented on their behalf by Mrs Nesfield at a gathering in Newcastle on Jan 4th, 1804. How proud the Chester Lads must have felt. Of course, the occasion had to be celebrated, and loyal toasts were drunk at the Lambton Arms or Cuthbertson's as it was known. The Earl's birthday and those of the commanding officers also provided excuses for a few drinks.

The Corps put in a good deal of hard work perfecting their marching and counter-marching as there was a strong belief that Napoleon would land an army in February 1804, at the mouth of the Tyne or Wear. The men showed such zeal that the magazine depot was permanently guarded by one officer, one sergeant, one corporal and twelve men every day. So faithfully did they fulfil their duty, not only from a possible enemy attack, but from the danger that a passing horse's hoof might create a spark on the cobbles and ignite the powder. On one occasion, the burning of some heather was mistaken for a signal that the invasion had started. The *Chester Volunteers* stood to arms for several nights while the whole population was preparing to evacuate to Waldridge Fell.

The diary states that the birthday of George III was celebrated by a Royal Salute on the Town Moor of Newcastle.

Among the seven-thousand present were the *Chester Volunteers* who marched there in the morning and back at night.

Regular inspections took place, sometimes at Palace Green and sometimes on South Shields sands. Their commanders, Sir Hew Dalrymple and Colonel Seddon expressed their satisfaction and in 1805, when Brigadier-General Ker made his inspection, he praised their discipline and military conduct, and proclaimed that they were a credit to the town. After the early death of Major Bell, Mr Carr Ibbetson took command and on taking up his position as a major, he gave each man sixpence to drink his health while he and his fellow officers dined at the Lambton Arms.

The Earl of Scarbrough continued to take an interest in the Volunteers. After entertaining the officers at dinner in Lumley Castle, it was the turn of the men. Nothing pleased his Lordship more after viewing their soldiering skills than to regale them with beer. So copiously did they quench their thirst and so belligerently did their spirits rise, that the Earl considered it expedient to confiscate their arms, thinking fists would do less damage. Tradition says that on their return through the Park and down Newbridge Bank, the rumble of distant carts and rustle of the wind in the trees combined with the rushing of the river waters, resembled a foreign tongue to some, that the cry went up: "Napoleon has landed!" and bedlam broke out. The town was alarmed by the shouts, causing wives and mothers to rush out to claim their wounded heroes.

Several times, rumours spread that Napoleon had arrived. In May 1805, the Chester Lads marched away to perform 21 days duty at South Shields. How the ladies in the villages through which they went cheered them on, offering draughts of ale.

On the Sunday when the heroes returned, they did the unexpected: they went on strike. No soldier could return home without a penny in his pocket, so at Broken Banks, arms were grounded and they refused to move. The officers were taken aback, but as there was money in the funds, and the men were due to some pay, it was agreed to pay the troops. This done, the Volunteers marched forward gallantly and proudly to their homes.

Following the great naval victory at Trafalgar on Oct 21st, 1805, when the English destroyed the French fleet, all fear of invasion ceased. The great rejoicing which followed was tempered by the news that Nelson had been killed.

After this, the Volunteer Corps was disbanded until, in 1859, the fear of the French led to its revival. The new Volunteers were organised as Rifle Clubs which eventually were absorbed into the Fourth Battalion (Chester-le-Street) Durham Light Infantry.

However, whenever Britain was in danger, the Chester Lads were ready to defend their country. This was demonstrated by the Home Guard in World War 2.

As Mr Harbottle said: "The History of Chester-le-Street is a history of England in miniature." The story of the Chester-le-Street Volunteers shows the attitude to Napoleon of the smaller towns in remote corners of England. To look at the broader picture, let us look at the war from the other side of the Channel:

In 1804 Napoleon Bonaparte had stared with frustration across *la* Manche towards the hated English. Everything was ready for his invasion. His *Grande Armée* comprised 200,000 crack veterans, and the host of sea transports and assault barges were to have been escorted by a fleet of warships. Ammunition, cavalry, artillery, ambulance wagons and even field-bakeries were all ready. Every logistical detail had been carefully planned. For months, Napoleon paced the beach at Boulogne trying to make up his mind and then he turned around and moved his army into the heart of Europe. The deterrent had been the Royal Navy. The Iberians (pre-Celts), Celts, Romans, Saxons, Vikings and Normans were now a unified nation and defended themselves with a formidable navy.

Britain would face a similar threat from another ex-corporal dictator on the other side of the Channel in 1940, but we will come to that in due course.

Now let us look at the target range, probably used from the Napoleonic war onwards:

On the east side of the River Wear a mile upstream from the new golf club, at the foot of the steep slope in Target Wood (also known as "Boat Wood"), can be seen a brick and concrete sunken emplacement from which once sprung the frames which supported targets for small arms firing practice. Riflemen and musketeers fired across the river from where the new nature reserve south of the county cricket ground, sits in the large loop of the river.

A recent metal detector search recovered much evidence. The high bank behind the target bunker is full of bullets of all kinds and calibres but some unusual ones have also come to light. Part of the lid of a metal ammunition box carries the logo: "St Mungo Target Ammunition." The origin of this ammunition is not yet known. Perhaps army historians can help.

A few very large-calibre lead bullets had us guessing for a while but we now have the answer. The bullets have a calibre of .577 inches and weigh 31 grams. Records tell us that these bullets were fired from a Snider .577 rifle of about 1867. Further records give us more information: In 1864 the British government set up the Russel Committee, charged with investigating the possibility of adopting a breech-loading rifle for the British Army. The basic factor which was to influence their decision was the fact that the army possessed tens of thousands old Enfield rifled muskets, and it would be preferable to have a system which allowed these to be converted rather than scrapped. Some fifty or more breech-loading systems were put forward, but in 1867, the proposals of Jacob Snider, an American, were accepted. The conversion consisted of cutting away the rear end of the Enfield barrel in order to fit a hinged breech-block which opened out to the right-hand side of the barrel. The block could then be slid back to actuate an extractor, and inside the block was a firing pin which was struck by the original Enfield outside hammer.

Snider produced a suitable self-contained cartridge for this rifle, but due to imperfections, it was redesigned by Colonel Boxer of the Royal Laboratory. With the redesigned cartridge, the Snider achieved considerable accuracy, and the Snider system was later adopted in various Balkan armies. Snider rifles were replaced in British service by Martini-Henry models.

In the centre of the Chester-le-Street Ropery Lane cemetery stands the obelisk of the Boer War memorial for those who fell in that conflict in South Africa (1899-1902). There were many rights and wrongs of that war. It is a pity that various racial factors such as British against Dutch Afrikaner and inequality of indigenous peoples prevented South Africa from becoming a successful British Commonwealth Dominion such as Canada, Australia and New Zealand. Such a democratic British Dominion would have brought stability to southern Africa. Unfortunately, it was not to be.

Our memorial in Chester-le-Street carries names of battles at Klipdrift, Uzerspruit, and Sterkstrom. Our Chester-le-Street soldiers are still lying in graves at these places with such strange-sounding names.

I was born in Chester-le-Street and some of my earliest memories are of my grandmother, Isabella Stephenson, singing to me songs of the Boer War. One, with a very haunting tune began with:

"The Boers have got my daddy, my soldier dad..."

Many years later, I was to work for an African airline and often flew in Southern Africa with South African airline crews. The Afrikaner pilots taught me their favourite song, "Sarie Marais" which tells of a Boer farmer-soldier who has left his girl far away and who waits for him in the meelie fields beside an old thorn tree by the Mooi River. My *Afrikaans* spelling and grammar may be very inaccurate. The tune is: *"The Old Transvaal."*

"O my Sarie Marais is so ver van my hart,(Oh my Sarie Marais is so far from my heart)

maar'k hoop om haar weer te sien. (But I hope to see her again)

Sy het in die wyk van die Mooirivier gewoon, (She lived down by the Mooi River)

Nog voor die oorlog het begin. (It was before the war began),

O bring my terug na die ou Transvaal, (Oh bring me back to the old Transvaal)

daar waar my Sarie woon, (there where my Sarie lives)

daar onder in die mielies by de groen doringboom,(down in the maize by the green thorn tree)

daa woon my Sarie Marais." (There lives my Sarie Marais)

My seafaring and flying careers had allowed me to view old wars from both sides. It would happen to me again many times at various places around the world.

World Wars.

There are hundreds of families in Chester-le-Street who contributed much to Britain's war efforts often without the slightest recognition. Some families had tragic losses. It is impossible for authors, even local ones, to list all those who deserve a mention. Time is marching on and memories are fading. Let us remember that for every decoration, there were many other deeds of bravery which received no mention because they were not witnessed.

I know little of all those Chester-le-Street families which deserve a mention, but the history of one family I do know, and that is my own. No members of my father's generation are left now but as I write about them, I am also thinking about all those other similar families.

My father William Caisley Selkirk was born 5 Oct 1898, in Red Rose Hall, Chester-le-Street, where now stands part of York Terrace. He was one of five brothers, the others being Louis, Norman, Percy and Arthur. There was also one sister, Dora. When World War 1 began in

1914, my father, aged 16, said he was 18 and joined the Durham Light Infantry. In the dreadful trench warfare of France he was wounded three times and gassed twice.

The eldest brother Louis joined the Royal Engineers and also served in France. Norman joined the Royal Flying Corps and remained an aircraft enthusiast for the rest of his life. He tried to form a Chester-le-Street flying club in the 1920s but he was away ahead of his time. He rejoined the RAF in 1935 and lived in Scotland after the war. When I was stationed at Edinburgh Airport many years later, I was requested by my family to try to find him. This I did, but I was too late. I discovered his home village but sadly, he had died just a few weeks previously. I was able to thank his friends who had carried him to his grave. Norman had no family and his friends did not know that he had a next of kin (myself), and that I was serving on a Scottish airfield just a few miles away.

Percy had joined the army and became Gunner P Selkirk, 72500, serving with 'A' Battery, 82nd Brigade, Royal Field Artillery. He was killed on 8th November 1917, aged 24, and is buried in Plot 6, Row B, Grave 28, in Bard Cottage Cemetery, Boesinghe, Belgium. Boesinghe is a village, north of Ypres, in the province of West Flanders. The cemetery is 2½ miles from Ypres and 1½ miles from Boesinghe. I am grateful to the Commonwealth War Graves Commission for furnishing me with this accurate information.

Arthur was too young for WW1, but joined the Royal Artillery in 1939 and was captured during the retreat of the BEF towards Dunkirk, and spent four years as a P.O.W. He escaped twice but was recaptured on both occasions. He said that the Germans treated him quite decently. He was a young athletic chap and on his second escape, he was dressed as a Hitler Youth leader, clad in leather-hose with all the trimmings. As he was striding confidently down a road, looking just the part, a German army lorry stopped to give him a lift. The Germans fell about with laughter at a Hitler Youth leader who could hardly speak German.

When I was a small boy in the 1930s, I was amazed at the conversation of my father and uncles. There were always "shells whizzing overhead." Some of my childhood drawings have survived and in these sketches, British and German stick & string biplanes are engaged in combat. The ones going down with smoke coming from their tails are always those decorated with the Iron Cross insignia.

My father became a reservist between the wars and had opted for armoured fighting vehicles in any future war. I remember conversations between my parents about the possibility of another World War, but who was this chap Hitler? Hadn't we just beaten the Germans?

A few months before the 1939 War started, I saw my first military funeral. Albert Donald from Chester-le-Street was killed in a flying accident at RAF Usworth on 2nd May 1939. I remember the smart RAF guard of honour and the coffin on a gun-carriage. The procession slow-marched from the church into the Front Street via High Chare and then down Ropery Lane to the cemetery. From there the volleys of rifle-fire echoed across Mains Park. There would be many more military funerals in the years to come but these would be carried out with less ceremony.

Upper: It was obvious that eventually, Germany would begin another European war. This statue is not the famous "Angel" to the north of Birtley. This one was in Berlin and commemorated the birth of the new Luftwaffe in 1935. Three Heinkel 51 fighters fly overhead.

Lower: One of the author's childhood sketches from the 1930s survives and this shows that even schoolchildren sensed that Germany would once again become an enemy.

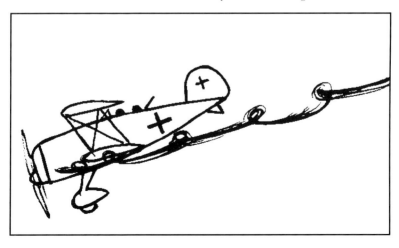

In World War 1, as in WW2, the sea was Britain's lifeline. Here a Royal Naval Air Service airship on convoy escort duties relieves another airship. The observer is signalling by semaphore in order to preserve W/T (wireless telegraphy) silence.

Albert Donald's grave is not in the war grave plot. The civilian-style marble headstone, decorated with pilot's wings, is about thirty yards south-east of the Boer War memorial.

Three weeks before war was declared in 1939, my father, being a reservist, had been called up and was already in France.

During the sudden and unexpected German *panzer* advance, the BEF were on the retreat towards the French coast. My father was wounded but got his tank to Cherbourg where he blew-up the vehicle before climbing on board a Dutch collier, the last ship to leave the port. He attended a hospital for walking wounded in Lambton Castle before rejoining his regiment in the south of England.

He was back in France again with the allied invasion of Normandy in 1944. This time, he managed to return from France without any German bullet-holes in him.

In the years before World War 2, I had some inkling of the preparations for war.

As a five-year-old, I had been taken in our old Morris Cowley, to a military tattoo in the grounds of Ravensworth Castle and I was astonished at the sight of army motor-cyclists leaping through burning wagons; and searchlights which illuminated objects miles away. Also, just about this time, I saw my first air display when the aviation pioneer, Alan Cobham (later Sir Alan) brought his air-circus to a large field at Bournmoor. There were mock dogfights between World War 1 surplus Avro 504s, demonstrations of wing-walking, parachute jumps

Westland "Wapiti" bombers of 607 Squadron (County of Durham) Auxiliary Air Force, based at RAF Usworth, over Tynemouth in 1936. Many Chester-le-Street men served with this squadron. This type of formation is used in order for each pilot to fly outside the turbulent wake of the aircraft in front. Migrating geese use the same technique.

A formation of Gloster "Gladiator" fighters from 607 Sqn AAF, Usworth over Roker shortly after the outbreak of war in 1939. The Squadron re-equipped with Hawker "Hurricanes" while based at Vitry-en-Artois during the Battle of France. Chester-le-Street resident, Squadron Leader, Joe Kayll, later Wing Commander, DSO, DFC, OBE, served in France with the squadron. The squadron shot down 73 enemy aircraft before returning to England at the end of May 1940. Joe Kayll took over command of 615 Squadron and fought in the Battle of Britain.

Wing Commander J R Kayll DSO, DFC, OBE, served with distinction in the Battle of Britain but was shot down and captured in 1941. In 1943, he was one of the masterminds of the famous "Wooden Horse" escape from Stalag-Luft III.

Sadly the Wing Commander has just died (March 2000), aged 86.

A vintage Battle of Britain Hawker Hurricane fighter lands at Usworth for an air display in 1967.

At the 1967 air display at Usworth, a WW2 Spitfire lands on Usworth's Runway Zero Five. In the foreground is a Sopwith "Pup" of WW1 vintage.

Prime Minister Winston Churchill in a defiant mood while inspecting North East defences in July 1940.

The British population prepares for a possible German onslaught.

**"Bison" concrete armoured vehicle
1940**

Britain did not have enough tanks and armoured cars for the army so for airfield defence, makeshift AFVs were made by putting concrete pillboxes onto the backs of commercial lorries and covering the engine and cab with concrete casings. This particular example, a Thorneycroft, was found by the author in a swamp near RAF Acklington. The vehicle was recovered by the RAF Regiment from Catterick and is now in the regiment's museum there.

In case of a German invasion, gun positions were constructed at strategic points right throughout England. This one is in the corner of a wood in the Hermitage grounds on the west side of the A167(T) road north of Chester Moor at NZ 271 498. It is thought that it was intended for a Blacker Bombard anti-tank weapon which was designed to guard road blocks. Neville Andison inspects the site. Just a few yards to the west of this gun position, on the night of 16th February 1942, a German parachute mine blew a huge crater in the eastern embankment of the hollow-way of the old medieval road. It was a narrow miss for the railway viaduct but that could not have been the target as a parachute mine could drift several miles on its way down from ten-thousand feet. The crater was filled in with ash and cinders long ago.

and aerobatic displays. An Airspeed Ferry trimotor took passengers around the local area at *"five bob"* (25p) a time. As the average weekly wage was about three pounds, five shillings was quite a lot of money for a ten minute *flip*. My mother wouldn't let me go for a flight but I was to make up for it in later years.

I remember being very puzzled by one aerial stunt: an old biplane, an Avro 504, I think, dropped a flimsy parcel or small sack from about two-thousand feet, directly above the crowd of spectators. The aircraft then went into a vertical dive and opened fire on the falling bag with its synchronised Vickers machine gun which fired through the propeller. The crowd cheered wildly as the target burst into flames. My small mind could not understand why the spent bullets were not hitting the crowd below. Neither the grown-ups nor myself realised that blank ammunition had been used in conjunction with a five-second fuse on the falling target!

The same field, or one close by, in which the pre-war air displays had been held was used during the war as an Air Training Corps gliding school. Gliders used were Kirby Kadet trainers and for instructor-officers' practice only, a beautifully streamlined "Slingsby Gull." Shortly after the war, the Gliding School moved to RAF Usworth, later to become Sunderland Airport, now the site of the Nissan car factory. The RAF hanger, built by a German company in the 1920s has survived in the middle of the factory complex. It is a geodetic "Lamella" building and is one of only two left in the world. If it is not a listed building, then it should be.

Usworth was the home of the pre-war 607 Squadron (County of Durham) Auxiliary Air Force (later Royal Auxiliary Air Force). The squadron was formed at Usworth in March 1930 as a light bomber squadron under the command of the Hon. Walter Leslie Runciman, son of Lord Runciman. The squadron was equipped at first with Westland "Wapitis" and then Hawker "Demons." The squadron was later converted to a fighter role and on the outbreak of war was using Gloster "Gladiators." The members of the squadron, except for permanent staff, were weekenders. One of the pilots who joined the squadron in 1933 at the age of 19 was Chester-le-Street resident Joe Kayll. Joe fought with distinction in the Battle of France and the Battle of Britain flying Hawker "Hurricanes" and winning both the DSO and DFC and shooting down nine enemy aircraft.

During this period, Joe was posted to the command of 615 Squadron but was shot down in 1941 and became a prisoner of war. In 1943, he helped mastermind the famous "Wooden Horse" escape from aircrew POW camp, *Stalag Luft III*. On his return from captivity, Wing Commander Kayll took over the command of his old 607 Squadron AAF which had reformed at Ouston, Northumberland. He held that post until 1951 when the weekend squadron re-equipped with DH "Vampire" and Gloster "Meteor" jet fighters. The Wing Commander has died just as this is being written (March 2000), aged 86.

During the war, the Germans knew exactly where Usworth was but their bombs fell short, and the infilled bomb craters can be seen from the air as crop marks near the new A19 motorway bridge.

A *Luftwaffe* target map marked *"Geheim"* (secret) shows that the German air force hit most of their planned targets in our area. It was said that the Germans missed the Tyne bridge and hit Spillers. On the target map, Spillers flour mill is shown as the genuine target. The Germans did not want to destroy the Tyne Bridge as they thought that their troops were going to use it in the months ahead. Manors Station, which was destroyed, was also marked on the German target map.

My schoolboy heroes prior to World War 2 were people like Alcock and Brown who had flown the Atlantic non-stop in an ex-wartime Vickers "Vimy" bomber; and Charles Kingsford Smith and his crew who had been first across the Pacific in their Fokker F.VIIb trimotor, *Southern Cross*.

I also admired the various explorers but it seemed that all the former unknown territories had already been found. I did not realise that half a lifetime later, I would become an explorer in my own home area, when, as an archaeological survey pilot, I would discover tell-tale marks which indicated traces of ancient civilisations just a few feet below the surface of my native northern English counties.

Just before World War 2, a significant train of events ocurred over the English Channel and southern North Sea. It has been widely held that in 1939, the British had invented radar and that the Germans had no knowledge of it. That is far from the truth; indeed the Germans were well ahead of the British and had precision sets which worked on metric radio frequencies and fired bursts of energy from rotating aerials at about a thousand times per second. This rate of fire is known as the "pulse repetition frequency" and as radio waves travel at 186,000 miles per second, a "PRF" of 1,000 gives the radar set a range of 93 miles, i.e. time for the pulse of waves to travel 186 miles - 93 miles out and 93 miles back before the next pulse goes out. The Germans wondered about the purpose of the large masts which were springing up along the English southern and eastern coasts and equipped the airship, *Graf Zeppelin,* as a flying radio laboratory, (this airship was LZ130, a replacement for the older *Graf Zeppelin,* which had been grounded). In 1938/39, this huge airship flew up and down the Channel and North Sea listening for a train of bursts of radio energy which would indicate that Britain had discovered the secrets of early warning of ships and aircraft by reflections of electro-magnetic waves. German scientists knew that about a thousand reflections per second was desirable to "paint" a target properly, and German technicians had developed an electronic trigger mechanism which fired these bursts of radio energy automatically at a 1,000 times per second. However, Britain had been carrying out experiments from a ramshackle wooden hut, funded by a few hundred pounds of Air Ministry money, using a lash-up of circuitry designed by Watson-Watt and his team. They used an old BBC metric transmitter shorn of its modulations of music and speech. Watson-Watt's team did not have time to develop a complex 1000 times/second electronic trigger, so fired their pulses by a simple improvised device synchronised with the British domestic mains AC frequency of 50 cycles per second. This "radar trigger" operated from a standard kitchen two-pin plug.

The German airborne scientists picked up transmissions of an unmodulated BBC radio frequency but put it down to BBC tests. No rapidly repeated bursts of a thousand cycles per second were detected but a fifty-cycle 'hum' was attributed to a faulty, leaky and slip-shod

British electicity grid distribution system. The Germans returned home, confident that Britain had no early warning system. Had the Germans known that the "50 cycle hum" was the firing of a radar set, the *Luftwaffe* would have attacked all the radar stations before the Battle of Britain had begun. RAF Fighter Command would have been blinded and the air battle over southern England could easily have been lost.

Later in the war, Britain developed radars far more efficient than the German ones due to the ability to produce "centimetric radio waves" which were generated by a resonant-cavity "magnetron" which was invented and developed by Birmingham University. British radar sets became smaller and could be carried in aircraft. The ensuing "Battle of the Wizards and Boffins" was won by Britain.

The war had started badly for Britain with the Fall of France. The only success had been the victory over the *Luftwaffe* in the Battle of Britain. The British thought that the Germans were lagging behind them in radar research but there were some worrying problems - how had the German navy achieved such expertise with gunnery? Often, broadsides from their capital ships hit targets with the first salvo.

When the German commerce raider *Admiral Graf Spee* was cornered in the South Atlantic and sought refuge in Montevideo in neutral Uruguay, the German high command had been fed misleading propaganda which led them to believe that a large British fleet sat outside awaiting the emergence of the high profile German battleship. The gentlemanly and honourable German captain, Hans Langsdorf scuttled the ship on Dec 17 1939, in the approaches to Montevideo, and he then shot himself. The British had won a victory by creating false rumours but the British admiralty received a stunning shock when photographs in an American news magazine showed the smoking wreck of the *Graf Spee* sitting on the bed of the River Plate. The masts and upperworks remained well out of the water. The British admirals were horrified to see clearly on the photograph that the ship's mast carried a sophisticated rotating-type radar antenna. The ship has been fitted with *"Seetakt"* radar in 1938. The wavelength could be calculated from the dimensions of the antenna and it was obvious that the German navy was far ahead of the Royal Navy in marine radar. Winston Churchill approached the Uruguayan government with a proposal to buy the German wreck but Uruguay stuck by the principles of neutrality and refused. The accuracy of German surface gunnery would again be shown when the *Bismarck* sunk HMS *Hood* with a so-called "lucky shot." Britain was shocked into top gear and subsequent rapid radar research left the Germans behind and also helped defeat the very dangerous U-boat packs which came close to knocking Britain out of the war in 1942. At this point, Britain had only three weeks' fuel left. Fortunately, German U-boats of the period used diesel engines while surfaced and electric while submerged. They had to spend several hours every night on the surface charging batteries. While charging batteries, the diesel engines were declutched from the propellers and turned the electric motors which, when so driven, became generators. During the night the surfaced U-boats were attacked by allied aircraft which used the new airborne miniature centimetric radar sets to locate them.

The RN had suffered a serious blow on 24 May 41, when the German battleship *Bismarck*, on a foray into the North Atlantic, sunk the elderly British 42,500 ton battleship HMS *Hood* with a shell into the magazine. There were only three survivors out of a crew of 1,419. The *Bismarck* and her consort *Prinz Eugen* escaped into the mists. *Prinz Eugen*, short of fuel, parted company to rendezvous with a tanker and then made it safely back to the French port of Brest.

On 26th May 41, patrolling as part of the massive search for the *Bismarck*, was United States built, Lend-Leased, "PBY Catalina" flying boat, No. AH545/WQ-Z of 209 Squadron, RAF Coastal Command. In the co-pilot's seat was US Navy pilot Ensign L B Smith, who as a neutral, was supposed to be merely familiarising RAF pilots with Catalinas: he had fiddled his way onto an operational flight against the German navy.

At 1010, a large warship was sighted and the Catalina sent a W/T (wireless telegraphy) message giving the position as 49.33N, 21.50W, course 150, speed 20 knots. While the RAF captain was busy attending to this in the radio compartment, Ensign Smith disengaged the autopilot and dodged in and out of cloud in a climbing turn to starboard. They emerged from cloud and were met by a hail of *flak* which fortunately did little damage. The PBY's W/T message sealed the fate of *Bismarck* and ancient single-engined 90 mph "Swordfish" torpedo-bomber biplanes from HMS *Ark Royal* went into action. The German battleship avoided four torpedoes by zig-zagging and exploded another with gunfire when the tell-tale track was spotted. It was however, the turn of the British to have a lucky shot and another torpedo hit the extreme stern of the German warship. This jammed the ship's rudders at 20 degrees to port and the ship went round in circles. Another torpedo hit amidships but had little effect on the hull's anti-torpedo blisters. German divers tried in vain to free the rudders and the ship had to be steered by differential power to its propellers.

British battleships *King George V* and *Rodney* sped to the scene and pounded the German ship. Soon, the *Norfolk* arrived and joined in the fray. Even though his ship was a flaming wreck, Admiral Lütjens refused to lower his ensign, and the cruiser *Dorsetshire* finished off the pride of the German navy with torpedoes.

Out of a crew of 2,404, over two-thousand German sailors were lost. The arrival of German U-boats on the scene forced the RN ships to abandon rescue operations and the German submarines picked up only a handful of survivors.

Ensign Smith's presence in the PBY was a clear violation of America's supposed neutrality and the story was censored by the British authorities. Smith never got his much deserved British flying cross though he had nearly earned a wooden one.

While we are discussing the war at sea in the 1940s this is an appropriate place to mention the deeds of a very brave Chester-le-Street merchant navy apprentice who won the George Cross, unfortunately posthumously.

Donald Owen Clarke of Osborne Road, Chester-le-Street was a 16 year old pupil at Chester-le-Street Secondary School (later Grammar School), when war was declared in 1939. He joined the merchant navy as an apprentice, (equivalent to a Navy midshipman).

*Apprentice Donald Owen Clarke
of Chester-le-Street, who was
awarded the George Cross,
posthumously, after his ship, the
tanker San Emiliano was
torpedoed and sunk near the
West Indies by a German U-boat
on Aug 8th 1942.*

In pre-war days, Donald had developed a love of the sea and during his holidays in a Northumberland seaside village, had piloted his home-made canoe up and down the coast.

Before he was seventeen, Donald had made many voyages to sea and was a veteran of the U-Boat war. At the age of 18, Donald performed an act of bravery. While Donald's ship was berthed in Liverpool, a dock gateman called John Taylor fell into the water near the ship. Donald shinned down a rope and got Taylor safely to the quayside. The very next night, Liverpool was suffering a raid from German bombers. Fires raged on shore and the ship's crew were ordered to take cover ashore but Donald volunteered to remain with the captain, as did dock gateman Taylor. To get the ship away from the fires, the Captain, Donald and Taylor severed the mooring ropes and the ship drifted down the dock away from the immediate danger. Donald was awarded the Liverpool Shipwreck and Humane Society's Silver medal for saving John Taylor's life. Donald also received a commendation signed by Winston Churchill for helping save his ship from fire. His name also appeared in the London Gazette of August 26th 1941 mentioning his brave conduct. The Mersey Docks and Harbour Board showed their appreciation with a cheque for five guineas!

A year later, Donald's ship, the tanker *San Emiliano* was homeward bound from Trinidad with a full cargo of gasoline. At 9.30 pm on August 8th 1942, two German torpedoes struck the after part of the ship which became an inferno. The starboard lifeboat well ablaze crashed into the sea. The port lifeboat was intact and hanging on its falls, and this was lowered by Radio Officer Dennis in spite of severe injuries. First Officer T D Finch managed to board the boat followed by Second Officer M Hudson, Third Steward Hancock and Apprentice Donald Clarke, the last two, both severely burnt. Radio Officer Franks and Seaman Hanham and Apprentice Brownrigg also scrambled into the boat and the falls were let go and the after painter cut. The boat was beginning to catch fire and was still attached to the ship by the forward painter. As the ship was still under way, the boat was towed by the painter but the helm was put over and the boat moved away from the fiercely burning ship's side. The painter was cut and uninjured Franks and Hanham got out the oars. Brownrigg with burnt legs took an oar and Donald Clarke, severely burnt did likewise. The boat was then blown back towards the burning water and the survivors had to row for their lives, heading into wind and sea. During this time further survivors were picked up, some uninjured but some badly burnt. Donald's hands were burnt to the bone although he made no complaints. After two hours it was realised how badly injured he was and his hands had to be cut away from the oars. Even so as he lay in the bottom of the board, he sang to try to keep up the spirits of his shipmates. Third Steward Hancock was found to be dead and was committed to the deep at 8am. At 11am a patrol plane spotted the boat and circled a few times. About this time, Greaser J Jackson died of his burns and was buried at sea. At noon, Donald Clarke, aged 19, died, and after a short service was also committed to the ocean.

At 3pm a patrol plane was again sighted and this dropped a water cask but although this was padded with life-jackets, it burst on impact with the sea. However, the boat's fresh water tanks were full with 36 gallons. Medical supplies were urgently needed.

A course had been set for Georgetown some 300 miles distant and at 4 pm, Second Officer Hudson died.

At 6.30pm an aircraft again approached and dropped stores and medical supplies by parachute. An attached note gave the boat's position. The next evening the US Army Transport *General Jessop* which had been sent out from Paramaribo, picked up the survivors.

Donald's George Cross and his Liverpool Society's silver medal for a previous act of bravery are on permanent display in Chester-le-Street's Civic Centre.

The German U-boats didn't get it all their own way, and later they were almost eliminated by advanced allied radar techniques and Churchill's ability to read German Navy top secret messages.

One Chester-le-Street man who was in the forefront of the battle against the U-boats was George Bell, a history teacher who served in the Royal Navy as an ASDIC (Allied Submarine Detection Investigation Committee) operator on U-boat hunting vessels. George served all over the North Atlantic and also on the convoys to Russia. Without these cargoes of Allied supplies, the Russians now admit that they would have lost the war against Nazi Germany. To help make amends for the wartime communists' failure to recognise the help the Allies provided, the Russians have recently awarded a medal to all those who served in the dreaded Arctic convoys. George went to Moscow to receive his long overdue award.

Anti-submarine frigate HMS *Domett in which Chester-le-Street historian, George Bell served as an ASDICs operator from Sept 1943 to June 1945. George's ships escorted Atlantic Convoys and Arctic convoys to Russia. He was recently awarded, by the Russians, a much belated Arctic Convoy Medal.*

While talking to George about warfare, he told me an interesting story about his headmaster, the late Tom Harker, who had won a Military Cross as a captain in the Durham Light Infantry in World War 1. In our church, on the north wall about half-way along, above the Lumley Warriors, is a plain wooden cross below which hangs a painting of a rocky outcrop or hillock near Bapaume, France, called the *Butte de* Warlencourt. The outcrop is covered in shell-craters and a few wooden crosses adorn the peak.

A bronze plaque on our church wall below the wooden cross tells us the following:

"This cross was originally on the Butte de Warlencourt, near Bapaume, France, during the Great War of 1914-18, as a memorial to the men of the 8th batallion, Durham Light Infantry, who fell in action at that place on Nov 5th 1916. A permanent memorial was erected on the Butte and the cross was transferred to this church on July 1st 1928.

George Bell told me that when Headmaster Tom Harker attended church services, he always sat in the seat right underneath this cross. Tom had survived the German onslaught on this hillock and had earned his Military Cross there.

A family story

My Aunt Dora had married a Belgian whom she had met while he was living at the Elizabethville Refugee Village in Birtley during World War 1. Alf had been in the diamond business in Antwerp and he and Dora set up home in that city at the end of the War. They enjoyed a happy marriage but with no children. The swift German advance of 1940 caught my aunt behind enemy lines but because of her marriage she had dual nationality. She died of an illness during the Nazi occupation but this had nothing to do with the Germans.

As a junior ship's officer, I was the first of the family to visit Belgium after the war. I sought out my uncle in Antwerp and asked if the Germans had mistreated my aunt. He said that they had not. Indeed, although she had to report to German Headquarters once a week together with other possible enemies of the Third Reich, my uncle said that a German officer had always brought a chair for her to sit on while other nationalities remained standing in a queue. My uncle also told me that whenever my aunt attended German HQ, she always wore a small Union Jack on her lapel. The Germans never made her remove it!

The Germans also informed Dora that her brother, Arthur Selkirk was in POW camp, *Stalag IXC,* and would she like to send him food parcels? This food and other regular Red Cross parcels helped Arthur survive captivity in a reasonable state of health.

The war was exciting for schoolboys and we followed the technology closely. The countryside was full of fascinating activity. Tanks and all kinds of military vehicles lay concealed under camouflaged netting in the Hermitage woods. Concrete pillboxes had sprung up to defend open spaces and road junctions. One such block-house in Lambton Park was disguised as a haystack. After USA entered the war, an American anti-aircraft gun and searchlight were positioned at NZ 291 499 beside the road up to Lumley. The searchlight was a master-light the beam of which had a blue tint. When it picked up a German aircraft which glittered like a silver-paper butterfly, all the other searchlights coned-in on the unfortunate bomber which entered convoluted manoeuvres to try to escape from the focal point of the blinding illumination

Arthur Selkirk of the Royal Artillery in German POW camp Stalag 1XC. Arthur escaped twice but on both occasions was recaptured. On his second attempt, he was dressed as a Hitler Youth leader and was making good progress until a German army lorry stopped to give him a lift.

which attracted a lot of anti-aircraft fire.

Red navigation beacons on RAF lorry-trailers were positioned around the countryside, their positions and codes being changed from day to day. The beacons flashed morse two-letter secret codes and the navigators of homeward-bound RAF aircraft knew the daily codes and locations. The signals meant nothing to enemy aircraft.

During the "invasion scare" of 1940, Chester-le-Street golf course sprouted spurious tree trunks and telegraph poles. These were meant to deter German troop-carrying aircraft from landing.

Even without the wooden obstructions, no pilot in his right mind would have attempted to land across the severe undulations of the remnants of medieval rig-and-furrow agriculture which cover the golf course. Our planners had also seriously miscalculated the range of the German Junkers 52 troop transports.

It was an exciting night when the presence of a convoy in the River Tyne coincided with a German air raid. The intense *flak* from the ships added to that of the army 3.7 AA guns. In addition to the bursts of high explosive anti-aircraft shells, multi-coloured tracer curved in huge arcs over the northern sky, all in clear view from Chester-le-Street. Most of the army's 3.7 AA ammunition was manufactured at the Royal Ordnance Factory at Birtley. Eighteen pounder anti-tank ammunition for the Desert Army was another major product of the same factory. The centre of the keep-left island at the east end of Ropery Lane at the crossing of the modern A167(T), was occasionally occupied by a Bofors anti-aircraft gun when military road convoys were expected through.

I read with great interest, the article in *Durham, Town & Country*, Autumn 96 issue, entitled: *St Cuthbert and the Lost Bombers*. One night in 1942, German bombers supposedly couldn't find Durham City because St Cuthbert's spirit had obscured the cathedral and city with a veil of mist. Instead, the confused German airmen bombed the river bend at Finchale in mistake for the Durham loop, so the story goes. That same night, I was camping in the Finchale Woods with the "Peewit Patrol" of the 2nd Chester-le-Street Boy Scouts. It was a clear night at Finchale because as we lay in our tent, we could see the flashes of the bursting anti-aircraft shells, through the thick canvas. There were also some very loud bangs, crumps and bumps in the woods. It looked to us as if the Germans were trying to hit the dozens of ammunition dumps on the hill above Finchale Abbey. These large earth-covered bunkers still exist today in a derelict condition. In the 1940s, they were crammed with all kinds of ordnance, and were a legitimate target for the *Luftwaffe*.

I remember that it was in the springtime, and the war records held in the library of Durham Constabulary HQ at Aykley Heads confirm that on the night of 30th April/1st May 1942, four high explosive bombs fell near Finchale Priory, two on the north side of the river and two on the south. One was unexploded and was defused by bomb disposal experts.

The official German news communique claimed their targets for that night had been Newcastle, Middlesbrough and Hull. There was no mention of Durham.

Ammunition dumps on the hill to the south-west of Finchale Priory. These magazines may have been the target for the Luftwaffe which dropped four high explosive bombs in the vicinity of the Priory during the early hours of 1st May 1942.

For whatever reason, I am pleased that Durham Cathedral was not destroyed. Blitzed central London's St Paul's escaped as did Cologne Cathedral. An RAF bomb aimer claimed that the latter's survival was because it had been used as the aiming point for a thousand bombers

Years later, I came across a bomb crater in the Cocken woods, not far from our wartime Finchale camp site, and I noticed that from the bomb hole, an elderberry tree had grown at about ten times its normal rate, presumably due to all the nitrates and other chemicals in the soil.

After the removal of fuses, British bomb-disposal squads steamed explosives from unexploded German delayed-action bombs, and the soldiers used to spread the recovered chemicals onto gardens. Rhubarb and other plants so treated, grew to immense sizes. The champion leek-growers missed an excellent opportunity.

It is unlikely that the *Luftwaffe* bombers couldn't find Durham City because of mist, as German aircraft were guided to their targets by intersecting directional radio beams from Germany and the occupied low countries. An example follows:-

On 10th May 1941, Winston Churchill, who was reading top secret *Luftwaffe* messages via broken "Enigma" codes, knew that the German pathfinder squadron, KG100, was going to drop marker flares on London for the guidance of the main force of bombers. That afternoon, the *Knickebein* radio beam, from Stollberg in central Germany, was remarkably late in swinging round onto London. For several hours, it pointed up the North Sea intercepting the British coast near Berwick upon Tweed. Riding up the beam, the pilot of a Messerschmitt Bf110 code letters, VJ+OQ, was none other than Rudolph Hess, the Second Deputy-*Führer* of Nazi Germany. His destination was the tiny private airstrip at Dunvagel which belonged to the Duke of Hamilton. This field was designed for light aircraft and was totally unsuitable for a fast fighter like the Me.110. The twin-engined Me.110 was faster than a Hurricane but slightly slower than a Spitfire. Almost out of fuel, Hess took to his parachute. Previously, Hess had made an abortive trip and had returned to base when a dislodged flare-pistol underneath his seat threatened to jam his controls. There was no crew-member to help; behind him, the radio operator's seat was empty.

It now seems fairly certain that Hess had been sent to Britain to sue for peace and even try to persuade Britain to join forces with Germany in Hitler's planned onslaught against the Soviet Union. After the failure of Hess's mission, Hitler claimed that Hess had suffered from mental disturbances and had left Germany without authorisation; but how about the assistance from the *Luftwaffe's* guidance beams? Germany attacked Russia in the following month on June 22nd 1941. The rest is well known history.

Important details of the two world wars can be found in Appx/A.

After the surrender of the Axis powers, smaller wars continued around the world. Those of us who were too young to fight in World War 2 thought that our generation was safe from hostilities. We were wrong.

The immediate post war years saw Britain getting back on her feet. German and Italian prisoners of war still worked in the fields. Many Italians and a few Germans elected not to return home at all.

The Prisoner of War camp at Featherstone Castle, near Haltwhistle still detained some hard-line German officers for de-Nazification treatment. The winter of 1947 was harsh and Newcastle upon Tyne was cut off by road from Alnwick for six weeks. My father was the first to get through in an American half-track military vehicle. Many Northumberland villages were isolated and were running out of food. An RAF Halifax bomber trying to drop food into Bellingham crashed into the Kielder forest where the mangled remains can still be seen. German officer prisoners at Haltwhistle Castle volunteered to relieve Bellingham. They quickly improvised skis in the camp workshops and crossed the hills without guards or escorts and delivered essential supplies.

This story never made the press. I only know about it because my father was finishing his army service at the POW camp as a member of the staff.

One evening, he was passing through Chester-le-Street in a jeep on his way south with a German general about to be released. As they entered the town, he said to the general: "This is my home town sir, would you like to stop for a drink?" The General thought that this was an excellent idea, so they parked behind the High Crown and went into the back room, the usual meeting place of all the old soldiers which included my uncles. The German general had a pleasant hour or so and carried out all conversations in perfect English.

No nations are either totally bad, or a hundred per-cent good. Every nation has its good men and wicked men. However, it will be a long time before Germany is allowed to forget its gas chambers and Japan its awful treatment of allied prisoners of war, and civilians in China. Nevertheless, these nations also contained honourable people even though they were swamped by evil regimes.

In World War 1, Japan was an ally of Britain. A British troopship was ploughing its way through the Mediterranean escorted by a Japanese destroyer. A German U-boat fired a torpedo at the troopship and scored a direct hit. A second torpedo was fired and in those days, compressed-air-driven torpedoes left a wake of bubbles on the surface. The Japanese destroyer captain steered his ship into the path of this second torpedo which exploded in his ship killing many of his crew. The Japanese captain had sacrificed his own seamen to save the British ship. There were several men from Chester-le-Street on that British troopship. The Japanese ship limped into an allied port where the dead Japanese sailors were quickly cremated. The caskets in which the Japanese sailors' ashes were placed for return to Japan, were made by British Royal Navy carpenters. This is a little-known story but it is surprising what unpublished information a military historian comes across from time to time.

The main theme of this chapter are the stories of Chester-le-Street people in wars and other duties around the world. Chester-le-Street is an international place and in every corner of the globe we often meet people from our home town. Due to my own careers, first as a ship's officer and then as an airline flyer, I have travelled the world extensively but have always returned to my home in the town. Stories from the two World Wars have already been told and more pictures will follow. The lesser wars such as the Falklands and Gulf War will also be mentioned.

My own sea and aviation careers put me in a good position to view many overseas events. After service on troopships, tankers,cargo ships and naval reserve ships, I changed to aviation and became an airline navigator/radio officer with various airlines in all parts of the world. I also received pilot training and flew an air survey aircraft, first in Central Africa and then elsewhere. On return to UK, after service with many colonial and foreign airlines, I joined the Ministry of Aviation (which later became the Civil Aviation Authority) as an air traffic control officer and worked at many major civil airports and also some military stations including one in Northern Ireland. After my retirement from the CAA, I attended university and took a BA (Hons) degree in archaeology, a subject which had been my hobby for many years. Also, during times of national emergencies, I returned to the sea on a temporary free-lance basis.

This book has concentrated on the importance of Chester-le-Street in history and the following pictures may show how some of the town's residents are truly "people of the wide world."

Flight Sergeant Jack Atkinson of North Lodge, who served as an RAF pilot in the Far East. Here he is seen climbing into his Republic P47 "Thunderbolt" fighter/ground attack aircraft.

(below) The British "Mulberry" Harbour at Arromanches, Normandy, June 1944. The Allied successful invasion of German occupied France was the turning-point of the war and led to the collapse of Nazi Germany.

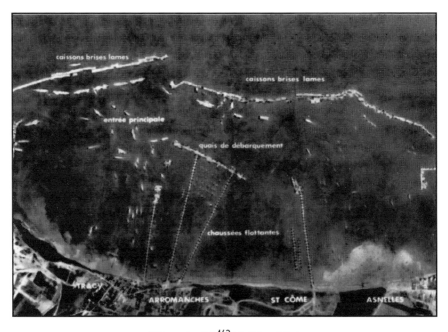

*Part of the structure of the floating causeways still lies on the beach at Arromanches.
Two of the breakwater caissons can be seen still in place in the distance.*

*In 1944, Jack Magee of Chester-le-Street, (hand on notice board),landed from LST
(Landing Ship Tank) No 67, on Juno Beach, Normandy, on 7th June, his 20th birthday.
This picture shows Jack and his comrades in the Ardennes in December 1944.*

Harry Dunn joined the Green Howards in 1940 as an infantryman and served in Cyprus during the fall of Crete, later in Iraq, and then with the Eighth Army "Desert Rats" in North Africa. During this period he fought from Bren-carriers. After the evacuation of the German "Afrika Korps" from Africa, Harry returned to UK to prepare for the Allied invasion of France. He landed on Gold Beach in Normandy on D-day. Having fought all the way across Europe, he ended the war in a Bremen hospital recovering from a shrapnel wound. He is pictured here in Alexandria with his sailor brother Raymond.

Harry is now in West House, Waldridge Road, Chester-le-Street.

William Selkirk (the author's father) on his return from Europe, 1945. The war is over. He served in both world wars for the entire durations. He was wounded three times and gassed twice in WW1, and wounded once in WW2.

(upper) 1507 (Chester-le-Street) Squadron, Air Training Corps on summer camp at RAF Pocklington in 1945.

The key to the cadets' names has been lost but in the back row are Alan Usher (later professor) and Derek Clarke. The author is in the centre row. The officers seated in the front row are:

left to right, Pilot Officer Murray (3), Flying Officer Hedley (4),

Flying Officer Foster (5), Flight Lieutenant Charlton (centre/6),

Flying Officer Davis (7), Flying Officer Taylor (8)and Warrant Officer Yarwood (9).

(lower) On a nostalgic visit to the camp site half a century later, the only evidence was a rusty and overgrown skeleton of a Nissen hut.

On the boat deck of trooper HMT Empire Ken.

This ship was the former German liner Ubena.

The author (left) met many Chester-le-Street soldiers who travelled to the Middle East in this former enemy luxury liner.

In the various messes, meals were eaten from crockery decorated with the Eagle and Swastika insignia of the Kreigsmarine.

HMT Empire Ken at anchor in Port Said after disembarking troops for service in the Suez Canal Zone.

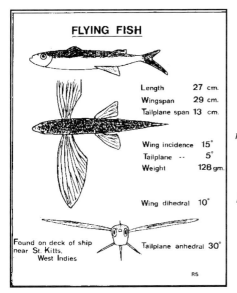

FLYING FISH

Length	27 cm.
Wingspan	29 cm.
Tailplane span	13 cm.
Wing incidence	15°
Tailplane --	5°
Weight	128 gm.
Wing dihedral	10°

Found on deck of ship near St. Kitts, West Indies

Tailplane anhedral 30°

RS

During the author's sea service (before he changed to flying),he carried out several research projects as a hobby. His interest in aviation led him to examine the little-known aeronautical characteristics of the remarkable flying fish which is a complex flyer and not a fish which merely makes extended leaps out of the water. The flying fish (Latin name Exocetus) gave its name to the French-built "Exocet" anti-ship sea-skimming missile which would give the author some anxious moments many years later.

The author left the sea in 1954 and became an airline navigator/radio officer. For a time he worked for Freddie Laker. Here the famous Freddie ...(left) is talking to the airline's chief pilot, Captain Norman Jennings. The aircraft is an Avro "Tudor."

Author's memories of service with Cyprus Airway, then a British subsidiary of British European Airways.

(upper) Many Chester-le-Street soldiers who served in Cyprus will remember the famous bus, seen here in Nicosia.

(lower) A Douglas DC3 "Dakota" of Arab Airways on a visit to Nicosia Airport. Cyprus Airways operated similar aircraft on routes all over the Middle East.

ARABIC	ARABIC

HINTS:—

1. Conduct when meeting Arabs

Remove footwear on entering tents. Ignore their women. If approaching a tent from the rear, proceed via the right side—the women live in the left section.

Be very courteous. A show of arms or bullying does not impress these people, but much politeness will certainly help you.

A personal present to the headman, say your watch, will create an atmosphere of friendliness and goodwill.

2. Useful words

English	Arabic	English	Arabic
English	... Ingilizi	Tired	— Ta'ban
Food	— Ta'am	Day	Nahar
Officer	— Dhabit	Water	Mai
Far	— Ba'id	Donkey	Himar
Police	Shurta	Near	Qarib
Friend	Sadiq	Night	Lail
Village	— Qarya	How far to	— Kam al musafa

What is your name? Shinu ismak

Take me to the British and Waddini ila al Ingiliz wa you will be rewarded. Isnak takhudh mukafat.

3. Give to the people who help you chits, stating:—
  (i) The man's name and tribe.
  (ii) What service he performed.
  (iii) Your name, rank and number.

4. Again—be very courteous and polite

GOOD LUCK!

These certificates were carried by aircrew when flying over remote regions in the Middle East. In the event of a forced landing in hostile territory, they were intended to help the holder reach safety and in one piece.

A Vickers "Viking" of Eagle Airways. During the author's leaves, he used to carry out free-lance flying on these aircraft, ferrying troops to and from the Middle East. Many Chester-le-Street soldiers travelled in these aircraft which sometimes carried RAF military markings for political reasons.

| Cunard Eagle Airways Ltd., London Airport, Hounslow, Middx. | Vickers Viking 3B 152 1946 | 2—Bristol Hercules 674 | 34,000 Transport (Passenger |

EAGLE VIKING

During the author's period of service with East African Airways, he took the opportunity to climb Kilimanjaro. This photograph, taken by Harry Tatton-Jones of EAA, shows the author holding the flag, with a British soldier who joined the airline team when his own comrades were forced to turn back with altitude sickness. Kilimanjaro is not a difficult climb but the rarified atmosphere at 19,000 feet (half that at sea level) can cause breathing problems for some.

The author's children, Elsie (left) and Christine (right) play in a derelict Avro "Anson" Nairobi West Airport, Kenya, 1956.

The author with an ex-French Air Force Junkers 52 trimotor transport on a delivery flight to a German aviation museum. If the Luftwaffe had gained air supremacy in the Battle of Britain in 1940, German paratroops would have been delivered to England in this type of aircraft. The Ju 52 was rugged and easy to fly although it had an unusual wheel-braking system. The operation of modern aircraft wheel brakes is usually via toe or heel pressure on the rudder pedals. In the Ju 52, the wheel brakes were operated by the three engine throttles: pull the left throttle right back to apply the left wheel brake. Pull the right throttle back for the right brake and the middle throttle back to operate both wheel brakes at the same time. In flight, oil thrown out from the central engine onto the windscreen could restrict forward vision. The Luftwaffe however had been very fond of this type of aircraft and had nicknamed it Tante Ju (Auntie Ju).

An air traffic control team at RAF Boulmer, Northumberland, in front of the huge Type 84 radar antenna. The occasion for this photograph by the RAF Air Clues magazine was when two French "Mystere" jet fighters en route from the Paris area to Teesside Airport for an air display, became lost, overshot their destination and declared a Mayday over the Irish Sea. The Boulmer team located them on the long range radar and shepherded them to a safe landing at Teesside. Both aircraft ran out of fuel as they taxied in from the runway. "Good show" awards were made to the team; left, Corporal Jackie Sagewood of Hordon, telephone operator, centre, the author (Civil Aviation Authority controller)and right, Pilot Officer Duncan Swift, military controller.

The author at work as a controller in the underground bunker of the RAF Boulmer radar station (call-sign "Border Radar").

This photograph was taken by the Sunderland Echo and used the caption: "Wearsiders help keep Britain's skies safe." The author also did a year's tour of duty at the RAF radar station at Bishop's Court, Ballyhornan, Northern Ireland, before being returned to civil airport duties in England.

Flying farmer Foster Ryle of High Flatts Farm, at the wingtip of a "Currie WOT" biplane. The Currie WOT resembled a World War 1 SE5 Scout and was often used as a replica for films and air displays. This photograph was taken at Sunderland Airport before its closure.

South Shields Ship Repair Company Managing Director Bob Fox, aircraft captain, left, and the author, copilot/navigator, right at Reykjavik Airport, Iceland, during the Paris - New York Air Race of 1981. The aircraft, Piper Aztec, G-BAVL, owned by Bob Fox came in fifth place in a field of 120 entries.

The race was from Paris to New York and return to the finishing line in France at Beauvais. Most aircraft routed via Iceland, Greenland and Labrador. While in the approach pattern just before the final landing at Beauvais, we crossed the burnt scar on the hillside, caused by the crash in October 1930, of the British airship R101, on its intended flight from Cardington to India.

Our Northumberland Cheviot Hills still carry traces of World War 2 casualties. Here on Cairn Hill, right beside the Pennine Way, the remains of a Vickers "Warwick" Coastal Command bomber lie in a swamp at NT 898 196. The photo shows a Pratt & Whitney Double Wasp engine. Five RAF crew members died when the aircraft struck the high ground. To the north, the remains of a USAAF B17 "Flying Fortress" are scattered around the rocky outcrop of Braydon Crag.
All but two of the B17's crew survived the crash and a local sheepdog, Sheila, from Southerknowe Farm, was awarded the Dicken Medal (the animal VC), for finding the survivors in the mist.

An American Good Year "Blimp" arrives at Sunderland Airport. During WW2, the US Navy escorted allied convoys around the American seaboard with similar airships which had a flight endurance of up to a week.

(upper) Port Stanley in East Falkland is a graveyard of interesting old ships. In the foreground is the beached wreck of the steam tug Plym, built in Plymouth in 1903 by Messrs Willoughby. To the left of the wreck of the Plym is the North-east-built sailing ship Lady Elizabeth.

She was built in 1879 by R Thompson of Sunderland. She arrived in the Falklands on March 13th 1913, under the Norwegian flag on a voyage from Vancouver to Delagoa Bay (Mozambique) with a cargo of lumber. She struck the Uranie rock in the entrance to Berkley Sound and was too badly damaged to return to sea. After serving many years as a floating warehouse, she was beached in Whalebone Cove where she still lies, just off the end of the old RAF runway. During the whole 74 days of the Argentine occupation, an SAS team hid in the wreck, reporting all enemy aircraft movements to the British task force offshore. Just to the left of the Plym can be seen one of the three huge floating barracks of the British forces. They are anchored in shallow water so that torpedoes cannot sink them.

(lower) On board the wreck of the Lady Elizabeth.
A whole book could be written about the Falklands wrecks and relics.

The author who was serving as a temporary ship's officer in the Falklands,inspects a wrecked Fuerza Aerea Argentina (Argentine air Force) IA-58 FAMA "Pucara" ground attack aircraft, shortly after the Argentine surrender. This excellent aircraft had two 1000 hp Garett TPE331 turboprops.

Care must be taken due to many unswept Argentine minefields. The plastic mines are difficult to find even with sensitive metal detectors. The mines take their toll of farm animals but fortunately the penguins seem too light to activate the pressure pads of the mines.

(upper) During the author's service in Port Stanley, he was invited by the ship's army liaison officer, Major Allen of the Royal Engineers, to search for any remains of the World War 1 Royal Navy narrow-gauge railway which ran from Navy Point to Moody Brook with coal for the generators of the RN radio station. Relics were required by the Falkland Islands Philatelic Bureau for subjects for a new set of stamps. After a search around Navy Point, the major and the author found a narrow-gauge steam locomotive underneath a huge scrap dump. A search was continued along the shore under Wireless Ridge and further information was obtained.

(lower) Two of a set of stamps produced as a result of the railway exploration. The locomotive is a Kerr-Stuart "Wren" saddle-back type. The railway also operated wind-propelled flat trucks.

While searching Wireless Ridge for evidence of the old railway, Argentine 30 mm anti-aircraft guns were inspected on the Ridge. The author removed this Hispano-Suiza insigna (left) from the abandoned gun (below).
The beautiful stork insignia now hangs in the author's kitchen.

Onze huwelijksdag is mede dankzij uw belangstelling onvergetelijk geworden

Bedankt

Kapitein Ruudi Verschoor of the Dutch Merchant Marine. He commanded the Dutch ammunition ship Singelgracht, which served in the Gulf War carrying several thousand tons of bombs, rockets and laser missiles for the RAF and USAF. The author served as a temporary officer under Ruudi. Two other Englishmen, Sergeant "Brad" Bradshaw and Corporal "Ash" Samuels found themselves on the same ship; they were RAF gunners.
War produces strange mixtures, in this case, Dutch merchant marine officers, Spanish seamen, two RAF gunners and a British reservist. After the war, the captain, Ruudi came on holiday to Chester-le-Street and was shown around the area. He was also taken for a flight from High Flatts airstrip, over Tyneside and Wearside in a Piper Vagabond, piloted by farmer Robert Ryle. The captain thought that Chester-le-Street was an excellent place.

Kapitein Verschoor is an excellent artist and amused himself drawing caricatures of his crew members. Here he has caught a conversation between one of the RAF gunners, Ash Samuels, and the author.

The new Durham County Cricket Ground at Chester-le-Street

Anatol Michaelovich Obolensky, the author's elder grandson who lives in Switzerland, on one of his frequent visits to Chester-le-Street.

The author's younger grandson,Christian Nicholas Alexander, on a visit to an Alpine ski slope. The future of our planet will shortly rest with this generation. They will be the caretakers of our Earth and I hope that they will realise that they must live with, and care for the environment and the animal species which travel with us at eighteen miles per second around our parent Star (the Sun). Our spaceship Earth, on which we live is in full flight at some 65,000 mph, and except for God and Mother Nature, it has neither pilot nor navigator.

Appendices

Important dates which affected the history of our countryside, our town, and our county, in the formation of our nation.

Appendix "A
ROMANS

BC= *(Before Christ)*

753   Rome founded.

510   Rome becomes a Republic.

55   Caesar's first invasion of Britain (unsuccessful).

54   Caesar's second invasion of Britain (partial failure).

4   True date of birth of Jesus. If this date is correct, and astronomical and other evidence seem to support it, then we have missed the second millennium by four years.

All dates from now on = AD *(Anno Domini)*
ROMANS, CELTS and SAXONS (continued)

14   Augustus dies.

30   Jesus crucified.

43   Roman Emperor Claudius successfully invades Britain. Roman army soon conquers South and bit by bit fights northwards.

49   Foundation of the *colonia* at Colchester.

61   Boadicea, Queen of the Iceni, revolts against the Romans, burns their settlement at London; but her army is annihilated and she takes poison.

78   Agricola reaches Britain.

82   Agricola, Roman Governor of Britain, begins conquest of Caledonia.

84   Agricola's victory at Mons Graupius.

93   Emperor Trajan adds Dacia (modern Romania) and Mesopotamia to Roman Empire, now at its largest.

117   Emperor Hadrian tries to keep barbarians out of Roman territories by building permanent frontier defences.

c122   Building of Hadrianic frontier.

c143   Building of Antonine frontier.

208   Severus in Britain, dies at York 211.

284   Diocletian, last Roman emperor to persecute Christians, re-organises the Empire with two joint emperors and two subordinate emperors.

312   Constantine defeats his joint Emperor, Maxentius and becomes sole Emperor in the West.

313   Constantine legalises Christianity; later makes it official State religion.

314   Constantine defeats emperor in the East, becomes sole ruler of Roman world.

328   To celebrate victory, Constantine founds 'new Rome' by enlarging ancient Greek city of Byzantium, and he calls this new capital 'Constantinople.'

398   St Patrick brought Christianity to Ireland.

407   As barbarians pour into the Roman Western Empire, Roman legions are withdrawn from Britain in a last attempt to defend Rome. Britain becomes an easy prey to Angles, Saxons and Jutes. Anglo-Saxon invasions of Britain begin.

410   Visigoths under Alaric plunder Rome. Waves of barbarians sweep into Spain, Portugal, Gaul, Italy and North Africa.

415   About this year, Newcastle still has the appellation of "Pons Aelius" (A Roman station: "Bridge of Aelius" [Emperor Aelius Hadrian]), where at that time a Roman cohort of auxiliaries was still in garrison. After a silence of two centuries, mention again occurs of this celebrated place, under the new name of "Ad Murus" (at the Wall), and was the residence of a Celtic British king.

THE SAXONS AND CELTS

Subsequently the Saxons drove the Celtic Britons totally from the province of Bernicia, which lay between the Tyne and at some periods as far as Edinburgh.

This unhappy state of the Celtic northern inhabitants of Britain, now totally deserted by the Romans, caused the Celts to seek foreign mercenary help. Because of the incursions on three sides by Celtic Irish Scots, Caledonian Celtic Picts and Saxon pirate sea raiders, the Celts recruited Saxon mercenary troops as had the Romans before them in their last years of rule.

c425   Reign of Vortigern in Britain begins.

449   Hengist and Horsa, Jutish chiefs invade Britain and set up Kingdom of Kent.

476   Last Emperor in Rome deposed, Western Roman Empire comes to an end; Eastern Roman Empire continues with capital, Byzantium (Constantinople).

547   IDA (Ida the flamebearer) founder of the Anglian Kingdom in Britain, now King of Northumbria. At the former Celtic fortified camp of Din Gairi (Bamburgh), Ida, an Anglian of high birth, erected a castle opposite the 'Fern' Islands, in a situation remarkably strong and conspicuous. Aethelric was the son of Ida and Aethelfrith, the son of Aethelric. The lineage of IDA is set down in its earliest surviving form in the *de Nodhumbrensium et Anglorum Regibus* entered by the Welsh writer Nennius c830. In the Northern History of the *Historia Brittonum:* Ida is traced back to the god, Woden.

>Woden begot Beldeg,
>begot Beornec,
>begot Gechbrond,
>begot Aluson,
>begot Inguec,
>begot Aedibrith,
>begot Ossa,
>begot Eobba,
>begot Ida.

560   Aelle, one of the chieftains who came over with Ida, conducted the Saxons against the province of Deira (North Yorkshire) from whence having expelled the Britons, he assumed the sovereignty thereof, and settled there with his followers. Aella having reigned in Deira for twenty-seven years, was elected king of Bernicia (approximating Northumberland plus Durham); the two provinces under him thus becoming united with the name, Northumbria (North-Humberland), continued so from 547 to 826, during which period it was governed by about thirty kings. It was one of the Heptarchy, or seven Saxon kingdoms.

565   Christianity brought to Iona from Ireland (St Columba).

585   Edwin born.

588   Aelle, King of Deira, died in the 13th year of his reign.

588   Athelric, Ida's son, reigned both provinces for 5 years.

590   Gregory the Great becomes Pope; declares Rome supreme centre of the Church.

593   Aethelfrith, King of Bernicia (north part of Northumbria). Bamburgh's name changed to Bebbanburh (OE) in honour of Aethelfrith's Queen Bebba.

597   Death of Columba; Arrival of Augustine Mission in Kent. Augustine baptises Aethelbert, King of Kent.

598   Anglo-Saxons defeated native Celtic Britons at Catterick.

601   Augustine becomes first Archbishop of Canterbury.

603   Battle of Degastan; Aethelfrith, King of Northumbria defeats Aedan, King of Scots. Aethelfrith marries Acha of Deira.

604   Oswald born.

612   Oswiu born.

614   Hild born.

616   Battle of Chester, North Celtic Britons isolated from South Celtic Britons.

616   Aethelfrith slain by Edwin, King of Deira's son, at Battle of Idle; Eanfrith, eldest son sought safety in Land of the Picts beyond the Forth. Oswald and Oswiu fled to Scotic Dalriada (Argyll). Oswald baptised later at Iona.

616   Edwin, King of Northumbria. King Edwin, some time between 617 and 633, erected on Tynemouth headland, a place of residence of wood for the religious of both sexes, in which his own daughter, Rosella, took the veil. Oswald, a succeeding King of Northumbria, in 634, pulled down this wooden structure and upon its site built another of stone.

619   Northumbrian conquest of Elfed.

625   Paulinus arrives in Northumbria.

625   Edwin married Christian Kentish Princess Aethelburga.

626   Eanflaed born and baptised, Edwin fought West Saxons.

626   Succession of Penda to Saxon Mercia.

627   Edwin baptised in wooden church (dedicated to St Peter) at York, Hild baptised. Conversion of Northumbria begins.

628   Benedict Biscop born, Edwin slain by his old enemy Cadwallon at Battle of Haethfield. One of Edwin's sons also killed. Cadwallon had joined with Penda, a heathen Mercian noble and they scattered Edwin's army and created havoc throughout Northumbria. Paulinus and Ethelburg fled by sea to Kent. Bernicia and Deira were split apart.

632   Eanfrith, King of Bernicia, Osric, King of Deira.

633   Deaths of Eanfrith and Osric, killed by Cadwallon.

633   After two years of confusion, Oswald, of the Royal house of Bernicia, turned the tables on Cadwallon in 633 and killed him in a battle fought at Deniseburn (Hefenfeld) near Chollerford. Oswald was greeted as the deliverer of his people and was accepted as king in all Northumbria: (combined Bernicia and Deira). Oswald, who had been baptised at Iona during his exile attributed his victory to his faith. After the defeat of Cadwallon, Oswald recovers his father's throne. Oswald asks Donald, King of Scotland, for a missionary to be sent from Iona to Northumbria.   Corman, a monk of Iona was sent, but he was not up to the task. He would be replaced by Aidan.

634   Wilfrid born.

635   Cuthbert born.

635   Aidan arrives in Northumbria from Iona. Aidan loved animals while his fellow Irishmen hunted them to death. Legend has it that as he sat reading on Connaught, where he was born, a desperate hunted stag sought refuge with him. Aidan baffled the pursuing hounds by making the stag invisible. Oswald gives Aidan Lindisfarne as his episcopal see. While Aidan who was not yet fluent in the Germanic language preached the gospel, King Oswald himself interpreted the word of God to his nobles and leaders. Thus was founded the Monastery of Lindisfarne, the "Iona of the East," with Aidan as its first bishop.

c639 Seige of Din Eidyn (Edinburgh).

640   The Monastery of Hartlepool was founded upon the first conversion of the Northumbrians to Christianity, about 640, by a religious woman named Hieu, or St Bega, whereof St Hilda, who was nearly allied to the kings of East Anglia and Northumbria, was sometime abbess.

c642 Northumbrian conquest of Manau (Forth). Battle of Strathcarron, death of Domnall Brecc. Battle of Maserfeld, death of King Oswald (St Oswald). His head which had been displayed on a pole was recovered and was taken to Lindisfarne. Later it would be placed in St Cuthbert's coffin when the monks evacuated Lindisfarne in 875. It would be found in 1827 when St Cuthbert's coffin was opened.

642   Oswiu, King of Northumbria.

643   Oswiu married Eanflaed. Oswine, sub-king of Deira.

644   Paulinus died.

645   Ecgfrith born.

647   Aethelburgh died.

c648 Cuthbert a shepherd on the Lammermuir Hills.

c650 Mercian attack on Northumbria, siege of Bamburgh.

c651 After a vision while working as a shepherd, Cuthbert entered Old Mailros (Old Melrose) where Eata was abbot.

651 This year, mention is made of a church at Bamburgh.

c653 Second Mercian attack on Northumbria.

653 Talcornan, King of Picts.

655 Death of Penda.

c655 Foundation of Gilling.

657 Foundation of Whitby.

c660 Cuthbert, Eata and other monks returned to Melrose after being transferred to Ripon but were unable to accept some practices of the Roman church. About this time, Cuthbert rode through Saxon Conceastre, ("Fort by the River Con"), the Saxon name for the old Roman fortified settlement of Concangis, later to become Chester-le-Street (Fort on the Road), so there must have been a Saxon settlement here long before 883 when the Lindisfarne monks established their wooden cathedral. Also about this time, according to Bede, Cuthbert visited Carlisle. Bede remarks in his *Life of St Cuthbert,* that while in Carlisle, the future saint drank from a Roman fountain which was still in working order. Because of the special links with Chester-le-Street, we must give Cuthbert a special mention:

Cuthbert, one of the greatest English saints and missionaries, became a monk of Melrose abbey under Abbot Eata, the gentlest and simplest of men, according to the Venerable Bede. The prior of Melrose, Boisil, taught Cuthbert the bible and the procedures of devout life. When Boisil died, Cuthbert became prior. He preached throughout the surrounding countryside, travelling on horseback and it was on one of these expeditions that he is recorded as having made a stop in Conceastre, the future Chester-le-Street. Bede comments:

"Cuthbert was so great a speaker and had such a light in his angelic face. He also had such a love for proclaiming his good news that none hid their innermost secrets from him. But the saint preferred the life of a hermit and secured Eata's permission to live as such on the Farne Islands for eight years. In 684, he was appointed, unwillingly, Bishop of Hexham but he preferred Lindisfarne where Eata had become bishop. The two men exchanged bishoprics. Cuthbert had two more years to live."

660 A monastery was established at Ebchester, by Ebba, daughter of Ethelred, King of Northumbria. It was afterwards destroyed by the Danes.

664 Cuthbert, now prior of Lindisfarne, soon became a monk-solitary.

664 Synod of Whitby. Differences between Celtic and Roman churches resolved. One difference was the hair styles of the monks. The Celtic monks shaved the front half of their heads whereas the Roman rule decreed the circular tonsure which represented Christ's crown of thorns. The Roman style was accepted by the Celtic Irish Church.

The other argument was the date of Easter celebrations.

The Celtic church used an old Jewish lunar calendar while the Roman church used the easier-to-handle solar system.

An agreement was reached and Easter was to be calculated as follows: Take the Spring Equinox when day equals night which is March 21st; predict the next full Moon on or after the equinox, and the following Sunday on or after the full Moon becomes Easter Sunday. If Easter Sunday coincides with the Jewish Feast of the Passover, Easter Sunday is delayed by one week.

Such seemingly trivial matters were apparently of great consequence to the two branches of the Christian church and the agreements healed the rift.

The Saxon name for Whitby was "Strenaeshalc." It is highly likely that Whitby had been a Roman port as a Roman dam was taken from the River Esk early in the twentieth century. On the site of the abbey, there was probably a Roman lighthouse. Mention has been made by historians of a Roman signal station at this point but this is a mis-translation: the 12th century monk, Symeon of Durham mentions a *pharos* at Whitby. A *pharos* is a *lighthouse* and not a signal station!

671 Death of Oswiu.

671 Ecgfrith, King of Northumbria.

671 Ecgfrith's fleet anchored in the mouth of the River Don at Jarrow (Portus Ecgfridi Regis). According to the antiquarian Leland, Ecgfrith also had an inland port at Bilton (Boldon) on the River Don; the latter is now just a small stream. A coin of Ecgfrith depicts the King's head surrounded by an Arabic legend. It seems that Ecgfrith's ships were trading with North Africa. Bede mentions that various

Saxon kingdoms were trading with the Continent. Many English coins of this period have been found on Frisian settlements. Coins of Offa of Mercia are near replicas of gold dinars struck by Kaliph Al-Mansor in 774 but they show Offa's head and the legend *"Offa Rex"* in Roman capitals. These coins must have been meant for direct trade between Mercia and the Kaliphate.

Communications between Offa and Charlemagne discuss the length of certain "cut black stones" being imported into England and with reference to reverse trade, Charlemagne complains that imports of English Saxon cloth was not of the promised lengths. There are references to English seagoing ships owned by monasteries being excused from tolls. The monks of Jarrow and elsewhere did not spend all their time at prayer!

The Anglo-Saxons had not lost completely their ability as seamen. In order to demonstate the ease of navigation in the ancient River Don, the following reports from later periods tell us that the river continued in use after the Saxon era: "The little River Don which winds round the hill on its way to the Tyne at Jarrow Slake, may in Bishop Pudsey's time (12th cent.) have been navigable as far as Brockley Whinns, close to Boldon Colliery's station. When the railway viaduct was built over the river in 1894, the framework of an old ship was discovered on the shingle bed." (from *The King's England* by Arthur Mee). William Fordyce in his *Northumberland & Durham*, makes a further mention about the navigability of the River Don: "The *Oliver*, a two-mast ship laden with timber sailed up the Don. Some years ago, two vessels, the *King* and the *Don*, of about 300 tons burthen each, were built in this river, and consequently sailed down the Don; but it is not on record that any other vessels sailed up the Don since the anchoring of King Ecgfrith's fleet in that river in the year 671."

672   Pictish uprising crushed by Ecgfrith. Foundation of "Hrypis" (Ripon) by Wilfrid; church built in Roman manner, Celtic monks having been sent back to Melrose. Church probably on ex-Roman site as many Roman stones found under floor recently during refurbishments.

c672   Bede born. Bede would later be called "The father of English History." When Ceolfrith's Jarrow Monastery was dedicated on Sunday 23rd April 685, Cuthbert the hermit-bishop of Lindisfarne had less than two years left to live, and Bede was only thirteen years old. Bede's ability as a writer and especially his *Historia Ecclesiasica gens Anglorum* (A History of the English Church and its People) gives us our main, but still very limited insight into the Anglo-Saxon period.

673   Foundation of "Hagustaldesia" (Hexham) by Wilfrid. Does the Saxon name contain a reference to "Augustus" which may point to a Roman fort under the early Saxon church? Archbishop of York, having obtained the land as a gift for religious uses, from Ethelfrida, Ecgfrid's queen. The church (not the present one) was erected by workmen brought from Italy and other distant countries, and dedicated to St Andrew. The crypt, constructed entirely of ex-Roman stones survives underneath the later abbey.

674   Ely founded.

674   Wulfhere's Mercian invasion crushed by Ecgfrith.

674   Foundation of Wearmouth. Monastery, dedicated to St Peter, was founded by Benedict Biscop; and when that building was nearly finished, he procured artificers from France skilled in the art of glass making, the manufacture of which the inhabitants of the British Isles were at that time strangers to, and this structure had the honour of being glazed with the first glass to be made in England since the time of the Romans.

676   Cuthbert on Islet of Hobthrush, later on Farne.

679   Battle of the Trent. Succession of Adomnan as abbot of Iona.

680   Bede enters monastery at Wearmouth.

680   Hild dies, succeeded at Whitby by Aelfled, the daughter of the late King Oswy.

682   Foundation of Jarrow by Benedict Biscop. Ceolfrith first Abbot. See also 672 above.

684   Northumbrian raid on Ireland.

684   Cuthbert, sixth Bishop of Lindisfarne at King Ecgfrith's request. Officiated from 684-687.

685   Battle of Nechtansmere. Death of Ecgfrith.

685   Aldfrith, King of Northumbria.

685   Dedication of Jarrow. Consecration of Cuthbert at York.

687   March, Cuthbert died on Inner Farne, buried on Lindisfarne.

690   Biscop died.
693?   Lindisfarne Gospels written during episcopacy of Eadfrith.
698   St Cuthbert's remains elevated. Body found to be undecayed.
698   Lindisfarne Gospels written 698-721.
704   Death of Aldfrith, in the twentieth year of his reign. Eadwulf siezed power but reigned for only two months.
705   Osred, Aldfrith's son (aged 8) King of Northumbria (reigned 11 years), Berhfrith regent.
709   Wilfrid died.
716   Osred slain by kinsmen due to his misconduct.
716   Ceowulf, King of Northumbria.
731   Bede's *Ecclesiastical History* completed.
735   Death of Bede (Baeda Venerabilis) at Jarrow on 25th May.
737   Ceowulf abdicated and entered church.
737   Eadbert, King of Northumbria.
740   Mercian warband invaded Northumbria while Eadbert was busy fighting Picts.
741   York monastery burned by the Mercian warband. Eadbert at peace with neighbours: Angles, Picts, Britons and Scots.
750   Eadbert conquers Kyle and Cyil (Ayrshire).
755   Offa, King of Mercia (to 797).
758   Offa built his Dyke to keep the Welsh out of Mercia.
758   Eadbert abdicates and joins church. Oswulf succeeds his father, Eadbert as King of Northumbria.
759   Oswulf put to death by his family at Mechil Wongtune (Market Weighton).
759   Ethelwald Moll, (not of any royal house) chosen by people as king.
761   Oswin of Bernicia murdered by Deiran called Aethelwald Moll of Catterick at Edwinscliffe (Coniscliffe). At this time the River Tees formed a boundary between the two Anglo-Saxon kingdoms of Bernicia (north), and Deira (south) rival dynasties.
764   The Great Winter. Symeon of Durham records: "In this year was the great winter. A usurper thane had siezed the kingdom of the dynasty of Ida and the last of the Idings died in the church of Cuthbert on Lindisfarne. The saga is told."
778   Chieftain called Ealdulf killed at High Coniscliffe.
781   Bishop installed at Sockburn. Hygebald has been ordained the new Bishop of Lindisfarne at Sockburn-on-Tees.
789   Synod at Aycliffe.

APPENDIX "A" (continued)
SAXONS & VIKINGS

c789   In the closing years of the Eighth Century, while Offa of Mercia was still alive, there occurred the first recorded Viking raid in Western Europe. Three longships, with about a couple of hundred rascals, landed somewhere on the peaceful coast of Dorset (part of Wessex). They killed the King's reeve who came to meet them and put back to sea probably with plundered property and slaves.
       No more Vikings were seen in those parts for many years but there followed in quick succession, a series of similar raids on the coasts of Northumbria, Scotland, Ireland and Wales. The pirates plundered the monasteries temptingly situated on islands and capes which were easy targets for seaborne assaults.
       Rumours must have spread throughout Norway and Denmark that the churches of the west were loaded with gold and jewellery and that there were no warships in the western seas.
793   June 8th, First Viking raids on Northumbrian coast. Lindisfarne Monastery plundered, many monks slain. These Vikings were from Norway. They were attracted by the wealth of the Northumbrian religious houses.
794   Vikings attack Jarrow, Hartlepool and Tynemouth monasteries.
800   Charlemagne crowned in Rome, Emperor of the Holy Roman Empire.
801   An Anglo-Saxon chieftain called Ida is said to have been buried at Gainford.

802	Egbert, King of Wessex, one of seven Anglo-Saxon kingdoms fighting for supremacy in Britain. Others are Northumbria, Mercia, Kent, Essex and East Anglia.
829	Egbert acknowledged as over-king in England.
839	Ethelwulf succeeds Egbert as over-king.
844	Frankish empire is divided between Charlemagne's sons and grandsons, whose quarrels lead to its breaking up.
844	Pictish and Scottish kingdoms united under Kenneth Macalpine. The name of Pict disappears slowly.
845	Danes plunder Paris and are bought off.
847	Danes capture and occupy Bordeaux.
855	Danes winter in Sheppey.
860	Ethelbert, King of England, many Danish raids.
866	Danish invasion begins.
867	Danish conquest of southern Northumbria.
868	Danes invade Mercia.
871	Danes defeated at Ashdown, Accession of Alfred.
871	Alfred the Great, King of Wessex, practically the only part of England not in Danish hands.
875	More onslaughts by Vikings; further damage to Jarrow. Lindisfarne Monastery community decided to evacuate, taking the body of their saint with them. After seven years of wandering around the north, they arrived at Conceastre (later to become Chester-le-Street), a Saxon settlement on the site of the old Roman fort of Concangis.
878	Alfred defeats Danes at Ethandune: compels them by Treaty of Wedmore to stay in their settlements in NE England and become Christians. Boundary of Wessex and "Danelaw," the old Roman road later called "Watling Street."
883	Bishop Eardulph and the monks and their families arrive at Conceastre (Chester-le-Street) with the coffin containing the body of St Cuthbert, the head of St Oswald and other relics. They built the first cathedral of timber. A piece of wood in the anchorage of the Chester-le-Street Parish Church of St Mary and St Cuthbert may be part of the original wooden Conceastre cathedral.

Guthred, a Danish prince of Northumbria, granted the bishop the land between the Tyne and the Tees as the diocese but the see extended from the Tees to the Firth of Forth and from the North Sea to the Irish Sea, including the towns which would become Edinburgh, Carlisle, Newcastle and Durham, and from Conceastre, the whole northern diocese of England was governed. King Alfred confirmed the grant and bestowed upon the Saint the other extensive privileges and immunities which eventually converted the patrimony of St Cuthbert into a county palatine. |
900	Eardulph, last bishop of Lindisfarne and first bishop of Conceastre, died.
900	Alfred dies.
918	Ragnald, King of the Dublin Norsemen has siezed York and established an Irish Viking-ruled kingdom in Yorkshire. York will now be ruled as a client kingdom of the great Norse stronghold of Dublin.
919	Henry I, King of Germany; completes the separation of the Frankish Empire into Germany and France.
925	Athelstane, King of England.
934	Visit of King Athelstane to Conceastre and bestowal of gifts. Later, Athelstane's brother, King Edmund, would bring more gifts. Writing of translation into the Saxon language of the *Lindisfarne Gospels* at Conceastre.
954	Eric Bloodaxe, Viking King of Yorkshire, killed on Stainmore by Maccus, an agent of Oswulf Ealdulfing, the High Reeve of Bamburgh. End of Northern independence; Yorkshire and the North-east now ruled by kings in the south.
987	Louis V, last Carolingian king of France, dies, and is succeeded by Hugh Capet, first modern French king.
991	Fresh Danish invasions and King Ethelred (the Unready) submitted to blackmail by paying tributes to the Danes.
993	Bamburgh sacked by Danes; lay desolate until the time of William the Conqueror who is thought to have built a strong wooden castle there.
995	Further Viking attacks (probably deep penetrations of River Wear) cause monks to evacuate Conceastre.

995 Removal of the bishop and monks temporarily to Ripon while in search for a safe refuge. After four months they arrived in Dunholme and selected the high peninsula-rock for their new home.

995 Makeshift refuge built of boughs erected on Dunholme (Durham peninsula) for the protection of St Cuthbert's remains.

995 A further timber church, the *Alba Ecclesia* (Saxon White Church), built on Dunholme. This church remained in use until the consecration of the great stone church, the *Ecclesia Major* (Saxon Cathedral).

995 First rectorial church at Chester-le-Street (995-1286).

998 *Ecclesia Major* (Saxon Major Church) consecrated (although unfinished). A list of the Bishops of Conceastre follows:

Eardulph.	Last bishop of Lindisfarne, first bishop of Conceastre, died 900.
Cutheard	900-915.
Tildred	915-928.
Wigred	928-944.
Uhtred	944-947.
Sexhelm	Expelled 947 for offences against the church.
Aldred	947-968.
Elfsig	968-990.
Aldune.	990 995, last bishop of Conccastre and first bishop of Durham.

1003 Sweyn Fork-Beard of Denmark invades and conquers England.

1013 Sweyn, King of England and Denmark.

1014 King Sweyn Fork-Beard has died. His son Canute has been elected King of Denmark and England by the Danish Army.

1015 Canute, Sweyn's son, defeats Edmund Ironside, son of last Anglo-Saxon king, and divides realm with him.

1016 Edmund dies, Canute becomes sole king.

1017 *Ecclesia Major* completed on Dunholme.

1022 Bede's remains stolen from the Benedictine Monastery Church at Jarrow by a monk called Aelfred, and taken to Durham and added to the collection of relics of Northern Saints accumulated there. In 1155, Bede's remains would be placed in a sumptuous shrine but this would be destroyed by Henry VIII. Bede's remains would later find a resting place in the Galilee Chapel of Durham Cathedral, where they still lie.

1028 Canute adds Norway to his Scandinavian empire.

1035 Canute died, Partition of his empire.

1035 William the Conqueror (aged eight), Duke of Normandy.

1035 King Duncan of Scotland laid seige to Durham but was eventually repulsed and the severed heads of some of his followers were displayed in the market place.

1042 Edward the Confessor, King of England. He returned from Normandy but left government to Earl Godwin and devoted himself to religion.

c1045 Saxon Bishop Egelric of Durham built the first stone church at Conceastre (Ch-le-Str). The lower part of the chancel may be part of this. A great Roman treasure was found, probably from the strong-room of the former Roman headquarters.

Egelric's church is believed to have consisted originally of a long chancel and nave, with a central tower within the church, the building having been brought to its present form by several subsequent additions. These include the two western bays of the nave and the lowest stage of the tower, the date of which is ascribed to the beginning of the thirteenth century; the octagonal upper stage and the 156 ft spire were added c1409 when the three old bells were presented.

1054 Eastern Orthodox Church breaks with Church of Rome.

1065 Westminster Abbey, rebuilt by Edward the Confessor, consecrated.

THE NORMAN CONQUEST

1066 Edward the Confessor dies. Harold, son of Earl Godwin elected king. William of Normandy invades England and kills Harold at the Battle of Hastings.

1066 William of Normandy crowned King William 1 of England at Westminster Abbey.

1069 Feudal system set up in England (Scotland in 1134).

1069 Jan 31st: massacre of Normans at Durham. Seven-hundred Norman soldiers killed by mob.

1069 Feb. Norman commander at York captured and killed.

1069 Dec. King burns the North and lays waste Durham and Yorkshire.

1069 Rebuilt parts of Jarrow Monastery razed by Conqueror.

1071 Norman conquest of England completed.

1071 King Malcolm of Scotland devastated the eastern part of the bishopric and carried hundreds of Durham folk away into captivity.

1071 Seljuk Turks, having siezed Baghdad, sweep across Asia Minor and take fortress of Niceaea opposite Constantinople.

1071 Norman construction of Durham Castle in stone commenced.

1073 Jarrow rebuilt by three monks, Aldwin, Elfwins and Reinfridus.

1075 Turks take Jerusalem and Holy places.

1080 William the Conqueror granted "palatine," or Royal powers to the Prince-bishop of Durham, William of St Calais. He was expected to be both a religious and military leader, and to exercise directly many of the King's own powers - a unique position for a baron in England at that time.
The bishops of Durham also had a mint. The silver pennies struck there were almost identical to the royal coinage, only distinguishable by minor marks, and the coins were accepted as legal tender. The Palatine became a frontier zone between the English and Scottish kingdoms. Palatine forces would fight against the Scots at Falkirk in 1296, Neville's Cross in 1346 and Flodden in 1513. The bishops held court, granted charters and administered justice. Much time was spent feasting and hunting but many contributions were made to the good of the Palatine by the building of churches, bridges and hospitals. Meanwhile, the spiritual side was left largely to the priors and monks of the Cathedral.
The Prince-bishops held control of the County Palatine until Tudor times when the first significant inroads began to be made into their power. There was a measure of recovery in the 17th century but the bishops' power fell into decline.

1083 Bishop St Calais replaced the hereditary guardians of St Cuthbert's shrine with a community of monks whose life was governed by the rule of St Benedict. The life of a monk was divided into three parts: prayer, worship, sacred reading and manual labour. The monks lived in Durham Cathedral Priory from its foundation in 1083 until the dissolution of the priory in 1539. The remains of the priory are incorporated into the south-western area of the cathedral. The monastic buildings were completed about the same time as the cathedral, the latter founded in 1093. Jarrow monks moved to Durham and Jarrow became a cell.

1086 *Domesday Book* compiled. This was the Record of Great Inquisition of the lands of England, their extent, value, ownership and liabilities, made by order of William the Conqueror. The North-east is not included and a separate survey, the *Boldon Book*, was made of the bishopric in the twelfth century by Bishop Pudsey of Durham. It is called the *Boldon Book* because a description of Boldon is its first entry.

???? Normans change name of Conceastre to Chester.

1092 Demolition of *Ecclesia Major* at Durham.

1093 Foundations of Norman cathedral laid at Durham. Stone from dismantled Saxon cathedral reused. Much stone quarried from cliffs below cathedral site and more floated upstream by barge from quarries below Kepier. Black marble rafted down River Wear from Frosterley. The construction of the Norman cathedral would take forty years. St Cuthbert's remains and associated relics inside an English oak coffin (dated to the late seventh century) were housed in a shrine behind the high altar in the Norman cathedral. During the reformation, the shrine was destroyed but the remains were buried under the floor of the feretory (chapel-shrine) on the same site.

1095 Pope Urban II, summons Christian nations to First Crusade.

1096 First Crusade.

1098 Crusaders take Antioch.

1099 Crusaders take Jerusalem.

1136 King David of Scotland invaded the north but was driven back.

1138 King David tried again but met a crushing defeat at the Battle of the Standard, just north of Northallerton.

1139 The archbishops of Canterbury and York met the bishops of St Andrews and Glasgow at Chester-le-Street for the purpose of drawing up a treaty between King Stephen of England and David of Scotland.

1149 Second Crusade ends in failure.

1160 Elvet Bridge built by Bishop Pudsey. Bishop Fox repaired it in 1495, and in 1805 it was widened.

1174 The Scots attempted yet another invasion under William the Lion, but his plans were foiled before his army had travelled far.

1174 Saladin proclaimed Caliph; launches a holy war of all Muslims against Christians.

1175 Galilee Chapel built onto west end of Durham Cathedral by Bishop Pudsey.

1183 *Boldon Buke* compiled by Bishop Pudsey.

1187 Saladin recaptures Jerusalem.

1189 Third Crusade, under Philip Augustus of France and Richard I, fails to retake Jerusalem. Siege of ACRE.

1192 Richard concludes armistice with Saladin.

1195 Hugh Pudsey died at Howden in Yorkshire while on his way to London, having been Bishop of Durham for 42 years.

1202 Fourth Crusade; Constantinople captured.

1215 King John is forced at Runnymede to accept *Magna Carta,* which lays down that no freedman may be imprisoned or punished except by the law of the land.

1218 Fifth Crusade captures Damietta, Egypt, but loses it 1221 again.

1228 Sixth Crusade recovers Jerusalem by negotiation.

1267 Most of Chester-le-Street church built.

1282 Edward I completes conquest of Wales.

1286 Bishop Bek made our church collegiate, the parish extending from Gateshead to Durham and Houghton-le-Spring to Lanchester. Collegiate Church 1286-1547.

1286 It is also known that a Chapelry at Lamesley (OE "lambs' pasture") was linked to the Collegiate Church of St Cuthbert at Chester-le-Street but the chapel existed before that date. There may have been a Saxon church on the site of Lamesley St Andrew's Church and as most Saxon St Andrew's churches are proving to have been located on ex-Roman sites, the Romans may have had a cross-road leading up to Old Ravensworth and beyond. The Romans may have also used the River Team for cargo punts.

1295 Edward I summons Model Parliament, so-called because for the first time, King, Lords and Commons meet.

1295 Marco Polo returned to Venice from China.

1296 Edward I attempts to annex Scotland.

1297 Sir William Wallace defeats Edward at Stirling.

1298 Edward defeats Wallace at Falkirk.

1304 Wallace captured and executed, but Robert Bruce raises another revolt against Edward.

1306 Robert Bruce crowned King of Scotland.

1309 Papacy falls into French control; residence of the Pope moved to Avignon.

1312 Robert Bruce of Scotland crossed the border and did great damage to the north of England. When he returned in 1313, he travelled with such speed that he was on the outskirts of Durham, creating havoc, before the inhabitants knew what was happening.

1314 Edward II defeated at Bannockburn by Robert Bruce. After the Scottish victory at Bannockburn, very few parts of the north escaped the raiding which followed. Stockton-on-Tees was destroyed and the port of Hartlepool burnt.

1316 Bishop Kellaw died. In the same year, Durham was overwhelmed by a disastrous flood which severely damaged the ancient weirs.

1327 Gunpowder first used by King Edward III against the Scots. The day of the castle and thick walls is almost over.

1327 A bridge is mentioned at Barnard Castle.

1328 Robert Bruce recognised by England as King of Scotland.

1337 Outbreak of Hundred Years War between England and France.

1340 English defeat French at sea at Sluys.

1346 Edward III defeats French at Crecy.

1346 Scottish army defeated at the Battle of Neville's Cross. King David of Scotland was captured and remained a prisoner for eleven years.

1348 Black Death, the bubonic plague, reaches England, killing nearly half of the population, and causing extreme shortages of labour and social unrest.

1378 Rival Popes elected in Rome and Avignon.

1380 Part of the north-west end of Chester-le-Street church was converted into an anchorage and two rooms added. The anchorage was occupied by hermits who had taken vows of obedience, and constancy of abode. The resident hermit was often consulted by people seeking spiritual guidance. The rooms were later used to house poor widows. On the exterior, an ancient weather-worn rectangular stone window frame may have come from a Roman building. Other reused Roman stones complete with lewis-holes are built into a buttress on the south side of the main entrance. The lewis hole was a dove-tailed hole which was cut into the top surface of a large Roman building-stone, and the Roman crane's normal hook was replaced by a double triangular device which was wedged into the dove-tail. In the reused position, the dove-tailed holes are on the sides of the stones and thus demonstrate that in the final building, cranes with lewis devices were not used.

1381 Heavily taxed and tied to the land, Wat Tyler organises peasants' revolt. Tyler is killed and the rising crushed, but from then on, serfdom gradually declines.

1382 The Bible translated into English by John Wyclif.

1385 Scots invade England but Richard II takes Edinburgh.

1388 Scots invade again and are victorious at Otterburn.

1388 Bishop Skirlaw builds Newton Cap bridge near Bishop Auckland and demolishes an old bridge to make way for it. This old bridge is thought to have been of Roman origin on "Proto Dere Street" from Fylands Bridge to Hunwick. The Roman road is still marked on some maps as "Mitchell's Causeway" and the loop-road from Fyland's Bridge which has gone through Binchester, rejoins Proto Dere Street at NZ 196 323 just to the west of the Hunwick Equestrian Centre.

1392 Sir Ralph Lumley obtained a licence from King Richard II, to convert Lumley Manor House into a castle. A considerable portion of the Manor House can be detected on the west side of the quadrangle.

1400 Welsh revolt under Owen Glendower.

1403 Scots defeated at Homildon Hill. Henry IV crushes revolt at Shrewsbury.

1409 The building of the spire of Chester-le-Street church.

1415 Henry V renews war against France, captures Harfleur and is victorious at Agincourt.

1429 At Orleans, English driven off by Joan of Arc's army.

1429 On Corpus Christi Day, when Durham was crowded with visitors, a terrific thunderstorm destroyed the central tower of Durham Cathedral.

1430 Repairs to central tower of Cathedral.

1431 Joan of Arc captured by English and burned at the stake.

1453 The Eastern Empire ends when Constantinople falls to the Ottoman Turks, who sweep into Greece and on to the Danube. Greek scholars fled to the West and so laid foundations for the Renaissance in the 16th century.

1455 The Hundred Years War ends. The Duke of York (White Rose) claims the throne from Henry VI, a Lancastrian (Red Rose). The Wars of the Roses begin. Yorkists win at St Albans but are then defeated. York flees to Ireland.

1460 York returns, is victorious at Northampton, but is defeated and killed at Wakefield.

1461 Edward, York's son, proclaimed King in London as Edward IV. He defeats the Lancastrians at Towton. Henry VI is captured and imprisoned.

1464 Lancastrians defeated at Hexham.

1465 The central tower of Durham Cathedral was rebuilt after further damage by fire.

1470 Yorkist Earl of Warwick quarrels with Edward IV; frees Henry VI. Edward flees to Flanders.

1471 Edward returns, defeats and kills Warwick at Barnet, and routs Lancastrians at Tewkesbury.

1483 Edward IV succeeded by 12-year-old son, Edward V. Richard, Duke of Gloucester, has himself proclaimed king as Richard III. Edward V and his brother are murdered in the Tower.

1485 Henry Tudor, Earl of Richmond, lands in England and defeats Richard III at Bosworth. As Henry VII, he founds the line of Tudors, breaks the power of the nobles and establishes a strong government.

APPENDIX "A" (continued)
Sixteenth to 20th centuries

1513 James IV of Scotland invades England and is defeated at Flodden.

1529 Cardinal Wolsey, Henry VIII's chief minister, fails to persuade the Pope to grant a divorce from Catherine of Aragon and Henry dismisses him.

1533 Archbishop Cranmer dissolves Henry's marriage and crowns Anne Boleyn as Queen.

1534 Henry VIII repudiates authority of the Pope and proclaims himself head of the Church and dissolves the monasteries, confiscating their property and wealth.

1536 Death of Catherine of Aragon; of Anne Boleyn. Henry marries Jane Seymour.

1536 Dissolution of the Monasteries carried through by Thomas Cromwell; brought much wealth to Henry, but had far-reaching consequences.

1538 IIcnry VIII excommunicated.

1539 The Reformation. St Cuthbert's shrine was broken up and coffin buried below where the shrine had stood. This was the reformers attempt to focus prayers on God instead of on saints.

1540 Henry VIII marries Anne of Cleves; later in the year marries Catherine Howard.

1542 Catherine Howard executed; Henry marries Catherine Parr.

1547 Dissolution of Kepier Hospital.

1547 Dissolution of collegiate church in Chester-le-Street.

1547 Ch-le-Str. Church under perpetual curacy (1547-1865).

1547 Ten-year old Edward VI succeeds Henry VIII.

1547 Foundations for Royal Navy laid and Merchant Navy prepared, the spacious days of Elizabeth.

1549 First Prayer Books in English are issued by Cranmer.

1553 Mary, Henry VIII's daughter and a catholic, becomes Queen. Lady Jane Grey, to whom Edward VI had bequeathed the crown to avoid a return to Catholicism, is also proclaimed Queen, but is arrested and executed. Cranmer burnt at the stake and replaced by a Catholic Archbishop of Canterbury. Supremacy of the Pope is acknowledged. Mary's persecution of Protestants gains her the nick-name, "Bloody Mary."

1558 Elizabeth I succeeds Mary and repudiates the authority of the Pope. To avoid religious conflict, a compromise is worked out with a mixture of Protestant and Catholic elements being worked into Church doctrines.

1568 Mary, Queen of Scots, Catholic and heir to Elizabeth forced to flee to England and there imprisoned by Elizabeth.

1569 Barnard Castle bridge built. It is thought to have replaced the bridge mentioned in 1327.

1574 An early bridge upstream of the later Prebends Bridge was built across the Wear to replace a ferry. The bridge was destroyed by the Great Flood of 1771 but the remains of the eastern abutment can still be seen.

1577 Sir Francis Drake being his voyage around the world in *Pelican,* later renamed *Golden Hind(e).*

1585 Elizabeth lands English army in the Netherlands to support Dutch in their revolt against Spanish rule, and this brings into the open the undeclared war between England and Spain as a result of trading conflicts and religious differences.

1587 Mary, Queen of Scots executed. Drake attacks Cadiz.

1588 Philip of Spain sends Great Armada with intention of invading England. Armada destroyed by British Navy.

1594 John Lumley revered his ancestors so much that he had imaginary portraits painted and hung in the castle. In 1594 he removed two effigies from Durham Cathedral churchyard and placed them in Chester-le-Street Church in the mistaken idea that they represented Lord Ralph Lumley, the builder of the castle, and his son. A third has an unknown provenance and the remaining eleven were made to order. None lie on top of tombs.

1603 Elizabeth dies. James VI of Scotland becomes King as James I. King's High Church views displease Puritans.

1605 The Gunpowder Plot: a Catholic-organised conspiracy to blow-up James and his Parliament fails when the explosives, already in place, were discovered by guards.

1609 Holland frees herself from Spain and becomes a great power.

1611 Settlement of English and Scottish protestants in Northern Ireland, with far-reaching effects.

1616 The "Queen's Head" is mentioned as a coaching inn. The *"Chester Volunteers"* patronised this inn and the Halmote Court met here three times a year before transferring to the "Lambton Arms." The Halmote Court ceased to function in 1925. Both the Lambton Arms and the Queen's Head sit back from the main street to allow access for coaches.

1618 Outbreak of the Thirty Years War. This was an unsuccessful attempt by the Catholics to stamp out the Reformation in Europe. Sweden's entry into the conflict in 1629 would swing the balance against the Catholics.

1620 Pilgrim Fathers sail from Plymouth in the *Mayflower* to found the first English colony in New England.

1640 Durham Cathedral damaged by Scottish invading troops.

1641 Irish rebel against England.

1642 Charles I goes to House of Commons to arrest his enemies but finds them gone. The Civil War begins. The first battle at Edgehill was indecisive.

1644 Royalists defeated by Cromwell at Marston Moor.

1645 Cromwell wins a resounding victory at Naseby.

1646 Charles surrenders to Scots.

1647 The Scots hand Charles over to Parliamentarians.

1648 The Scots change their policy and invade England and are defeated by Cromwell at Preston.

1648 The afore-mentioned Thirty Years War ends in a stalemate.

1649 Charles I executed. England becomes a republic with the name 'Commonwealth.' Cromwell, using a heavy hand, restores English rule in Ireland.

1650 Charles I's son, later Charles II, lands in Scotland and is crowned King of Scotland.

1650 Three-thousand Scottish prisoners of war were taken by Oliver Cromwell at the Battle of Dunbar on 3rd September. They were imprisoned in Durham Cathedral where they vandalised the fabric of the building. They were half starved and many had died on the march south. They were hungry and cold and burned anything they could find including choir stalls and priceless artwork. Only the wooden clock was spared because, it is said, of the thistle carved on it. The citizens of Durham were so upset that for centuries to come, city guilds refused to accept Scotsmen as apprentices to their trades.

c1651 The great lead-covered timber spires on Durham Cathedral's western towers were taken down and the materials sold.

1651 Charles invades England and is defeated by Cromwell at Worcester. Charles escapes to the continent.

1652 England and the Netherlands enter naval war over trade.

1653 Cromwell becomes Lord Protector.

1655 Cromwell siezes Jamaica from Spain.

1658 Cromwell dies and is succeeded by son, Richard.

1659 Richard Cromwell resigns.

1660 General Monk, Commonwealth commander in Scotland, occupies London and invites Charles to return to England as Charles II.

1664 Further war between Britain and Holland. British capture New Amsterdam and rename it New York.

1665 Great Plague of London.

1666 Great Fire of London.

1667 Dutch navy sails up Medway and destroys British squadron. Britain makes peace but does not give back New York.

1685 Charles II dies. James, a Catholic becomes King James II, Monmouth, illegitimate son of Charles II, and a Protestant, tries to sieze the throne but is executed after being defeated at Sedgemoor.

1688 William of Orange, married to Mary, James' Protestant daughter, is invited to come to England with an army to save the English Church and Constitution. James II flees to France after William lands at Torbay.

1689 The Crown is accepted by William with Mary as Queen. They agreed to the Bill of Rights, which limited Royal power. James II lands in Ireland and leads an Irish rebellion.

1690 William of Orange, at the Battle of the Boyne, defeats James II.

1701 Parliament passes the Act of Settlement confining the succession of the Throne to Protestants. Louis XIV plans to make France the strongest power in Europe. William forms a 'Grand Alliance' of Britain, Holland and Austria, to stop him.

1702 William dies, succeeded by Anne.

1704 Marlborough's victory over French at Blenheim saves Vienna. Admiral Rooke captures Gibraltar.

1706 Marlborough defeats French at Ramillies.

1707 Act of Union between England and Scotland.

1708 Marlborough defeats French at Oudenarde.

1709 Marlborough victorious at Malplaquet.

1713 War ends. Britain receives Newfoundland and Hudson Bay from France, Gibraltar and Minorca from Spain.

1714 Anne dies, and Elector of Hanover becomes king as King George I. He cannot speak English and has no interest in English affairs.

1715 The 'Old Pretender,' son of James II, lands in Scotland to find his supporters have already been defeated.

1733 The antiquarian, Dr Christopher Hunter published the first local guide-book of County Durham. Present day archaeologists are indebted to him.

c1742 Toll Bar at NZ 273 498 operating on Toll Road which led down from what is now, modern A167 into Southburn Dene (underneath later railway viaduct). The toll charges were a penny for a horse, a half penny for a score of sheep, a shilling for a score of hogs and a shilling for a stage coach. A team of cattle from Chester Moor Farm assisted coaches up the relatively gentle incline to the south of the South Burn.

1743 George II defeats French at Dettingen; the last time a British king is personally in command in a battle.

1745 Prince Charles Edward, the 'Young Pretender,' lands in Scotland and wins a victory at Prestonpans. He invades England but finds little support and his army returns to Scotland.

1746 The Jacobites defeated at Culloden. The 'Young Pretender' escapes to the continent.

1755 Stocks finally removed from just inside our church gate.

1760 George II succeeded by his grandson, George III, first Hanoverian king to speak English and regard himself as King of England rather than Elector of Hanover.

1771 Nov 17th, The Great Flood. Many bridges destroyed.

1772 Prebend's bridge designed. The weir below Prebend's Bridge was constructed in ancient times.

1773 'Boston Tea Party' brings to a head the long quarrel between George III and English colonists in America. Colonists, disguised as Indians board ships in Boston and throw cargoes of tea into harbour as a protest against taxes on tea.

1774 Building of replacement Tyne bridge at Newcastle began after destruction of the old one in flood of 1771.

1775 First shots exchanged between colonists and British troops at Lexington. George Washington made American Commander-in-Chief.

1776 The 13 American colonies issue *Declaration of Independence* on July 4th.

1777 France and Spain declare war on Britain.

1781 British army forced to surrender at Yorktown, Virginia.

1783 Britain recognises American independence.

1793 French occupy Austrian Netherlands (now Belgium).

1796 George Watson born in Durham. He came to Chester-le-Street at age of nine to work in Pickerings' shop. He was press-ganged into navy when 19 (1815) but after serving his time returned to Chester-le-Street and opened a school where navigation and mathematics were part of the curriculum. A former pupil, Sir George Elliot, M.P. erected the headstone on his grave which is behind the war memorial in the north east corner of the churchyard.

1797 Napoleon threatens Vienna; Austria makes peace. Jarvis and Nelson defeat Spanish fleet at Cape St Vincent. Duncan defeats Dutch fleet at Camperdown.

1798 Nelson destroys French Fleet at Aboukir in *Battle of the Nile*.

1799 Britain, Turkey, Austria and Russia combine against France. Bonaparte abandons army in Egypt and returns to France where he makes himself First Consul.

1800 Bonaparte defeats Austrians at Marengo. Ireland made part of UK.

1801 Austria sues for peace. Nelson smashes Danish fleet at Copenhagen.

1802 Peace returns for a time. Britain restores Cape of Good Hope to Dutch, but keeps Ceylon (formerly Dutch) and Trinidad (formerly Spanish). Bonaparte made First Consul for life.

1803 War between Britain and France renewed, with Spain on French side. Bonaparte sells Louisiana to the USA.

1804 Bonaparte becomes Emperor Napoleon.

1804 Napoleon gathers army at Boulogne to invade England. He is deterred by threat of Royal Navy.

1805 Nelson defeats French and Spanish fleets at Trafalgar. Napoleon defeats Austrians and Russians at Austerlitz.

1806 Austria again sues for peace.

1807 Napoleon defeats Russians and forms an alliance with them. Britain is now his only enemy.

1807 Abolition of the Slave Trade due to the efforts of William Wilberforce.

1809 Sir Arthur Wellesley (later Duke of Wellington) defeats French at Talavera.

1812 Napoleon invades Russia and occupies Moscow which the Russians have burnt. Napoleon is forced to retreat during the harsh winter and his *'Grande Armée'* is destroyed. Dispute arising out of Britain's insistence on searching neutral ships, sparks off war between Britain and USA. British troops occupy and burn Washington.

1812 The Round School in Chester-le-Street, formerly the oast house of the Deanery, was in operation at the north end of Church Chare. Birch Kirby was the master and also the publican of the King's Head inn. Thomas Wilkinson, his successor, in 1832, introduced Greek and Latin into the curriculum. The Round School closed in 1860; its last master was Peter Purvis, a Scotsman who had served with Napoleon's army and became a prisoner of war. All that is left of the Round School is the curved wall, opposite the old school which became St Mary's Hospice.

1813 Prussia and Austria drive Napoleon from Germany. Wellington defeats French at Vittoria and drives them out of Spain.

1814 Britain and America make peace. Austria, Russia and Prussia invade France, occupy Paris. Wellington marches into southern France. Napoleon abdicates and is banished to Elba. Bourbon dynasty restored.

1815 Napoleon escapes, resumes power but is defeated at Waterloo and is banished to St Helena. Louis XVIII returns to Paris.

1821 Greeks revolt against Turkish rule. Death of Napoleon on St Helena.

1822 Lord Byron (poet) joins Greek forces to assist with war of independence.

1823 Criminal law reform. Abolition of the death penalty for petty crimes.

1826 Mechanics' Institute built in Chester-le-Street.

1827 St Cuthbert's coffin was once more unearthed, the relics this time being removed and the bones reburied. More fragments of the coffin were found in the grave in 1899, and in 1939 all the pieces were reassembled and mounted on new oak boards. The coffin was five-feet-six-inches long and covered with pictorial carvings.

1833 Monastery site found at Hartlepool.

1833 Slavery abolished throughout British Empire.

1835 *Boers* undertake their *'Great Trek'* to escape from British rule in the Cape; set up republic in Transvaal.

1837 Queen Victoria ascends the throne.

1838 St Cuthbert's beloved Farne Islands are in the news. On Sept 7th, the Dundee, Perth and London steam Paddle-wheeler *cum* sailing ship *Forfarshire* was wrecked on the west point of the Harcar Rock near Longstone. The 400-ton steam-sailer had departed Hull bound Dundee, but off Berwick, the boilers became leaky causing a loss of steam. Captain Humble turned downwind and set sail for South

Shields in a northerly gale and poor visibility. At 4am the ship struck the rock. In 15 minutes the ship had broken in two at the paddle axle and 43 people were drowned. Nine people who had left by boat were later picked up by a Montrose vessel and taken to Shields but nine others held onto the wreck. The Lighthouse keeper on Longstone, Mr William Darling and his daughter, Grace manned a coble in the dreadful conditions of wind and sea and rowed to the wreck. Some passengers were taken off and the coble returned for the rest, with rescued men replacing Grace at the oars. Grace Horsley Darling, was born in Bamburgh on 24 Nov 1815 and died on 20 Oct 1842. Her ornate grave, fitting for such a heroine is in Bamburgh churchyard.

1839 Roman ford found at Barnard Castle. Startforth = "Street Ford."
1840 Penny Post established.
1840 Annexation of New Zealand.
1841 Capture of Hong Kong.
1852 Louis Napoleon (Bonaparte's nephew) makes himself French Emperor as Napoleon III.
1853 Britain, France and Turkey declare war on Russia and land forces in Crimea. Very harsh winter, Nurse Florence Nightingale becomes heroine.
1856 Crimean war ends.
1857 Indian Mutiny breaks out.
1860 Abraham Lincoln elected US President. Eleven southern states break away from the Union; American Civil War breaks out.
1863 General Robert E Lee defeated at Gettysburg; Lincoln proclaims abolition of slavery.
1865 Saxon finds at Darlington. Saxon foundations have been discovered at Darlington during restoration of the historic parish church of St Cuthbert.
1865 The Second Rectorial Church at Chester-le-Street.
1865 General Lee surrenders to General Grant and American Civil War is over. Abraham Lincoln assassinated.
1867 Canada becomes Dominion.
1867 Railway viaduct over Cong Burn valley completed.
1868 Chester-le-Street Railway Station opened.
1869 Suez Canal opened. Verdi writes "Aida" for grand opening ceremony.
1870 Elementary Education Act. Education to be provided throughout the country. (Scotland 1872). Later Acts - 1880 attendance compulsory and 1896, free.
1870 Napoleon III declares war on Prussia. French army defeated; Napoleon's Empire collapses and is followed by Third Republic.
1871 United Germany proclaimed with King of Prussia as Emperor.
1872 Voting becomes secret in Britain.
1872 Matthew Richley in his *History of Bishop Auckland,* noticed that the original Roman road north from Fyland's Bridge did not turn up into Newgate Street, but went straight ahead to Newton Cap. It is very likely therefore that the old bridge which Bishop Skirlaw pulled down in 1388 was a Roman bridge on the direct line from Fyland's Bridge to Hunwick. This Roman road has been rediscovered recently by the Northern Archaeology Group. There is a possible Roman site at Newton Cap and the Binchester Roman site may be an afterthought on a later loop road. The implications of this are that Binchester may not be "Vinovia." A hitherto unknown Roman fort at Newton Cap may prove to have that identity. Bishop Skirlaw's 1388 bridge looks as if it is standing on the remains of an older structure. The original northbound road is easily found from Newton Cap to Hunwick where the later Roman loop road from Binchester rejoins it.
1875 Disraeli buys bankrupt Khedive's shares of the Suez Canal for Britain with money borrowed from Rockerfeller.
1877 Queen Victoria becomes Empress of India.
1881 *Boers* (farmers) defeat British force trying to occupy Transvaal. Scramble for Africa by European powers becomes intense.
1882 Britain occupies Egypt and is drawn into the affairs of the Sudan, where Mohammed Ahmed has proclaimed himself *Mahdi* (Messiah) and declared a holy war against Egypt and all non-Moslems.
1883 Millenary Festival and Restoration at Chester-le-Street.
1884 Germany joins "Scramble for Africa" and takes SW Africa, Cameroons, Togoland and Tanganyika.

1885 General Gordon sent to evacuate British and Egyptian garrisons in the Sudan, is killed in Khartoum by *Mahdi's* forces.
1888 British East Africa Company secures EA territories.
1890 Cecil Rhodes, founder of Rhodesia, who hopes to see British territory extend from the Cape to Cairo, becomes Prime Minister of the Cape Colony.
1894 Chester-le-Street's gasworks beside the railway viaduct used 27 retorts to fill three gasholders which supplied the township and 74 public lamps.
1896 Jamieson's raid into Transvaal.
1898 General Kitchener defeats *Mahdi* and recaptures Khartoum.
1899 South African War begins as *Boers* invade Natal.

APPENDIX "A" (continued)
The 20th Century

1900 Lord Roberts wipes out main *Boer* forces, but *Boer* guerilla units continue war.
1901 Queen Victoria dies. Australia becomes self-governing dominion.
1902 *Boer* War ends; *Boer* republics annexed by British Crown.
1904 *Entente Cordiale* (warm understanding) established between Britain and France.
1907 New Zealand becomes dominion. Alliance between Britain and France extended to include Russia. Germany and Austria on one hand and Britain, France and Russia on the other, begin an arms race.
1908 Austria annexes Bosnia and Herzogovina, offending Serbia and Russia, since both provinces have large Serb(Slav) populations.
1910 Union of South Africa, formed from Cape of Good Hope, Natal, Orange Free State, and Transvaal, becomes a dominion.
1911 National Insurance Act.
1912 Cunard White Star 60,000 ton liner, SS *Titanic* sinks after collision with iceberg; 1,517 passengers drowned.
1914 Panama Canal opened.
1914 Assassination of heir to Austrian throne at Sarajevo, triggers off World War 1. Germans sweep through neutral Belgium and are halted just short of Paris. Struggle settles down into stalemate of trench warfare. Immense casualties in return for few gains. Russians invade East Prussia but are stopped by Hindenburg at Tannenberg.
1915 Turkey, fighting on the German side, tries to cut the Suez Canal but fails. The British fail to open communications with Russia via the Dardanelles because a British Commonwealth and allied invasion of the Gallipoli peninsula evacuates in the face of fierce and intense Turkish resistance.
1915 Cunard 40,000 tons passenger liner, SS *Lusitania* sunk by German U-boat. 1,198 people drowned including many Americans and other neutrals.
1916 Trench warfare continues with tremendous losses on both sides. British and German fleets meet off Jutland: German fleet so battered that it remains in port for the rest of the war.
1916, Germans' unrestricted U-boat warfare against all merchant ships in British waters continues. Germans temporarily abandon policy of sinkings without warning.
1917 Anti-war feeling in Russia leads to overthrow of the Czar, but the provisional government's attempts to continue the war enables Lenin and the Bolsheviks to sieze power. The Germans renew unrestricted submarine attacks and in April, USA declares war on Germany.
1918 The Germans launch their final offensive which fails. The Germans sue for armistice in November. The German Kaiser, Wilhelm II abdicates; Germany becomes a republic. Hapsburg monarchy in Austria comes to an end.
1919 Under peace treaties, France regains Alsace-Lorraine; Germany loses the 'Polish Corridor' to the new Polish Republic; Austria and Hungary are separated; Serbia is enlarged and becomes Yugoslavia; Czechoslovakia is created; the Ottoman Empire is broken up leaving only Turkey which becomes a republic. The League of Nations is created; Germany's colonies become League of Nation's mandates and Germany has limits put on the size of her armed forces.
1920 League of Nations inspired by President Wilson of USA, but America never became a member state.

1921 Ireland, with the exception of Northern Ireland, which remains linked to UK, becomes a dominion after almost three years of unrest.

1924 Lenin, having established Communist rule in Russia dies. Stalin emerges as his successor, becomes virtual dictator in 1929.

1933 Hitler appointed Chancellor of German Republic.

1934 Cunard 81,327 ton liner, *Queen Mary* launched. (put into service 1936).

1934 Italians invade and conquer Abyssinia.

1935 Hitler denounces the terms of the *Versailles Treaty* which limits the size of the German forces. Had the weak western leaders been firm with Hitler at this point, millions of lives would have been saved and World War II avoided. It was not to be.

1936 Hitler occupies the Rhineland. Weak Allies take no action.

1936 Outbreak of Spanish Civil War. Germans and Italians fight openly on fascist Franco's side; and the left wing government receives aid from Russia.

1938 Hitler occupies Austria and claims the Sudetenland in Czechoslovakia.

1939 Cunard 83,673 liner SS *Queen Elizabeth* launched. Put into service 1940.

1939 The Spanish Civil War ends with the surrender of Madrid. General Franco becomes dictator. Hitler siezes the rest of Czechoslovakia. Mussolini siezes Albania. Hitler makes a pact with Stalin, and Germany and Russia invade, divide and crush Poland. Britain and France honour their treaty with Poland and declare war on Germany. Thus began the Second World War. Russia makes war on Finland for territorial gains but Russian armies beaten by smaller Finnish forces in winter campaign.

1940 Russians break through; Finland sues for peace. Hitler occupies Norway and Denmark. In Britain Chamberlain is brought down, and Winston Churchill forms a coalition government. German forces sweep through Holland, Belgium and Luxembourg. France sues for armistice. Britain, having extricated her army from France at Dunkirk, fights on alone. Hitler's plan to invade Britain receives great setback when *Luftwaffe* is defeated over southern England in Battle of Britain by Royal Air Force Fighter Command. Churchill who is reading top secret German radio messages via broken *Enigma* codes and brilliant scholars working as crypto-analysists, realise that German invasion plans have serious logistical flaws. German admirals advise Generals that *Wehrmacht* plans for crossing Channel with strings of unpowered low-freeboard canal barges towed by captured Dutch tugs are unworkable. German admirals express fears that *Kriegsmarine's* depleted fleet of 19 destroyers cannot cope with Royal Navy's 79 destroyers. German admirals tell army that British destroyers will race through strings of unpowered and underpowered canal-craft and swamp them, drowning troops and horses which at that time still supplied the motive power for half of German transport.
German generals tell German navy to place two minefields across Channel to protect sea corridor. German admirals inform army of thirty feet tides in English Channel and ask if mines should be set for high tide or low tide? If set for high tide, mines will flop around on surface at low tide and British ships will destroy them with gunfire. If mines set for low tide, destroyers will cross them unharmed at high tide. *Luftwaffe* also reveals that only 365 Junkers 52 transport aircraft, each carrying 12 parachutists are available for an airborne invasion. With such a small airborne force, an aerial invasion was impossible. Also 300+ mph Spitfires and Hurricanes still control skies over Britain. Churchill realises that Germans cannot invade and diverts tanks and guns to North Africa where he realises that soon the battle for Suez Canal will commence. A loss of the canal would cut the British Empire in two. Churchill is also in process of borrowing from his friend, President Franklin D Roosevelt, 50 mothballed US Navy destroyers from World War 1. Britain has spent most of its cash on American arms. Roosevelt is trying to bring in legislation so that Britain can borrow weapons without paying as long as those not destroyed are returned to USA at the end of the war. This will be known as *"lend lease"* and will become effective in March 1941. The WW1 American destroyer deal was agreed between Churchill and Roosevelt on Aug 14th 1940. On that very same day, German General Halder recorded in his diary that the German army was looking for a site in East Prussia which could serve as Hitler's headquarters during the invasion of Russia. Hitler had therefore given up his plans for the invasion of England as early as Aug 14th 1940.
Royal Navy sank the French fleet in Oran, killing a thousand French sailors. The French ships had been given the option of coming over to Britain or sailing to neutral bases beyond Axis control.

Roosevelt realised that the British were in the war to the finish if they took such drastic steps. As Roosevelt realised from the killing of their former allies, Britain could be relied on not to negotiate with Hitler. Roosevelt resolved to give Britain as many arms as possible and free of charge into the bargain, and to get USA into the war as soon as an opportunity presented itself. The Japanese would provide this opportunity.

Roosevelt makes wonderful speech in support of *"lend lease"* and tells American people that: "When your neighbour's house is on fire, you do not need to beat out the flames but you can easily lend the neighbour your hosepipe." This speech carries the American people and without doubt saved Britain.

Hitler has abandoned ambitions of invading Britain and his plans for an invasion of Russia are already complete.

Italy enters war on German side and attacks Greece. British troops begin the captures of Italian colonies in East Africa and occupy Ethiopia.

1941 Hitler conquers Yugoslavia and Greece and attacks Russia. Germans sweep to gates of Moscow and Leningrad but are caught by Russian winter. The German supply lines are too long and only tracked vehicles are of any real use. Russian rivers run north-south and are useless for west-east army logistics.

The German *Afrika Korps* under Rommel arrives to strengthen Italians in North Africa. This German army becomes a dangerous threat to Egypt, the Suez Canal, and the whole of the oil-producing Middle East.

In December, Japan attacks the US Pacific Fleet at Pearl Harbor. Roosevelt knew an attack was coming but not exactly where and when. Fortunately, the most important ships, the aircraft carriers, are out at sea on exercise and escape destruction. They would play an important role in the subsequent defeat of the Japanese Navy in the Pacific sea battles. Another important factor missed by most historians is the development by the allies of the proximity-fused anti-aircraft shell. This capacitance-activated device exploded the shell when in close proximity to the metal mass of an aircraft in a "near-miss situation." The weapon would be used by American ships to destroy Japanese *"Kamikaze"* suicide bombers and by the British anti-aircraft gunners to shoot down Hitler's "V1 flying bombs" (doodlebugs) in 1944.

1942 The Germans experience another winter in Russia and a German army of 300,000 is surrounded and destroyed at Stalingrad.

In North Africa, Rommel defeats the British and gets within 60 miles of Alexandria. Rommel then runs out of fuel for his excellent diesel tanks. Although the *Afrika Korps* was superior to the Eighth Army, the German planners suffered a logistical failure. Malta was the thorn in the Germans' side. Royal Air Force and Royal Navy Torpedo bombers were sinking Italian tankers bound for North Africa. Hitler should have taken Malta with his excellent parachute regiment which had conquered the allies in Crete.

The British and Commonwealth forces which had defended Crete had however inflicted such severe casualties on Hitler's favourite regiment, that he never used it again in its parachute role. The failure to take Malta was a tactical/logistical error and probably cost Germany the war.

The British Eighth Army, well-supplied via the Cape, regrouped at El Alamein and begin the advance which drove the Germans out of Africa.

Britain lost Singapore to the Japanese but American naval and carrier-aircraft battles in the Coral Sea and at Midway halted the Japanese onslaught in the Pacific and the Americans began to roll the Japanese back, capturing Guadalcanal in 1943, the Gilbert, Marshall and Mariana Islands in 1943 and 1944, the Philippines in 1944 and Iwo-Jima and Okinawa in 1945.

1943 Italy changes sides.

1944 The Russians push the Germans out of Russia and advance into Europe. The Western allies land in Normandy with the greatest military logistics operation the world has ever seen. A group of German officers attempt to assassinate Hitler, without success.

1945 The Allies cross the Rhine: the Russians invade Germany from the east. Hitler commits suicide as the Russians take Berlin. Germany surrenders. Japan surrenders after two nuclear weapons have been dropped on Hiroshima and Nagasaki. Strangely, some of the scientists who developed the nuclear weapons in USA were driven out of Fascist Germany and Italy on racial grounds. The war dead are estimated at 35 million apart from the 10 million civilian atrocities in concentration camps and elsewhere.

The British obey their *"lend lease"* obligations. In many cases, USA says destruction of "lend lease" weapons is acceptable instead of return. Royal Navy pushes hundreds of American built aircraft overboard from aircraft-carriers. The British have kept their promise and the world is not flooded with surplus aircraft, thus putting American manufacturers at risk.

1945 Allies occupy Germany and divide the country into zones of responsibility. If Germany had won the war, the plan was to reduce Britain's population to 13 million, the German language made mandatory and the only industry, agriculture. Britain did not retaliate with the harsh treatment the Germans expected. The Germans were astonished that Britain between 1945 and 1950 spent 200 million pounds on food for Germany. This is equivalent to several billion pounds today (2,000). Rationing was eliminated in Germany years before ration cards were no longer necessary in Britain. The older generations in Germany still praise Britain for her forgiving and humanitarian administration.

1946 Civil War in Greece. The United Nations organisation is formed. The communists seem intent on taking over the world and sieze every opportunity to cause conflict. The threat of nuclear weapons limits the aggression.

1947 Nationalisation of British coal industry, followed by the railways and electricity in 1948.

1948 The Russians blockade Berlin but the allies astonish the Russians by supplying the city by air.

1949 The USA, Canada, Britain, France and eight other western European countries join together for mutual defence in the North Atlantic Treaty Organisation (NATO).

1950 The Korean war commences when communist North Korea invades South Korea. American, British and other UN forces land just in time to prevent South Korea from being overrun. The communists are driven back into North Korea but the Chinese intervene and push the UN forces back across the frontier. British and UN forces are confronted by Russian and Chinese aircraft which are powered by Rolls Royce jet engines. This is a result of a post-war British government giving or selling technology to the communists.

1951 Egypt abrogates the 1936 Treaty with Britain; British troops occupy the Canal Zone.

1952 Cyprus Emergency begins; lasts to 1959.

1952 Mau Mau rebellion in Kenya; state of emergency lasts to 1959.

1953 Rising in East Germany supressed by Soviet troops.

1953 The Korean war ends in a stalemate. Stalin dies and there is a struggle for power in Russia. The old Imperial empires have collapsed into dozens of newly independent states but the Communist Empire will also begin its rapid disintegration with communism being rapidly replaced by democracy.

1956 Suez Crisis; Nasser nationalises the Suez Canal; Israel invades Sinai; Britain and France invade Egypt. American president does not back Britain; regrets it later when USA has problems in Middle East. Britain ceases to rely on American protection and brings her armed forces up to scratch.

1957 First satellite in space launched by Russia. Shocks America into a space race which results in America being first to the moon, and space race, together with arms race helps bankrupt Soviet Union with a subsequent collapse of communism. Escalating arms race also reduced.

1960 The 1960s were described by some as "a time of change". The so-called change was a change of social attitudes camouflaged by strange new types of music. Politicians in order to attract the votes of the young, issued honours and decorations in a frivolous manner. Acceptance of responsibility declined, as did discipline in schools. Teaching became as stressful as air traffic control and a recent poll shows that 55% of teachers wish to leave the profession. If education fails, then our nation is doomed. It is to be hoped that the new millenium will bring a climb back to our former levels.

1963 New universities are established at Newcastle, York and Guyana. Kenya becomes independent. Britain dissolves the Central African Federation. Sadly the Beeching report leads to the rundown of the British Railway system. We could do with the old system right now to take the pressure off the roads.

1982 Argentina invades Falkland Islands. Britain sends expeditionary force. Argentinian occupation lasts only 74 days; ends with Argentinian surrender.

1991 Gulf War begins when coalition forces attack Iraq after the latter's refusal to withdraw its invading forces from Kuwait. Iraq's army quickly defeated.

1999 Huge Roman inland port found at Pisa while building an underground station. Over thirty intact medium-sized Roman ships found. A canal has connected the inland port with the sea.

1999 The Roman port of "Portus" north of Ostia has been relocated under the Leonardo Da Vinci Airport near the mouth of the Tiber. Archaeologists of the British School of Rome and Southampton University now talk of a constant stream of barges plying the Tiber between Portus and Rome in order to feed the million inhabitants of the capital. All this was told to the authorities in 1983 in the Chester-le-Street produced book, *The Piercebridge Formula*.

1999 A huge Roman inland port has been found at Wroxeter on the River Severn. It was known that there was a Roman port at Gloucester but Wroxeter is 70 miles further upstream. Now a Piercebridge-type exploration should be able to find signs of Roman barge navigation all the way between Gloucester and Wroxeter. This is in addition to the recent finds of a Roman villa on the dried-up channel of the River Og, a former tributary of the River Kennet. The latter is now also almost dry. There was much more water around in Roman times. The "Og" Roman villa has jetties and a boathook was among the artefacts found.

1999 We have all know for many years that there was a huge amount of Roman transport on all the rivers of the Roman Empire. The evidence was ignored by many members of the establishment because they had written about the importance of ox-wagon transport. Now the huge inland port of the City of Rome has been found in the Trastevere area of Rome. All the capital's supplies came up the Tiber from Portus at the river's mouth. (*The Times*, Feb 21, 2000).

2000 Millennium celebrations in Britain and around the world. Chester-le-Street, the "City of the World" has played its part.

Maps of Chester-le-Street

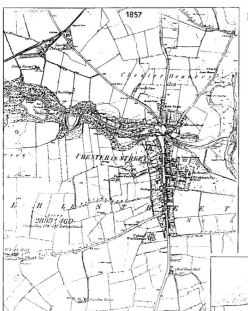

Map1 A map of Chester-le-Street of 1857. The old loop of the River Wear in which the sewage works would be built in 1930, shows "Ruins of a stone pier".Red Rose Hall, the birthplace in 1898 of the author's father, William Selkirk, is shown at the south end of the town.

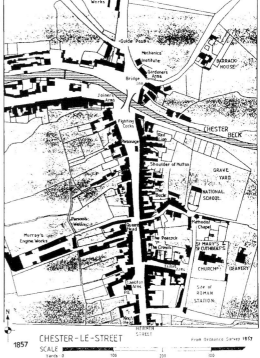

Map 2 An enlarged map of 1857 of the town centre. Inns shown are from north to south: Gardeners' Arms, Bridge Inn, Joiners'Arms, Fighting Cocks, Red Lion, Shoulder of Mutton, The Buck, Queen's Head, The Peacock, The Crown, Tailors' Arms, Lambton Arms, and King's Head. Others not shown are The Black Horse, The High Crown, The Boat, Grey's Arch, The Leopold, Letters, and The Shovel and Broom.

Map 3 A map of the town of 1898. The old Roman loop of the river   is now a sand pit.

Map 4 A map c1930. The bypass has not yet been built. Hinegan's Pond and the old course of the Cong Burn are shown and the sewage works in the old river loop are under construction.

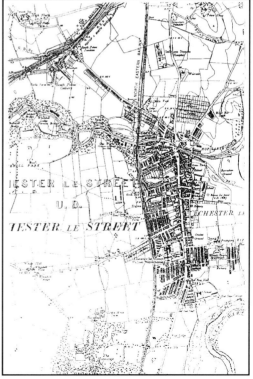

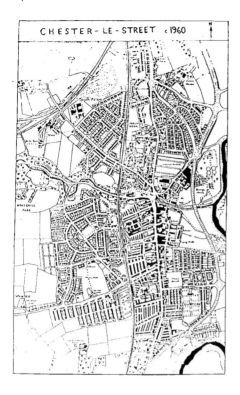

Map 5 Map of c1960. The Sewage works are in the old Roman river loop. Lindisfarne and Crichton Avenues are complete

Map 6 A map of c1840 showing old mine shafts. Lambton Castle is marked so the map is post 1833. The main LNER railway line is not marked, the Cong Burn is in its old bed and the old loop of the River Wear still has water in both channels.

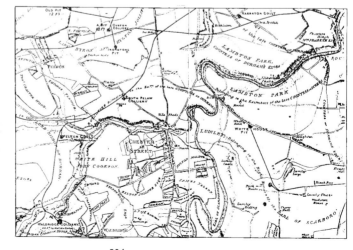

Addendum to Chester-le-Street and its Place in History.

Since the main script of this book was finished, other important pieces of evidence have come to light, hence this Addendum.

Proto-Dere Street and the Binchester loop road at Bishop Auckland; suspected Roman sites at Toronto/Newton Cap and a Roman short cut to Helmington Hall.

In Chapter 8 (The Lost Roman Roads of County Durham), it was explained that the Roman road from Fyland's Bridge up Newgate Street in Bishop Auckland, heading for Binchester, seemed to be an afterthought and that the original Roman road from Fyland's Bridge had gone due north crossing the River at Newton Cap on the same point as the later medieval (1388) bridge. Earthworks beside Newton Cap Farm looked like the remains of a Roman site. A small Hall called Newton Cap Hall had existed here but the earthworks were far too large for such a modest building. Also the NAG team discovered the original Roman road all the way from Newton Cap to the Hunwick Equestrian Centre where the loop-road from Binchester rejoined the original "Proto Dere Street." This suspected "Proto Dere Street" is still marked on some old maps as "Mitchell's Causeway." An inspection of the line shows that it is a perfect Roman road.

Further information has come to light and this authenticates the findings of the NAG team. On page 186 of Matthew Richley's book the *History of Bishop Auckland*, published in 1872, the author says:

"On reaching the high ground at Brusselton, we there find the road runs about 200 yards on the east of the Tower, and thence down the hill, where there are still distinct traces of its existence. It crosses the Gaunless at Fyland's Bridge, about 130 yards on the east of the present bridge, and continues nearly in a straight line to Bishop Auckland, where it enters the town by Newgate Street. In the short lane between Fyland's Bridge and its junction with the West Auckland lane, we still find traces of the road remaining at the present day. In the town of Auckland all traces (at least on the surface) are entirely lost, but a few years ago the Board of Health, in laying down the sewers at Newgate End, came upon a portion of it a few feet below the surface. More recently, when digging for the same purpose at the lower end of Fenkle Street, evident remains of the road were found about six feet below the surface.

Leaving the town and following in the same direction, we find a portion of the top pavement of the road exposed in the fields on the foot-road to the village of Hunwick. These vestiges seem to infer pretty clearly that the main road crossed the River Wear in the vicinity of the present bridge at Newton Cap, and in all likelihood, the old bridge pulled down in the year 1388 was a Roman structure, and that the road passed over it. It seems probable that a branch road to the camp at Binchester turned off the main road at the south end of the town and, taking the line of Newgate Street, crossed the present site of the Market Place in the vicinity of the Town Hall, and thence descending the hill in an angular direction behind Silver Street, entered the camp ground through the narrow neck of land between the stone bridge in the Park and Jock's Row. The branch road from Binchester seems to have left the camp at the north-east corner, and descending the hill, crossed the river near the Hind's house. It again becomes distinctly visible at the opposite side of the river, and runs up past Old Birtley, where at a distance of about 1,000 yards it enters a blind lane, and in all probability joined the main road again, about 200 yards below the Church at Hunwick. A little further on we find the main road in the lane leading to Helmington Hall, and the cottage and garden situated a little to the west of the Hall are upon it, its traces being clearly seen as it descends to the brook."

Addendum

On the same page, author Matthew Richley has added a footnote:

"In thus giving the route of the Roman road, the author is well aware that he is running counter to the pre-conceived notions of many of his readers, who assert that it went direct to the camp at Binchester. Existing evidence however, seems very strong in support of the above theory which is submitted with all due deference."

It seems that in Matthew Richley's time, as today, pre-conceived notions of Roman activities were difficult to eliminate. It also looks as if new evidence was just as unpopular in some quarters then as it is today. Nevertheless, Richley's observations have given a boost to our own findings.

Aerial view of the Toronto/Newton Cap area. Bishop Skirlaw's bridge of 1388 is just beyond the viaduct. This view is to the west. Centre right, just above the main road is a square which is thought to be an unknown Roman fort. There are further earthworks on the other side of the medieval road, which winds northwards up the hill from the 1388 bridge. Bishop Skirlaw pulled down an old bridge, thought to have been Roman, in order to build his own bridge on the same site, using the base of a Roman central pier. Investigations continue.

Bishop Skirlaw's bridge of 1388 on the suspected site of an earlier Roman bridge.

NEWTON CAP
BRIDGE
1388

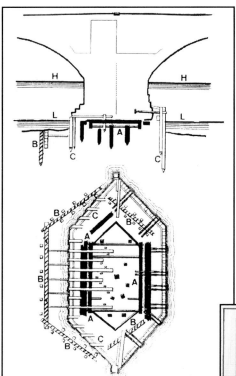

When the Swing Bridge was built at Newcastle upon Tyne, the remains of three earlier bridges were found on the bed of the Tyne.

A =   the timbers of a Roman bridge pier. Roman coins and other artefacts were also found.

B =   the remains of the medieval bridge (built 1250) which was washed away during the Great Flood of 1771.

C =   the remains of the bridge built in 1775, later dismantled to allow navigation upstream.

H =   level of High Spring Tide.

L =   level of Low Spring Tide.
       Tidal range = 16 feet.

At Newton Cap, it is thought that Bishop Skirlaw's central bridge pier of 1388 encapsulated the remains of a Roman bridge pier in a similar manner to the 1250 bridge-work in the Tyne.

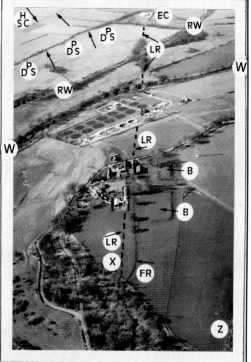

Aerial view of Binchester Roman fort and surrounds, looking north-west. Binchester Farm is in the centre of the photograph.

B   =   earthworks of Binchester Roman fort.

W   =   River Wear.

RW =   dismantled railway line.

FR =   False road, which has caused so much confusion.

Z   =   bypass Roman road around edge of plateau and then across canal, after that heading north towards Byers Green, Page Bank and Old Durham.

PDS =   Proto Dere Street from Newton Cap to Hunwick Equestrian Centre, also marked as "Mitchell's Causeway" & "Birtley Lane."

EC =   Hunwick Equestrian Centre.

LR =   Loop road from Fylands Bridge via Binchester to Hunwick.

HSC =   Hunwick Roman Short Cut.

X   =   position where the Rev Hooppell excavated the Binchester loop road c1880. There is also a Roman well close by at the top of the wood.

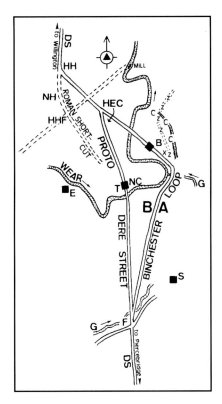

Proto Dere Street, the Binchester Loop and a Roman short cut.

F	=	Fylands Bridge.
BA	=	Bishop Auckland
HEC	=	Hunwick Equestrian Centre.
DS	=	Dere Street.
B	=	Binchester Roman fort.
X	=	Hooppell's excavation site c1880, of Roman road.
CCC	=	Roman canal from dammed Gaunless to River Wear via valley on east side of Binchester Roman fort,
ZZZ	=	Roman bypass road around plateau, then across canal and northwards to Byers Green, Page Bank and Old Durham.
T	=	Toronto, suspected Roman earthworks to south of Newton Cap Farm on west side of medieval road up from 1388 bridge.
NC	=	Newton Cap suspected Roman fort and quarry to east side of medieval road.
HHF	=	Hunwick Hall Farm on Hunwick Roman Short-cut.
NH	=	New Hunwick on Hunwick Roman Short-cut.
HH	=	Helmington Hall, at junction of Hunwick Short-cut and the reunited Dere Street and Proto Dere Street.
E	=	Escomb, suspected site of unspecified Roman building.
G	=	River Gaunless.
S	=	Southchurch St Andrews, suspected Roman site.

A hitherto unknown Roman road also crosses the Roman short-cut at HHF (Hunwick Hall Farm) and heads down to to the River Wear at Furness Mill. This watermill looks as if it may have reused an old Roman navigation weir as its mill-dam.

The above evidence undermines the postulated history of Binchester, which may not be "Vinovia" after all, as this title depends on Binchester being located on Dere Street. The 1872 evidence and our own observations show clearly that it is not. It is on a side loop. Vinovia is therefore most likely to be at Newton Cap. This also has implications for the history of the Saxon church at Escomb. Most history books claim, without the slightest evidence, that the reused Roman stones in Escomb Church were robbed from Binchester. There was a much closer Roman fort than Binchester (Newton Cap?), but even so, it is obvious from the air that Escomb Church sits on a Roman-looking earthwork. The farmer tells us that in the fields to the north of the church, his potato-pickers find dozens of Roman coins. Also, gravediggers in Escomb churchyard find Roman pottery and coins at a depth of six feet. Did the Saxon monks who were supposed to rob Roman stones from Binchester, also bring coins and broken pottery back with them?

The Newton Cap Roman site may have been river supplied. At the foot of the steep slope to the river below Newton Cap, the vestiges of a possible canal can be seen from the air. As part of such a navigation system, the long dismantled old dam at Damhead just upstream may have had Roman origins. It seems that the history of the Bishop Auckland area has gone back to square one. This may not be popular with diehard historians but for the new generation, many Ph.D degrees are just awaiting the taking. The evidence is all there right in front of our noses.

Our investigations have revealed yet another Roman road in the Hunwick area. The above-mentioned

Proto Dere Street from Newton Cap to Hunwick, passing just to the west of the Equestrian Centre, has itself been short-circuited by a short-cut Roman road which ran from Newton Cap, under a modern footpath, direct to Hunwick Hall Farm (NZ 190 323), and then north of Hunwick to New Hunwick, joining the combined Proto Dere Street and the Binchester Loop, at Helmington Hall (NZ 187 334).

Yet a further Roman road crosses both the Hunwick short cut at Hunwick Hall Farm where some kind of Roman site is suspected. This cross road then heads north-east crossing Proto Dere Street on the north side of Hunwick Gill, and proceeds to Furness Mill on the River Wear. It is suspected that the mill has reused a Roman navigation weir for its mill-dam.

It is also now known that a Roman road ran past Southchurch St Andrew's, NZ 217 284, from Dere Street at NZ 205 264. It has been stressed several times in this book that St Andrew's churches are invariably located on Roman sites, for reasons as yet not fully understood. A possibility is that one of Pope Gregory's assistants was called Andrew. Southchurch St Andrew is located on a former Saxon place of worship.

Map refs of 1872 evidence plus recent observations.

Fyland's Bridge, NZ 205 267.

Bishop Skirlaw's 1388 bridge at Newton Cap, NZ 205 303.

Newton Cap suspected Roman sites, NZ 203 303 & NZ 204 304.

Mitchell's Causeway, also called "Birtley Lane" (Proto Dere Street, NZ 200 310 to NZ 196 323).

Junction of Proto Dere Street with Binchester Loop, NZ 196 323.

Escomb Saxon Church, NZ 189 303.

Further Roman road, Newton Cap to Hunwick Hall Farm (NZ 190 323), through Hunwick to New Hunwick and then to junction with Proto Dere Street at Helmington Hall (NZ 187 334).

A Roman road through Quaking Houses

We have long thought that the north-south straight road from Oxhill, West Stanley south through Quaking Houses was on top of an unknown Roman road. Now we have proof. Just to the east of Wheatley Hill, the modern road leaves the Roman line and bends to the east at NZ 193 496. The Roman road has carried on almost due south across the fields. It can be seen clearly as it passes to the west of the old rectory, along the public footpath at NZ 195 487. It then crosses underneath the modern road from Holmside to Burnhope and continues southwards underneath a public footpath to the Whiteside Burn which it crosses at NZ 196 483. It then runs up the west side of a wood and crosses a farm track at NZ 196 480. The surface of the Roman road can then be seen sticking out of a grass track all the way to the known Roman road of Long Edge at NZ 198 474. On the south side of the Long Edge Roman road, the fields have been open-cast mined, but an RAF vertical aerial photograph taken about 1950 before open-casting, show the Roman road, after a change of heading of five degrees to the west, crossing the fields. The road is showing as a snow mark. It seems to be heading for Blackburn, at the west end of Langley Park. This Roman road is only one of a huge network which is slowly coming to light across the whole of north-eastern England.

The Bishop Middleham, Bradbury and Morden ancient lakes are trying to form again after heavy winter rainfall.

After flying over southern County Durham very recently, I was amazed to see that the ancient lakes of County Durham were trying to reform after the heavy winter rains. Most evident was the former lake to the south of Bishop Middleham. The ancient water-route between the Tees and the Wear was via a very much larger River Skerne, the ancient lakes, the Ferryhill Gap and various streams to Croxdale. At Sunderland Bridge, a Roman camp has been found near the confluence of the River Wear and the Croxdale Burn. There was obviously much more water around in Roman times.

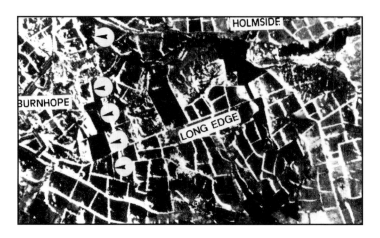

The Quaking Houses Roman Road.

There is a suspected Roman road from Oxhill, West Stanley, south through Quaking Houses and then across the fields, past the rectory at NZ 195 487, then over the Whiteside Burn and up to the known Roman road of Long Edge at NZ 197 473.
On this photograph, the suspected Roman road is arrowed. Long Edge runs from near bottom left to near top right. The land to the south of Long Edge has been open casted and the suspected newly discovered Roman road has been lost. This photograph is however, an old RAF one taken before open casting. The Roman road can be seen heading south in the direction of the A691 modern road, and then probably went to Blackburn to the west of Langley Park and then up to Esh Cross or possibly to Flass Hall. In the woods to the north of Long Edge, a Roman-type surface can be seen sticking out of a grass double-ditched modern farm track.

A lost Roman road under the Derwent Reservoir

We have long suspected that the modern road which heads south from Barleyhill (NZ 023 549) and disappears into the Derwent Reservoir at Millshield (NZ 013 532) is on top of a lost Roman road. We are now sure: the road has come north across Edmundbyers Common, crossed the B6306 and disappeared into the reservoir in the vicinity of Hunter House, emerging again at Millshield. The Roman road runs north up the west side of the Minsteracres estate and can be clearly seen from NZ 023 555, running up the west side of a strip wood. A boundary wall has been built on top of the Roman road and this wall has utilised some of the Roman stones. At NZ 023 564, the Roman road, still with its modern wall on top, comes to the top of a bank before descending to the crossing of the Stocksfield Burn. On the crest, just inside the plantation are the square ditches of a Roman fortlet. The Roman road crosses the stream and can be traced to the north, passing up a strip wood to the east of High Fotherly Farm. The Roman road is underneath a farm track north of Lingey Field Farm and seems to be heading for Broomhaugh where it will join Dere Street coming in from the south-east. To the north of Broomleyfell Plantation, it should cross the recently found Roman road which runs direct from Ebchester to Hexham Abbey, leaving Dere Street at Apperley Dene, crossing the March Burn at NY 998609 and the Devil's Water at NY 967 626. The crossing of the Ebchester-Hexham road and the Minsteracres road has not yet been found but searches are being conducted.

More Roman roads in western Durham

There are more Roman roads in the Derwent/Stanhope area. The B6278 south-west from Edmundbyers is on top of a Roman road and this meets yet another Roman road at NY 998 436, which has come from

After the heavy winter rains, the lost ancient lakes of County Durham are trying to form again. Here, south of Bishop Middleham, one of the lakes is very evident. At the top end of the lake, the Roman earth dam is still almost intact. In the distance, another of the former string of lakes is also holding water. A causeway from the site of Bishop Middleham medieval castle to "Island Farm" is thought to be a reused Roman dam. There is thought to be a Roman barge basin at Mordon and another on Great Isle Farm. Access to the former lakes from the south has been by a much larger ancient River Skerne, and from the north, via the Ferryhill Gap and thence by various streams to the River Wear.

Corbridge via Slaley Forest, Bay Bridge and Pennypie House. This road is mentioned in old documents hitherto ignored. At Stanhope, the Roman road continues over Bollihope Common, approximating to the modern B6278 to Eggleston and is then believed to pass Romalkirk en route to Bowes, with another branch via Cotherstone to Barnard Castle.

Other Roman roads also head south from the River Wear. The Road from Westgate over Westernhope Moor and Newbiggin Common to Newbiggin shows Roman features. Another is from St John's Chapel to Langdon Beck.

Wolsingham is also producing Roman evidence. The old road called Doctor's Gate from Wolsingham to Hamsterley Forest is Roman but a whole network of hitherto unknown Roman roads converge on Wolsingham. Old antiquarians thought that there was a Roman site at Chapel Walls in Wolsingham. They were correct. The Roman site appears to be underneath the council builder's yard at NZ 076 377. Several Roman roads converge on this point. The footpath to the north of Chapel Walls, past Holy Well and then up the hedge line is on a Roman road which joins up with Drovers' Road to the south-west of Satley. Another suspected Roman road comes into Wolsingham from the north-west and is called "Long Dyke." This is also lined-up on Chapel Walls and fieldwork is being carried out in order to provide proof of the road's origins. We have already located its crossing of the Waskerley Beck at NZ 073 380.

The Roman coast road south from Sunderland

We have picked up evidence of the Roman coast road here and there such as the crossing of Hawthorn Dene, passing Dalton-le-Dale St Andrew's Church, and Yoden Saxon village. Further information has come

Addendum

to light: In Sunderland's Grangetown district, in 1940, Anderson-type air raid shelters were being sunk into the gardens of St Aidan's Avenue and Askrigg Avenue. In the garden of No 17 St Aidan's Avenue, a Roman road lined up NNW-SSE was the same road which was cut into the garden of No. 26 Askrigg Avenue. It is interesting to note that on the Tithe map the site of the later cemetery on the opposite side (west) of Ryhope Road, would be built on three fields, numbers 71, 72 and 73. These fields are called "Chester Stones" on the Tithe map, so it looks as if there was some ancient fortification here.

The Roman coast road also appears to have linked Sunderland to South Shields. The ecclesiastical experts in our society are fairly sure that Whitburn St Mary's & St Andrew's Church stands on the site of an old monastery. A Roman road is also suspected in the vicinity. Further to the north, the mark of a Roman road can be seen to the north-east of the Cleadon Mill, running across the golf course in the direction of the South Shields Roman fort. A search is also being made in this area for a Roman lighthouse. Such a beacon at the spot-height of 83m at NZ 395 639 would have been visible from long distances to both north and southbound Roman ships as well as those bound for the Tyne and the Wear from the Rhine. Roman coins have been found on the Cleadon Hill. It is now well known that there was a regular Roman shipping route across the North Sea from the Rhine. When a new Roman ship sailed on its maiden voyage from the Rhine, an altar was thrown overboard. Dutch fishermen have recovered over a hundred such altars from the sea-bed.

Roman ships from across the North Sea bound for the Rivers Tees, Esk and Humber would have been assisted by a lighthouse on the site of Whitby Abbey. The chronicler-monk Symeon of Durham tells us that there was a Roman pharos on the site of the later abbey. This has been incorrectly translated by historians as a 'signal station.' No doubt however, the known Roman signal stations down the Yorkshire coast such as Filey Brigg and Scarborough were ideally placed to have performed secondary duties as lighthouses.

This book has devoted much space to Chester-le-Street's strategic importance in the Roman Empire when the town was connected by army occupation roads to all parts of Roman Britain. The huge network of roads were also used by the Roman tax-collectors who visited the thousands of Romano-Celtic farmsteads to collect the tributes of corn or money. The corn would have been transported to the nearest navigable

There is a whole network of little known and unknown Roads in the Corbridge, Dilston, and Hexham area.

P   =   *Portgate, on Hadrians Wall.*
HC =   *Halton Chesters (Hunnum)Roman Wall fort.*
H   =   *Halton Castle.*
A   =   *Anick. Stanegate passes just to the south of this hamlet.*
RH =   *Red House early Roman fort, now under A69 (T).*
C   =   *Corstopitum (Corbridge) Roman Town.*
HX =   *Hexham, Roman site suspected under abbey.*
SI   =   *Sam's Island, suspected Roman ford.*
5G =   *Five Gates, suspected Roman crossroads*
DP =   *Dilston Park Farm, at Roman road fork.*
D   =   *Dilston, Roman crossroads, Roman bridge, Roman fortlet.*
E   =   *Earthwork of suspected Roman signal station.*

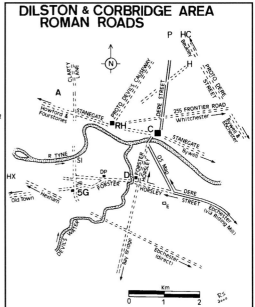

DILSTON & CORBRIDGE AREA ROMAN ROADS

river or stream by pack animals along farm tracks and paths. Our town's position at the tidal limit of the River Wear also tells us that Concangis was in contact by river and sea to the whole of the rest of the Roman Empire. Even as this is being written, further pieces of information on Roman communications are being discovered. The little-known hamlet of Dilston to the south of Corbridge has recently produced a whole network of Roman roads.

In 1881, Robert Forster mentioned in his book, *The History of Corbridge*, a Roman road leaving the southern end of the Corstopitum Roman bridge heading due south to Dilston before turning a right-angle west towards Dilston Park Farm and Five Gates, on its way to Old Town. Forster's Road is there for all to see.

Acca's Cross was found at Dilston. Forster's right-angled turn of a Roman road at Dilston was actually two arms of a crossroad. The southern arm went via Pennypie to Bay Bridge near Blanchland and according to Horsley's *Britannia*, the eastern arm was Dere Street itself. There appears to be the earthwork of a small Roman building on the hillock to the south of Dilston Farm. A Roman gravestone is built into the east wall of Dilston chapel and like any other unexplained stones in the area was said "to have come from Corbridge."

A Roman bridge crossed the Devil's Water here just a few yards downstream from the site of the medieval bridge. The remains of one pier of the latter still stands in the garden of Dilston Mill close to the waterfall. A map of 1810 shows an aqueduct upstream fom the medieval bridge. The aqueduct was modern and carried water from Dilston Mill across the river to Dilston Farm to power an hydraulic threshing machine. See the map for details of the huge network of Roman roads in the area. More Roman roads remain undiscovered.

Yet another Roman riverboat found

Information has just reached me about the find of a small Roman boat which has been found in South Wales near the town of Magor, near Caerleon, during the development of a Tesco Supermarket. The flat lands in which the boat was found had once been part of the Severn Estuary before the building of sea walls. The remains of a Roman bridge or jetty consisting of large stones and driven oak piles was uncovered, and alongside, the remains of a Roman boat were found. Pottery, coins and dendrochronology dated the ship to the fourth century.

The boat was 9.5m long with a beam of 2.5m. This type of boat could not only have navigated the River Wear into its high reaches, but also up the lower reaches of lesser streams such as the Cong Burn.

A book on archaeology is never complete and this one is out of date before it has even got to the printers. It is obvious that there is a whole mass of new information to be found and I hope that one or more of my brilliant pupils will write a comprehensive book with such a title as *"The Lost Roman Roads of North-eastern England."*

Yet another Roman boat used for inland navigation has come to light. This one was found near the South Wales town of Magor, near Caerlon, during the development of a supermarket.

Stop Press

Even while the Addendum was being prepared, more inportant information has come to light. The following "STOP PRESS" gives very brief mentions. Even so, a vast amount of unknown historical evidence still remains to be discovered in our countryside.

The Roman dam at Hylton. University of Sunderland thesis.

The Northern Archaeology Group found about two-thousand tons of ex-Roman stones dumped at Roker on the north side of the river mouth and around the Napoleonic defences on the south side. These stones were thought to have been used as sea erosion defences when the great Roman dam at Hylton was dismantled in the early 1800s.

A geology student at Sunderland University, Ian McCarrison, has just completed his thesis, the subject of which was the examination of these ex-Roman stones dumped at the river mouth. The thesis compares specimen slivers taken from the Roman stones and from various ancient quarries in the area.

The conclusions are that the river mouth dumped stones are

(a), Definitely ex-Roman as they contain evidence of Roman building techniques and:

(b), Most of the stones show all the characteristics of having been quarried in the Hylton area.

A Roman dam on the River Eden at Armathwaite

In *The Piercebridge Formula* of 1983, the present author predicted a Roman navigation dam at Armathwaite on the River Eden. The search has been taken up by Cedric Bell, a resident of Penrith, and a retired chief engineer of the Blue Funnel Line. Cedric has found the Roman dam at NY 5002 4543. The Romans have improved a natural rock sill across the river, blocking the gaps with typical Roman lewis-holed huge stone blocks.

More evidence of Roman inland waterways trade and navigation.

Cedric is a very skilled and industrious chap and is an honorary warden of public footpaths of the Lake District. His knowledge of the area is second to none. He has also found a suspected Roman barge basin in Ullswater and several associated Roman lead mines with hitherto unknown Roman roads and defences.

His interest in the Roman navigation of the River Eden was sparked off by *"On the Trail of the Legions"* (R. Selkirk, Anglia 1995) which described a possible Roman flash lock at Wetheral. This was described by local historians as a fish-trap built by the monks of Wetheral Priory. The features however showed Roman characteristics. Cedric has investigated the river further and found the post-holes of a suspected Roman dam and also relocated a forgotten Roman inscription carved by soldiers of the XXth Legion.

Cedric has also found that when the king granted the land to the monks for Wetheral Abbey, the dam was already in existence in the river. This also points to the construction having had a Roman origin. Between the artificial linear island in the river and the east bank are several stone piers of the type described by Dr MJT Lewis in a paper entitled *Flashlocks on English Waterways* (a survey).

The Wetheral evidence is at NY 4678, 5370, just downstream from St Constantine's Cells, which are artificial caves cut into the cliffs and according to Charlie Emett in his *The Eden Way*, (Cicerone Press), are thought to date from pre-Roman times.

The Romans have certainly used the River Eden as a major supply line.

A Roman road along the south bank of the River South Tyne and a possible Roman *"Limes"* grid system of patrol roads.

A Roman road has just been found along the south bank of the South Tyne, from Beltingham Church (NY 790 640) through Willimoteswick (NY 771 636) and westwards to Unthank (NY 723 633).

Roman altars in the grounds of St Cuthbert's Church at Beltingham were found many years ago and we have just located another one. Beltingham Church sits on a typical Roman fortlet platform. St Cuthbert's body rested here for a while during the monks flight from Lindisfarne to Concangis (Chester-le-Street).

The Roman road passes the ancient farm at Willimoteswick and in a riverside wood to the west, a typical Roman culvert (NY 763 633) passes under the Roman way. There is more evidence at Unthank Hall but it is extremely likely that the Beltingham to Unthank road is merely part of a much longer road which defended the south bank of the South Tyne, perhaps even before Agricola's troops crossed the river. Mention has been made in Chapter 10 of a pre-Hadrianic defence line across northern England. This "255 Line" is not far south of the South Tyne and has been excavated by one of our teams, at Staward Manor (NY 810 603). Between the "255 suspected early frontier" and the South Tyne are probable Roman patrol roads, of which the Beltingham to Unthank road must be one. A mile south of Willimoteswick is a suspected Roman ridge road. How this has not been noticed before now is difficult to understand. The road is part of a defensive linear complex very similar to Hadrian's *Vallum*. The line runs from NY 769 624 to NY 771 621, and in the eastern sector, the Roman road runs along the north mound and then switches to the south mound at NY 779 623. There is a precedent for this as the Military Way of Hadrian's Wall (nothing to do with Wade's 1750 Military Road) runs along the north mound of Hadrian's *Vallum* for a considerable distance.

A Roman road north through the Dotland DMV.

About forty Roman coins have been found by a metal detectorist close to the Deserted Medieval Village of Dotland (NY 923 595). A close ground scrutiny reveals the shape of the corner of a Roman fortlet and part of the defensive ditch at the south side of the "humps and bumps" of the grass-covered medieval buildings. The suspected Roman road runs south to Whitley Mill (NY 925 582).

To the north of the Dotland DMV, the Roman road is under the modern road but shows its Roman characteristics down a farm track immediately to the west of Channel Well Farm (NY 921 603). At the north end of this steeply descending cart-track, the Roman road disappears once again under a modern road to position NY 918 609, where it becomes a rough path. A sudden bend to the west takes the Roman road which is now just a stony track, down a steeply-angled incline which is the typical method the Romans used to descend a cliff. The turns are always in the upstream direction of the stream at the bottom of the cliff. At the stream crossing, the road turns north and has crossed a large Roman bridge over the West Dipton Burn. The bottom courses of the huge Roman abutments are visible at NY 915 612. The tiny modern footbridge looks out of place resting on these massive rough stone abutments. Roman roads can be traced from the bridge to the north in the vicinity of Hexham race-course and to the east to Diptonmill, turning there to Black House, High Shield and Hexham.

Roman defensive roads along the ridges of County Durham.

As in Northumberland, the Romans have placed defensive roads along the east-west ridges of County Durham. These form part of a huge "limes system" across our two northern counties. One ridge road crosses Dere Street at the top of Ragpath Wood (NZ 421 205). Another to the north lies along the Esh Ridge and continues to the west along the Hedley ridge and to Tow Law (Tower Hill).

To the east of the Esh Ridge, the Roman road runs down to the River Browney and past Beaurepaire (NZ 243 438) to Stotgate, Arbour House and Crossgates Moor.

The medieval ruin at Beaurepaire has a sewage system which resembles a copy of Roman technology. It is too technically advanced for medieval flushing methods. In the building which is taken to be the medieval lavatory, a Roman stone toilet seat has been reused as a window frame.

Roman fortifications in the early period were merely turf and timber. About AD120, some of these were rebuilt in stone. The redundant turf & timber forts eroded away as did the temporary work camps. Some of them can still be seen from the air, but the Roman sites are often reoccupied by farms and very frequently by churches. Witton Gilbert church looks as if it standing on a Roman-type platform, as does Beltingham church, and many other early Christian religious sites. Esh Hall and Flass Hall show evidence of standing on hitherto unknown Roman sites. Flass Hall sits enclosed in a triangle of three Roman roads, two of which were previously unknown. Esh Hall is located on the intersection of an east-west Roman ridge road, and a north-south Roman road.

Chester-le-Street in Roman times was not in a relatively uninhabited desert as has been portrayed by some historians in the past. It was a major supply base in a territory which had the major frontier *limes* across Northumberland to the north and also the policed ridges of County Durham to the south and west. All those who wish to take part in the exciting exploration of an ancient civilisation only two or three feet down under our pleasant countryside are welcome to do so. In addition to the exploration of our home area, vast tracts of moorland between Hexham and Allendale need to be explored. Some of the rough paths are showing Roman road identification characteristics. An excellent example is the path across Burntridge Moor from Burnt Ridge (NY 894 559) to Sinderhope Gate (NY 848 524), the latter two miles south of Allendale Town. Several more suspected Roman roads remain to be investigated. Let us get rid of those large open white spaces on our maps of Roman Britain.

The very recent discovery of a Roman bridge in Yorkshire.

Our archaeological divers have also been busy with various underwater searches. They have just discovered a Roman bridge at Newton Kyme near Tadcaster, which carried the Roman road, the "Rudgate" over the River Wharfe at SE 453 456. Experts said that the Romans crossed here via a ford but our divers Rolfe Mitchinson and Bob Middlemass have discovered the huge southern abutment of a bridge hidden in the southern river bank. Many more Roman bridges lie undiscovered. The Roman army marched in all weathers and at all times of the year. They could not afford to be delayed by flooded fords.

The searches of the Northern Archaeology Group continue throughout the year but now it is time to finally close this book. Any further information will have to wait for the next publication, but in the meanwhile, our newsletters are available to members and visitors at our monthly meetings in Washington, and worldwide on the internet. For further information, contact Chairman Alan Richardson Tel/Fax 0191 5840791; E-mail: alan.richardson@n-a-g.co.uk ; Vice-chairman Tom Wright 0191 5843464 or Secetary Raymond Selkirk, 0191, 3883198.

Bibliography

Adam, JP,   Le Chantier Antique, in Dossiers de l´Archeol. 1977
Anonymous,   Anecdotes of American Horses, in Penny Magazine 1840.
Astbury, AK,   The Black Fens.
Bailey, R,   Dowsing and Church Archaeology.
Baines, T,   Yorkshire Past and Present,
Baradez   Fossatum Africae - Vue Aérienne de l'organisation romaine dans le sud-Algérien 1949.
Bede,   A History of the English Church and People.
Birley, E,   Corbridge Roman Station, A Roman Altar from Staward Pele, and Roman Remains in Allendale, in Archaeologia Aeliana, 1950.
Boyles,   Jarrow Church and Monastery, in Archaeol Aeliana, 1885.
Bruce, JC,   The Roman Wall, 1867, & Roman Hexham, in Archaeologia Aeliana, 1861.
Burton, A,   The Changing River.
Camden,   Britannia, 1637.
Campbell, J,   The Anglo-Saxons.
Casey, J,   A Votive Deposit from the River Tees at Piercebridge, County Durham, in Durham Archaeological Journal 5.
Chevalier, R,   Roman Roads.
Churchill, W,   A History of the English Speaking Peoples.
Cintas, P,   Manuel d'Archéologie Punique.
Codrington, T,   Roman Roads in Britain 1919.
Crawford, OGS,   Wessex from the Air, 1928.
Deuel, L,   Flights into Yesterday.
Dickinson, G,   Allendale and Whitfield.
Duckham, BF,   Inland Waterways, in Amateur Historian, v6 No 1.
Eckholdt, M,   Navigation on Small Rivers in Central Europe in Roman and Medieval Times, in The International Journal of Naut. Archaeol & Underwater Expl. 84.
Eden, T,   Durham.
Engels, DW,   Alexander the Great and the Logistics of the Macedonian Army.
Fordyce, W,   Local Records of Northumberland and Durham.
Forster, R,   History of Corbridge, 1881.
Frere, SS,   Britannia.
Frontinus,   The Strategems and Aqueducts of Rome.
Garrett, WE,   George Washington's Patowmack Canal, in National Geographic Magazine, Vol 171 No 6, June 1987.
Glover, M,   Invasion Scare 1940.
Graham, F,   Bridges of Northumberland and Durham.
Grenier, A,   Manuel D'archéologie Gallo-romaine.
Hall, GR,   Roman Way Across Wark's Ford, in PSAN 1866.
Hastings, M   The Battle for the Falklands.
Hildyard, E   A Possible Roman Road, in Archaeology of Weardale.
Hersey, J,   A Single Pebble.
Hippisley Coxe,   Haunted Britain.
Hodges, H,   Technology in the Ancient World.
Hodgson, JC,   A History of Northumberland, 1839.
Horsley, J,   Britannia Romana, 1732.
Hoskins, WG,   Fieldwork in Local History.
Hutchinson, W,   History and Antiquities of the County Palatine of Durham, 1785, & Views of Northumberland.
Johnston, DE,   Roman Roads in Britain.

Bibliography

Jones, HS,	Companion to Roman History, Oxford, 1912.
Jones, P,	Flash Locks and Flashing, in Waterways World, April 1991.
Longstaffe, W	Before the Conquest, & History and Antiquities of Northumberland.
Mackenzie, E,	History of Northumberland, 1825.
Mackenzie/Ross	Durham, 1834.
Maclauchlan, H,	Survey of the Watling Street, 1852.
Margery, ID,	Roman Roads in Britain, 1967.
Massie, WH,	A Roman Bridge at Birkenhead, in Journal of the Architect., Archaeol. & Hist. Soc. of Chester, 1850.
Mitchell, WC,	History of Sunderland, 1919.
Mocsy, A,	Pannonia and Upper Moesia.
Moore, RW,	The Romans in Britain.
Mothersole, J	Agricola's Road into Scotland.
Murray,	Handbook for Travellers in Durham and Northumberland.
Nelson/Norris	Warfleets of Antiquity.
Ordnance Survey,	Roman Britain.
Palmer,	The Tyne and its Rivers, 1862.
Pliny (Elder),	Natural History.
Pliny (Younger),	Letters to Trajan.
Poidebard, RPA,	La Trace de Rome dans le désert de Syrie, 1934. Le Limes de Chalcis, 1945, & Le Limes de Trajan, la conquête arabe.
Pollen, JH,	Trajan's Column Described
PSAN,	Proceedings, 1839.
Richley, M	History of Bishop Auckland, 1872.
Ripon Boat Club,	Cruising Guide to the North East Waterways.
Rivet, A	The Place-names of Roman Britain.
St Joseph/Frere,	Roman Britain from the Air.
Salzman, LF,	Building in England Down to 1540.
Selkirk, R,	The Piercebridge Formula, 1983.
Selkirk, R,	On the Trail of the Legions,
Shirley Smith,	The World's Great Bridges.
Sitwell, NHH,	Roman Roads of Europe.
Smith, NAF,	A History of Dams.
Stukeley, W,	Itinerarium Curiosum, Centuria .
Summer,	History of Sunderland.
Surtees, R,	History of the County of Durham.
Sykes, J,	Local Records, 1866.
Tacitus,	Agricola, Annals, & Histories.
Testaguzza, O,	Port of Rome, in Archaeology, Vol 17 No 3.
Tomlinson, WW,	Comprehensive Guide to Northumberland.
Tudor, D,	Les Ponts Romains du Bas-Danube.
Vegetius,	De Re Militari.
Venedikov,	Trakijskate Kolesniza.
Von Hagen, V,	Roman Roads.
Warburton,	Vallum Romanum, 1753.
Whellan, W,	Various pieces of info on Roman roads.
Willan, TS,	River Navigation in England 1600-1750.
Wright, RP,	The Wrekendike and Roman Road Junction on Gateshead Fell, in Archaeologia Aeliana, 1940.

Index

For ease of reference, the index has been subdivided under the following headings:

A page number preceded by an asterisk* indicates an illustration.

Index

Index

Index

Index

14. Rivers, canals, lakes and seas

Index

15. Roads and cross-country transport

16. Ships and water transport

Index

Appendices,
Important events and dates from 753BC to AD2000

Subjects in Stop Press:

Roman stones of Hylton dam identified.

Roman dam discovered at Armathwaite on River Eden.

Roman inscription found beside dam at Wetheral on River Eden.

Grid of Roman *limes* roads across Northumberland.

Roman road found through Dotland DMV (near Hexham).

Grid of Roman *limes* roads across County Durham.

Roman bridge abutment found in River Wharfe near Tadcaster.

List of Illustrations

List of Illustrations

List of Illustrations

Authors Comments

It would not be fair to close without recording the importance of a chance meeting which played such an importance part in the final publishing of this book, "chance" being such an important part of all archaeological search.

In 1999 I was giving a talk to Chester-le-Street Rotary Club and as part of that talk I mentioned the research on which the book was based and the fact we were to publish and that my last book had been published in Ipswich, and the difficulties involved with distance. At the end of the talk Tom Moffat came up to me and said that Casdec, his family publishing and printing company, would help if needed.

The quality of the final product is testimony to the help that Tom's daughter, Mrs Carole Shotton (Managing Director of Casdec Ltd.), gave to myself and our team at every stage of the final preparations and subsequent publishing of the book.

I do wish to recognise our thanks for all that help we were given by Carole, George (the Designer) and the whole Casdec team, always without question. I am sure that readers will see for themselves the quality of the end result, and enjoy the book.

Raymond Selkirk
January 2001